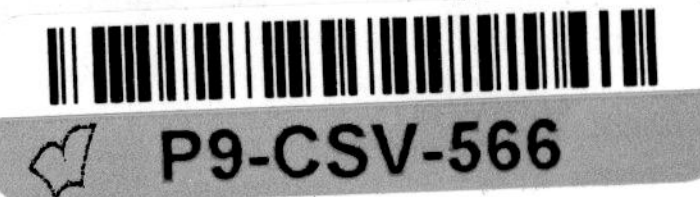

EUROPE & THE MEDITERRANEAN

Turn to the page shown for the start of each country

Atlantic Ocean
North Sea
English Channel
Baltic Sea
Black Sea
Mediterranean Sea
Norway
Sweden
Finland
Denmark
Germany
Russia
Belarus
Ukraine
Moldova
Romania
Bulgaria
Hungary
Serbia
Bosnia-Herzegovina
Macedonia
Albania
Geo
Syria
Lebanon
Cyprus
Crete
Malta
Sicily
Sardinia
Corsica
Balearic Islands
Tunisia
Algeria
Madeira Islands
Atlantic Ocean
Canary Islands

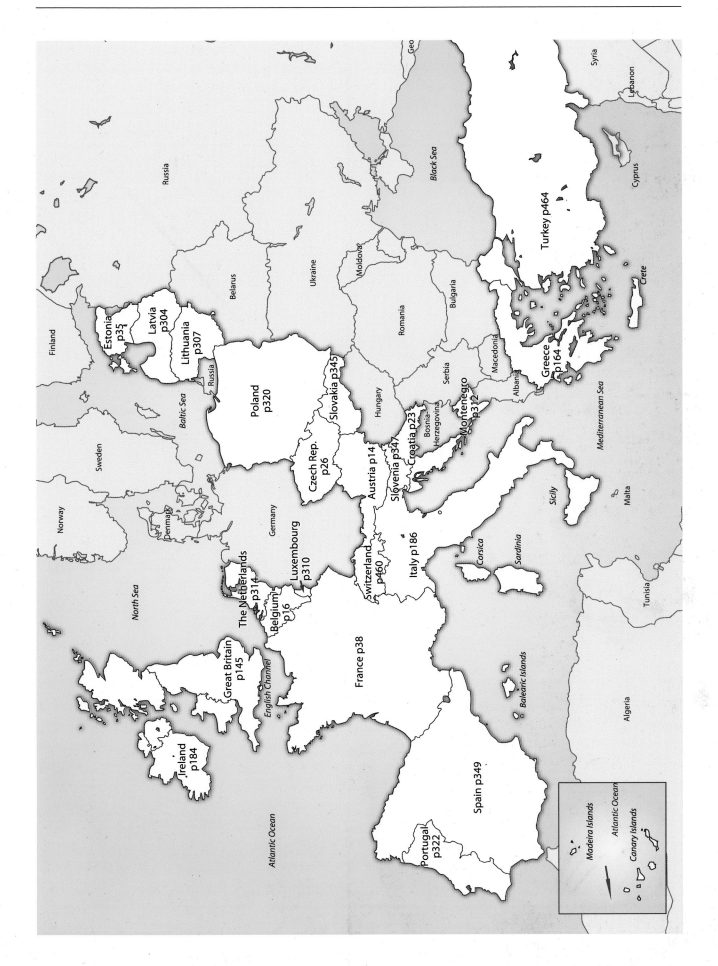

How to use this Guide / Comment utiliser ce Guide / Cómo utilizar esta Guía

To find a hotel by location:

- Turn to the Map of Europe overleaf to identify the country you wish to search.
- Turn to the relevant country section where properties are featured alphabetically by region and/or by place names.
- Alternatively, turn to the title page of the country required where you will find a country map. The location of each property appears in red (hotel) or purple (spa hotel) with a number corresponding to the page on which the establishment entry is published.

To find a property by name look for it in the index from pages 506-510.

The indexes also list our Recommendations by their amenities such as SPA, Golf course on-site etc.

The Recommendations are split into 3 categories:

- **Hotels**: properties providing a high standard and wide range of services and facilities.
- **Charming Hotels**: properties with a more homely and intimate atmosphere.
- **Guest Houses**: properties which are usually owner managed and only serve breakfast.

Once you have made your choice please contact the property directly. Rates are correct at the time of going to press but should always be checked with the hotel before you make your reservation. When making a booking please mention that Condé Nast Johansens was your source of reference.

We occasionally receive letters from guests who have been charged for accommodation booked in advance but later cancelled. Readers should be aware that by making a reservation with a hotel, either by telephone, e-mail or in writing, they are entering into a legal contract. Under certain circumstances, a hotelier is entitled to make a charge for accommodation when guests fail to arrive, even if notice of the cancellation is given.

All Guides are obtainable from bookshops or by calling Condé Nast Johansens direct on 0800 269397 (UK) or +44 1323 649 349 (Europe & US). Alternatively, use the Order Forms on pages 523 (English), 525 (French) and 527 (Spanish). Guides may also be ordered via the Internet at www.johansens.com/bookshop

Si vous souhaitez trouver un hôtel dans un emplacement spécifique:

- Reportez-vous à la carte d'Europe au verso pour identifier le pays que vous souhaitez rechercher.
- Reportez-vous à la section du pays désiré, où les hôtels sont présentés par ordre alphabétique par région et/ou nom de la ville.
- Autrement, reportez-vous à la première page du pays désiré, où vous trouverez une carte. L'emplacement de chaque hôtel est marqué d'un point rouge (hôtel) ou un point violet (hôtel spa/centre thermal) avec un chiffre correspondant à la page à laquelle l'hôtel est présenté.

Si vous souhaitez trouver un hôtel dont vous connaissez le nom, reportez vous à l'index aux pages 506-510.

L'index offre aussi la liste des hôtels recommandés classés par leurs aménagements, par exemple Centre thermal, Golf sur site etc.

Les Recommandations se divisent en 3 catégories:

- **Hotels**: établissements offrant une prestation haut de gamme ainsi qu'un vaste choix de services.
- **Charming Hotels (Hôtels de charme)**: établissements à l'atmosphère plus intime et chaleureuse.
- **Guest Houses (Maison d'Hôtes)**: établissements généralement gérés par les propriétaires et ne servant que le petit-déjeuner.

Quand vous avez fait votre choix, veuillez contacter l'hôtel directement. Les tarifs indiqués sont corrects au moment de l'impression mais il vous est recommandé de les vérifier auprès de l'établissement concerné avant de réserver. N'oubliez pas de mentionner Condé Nast Johansens comme référence lors de votre réservation.

Il nous arrive parfois de recevoir des lettres de clients qui ont dû payer des chambres réservées à l'avance puis annulées. Les lecteurs doivent savoir qu'en effectuant une réservation auprès d'un hôtel, que ce soit par téléphone, courrier électronique ou lettre, ils passent un contrat légal avec cet hôtel. Dans certaines circonstances, un hôtelier est en droit de facturer une chambre lorsque le client ne se présente pas à l'hôtel même s'il a été avisé de l'annulation.

Tous les Guides peuvent être obtenus en librairies ou en appelant directement Condé Nast Johansens au +44 1323 649 349 Vous pouvez également utiliser les bons de commande fournis dans ce guide aux pages 523 (anglais), 525 (français) et 527 (espagnol). Vous pouvez commander nos Guides sur Internet www.johansens.com/bookshop

Si desea encontrar un hotel en un lugar específico

- Vaya al mapa de Europa en la página anterior para identificar el país.
- Vaya a la sección del país que elegido, donde los hoteles aparecen en orden alfabético por región y / o por el nombre de la ciudad.
- Alternativamente, vaya a la primera página del país elegido donde encontrará un mapa. La localización de cada hotel aparece como un punto rojo (hotel) o violeta (hotel spa) con un número que corresponde a la página del hotel en cuestión.

Para buscar un hotel por nombre, vaya al índice en las páginas 506-510.

También hay un índice donde los hoteles aparecen catalogados por sus instalaciones, tales como spa, campo de golf in situ etc.

Los hoteles recomendados se dividen en 3 categorías::

- **Hotels:** establecimientos que ofrecen un alto nivel de comodidad y una variedad amplia de servicios y de instalaciones.
- **Charming Hotels (Hoteles con encanto):** establecimientos con una atmósfera más íntima y acogedora.
- **Guest Houses:** establecimientos que son dirigidos generalmente por los propietarios y sirven solamente el desayuno.

Cuando haya hecho su selección, por favor contacte con el hotel directamente.

Los precios indicados son correctos en el momento de ir a la prensa, pero recomendamos que los verifique con el hotel antes de confirmar su reserva. No olvide de mencionar que Condé Nast Johansens fue su referencia para la reserva.

A veces, recibimos cartas de clientes a los cuales se les ha cobrado por una habitación reservada de antemano y luego cancelada. Advertimos a nuestros lectores que cuando confirman una reserva con el hotel por teléfono, e-mail o carta, entran en un contrato legal. Bajo ciertas circunstancias, el hotelero tiene el derecho de facturar una habitación cuando el cliente no se presenta, incluso si ha avisado para cancelar.

Todas las guías se pueden comprar en librerías o llamando directamente a Condé Nast Johansens al +44 1323 649 349 Alternativamente, puede utilizar los formularios de pedido en las páginas 523 (inglés), 525 (francés) y 527 (español) de esta guía. Nuestras guías también se pueden comprar por Internet en www.johansens.com/bookshop

Contents / Sommaire / Contenido

Key to Symbols / Signification des Symboles / Símbolos

Total number of rooms / Nombre de chambres / Numero de habitaciones

Credit cards not accepted / Cartes de crédit pas acceptées / No se aceptan tarjetas de crédito

Exclusive use available / Utilisation exclusive possible / Uso exclusivo disponible

Access for wheelchairs to at least 1 bedroom and public rooms / Accès handicapé dans au moins une chambre et salles communes / Habitaciones para minusválidos

Gastronomic restaurant (holds at least 1 Michelin star or mark above 14/20 GaultMillau) / Restaurant gastronomique (au moins 1 étoile Michelin ou note supérieure à 14/20 au GaultMillau) / Restaurante gastronómico (por lo menos 1 estrella Michelin o superior a 14/20 GaultMillau)

Restaurant / Restaurant à l'hôtel /Restaurante

24-hour room service / Service en chambre à toutes heures / Room-Service 24 horas

Meeting/conference facilities with maximum number of delegates / Salle(s) de conférences – capacité maximale / Salon(es) de reunion(es) – capacidad maxima

Dogs accommodated in rooms or kennels / Chiens autorisés / Se admiten perros

At least 1 room has a four-poster bed / Lit à baldaquin dans au moins 1 chambre / Camas con dosel disponibles

Cable/satellite TV in all bedrooms / TV câblée/satellite dans toutes les chambres / TV cable/satelite en todas las habitaciones

CD player in all bedrooms / Lecteur CD dans toutes les chambres / Lector de CD en todas las habitaciones

DVD/video player in all bedrooms / Lecteur vidéo/DVD dans toutes les chambres / DVD en todas habitaciones

ISDN/modem point in all bedrooms / Ligne ISDN/ligne modem dans toutes les chambres / Linea ISDN/Modem en todas habitaciones

Wireless Internet connection available in part or all rooms / Connection Internet sans-fil disponible dans certaines ou toutes les chambres / Conexión a Internet sin cable en algunas o todas las habitaciones

At least 1 non-smoking bedroom / Au moins 1 chambre non-fumeur / Habitaciones para no-fumadores

Lift available for guests' use / Ascenseur / Ascensor

Air conditioning in all bedrooms / Climatisation dans toutes les chambres / Aire acondicionado en todas las habitaciónes

Gym facilities / Facilités de remise en forme / Instalaciones de gimnasio

SPA Dedicated spa with an on-site qualified staff and indoor pool - offering extensive body, massage, beauty and water treatments / Un spa dans l'hôtel avec personnel qualifié sur place et une piscine intérieure - offre une variété de massages, soins de beauté et traitements thermaux / Zona dedicada a spa, con personal cualificado permanente y piscina interior, donde se ofrecen extensivos tratamientos de agua, corporales, de belleza y masajes.

Wellness area – offering body, massage and beauty treatments / Centre Wellness - Offre une variété de massages, soins de beauté et traitements thermaux / Zona Wellness - Donde se ofrecen tratamientos corporales, de belleza y masajes

Indoor swimming pool / Piscine couverte / Piscina interior

Outdoor swimming pool / Piscine en plein air / Piscina exterior

Fishing on-site / Pêche sur place / Pesca in situ

Fishing can be arranged / Pêche peut être organisé / Se puede organizar pesca

Golf course on-site / Golf sur site / Campo de golf in situ

Golf course nearby, which has an arrangement with the hotel allowing guests to play / Golf sur site ou à proximité, arrangement avec l'hôtel / Campo del golf cerca con acuerdo de green fee

Shooting can be arranged / Tir peut être organisé / se pueden organizar sesiones de tiro

Hosre riding can be arranged / Équitation possible / Equitación posible

Located in a ski resort / Situé à une station de ski / Situado en una estación de esquí

Skiing nearby (within 50km) / Ski / Esquí cerca

Property has a helicopter landing pad / Hélipad / Helipuerto

Licensed for wedding ceremonies / Licencé pour cérémonies de mariage / Licencia para celebrar bodas

Introduction / Introducción

Andrew Warren, Managing Director, Condé Nast Johansens Ltd.

September 2006 marked the 25th Anniversary of the Johansens Guides. In recognition of this milestone, Condé Nast Johansens has published special anniversary editions of its 2007 Recommended Hotels Guides.

Today, more than ever, the sophisticated traveller has the opportunity to select a hotel to match the experience they seek: a romantic city break, a weekend escape, a holiday in the sun, skiing or an indulgent spa treatment.

Our Recommendations offer a breadth of variety and value yet all ensure that the high standards expected of a Condé Nast Johansens Recommendation are never compromised.

Please spare a moment to complete the Guest Survey Report at the back of this Guide. Your comments will help to maintain the standards of excellence expected by our readers and are equally important when we nominate establishments for our Annual Awards.

Above all, please remember to mention "Condé Nast Johansens" when you make an enquiry or reservation and again when you arrive. You will be made especially welcome.

Septembre 2006 marque le 25ème Anniversaire des Guides Johansens. Pour célébrer cette date importante, les guides d'hôtels recommandés en 2007 par Condé Nast Johansens ont été publiés en édition spéciale anniversaire.

Aujourd'hui plus que jamais, le voyageur sophistiqué à la possibilité de choisir un hôtel qui satisfasse l'expérience qu'il recherche: une escapade romantique en ville, une évasion le temps d'un week-end, des vacances au soleil, à la neige ou un indulgent soin dans un spa.

Nos recommendations offrent une grande variété d'hôtels et de prix ; tous garantissent que les plus hauts standarts de qualité, attendus de la part d'un hôtel Condé Nast Johansens, soient maintenus.

Merci de prendre une minute pour compléter l'Enquête de Satisfaction à la fin de ce Guide. Vos commentaires nous aide à maintenir les standards d'excellence attendus par vous, nos lecteurs, et sont également importants pour la nomination des établissements lors de notre remise de Prix Annuels.

Surtout, souvenez-vous, s'il vous plait, de mentionner "Condé Nast Johansens" lorsque vous contactez l'hôtel pour des renseignements ou une réservation ainsi qu'à votre arrivée à l'hôtel. Vous serez chaleureusement reçu.

El 25 aniversario de las Guías Johansens se celebro en septiembre del 2006. Para distinguir esta importante fecha, las guías de hoteles recomendados para el año 2007 han sido publicadas por Condé Nast Johansens en edición especial conmemorativa.

Hoy mas que nunca, el viajero sofisticado tiene la oportunidad de elegir un hotel que haga eco con la experiencia que busca: escapada romántica en una ciudad, evasión de fin de semana, vacaciones al sol, algunos días de esquí o tratamientos gratificantes en un Spa.

La colección de hoteles que recomendamos ofrece una amplia gama en variedad y en calidad, pero todos se comprometen en mantener el alto nivel que se exige a un hotel recomendado por Condé Nast Johansens.

Por favor, dedique unos minutos para completar el "Cuestionario de Calidad" que se encuentra en las últimas paginas de esta Guía. Sus comentarios nos ayudan a mantener los niveles de excelencia a los cuales nuestros lectores están acostumbrados y también son importantes en el momento de nominar establecimientos para nuestros Premios de Excelencia Anuales.

Sobre todo, no olvide de mencionar "Condé Nast Johansens" al pedir información, al hacer una reserva y de nuevo a su llegada al hotel. De esta manera su recibimiento será aún más cálido.

Andrew Warren

The Condé Nast Johansens Promise

Condé Nast Johansens is the most comprehensive illustrated reference to annually inspected, independently owned hotels throughout Great Britain, Continental Europe, The Americas, Atlantic, Caribbean and Pacific.

It is our objective to maintain the trust of Guide users by recommending, through annual inspection, a careful choice of accommodation offering quality, excellence and value for money.

Our team of over 50 dedicated Regional Inspectors have visited almost 3,000 hotels, country houses, inns and resorts throughout the world to select only the very best for Recommendation in the 2007 editions of our Guides.

No hotel can appear in our Guides unless it meets our exacting standards.

L'Engagement de Condé Nast Johansens

Condé Nast Johansens est la référence de guides illustrés la plus complète en matière d'hôtels indépendants, inspectés annuellement en Grande-Bretagne, Europe, Les Amériques, Atlantique, Caraïbes et Pacifique.

C'est notre objectif de maintenir la confiance de nos lecteurs en continuant à recommander, par le biais de nos inspections annuelles, une sélection d'établissements offrant qualité, excellence et un bon rapport qualité-prix.

Notre équipe de plus de 50 inspecteurs régionaux a visité près de 3000 hôtels, country houses, inns et resorts partout dans le monde, pour ne sélectionner que le meilleur en recommandation dans les éditions 2007 de nos Guides.

Aucun hôtel ne peut apparaître dans nos Guides sans répondre exactement à nos standards.

El Compromiso de Condé Nast Johansens

Condé Nast Johansens es la relación más extensa de hoteles independientes e inspeccionados anualmente en Gran Bretaña, Europa, Las Américas y las islas del Atlántico, Caribe y Pacífico.

Es nuestro objetivo de mantener la confianza de nuestros lectores al seguir recomendando, gracias a nuestras inspecciones anuales, una cuidada selección de hoteles que ofrecen variedad, excelencia y buena relación calidad-precio.

Nuestro equipo de más de 50 inspectores regionales ha visitado unos 3.000 hoteles y resorts en muchos países del mundo y ha seleccionado solo los mejores para ser incluidos en nuestras guías del 2007.

Ningún hotel puede aparecer en nuestras guías sin someterse a nuestros altos niveles de inspección.

With over 1,300 Recommendations across The Americas, the UK and Europe, our website is a great reference point to source a property that fits the experience you're after, be it a luxury hotel, a coastal hideaway, a traditional inn, country house or resort. Each one is annually inspected and you can feel confident that we have taken care in helping you to select a place to stay.

You can search for a place by location, see what special breaks are on offer and send an enquiry. The on-line Bookshop offers great gift ideas - Guides and gift vouchers to use in any of our worldwide destinations. You can also register on-line to receive our monthly Newsletter.

For a great source of inspiration...

johansens.com

From top, left to right: Cliveden, England; One & Only Palmilla, Mexico; Lake Vyrnwy Hotel, Wales; Fawsley Hall, England; Sorrel River Ranch Resort & Spa, U.S.A.; Elounda Peninsula All Suite Hotel, Greece; Dalhousie Castle and Spa, Scotland; Lainston House Hotel, England; Qamea Resort & Spa; Fiji Islands.

The King and I

Condé Nast Johansens

Condé Nast Johansens Ltd, 6-8 Old Bond Street, London W1S 4PH, UK
Tel: +44 (0)20 7499 9080 Fax: +44 (0)20 7152 3565
Find Condé Nast Johansens on the Internet at: **www.johansens.com**
E-mail: info@johansens.com

Publishing Director:	Charlotte Evans
PA to Publishing Director:	Sophie Lanfranc de Panthou
Inspectors:	Ana María Brebner
	Suzanne Flanders
	Paz García
	Gianna Illari
	Tunde Longmore
	Barbara Marcotulli
	Stéphanie Court
	Murat Özgüç
	Seamus Shortt
	Agnes Szent-Ivanyi Exton
	Danielle Taljaardt
	Christopher Terleski
Production Manager:	Kevin Bradbrook
Production Editor:	Laura Kerry
Senior Designer:	Michael Tompsett
Copywriters:	Sasha Creed
	Norman Flack
	Sarah Koya
	Debra O'Sullivan
	Rozanne Paragon
	Leonora Sandwell
Translators:	Ana María Brebner
	Stephanie Cook
	Eroulla Demetriou
	Stéphanie Court
	Carmen Saliba
	Peter Saliba
Marketing & Sales Promotions Executive:	Charlie Bibby
Client Services Director:	Fiona Patrick
Managing Director:	Andrew Warren

Condé Nast Johansens Ltd. is part of The Condé Nast Publications Ltd.
ISBN 1 903665 30 2

Printed in England by St Ives plc
Colour origination by Wyndeham Graphics

Distributed in the UK and Europe by Portfolio, Greenford (bookstores).
In North America by Casemate Publishing, Havertown (bookstores).

2006 Awards For Excellence

The winners of the Condé Nast Johansens 2006 Awards for Excellence

The winners of the Condé Nast Johansens 2006 Awards for Excellence

The Condé Nast Johansens 2006 Awards for Excellence were presented at the Condé Nast Johansens Annual Luncheon held at Jumeirah Carlton Tower on November 14th, 2005. Awards were made to properties from all over the world that represented the finest standards and best value for money in luxury independent travel. An important source of information for these awards was the feedback provided by guests who completed Condé Nast Johansens Guest Survey Reports. Guest Survey Reports can be found on page 524.

Les vainqueurs des Conde Nast Johansens 2006 Awards for Excellence

Les Condé Nast Johansens 2006 Awards for Excellence ont été remis lors du déjeuner de gala annuel de Condé Nast Johansens à l'hôtel Jumeirah Carlton Tower à Londres le 14 novembre 2005. Ces prix ont été créés afin de récompenser les établissements qui, à travers le monde, offrent les meilleurs standards et rapport qualité~prix dans l'hôtellerie de luxe indépendante. Une source d'information et de sélection importante pour ces prix provient des questionnaires de satisfaction renvoyés par les clients. Les questionnaires de satisfaction sont disponibles page 526.

Los ganadores de los Condé Nast Johansens 2006 Awards for Excellence

Los Condé Nast Johansens Awards for Excellence del 2006 fueron presentados durante el almuerzo anual de Condé Nast Johansens en el Hotel Jumeriah Carlton Tower de Londres, el 14 de noviembre del 2005. Han sido premiados aquellos establecimientos de todas partes del mundo que ofrecen el más alto estándar y la mejor relación calidad-precio dentro del sector de turismo de lujo independiente. Una fuente de información importante para la adjudicación de estos premios proviene de los Cuestionarios de Calidad que nos envían los clientes. Estos cuestionarios se pueden encontrar en la página 528 de esta guía.

Most Excellent Value For Money

Romantik Hotel le Silve di Armenzano

– Umbria, Italy, p274

"High professionalism, excellent service and extremely helpful staff make this hotel a true discovery."

«Un trés grand professionalisme, un service de premier ordre et un personnel extrêmement serviable font de cet hôtel une vraie découverte.»

„Un profesionalismo total, un servicio excelente y un personal atentísimo hacen que este hotel sea un verdadero hallazgo."

Most Excellent Service

Château des Alpilles – Provence, France, p131

"The décor, the welcome, the bedrooms, the furniture, the food and the atmosphere are a pure delight."

«Le décor, l'accueil, les chambres, le mobilier, la cuisine et l'atmosphère sont un ravissement.»

„La decoración, la acogida, las habitaciones, los muebles, la comida y la atmósfera son una pura delicia."

2006 Awards For Excellence

The winners of the Condé Nast Johansens 2006 Awards for Excellence

Most Excellent Guest House

Marignolle Relais & Charme - Tuscany, Italy, p253

"The warm hospitality, the immaculate interiors and proximity to the historical city centre are just a few of the reasons to visit this hidden gem in the Tuscan countryside."

«L'accueil chaleureux, les intérieurs impeccables, le sentiment de tranquilité et la proximité du centre historique de la ville ne sont que quelques uns des atouts de ce joyau caché dans la campagne Toscane.»

„La cálida acogida, los interiores perfectos y la cercanía al centro histórico de la ciudad son algunas de las razones para visitar esta joya escondida en la campaña toscana."

Most Excellent Charming Hotel

Divan Bodrum Palmira - Bodrum, Turkey, p466

"Homely and romantic in a charming setting and atmosphere.""

«Accueil et romance dans un cadre et une atmosphère de charme.»

„Acogedor y romántico con una ubicación y un ambiente encantadores."

Most Excellent Hotel

Hospes Maricel - Mallorca, Balearic Islands, Spain, p393

"This modern hotel, with its beach-front location, boasts contemporary interior design and friendly young staff."

«Cet hôtel moderne avec son emplacement en bord de mer offre une décoration intérieure moderne et le jeune personnel est acceuillant.»

„Este moderno hotel, situado a la orilla del mar, hace alarde de interiores de diseño contemporáneo y un personal joven amabilísimo."

Most Excellent Business Venue

Antiguo Convento - Madrid, Spain, p443

"This 17th-century convent has been carefully restored, with no expense to detail, charm or quality spared."

«Ce couvent du 17ème siècle a été restauré à grands frais, les détails, le charme et la qualité sont soignés.»

„Este convento del siglo 17, ha sido cuidadosamente restaurado sin reparar en gastos de detalle, encanto y calidad."

Most Excellent Resort

Hotel Jardín Tropical - Tenerife, Canary Islands, Spain, p411

"Whether enjoying a leisurely stroll through the sub-tropical gardens or a gourmet dinner in the restaurant, hotel staff are on-hand to guarantee you an unforgettable stay."

«Que vous profitiez d'une promenade dans les jardins sub-tropicaux ou d'un dîner gastronomique au restaurant, le personnel de l'hôtel est à votre disposition pour vous garantir un séjour mémorable.»

„Mientras se pasea tranquilamente por los jardines subtropicales, o disfruta de una cena gourmet en el restaurante, el personal de este hotel esta siempre a mano para asegurar que su estancia sea inolvidable. "

2006 Awards For Excellence

The winners of the Condé Nast Johansens 2006 Awards for Excellence

Most Excellent Romantic Hotel

Hotel Vis à Vis - Liguria, Italy, p210

"A romantic escape in a spectacular and unrivalled stretch of nature where the mountains plunge into the sea."

«Une escapade romantique dans un environnement natural spectaculaire où la montagne plonge dans la mer.»

„Una escapada romántica perfecta, en un lugar espectacular e incomparable donde las montañas se hunden en el mar."

Most Excellent Spa Hotel

Romantik Hotel Turm - Trentino - Alto Adige / Dolomites, Italy, p241

"Marvellous environment, excellent cuisine and a spa which is like something out of the 'Arabian Nights'." ""

«Un superbe environnement, une délicieuse cuisine et un spa tout droit sorti des Mille et Une Nuits.»

„Ambiente maravilloso, cocina excelente y un spa que parece que sale de Las Mil y Una Noches."

Most Excellent Hotel Restaurant

Read's Hotel & Spa - Mallorca, Baleric Islands, Spain, p401

"Chef Marc Fosh has deservedly earned his Michelin star for his intriguing mixtures of flavours and artistically presented dishes."

«Le Chef Marc Fosh a largement mérité son étoile Michelin pour son intriguant mélange de saveurs et la présentation artistique de ses plats.»

„El chef, Marc Fosh, se ha ganado su merecida estrella Michelin por sus intrigantes mezclas de sabores y la presentación artística de sus platos."

Most Excellent Hotel For Design & Innovation

Hotel Omm - Barcelona, Spain, p429

"The innovation is apparent beyond the interior décor: it is also seen on the menu, which has made the hotel as popular with locals as with guests."

«L'innovation est visible au delà de la décoration intérieure; elle est également visible sur les menus, ce qui a rendu l'hôtel populaire autant auprès des locaux que des clients.»

„La innovación es aparente mas allá de la decoración; también está presente en el menú, lo que hace que este hotel sea concurrido tanto por los barceloneses como por los huéspedes de fuera."

Condé Nast Johansens European Reader Award

Pieve di Caminino - Tuscany, Italy, p266

"With views of the sea and the Tuscan hills, this luxury guest house is a hidden treasure.""

«Avec vues sur la mer et sur les collines Toscanes, cette maison d'hôtes de luxe est un véritable trésor caché .»

„Con vistas al mar y a las colinas de Toscana, esta lujosa casa de huéspedes es un verdadero tesoro escondido."

Condé Nast Johansens Guides

Recommending only the finest hotels in the world

As well as this Guide, Condé Nast Johansens also publishes the following titles:
En plus de ce Guide, Condé Nast Johansens publie également les titres suivants:
Además de esta Guía, Conde Nast Johansens también publica los siguientes títulos:

Recommended Hotels & Spas, Great Britain & Ireland

Unique and luxurious hotels, town houses, castles and manor houses chosen for their superior standards and individual character.

Hôtels luxueux et uniques, hôtels particuliers, châteaux et manoirs sélectionnés pour leurs standards supérieurs et leur caractère individuel.

Hoteles lujosos y únicos, hoteles boutique, castillos y mansiones elegidos por su alto estándar y su carácter particular.

Recommended Country Houses, Small Hotels, Inns & Restaurants, Great Britain & Ireland

Smaller, more rural properties, ideal for short breaks or more intimate stays.

Établissements plus petits et le plus souvent à la campagne. Idéal pour des courts séjours ou des escapades romantiques.

Establecimientos más pequeños, sobre todo rurales. Ideales para estancias en el campo o escapadas románticas.

Recommended Hotels, Inns, Resorts & Spas The Americas, Atlantic, Caribbean & Pacific

A diverse collection of properties across the region, including exotic ocean-front resorts, historic plantation houses and traditional inns.

Une collection variée d'établissements à travers le pays, comprenant des resorts éxotiques en bord de mer, des maisons de plantations historiques et des inns traditionnels.

Una variada colección de establecimientos que cubre toda esta zona e incluye exóticos resorts al borde del mar, históricas casonas en plantaciones, e "inns" tradicionales americanos.

International Recommended Venues, For Conferences, Meetings & Special Events

Venues that cater specifically for business meetings, conferences, product launches, events and celebrations.

Des lieux spécifiquement dédiés aux réunions d'affaires, conférences, lancements de produits, évènements et festivités.

Lugares dedicados específicamente, o que tienen instalaciones para reuniones de negocios, conferencias, presentaciones de productos y otros eventos.

To order any Guides please complete the order form on page 523 or call FREEPHONE 0800 269 397

Pour commander les Guides, merci de compléter le bon de commande situé en page 525 ou appelez +44 208 655 7810

Para pedir estas Guías, rellene, por favor, la hoja en la página 527 o llame al teléfono +44 208 655 7810

The Perfect Gift...

Condé Nast Johansens Gift Vouchers

Condé Nast Johansens Gift Vouchers make a unique and much valued present for birthdays, weddings, anniversaries, special occasions or as a corporate incentive.

Vouchers are available in denominations of £100, £50, €140, €70, $150, $75 and may be used as payment or part payment for your stay or a meal at any Condé Nast Johansens 2007 Recommended property.

To order, call +44 (0)207 152 3558

or purchase direct at www.johansens.com

AUSTRIA

Hotel location shown in red (hotel) or purple (spa hotel) with page number

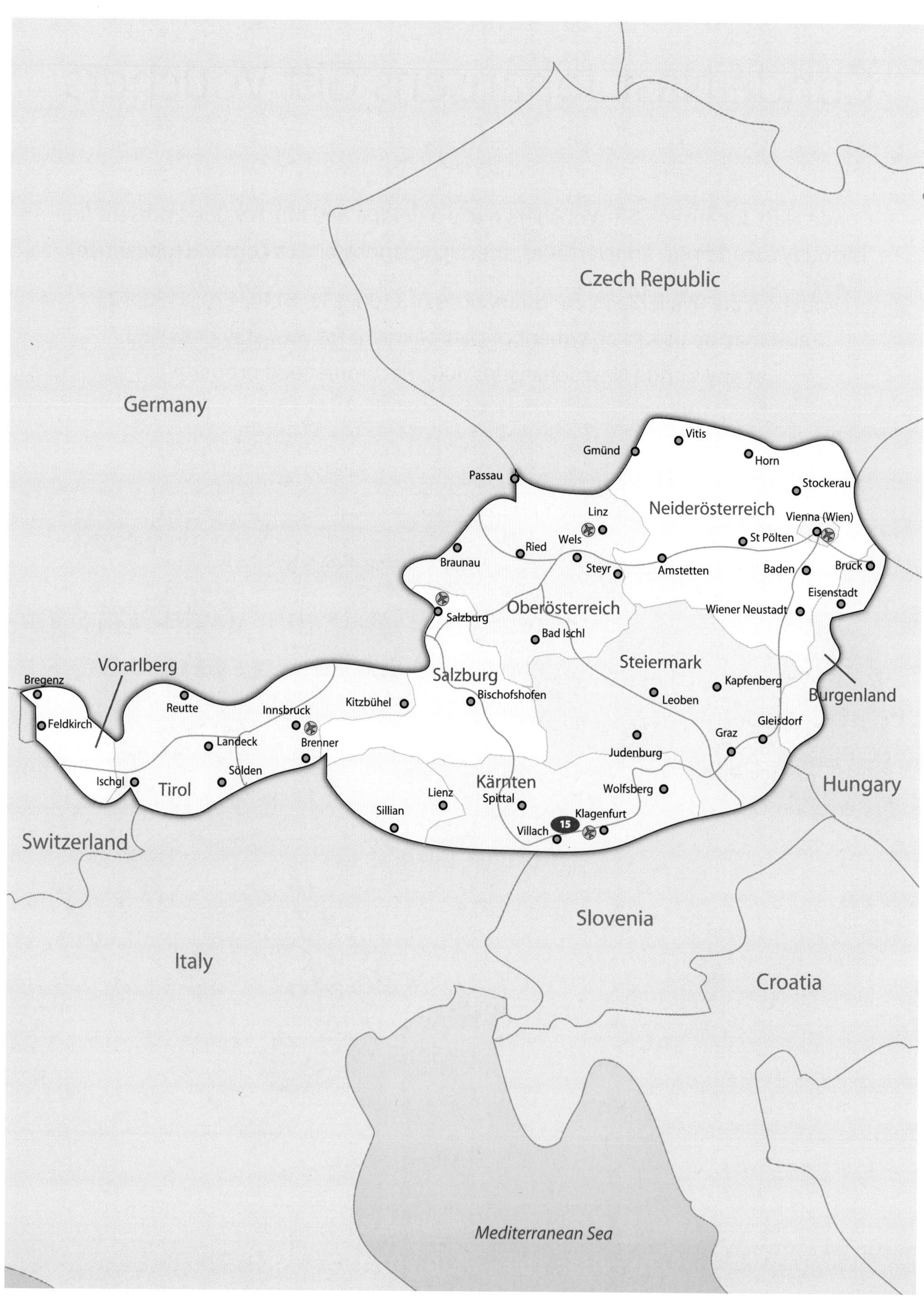

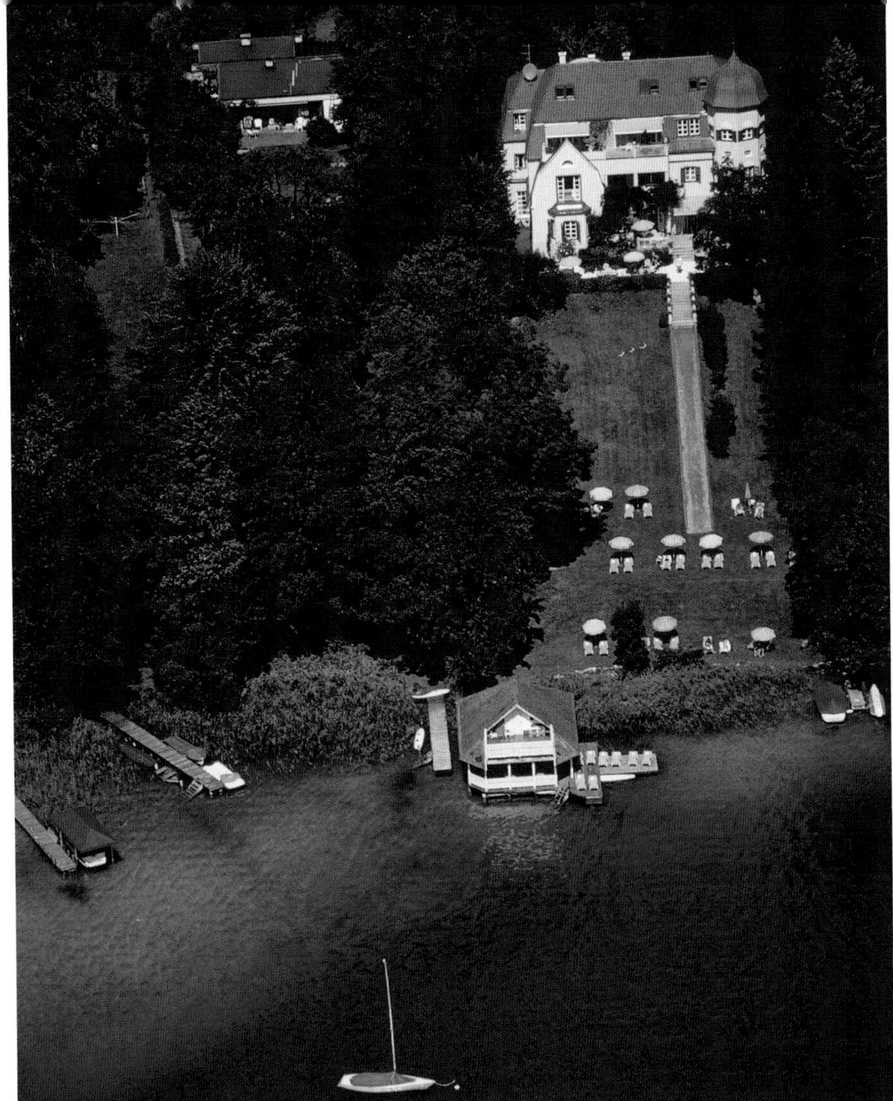

SEESCHLÖSSL VELDEN

KLAGENFURTER STRASSE 34, 9220 VELDEN, AUSTRIA

With its own private water front and pier, and shielded by a thick wall of imposing trees, this friendly secluded hotel is a mere 5 minutes from Velden's bustling town centre. The public rooms are luxuriously appointed with their panelled walls, polished wooden floors and delightful rustic furnishings. This high level of comfort extends to the bedrooms – all individually designed – some of which have scenic views over the waterfront.

Bénéficiant de son propre quai d'amarrage et entouré d'un mur épais de superbes arbres, cet hôtel sympathique est très calme, tout en étant à 5 minutes du centre bruyant de Velden. Les pièces communes sont luxueusement décorées avec des murs en lambris, des parquets polis et un ameublement délicieusement rustique. Le haut niveau de confort s'étend aux chambres – toutes individuellement décorées – dont certaines ont une vue scénique sur le bord de l'eau.

Con su propia ribera y embarcadero, protegido por un ancho muro de majestuosos árboles, este apartado y cordial hotel está a unos 5 minutos del centro del bullicioso Velden. Las paredes de los salones están tan lujosamente revestidas con madera, lo mismo que los lustrosos suelos y el mobiliario rústico es precioso. El alto nivel de confort se extiende a las habitaciones, todas ellas diseñadas individualmente y algunas ofrecen vistas panorámicas de la ribera.

Our inspector loved: *The very warm and distinctive welcome.*

Directions: Near Velden town centre.

Web: www.johansens.com/seeschlosslvelden
E-mail: seeschloessl@aon.at
Tel: +43 4274 2824
Fax: +43 4274 2824 44

Price Guide:
single/double €120–260
junior suite €300

Belgium

Hotel location shown in red (hotel) or purple (spa hotel) with page number

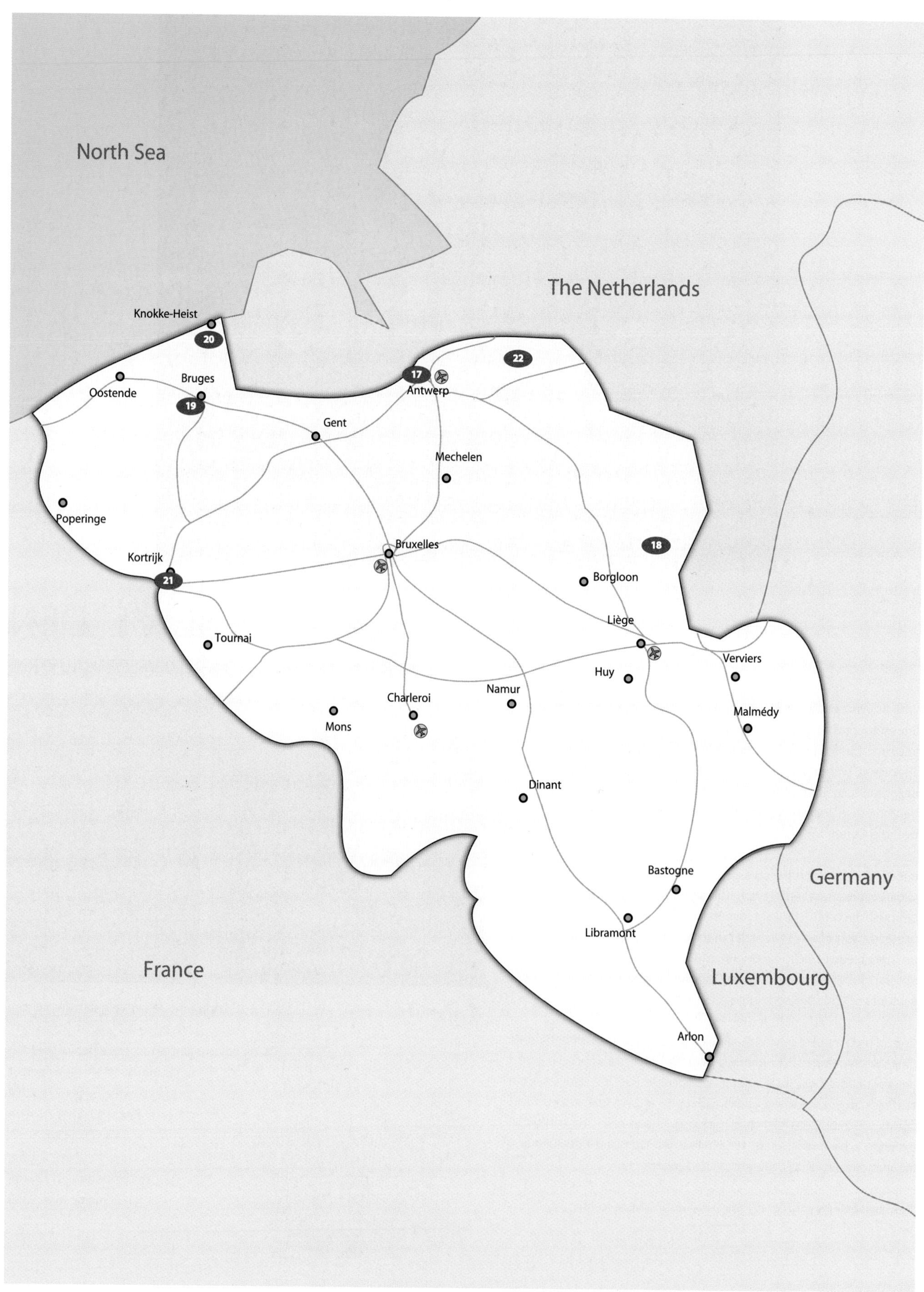

FIREAN HOTEL

KAREL OOMSSTRAAT 6, 2018 ANTWERP, BELGIUM

Set in a quiet residential street minutes away from the centre of picturesque Antwerp, this art deco hotel is a genuine original. Ideally suited for the traveller weary of homogeneous hotel chains, its suave style is all-pervasive, from the stunning entrance right through to the Tiffany enamel and glass in the bedrooms. Renowned for the courtesy of its staff, the Firean's restaurant combines excellent service with the finest of cuisine.

Situé dans une rue résidentielle calme à quelques minutes du centre de la pittoresque ville d'Anvers, cet hôtel art déco est très original. Situé idéalement pour le voyageur lassé des chaînes d'hôtels, son style est suave et partout présent, de l'entrée étonnante à l'émail de Tiffany et aux glaces des chambres. Renommé pour la courtoisie de son personnel, le restaurant du Firean combine un excellent service avec une cuisine raffinée.

Situado en una tranquila calle residencial a sólo unos minutos del centro de la pintoresca ciudad de Amberes, este hotel art deco es realmente original. Resulta ideal para el viajero cansado de las homogéneas cadenas hoteleras. Su afable estilo lo invade todo, desde su impresionante entrada hasta el esmalte de Tiffany y el vidrio de sus habitaciones. Célebre por la amabilidad de su personal, el restaurante del Firean combina excelente servicio con la mejor cocina.

Our inspector loved: *The art deco stained-glass windows and gates.*

Directions: From the coast > Kennedy Tunnel > second exit turn left > over freeway > the hotel is on the left-hand side across the square.

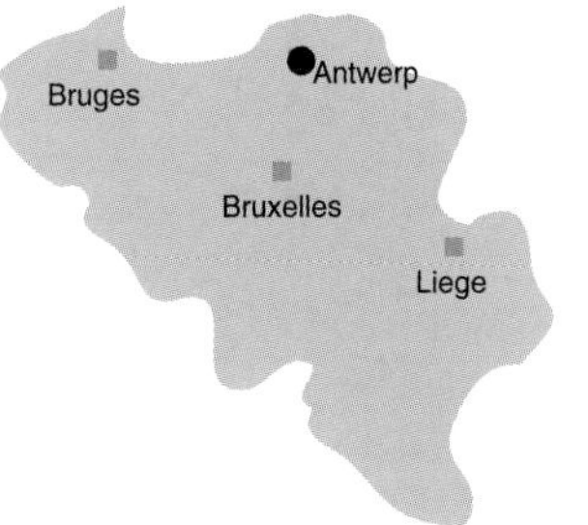

Web: www.johansens.com/firean
E-mail: info@hotelfirean.com
Tel: +32 3 237 02 60
Fax: +32 3 238 11 68

Price Guide:
single €143-149
double/twin €167-178
suite €180-221

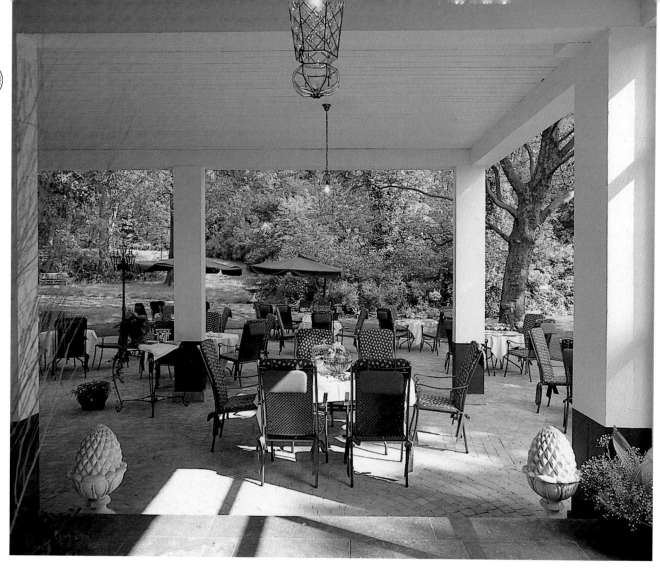

HOSTELLERIE MARDAGA

121 STATIONSSTRAAT, 3665 AS, BELGIUM

Directions: The nearest regional airport is Maastricht/Aachen. The nearest international airport is Brussels, in Zaventem.

Web: www.johansens.com/mardaga
E-mail: mardaga.hotel@skynet.be
Tel: +32 89 65 62 65
Fax: +32 8965 62 66

Price Guide:
single €89-96.50
double €131-146
suite €146

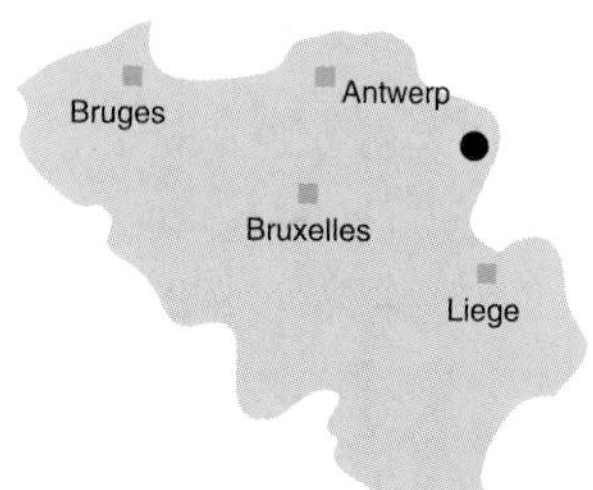

This stylish, tall hostellerie, with 2 handsome roof gables, is ideally situated for a relaxing break and centrally situated for sightseeing and visiting such attractions as Belgium's First National Park and the beautiful village of Bokryk with its historic museum and extensive children's amusement park. Built in the early 20th century it is charmingly appointed, elegantly furnished and has exquisite bedrooms, which offer all modern facilities and panoramic views of over 2½ acres of parkland. An excellent restaurant serves memorable dishes.

Cette auberge de style, haute avec ses 2 combles sur pignons, a une situation géographique idéale tout aussi bien pour un séjour de détente que pour des excursions et visites d'attractions telles que le Premier Parc National belge et le beau village de Bokryk, son musée historique et son grand parc d'amusement pour enfants. Construit au début du XXe siècle, l'hôtel est joliment aménagé avec des meubles élégants et des chambres raffinées, qui offrent tout le confort moderne et des vues panoramiques sur près d'un hectare de parc. L'excellent restaurant sert des mets inoubliables.

Esta elegante y magnífica hostellerie de bellos techos inclinados es un lugar ideal para el relax y está céntrico para los que desean hacer turismo y visitar lugares de interés tales como el Primer Parque Nacional de Bélgica o la bella aldea de Bokryk, donde puede admirarse su museo histórico y su gran parque de atracciones para niños. Construida a principios del siglo XX, esta hostellerie de bello acabado y elegante mobiliario cuenta con refinadas habitaciones, todas ellas provistas de modernas instalaciones y vistas panorámicas a una zona verde de 1 ha. Los platos de su excelente restaurante son realmente memorables.

Our inspector loved: *The relaxing park-like setting.*

Hotel Die Swaene

1 STEENHOUWERSDIJK (GROENE REI), 8000 BRUGES, BELGIUM

Overlooking one of Bruges' picturesque canals, this luxurious hotel offers a relaxing and romantic ambience. Each of the bedrooms is individually decorated and the hotel's candle-lit restaurant serves cuisine created from regional and organic ingredients. The 18th-century lounge, the former meeting room for the Tailors Guild, features fine tapestries and the 15th-century attic room is ideal for conferences accommodating up to 25 delegates. To relax, guests may use the hotel's indoor swimming pool, sauna and cold bath. Alternatively, drinks can be taken in the cosy bar.

Donnant sur un canal pittoresque, cet hôtel luxueux propose une ambiance romantique et relaxante. Chacune des chambres est décorée de façon unique et le restaurant éclairé à la bougie, sert des plats aux ingrédients régionaux. Le salon, datant du XVIIIe siècle et orné de tapisseries, est l'ancienne salle de réunion pour la guilde de tailleurs. La mansarde date du XVe siècle et offre un endroit idéal pour des conférences pour jusqu'à 25 délégués. Pour se détendre, les hôtes peuvent profiter de la piscine intérieure, la sauna et les bains froids ou prendre un verre dans le bar intime.

Este lujoso hotel con vistas a uno de los típicos canales de Brujas ofrece un ambiente relajante y romántico. Cada una de sus habitaciones está decorada con un estilo diferente y el restaurante sirve comida preparada con ingredientes regionales y ecológicos a la luz de las velas. El gran salón del siglo XVIII, anteriormente sala de reuniones para el Tailors´ Guild, se caracteriza por sus magníficos tapices y el ático del siglo XV es ideal para celebrar congresos de hasta 25 delegados. Para relajarse los huéspedes pueden hacer uso de la piscina climatizada, de la sauna y del baño frio. Alternativamente pueden disfrutar de sus bebidas en el bar acogedor.

Our inspector loved: *The newly decorated entrance, and elegant dining room.*

Directions: Take the E40 to Bruges in the direction of Ostend. Brussels (Zaventem) is the nearest airport.

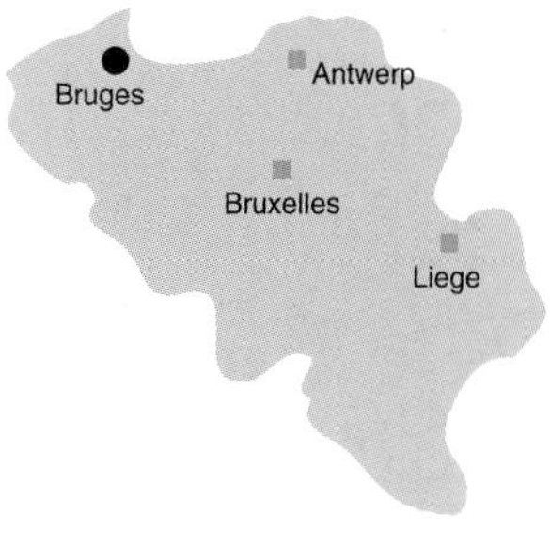

Bruges
Antwerp
Bruxelles
Liege

Web: www.johansens.com/swaene
E-mail: info@dieswaene-hotel.com
Tel: +32 50 34 27 98
Fax: +32 50 33 66 74

Price Guide: (breakfast included only for Condé Nast Johansens guests)
single €170
double €195-295
suite €360-460

Romantik Hotel Manoir du Dragon

ALBERTLAAN 73, 8300 KNOKKE~HEIST, BELGIUM

Overlooking the Royal Zoute Golf, this luxury, romantic manor, dating back to 1927, has a wonderful ambience. Rooms and suites offer unequalled comfort; each has a terrace, air conditioning, Jacuzzi bath, flat-screen TV and WiFi. The buffet breakfast is served in the garden during summer. The central location is ideal for walking/cycling tours; bicycles can be rented from the hotel. The nature reserve ZWIN, beach, shops and art galleries are close by. 3 golf clubs are within 15km, Bruges is 18km away and Damme, a 16th-century village, is 12km.

Situé aux bords du Royal Zoute Golf, ce manoir romantique datant de 1927, se caractérise par une ambiance de charme et de distinction. Ses chambres et suites luxueuses offrent un confort inégalé: terrasses, climatisation, jacuzzi, télévision à écran plat, WIFI, ainsi que les petits déjeuners servis au jardin en été. Une situation centrale idéale pour les promenades à pied ou en bicyclettes (location à l'hotel), non loin de la réserve naturelle le Zwin, la plage, les boutiques et les galeries d'art. 3 clubs de golf se trouvent à moins de 15 km de l'hotel; Bruges à 18 km, Damme, village du XVIe siècle, à 12 km.

Con vistas al campo de golf Royal Zoute, este lujoso, romantico y encantador hotel del año 1927 tiene un ambiente maravilloso. Las habitaciones y suites ofrecen un confort sin par, cada una con terraza, aire acondicionado, bañera con jacuzzi, televisor de pantalla plana, DVD y WIFI. El desayuno-buffet se sirve en el jardin durante todo el verano. Su ubicación central es ideal para hacer giras a pie o en bicicleta y estas se pueden alquilar en el hotel. La reserva natural ZWIN, la playa, tiendas y varias galerias son de facil acceso, 3 clubes de golf se encuentran en un radio de unos 15 km, Bruges queda a 18 km de distancia y Damme, bonito pueblo del siglo XVI, a solo 12 km.

Directions: Follow signs to centre of Knokke-Heist > signposted.

Web: www.johansens.com/dudragon
E-mail: info@manoirdudragon.be
Tel: +32 50 63 05 80
Fax: +32 50 63 05 90

Price Guide:
room €195–260
suite €320–475

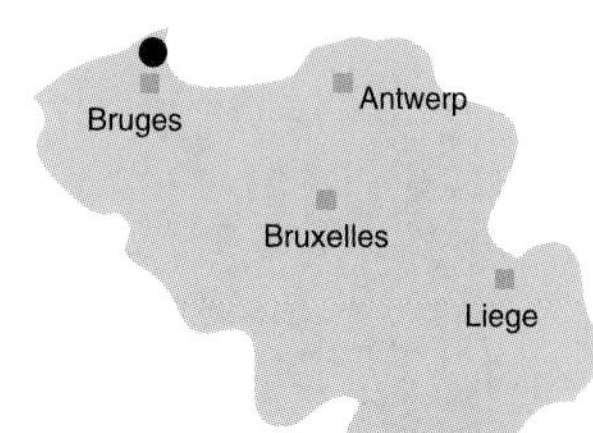

Our inspector loved: *The recently refurbished suite overlooking the golf course.*

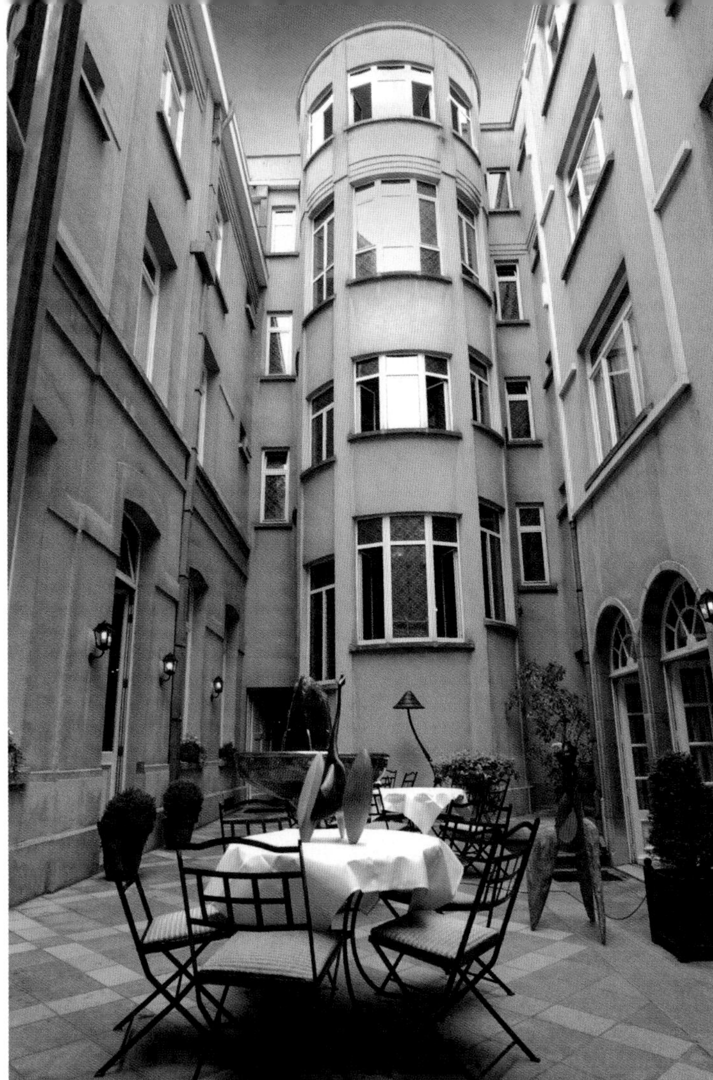

GRAND HOTEL DAMIER

GROTE MARKT 41, 8500 KORTRIJK, BELGIUM

This exquisite Rococo building is right in the town centre and ideally located for sightseeing, shopping and visiting the city museums. The hotel is one of the oldest in Belgium and is charmingly appointed with period features, elegant bedrooms and marble bathrooms. Its previous guests include Margaret Thatcher and President George Bush, who would have sampled the hotel's legendary silver service that takes place during functions in the dining room.

Ce immeuble raffiné de style rococo est situé en plein centre de ville, dans une location idéale pour visiter la ville et ses musées, et pour faire du shopping. Cet hôtel, l'un des plus vieux de Belgique, est aménagé de manière charmante avec des décors d'époque, de chambres élégantes et des salles de bain en marbre. Parmi ses hôtes précédents, on trouve Margaret Thatcher et le Président George Bush, qui ont pu apprécier le célèbre service stylé des grandes fonctions qui se tiennent dans la salle à manger.

Este distinguido edificio de estilo rococó se encuentra justo en el centro de la ciudad. Su localización es ideal para quienes deseen hacer turismo, ir de compras o visitar los museos de la ciudad. El hotel, uno de los más antiguos de Bélgica, exhibe un encantador acabado a base de motivos de época, elegantes habitaciones y cuartos de baños de mármol. Entre los clientes que han pasado por él están Margaret Thatcher y el Presidente George Bush, quienes pudieron apreciar la suprema calidad del servicio del hotel durante las recepciones celebradas en su comedor.

Our inspector loved: *This unique boutique hotel that successfully balances its cultural heritage with innovative displays of modern art.*

Directions: 42km from Bruges. Take the E40 from Bruges to Kortrijk centre, the hotel is in the market square.

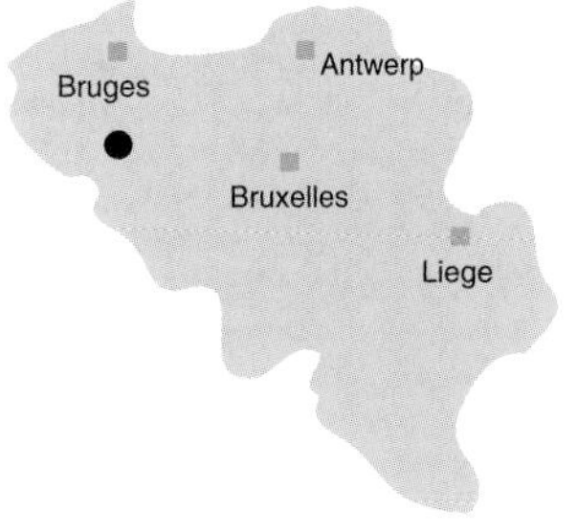

Web: www.johansens.com/damier
E-mail: info@hoteldamier.be
Tel: +32 56 22 15 47
Fax: +32 56 22 86 31

Price Guide:
single €119-180
double €139-195
suites €199-359

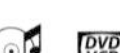

HOSTELLERIE TER DRIEZEN

18 HERENTALSSTRAAT, 2300 TURNHOUT, BELGIUM

Formerly the official residence of the mayor of Turnhout, today this 18th-century house offers modern accommodation alongside professional service managed by Gust and Liesbeth Keersmaekers, owners for 28 years. Public rooms feature classic furnishings, crystal chandeliers, Oriental rugs and wooden floors and bedrooms provide relaxing havens in warm tones. Enjoy pre-dinner drinks by the fireplace before dining in one of the 8 fine restaurants within 5 minutes, walk in the centre of town. During summer, breakfast is served in the garden.

Ancienne résidence officielle du maire de Turnhout, cette maison du XVIIIe siècle est aujourd'hui un hôtel moderne bénéficiant du service professionnel de Gust et Liesbeth Keersmaekers, propriétaires depuis 28 ans. Les pièces communes sont aménagées avec un mobilier classique, des chandeliers en cristal, des tapis orientaux et des planchers et les chambres sont des havres de paix dans des tons chaleureux. Dégustez un apéritif près de la cheminée avant de dîner à l'un des 8 restaurants excellents au centre ville. Pendant l'été, des petits-déjeuners sont servis dans le jardin.

Anteriormente fue residencia oficial del alcalde de Turnhout, hoy este edificio del siglo XVIII ofrece alojamiento moderno junto con un servicio profesional dirigido por Gust y Liesbeth Keersmaekers, dueños desde hace 28 años. En las zonas comunes destaca un mobiliario clásico, arañas de cristal, alfombras orientales y suelos de madera. Las habitaciones proporcionan un ambiente relajante en tonos cálidos. Disfrute de los aperitivos junto a la chimenea antes de cenar en uno de los 8 excelentes restaurantes a sólo 5 minutos andando del centro de la población. Durante el verano el desayuno se sirve en el jardín.

Directions: Antwerp > E34 > Turnhout. From Brussels > A1 > E19 to Antwerp.

Web: www.johansens.com/terdriezen
E-mail: terdriezen@yahoo.com
Tel: +32 14 41 87 57
Fax: +32 14 42 03 10

Price Guide:
single €110
double €135-145

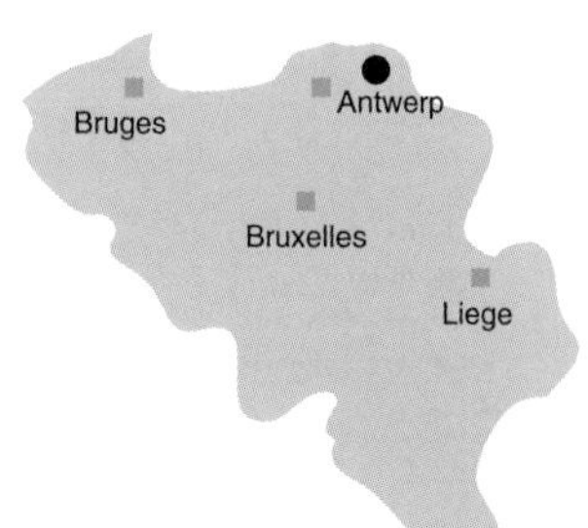

Our inspector loved: *The warm hospitality of the owner.*

Croatia

Hotel location shown in red (hotel) or purple (spa hotel) with page number

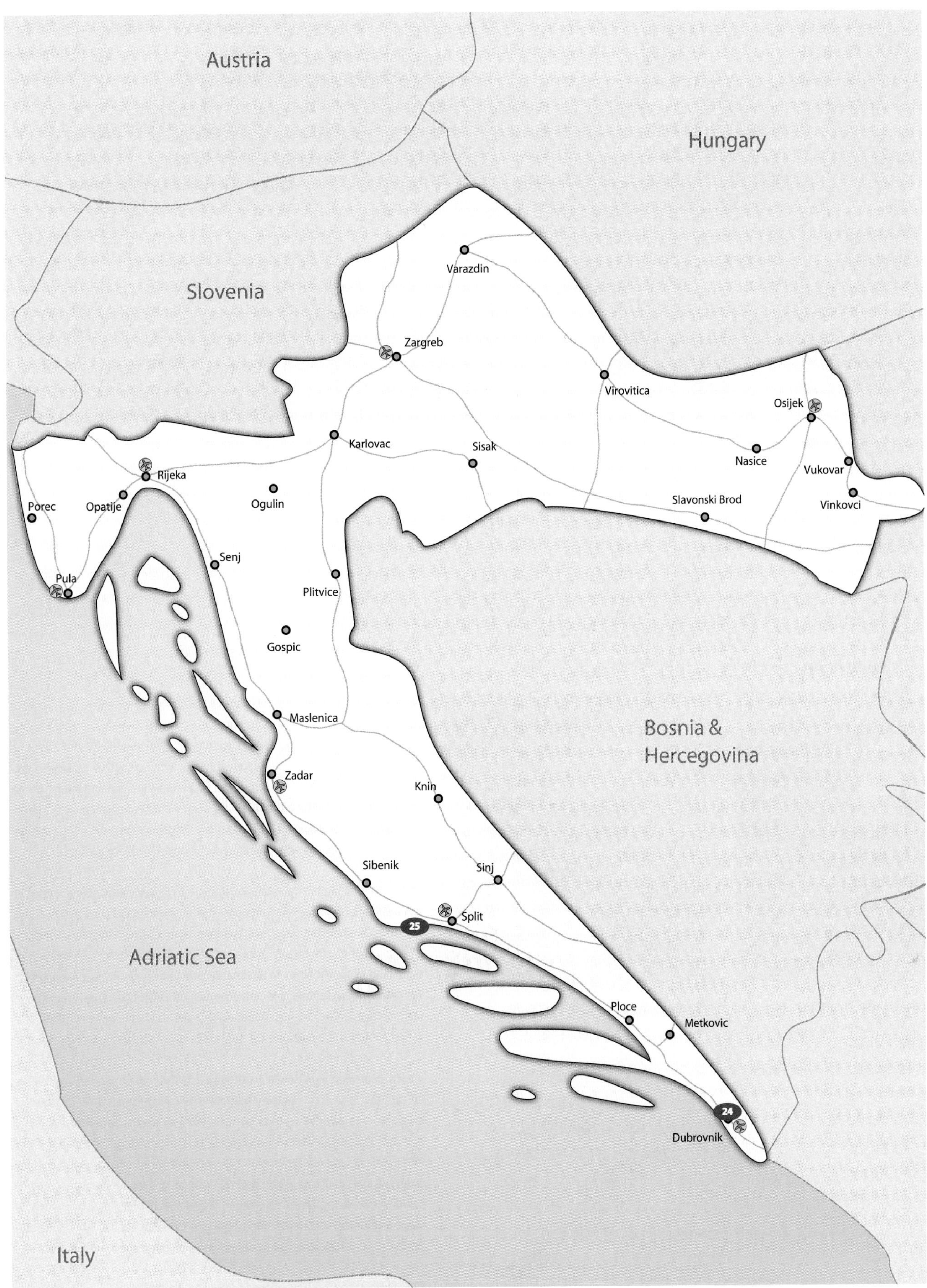

Grand Villa Argentina

FRANA SUPILA 14, 20000 DUBROVNIK, CROATIA

Directions: 20 minutes from Dubrovnik International Airport. Follow city centre > the hotel is signposted.

Web: www.johansens.com/grandvillaargentina
E-mail: sales@gva.hr
Tel: +385 20 44 0555
Fax: +385 20 43 2524

Price Guide: (excluding VAT)
single €160-270
double €180-360
suite €420-520

4 exclusive villas and a hotel comprise this unique property, which reflects the spirit, history and cultural heritage of Dubrovnik. Surrounded by charming terraced gardens, each villa is tastefully appointed; standard guest rooms are spacious, and the sea view rooms look across the gardens to the Island of Lokrum. The restaurants serve gourmet Dalmatian and international cuisine, and the Wellness Centre offers health and beauty treatments. Grand Villa Argentina is the ideal place to discover the old city, only a 10-minute walk away. Versatile congress and banqueting facilities are available.

Cette propriété unique qui reflète parfaitement l'héritage spirituel, historique et culturel de Dubrovnik, est composée de 4 villas exclusives et d'un hôtel. Entourées de charmants jardins en terrasses, chaque villa est décorée avec goût. Les chambres standard sont spacieuses, et les chambres côté mer offrent des vues allant du jardin à l'île de Lokrum. Les restaurants servent cuisine gourmet dalmate et internationale et le centre de bien-être offre des soins de santé et de beauté. C'est l'endroit idéal pour découvrir la vieille ville, seulement à 10 minutes a pied. L'interieur de salons de banquets et réunions s'adapte selon vos besoins.

4 exclusivas villas y un hotel constituyen esta singular propiedad, que refleja el espíritu, historia y patrimonio cultural de Dubrovnik. Rodeadas de encantadores jardines en terraza, cada villa está decorada con sumo gusto. Las habitaciones estándar son amplias, y las con vista al mar admiran los jardines y la Isla de Lokrum. Los restaurantes sirven cocina gourmet internacional y Dalmata, y el centro de wellness proporciona tratamientos de salud y de belleza. Grand Villa Argentina es el lugar ideal para descubrir la ciudad antigua, a sólo 10 minutos a pie de distancia. El hotel dispone también de instalaciones polivalentes para congresos y banquetes.

Our inspector loved: *The romantic ambience in Villa Orsula.*

Villa Lavandula

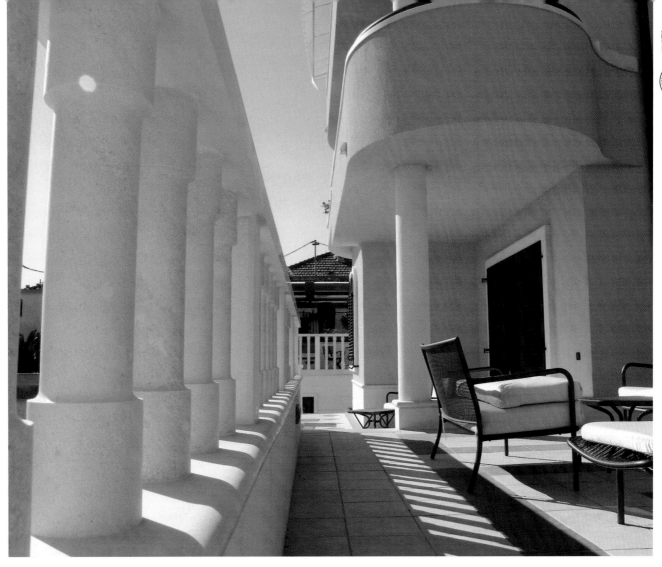

PUT SALDUNA 3, 21220 TROGIR, CROATIA

This delightful, pastel coloured modern villa, with a hillside backdrop of deep green woodland, stands in a residential area in the western part of the islet of Ciova. 50 metres from a sun trap beach and a short walk from the World Heritage medieval town of Trogir, it is a cool and welcoming guest house of elegance, good taste and excellent, traditional dining. The accommodation is bright and stylishly furnished with every facility from a fully-fitted kitchen to air conditioning.

Cette ravissante villa moderne dans les tons pastel, avec en toile de fond un coteau boisé verdoyant, se dresse dans un quartier résidentiel de la partie occidentale de l'île de Ciovo. A 50 mètres d'une plage ensoleillée et à quelques minutes de la ville médiévale de Trogir, Patrimoine Mondial, c'est une maison d'hôtes accueillante, élégante, de bon goût et ou l'on sert une excellente cuisine traditionnelle. L'hébergement est clair et meublé avec style avec tous les équipements allant de la cuisine entièrement équipée à la climatisation.

Esta deliciosa y moderna villa de color pastel al fondo de la cual puede verse una colina de verde bosque se encuentra en una zona residencial del oeste del islote de Ciova. A 50 metros de una soleada playa bien resguardada del viento y la corta distancia que la separan andando de la ciudad medieval de Trogir, nombrada Patrimonio de la Humanidad, Villa Lavandula resulta ser un hotel elegante, tranquilo y acogedor, de excelente cocina tradicional. El alojamiento derrocha luz y está amueblado con gran estilo. Cuenta con todas las comodidades, desde una cocina completamente equipada hasta aire acondicionado.

Our inspector loved: *The delightful dinner, chosen with the aid of the owner's knowledge of the freshly caught fish from the market of Trogir.*

Directions: The nearest airport is Split. The hotel has a garage for guests.

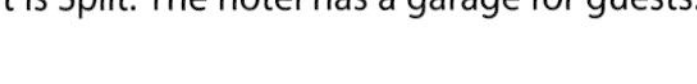

Web: www.johansens.com/lavandula
E-mail: villa@villalavandula.com
Tel: +385 21 798 330
Fax: +385 21 798 331

Price Guide:
double €135-195
suite €185-235

Czech Republic (Prague)

Hotel location shown in red (hotel) or purple (spa hotel) with page number

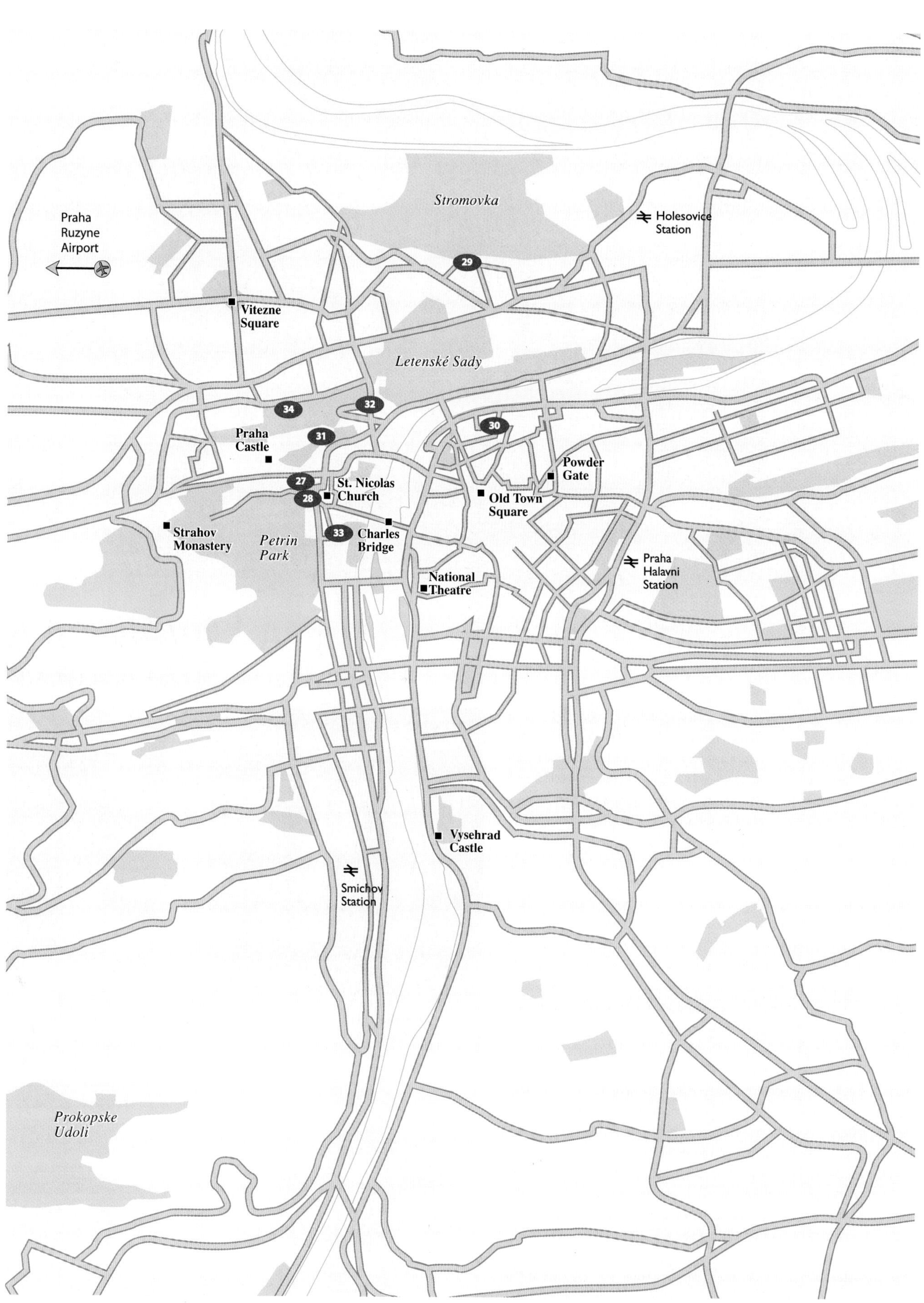

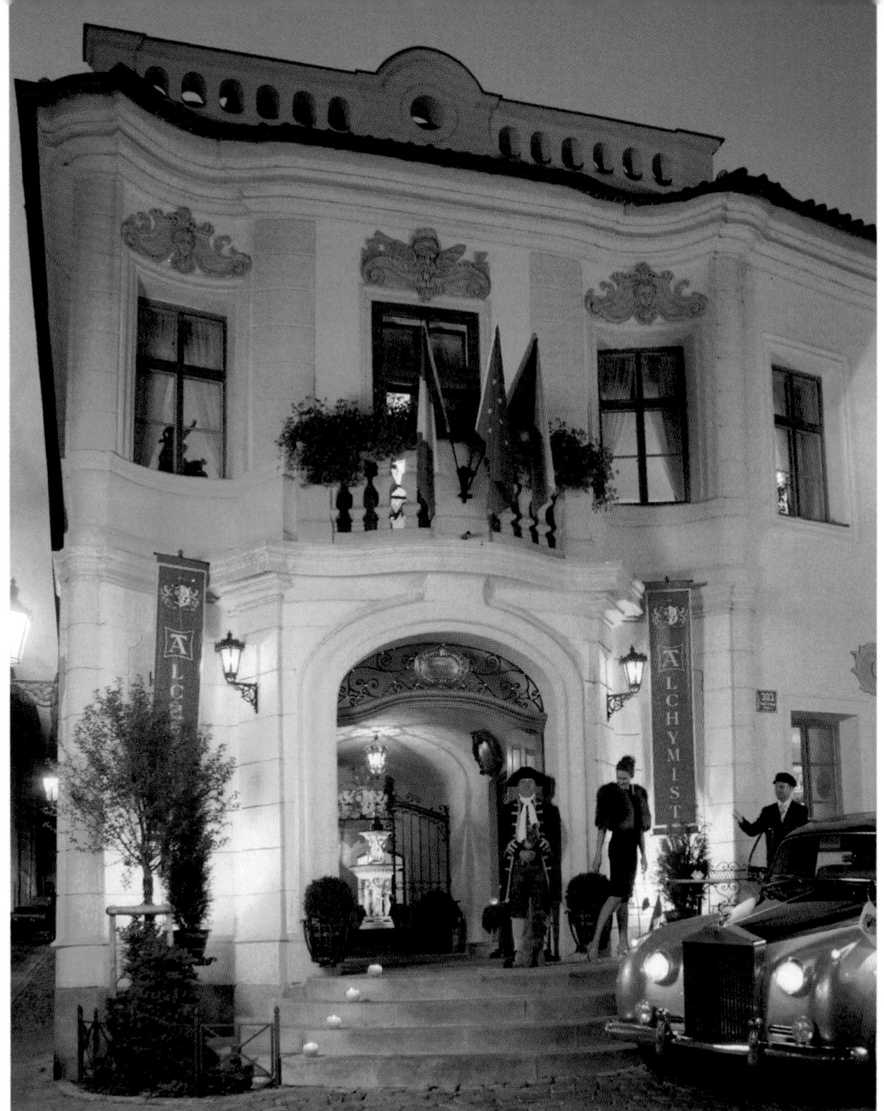

ALCHYMIST GRAND HOTEL AND SPA

TRZISTE 19, MALÁ STRANA, 11800 PRAGUE, CZECH REPUBLIC

This intimate retreat, in the heart of Malá Strana, is minutes from Charles Bridge and Prague Castle. The interior emulates Italian chic and the Renaissance frescoes and vaulted ceilings exude romance. Bedrooms cleverly combine modern luxuries such as plasma TVs and DVD players alongside 19th-century paintings and exquisite sculptures. Café Barocco Veneziano is an ideal location to meet before taking dinner in the hotel's restaurant, which serves an Italian-European menu. Ecsotica Spa and Sushi Bar is now open.

Cette adresse intime, au coeur de Malá Strana, n'est qu'à quelques minutes du Pont Charles et du Château de Prague. L'intérieur respire le chic italien, les fresques de la Renaissance et les plafonds voûtés inspire la romance. Les chambres mélangent le confort moderne, tels qu'écrans plasma et lecteurs DVD, et les superbes sculptures et peintures du XIXe siècle. Le Café Barocco Veneziano est l'endroit idéal pour se retrouver avant de dîner au restaurant et servira une cuisine italo-européenne. Le Spa Ecsotica et le Bar à Suschi sont dorénavant ouverts.

Este íntimo refugio, sito en el corazón de Malá Strana, está a sólo unos minutos del Puente Carlos y del Castillo de Praga. Su interior emula el chic italiano y los frescos renacentistas y sus techos abovedados emanan romanticismo. Sus habitaciones combinan los lujos modernos tales como la televisión de plasma y los equipos de DVD con los lienzos y las refinadas esculturas del siglo XIX. El Café Barocco Veneziano es el lugar ideal para reunirse antes de cenar en el restaurante el cual le podrá servir su carta italiana-europea. El hotel cuenta ahora también con el Spa Exótica y Sushi Bar.

Our inspector loved: *The traditional and relaxing Malaysian treatment in the spa.*

Directions: In the heart of Malá Strana beneath the Old Castle Hradcany, the historic centre of Prague.

Web: www.johansens.com/alchymist
E-mail: info@alchymisthotel.com
Tel: +420 257 286 011/016
Fax: +420 257 286 017

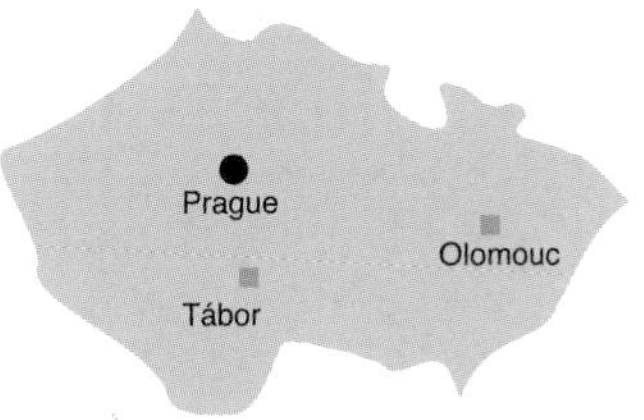

Price Guide:
de luxe suite €240-280
junior suite €340-420
1 or 2-bedroom suite €750-1,100

Aria Hotel Prague

TRZISTE 9, 118 00 PRAGUE 1, CZECH REPUBLIC

Directions: A transfer to and from the airport is complimentary to guests.

Web: www.johansens.com/aria
E-mail: stay@aria.cz
Tel: +420 225 334 111
Fax: +420 225 334 666

Price Guide: (excluding VAT,
a 27-place garage is at guests' disposal)
single €205-360
double €235-360
suite €450-1,200

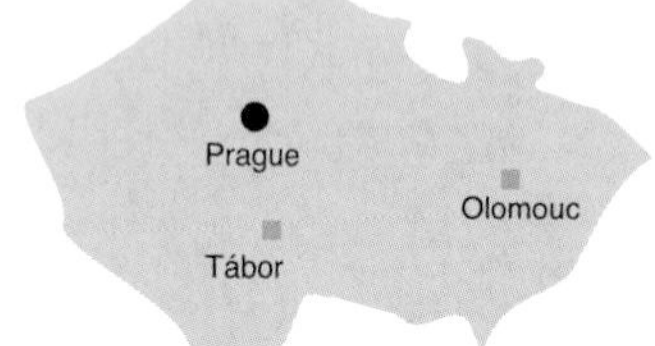

Enjoy the sense of space and tranquillity in this delightful hotel located minutes from Charles Bridge and Prague Castle. Decorated by Italian designers Rocco Magnoli and Lorenzo Carmelini, each floor represents a style of music, and each guest room is devoted to a musician or composer. Relax by the fire in the Winter Garden, with its grand piano and water feature, or on the rooftop terrace with bird's eye view of the city. A fully-equipped business centre is available.

Appréciez ce sentiment d'espace et de tranquillité dans ce charmant hôtel quelques minutes du Pont Charles et du château de Prague. Décoré par les designers italiens Rocco Magnoli et Lorenzo Carmelini, chaque étage est consacré à un genre de musique et chaque chambre d'hôte honore un musicien ou un compositeur. Relaxez vous auprès du feu dans le Jardin d'Hiver, avec son grand piano à queue et sa fontaine ou sur la terrasse sur le toit, qui offre une vue panoramique sur la ville. Un centre d'affaire tout équipé est disponible.

Disfrute de la sensación de espacio y tranquilidad que se respira en este encantador hotel, situado a pocos minutos de Charles Bridge y el Castillo de Praga. Decorado por los diseñadotes italianos Rocco Magnoli y Lorenzo Carmelini, cada piso representa un estilo de música y todas las habitaciones están dedicadas a un músico o compositor. Descanse al lado de la chimeneo en el Jardín de Invierno, con su piano de cola, y fuente de agua, o en la terraza del ultimo piso, para disfrutar de vistas de pájaro sobre la ciudad. El hotel también dispone de un centro de negocios totalmente equipado.

Our inspector loved: *The Music Library for after-dinner drinks.*

Art Hotel Prague

NAD KRÁLOVSKOU OBOROU 53, 170 00 PRAGUE 7, CZECH REPUBLIC

2 famous artists, Jan and Pravoslav Kotik, provided the inspiration for this artistic hotel, which is located only a 10-minute walk from the city centre. The hotel was recently designed and built by the architect Martin Kotik, ensuring that its long artistic tradition is kept within this well-known family, but made available to guests. Each floor of the 6-storey building presents a thematic mini collection of works by the Kotiks, as well as Pavel Stecha, famous for photographs of architectural detail, and Pavel Roucka, a painter and graphic artist.

2 artistes de renom, Jan et Pravoslav Kotik, sont à l'origine de cet hôtel artistique, situé à quelques minutes à pied du centre ville. L'hôtel à été récemment conçu et construit par l'architecte Martin Kotik, garantissant ainsi que la tradition artistique reste dans cette célèbre famille tout en en faisant profiter les clients. Chaque étage, de cet immeuble de 6 niveaux, présente une mini collection thématique des œuvres des Kotiks ainsi que de Pavel Stecha, photographe reconnu de détails d'architecture, et de Pavel Roucka, un peintre et artiste graphique.

Este artístico hotel a sólo 10 minutos a pie del centro de la ciudad es fruto de la inspiración de los 2 célebres artistas, Jan y Pravoslav Kotik. El hotel, diseñado y construido recientemente por el arquitecto Martin Kotik, da continuidad a la larga tradición artística iniciada por esta conocida familia y al mismo tiempo la pone a disposición de los clientes. En cada una de las 6 plantas del edificio se presenta una mini colección temática de obras de los Kotiks, así como de Pavel Stecha, famoso por sus fotografías de detalles arquitectónicos, y de Pavel Roucka, pintor y artista gráfico.

Our inspector loved: *The newly decorated breakfast area, and the conference facility which opens out to the courtyard.*

Directions: The hotel is 12km from Prague Ruzyne Airport. Travel through Stefanikuv Bridge and tunnel and at the traffic lights on Korunovachi take the fourth street on the left.

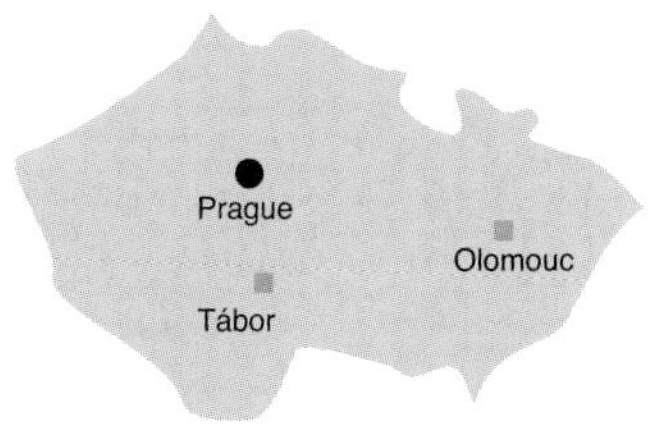

Web: www.johansens.com/arthotel
E-mail: johansens@arthotel.cz
Tel: +420 233 101 331
Fax: +420 233 101 311

Price Guide:
single €100-160
double €120-180
suite €180-215

Bellagio Hotel Prague

U MILOSRDNYCH 2, 110 00 PRAGUE 1, CZECH REPUBLIC

Located in a quiet yet central part of historical Prague, within walking distance of the Old Town Square, the impressive Hotel Bellagio underwent a complete refurbishment in winter 2006. Guest rooms are comfortable and provide every modern convenience. Guests find the convivial staff helpful and courteous, in particular Swedish chef Lars Sjostrand is on hand to fulfil any unique request from gourmet guests!

Situé dans un endroit calme mais accessible de la ville historique de Prague, et seulement à quelques minutes à pied du cœur de la vieille ville, l'impressionnant Hôtel Bellagio a été complètement rénové pendant l'hiver 2006. Les chambres sont confortables et offrent tout l'équipement moderne. Le personnel est convivial, courtois et serviable, en particulier le Chef suédois Lars Sjostrand toujours prêt à répondre à toutes les demandes de ses hôtes gastronomes.

Situado en una zona tranquila pero accesible de la Praga histórica, a escasa distancia a pie de la Plaza del Casco Antiguo, el impresionante Hotel Bellagio ha sido totalmente renovado en el invierno del 2006. Las habitaciones son cómodas y proporcionan todas las modernas instalaciones posibles. Los clientes encontrarán su agradable personal de lo más servicial y cortés, sobre todo al chef sueco Lars Sjostrand, que está a disposición de los huéspedes gourmets que deseen hacer cualquier petición particular.

Our inspector loved: *The friendly and welcoming staff, and the central location of the hotel in the old city centre.*

Directions: Situated in the old city centre, in the old Jewish district between Cechuv and Stefanikuv bridge.

Web: www.johansens.com/bellagio
E-mail: info@bellagiohotel.cz
Tel: +420 221 778 999
Fax: +420 221 778 900

Price Guide:
single €158-208
double €180-232
suite €207-285

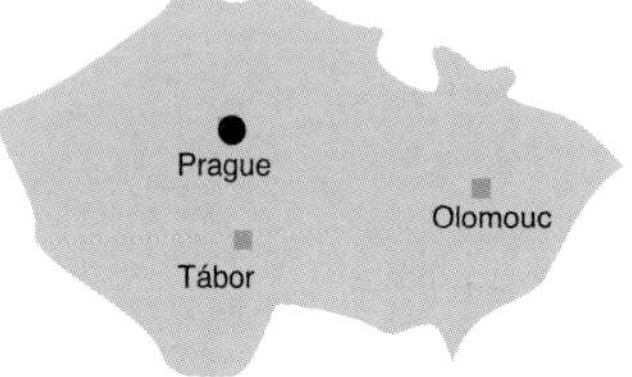

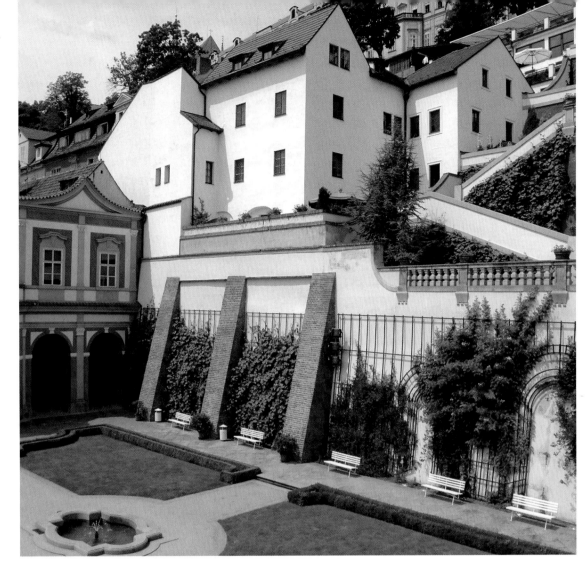

Golden Well Hotel

U Zlaté Studne 166/4, 118 00 Prague 1, Czech Republic

Discretely tucked away in a hidden road below the Castle, this romantic haven offers spectacular views of magical Prague. This 16th-century Renaissance building was originally owned by Emperor Rudolph II, and now comprises 20 guest rooms including 3 suites. Rooms are spacious and look out to the Ledeburg gardens filled with Baroque fountains and the rooftops of the city. The hotel's rooftop restaurant boasts fantastic panoramic views and delicious international cuisine with a French influence.

Discrètement à l'abri dans une rue cachée sous le château, cet havre romantique offre de somptueuses vues sur la ville de Prague. Jadis la propriété de l'Empereur Rudolph II, ce bâtiment Renaissance du XVIe siècle propose aujourd'hui 20 chambres dont 3 suites. Les chambres sont spacieuses et donnent sur les jardins remplis de fontaines de Ledeburg et sur les toîts de la ville. Le restaurant de l'hôtel situé sur le toit offre d'incroyables vues panoramiques et sert une délicieuse cuisine internationale aux accents français.

Discretamente apartado en una carretera escondida bajo el Castillo, este romántico remanso de paz proporciona espectaculares vistas a la mágica Praga. Este edificio renacentista del siglo XVI fue originalmente propiedad del emperador Rodolfo II, y ahora cuenta con 20 habitaciones, entre las que se incluyen 3 suites. Las habitaciones son amplias, tienen vistas a los jardines Ledeburg, repleto de fuentes barrocas, y a los tejados de la ciudad. El restaurante, situado sobre el tejado del hotel, goza de fantásticas vistas panorámicas y una deliciosa carta internacional con influencia francesa.

***Our inspector loved:** The romantic view of Prague lit up at night while tasting exquisite food and wine.*

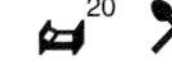

Directions: Located between the Castle and Ledeburg gardens.

Web: www.johansens.com/zlatestudna
E-mail: hotel@zlatastudna.cz
Tel: +420 257 011 213
Fax: +420 257 533 320

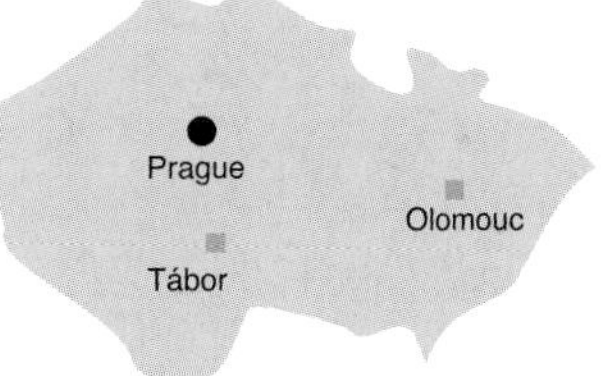

Price Guide: (excluding VAT)
single €175-245
double €175-245
suite €295-385

Hotel Hoffmeister & Lily Wellness and Spa

POD BRUSKOU 7, MALÁ STRANA, 11800 PRAGUE 1, CZECH REPUBLIC

This charming hotel has recently undergone extensive refurbishment. Great thought has been paid to 3 superbly designed new suites, furnished with beautiful antique effects and situated in a medieval house opposite the main building. The original restaurant has been divided in 2 and replaced by a coffee lounge, ideal for light lunches, and an elegant dining room, complete with Bohemian crystal glassware. Guests can take advantage of the relaxing spa, which incorporates the walls of ancient Prague in its design.

Cet hôtel de charme vient juste d'être entièrement rénové. Une attention toute particulière à été portée au design des 3 magnifiques nouvelles suites, meublées avec de superbes antiquités et situées dans une maison médiévale en face du bâtiment principal. Le restaurant d'origine a été séparé en 2 et remplacé par un café lounge, idéal pour les déjeuners légers, et par une salle à manger très élégante avec un service en cristal de Bohême. Les hôtes peuvent profiter du spa, qui comprend, dans sa conception, les murs de l'ancien Prague.

Este encantador hotel ha sido ampliamente renovado en fecha reciente. Se ha puesto gran esmero en sus 3 nuevas suites de magnífico diseño. Están provistas de bellas piezas de anticuario y ubicadas en una casa medieval frente al edificio principal. El restaurante original se ha dividido en 2 partes, un café lounge, ideal para un almuerzo ligero, y un elegante comedor complementado con servicio en cristal de Bohemia. Los clientes pueden disfrutar del relajante balneario, el cual incorpora a su diseño las murallas de la Praga antigua.

Our inspector loved: *The Lily Wellness and Spa, and the new luxurious apartments opposite the main building with their extraordinary bathrooms.*

Directions: The hotel is situated between Mánesu bridge and Prague castle.

Web: www.johansens.com/hoffmeister
E-mail: hotel@hoffmeister.cz
Tel: +420 251 017 111
Fax: +420 251 017 120

Price Guide:
single €170-260
double/twin €200-350
suite €290-600

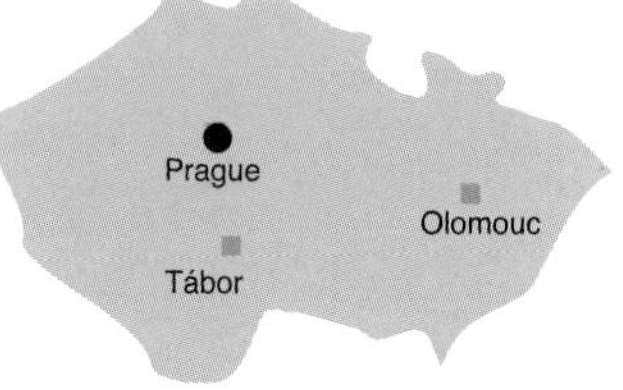

SPA

Nosticova Residence

NOSTICOVA 1, MALÁ STRANA, 11800 PRAGUE, CZECH REPUBLIC

Providing complete privacy within the heart of Prague, Nosticova Residence stands in Mala Strana, 2 minutes from Charles Bridge. Warm, inviting décor features Central European furnishings and beautiful paintings. Careful consideration has been taken to adorn each apartment with art that reflects their individual styles. Each has a fully-equipped kitchen, WiFi, and a full range of services such as baby-sitting and room service is available. A Continental menu with a Italian influence is served in the unique Alchymist Restaurant.

Offrant une intimité totale au cœur de Prague, la Résidence Nosticova se situe sur Mala Strana, à 2 minutes du Pont Charles. La décoration chaleureuse et accueillante met en avant de superbes meubles d'Europe Centrale et de magnifiques tableaux. Chaque appartement a été soigneusement décoré d'arts reflétant son style. Tous ont une cuisine complètement équipée, WiFi et de nombreux services tels que baby-sitting et room service sont disponibles. Une carte continentale aux influences françaises est servie à l'Alchymist Restaurant.

Situada en Mala Strana, a 2 minutos del Puente Charles, Nosticova Residence le proporciona absoluta intimidad en pleno corazón de Praga. Su acogedor y cálido ambiente se lo proporcionan los muebles y bellos lienzos centroeuropeos. Especial cuidado se ha prestado a los adornos de cada apartamento, de individual estilo artístico. Cada apartamento dispone de cocina totalmente equipada, de WiFi, así como de una amplia variedad de servicios tales como cuidado de niños pequeños y servicio de habitación. Su carta continental de influencia francesa se sirve en el singular Alchymist Restaurant.

Our inspector loved: *The pan-fried scallops with fresh spinach and carrots prepared by Master Chef Fulvio Lanuti.*

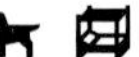

Directions: Prague Airport > Malá Strana > Karmelitska Street > Harantova > Nebovidska > Nosticova.

Web: www.johansens.com/nosticova
E-mail: info@nosticova.com
Tel: +420 257 312 513/516
Fax: +420 257 312 517

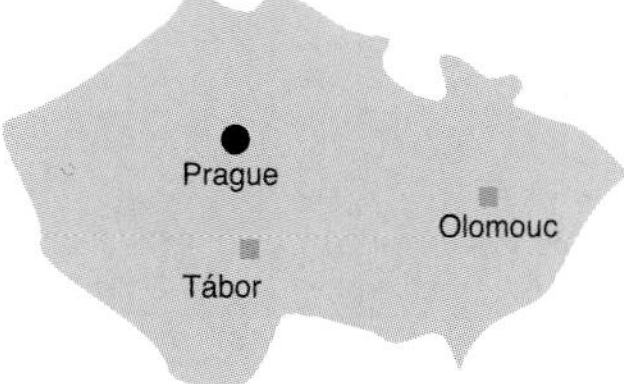

Price Guide:
standard suite €215-245
luxury suite €285-565

Romantik Hotel U Raka

CERNÍNSKÁ 10/93, 11800 PRAGUE 1, CZECH REPUBLIC

Located on the castle hill in the Hradcany area, this enchanting hotel in the centre of Prague is an oasis of peace and seclusion – the ideal place for those who wish to escape the hustle and bustle of modern life, withdraw with a book and discover the city on a leisurely walk. With its cosy bedrooms and warming fireplaces, the atmosphere is more that of a private home than a hotel. The hotel serves snacks and drinks, whilst for dinner, guests will find numerous restaurants in the vicinity.

Situé sur la colline du château dans le quartier de Hradcany, cet hôtel enchanteur du centre de Prague est un havre de paix et d'isolement – l'endroit idéal pour ceux qui veulent échapper au tourbillon de la vie moderne, se retirer avec un livre et découvrir la ville au rythme d'une promenade. Avec ses chambres douillettes et de chaleureux coins cheminée, l'atmosphère ressemble plus à celle d'une maison privée que d'un hôtel. L'hôtel sert des en-cas et boissons, alors que pour le dîner les hôtes pourront faire leur choix parmi les nombreux restaurants du voisinage.

Situado en la colina del castillo dentro de la región de Hradcany, este encantador hotel del centro de Praga constituye un apartado oasis de paz, el lugar ideal para quienes desean dejar atrás el ajetreo de la vida moderna, disfrutar a solas de un buen libro y descubrir la ciudad paseando tranquilamente. La calidez de sus habitaciones y chimeneas hacen que el ambiente sea más propio de un hogar que de un hotel. Este hotel sirve aperitivos y bebidas. Los clientes que deseen cenar podrán hacerlo en los numerosos restaurantes de los alrededores.

Our inspector loved: *Enjoying a Czech beer in the flower-filled, quiet garden.*

Directions: In the centre of Prague's Castle area, near Loretta.

Web: www.johansens.com/uraka
E-mail: info@romantikhotel-uraka.cz
Tel: +420 2205 111 00
Fax: +420 2333 580 41

Price Guide:
single €160-190
classic double €180-220
superior €180-240
triple bed €190-240
superior luxury €220-260

Estonia

Hotel location shown in red (hotel) or purple (spa hotel) with page number

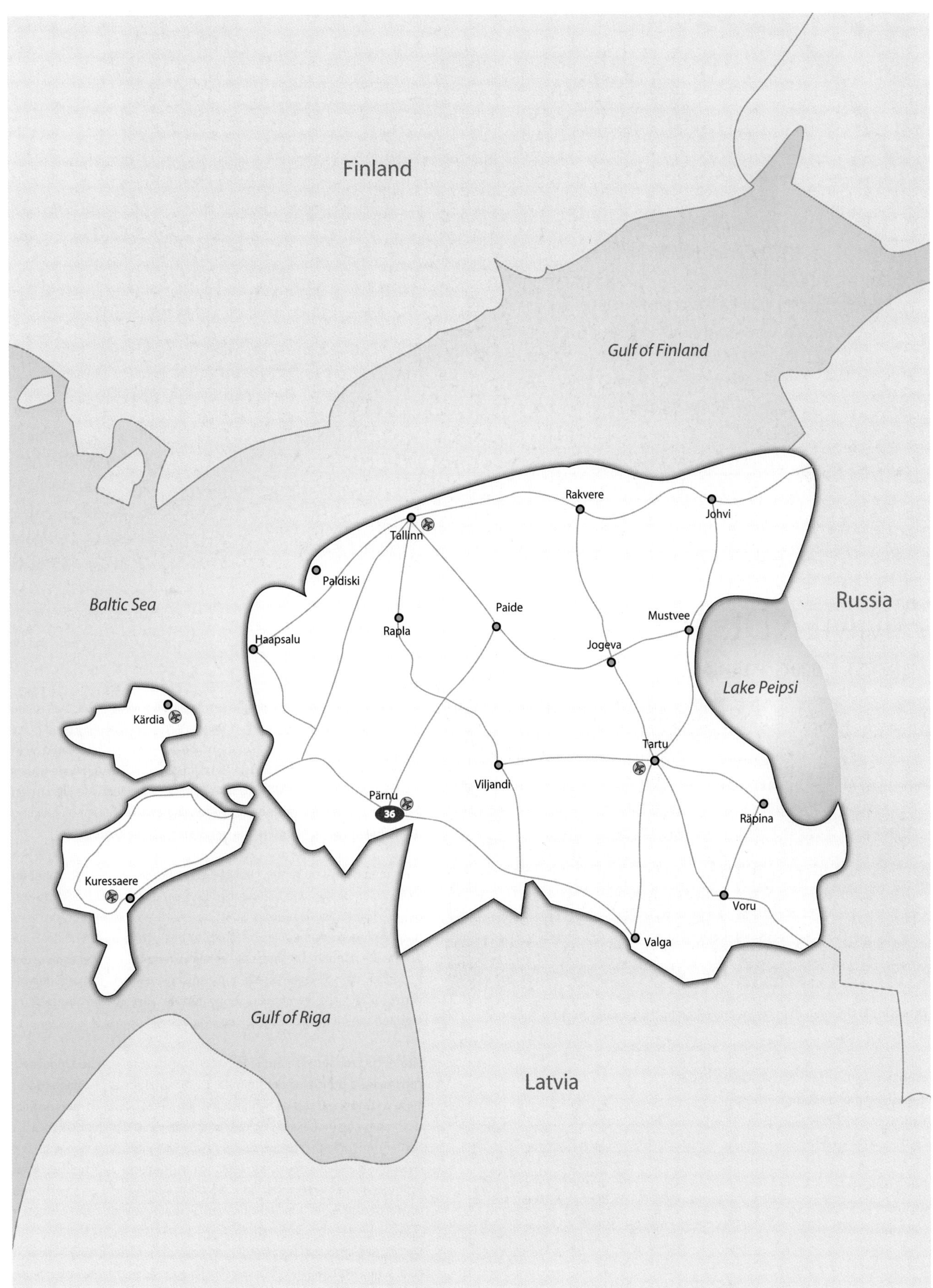

Ammende Villa

MERE PST 7, 80010 PÄRNU, ESTONIA

Directions: On main road between Tallinn and Riga. 2 hours from Tallinn, 3 hours from Riga.

Web: www.johansens.com/villaammende
E-mail: ammende@ammende.ee
Tel: +372 44 73 888
Fax: +372 44 73 887

Price Guide:
de luxe €135–225
suite €212–500

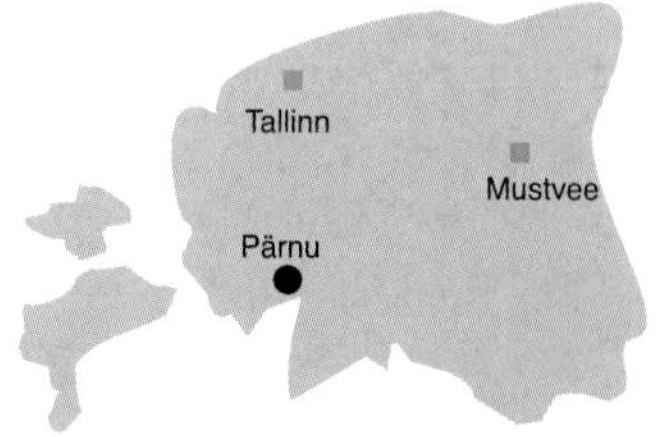

Set in a romantic park close to the sea, this art nouveau hotel, built at the beginning of the 20th century, is Estonia's most fascinating building of its kind. All bedrooms are suites or de luxe rooms decorated with restored original furniture and period details. The Suite Ammende boasts a sauna and whirlpool bath. Guests can enjoy French and Mediterranean cuisine accompanied by fine Old World wines in the elegant blue dining room, the green "wine room" or the crimson "hunting room".

Dans un pareprès de la mer, cet hôtel art nouveau construit au début du XXe siècle, est l'un des bâtiments d'Estonie les plus fascinants de son genre. Toutes les chambres sont des suites ou chambres de luxe, décorées avec des meubles restaurés et des détails d'époque. La Suite Ammende contient un sauna et un bain à remous. Les invités peuvent apprécier, dans l'élégante salle à manger bleue, dans la "salle de vin" verte ou la "salle de chasse" rouge foncée, une cuisine française et méditerranéenne accompagnée de vins fins.

Sito en un romántico parque cercano al mar, este hotel art nouveau, construido a principios del siglo XX, es el edificio más fascinante de su clase en Estonia. Todas las habitaciones son suites o habitaciones de lujo, decoradas con mobiliario original restaurado y con detalles de época. La Suite Ammende dispone de sauna y baño con efectos de remolino. Los clientes pueden degustar la cocina francesa y mediterránea acompañada de excelentes vinos de crianza tradicional en su elegante comedor azul, en la "sala del vino" verde o en la "sala de caza" carmesí.

Our inspector loved: *Savouring a candle-lit dinner after a long walk on a cold, sunny winter's day whilst watching the ice-fishers on the frozen Baltic Sea.*

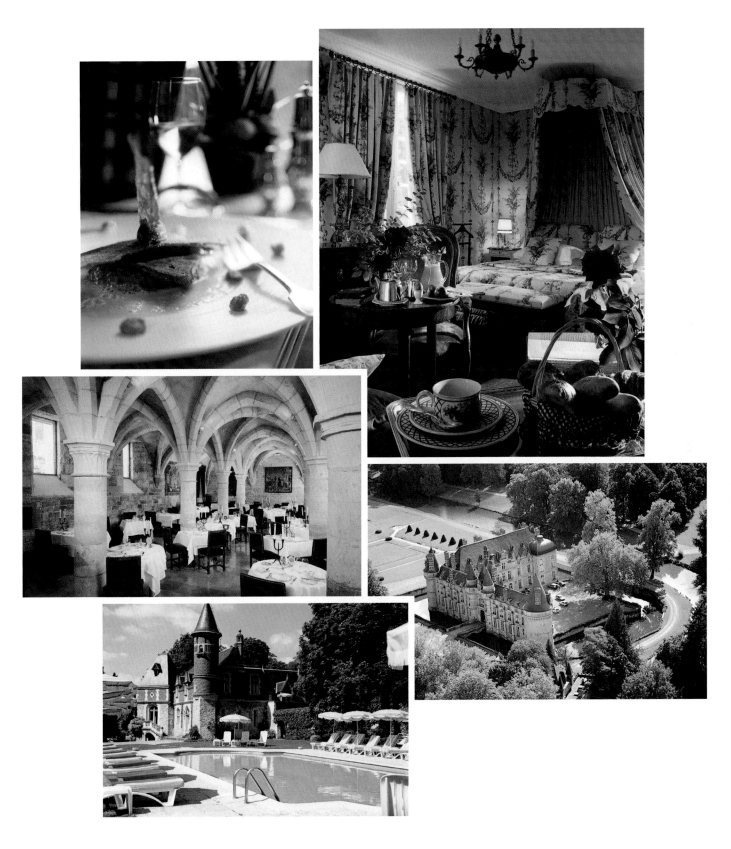

FRANCE

Hotel location shown in red (hotel) or purple (spa hotel) with page number

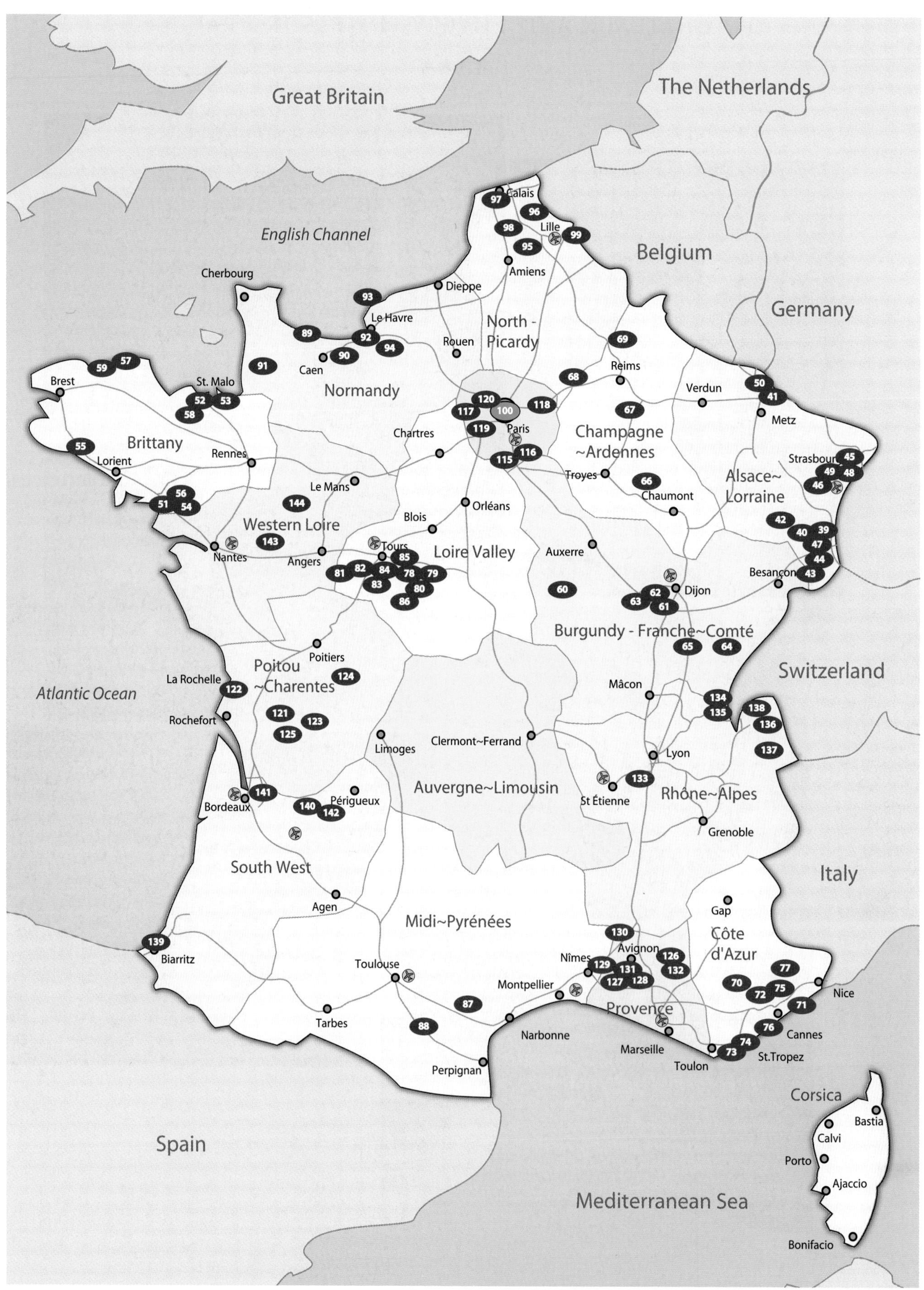

HÔTEL LES TÊTES

19 RUE DES TÊTES, BP 69, 68000 COLMAR, FRANCE

Situated at the heart of this labyrinthine cathedral town, this beautiful Renaissance hotel is truly unique. Covered by 105 grotesque masks, the Baroque theme extends into the interior, where an intimate courtyard allows guests to relax over coffee and cool drinks in summer. The bedrooms, complete with ancient beamed ceilings and attractive stonework, are highly atmospheric. The hotel's welcoming owner, Marc Rohfritsch, prepares sumptuous dishes served under glittering chandeliers in the restaurant La Maison des Têtes.

Situé au coeur de cette ville labyrinthique avec sa cathédrale, ce magnifique hôtel Renaissance est vraiment exceptionnel. Décoré de 105 masques de style grotesque, le thème baroque s'étend à l'intérieur, où une cour intime permet aux clients de se détendre autour d'un café ou de boissons rafraîchissantes en été. Les chambres, avec leurs poutres anciennes et leurs beaux murs en pierre, dégagent une ambiance extraordinaire. L'accueillant maître des lieux, Marc Rohfritsch, prépare de somptueux repas dans son restaurant La Maison des Têtes.

Situado en el corazón de esta ciudad laberinto con catedral, el hermoso hôtel renacentista es verdaderamente único. Cubierto por 105 máscaras grotescas, el tema barroco se extiende también a su interior, donde un íntimo patio permite a los huéspedes relajarse tomando un café o una refrescante bebida en verano. Las habitaciones con techos de vigas antiguas y atractiva piedra proporcionan un ambiente admirable. Marc Rohfritsch, simpático dueño del hôtel, prepara suntuosos platos que se sirven bajo el encanto de los deslumbrantes candelabros en el restaurante La Maison des Têtes.

Our inspector loved: *The courtyard area for a cool summer's drink in the shade.*

Directions: Colmar city centre.

Web: www.johansens.com/lestetes
E-mail: les-tetes@calico.net
Tel: +33 3 89 24 43 43
Fax: +33 3 89 24 58 34

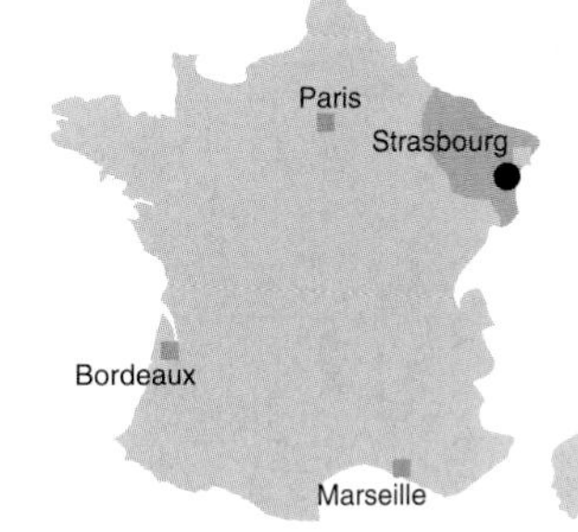

Price Guide: (room only, closed during February)
single €95-168
double/twin €95-168
suite €230

Romantik Hotel le Maréchal

4 PLACE SIX MONTAGNES NOIRES, PETITE VENISE, 68000 COLMAR, FRANCE

Directions: From Strasbourg turn off the highway for Colmar Sud. Then follow the directions to Petite Venise.

Web: www.johansens.com/marechal
E-mail: info@le-marechal.com
Tel: +33 3 89 41 60 32
Fax: +33 3 89 24 59 40

Price Guide: (room only)
single €85–190
double €105–225
suite €255

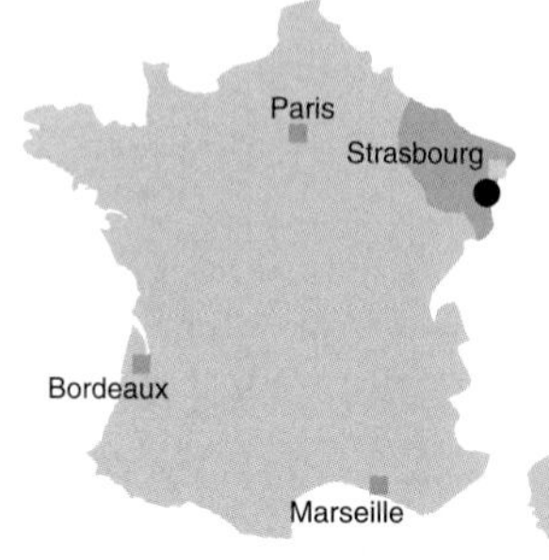

Set beside a canal in Colmar's most beautiful quarter, "Little Venice", this charming house is renowned for its exquisite cuisine, superb Alsatian wines and warm hospitality. After 2 years of renovation, the 4-star hotel now provides 30 delightful bedrooms, all named after famous musicians and equipped with air conditioning, satellite television and comfortable bathrooms. L'Echevin serves Alsatian delicacies by candlelight and classical music. This is the perfect place for a romantic weekend!

Située en bordure d'un canal dans le plus beau quartier de Colmar, "La Petite Venise", cette maison charmante est réputée pour sa cuisine, ses vins alsaciens et sa chaleureuse hospitalité. Après 2 ans de rénovation, cet hôtel 4 étoiles a 30 chambres superbes, qui portent toutes le nom d'un musicien célèbre. Elles possèdent la climatisation, la télévision et par satellite ainsi que des salles de bain confortables. L'Echevin sert les plats fins alsaciens à la lueur des chandelles et au son de la musique classique. L'endroit idéal pour un week-end romantique!

Ubicada junto a un canal en el barrio más bonito de Colmar, "Pequeña Venecia", esta encantadora casa es famosa por su exquisita cocina, destacados vinos alsacianos y sa cálida hospitalidad. Después de 2 años de renovación, este hotel de 4 estrellas ofrece hoy día 30 encantadoras habitaciones, todas ellas denominadas con famosos músicos y equipadas con aire acondicionado, televisión por satélite y cómodos cuartos de bano. L'Echevin sirve delicias alsacianas acompañadas por luz de velas y música clásica. Es el perfecto lugar para pasar un romántico fin de semana.

Our inspector loved: *Taking dinner on the new outdoor waterside terrace.*

Domaine de la Grange de Condé

41 RUE DES DEUX NIED, 57220 CONDÉ NORTHEN, FRANCE

This brand new hotel has been designed with attention to every detail. Spacious rooms have luxurious carpets and opulent solid wood furniture; some have terraces overlooking idyllic landscaped grounds. Outdoor barbecues are extremely popular by the poolside and the hotel's 6 dining rooms serve a wide variety of gastronomic treats. There is a wonderful little spa with Jacuzzi, sauna, hammam and a range of massages.

Ce tout nouvel hôtel a été conçu avec une grande attention du détail. Les chambres spacieuses ont de superbes moquettes et du beau mobilier en bois massif; certaines ont des terrasses surplombant les environs paysagers. Les barbecues près de la piscine sont très appréciés et les 6 salles à manger de l'hôtel offre un large choix de délices gastronomiques. L'hôtel possède également un ravissant petit spa avec jacuzzi, sauna, hammam et un choix de massages.

Es de nueva creación y ha sido diseñado con todo lujo de detalles. Sus espaciosas habitaciones poseen alfombras de calidad y el mobiliario es de opulenta madera sólida, algunas de ellas poseen terrazas con vistas a idílicos paisajes. Las barbacoas al aire libre junto a la piscina son realmente populares y los 6 comedores del hotel sirven gran variedad de delicias gastronómicas. Hay también un maravilloso y pequeño spa con jacuzzi, sauna, hammam y variedad de masajes.

Our inspector loved: *The rotisserie in the restaurant.*

Directions: A4 > exit 38 > turn right after péage to Varize > turn right towards Vaudoncourt > turn right to Condé > hotel is in the village centre. The nearest airports are Metz/Nancy and Luxembourg.

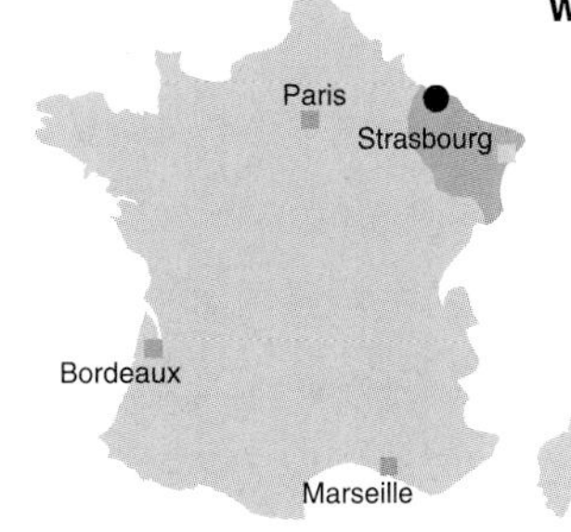

Web: www.johansens.com/grangedeconde
E-mail: lagrangedeconde@wanadoo.fr
Tel: +33 3 87 79 30 50
Fax: +33 3 87 79 30 51

Price Guide: (room only)
single €95
double €95
suite €230-250

Hostellerie les Bas Rupts Le Chalet Fleuri

181 ROUTE DE LA BRESSE, 88400 GÉRARDMER, VOSGES, FRANCE

Close to Lake Gérardmer, in the heart of Les Vosges Mountain region, the Hostellerie and its adjoining Chalet Fleuri is a magical retreat all year round. A homely and welcoming ambience is accompanied by warm hospitality - the bedrooms are comfortable and uniquely attractive, with hand-painted flowers adorning the walls and doors. The succulent dishes, an inspired interpretation of local specialities, are complemented by fine wines and served in the panoramic restaurant. Facilities include an indoor pool, sauna, hammam and fitness rooms.

Tout près du lac de Gérardmer, au coeur des Vosges, l'Hostellerie Les Bas Rupts et son annexe, le Chalet Fleuri, offrent une retraite idyllique tout au long de l'année. L'accueil cordial est complété par une atmosphère intime et chaleureuse - les chambres sont confortables et très jolies, avec des portes et des murs ornés de fleurs peintes à la main. Des plats succulents, une brillante interprétation des spécialités locales, accompagnés de vins exceptionnels sont servis dans le restaurant panoramique. L'hôtel offre une piscine couverte, un sauna, un hammam et des salles de gym.

Situada junto al lago Gérardmer, en el corazón de la región montañosa de Los Vosgos, esta Hostellerie, que cuenta con el chalet aledaño Fleuri, es un mágico y recóndito lugar para el descanso durante todo el año. El ambiente hogareño y acogedor se une a una cálida hospitalidad. Las habitaciones son confortables y de inigualable belleza con flores decorativas pintadas a mano en paredes y puertas. Sus suculentos platos, inspirados con acierto en las especialidades gastronómicas de la zona, se complementan con unos excelentes vinos, todo ello servido en su restaurante de panorámicas vistas. Las instalaciones del hotel incluyen una piscina interior, hammam, sauna y gimnasio.

Our inspector loved: *The new indoor swimming pool*

Directions: Paris > Nancy > Remiremont > Gérardmer.

Web: www.johansens.com/lesbasrupts
E-mail: basrupts@relaischateaux.com
Tel: +33 3 29 63 09 25
Fax: +33 3 29 63 00 40

Price Guide: (room only)
single €140-205
double/twin €140–205
suite €250-500

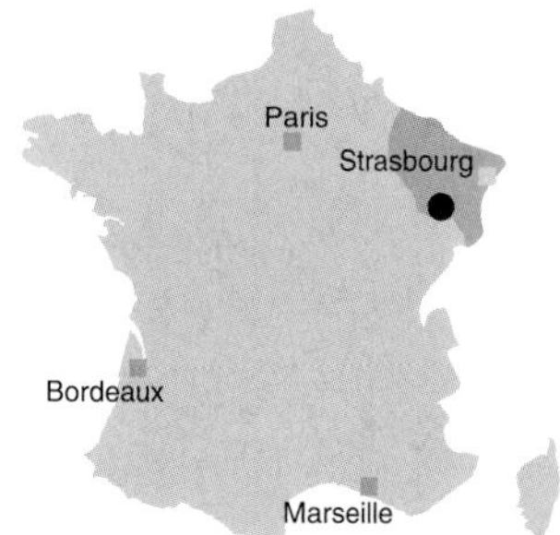

Hostellerie St Barnabé

68530 Murbach – Buhl, Guebwiller, France

The warmest of welcomes and the chance to really get away from it all are offered by this marvellous hostellerie in the heart of the Alsace. Set amidst spectacular forest scenery and beside a meandering mountain stream, each of the charming beamed bedrooms is named after one of the Alsatian grand cru wines. One of the cosy chalets has its own wood-burning stove. The hosts are true professionals and will ensure guests of impeccable service and breathtaking views.

Un accueil des plus chaleureux vous attend dans cette merveilleuse hostellerie alsacienne où vous pourrez vous reposer loin de tout. Construite au milieu d'une magnifique forêt et au bord d'un ruisseau de montagne, elle offre de ravissantes chambres aux poutres apparentes, qui portent toutes des noms de grands crus d'Alsace. Un poêle à bois chauffe l'un des chalets douillets. Les patrons sont de vrais professionnels, qui garantissent aux visiteurs un service impeccable, dont ils peuvent profiter en admirant des vues à couper le souffle.

Esta maravillosa hostellerie situada en el corazón de Alsacia le ofrece una calurosa bienvenida y la oportunidad de escapar de todo. Rodeado de espectaculares bosques y junto a un montañoso arroyo errante, cada una de sus encantadoras habitaciones con vigas recibe el nombre de un vino gran cru de Alsacia. Uno de sus acogedores chalets tiene su propia estufa con troncos. Los dueños son verdaderos profesionales que se preocupan de que sus huéspedes reciban un servicio impecable y disfruten de unas vistas impresionantes.

Our inspector loved: *The views of the wooded hillsides.*

Directions: D429 to Guebwiller > Murbach D429II.

Web: www.johansens.com/stbarnabe
E-mail: hostellerie.st.barnabe@wanadoo.fr
Tel: +33 3 89 62 14 14
Fax: +33 3 89 62 14 15

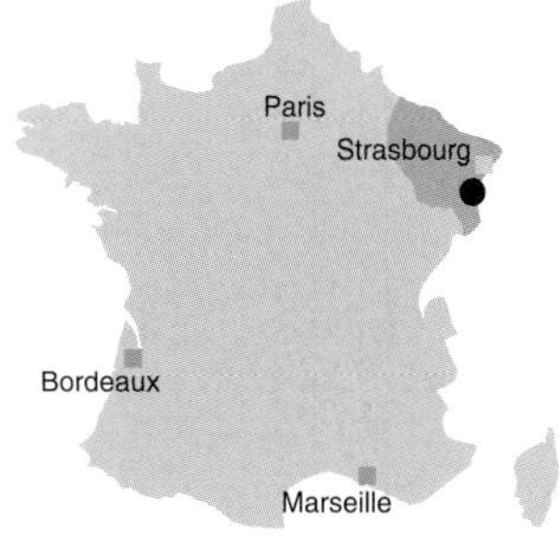

Price Guide: (room only, closed 24th-26th December)
single €95-190
double €95–190

27

Romantik Hotel les Violettes

THIERENBACH, BP 69, 68500 JUNGHOLTZ, FRANCE

This stunning newly built mountain chalet hotel could have existed for centuries. Bedrooms feature rich colours and furnishings, romantic bathrooms and ready-to-light log fires. In the Honeymoon Suite a ceiling mounted mirror appears at the flick of a button! The lounge and first dining room are wood clad and cosy, whilst the second dining room is a veranda, which gives beautiful views across the mountains and valley.

Ce superbe hôtel-chalet de montagne tout neuf pourrait avoir été là depuis des siècles. Les chambres présentent des couleurs riches, des salles de bain romantiques et des feux de bois prêts à allumer. Dans la suite Lune de Miel, un miroir au plafond apparaît sur simple pression d'un interrupteur! Le salon et la première salle à manger en lambris sont douillets, alors que la seconde salle à manger est une véranda qui offre de fantastiques vues sur la montagne et la vallée.

Este sorprendente hôtel chalet de montaña recientemente construido podía haber existido durante siglos. En las habitaciones destacan sus ricos colores y su mobiliario, sus románticos cuartos de baño y sus chimeneas de leña listas para ser encendidas. En la suite Luna de Miel, un espejo montado en el techo aparece ¡con el simple toque de un botón! El salón y el primer comedor son acogedores y están recubiertos de madera, mientras que el segundo comedor es una terraza, desde donde se pueden observar maravillosas vistas a través de montañas y valle.

Our inspector loved: *The incredibly romantic atmosphere.*

Directions: Mulhouse Basel Airport > D430 > exit 3 towards Guebwiller > Soultz > Jungholtz > Thierenbach > left after the church.

Web: www.johansens.com/lesviolettes
E-mail: lesviolettes2@wanadoo.fr
Tel: +33 3 89 76 91 19
Fax: +33 3 89 74 29 12

Price Guide: (room only)
single €150-195
double €150-195
suite €210-300

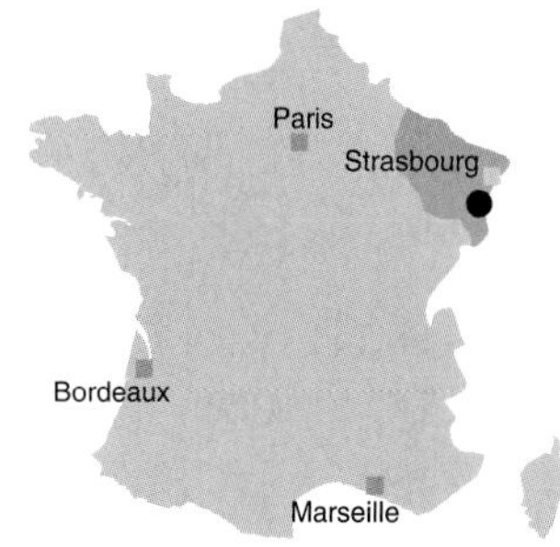

9 500

Romantik Hotel Relais de la Poste

21 RUE DU GÉNÉRAL~DE~GAULLE, 67610 LA WANTZENAU, FRANCE

This former post office in the heart of La Wantzenau village is the height of Alsace charm. With low beamed ceilings and carved wood furnishings, this cosy retreat is a delight for tourists wishing to discover the surrounding countryside. Chef proprietor Jerome Daull's warm welcome ensures that guests in this 18-bedroomed property are treated to home comforts and fine dining in the Michelin-starred restaurant. The slopes of the Vosges are nearby whilst Strasbourg and its magnificent architecture provides a perfect day trip.

Cet ancien relais de poste situé au cœur du village de La Wantzenau, est un excellent représentant du charme alsacien. Avec ses poutres basses et son mobilier en bois sculpté, cette retraite est un ravissement pour les touristes souhaitant découvrir la campagne environnante. Grâce à l'accueil chaleureux du chef et propriétaire Jérôme Daull, les hôtes de cette demeure sont assurés de bénéficier du meilleur confort et d'une excellente table au restaurant étoilé Michelin. Les pentes des Vosges sont toutes proches alors que Strasbourg et son architecture magnifique propose des sorties idéales pour la journée.

Situado en el corazón del pueblo de La Wantzenau, fue anteriormente la oficina de correos y hoy representa la cima del encanto alsaciano. Con sus techos bajos de vigas y muebles de madera tallada, este acogedor refugio es un deleite para los turistas que deseen descubrir el paisaje circundante. Jérome Daull chef y dueño en su cálida acogida se asegura de que los huéspedes de sus 18 habitaciones son tratados como si estuviesen en su casa y disfrutan de una excelente cena en el restaurante galardonado con una estrella Michelin. Cercanos al hotel encontrará las laderas de los Vosges y Estrasburgo con su magnífica arquitectura, lugar perfecto para pasar un día.

Our inspector loved: *The cosy chalet-like bedrooms.*

Directions: The nearest airport is Strasbourg. A4 > A35 from Strasbourg > exit 49 Reichstett > village centre.

Web: www.johansens.com/relaisposte
E-mail: info@relais-poste.com
Tel: +33 3 88 59 24 80
Fax: +33 3 88 59 24 89

Price Guide:
(room only, closed 2nd - 21st January)
single €80-90
double €80-130
suite €135

Hotel à la Cour d'Alsace

3 RUE DE GAIL, 67210 OBERNAI, FRANCE

Within the medieval old town of Obernai, 23 carefully restored houses surround a central courtyard to create this unique hotel. Light and airy guest rooms feature original beamed ceilings and overlook the courtyard or garden. Traditional Alsatian cuisine is served in the hotel's restaurants whilst dinner may be enjoyed in the garden during the summer. This is an ideal base from which to explore Alsace and its vineyards; alternatively the hotel's wine tavern boasts many regional specialities to sample.

Situé dans la ville médiévale d'Obernai, 23 maisons rénovées avec le plus grand soin entourent une cour centrale afin de créer cet hôtel unique. Les chambres claires et spacieuses aux poutres originales apparentes donnent sur la cour ou sur le jardin. Une cuisine traditionnelle alsacienne est servie dans les restaurants et le dîner peut-être servi dans le jardin en été. Cet hôtel est une base idéale pour explorer l'Alsace et ses vignes. La taverne de l'hôtel propose de nombreux vins régionaux à déguster.

Dentro del antiguo pueblo medieval de Obernai, 23 casas restauradas cuidadosamente rodean un patio central para crear este hôtel único. Las habitaciones luminosas y espaciosas en las que destacan techos con vigas que dan al patio o al jardín. Los restaurantes del hôtel sirven cocina tradicional alsaciana y en verano se puede cenar en el jardín. Es base ideal para explorar Alsacia y sus viñedos; alternativamente la vinoteca del hôtel ofrece muchas especialidades regionales para degustar.

Our inspector loved: *The feeling of being in a private village.*

Directions: A35 > exit 11 > Obernai town centre > top of the town. The nearest airport is Strasbourg.

Web: www.johansens.com/couralsace
E-mail: info@cour-alsace.com
Tel: +33 3 88 95 07 00
Fax: +33 3 88 95 19 21

Price Guide: (room only, closed 24th December - 25th January)
single €109-132
double €123-179
suite €273

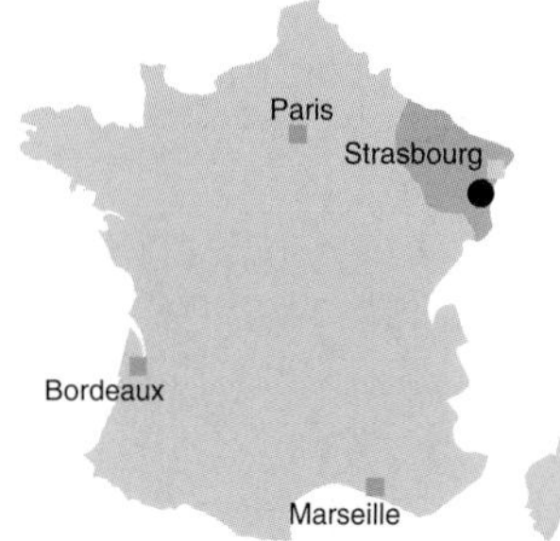

40 140

Château d'Isenbourg

68250 Rouffach, France

Peace, comfort, luxury, discreet charm and attentive service are the hallmarks of this imposing, hillside château-hotel overlooking colourful gardens, vineyards at the foot of the Vosges forest, the Rhine Valley and Black Forest. Built on 12th and 14th-century cellars d'Isenbourg is a superb historical and gourmet retreat on the Alsace wine route. Its restaurant is famed, its bedrooms elegantly spacious and leisure facilities are excellent.

Paix, confort, charme discret et service attentif sont les marques de cet imposant château-hôtel, posé sur les coteaux et surplombant des jardins colorés et des vignobles derrière les contreforts des Vosges, en face du Rhin et de la Forêt Noire. Construit sur les celliers d'Isenbourg datant des XIIe et XIVe siècles, c'est une superbe halte historique et gastronomique sur la route des vins d'Alsace. Son restaurant est connu des gastronomes, ses chambres élégantes sont spacieuses et ses équipements de loisirs sont excellents.

Paz, confort, lujo, encanto discreto y servicio esmerado son los sellos distintivos de este château-hotel situado en la ladera de una colina desde donde se divisan coloridos jardines y viñedos hacia el bosque Vosges, y vistas al valle del Rhine y la Selva Negra. Construido entre los siglos XII y XIV en las bodegas de Isenbourg es un excelente refugio histórico y gastronómico- en la ruta vinícola de Alsacia. Su restaurante goza de una gran fama, sus habitaciones son elegantemente espaciosas y sus instalaciones del ocio son excelentes.

Our inspector loved: *Taking lunch on the lawn overlooking the vineyards.*

Directions: A35 > exit Colmar.

Web: www.johansens.com/isenbourg
E-mail: isenbourg@grandesetapes.fr
Tel: +33 3 89 78 58 50
Fax: +33 3 89 78 53 70

Price Guide: (room only)
single €118–380
double €118–380
suite €422–545

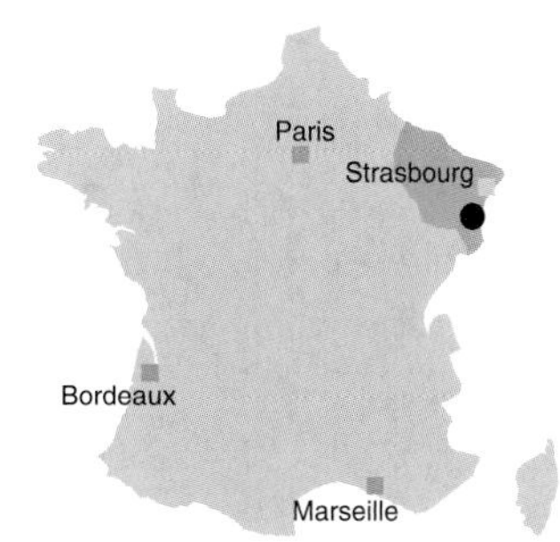

41 200 SPA

Château de L'Ile

4 QUAI HEYDT, 67540 STRASBOURG - OSTWALD, FRANCE

Here is total luxury and absolute quality. Nestling in 10 acres of parkland in a loop of the river Ill, this gorgeous château is elegant and spacious while at the same time being intimate and cosy. Individually decorated guest rooms with their refined bathrooms and air conditioning, some with balconies, are simply a dream. Diners enjoy views over river and woods. Spa treatments are available by arrangement. There is a large spa.

Tout ici est synonyme de luxe et de complète qualité. Niché au cœur de 4 ha de parc dans un méandre de l'Ill, ce superbe château est élégant et spacieux tout en bénéficiant d'une atmosphère intime et douillette. Les chambres sont toutes decorées differement, possèdent des salles de bain raffinées, disposent de l'air conditionné, certaines sont même équipées un balcon, ce sont de vraies merveilles. Les dîneurs peuvent profiter de la vue sur la rivière et les bois. Le spa offre des traitements sur demande, et il y a une grande spa.

He aquí el lujo y la calidad en grado absoluto. Enclavado en un recodo del río Ill y rodeado por 4 ha de zona verde, este magnífico château alterna la elegancia y la amplitud de sus espacios con un ambiente íntimo y acogedor. Sus habitaciones tienen aire acondicionadio, una dcoracio exclusiva, alginos con balcones, elegantes baños y son sencillamente de ensueño. Los diners podrán disfrutar de vistas al río y a zonas de bosque. Diversos tratamientos curativos del spa se pueden arreglar a pedido. El hotel cuenta además con una gran spa.

Our inspector loved: *The underwater massage in the wellness centre.*

Directions: A35 > exit Ostwald.

Web: www.johansens.com/chateaudelile
E-mail: ile@grandesetapes.fr
Tel: +33 3 88 66 85 00
Fax: +33 3 88 66 85 49

Price Guide: (room only)
single €190–450
double €190–450
suite €715

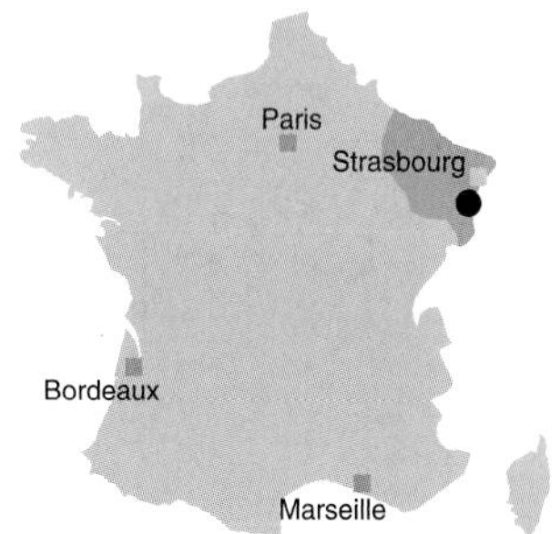

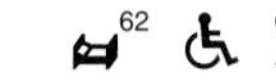

Romantik Hotel Beaucour-Baumann

5 RUE DES BOUCHERS, 67000 STRASBOURG, FRANCE

Just a stone's throw from the cathedral, this authentic timber-framed hotel is ideally situated for discovering Strasbourg. Built around plant-filled courtyard, its exposed beams, warm colours and hand-painted frescoes create a homely and comfortable Alsatian ambience. Bedrooms are individually decorated and have Jacuzzi baths. A sumptuous breakfast is served daily, and guests can relax in the cosy lounge with its log fire. All visitors are given a hearty welcome from the staff and also the resident talking parrot!

A deux pas de la cathédrale, cet hôtel en style typique de la région est parfaitement situé pour découvrir Strasbourg. Construit autour d'une cour intérieure arborée, ses poutres apparentes, des couleurs chaudes et des fresques peintes à la main créent une ambiance confortable et alsacienne. Les chambres sont décorées de façon individuelle et disposent d'un Jacuzzi. Un petit déjeuner somptueux est servi tous les jours et les hôtes peuvent se détendre dans le salon intime autour du feu de bois. Le personnel, ainsi que le perroquet parlant, attend tous les visiteurs avec un accueil chaleureux!

A un paso de la catedral y construido en auténtica madera, el hôtel está idealmente situado para descubrir Estrasburgo. Construido alrededor de un enanbola patio abundantemente plantado, sus vigas vistas, sus cálidos tonos y frescos pintados a mano crean un ambiente alsaciano cómodo y hogareño. Las habitaciones están decoradas individualmente y poseen baños con jacuzzi. Diariamente se sirve un suntuoso desayuno y los huéspedes pueden relajarse en el acogedor salón con chimenea de leña. Todos los visitantes son recibidos con una cordial bienvenida por el personal y ¡también por el loro parlante residente!

Our inspector loved: *The wonderful breakfast, and pretty courtyard.*

Directions: The hotel is in the town centre, near the old customs house. The nearest airport is Strasbourg. Parking available opposite the hotel, €7 per day.

Web: www.johansens.com/beaucour
E-mail: info@hotel-beaucour.com
Tel: +33 3 88 76 72 00
Fax: +33 3 88 76 72 60

Price Guide: (room only)
single €98-121
double €139
junior suite €167-186

Romantik Hotel L'Horizon

50 ROUTE DU CRÈVE~CŒUR, 57100 THIONVILLE, FRANCE

Directions: A31> exit 40 > follow signs for Crève-Cœur.

Web: www.johansens.com/lhorizonfrance
E-mail: hotel@lhorizon.fr
Tel: +33 3 82 88 53 65
Fax: +33 3 82 34 55 84

Price Guide: (room only,
closed 24th December - 24th January)
single €92–145
double €92–145
suite €195

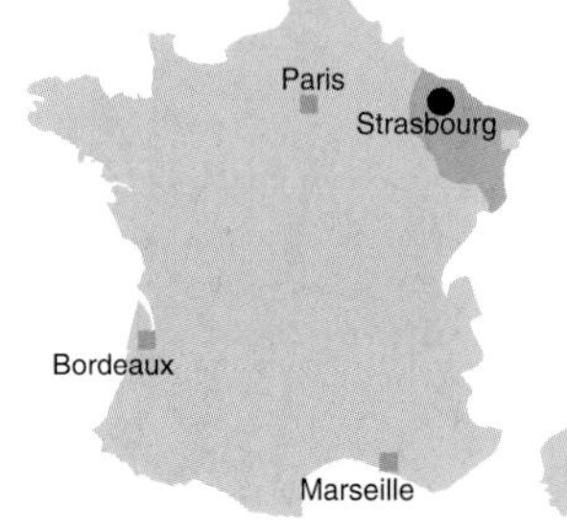

Set on the Crève-Cœur hill overlooking Thionville and the surrounding countryside, this 3-star hotel is the perfect base from which to explore the beautiful Lorraine region. The individually decorated bedrooms are furnished with antiques and offer all modern comforts. Panoramic views can be enjoyed from the terrace and the popular restaurant where guests can sample delicious, simple dishes complemented by excellent wines. Luxembourg is within easy reach and guests can visit several Maginot Line forts nearby.

Situé sur la colline de Crève-Cœur surplombant Thionville et la campagne environnante, cet hôtel 3 étoiles est la base idéale pour explorer la belle région de Lorraine. Les chambres décorées individuellement sont meublées avec des antiquités et offrent tout le confort moderne. Les vues panoramiques peuvent être appréciées de la terrasse et le restaurant reputé ou les hôtes peuvent déguster des plats délicieux quoique simples, accompagnés d'excellents vins. Le Luxembourg est facile d'accès et les hôtes peuvent visiter la ligne Maginot toute proche.

Este hôtel de 3 estrellas ubicado en la colina Crève-Cœur con vistas a Thionville y al paisaje colindante es base perfecta para explorar la encantadora región de Lorena. Sus habitaciones decoradas individualmente están amuebladas con antigüedades al mismo tiempo que ofrecen todas las modernas comodidades. Desde las terrazas se pueden disfrutar vistas panorámicas y también en el popular restaurante los huéspedes pueden saborear deliciosos y sencillos platos complementados por excelentes vinos. Luxemburgo está muy próximo y los huéspedes podrán visitar varias cercanas fortalezas de la Línea Maginot.

Our inspector loved: *The Maginot Line packages organised by the hotel.*

MANOIR DE KERTALG

ROUTE DE RIEC~SUR~BELON, 29350 MOËLAN~SUR~MER, FRANCE

Set in a huge park filled with a variety of trees, this country house offers tranquillity, discreet luxury and a truly warm welcome. The owner's paintings adorn the walls, and fresh flowers can be found everywhere. The hotel has recently been elegantly refurbished, including bedrooms and bathrooms. Breakfast is served in the conservatory or on the sun terrace overlooking the park. Although there is no restaurant at the hotel, numerous gastronomic venues can be found in the vicinity.

Blotti au milieu d'un parc peuplé de différentes espèces d'arbres, ce manoir vous accueille cordialement dans un cadre au luxe discret baigné d'une douce tranquillité. Les tableaux du propriétaire ornent les murs, et des fleurs fraîches égayent toute la demeure. L'hôtel a récemment été remis à neuf de manière très élégante, incluant les chambres et salles de bains. Le petit déjeuner est servi dans le jardin d'hiver ou sur la terrasse avec vue sur le parc. L'hôtel n'a pas de restaurant, mais les environs regorgent d'établissements gastronomiques.

Enclavada en un enorme parque repleto de gran variedad de árboles, esta casa de campo ofrece paz, sobriedad en el lujo y una bienvenida realmente cálida. Los cuadros de su propietario adornan las paredes y las flores recién cortadas alegran el lugar. El hotel, incluidos sus cuartos de baños y habitaciones, han sido objeto recientemente de elegantes restauraciones. El desayuno se sirve en el jardín de invierno o en la terraza con vistas al parque. Aunque el hotel carece de restaurante, sus clientes podrán disfrutar de la gastronomía en numerosos lugares de los alrededores.

Our inspector loved: *The beautifully kept parklands and garden.*

Directions: N165 > exit at Quimperlé centre.

Web: www.johansens.com/manoirdekertalg
E-mail: kertalg@free.fr
Tel: +33 2 98 39 77 77
Fax: +33 2 98 39 72 07

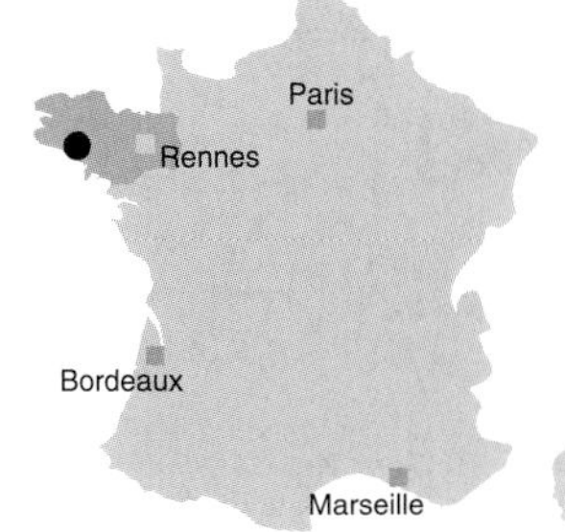

Price Guide: (breakfast €13, closed 12th November - 25th March) single/double/twin €105–198 suite €240

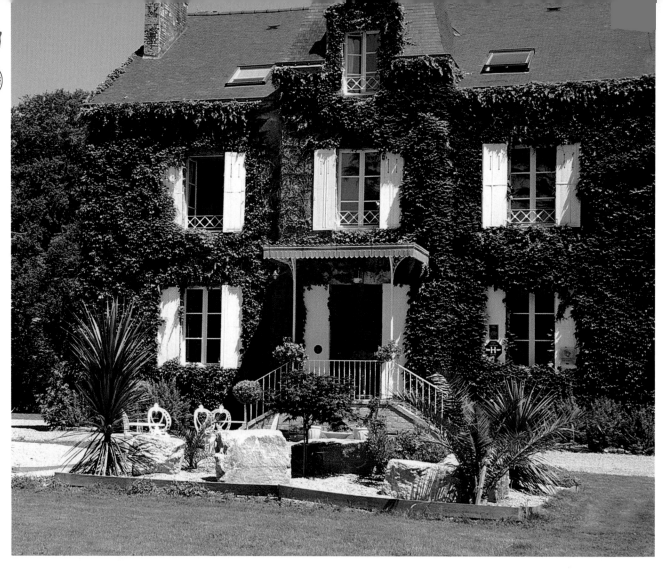

Domaine de Bodeuc

ROUTE DE SAINT~DOLAY, 56130 NIVILLAC, LA ROCHE BERNARD, FRANCE

This beautiful, recently renovated 19th-century manor house stands in 35 acres of parkland, 20 minutes from Atlantic beaches and 5 minutes from the port city of La Roche Bernard. This tranquil haven offers intimate public rooms and 14 individually decorated en-suite bedrooms, 4 of which are located in the old stable block. A first-class French menu is prepared from fresh ingredients bought from the local market. For leisure, guests may wish to use the heated pool, go cycling, take walks in the park and have picnics in the grounds.

Ce magnifique manoir du XIXe siècle, récemment rénové, se dresse dans un parc de 15 ha, à 5 minutes du port de la Roche Bernard et à 20 minutes des plages de l'Atlantique. Ce havre de paix offre une atmosphère intime qui se retrouve dans les 14 chambres, toutes décorées individuellement; 4 d'entre elles sont situées dans les anciennes écuries. Le restaurant propose une cuisine française de qualité qui est préparée à partir de produits frais du marché local. Pour les loisirs, les clients ont accès à la piscine chauffée et peuvent faire du vélo, se promener ou pique-niquer dans le parc.

Esta bella casa solariega del siglo XIX, recientemente renovada, se erige entre 15 ha de parque, a 20 minutos de las playas del Atlántico y a 5 minutos de la ciudad portuaria de La Roche Bernard. Este tranquilo remanso de paz dispone de acogedores salones comunes y 14 habitaciones en-suite individualmente decoradas, 4 de las cuales están situadas en el antiguo edificio del establo. El restaurante prepara un menú francés de primera con ingredientes naturales recién adquiridos en el mercado local. Para el ocio los huéspedes pueden hacer uso de la piscina climatizada, montar en bicicleta, pasear por el parque o hacer picnics en sus terrenos.

Our inspector loved: *The relaxed atmosphere, and the attentive proprietors.*

Directions: The nearest airport is Nantes. From Nantes or Vannes leave the N165 at exit 16 toward St Dolay. After 3 kilometres turn left to Izernac, continue for 500 metres then turn right.

Web: www.johansens.com/hotelbodeuc
E-mail: contact@hotel-bodeuc.com
Tel: +33 2 99 90 89 63
Fax: +33 2 99 90 90 32

Price Guide: (room only)
single €75-175
double €75-175
suite €120-175

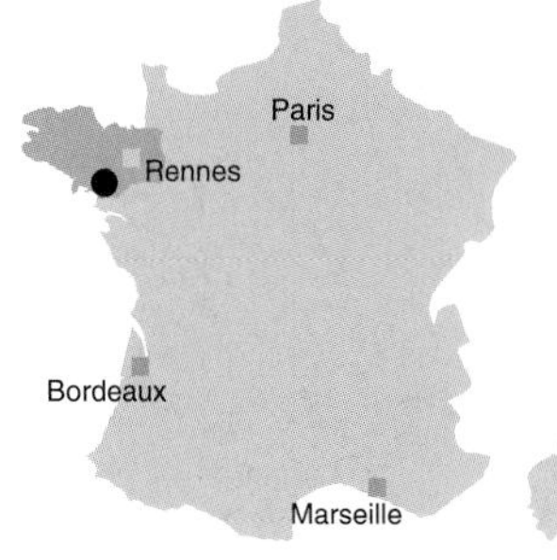

HOTEL L'AGAPA & SPA

12, RUE DES BONS ENFANTS, 22700 PERROS~GUIREC, FRANCE

Set high above the rocks of the Granite Rose Coast, overlooking the sea and Seven Islands, this hotel is surrounded by wild and unspoilt land. The ultra modern, designer décor has used minerals and plants in spacious rooms with huge panoramic windows looking out to the ocean. All bedrooms are fitted with high-tech lighting, flat-screen TVs and thermostatic floor heating whilst maintaining a reminiscent elegance of the 1930s. Contemporary cuisine prepared from the finest local produce is served in Le Belouga restaurant.

Situé au-dessus des rochers de la Côte de Granite Rose, surplombant la mer et les Sept Iles, cet hôtel est entouré de terres sauvages et intactes. Le décor design ultra moderne est composé de minéraux et de plantes dans des pièces spacieuses offrant des vues panoramiques sur l'océan. Toutes les chambres sont équipées d'éclairages high-tech, de téléviseurs à écrans plats et de sols chauffants à thermostat tout en gardant une trace de l'élégance des années 1930. Une cuisine contemporaine créée à partir des meilleurs produits locaux est servie au restaurant Le Belouga.

Este hotel, situado por encima de las rocas de Costa de Granite Rose y con vistas al mar y a las Siete Islas, se encuentra rodeado de tierra virginal y salvaje. Su decoración de diseño ultramoderno utiliza minerales y plantas en espaciosas habitaciones con enormes ventanas panorámicas que dan al océano. Todas las habitaciones cuentan con los últimos avances en iluminación, televisión de pantalla plana y calefacción termostática por el suelo al tiempo que conservan una elegancia que recuerda a los años 30. La cocina moderna basada en productos locales de primera calidad se sirve en el restaurante Le Belouga.

Our inspector loved: *The quality of the spa.*

Directions: The nearest airport is Lannion. From the centre of Perros-Guirec head for Trégastel and fork right towards Trestraou.

Web: www.johansens.com/lagapa
E-mail: hotel@lagapa.com
Tel: +33 2 96 49 01 10
Fax: +33 2 96 91 16 36

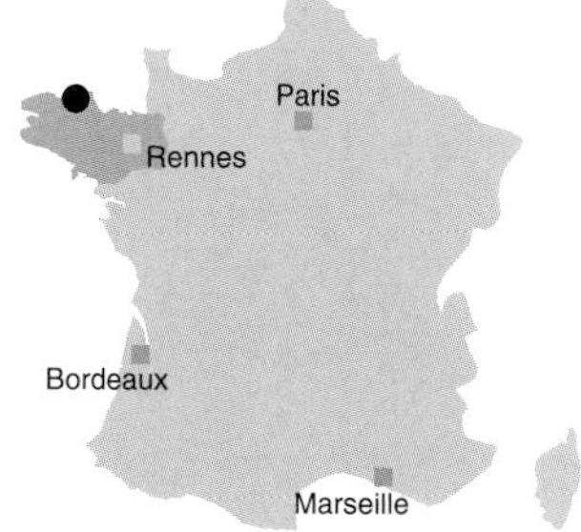

Price Guide:
double €160-380
suite €410-490

          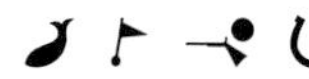

Manoir du Vaumadeuc

22130 PLEVEN, BP 69, FRANCE

The magnificent Hunaudaye forest encompasses this luxurious former 15th-century manor house, which fuses modern comfort and medieval grandeur. Sculpted beams, ornate fireplaces and wooden floors set the tone in the public rooms, whilst an imposing granite staircase leads to the individually decorated rooms. Exclusive use of the château is available; this is an ideal venue for a special family function.

La somptueuse forêt de Hunaudaye abrite ce luxueux et ancien manoir du XVe siècle, qui allie un cadre médiéval authentique avec le confort moderne. Des poutres sculptées, des cheminées ornées et des parquets en bois plantent le décor des salons, alors qu'un magnifique escalier en granit vous amène aux chambres décorées de manière individuelle. L'utilisation exclusive du château est disponible; c'est l'endroit idéal pour des fêtes en famille.

El magnífico bosque Hunaudaye rodea esta lujosa mansión señorial del siglo XV en la que se funden el confort moderno con el esplendor medieval. Vigas esculpidas, chimeneas vistosas y suelos de madera asignan el tono a los salones comunes, al mismo tiempo que una majestuosa escalera de granito le lleva a las habitaciones individualmente decoradas. El uso exclusivo del château está disponible, lugar ideal para celebrar una reunión familiar especial.

Our inspector loved: *The glorious rose garden.*

Directions: N168 > Plancoet > Lamballe > Pleven.

Web: www.johansens.com/manoirduvaumadeuc
E-mail: manoir@vaumadeuc.com
Tel: +33 2 96 84 46 17
Fax: +33 2 96 84 40 16

Price Guide: (room only)
single €90-195
double/twin €90–195
suites €205

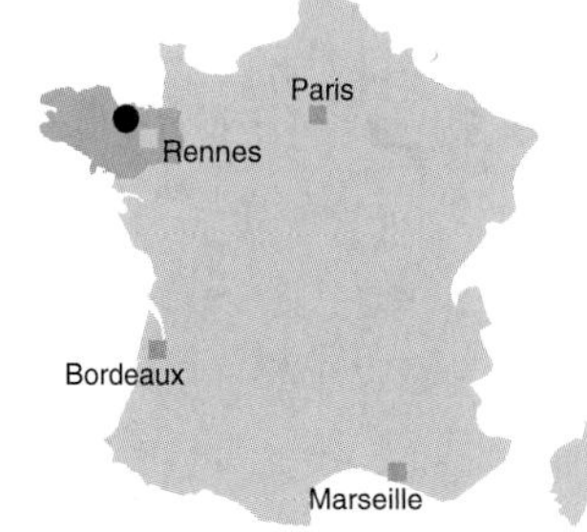

Ti al Lannec

14 ALLÉE DE MEZO~GUEN, 22560 TREBEURDEN, FRANCE

This Breton manor house commands imposing views, perched high on a cliff top overlooking the Rose Granite Coast – one of the most spectacular reaches of Brittany. Professionalism is key here with a warm welcome from the attentive staff and a keen eye for detail. The public rooms are well-appointed and inviting, whilst the bedrooms are luxurious; many having private balconies and sea views. A wide range of spa treatments are available.

Ce manoir breton, à la vue incroyable, est solidement posé sur la colline surplombant la Côte de Granite Rose - l'une des plus spectaculaires de Bretagne. Ici le professionnalisme est de mise, accompagné d'un accueil chaleureux de la part d'un personnel attentif et d'une attention particulière pour le détail. Les salles communes sont bien équipées et accueillantes, et les chambres sont luxueuses, avec pour beaucoup d'entre elles un balcon privé et vue sur la mer. De nombreux soins Spa à l'hôtel.

Esta mansión bretona dominando impresionantes vistas se ubica al borde de un acantilado desde donde se divisa la Costa de Granite Rose, una de las más espectaculares zonas de Bretaña. Aquí la profesionalidad es la clave del éxito, desde la cordial bienvenida del atento personal hasta el cuidado del más mínimo detalle. Las zonas comunes son atractivas y bien equipadas, y muchas de las lujosas habitaciones tienen balcones privados y vistas al mar. Una gran variedad de tratamientos de spa está a disposición de los huéspedes.

Our inspector loved: *The gastronomic fare, and the views from the restaurant.*

Directions: From north > towards Lannion > towards Trebeurden.

Web: www.johansens.com/tiallannec
E-mail: resa@tiallannec.com
Tel: +33 2 96 15 01 01
Fax: +33 2 96 23 62 14

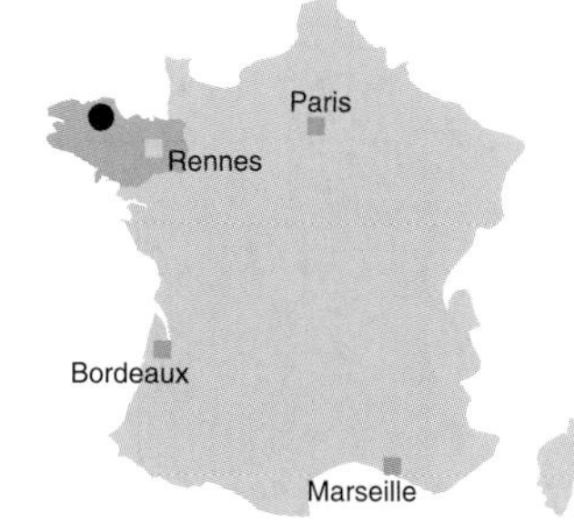

Price Guide: (room only, closed 11th November - 9th March)
single €85-110
double €157-270
suite €325-355

Château de Vault de Lugny

11 RUE DU CHÂTEAU, 89200 VAULT DE LUGNY, FRANCE

Dating from the 16th century, this magical rural hideaway is surrounded by an authentic 13th-century moat weaving its way through the verdant estate. The interior is no less dramatic, with its marvellous panelling, elaborate fireplaces and ornate ceilings. Some of the splendid bedrooms have four-poster beds and fireplaces. The château is renowned for the variety of its food, which is taken around a large table exclusively for hotel residents (closed on Tuesdays), and its magnificent 100-acre garden and vegetable garden. There is also a terrace overlooking the river.

Ce ravissant château du XVIe siècle est encerclé de ses douves authentiques du XIIIe siècle. L'intérieur est tout aussi impressionnant, avec ses lambris magnifiques, ses cheminées élaborées et ses plafonds à la Française. Certaines chambres splendides ont des lits à baldaquins et des cheminées. Le château est renommé pour sa table d'hôte (restauration exclusivement pour résidents de l'hôtel, fermé le mardi) et son magnifique jardin de 40 ha et potager. Terrasse sur la rivière.

Este mágico apartado rincón rural que data del siglo XVI está cercado por un auténtico foso del siglo XIII que se abre zigzagueante camino por entre la frondosa finca. No menos espectacular es su interior, con maravillosos paneles, elaboradas chimeneas y ornamentados techos. Algunas de sus espléndidas habitaciones disponen de camas con baldaquino y chimeneas. El château no sólo es célebre por la variedad de su carta, la cual se sirve en una gran mesa exclusivamente a residentes (cerrados los martes), sino también por su magnífico jardín de 40 ha y huerto. El lugar cuenta también con una terraza con vistas al río.

Our inspector loved: *The beautiful lawn and park where ducks, peacocks and hens roam freely.*

Directions: A6 > Avallon > Vezelay > Pontaubert.

Web: www.johansens.com/vaultdelugny
E-mail: hotel@lugny.fr
Tel: +33 3 86 34 07 86
Fax: +33 3 86 34 16 36

Price Guide:
(closed 12th November - 30th March)
double/twin €160-510
suite €450

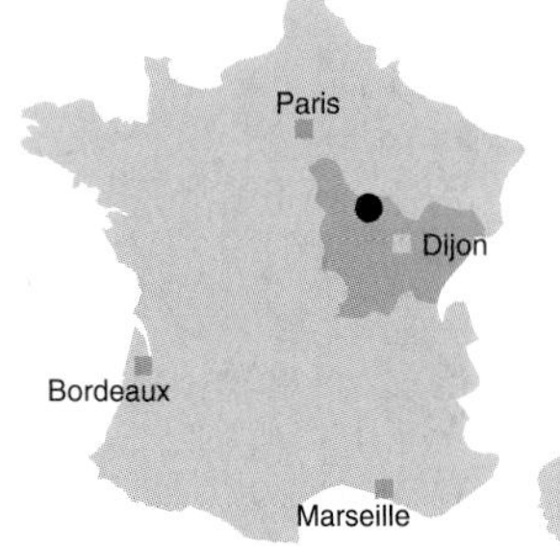

Ermitage de Corton

R.N. 74, 21200 CHOREY~LES~BEAUNE, FRANCE

Set within glorious vineyards, this Burgundy-style mansion provides comfortable accommodation and warm hospitality. The hotel has undergone a complete refurbishment, creating a simple yet elegant style and offering spacious bedrooms and suites. The restaurant, which serves traditional cuisine, is undoubtedly the centre-point; guests may bring their own wine or pick from the superb wine list. The new, welcoming bar is decorated in warm woods and red tones, and the redesigned swimming pool is a relaxing retreat.

Entouré d'hectares de merveilleux vignobles, ce vieux manoir de style bourguignon offre des séjours confortables et un acceuil chaleureux. L'hôtel a subi une renovation complète, créant un style simple et élégant qui offre des chambres à coucher et des suites spacieuses. Le restaurant qui sert une cuisine traditionnelle est sans conteste le centre d'attraction de l'hôtel; les clients peuvent apporter leur propre vin ou choisir parmi l'impressionnante carte des vins. Le nouveau bar, trés accueillant, est décoré dans des tons chauds de bois et de rouge. La nouvelle piscine est un refuge relaxant.

Rodeada de fabulosos vinedos, esta mansión de estilo borgonés ofrece una confortable estancia con calurosa hospitalidad. El hotel ha sido renovado para crear un estilo simple y elegante, y ofrecer unas habitaciones y suites espaciosas. El restaurante, donde se sirve cocina tradicional, es sin duda el punto central del hotel. Los clientes pueden llevar su propio vino, si prefieren, o pueden escoger alguno de la estupenda lista. El nuevo y acogedor bar esta decorado en tonos cálidos con madera y rojo, y la piscina se ha reestructurado para convertirla en un tranquilo refugio.

Our inspector loved: *The location: ideal for exploring the nearby vineyards.*

Directions: A6 > Beaune > exit 24 > Dijon.

Web: www.johansens.com/ermitagedecorton
E-mail: ermitage.corton@wanadoo.fr
Tel: +33 3 80 22 05 28
Fax: +33 3 80 24 64 51

Price Guide:
(Continental breakfast €25, lunch €40, dinner €40, à la carte menu €65-100, excluding VAT, closed during February)
double/twin €100-150
suite €150-250

Abbaye de la Bussière

21360 LA BUSSIÈRE~SUR~OUCHE, CÔTE D'OR, FRANCE

Directions: Take the A38 from Dijon or the A6 to Paris from Beaune.

Web: www.johansens.com/abbayedelabussiere
E-mail: info@abbayedelabussiere.fr
Tel: +33 3 80 49 02 29
Fax: +33 3 80 49 05 23

Price Guide: (room only)
disabled €150
de luxe €350
superior €220

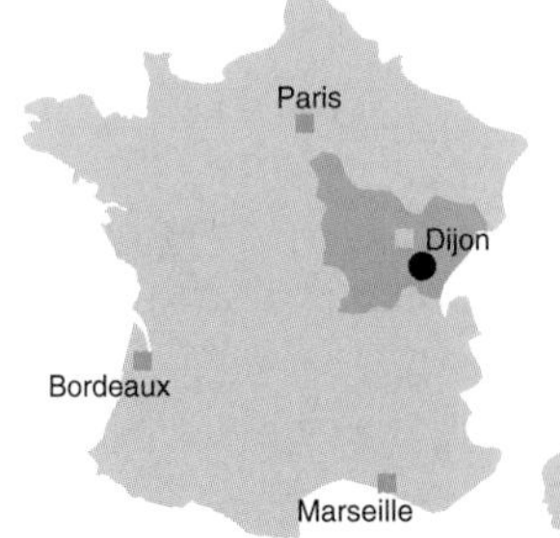

Built in the early 12th century by Cistercian monks, this magnificent abbey has been transformed into a luxurious hotel, which revealed hidden frescoes during its restoration by local craftsmen. The restaurant offers gastronomic delights created from local and regional produce, complemented by a well-stocked wine cellar viewed through glass under a gothic arch. This is a romantic place, where no 2 bedrooms are quite the same but they all enjoy a lofty perspective of the surrounding park.

Construite au début du XIIe siècle par des moines cisterciens, cette magnifique abbaye transformée en hôtel de luxe se dote de fresques anciennes révélées lors de la restauration par des artisans locaux. Le restaurant sert de délicieux mets gastronomiques créés à partir de produits locaux et régionaux, parfaitement complétés par une cave sous verre bien remplie située sous les voutes gothiques. C'est un endroit trés romantique, toutes les chambres sont différentes mais toutes offrent de superbes vues sur le parc environnant.

Esta abadía construida por monjes cistercienses a comienzos del siglo XII ha sido transformada en un lujoso hotel donde artesanos locales descubrieron al restaurarla frescos escondidos. El restaurante ofrece delicias gastronómicas creadas con productos locales y regionales, se complementa con una bodega repleta que se admira por una vidriera bajo un arco gótico. En este romántico lugar no hay 2 habitaciones iguales y todas ellas disfrutan de una elevada perspectiva del parque circundante.

Our inspector loved: *The amazing restoration work accomplished by the owners, Clive and Tanith Cummings.*

Château Les Roches

RUE DE GLANOT, 21320 MONT~SAINT~JEAN, FRANCE

Perfectly situated for exploring Burgundy and Morvan National Park, this boutique bed and breakfast is surrounded by a small private park filled with mature trees and provides 6 spacious double rooms and a self-catering cottage for week-long stays. Breakfast is served in the dining room, on guest room balconies or on the terrace, which looks out to the valley. Locally sourced, 4-course dinners are served on Fridays and Saturdays. Wine tasting, hiking and cycling can be arranged, alternatively there is an ever-changing art exhibition in the salon.

Idéalement situé pour explorer la Bourgogne et le Morvan, cette charmante maison d'hôte est entouré des grands arbres du parc privé. Le bâtiment compte 6 spacieuses chambres doubles et un gîte annexe pour des séjours de plus d'une semaine. Le petit déjeuner est servi dans la salle à manger, sur les balcons des hôtes ou sur la terrasse, qui a vue sur la vallée. Des dîners de 4 plats régionaux sont servis les vendredis et samedis. Dégustation de vins, randonnées pédestres et cyclistes peuvent être arrangées. Dans le salon, une exposition d'art est sans cesse renouvelée.

Perfectamente ubicado para explorar Borgoña y el Parque Nacional Morvan, este bed and breakfast boutique está rodeado de un pequeño parque repleto de árboles maduros con 6 espaciosas habitaciones dobles y una casita rural self catering para estancias semanales. El desayuno se sirve en el comedor, en los balcones de las habitaciones o en la terraza con vistas al valle. Viernes y sábados se sirven cenas de 4 platos con productos locales. Degustación de vinos, senderismo y ciclismo se pueden gestionar o bien hay en el salón una exposición de arte que se renueva con frecuencia.

Our inspector loved: *The superb art exhibition throughout the house.*

Directions: A6 > exit 23 > head toward Precy-sous-Thil > head towards Pouilly-en-Auxois / Missery > signs for Mont-Saint-Jean > turn right at Le Medieval restaurant > Les Roches will shortly be on the left.

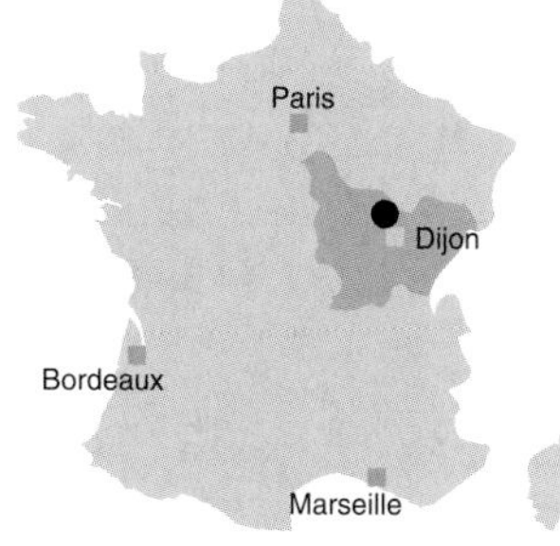

Web: www.johansens.com/lesroches
E-mail: info@lesroches-burgundy.com
Tel: +33 3 80 84 32 71

Price Guide:
(closed during January and February)
single €95
double €105
suite €130

Hostellerie des Monts de Vaux

LES MONTS DE VAUX, 39800 POLIGNY, FRANCE

Directions: N5 from Poligny towards Switzerland.

Web: www.johansens.com/montdevaux
E-mail: mtsvaux@hostellerie.com
Tel: +33 3 84 37 12 50
Fax: +33 3 84 37 09 07

Price Guide: (breakfast €13.50, closed 25th October - 27th December) rooms and apartments €145-220

This wonderful family-run coaching inn perched high on a mountain top is of beautifully old-fashioned charm. With its traditional décor and furnishings, it takes you back into a bygone era. It is a true home from home, with warming logfires in the lounges creating a cosy and welcoming atmosphere. After a day spent exploring the breathtaking surroundings by bicycle or on foot, guests can enjoy the extensive menu featuring delicious regional cuisine, complemented by an extraordinary wine list.

Perchée au sommet d'une montagne, cette superbe auberge familiale dégage un charme merveilleusement ancien. Son décor et son mobilier traditionnels vous transportent dans l'ancien temps. On se sent vraiment chez soi à la lueur des feux de bois qui réchauffent les salons en créant une atmosphère douillètte et accueillante. Après une journée passée à explorer les alentours pittoresques à vélo ou à pied, les clients pourront apprécier le menu complet qui propose une délicieuse cuisine régionale, accompagné d'une carte des vins extraordinaire.

Esta maravillosa posada familiar que se encuentra en la cima de una montaña refleja el hermoso encanto de un pasado perdido. Nos lleva a una época pasada con su decorado y mobiliario tradicionales. Se siente totalmente en el hogar donde las chimeneas cálidas de los salones crean un ambiente acogedor y de gran bienvenida. Después de haber pasado un día explorando los alucinantes alrededores en bicicleta o a pie, los clientes pueden disfrutar de un menú extenso donde destaca una cocina regional deliciosa que se complementa con una extraordinaria lista de vinos.

Our inspector loved: *The family welcome.*

Château de Gilly

GILLY~LES~CÎTEAUX, 21640 VOUGEOT, FRANCE

With its moats, parkland gardens and magnificent 14th-century vaulted dining room this former residence of the Priors of the Cistercian Abbey in the heart of Burgundy is a superb hotel of history. Restoration, refurbishment, modernisation in no way diminished its authenticity and charm. The architecture is superb, the interior décor and furnishings stunning and guest rooms are of the highest standard.

Avec ses douves, son parc et sa magnifique salle à manger sous voûtes, cette ancienne résidence des moines de l'abbaye cistercienne au cœur de la Bourgogne est un splendide monument historique. Restauration, redécoration et modernisation n'ont en rien diminué son authenticité et son charme. L'architecture est superbe, les intérieurs et le mobilier magnifiques et les chambres d'un niveau exceptionnel.

Fosos de agua, zonas verdes ajardinadas y un espléndido salón comedor abovedado del siglo XIV convierten esta antigua residencia de los Priores de la Abadía cisterciense sita en el corazón de la Borgoña en un hotel repleto de historia. Tanto las restauraciones como las remodelaciones y las modernizaciones que se les ha hecho no deslustran lo más mínimo su verdadera identidad y encanto. Su arquitectura es magnífica, como deslumbrante su decoración interior y mobiliario, a la vez que sus habitaciones están al más alto nivel.

Our inspector loved: *The very impressive vaulted dining room, and the many activities organised for children.*

Directions: A6 > A31 > exit Nuits-Saint-Georges > follow signs to Gilly-Les-Cîteaux.

Web: www.johansens.com/gilly
E-mail: gilly@grandesetapes.fr
Tel: +33 3 80 62 89 98
Fax: +33 3 80 62 82 34

Price Guide: (room only, excluding VAT)
double €156–300
junior suite €405
suite €715

48 200

Le Moulin du Landion

5 RUE SAINT~LÉGER, 10200 DOLANCOURT, FRANCE

This beautifully restored 17th-century watermill idyllically situated in the south of the Champagne region is within easy reach of the A5 motorway. The Heckmann-Aubertin Family have lovingly converted this attractive stone-built building into an elegant haven of peace and tranquillity where the best of the original features combine superbly with modern-day facilities. Bedrooms are smart and comfortable, and excellent regional cuisine is served in the beamed dining room, which looks out onto, and beyond, a slowly revolving waterwheel.

Ce Moulin à eau du XVIIe siècle, joliment restauré, est idéalement situé dans le sud de la Champagne avec un accès facile à l'autoroute A5. La famille Heckmann-Aubertin a converti avec soin ce beau bâtiment de pierre situé dans un havre de paix et de tranquillité, où le meilleur des caractéristiques originales se marient parfaitement aux commodités d'aujourd'hui. Les chambres sont élégantes et confortables; l'excellente cuisine régionale est servie dans la salle à manger aux poutres apparentes, surplombant la roue à aubes à lente révolution.

Este molino de agua del siglo XVII de bella restauración e idílico emplazamiento en el sur de la región de la Champaña es de fácil acceso desde la autopista A5. La familia Heckmann-Aubertin han puesto todo su cariño en convertir este atractivo edificio de piedra en un elegante remanso de paz y tranquilidad donde se combina perfectamente lo mejor de sus rasgos originales con las instalaciones modernas de hoy en día. Las habitaciones son elegantes y cómodas y su excelente cocina regional se sirve en el comedor, cubierto de vigas, con vistas tanto al suave movimiento de la rueda del molino como a sus alrededores.

Our inspector loved: *Watching the mill wheel turning from the dining room.*

Directions: Troyes Est > A26 > exit 23 > Vendeuvre > Dolancourt (30 minutes). Troyes > A5 > exit 22 > Vendeuvre > Dolancourt (15 minutes). Chaumont > A5 > exit 23 > Bar sur Aube > Dolancourt (20 minutes).

Web: www.johansens.com/moulindulandion
E-mail: contact@moulindulandion.com
Tel: +33 3 25 27 92 17
Fax: +33 3 25 27 94 44

Price Guide: (room only)
single/double/twin €75-86

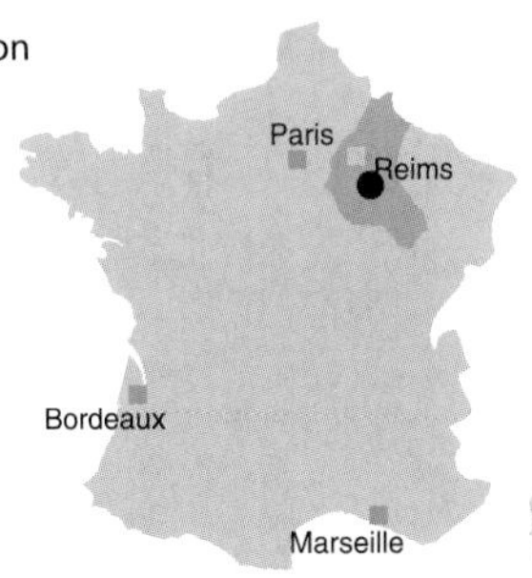

CHÂTEAU D'ETOGES

51270 ETOGES~EN~CHAMPAGNE, FRANCE

Set in the glorious Champagne Region, Château d'Etoges has recently been enhanced with the addition of 9 new bedrooms; all are individually appointed. Located in the Orangerie by the moat, the rooms are complemented by 2 new dining rooms overlooking the gardens, and décor includes an imposing fireplace. Steeped in history featuring tales of banquets, confidential meetings and celebrations this medieval fortress has been successfully renovated to enable its doors to once again welcome larger groups.

Situé dans la magnifique région de Champagne, le Château d'Etoges a récemment vu l'addition de 9 nouvelles chambres, toutes individuellement décorées. Situées dans l'Orangerie, près des douves, les chambres sont complétées par 2 nouvelles salles à manger surplombant les jardins et ornées d'une imposante cheminée. Imprégnée d'histoire relatant des récits de banquets, de réunions secrètes et de célébrations, cette forteresse médiévale a été rénovée avec succès afin de pouvoir accueillir à nouveau des groupes.

Ubicado en la gloriosa región de la Champaña, el Château d'Etoges ha sido recientemente mejorado al añadírsele 9 nuevas habitaciones a los que se la dado nombre. Situados en el Orangerie junto al foso, las habitaciones se complementan con 2 nuevos comedores con vistas al jardín, y la decoración incluye una imponente chimenea. De gran riqueza histórica gracias a los numerosos relatos de banquetes, reuniones confidenciales y celebraciones vinculadas a ella, esta fortaleza medieval ha sido espléndidamente renovada para abrir sus puertas y acoger de nuevo a grupos más numerosos.

Our inspector loved: *The new and spacious restaurant.*

Directions: The hotel is situated beside the D933 Montmirail, Chalons en Champagne road. The nearest airport is Paris Roissy.

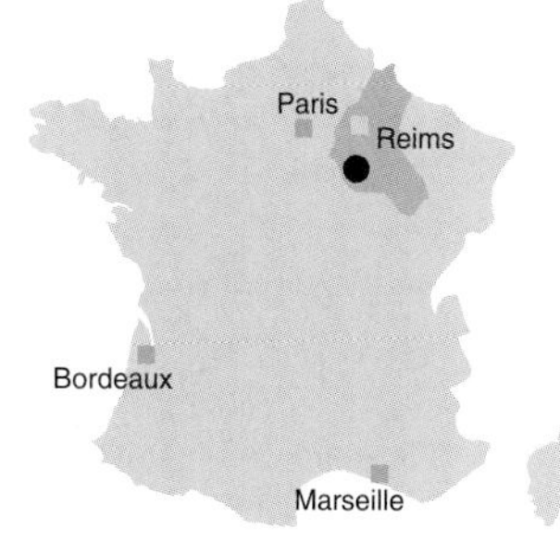

Web: www.johansens.com/etoges
E-mail: contact@etoges.com
Tel: +33 3 26 59 30 08
Fax: +33 3 26 59 35 57

Price Guide: (room only, closed 12th January - 15th February)
single €80-120
double €120-200

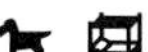

Château de Fère

02130 FÈRE~EN~TARDENOIS, FRANCE

Side by side with the impressive ruins of a medieval castle, this grand and exclusive 18th-century château is situated in beautiful, wooded countryside just 1 hour's drive from Paris. The guest rooms are tastefully furnished, maintained to the highest standard and offer spectacular views. Excellent gourmet meals are served in 3 individual and stylishly designed dining rooms where the service is impeccable. The treasures of the Champagne region can be enjoyed on a tour of the Château's cellars.

Dominé par les ruines impressionnantes d'un château fort, cet hôtel de luxe occupe un magnifique château du XVIIIe siècle, au milieu d'un beau parc boisé, à une heure seulement de Paris. Des chambres de premier ordre, meublées avec goût, offrent des vues spectaculaires sur les environs. 3 salles à manger différentes proposent des menus gourmands dans un cadre élégant. Le service est d'une qualité irréprochable. Un tour des caves du château permet aux œnophiles de savourer les délices de la région champenoise.

A la vera de las impresionantes ruinas de un castillo medieval, este grandioso y exclusivo château del siglo XVIII está situado en un bello paisaje de bosques a sólo una hora en coche de París. Las habitaciones, amuebladas con gusto y cuidadas al más exquisito nivel, ofrecen vistas espectaculares. Su excelente carta de gourmet se sirve en 3 comedores, cada uno de ellos decorados con estilo propio, siendo además el servicio impecable. Los tesoros de la Champaña pueden disfrutarse en un tour por las bodegas del château.

Our inspector loved: *The consistent high quality.*

Directions: From Paris on the A4 > exit at Château-Thierry. From Calais on the A26 > exit at Reims.

Web: www.johansens.com/chateaudefere
E-mail: chateau.fere@wanadoo.fr
Tel: +33 3 23 82 21 13
Fax: +33 3 23 82 37 81

Price Guide: (breakfast €20,
closed 2nd January - 10th February)
single/double/twin €150–350
suite €230–400

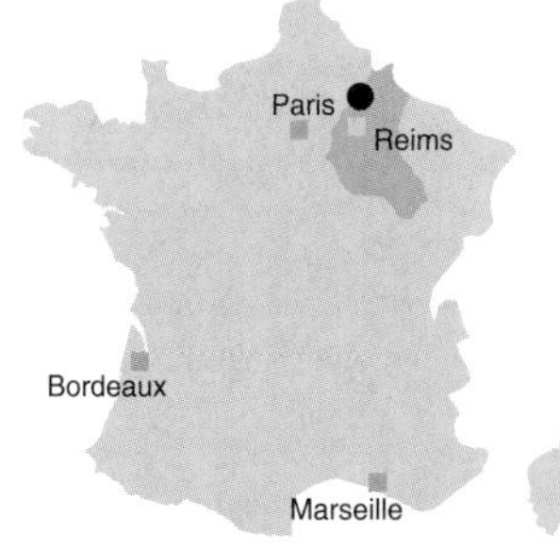

Domaine du Château de Barive

02350 SAINTE~PREUVE, FRANCE

This perfectly restored stone built hotel is accessed through an ornamental gateway, which gives way to a manicured garden and courtyard area. Although the atmosphere is one of relaxed elegance, there is amazing attention to detail. Public rooms are furnished in a modern style in contrast with the historic ambience, and bedrooms are light, spacious and airy. Classic French cooking can be sampled in the restaurant, and guests may enjoy the pool, sauna and gymnasium. Ideally located for exploring the World War I battlefields and numerous champagne cellars.

Cet hôtel, magnifiquement restauré, est accessible par une entrée ornementale qui s'ouvre sur des jardins et une cour très soignés. L'atmosphère décontractée mais élégante n'empêche pas une impressionnante attention du détail. Les pièces communes sont meublées avec une touche moderne dans cette ambiance historique. Les chambres sont claires et spacieuses. Une cuisine classique est servie au restaurant et les clients ont accès à la piscine, au sauna et à la salle de gym. Idéalement situé pour explorer les champs de bataille de la 1ère guerre mondiale et les caves de champagne.

A este perfectamente restaurado hotel de piedra se llega a través de una ornamental verja, por la que se accede a un cuidadísimo jardín y patio interior. El ambiente es de relajada elegancia y se cuida también al máximo detalle. Los salones comunes están amueblados con un estilo moderno que contrasta con el sabor histórico. Las habitaciones son luminosos y amplios. El restaurante sirve la cocina clásica francesa y los clientes disfrutan de la piscina, sauna y gimnasio. Un emplazamiento ideal para explorar los campos de batalla de la I Guerra Mundial así como las numerosas bodegas de champaña.

Our inspector loved: *The friendly and efficient staff.*

Directions: A26 > exit 13 > N2 towards Laon > D977 to Chivres en Laonnais. The nearest airport is Rheims.

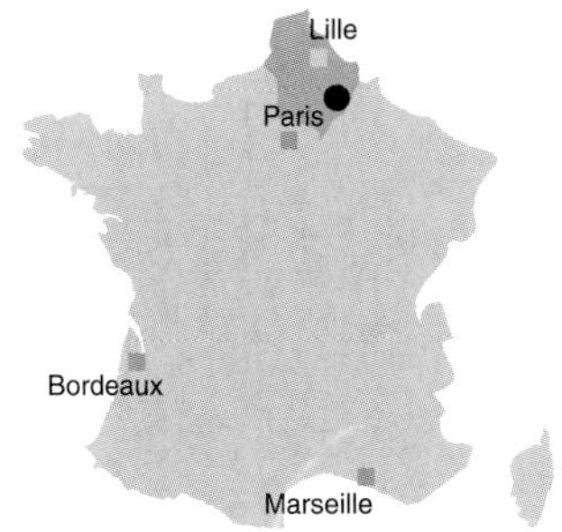

Web: www.johansens.com/barive
E-mail: contact@lesepicuriens.com
Tel: +33 3 23 22 15 15
Fax: +33 3 23 22 08 39

Price Guide: (breakfast €16)
single €120-180
double €140-250
suite €220

Bastide du Calalou

VILLAGE DE MOISSAC-BELLEVUE, 83630 AUPS, FRANCE

Directions: From the A8 > exit either Saint-Maximin or Le Muy.

Web: www.johansens.com/calalou
E-mail: info@bastide-du-calalou.com
Tel: +33 4 94 70 17 91
Fax: +33 4 94 70 50 11

Price Guide: (room only, excluding VAT)
double €95-195
apartment €184-234

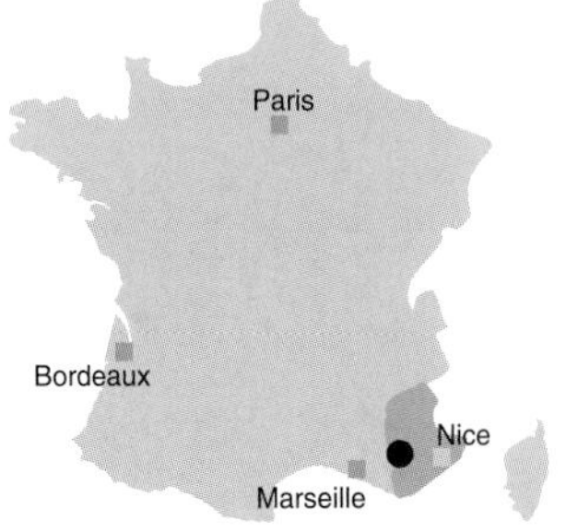

Perched on a hill, within the Nature Park of Verdon and amidst 10 acres of century-old olive trees, Bastide du Calalou is a delightful retreat. The lounges, library, bar and restaurant are all decorated with antiques and family pictures, as are the bedrooms, which overlook the garden, swimming pool or surrounding valley. Breakfast, lunch and dinner are served on the terrace under olive trees, and refined Provençale cuisine can be enjoyed in the restaurant. Numerous attractions of the Var region include the Gorges du Verdon and St-Tropez.

Perché sur le flanc d'une colline, au milieu de 4 ha d'oliviers multicentenaires au milieu du Parc Naturel Régional du Verdon, la Bastide du Calalou est synonyme de charme. Elle est décorée de meubles antiques et tableaux de famille depuis les salons TV, bibliothèque, bar, restaurant jusqu'aux chambres qui font toutes face au jardin, à la piscine et à la vallée environnante. Le petit-déjeuner, le déjeuner et le dîner sont servis en terrasse, sous les oliviers, et le restaurant propose une cuisine provençale raffinée. La région du Var comporte de nombreux sites à visiter, comme les Gorges du Verdon et St-Tropez.

En lo alto de un monte, dentro del parque natural de Verdon y rodeado de 4 ha de olivos milenarios, Bastide du Calalou es un refugio encantador. Los salones, librería, bar y restaurante están decorados con antigüedades y cuadros de la familia, así como las habitaciones, que tienen vistas al jardín, a la piscina o a el valle que les rodea. El desayuno, almuerzo y cena se pueden tomar en la terraza, debajo de los olivos, y en el restaurante se puede degustar una refinada cocina provenzal. Los Gorges du Verdon y St. Tropez son algunas de las atracciones que ofrece la región de Var.

Our inspector loved: *The feeling of serenity and relaxation.*

Château Eza

RUE DE LA PISE, 06360 ÈZE VILLAGE, FRANCE

From its vantage point, 1,300ft above the Mediterranean Sea, Château Eza enchants its guests as its location and history suggest. Completely refurbished in a contemporary style, original stone walls, oak beams and fireplaces of several 13th-century houses have been preserved. 10 sumptuous suites have all been tastefully redecorated with superb fabrics and feature every modern facility. Breathtaking views are guaranteed as an accompaniment to the award-winning meals served on the terrace or panoramic restaurant.

Perché à plus de 400 mètres au-dessus de la Méditerranée, Château Eza émerveille les visiteurs par sa situation et son histoire privilégiées. Complètement remis à neuf au style contemporain, la propriété a gardé les murs de pierre originaux, les poutres en chêne et les cheminées de plusieurs maisons du XIIe siècle. Les 10 suites somptueuses, ont été redécorées avec goût utilisant des tissus superbes et offrant tout le confort moderne. Des vues spectaculaires accompagnent la dégustation des plats primés servis sur la terrasse ou dans le restaurant panoramique.

Desde su posición, a 400 m por encima del nivel del Mediterráneo, el Château Eza deja encantados a sus clientes por su situación y por su historia. Aunque ha sido completamente remodelado respetando al estilo contemporáneo, para lo cual se han respetado y conservado los muros de piedra originales, vigas de roble y chimeneas de varias casas del siglo XIII. 10 suntuosas suites, han sido todas redecoradas con gusto con espléndidas telas, y ofrecen todas las modernas instalaciones. Sus sobrecogedores paisajes resultan ser el perfecto acompañamiento a sus galardonados platos servidos en la terraza o en su panorámico restaurante.

***Our inspector loved:** The breathtaking views, ideal for a romantic getaway.*

Directions: On Moyenne Corniche between Nice and Monaco.

Web: www.johansens.com/eza
E-mail: info@chateaueza.com
Tel: +33 4 93 41 12 24
Fax: +33 4 93 41 16 64

Price Guide: (room only, excluding VAT)
double/twin €150–575
suite €425–1,050

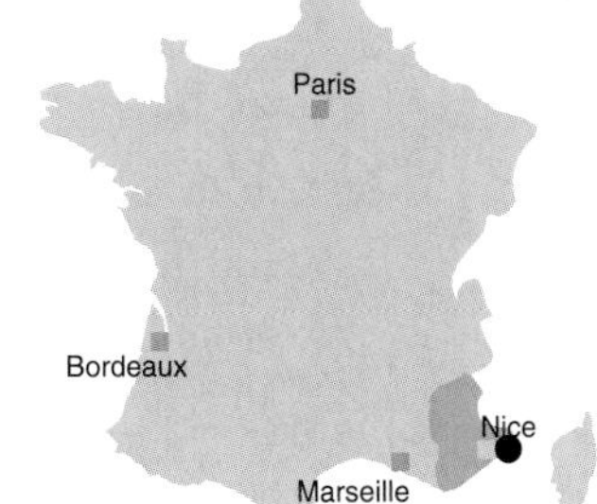

    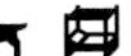   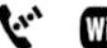  

BASTIDE SAINT~MATHIEU

35 CHEMIN DE BLUMENTHAL, 06130 SAINT~MATHIEU, GRASSE, FRANCE

Directions: A8 > exit at 42 Cannes / Mougins / Grasse > Grasse > exit Grasse Sud. The nearest airport is Nice, Côte d'Azur.

Web: www.johansens.com/saintmathieu
E-mail: info@bastidestmathieu.com
Tel: +33 4 97 01 10 00
Fax: +33 4 97 0110 09

Price Guide:
single €250-360
double €250-360

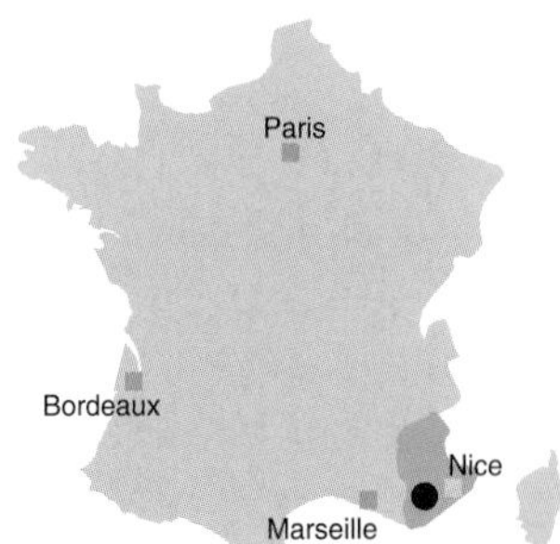

This 18th-century Provençal bastide is in the heart of the "Golden Triangle," south east of the perfume town, Grasse. Owners Mr and Mrs van Osch personally welcome guests into this exclusive yet homely country residence. Each individually decorated, spacious suite features exquisite antiques and luxurious cashmere blankets. Breakfast may be taken on the terrace overlooking the hills of Mougins and Cannes or in the intimate stone breakfast room. Within the pretty, extensive gardens the secluded pool is a relaxing haven.

Cette bastide provençale, datant du XVIIIe siècle est située au coeur du "triangle d'or" au sud-est de la ville de Grasse, célèbre pour le parfum. Les propriétaires, M et Mme van Osch, accueillent leurs hôtes personnellement dans cette résidence de campagne, qui est également exclusive et confortable. Toutes les suites, spacieuses et décorées de manière individuelle, sont parées d,antiquités et de couvertures luxueuses de cachemire. Le petit déjeuner est servi sur la terrasse donnant sur les collines de Mougins et de Cannes, ou dans la petite salle à manger construite en pierre. Dans les beaux jardins vastes, la piscine isolée offre un havre relaxant.

Este Bastide Provençal del siglo XVIII se encuentra en el corazón del llamado "Triángulo Dorado", al sudeste de Grasse, la ciudad del perfume. Sus propietarios, el matrimonio van Osch recibe personalmente a los huéspedes en esta hogareña y al mismo tiempo distinguida residencia rural. Cada una de sus amplias suites cuenta con un diseño propio así como con finas piezas de anticuario y mantas de cachemir. El desayuno puede tomarse en la terraza con vistas a las colinas de Mougins y Cannes o en su intimista salón de piedra. La piscina cubierta, situada entre grandes y bellos jardines, ofrece un relajante remanso.

***Our inspector loved:** The superb and original toiletries.*

LE BAILLI DE SUFFREN

AVENUE DES AMÉRICAINS, GOLFE DE SAINT~TROPEZ, 83820 LE RAYOL – CANADEL~SUR~MER, FRANCE

This superb hotel facing the islands of Port-Cros and Levant is located in one of the most beautiful coves of the Saint-Tropez Gulf. Spacious and cosy lounges overlook the sea and the 53 junior suites are tastefully decorated in a Provençal style with balconies and terraces which boast views of the islands. There is a heated swimming pool overlooking the sea, fitness room, sauna, private beach and yacht; all the ingredients for a fantastic holiday. The gastronomic restaurant La Praya, the beach restaurant L'Escale, as well as the poolside buffet are ideal for dining by the sea.

Ce superbe hôtel est situé face aux îles de Port-Cros et du Levant, au bord d'une des criques les plus séduisantes du Golfe de Saint-Tropez. Vastes salons ouverts sur la mer, 53 suites junior décorées avec goût dans le style provençal avec balcons et terrasses orientés vers les îles, piscine chauffée surplombant la mer, salle de fitness, sauna, plage privée, splendide voilier; tous les ingrédients sont réunis pour des vacances fantastiques. Le Restaurant gastronomique La Praya, le restaurant de plage L'Escale et le buffet à la Terrasse Piscine sont parfaits pour se restaurer au bord de la mer.

Este magnífico hotel situado frente a las islas de Port-Cros y Levant se encuentra en una de las calas más bellas del golfo de Saint-Tropez. Sus amplios y acogedores salones tienen vistas al mar y las 53 suites junior están decoradas con sumo gusto al estilo provenzal con balcones y terrazas desde donde se pueden contemplar las islas. El hotel dispone de piscina climatizada con vistas al mar, gimnasio de fitness, sauna, playa privada y yate; todos los ingredientes para unas vacaciones fantásticas. El refinado restaurante La Praya, el restaurante de playa L'Escale, así como el buffet al lado de la piscina son ideales para cenar junto al mar.

Our inspector loved: *The feeling of being disconnected from the world.*

Directions: A8 > exit Le Muy > Saint-Tropez > Cavalaire > Le Rayol - Canadel.

Web: www.johansens.com/lebaillidesuffren
E-mail: info@lebaillidesuffren.com
Tel: +33 4 98 04 47 00
Fax: +33 4 98 04 47 99

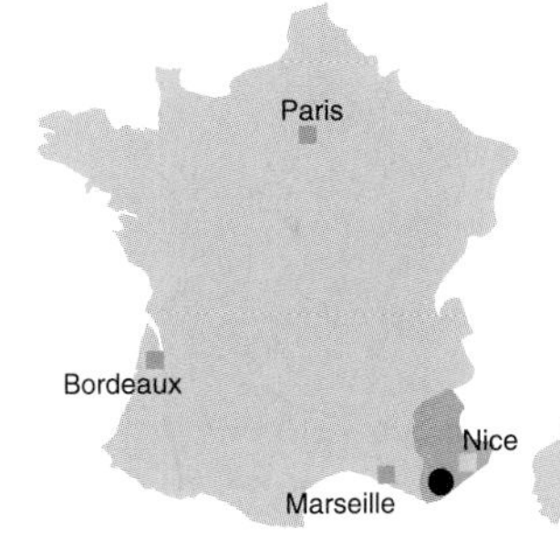

Price Guide: (room only, excluding VAT, closed 15th October - 15th April)
double €184–430
suite €184–430

La Ferme d'Augustin

PLAGE DE TAHITI, 83350 RAMATUELLE, NEAR SAINT~TROPEZ, FRANCE

This delightful family-run hotel combines traditional French charm with modern hospitality to create an idyllic retreat from the buzzing pace of the Côte d'Azur. The pretty bedrooms and suites are furnished with antiques and have whirlpool baths – some even have private gardens. A hydrotherapy pool in the charming gardens and wonderful homemade cooking create a sense of luxury and complement the impeccable standards set by the owners, the Vallet family.

La famille Vallet a complété le charme français traditionnel de cet hôtel séduisant par un accueil moderne pour créer un havre de paix idyllique, à l'écart de la vie trépidante de la Côte d'Azur. Les jolies chambres et suites sont pourvues de meubles anciens et d'un bain bouillonnant, parfois même d'un jardin privatif. La piscine hydrothérapique aménagée dans le ravissant jardin et la cuisine maison succulente soulignent le caractère luxueux et la qualité exceptionnelle de cet établissement.

Este encantador hotel de regencia familiar combina el tradicional encanto francés con el sentido moderno de la hospitalidad para lograr crear un lugar de descanso idílico alejado del bullicioso estilo de la Costa Azul. Sus preciosas habitaciones y suites están amuebladas con antigüedades y disponen de baños con remolinos; algunas incluso tienen jardines privados. Tanto la piscina de hidroterapia en sus primorosos jardines así como su maravillosa cocina casera aportan una sensación de lujo que se complementa con el elevado estándar que se han impuesto lograr sus propietarios, la familia Vallet.

Our inspector loved: *The friendliness of the staff and the relaxed atmosphere.*

Directions: A8 > exit Le Muy > Saint-Tropez > Plage de Tahiti.

Web: www.johansens.com/fermedaugustin
E-mail: info@fermeaugustin.com
Tel: +33 4 94 55 97 00
Fax: +33 4 94 97 59 76

Price Guide: (breakfast €14, excluding VAT, closed end of October - beginning of April)
double/twin €125–230
suite €200-560

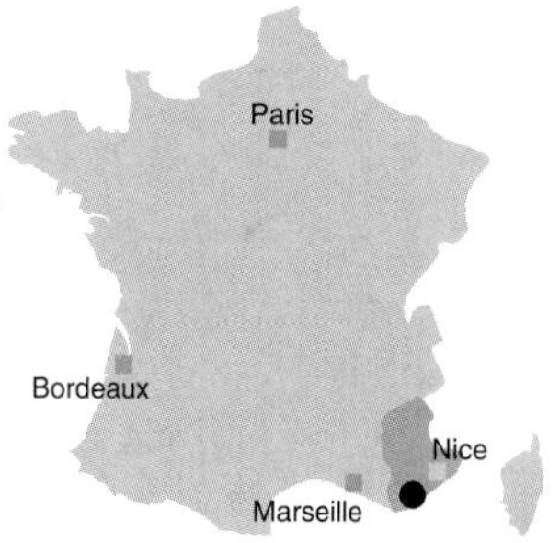

Paris
Bordeaux
Nice
Marseille

Le Mas d'Artigny

ROUTE DE LA COLLE, 06570 SAINT~PAUL~DE~VENCE, FRANCE

Le Mas d'Artigny stands in 20 acres of hillside pine forest overlooking the Mediterranean and the medieval city of Saint-Paul-de-Vence between Nice and Cannes. Guests have the choice of bedroom, apartment or 2 to 8-bedroom villa with garden. All are spacious and individually decorated. Award-winning cuisine is served in an elegant restaurant with panoramic views. Extensive leisure and sport facilities are available.

Le Mas d'Artigny se tient au sein de 8 ha de forêt de pins sur les côteaux des collines surplombant la Méditerranée et la cité médiévale de Saint-Paul-de-Vence entre Nice et Cannes. Les hôtes ont le choix entre chambres, appartements ou villas de 2 à 8 chambres avec jardin. Tous ces logements sont spacieux et décorés individuellement. Une cuisine primée est servie dans un restaurant élégant avec vue panoramique. De nombreux loisirs et sports sont disponibles.

Le Mas d'Artigny se levanta sobre una ladera de 50 ha de pinar con vistas a la ciudad medieval de Saint-Paul-de-Vence situada entre Niza y Cannes. Los clientes pueden elegir entre una habitación, un apartamento o una villa con jardín de 2 a 8 dormitorios. Todos son amplios y cuentan con una decoración propia. Un elegante restaurante con vistas panorámicas sirve platos de su galardonada cocina. Los clientes podrán disfrutar asimismo de las numerosas instalaciones deportivas y de ocio.

Our inspector loved: *The beautiful spa and its amazing treatments.*

Directions: A8 from Nice > exit Cagnes-sur-Mer > follow signs to Vence > Saint-Paul.

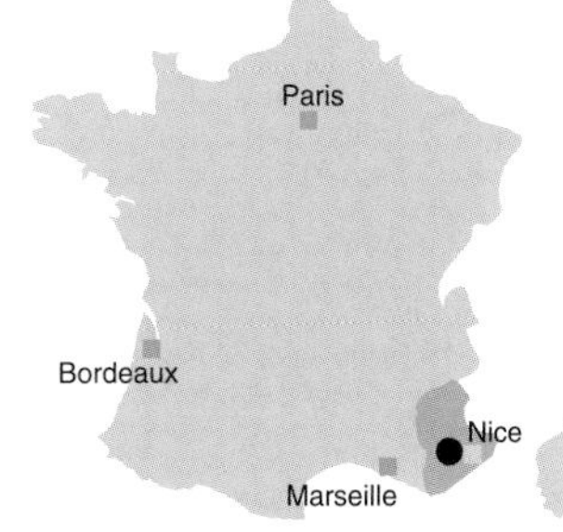

Web: www.johansens.com/masdartigny
E-mail: mas@grandesetapes.fr
Tel: +33 4 93 32 84 54
Fax: +33 4 93 32 95 36

Price Guide: (room only, excluding VAT)
single €159–469
double €159–469
suite €670–1,400

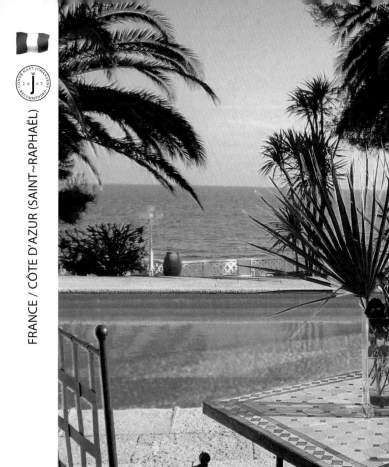

La Villa Mauresque

1792 ROUTE DE LA CORNICHE, 83700 SAINT~RAPHAËL, FRANCE

Located directly on the seafront with breathtaking views of the Mediterranean and the Bay of St Tropez, this superb property was built in 1860 by Chapoulard. A luxurious and romantic escape from the bustle of St Tropez, the hotel offers 17 individually designed bedrooms and suites within 2 villas. The French chef caters for guests' every desire, and for relaxation, massages and beauty treatments can be arranged. Enjoy the heated swimming pools, private boathouse and this sublime stretch of the Côte d'Azur perfect for kayaking, motor boat activities and water sports.

Les pieds dans l'eau, avec des vues à couper le souffle sur la Méditerranée et la Baie de St Tropez, cette superbe propriété a été construite en 1860 par Chapoulard. L'hôtel propose une escapade luxueuse et romantique à la vie agitée de St Tropez, offrant seulement 17 chambres et suites individuellement décorées au sein de 2 somptueuses demeures de style mauresque, aux magnifiques vues sur la mer et les jardins. Sur place : un chef privé s'occupe de tout vos envies, un spa, piscines chauffées et le petit port privé avec yacht, bateaux à moteur et voiliers pour découvrir cette sublime partie de la Côte d'Azur.

Situado al borde del mar, con vistas espectaculares del mediterráneo y la bahía de St. Tropez, este magnifico edificio fue construido en 1860 por Chapoulard. Para huir del bullicio de Sr. Tropez, este lugar lujoso y romántico dispone de 17 habitaciones y suites de diseño individual ubicadas dentro de 2 villas. El chef francés cumple con todos los caprichos de los huéspedes, y para la relajación, hay servicios de masajes y tratamientos de belleza. Disfrute de las piscinas climatizadas, cobertizo privado para botes, y de este maravilloso tramo de la Costa Azul donde puede recrearse con kayak, embarcaciones de motor y otros deportes acuaticos.

Our inspector loved: *The superb Moorish architecture, and views of the sea.*

Directions: A8 > exit Fréjus/Saint-Raphaël > follow Saint-Raphaël centre > signs to Cannes via Bord de Mer > hotel is on the right.

Web: www.johansens.com/mauresque
E-mail: contact@villa-mauresque.com
Tel: +33 494 83 02 42
Fax: +33 494 83 02 02

Price Guide: (room only, excluding VAT)
double €160-580
suite €260-880

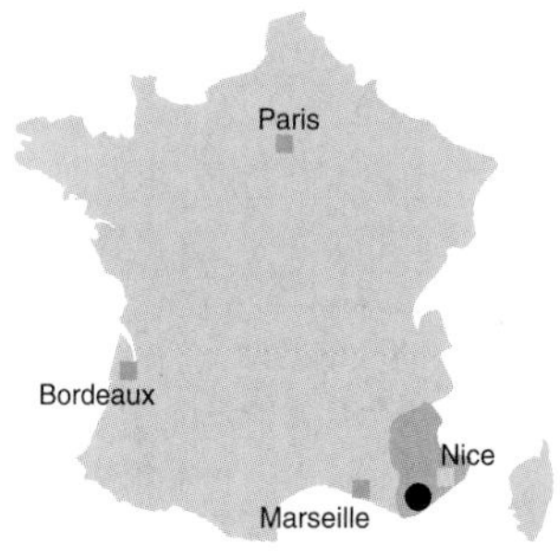

Hôtel Cantemerle

258 CHEMIN CANTEMERLE, 06140 VENCE, FRANCE

Nestling on a wooded hillside, this hotel is a haven of peace. Everything seems far away, yet Cannes, Nice and the airport, the sea and a few museums are within easy reach, and the towns of Vence and Saint-Paul, whose Provençal charm has inspired great artists such as Matisse and Chagall, are nearby. The comfortable rooms and suites have private terraces and each has its own individual style. Large lawns border the pool and the solarium, overlooking the Mediterranean. The indoor pool and Turkish bath, the lounges, the bar and the restaurant open onto large terraces.

Cet hôtel se niche sur une colline boisée et est un vrai havre de calme. Tout semble très loin, quand tout n'est qu'à quelques minutes: Cannes, Nice et son aéroport, la mer, les musées, et, à deux pas, Vence et Saint-Paul, petites cités dont le charme provençal a inspiré les plus grands artistes, comme Matisse ou Chagall. Les chambres et les duplex confortables avec terrasse privée offrent une grande diversité de décors raffinés. Une grande pelouse borde la piscine et le solarium, face à la Méditerranée. La piscine couverte et son hammam, les salons, le bar et le restaurant s'ouvrent sur de vastes terrasses.

Ubicado en una colina de bosques, este hotel es un remanso de paz. Todo parece estar alejado; sin embargo, Cannes, Niza y el aeropuerto, el mar y varios museos son de fácil acceso y las localidades de Vence y Saint-Paul, cuyo encanto provenzal ha inspirado a artistas tales como Matisse y Chagall, se encuentran asimismo cercanas. Las cómodas habitaciones y suites tienen terrazas privadas y cada una de ellas tiene su propio estilo. La piscina y el solarium, con vistas al Mediterráneo, se encuentran en medio de grandes extensiones de césped. La piscina cubierta y baño turco, los salones, el bar y el restaurante dan todas a amplias terrazas.

Our inspector loved: *The delightful garden and pool; a relaxing haven.*

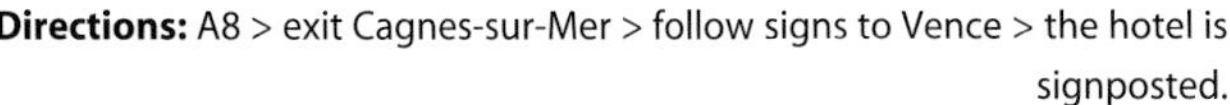

Directions: A8 > exit Cagnes-sur-Mer > follow signs to Vence > the hotel is signposted.

Web: www.johansens.com/hotelcantemerle
E-mail: info@hotelcantemerle.com
Tel: +33 4 93 58 08 18
Fax: +33 4 93 58 32 89

Price Guide: (breakfast €15, excluding VAT)
double €180-200
duplex €205-225

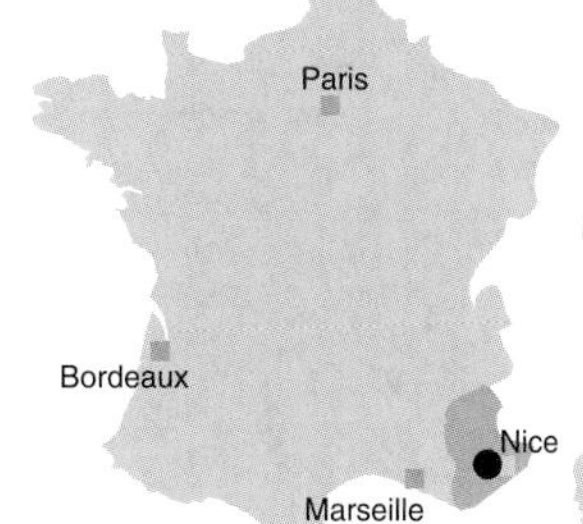

Château de Pray

ROUTE DE CHARGÉ, 37400 AMBOISE, FRANCE

Nestled on the sunny terraced slopes overlooking the tranquil Loire river, Château de Pray is simply steeped in history. Surrounded by peaceful gardens, the imposing round towers bear witness to its Renaissance origins. The traditional ambience extends to the interior, where wood panelling, heavy beams and rich fabrics abound. The en-suite bedrooms, many of which have stunning views, are tastefully furnished. Award-winning gourmet cuisine is served in the restaurant.

Niché sur les côteaux ensoleillés des collines des eaux tranquilles de la Loire, Le Château de Pray est imprégné d'histoire. Entouré de jardins paisibles, ses tours rondes sont témoins de son origine Renaissance. L'ambiance traditionnelle s'étend à l'intérieur où les boiseries, les lourdes poutres et riches étoffes abondent. Les chambres en-suite dont la plupart ont de superbes vues, sont meublées avec goût. La cuisine y est gourmande et soignée.

Abrigado por las soleadas laderas en terraza que miran al sereno río Loira, el Château de Pray es de una gran riqueza histórica. Rodeado de apacibles jardines, los imponentes torreones de planta circular dan debida cuenta de su origen renacentista. El ambiente tradicional es extensible a su interior, donde abundan los paneles de madera, las pesadas vigas y las telas suntuosas. Las habitaciones en-suite, muchas de ellas con sorprendentes vistas, están amuebladas con gusto y estilo. La cocina gourmet que sirve el restaurante ha sido merecedora de galardones.

Our inspector loved: *The welcome from the resident owners.*

Directions: D31 > Blois.

Web: www.johansens.com/chateaudepray
E-mail: chateau.depray@wanadoo.fr
Tel: +33 2 47 57 23 67
Fax: +33 2 47 57 32 50

Price Guide: (room only,
closed 12th November - 1st December and 2nd - 20th January)
single €98-180
double/twin €98-180
suite €185-240

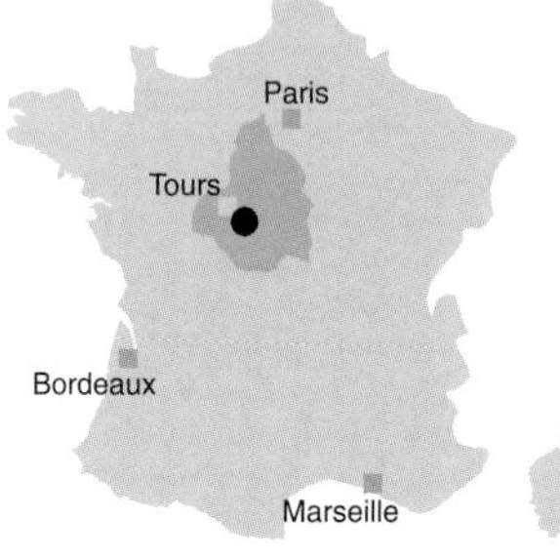

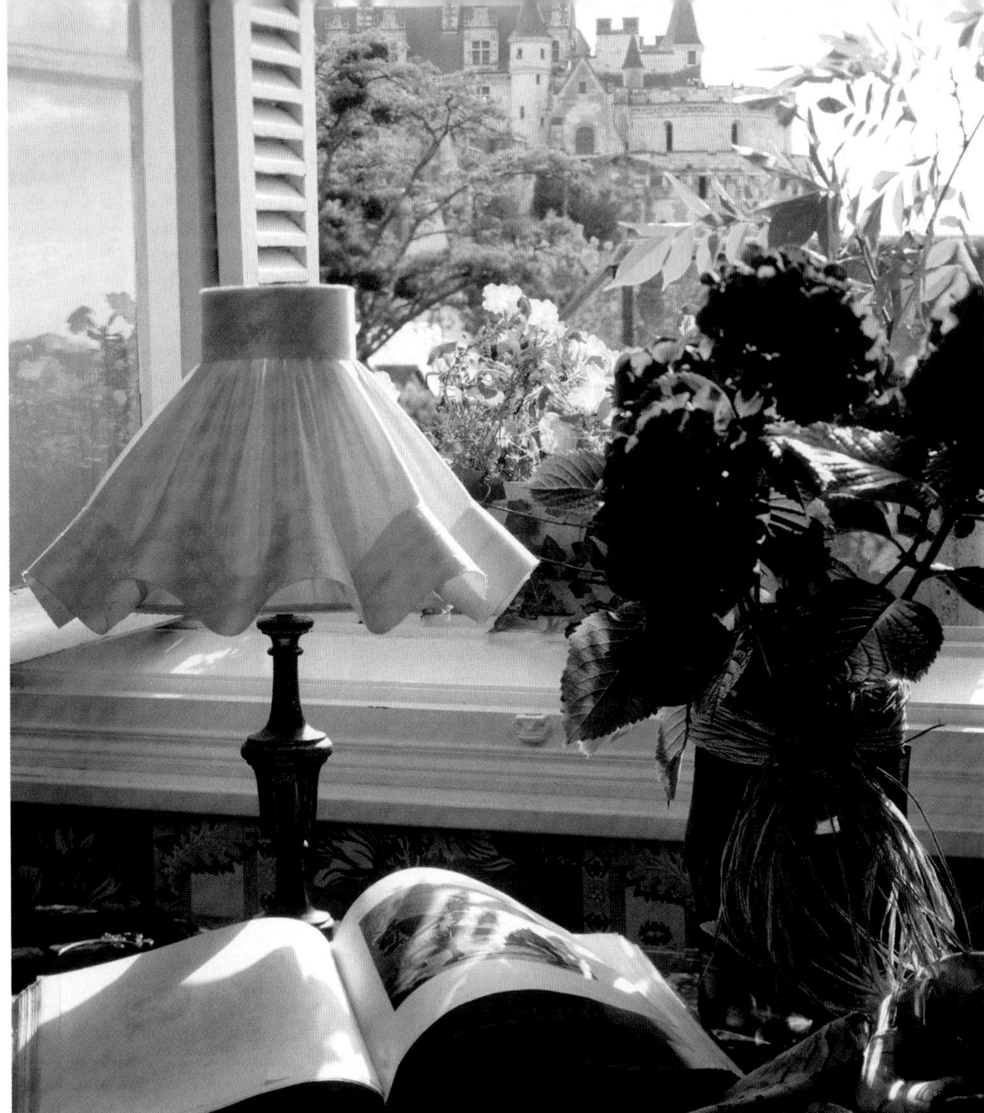

Le Choiseul

36 QUAI CHARLES GUINOT, 37400 AMBOISE, FRANCE

Below the ramparts of the Amboise Castle, Le Choiseul lies tucked between the hillside and the Loire river. The surrounding grounds of this ensemble of 3 delightful 18th-century houses feature a labyrinth of superb Italian-style terraced gardens. 32 tastefully decorated guest rooms with elegant bathrooms offer every comfort and there is excellent dining in a refined restaurant with panoramic views.

En contrebas des remparts du Château d'Amboise, le Choiseul est blotti entre les flancs de côteaux et la Loire. Sur les terrains environnants de ce complexe de 3 demeures charmantes du XVIIIe siècle, existe un labyrinthe de jardins en terrasses, dessiné dans un style italien superbe. Les 32 chambres décorées avec goût et disposant d'élégantes salles de bain offrent tout le confort et les dîners servis dans un restaurant raffiné avec vue panoramique sont délicieux.

Debajo de los terraplenes del Castillo d'Amboise, Le Choiseul se encuentra encajado entre la ladera y el río Loira. Los terrenos que circundan este complejo formado por 3 encantadoras casas del siglo XVIII incluyen un laberinto de esplendidos jardines en terraza al estilo italiano. 32 habitaciones decoradas con sumo gusto y provistas de elegantes cuartos de baño ofrecen todo el confort. Le Choiseul cuenta también con un exquisito restaurante de excelente carta y vistas panorámicas.

Our inspector loved: *The newly refurbished bedrooms.*

Directions: D751 east of town centre.

Web: www.johansens.com/lechoiseul
E-mail: choiseul@grandesetapes.fr
Tel: +33 2 47 30 45 45
Fax: +33 2 47 30 46 10

Price Guide: (room only)
single €125–275
double €125–275
suite €290–335

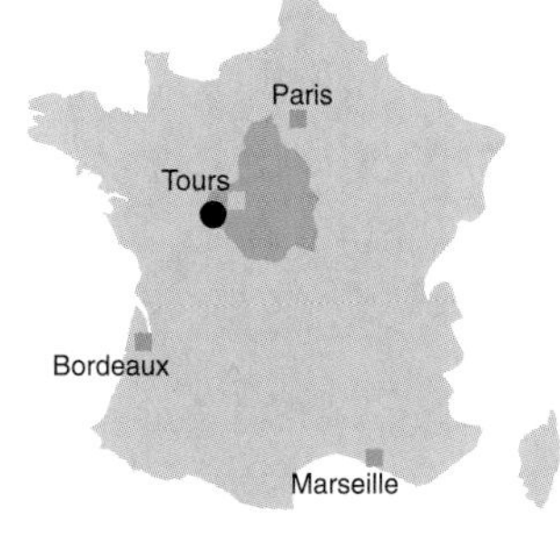

32 200

Le Manoir les Minimes

34 Quai Charles Guinot, 37400 Amboise, France

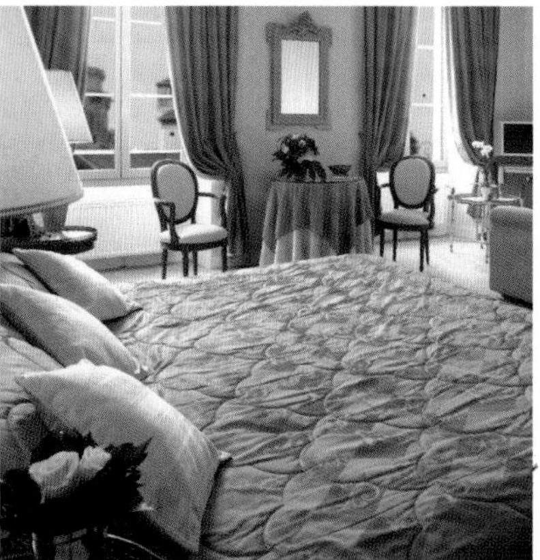

This authentic 18th-century manor house was built on the foundations of the ancient medieval Monastère des Minimes and is situated in proximity of the old town. It is the ideal place from which to explore the châteaux and vineyards of the Loire Valley. This selected stopping place offers its visitors comfort "à la française," a harmonious blend of sophistication and intimacy, whilst affording glorious views of the Château Royale d'Amboise and the River Loire. Air-conditioned rooms; private enclosed parking; no restaurant.

Authentique demeure du XVIIIe siècle, érigée sur les fondations de l'ancien monastère médiéval des Minimes, située à proximité immédiate de la vieille ville. Le Manoir les Minimes est un lieu de villégiature rêvé pour découvrir les châteaux et les vignobles de la Loire. Cette halte de choix offre à ses visiteurs ce confort "à la française", harmonieux dosage de délicatesse et d'intimité, avec une vue exceptionnelle sur le Château Royale d'Amboise et la Loire. Chambres climatisées et parking privé clos. Sans restaurant.

Esta auténtica casa solariega del siglo XVIII, situada cerca del casco viejo de la ciudad, fue construida sobre los cimientos del antiguo monasterio medieval de Minimes. Es el lugar de partida ideal para explorar los castillos y los viñedos del Valle del Loira. Esta sublime parada ofrece a sus visitantes confort "à la française", una combinación armoniosa de sofisticación e intimidad, mientras se disfruta de las maravillosas vistas que proporcionan tanto el Château Royale d'Amboise como el río Loira. Las habitaciones tienen aire acondicionado. El lugar cuenta con una zona de aparcamiento cercada de uso privado. No dispone de restaurante.

Our inspector loved: *The total attention to detail.*

Directions: A10 > exit Amboise > D751 on the south bank of the river.

Web: www.johansens.com/lemanoirlesminimes
E-mail: reservation@manoirlesminimes.com
Tel: +33 2 47 30 40 40
Fax: +33 2 47 30 40 77

Price Guide: (room only,
closed mid-November - mid-February)
single €118–185
double €118–185
suite €260

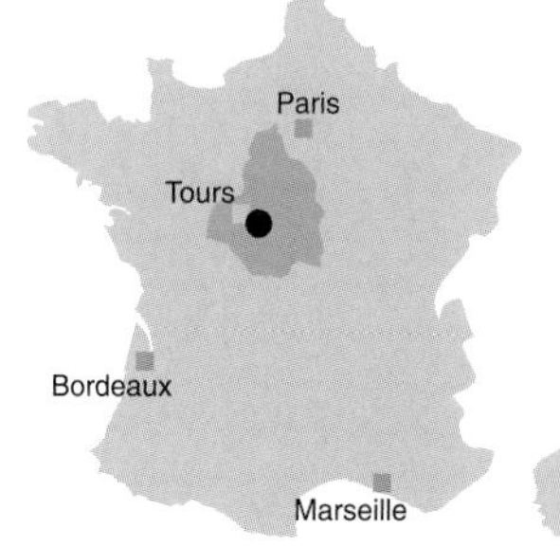

LE PRIEURÉ

49350 CHÊNEHUTTE~LES~TUFFEAUX, FRANCE

This historic, local stone built former priory stands majestically in 17 acres of magnificent parkland featuring centuries-old trees just 7km from Saumur, the Loire Valley's capital city of horse riding. Guests are accommodated in the elegant château or small, modern chalets in the grounds. All are extremely comfortable and offer stunning views. There is an excellent restaurant with equally good, friendly service. Heated pool.

Cet ancien prieuré historique construit en pierre locale, se tient majestueusement dans les 7 ha d'un parc magnifique aux arbres centenaires et à seulement 7 km de Saumur, la capitale de l'équitation de la vallée de la Loire. Les hôtes sont logés dans l'élégant château ou dans des petits pavillons modernes. Tous sont extrêmement confortables et offrent une vue imprenable. Le restaurant est excellent avec un service amical. Piscine chauffée.

Este histórico antiguo priorato construido en piedra local se erige majestuosamente sobre una espléndida zona verde de 7 ha con árboles centenarios a tan sólo 7 km de Saumur, la capital de la equitación del Valle del Loira. Los clientes pueden alojarse o bien en el elegante château o bien en los pequeños y modernos chalets. Todos son enormemente cómodos y generosos en sobrecogedores paisajes. Hay un excelente restaurante atendido por un personal igualmente afable y competente, así como una piscina climatizada.

Our inspector loved: *The views from the restaurant.*

Directions: On the D751 between Saumur and Gennes.

Web: www.johansens.com/leprieure
E-mail: prieure@grandesetapes.fr
Tel: +33 2 41 67 90 14
Fax: +33 2 41 67 92 24

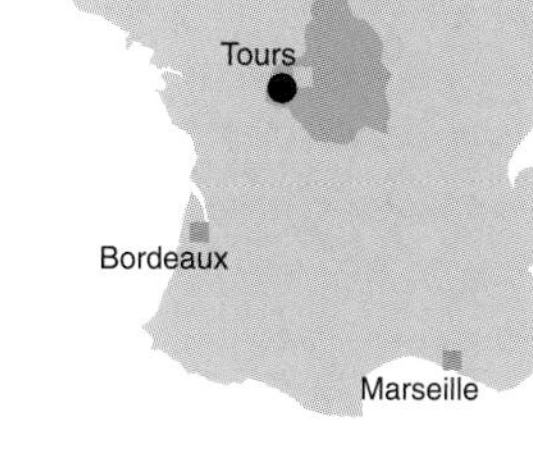

Price Guide: (room only)
single €140-280
double €140-280
suite €295-335

36 50

Domaine de Beauvois

LE PONT CLOUET, ROUTE DE CLÉRÉ~LES~PINS, 37230 LUYNES, FRANCE

Situated on the banks of Lake Briffaut, in the heart of peaceful Tourain countryside, this gracious former manor house offers stunning views over beautiful gardens and 350 acres of glorious woodland. It is a true and historically attractive getaway hotel providing visitors with every comfort and excellent cuisine and service. Lounges are intimate, dining rooms elegant, bedrooms superb – and silence almost absolute.

Situé sur les rives du Lac Briffaut, au cœur de la paisible Touraine, cet élégant ancien manoir offre une vue imprenable sur des beaux jardins et plus de 140 ha de bois magnifiques. Cet hôtel procure un véritable échappatoire à ses visiteurs dans un confort total, une cuisine et un service excellents, avec des salons à l'atmosphère feutrée, des salles à manger élégantes et des chambres superbes – le tout dans un silence presque absolu.

Situada a orillas del lago Briffaut y en pleno corazón de la apacible Tourain, esta encantadora antigua casa solariega proporciona deslumbrantes vistas a sus bellos jardines así como a una maravillosa arboleda de 140 ha. Es un verdadero lugar de retiro de atractivo histórico capaz de proporcionar a sus visitantes todo tipo de comodidades así como de un servicio y una cocina excelentes. Sus salones son acogedores, sus comedores elegantes, sus habitaciones magníficas, y casi absoluto el silencio.

Our inspector loved: *The buffet luncheon beside the pool.*

Directions: N152 Tours - Langeais > exit at Luynes > direction Cléré.

Web: www.johansens.com/domainedebeauvois
E-mail: beauvois@grandesetapes.fr
Tel: +33 2 47 55 50 11
Fax: +33 2 47 55 59 62

Price Guide: (room only)
single €130–275
double €130–275
suite €300

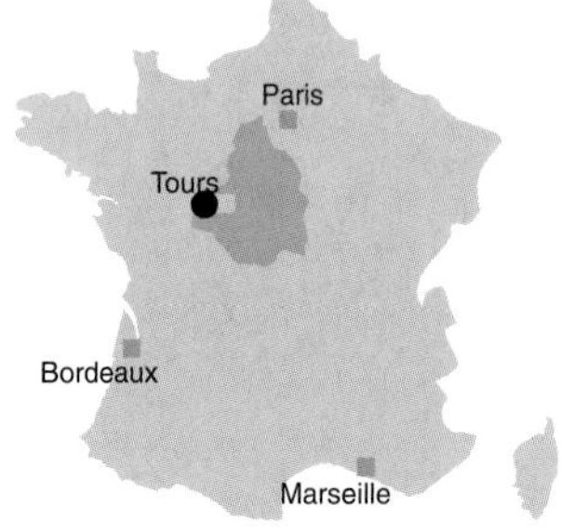

34 90

Château d'Artigny

37250 MONTBAZON, FRANCE

Built by the perfumer Coty in 18th-century style, this palatial hotel creates an immediate impression. Its startling white exterior with soaring entrance pillars is in striking contrast to the lush greens of the surrounding 25 acres of parkland and formal gardens. The interior is equally majestic with imposing stone staircase, stunning public rooms, superb spacious bedrooms and 2 elegant gourmet restaurants.

Construit par le parfumeur Coty dans un style du XVIIIe siècle, cet hôtel magnifique fait une impression immédiate. Ses saisissants extérieurs blancs et l'entrée aux piliers élancés créent un contraste frappant avec les verts luxuriants des 10 ha de parc et jardins alentours. L'intérieur est tout aussi majestueux avec d'impressionnants escaliers de pierre, d'incroyables salles communes, des superbes chambres spacieuses et 2 élégants restaurants gastronomiques.

Construido por el perfumista Coty al estilo del siglo XVIII, este palacio-hotel causa en el visitante una impresión inmediata. Su llamativo exterior blanco con altísimos pilares a la entrada contrasta llamativamente con las exuberantes zonas verdes de sus 10 ha de parque y cuidados jardines. Su interior es igualmente majestuoso, con su imponente escalera de piedra, sorprendentes salones comunes, inmejorables y amplias habitaciones y 2 restaurantes gourmet.

***Our inspector loved:** The circular dining room and the views.*

Directions: A10 > exit 23 > direction Montbazon > in the centre of the village turn right.

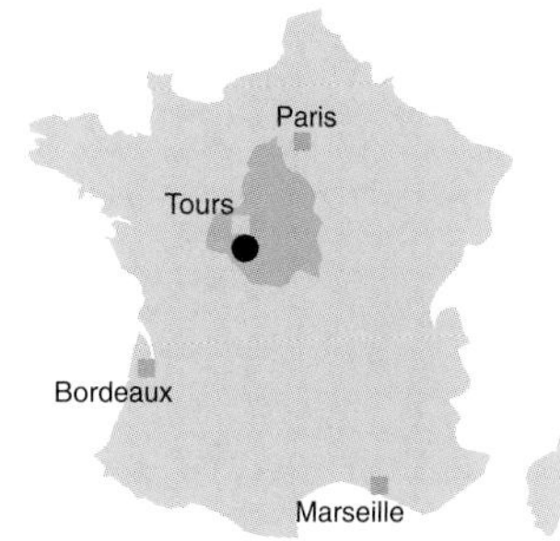

Web: www.johansens.com/dartigny
E-mail: artigny@grandesetapes.fr
Tel: +33 2 47 34 30 30
Fax: +33 2 47 34 30 39

Price Guide: (room only)
single €160–330
double €160–330
suite €420

Domaine de la Tortinière

ROUTE DE BALLAN~MIRÉ, 37250 MONTBAZON, FRANCE

Directions: A10 > exit 23 direction Montbazon > turn right in the direction of Ballan-Miré.

Web: www.johansens.com/domainetortiniere
E-mail: domaine.tortiniere@wanadoo.fr
Tel: +33 2 47 34 35 00
Fax: +33 2 47 65 95 70

Price Guide: (room only,
closed 20th December - 28th February)
single €150-205
double €150-205
suite €325

This 4-star, fairytale château lies in the very heart of the Loire Valley and has breathtaking views over the Indre River. The welcome is warm and genuine and indicative of a winning formula that creates a sense of intimacy amongst classically elegant high ceilings, moulded doors and grand mirrors. Each of the bedrooms is individually decorated, whilst the "cottage rooms" in the park outbuildings are enchanting and even older than the château itself.

Ce château de conte de fées 4 étoiles se situe au cœur de la Vallée de la Loire et a une vue à couper le souffle sur l'Indre. L'accueil est chaleureux, sincère et indicatif de la recette gagnante qui crée une sensation d'intimité au sein de hauts plafonds classiques et élégants, de portes à moulures et de grands miroirs. Chaque chambre est décorée de façon differente, alors que les pavillons dans le parc, plus anciens que le château lui-même, sont absolument enchanteurs.

Este château de cuento de hadas 4 estrellas se ubica en el mismo corazón del valle del Loira, ofreciendo espectaculares vistas del rio Indre. Una bienvenida cálida y genuina, indicativo de un ambiente íntimo creado entre otros elementos por los elegantes, altos y clásicos techos, puertas moldeadas y grandes espejos. Cada una de las habitaciones ha sido decorada de forma diferente mientras que los bungalows anexos al château son encantadores e incluso más antiguos que éste.

Our inspector loved: *The new swimming pool area.*

CHÂTEAU DE LA BARRE

72120 CONFLANS~SUR~ANILLE, FRANCE

Home to the Vanssay family for more than 600 years, the Count and Countess welcome guests into their 14th to 18th-century residence set in the centre of a 100-acre park. Each of the bedrooms and the suite is elegantly furnished; all the rooms are filled with antiques, original oil paintings, tapestries and sumptuous fabrics. Candle-lit dinner, served in the grand dining hall, is enjoyed together with the Comte and the Comtesse de Vanssay. The Comte is happy to organise wine tasting sessions and various country pursuits.

Le Comte et La Comtesse de Vanssay accueillent leurs hôtes dans leur demeure datant du XIVe au XVIIIe siècle. Celle-ci, située au coeur d'un parc privé de 40 ha, est la résidence de la famille depuis plus de 600 ans. Chacune des chambres et suites bénéficient d'une décoration élégante et toutes les pièces sont ornées de meubles d'époque, de tableaux d'ancêtres, de tapisseries et de superbes étoffes. Le dîner aux chandelles est servi dans la grande salle à manger, et dégusté en compagnie du Comte et de la Comtesse de Vanssay. Le Comte organise avec plaisir des dégustations de vins ou des séjours découvertes.

Hogar de la familia Vanssay pur más de 600 años, el Conde y la Condesa dan una bienvenida a los huéspedes en su residencia, construida entre los siglos XIV y XVIII y situada en el centro de 40 ha de parque privado. La decoración de las habitaciones y la suite es elegante y las salas están repletas de antigüedades, óleos originales, tapices y suntuosas telas. La cena, a la luz de las velas y servida en el grandioso comedor, se disfruta en compañía del Conde y la Condesa de Vanssay. El Conde organiza pruebas de vinos y otras actividades campestres a petición de sus huéspedes.

Our inspector loved: *The exceptional collection of antique furniture.*

Directions: The nearest airport is Tours. Located just outside Saint-Calais on the D1 towards Vibraye.

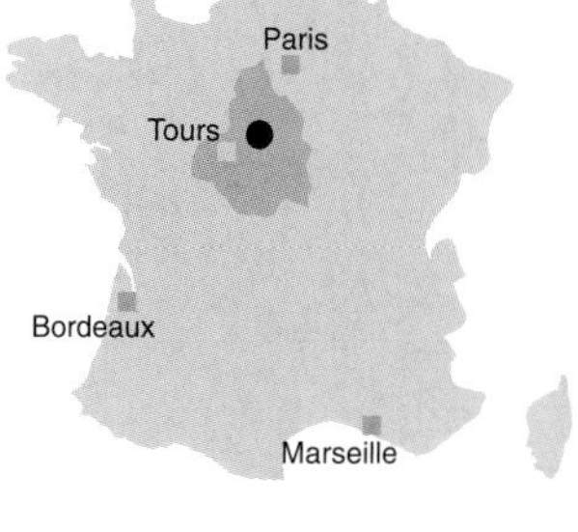

Web: www.johansens.com/delabarre
E-mail: info@chateaudelabarre.com
Tel: +33 2 43 35 00 17

Price Guide:
single €130
double €150-220

HOSTELLERIE DES HAUTS DE SAINTE~MAURE

2-4 AVENUE DU GÉNÉRAL~DE~GAULLE, 37800 SAINTE~MAURE~DE~TOURAINE, FRANCE

This charming, former 16th-century coaching inn has been sympathetically restored to its former glory. Encircling a peaceful courtyard and surrounded by a flower-filled garden with secluded, heated swimming pool, it is situated on the main Paris to Bordeaux road and is an ideal base for touring the Loire Valley. Modern bathrooms and spacious, air-conditioned bedrooms are intimate and delightful; some have four-poster beds. The beamed restaurant prides itself on offering authentic regional cuisine.

Ce charmant relais du XVIe siècle a été agréablement restauré dans sa gloire ancienne. Au sein d'une cour paisible et entouré d'un jardin de fleurs avec une piscine chauffée et à l'écart, il est situé sur l'axe principal Paris-Bordeaux et est la base idéale pour explorer la Vallée de la Loire. Les salles de bain sont modernes et spacieuses, les chambres avec climatisation, intimes et délicieuses; certaines ont même des lits à baldaquins. Le restaurant à poutres apparentes se glorifie d'offrir une cuisine régionale authentique.

Una encantadora posada del siglo XVI que ha sido restaurada conservando su pasado glorioso. Está rodeada por un tranquilo patio y un jardín lleno de flores, con piscina climatizada e íntima, que se encuentra en la carretera principal París-Burdeos, lo que la convierte en un lugar ideal para visitar el Valle del Loira. Los cuartos de baño son modernos y las habitaciones espaciosas y con aire acondicionado, algunas teinen camas con dosel. El acogedor restaurante con vigas ofrece una auténtica cocina regional.

Our inspector loved: *The picturesque garden.*

Directions: N10 south from Tours >the hotel is on the right. Maure or A10 > exit 25 > turn left at lights > hotel is on the hill, on the left. The nearest airport is Tours.

Web: www.johansens.com/saintemaure
E-mail: hauts-de-ste-maure@wanadoo.fr
Tel: +33 2 47 65 50 65
Fax: +33 2 47 65 60 24

Price Guide: (room only, closed during January)
single €119-160
double €119-160
suite €180-215

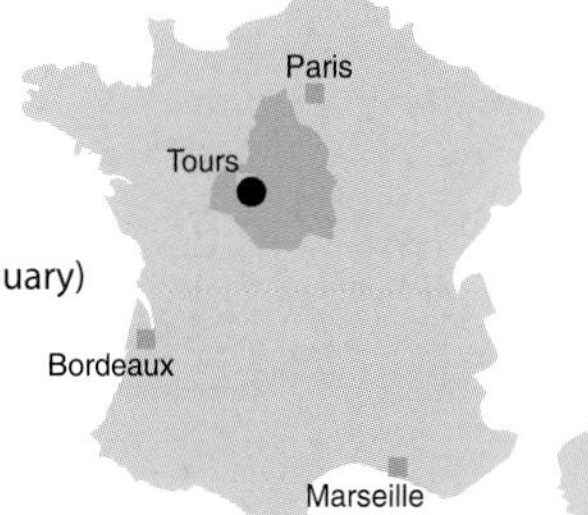

Château de Floure

1, ALLÉE GASTON BONHEUR, 11800 FLOURE, FRANCE

Only 10 minutes from Carcassonne, facing the majestic Mount Alaric, this beautiful château, which was formerly the residence of French writer Gaston Bonheur, lies peacefully within a lush park, surrounded by vineyards and exquisite traditional French gardens. Charming bedrooms are the ultimate in comfort whilst irresistible French cuisine and superb wines are served in the 17th-century restaurant, featuring impressive original woodwork. Guests can stroll through the grounds, play tennis or swim in the pool.

A seulement 10 minutes de Carcassonne, face au mont Alaric, le beau Château de Floure, ancienne résidence de Gaston Bonheur l'écrivain, se niche au cœur d'un parc luxuriant entouré de vignobles et d'adorables jardins typiques de la région. Les chambres charmantes sont ultra confortables et une cuisine succulente accompagnée de vins délicieux est servie au restaurant dans un cadre du XVIIe siècle à l'ébénisterie impressionnante. Les hôtes peuvent se promener dans le parc, jouer au tennis ou profiter de la piscine.

A solo 10 minutos de Carcassonne, mirando al majestuoso monte Alaric, este precioso château, que fue en su día la residencia del escritor francés Gaston Bonheur, se encuentra en el corazón de un parque frondoso, rodeado de viñedos y exquisitos jardines tradicionales franceses. Las encantadoras habitaciones son de los más confortable y una cocina francesa irresistible, acompañada de buenísimos vinos, se sirve en el restaurante del siglo XVII con su impresionante artesanía en madera de la época. Los clientes pueden pasear por la finca, jugar al tenis o refrescarse en la piscina del hotel.

Our inspector loved: *The new swimming pool and Jacuzzi.*

Directions: A61 > exit Carcassonne Est, no. 24 > RN113 towards Narbonne.

Web: www.johansens.com/floure
E-mail: contact@chateau-de-floure.com
Tel: +33 4 68 79 11 29
Fax: +33 4 68 79 04 61

Price Guide: (room only, closed 1st January - mid-February)
double €110-170
suite €230

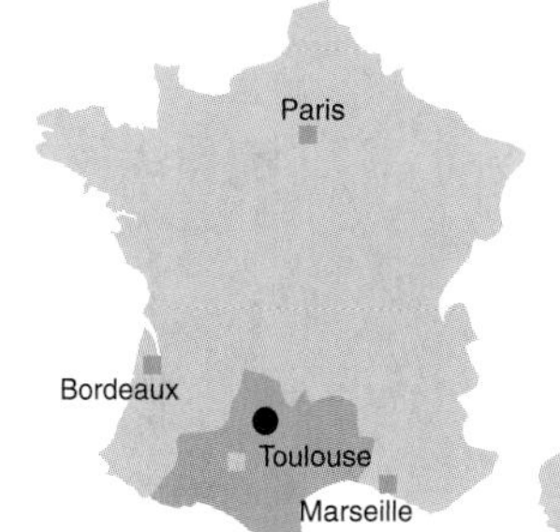

Relais Royal

8 RUE MARÉCHAL CLAUZEL, 09500 CARCASSONNE - MIREPOIX, FRANCE

At the foot of the Pyrenean Mountains stands this historical 18th-century building, completely renovated to maintain original features such as terracotta tiled floors and natural stone fireplaces. Bygone luxury combines with modern comfort in the guest rooms. Le Ciel d'Or serves creative French cuisine complemented by an expertly chosen wine list from the hotel's arched wine cellar. Customised menus for events can be arranged. Explore the medieval town of Mirepoix, sail on the Montbel Lake or relax in the courtyard.

Cette demeure historique du XVIIIe siècle, complètement rénovée tout en gardant ses beaux éléments d'origine tels que ses sols en terre cuite et ses cheminées en pierre, se situe au pied des Pyrénées. Dans les chambres, le luxe d'autrefois est harmonieusement mélangé au confort moderne. Le restaurant "Le Ciel d'Or" sert une cuisine créative française accompagnée par des vins habilement choisi dans la cave voûtée de l'hôtel. Des menus adaptés aux événements sont disponibles. Les hôtes peuvent visiter la ville médiévale de Mirepoix, le lac de Montbel ou se relaxer dans la cour de l'hôtel.

Al pie de los Pirineos se erige este histórico edificio del siglo XVIII, completamente renovado para mantener sus rasgos originales, tales como los suelos de baldosas de terracota y las hogares de chimenea de piedra natural. En las habitaciones se combina el lujo de épocas pasadas con el moderno confort. Le Ciel d'Or sirve platos de la cocina creativa francesa que se complementan con una selecta lista de vinos procedentes de la bodega en arco del hotel. Se pueden concertar cartas a gusto del cliente para ocasiones especiales. Podrá explorar la localidad medieval de Mirepoix, navegar en el lago Montbel o relajarse en su patio interior.

Our inspector loved: *The perfect location of the hotel in the heart of the lovely town of Mirepoix, and the warm welcome from the owners.*

Directions: From A61 > exit Mirepoix/Bram. From A66 > exit Foix/Andorre/Mirepoix. Located in the centre of Mirepoix, Ariége, 40km from Carcassonne. Carcassonne Airport is nearby.

Web: www.johansens.com/relaisroyal
E-mail: relaisroyal@relaischateaux.com
Tel: +33 5 61 60 19 19
Fax: +33 5 61 60 14 15

Price Guide: (room only)
de luxe €150-220
suite €220-350

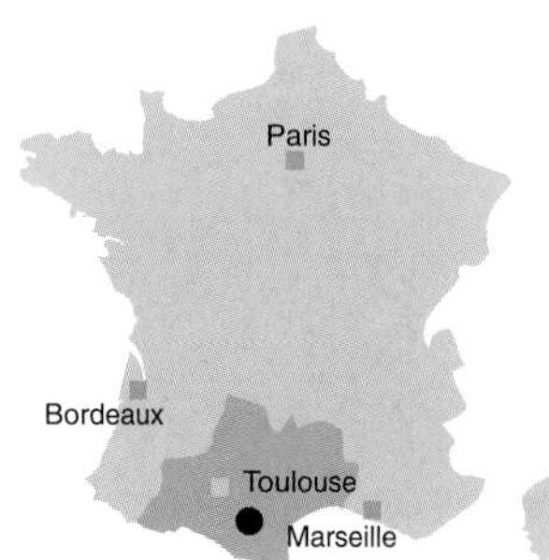

Château La Chenevière

ESCURES-COMMES, 14520 PORT~EN~BESSIN, FRANCE

Ideally located for exploring the Normandy coasts and landing beaches, as well as historic Bayeux, this classical French château offers the very highest quality of traditional hospitality. Individually designed bedrooms overlook the hotel's beautiful parklands, and the stylish and spacious public rooms create an atmosphere of relaxed elegance. The dining room is a beautiful setting in which to enjoy a range of regional gastronomic cuisine, whilst the Zanzibar cellar bar is both characterful and intimate, ideal for pre or post-dinner drinks.

Idéalement situé pour explorer les côtes Normandes, les plages du Débarquement et la ville historique de Bayeux, ce château classique français offre le summum de l'hospitalité traditionnelle. Les chambres décorées individuellement surplombent les magnifiques jardins et les salons spacieux et élégants créent une atmosphère douillette. Une large variété de mets régionaux gastronomiques est servie dans le superbe décor de la salle à manger et le bar feutré du Zanzibar est idéal pour un apéritif ou un digestif.

Situado en un emplazamiento ideal para explorar tanto las costas y las playas del desembarco de la Normandía como la histórica ciudad de Bayeux, este clásico château francés ofrece la mayor calidad en hospitalidad tradicional. Sus habitaciones individuamente diseñadas tienen vistas a los bellos campos de césped del hotel y sus refinadas y amplias salas comunes proporcionan un ambiente de relajada elegancia. El comedor constituye un bello entorno en el que se puede disfrutar de gran variedad de platos de la gastronomía regional, a la vez que su bar-bodega Zanzibar resulta tanto pintoresco como intimista, ideal por tanto para tomarse unas copas antes o después de la cena.

Our inspector loved: *The Zanzibar: the original and intimate cellar bar.*

Directions: From Bayeux head towards Port-en-Bessin D6. The hotel is on the right before reaching Port-en-Bessin. The nearest airport is Caen Carpiquet.

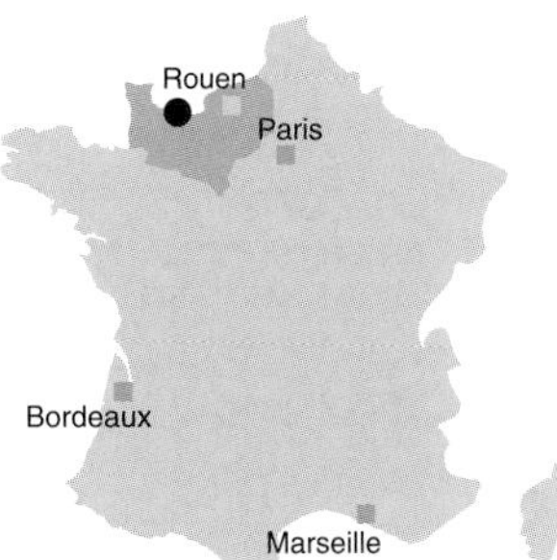

Web: www.johansens.com/cheneviere
E-mail: reservation@lacheneviere.fr or cheneviere@lacheneviere.fr
Tel: +33 2 31 51 25 25
Fax: +33 2 31 51 25 20

Price Guide: (closed during January)
single €200-295
double €250-400
suite €400-500

Château Les Bruyères

ROUTE DU CADRAN, 14340 CAMBREMER, FRANCE

Directions: From Deauville Saint-Gatien Airport > A13 > exit 29 > direction Beuvron en Auge > Cambremer > village centre > D851 > 1 km.

Web: www.johansens.com/lesbruyeres
E-mail: contact@chateaulesbruyeres.com
Tel: +33 2 31 32 22 45
Fax: +33 2 31 32 22 58

Price Guide: (room only)
single €85
double €215
suite €200-250

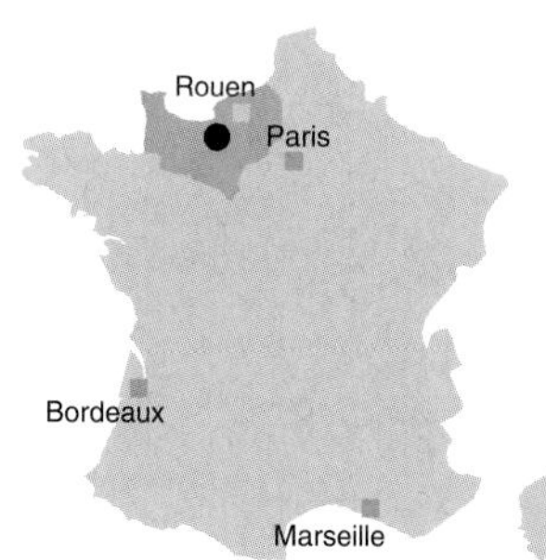

Set on the outskirts of a picturesque village, just 20 minutes from the Normandy coast, a long leafy drive leads guests to this inviting Château. Completely restored by its new resident owners, Madame Harfaux is in charge of looking after guests and Monsieur prepares the innovative, delicious meals. The hotel offers spacious rooms with views over the beautifully kept grounds, and there is a bar and cosy lounge complete with log fire. The gardens house a delightful swimming pool area.

Situé au bord d'un village pittoresque, à 20 minutes de la côte normande, une longue allée bordée d'arbres mène les hôtes à cet accueillant château. Entièrement restauré par ses nouveaux propriétaires, Madame Harfaux est au petit soin pour ses clients tandis que Monsieur, aux fourneaux, prépare une cuisine inventive et délicieuse. L'hôtel propose des chambres spacieuses qui surplombent le domaine superbement entretenu. Un bar et un salon confortable accueille les clients autour d'un feu de bois. Une ravissante piscine se trouve dans les jardins.

A las afueras de una pintoresca aldea y a sólo 20 minutos de la costa de Normandía se encuentra este acogedor Château al que se accede a través de un largo y frondoso camino privado. Está completamente restaurado por sus nuevos propietarios residentes: Madame Harfaux se encarga de atender a los clientes y su marido se ocupa de cocinar los deliciosos y originales platos. El hotel dispone de habitaciones espaciosas con vistas a zonas verdes primorosamente cuidadas, además de un bar y un acogedor salón provisto de una chimenea de leña. Entre los jardines los clientes podrán disfrutar de una preciosa piscina.

Our inspector loved: *Taking a stroll in the beautiful, tranquil park.*

Le Castel

50210 MONTPINCHON, FRANCE

English owners Jon Barnsley and Nicholas Hobbs provide guests with a warm and hospitable welcome to their superb Napoleon III château in the heart of 4 acres of parkland near the beautiful cathedral city of Coutances. Peace and quiet abound. Each of the 6 bedrooms is the height of comfort. Breakfast is taken in the kitchen and table d'hôte dinners can be savoured in the dining room or al fresco on the terrace. Ideal for family parties or small corporate events. Extra accommodation is available in a cottage within the grounds.

Les propriétaires anglais, Jon Barnsley et Nicholas Hobbs offrent à leurs hôtes un accueil chaleureux dans leur superbe château Napoléon III situé au cœur de 2 ha de parc, près de la belle ville de Coutances et sa cathédrale. Calme et tranquillité sont à l'honneur. Chacune des 6 chambres est un must de confort. Le petit-déjeuner est servi dans la cuisine et les dîners table d'hôtes peuvent être dégustés dans la salle à manger ou au frais sur la terrasse. Le Castel est parfait pour les réunions de famille et les petites conférences d'entreprises. Des logements supplémentaires sont disponibles dans une petite maison sur le domaine.

Sus propietarios ingleses Jon Barnsley y Nicholas Hobbs ofrecen a sus clientes una cariñosa bienvenida en su magnífico château de Napoleón III, situado en el corazón de una zona de 2 ha de césped cerca de la bella ciudad catedralicia de Coutances. La paz y la tranquilidad son las sensaciones dominantes. Cada una de las 6 habitaciones alcanzan altas cotas de confort. El desayuno se sirve en la cocina, y las excelentes cenas pueden degustarse en el comedor, o al aire libre en la terraza. Le Castel es el lugar ideal para organizar fiestas familiares o pequeñas reuniones de negocios. Un alojamiento adicional está disponible en una casa en los jardines.

Our inspector loved: *The proprietors' 2 llamas and 4 Burmese cats.*

 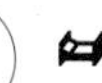 6    16   

Directions: The nearest ferry ports are Cherbourg, Caen or St Malo. The nearest airports are Dinard, Cherbourg or Rennes. From Coutances take the D972 to Belval Gare> turn right> 4.1km > turn right> 0.6km.

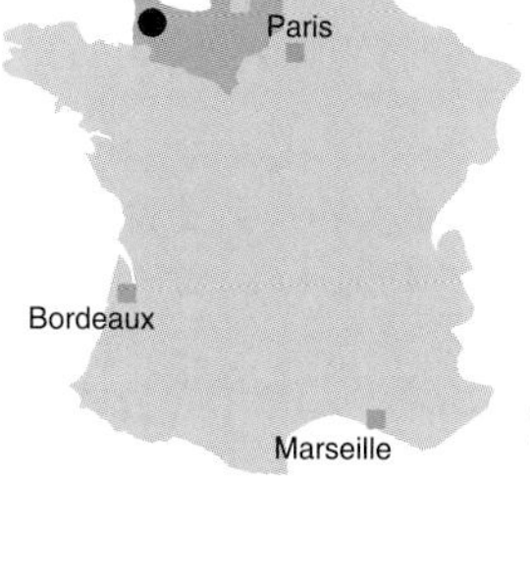

Rouen
Paris
Bordeaux
Marseille

Web: www.johansens.com/lecastelnormandy
E-mail: enquiries@le-castel-normandy.com
Tel: +33 2 33 17 00 45

Price Guide:
double/twin €100-140

Manoir de la Poterie, Spa "Les Thermes"

CHEMIN PAUL RUEL, 14113 CRICQUEBOEUF, FRANCE

Ideally located between Deauville and Honfleur along the coast, this typical Norman hotel, with Louis XVI-style furniture, provides generously sized, comfortable bedrooms with sea or countryside views. The large lounge is the perfect retreat to curl up in front of the log fire and read a good book. Guests may enjoy the gastronomic cuisine in the elegant restaurant. Relax in Les Thermes spa, which includes massage and beauty treatments, a heated pool, Jacuzzi, hammam, sauna, jet streams, balneo seat, herbal tea lounge and LCD screen.

Idéalement situé sur la côte entre Deauville et Honfleur, ce charmant hôtel Normand, avec des mobiliers de style Louis XVI, offre des chambres confortables et spacieuses avec des vues mer ou campagne. Le grand salon est le refuge parfait pour profiter d'un bon livre devant l'âtre de la cheminée. Les menus proposent une cuisine gastronomique à déguster dans l'élégante salle à manger. Les hôtes peuvent se relaxer dans Les Thermes spa, comprenant massages et traitements de beauté, une piscine chauffée, jacuzzi, hammam, sauna, siège balnéo, lounge dédié aux tisanes et écran LCD.

Este encantador hotel normando provisto de elementos del estilo de Luis XIV y de ideal emplazamiento en la costa entre Deauville y Honfleur, proporciona cómodas habitaciones de generosas dimensiones con vistas al mar o al campo. Su amplio salón es el retiro perfecto a relajar delante de la chimenea y para leer un buen libro. Los clientes pueden apreciar la cocina gastronomica en el restaurante elegante. Podrá relajarse en el spa Les Thermes, que incluye masajes y tratamientos de la belleza, una piscina climatizada, jacuzzi, hammam, sauna, baños a chorro (jet streams), asiento-balneo, salón de infusiones y pantalla LCD.

Our inspector loved: *The new indoor pool area.*

Directions: Detailed directions are available from the hotel.

Web: www.johansens.com/manoirdelapoterie
E-mail: info@honfleur-hotel.com
Tel: +33 2 31 88 10 40
Fax: +33 2 31 88 10 90

Price Guide: (room only)
single €116–230
double €230
suite €185–250

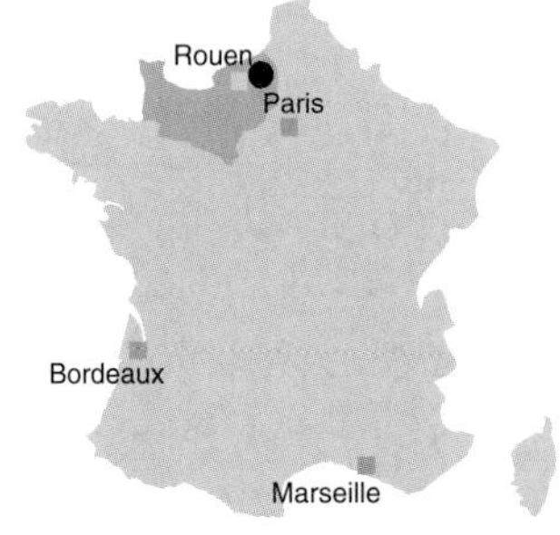

Domaine Saint~Clair, Le Donjon

Chemin de Saint~Clair, 76790 Etretat, France

The colour and character of this ivy-clad château are as inspiring as its breathtaking coastal views. Rooms are cosy and intimate with antique furnishings, and each of the superb newly decorated bedrooms in the adjoining villa are themed after a person who lived as a house guest between 1890 and 1920. After a delicious dinner in one of 3 unique dining rooms guests can retire to the cigar lounge, relax in the pretty courtyard or enjoy a drink on the poolside terrace.

La couleur et le caractère de ce château couvert de vigne vierge sont tout aussi inspirants par leur beauté qu'est la vue à couper le souffle sur la côte. Les pièces sont douillettes et intimes avec des antiquités pour mobilier, et chaque chambre de la villa adjacente, a été superbement décorée récemment selon quelqu'un qui a séjourné dans la maison entre 1890 et 1920. Après un délicieux dîner dans l'une des 3 salles à manger, les hôtes peuvent se retirer dans le salon, se détendre dans la petite cour intérieure ou déguster un verre sur la terrasse près de la piscine.

El colorido y carácter de este château revestido de hiedra son tan sugerentes como su imponente paisaje costero. Sus habitaciones, de mobiliario antiguo, son cálidas y acogedoras y todas las que se encuentran en la villa contigua han sido magníficamente decoradas en fecha reciente con temas relacionados con alguna persona alojada en ellas entre 1820 y 1920. Tras una deliciosa cena en cualquiera de sus 3 excelentes comedores, los huéspedes pueden retirarse al salón de fumadores, disfrutar de una copa en la terraza junto a la piscina o descansar en su precioso patio.

Our inspector loved: *The pool area in the gardens.*

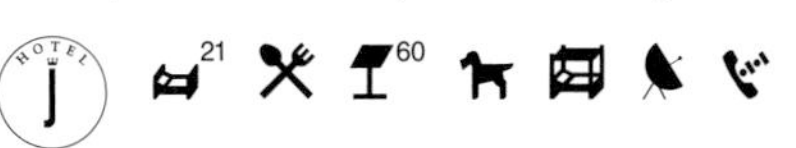

Directions: Town centre > follow signs.

Web: www.johansens.com/donjon
E-mail: info@hoteletretat.com
Tel: +33 2 35 27 08 23
Fax: +33 2 35 29 92 24

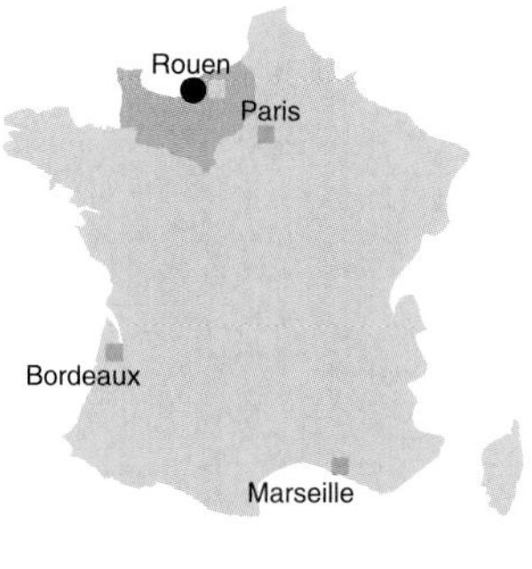

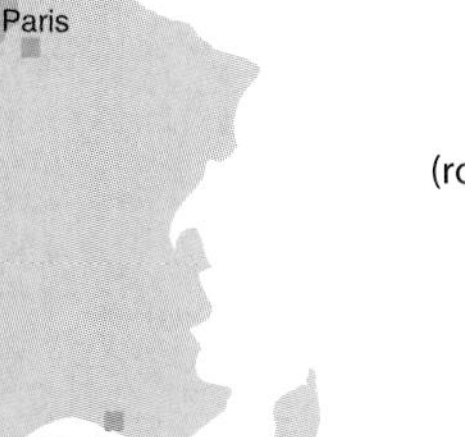

Price Guide:
(room only, closed during January)
single €90-250
double/twin €90–250
suites €255-300

Château la Thillaye

27450 SAINT~CHRISTOPHE~SUR~CONDE, FRANCE

Directions: Leave Pont-Audemer by the D-810 in the direction of Lieurey, then take the D-29 towards Campigny and follow signs for La Thillaye.

Web: www.johansens.com/thillaye
E-mail: chateaulathillaye@wanadoo.fr
Tel: +33 2 32 56 07 24
Fax: +33 2 32 56 70 47

Price Guide:
single €165-220
double €185-230

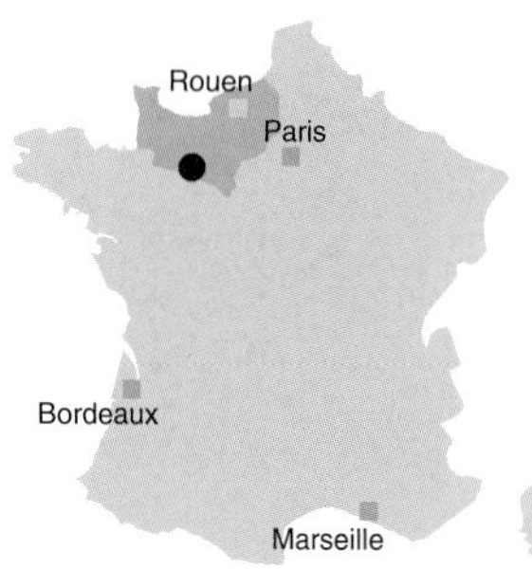

This remarkable 17th-century château has been fully refurbished with all modern conveniences yet retains the traditional, opulent atmosphere of its venerable roots. Perfectly manicured gardens and wooded parklands create an idyllic space in which to relax, whilst the sumptuous interior is cosy with open fireplaces, a grand lounge and delightfully spacious bedrooms. A generous breakfast is scrumptious and is the perfect start to a delightful day. Every evening a menu of gastronomic delights awaits guests.

Ce magnifique château du XVIIe siècle a été complètement rénové avec tout le confort moderne mais en gardant l'atmosphère traditionnelle et opulente des ses vénérables origines. Les jardins et espaces boisés parfaitement entretenus créent un endroit idyllique où se reposer. Les somptueux intérieurs sont douillets avec cheminées, un grand salon et de grandes et ravissantes chambres. Le délicieux et copieux petit-déjeuner est idéal pour bien commencer la journée. Le soir, un menu gastronomique vous attend.

Este magnífico château del siglo XVII ha sido completamente renovado con todas las modernas comodidades de hoy en día sin perder el ambiente opulento y tradicional de su rancio abolengo. Tanto los jardines, perfectamente cuidados, como sus zonas verdes arboladas crean un entorno idílico donde poder relajarse. El suntuoso interior es acogedor y dispone de chimeneas, de un gran salón así como de amplias habitaciones que son una delicia. El desayuno, copioso y exquisito, es el comienzo ideal de un día maravilloso. Cada tarde, los clientes pueden elegir del menú gastronómico delicioso.

Our inspector loved: *The incredibly comfortable beds.*

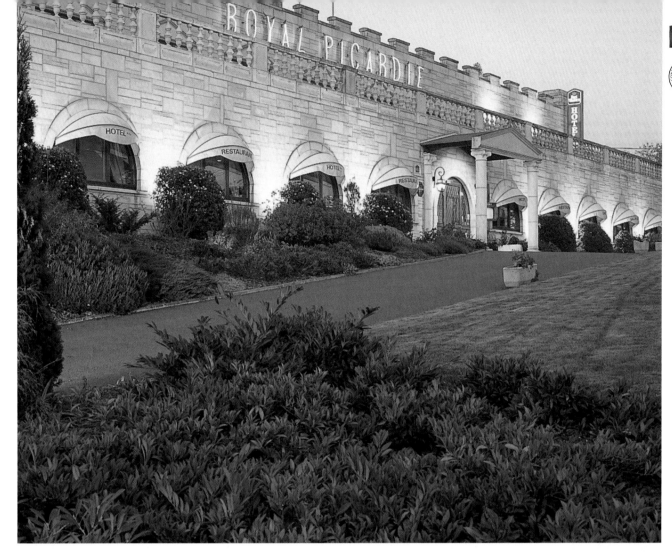

Hôtel Royal Picardie

AVENUE DU GÉNÉRAL LECLERC, 80300 ALBERT, FRANCE

With its location close to Lille and Arras, in the heart of Picardy and its history, just 1 hour from the bay of Somme, Hôtel Royal Picardie offers elegant and refined surroundings. Bedrooms are very comfortable and feature marble bathrooms. Sample excellent French cuisine, with its abundance of flavours, in the hotel's restaurant, "Le Royal". The Bar is an ideal location for informal business meetings or to enjoy a drink with friends. Private lounges and conference rooms accomodating up to 70 are available. The property is air-conditioned throughout.

Tout proche de Lille et Arras, au coeur de la Picardie et de son histoire, à une heure de la Baie de Somme, l'hotel Royal Picardie vous accueille dans un cadre élégant et raffiné. Les chambres sont de grand confort avec salle de bain en marbre. Découvrez les milles et une saveur de la cuisine française au restaurant "Le Royal". Le Bar lieu idéal pour un rendez vous d'affaire ou pour un verre entre ami. Les salons privés et les salles de séminaires adaptant à jusquà 70 personnes sont disponibles. Etablissement entièrement climatisé.

Por su cercanía a Lille y Arras, en el corazón de Picardía, y sólo a 1 hora de la bahía de Somme, Hôtel Royal Picardie ofrece una atmósfera elegante y refinada. Las habitaciones son muy confortables y tienen cuartos de baños en mármol. Pruebe la cocina francesca excelente con sus muchos sabores en el restaurante "Le Royal". El Bar es el lugar ideal para realizar una reunión de negocio informal o para tomar una copa entre amigos. Los salones privados y las salas de conferencias que acomodan a hasta 70 personas están disponibles. La propiedad entera está condizionada.

Our inspector loved: *The dynamic and welcoming proprietors.*

Directions: A1 > Paris > Lille exit 14 > D929 Amiens/Albert. The hotel is immediately south west of Albert. The nearest airports are Lille, Charles de Gaulle and Beauvais Tillé.

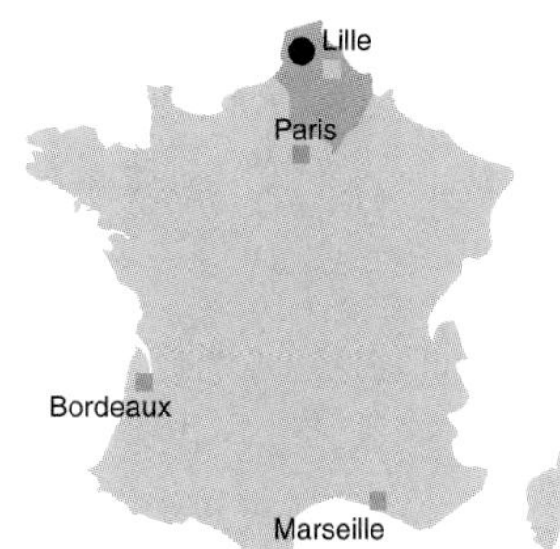

Web: www.johansens.com/royalpicardie
E-mail: reservation@royalpicardie.com
Tel: +33 3 22 75 37 00
Fax: +33 3 22 75 60 19

Price Guide: (breakfast €10)
single €97
double €97-153

La Chartreuse du Val Saint~Esprit

62199 GOSNAY, FRANCE

Set in the heart of the Artois region, the hotel La Chartreuse du Val Saint-Esprit is the prestigious remainder of a past where elegance and refinement were intrinsically linked. This beautiful property has just been completely renovated, and its various lounges and bedrooms are equipped to a very high standard and offer unique character. Local gastronomic delights may be sampled in one of the 3 restaurants where guests can enjoy a truly calm and serene environment.

Situé au cœur de l'Artois, l'hôtel de La Chartreuse du Val Saint-Esprit est le témoin prestigieux d'un passé où l'élégance et le raffinement ètaient indissociables. Cette demeure vient d'être entièrement rènovée, les chambres et les différents salons vous séduiront par la qualité de leur équipement, et de leur personnalité. Une gastronomie locale peut être appréciée dans chacun des 3 restaurants - calme et sérénité vous attendent.

Sito en el corazón de la región del Artois, el hotel La Chartreuse du Val Saint-Esprit es el prestigioso vestigio de un pasado donde la elegancia y el refinamiento estaban intrínsecamente unidos. Esta bella propiedad acaba de ser totalmente renovada y sus variados salones y dormitorios están acondicionados al más alto nivel, lo que les confiere una irrepetible personalidad. Pueden degustarse las delicias gastronómicas locales en alguno de sus 3 restaurantes, donde los huéspedes podrán disfrutar de un entorno verdaderamente sereno y tranquilo.

Our inspector loved: *The quality of the gastronomic cuisine.*

Directions: A26 > exit 6 for Bethune.

Web: www.johansens.com/lachartreuse
E-mail: levalsaintesprit@lachartreuse.com
Tel: +33 3 21 62 80 00
Fax: +33 3 21 62 42 50

Price Guide: (breakfast €14)
standard €89–108
superior €109–135
de luxe €128-159
family room €210
suite €380

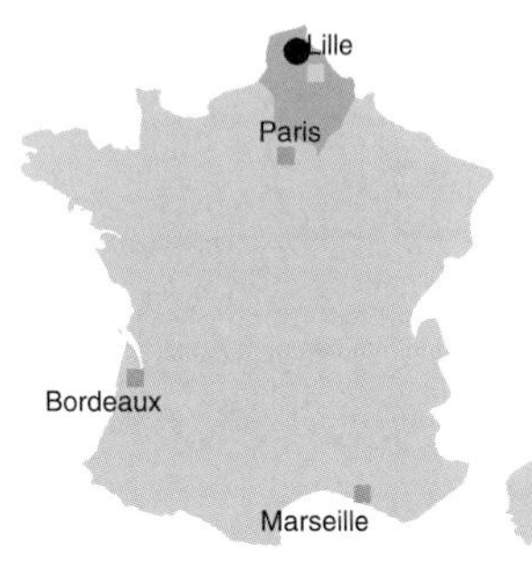

Château de Cocove

62890 RECQUES~SUR~HEM, FRANCE

This classically proportioned château nestles within 11 hectares of its own pretty parkland and is an idyllic setting in which to enjoy fine regional cuisine. The elegant and panoramic dining room is the backdrop for romantic candle-lit dinners, whilst afternoon tea and apéritifs served by attentive staff can be savoured from the terrace. A carefully planned menu and fine wine selection ensure a gastronomic delight.

Ce château de style XVIIIe niché au sein des 11 ha de son joli parc, est l'endroit idéal où apprécier une cuisine régionale raffinée. La salle à manger panoramique élégante est la toile de fond pour des dîners romantiques aux chandelles, alors que le thé de l'après-midi et les apéritifs servis par un personnel attentif peuvent être dégustés sur la terrasse. Un menu soigneusement planifié et une sélection de vins fins sont la garantie d'un régal gastronomique.

Este château de proporciones clásicas está enclavado dentro de las 11 ha que ocupan sus bellos jardines. Posee un idílico emplazamiento en el que se puede disfrutar de una excelente cocina regional. Su elegante y panorámico comedor constituye el perfecto telón de fondo para románticas cenas a la luz de las velas, mientras el té de la tarde y los aperitivos, servidos por su atento personal, se saborean en la terraza. Una carta cuidadosamente elaborada y una excelente selección de vinos le aseguran todo un placer gastronómico.

Our inspector loved: *The wine cellar, which is open to visitors.*

Directions: A26 > Calais > Paris exit No 2 > Cocove.

Web: www.johansens.com/chateaudecocove
E-mail: chateaudecocove@hotmail.com
Tel: +33 3 21 82 68 29
Fax: +33 3 21 82 72 59

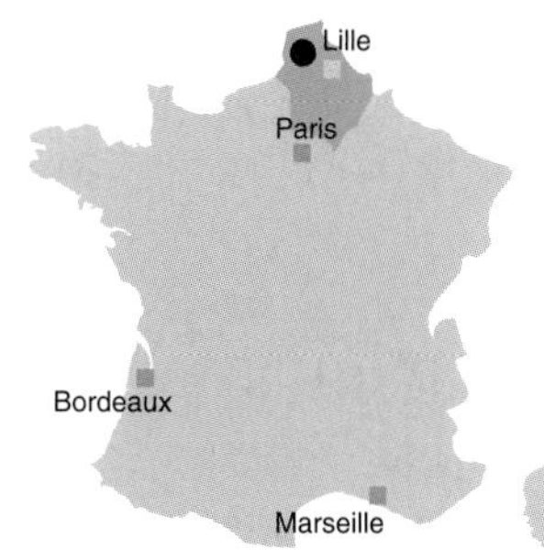

Price Guide: (room only, closed 24th-25th December)
single €80–100
double €90–162

22 25

Château de Remaisnil

80600 REMAISNIL, FRANCE

Formerly owned by Laura Ashley, this historic hideaway in North-Picardy is elegant, welcoming and romantic. Run by the affable Carroll family, this stone and brick château is a striking example of Rococo architecture and features period furnishings throughout. Log fires burn in the public rooms, and in the evening guests can enjoy a pre-dinner drink in the drawing room before a candle-lit meal with an exquisite selection of wines in the intimate dining room.

Ancienne propriété de Laura Ashley, ce refuge historique en Nord Picardie est élégant, accueillant et romantique. Géré par la très courtoise famille Carroll, ce château de pierres et de briques est une exemple frappant de l'architecture Rococo et de superbes et nombreux meubles antiques en ornent les pièces. Des feux de bois crépitent dans les pièces communes et le soir, les hôtes peuvent apprécier un apéritif dans le salon avant de déguster un repas aux chandelles agrémenté de délicieux vins, dans l'intime salle à manger.

Este rincón histórico del Norte-Picardy, antigua propiedad de Laura Ashley es elegante, acogedor y romántico. Regentado por la familia Carroll tan afable, este château de piedra y ladrillo resulta ser un magnífico ejemplo de arquitectura rococó, haciendo gala de un mobiliario de la época. Tanto los salones comunes disponen de chimeneas de leña. Por la noche los clientes pueden disfrutar de una copa previa a la cena en el salón, para luego pasar a cenar a la luz de las velas con una exquisita selección de vinos en su íntimo comedor.

***Our inspector loved:** The wonderful welcome from Jérôme, the resident owner.*

Directions: Airport > Lille > Beauvais > Charles de Gaulle.

Web: www.johansens.com/remaisnil
E-mail: charles.carroll@wanadoo.fr
Tel: +33 3 22 77 07 47
Fax: +33 3 22 77 41 23

Price Guide: (room only
closed 1st December - 1st February)
single €150-250
double €195-295
suite €350

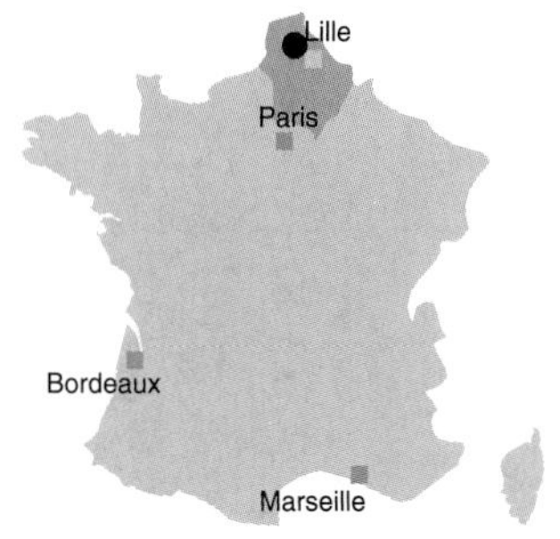

Carlton Hotel

RUE DE PARIS, 59000 LILLE, FRANCE

A new health and fitness facility and solarium as well as stunning new double floor luxury suite are the latest additions to this historic city centre hotel. Situated in the Cupole, the suite has its own lounge, bar and bathroom, and is the ideal place in which to relax after a day enjoying Lille's shopping, museums and opera. The hotel is furnished in Louis XV and XVI styles and is easily accessible by plane or rail.

Un centre de remise en forme et un solarium ainsi qu'une superbe suite luxueuse sur deux niveaux sont les dernières nouveautés de cet hôtel historique du centre ville. Située dans la coupole la suite a son propre salon, bar et salle de bain et est l'endroit idéal pour se détendre après avoir profiter d'une journée de shopping, de musées et d'opéra à Lille. L'hôtel est meublé en style Louis XV et Louis XVI et est d'accès facile par avion ou train.

Las nuevas instalaciones del centro de la salud y solarium, así como una impresionante suite de lujo de dos pisos constituyen las últimas mejoras realizadas en este hotel del centro histórico de la ciudad. Situado en el Cupole, la suite tiene su propio salón, bar y cuarto de baño; es el lugar ideal para relajarse tras disfrutar de un día de compras en Lille, en sus museos y ópera. El hotel está amueblado con los estilos Luis XV y Luis XVI y es de fácil acceso por vía aérea o por ferrocarril.

Our inspector loved: *The luxury suite in the domed tower of the hotel.*

Directions: In the heart of Lille, near the opera, in the main square. The nearest airport is Lille Lesquin.

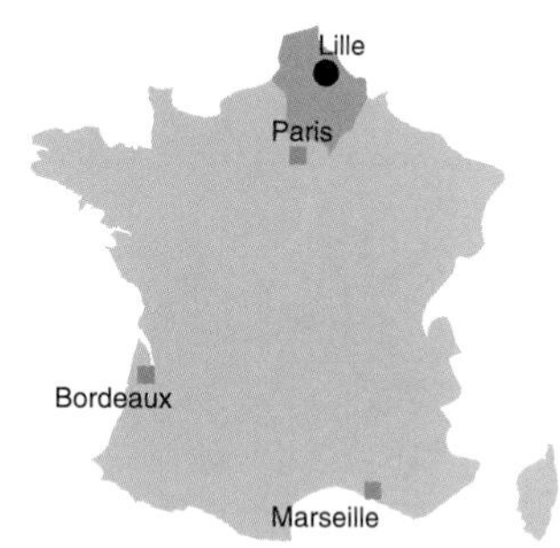

Web: www.johansens.com/carltonlille
E-mail: carlton@carltonlille.com
Tel: +33 3 20 13 33 13
Fax: +33 3 20 51 48 17

Price Guide: (breakfast €17)
single €173-230
double €265
suite €455-1,240

Paris

Hotel location shown in red (hotel) or purple (spa hotel) with page number

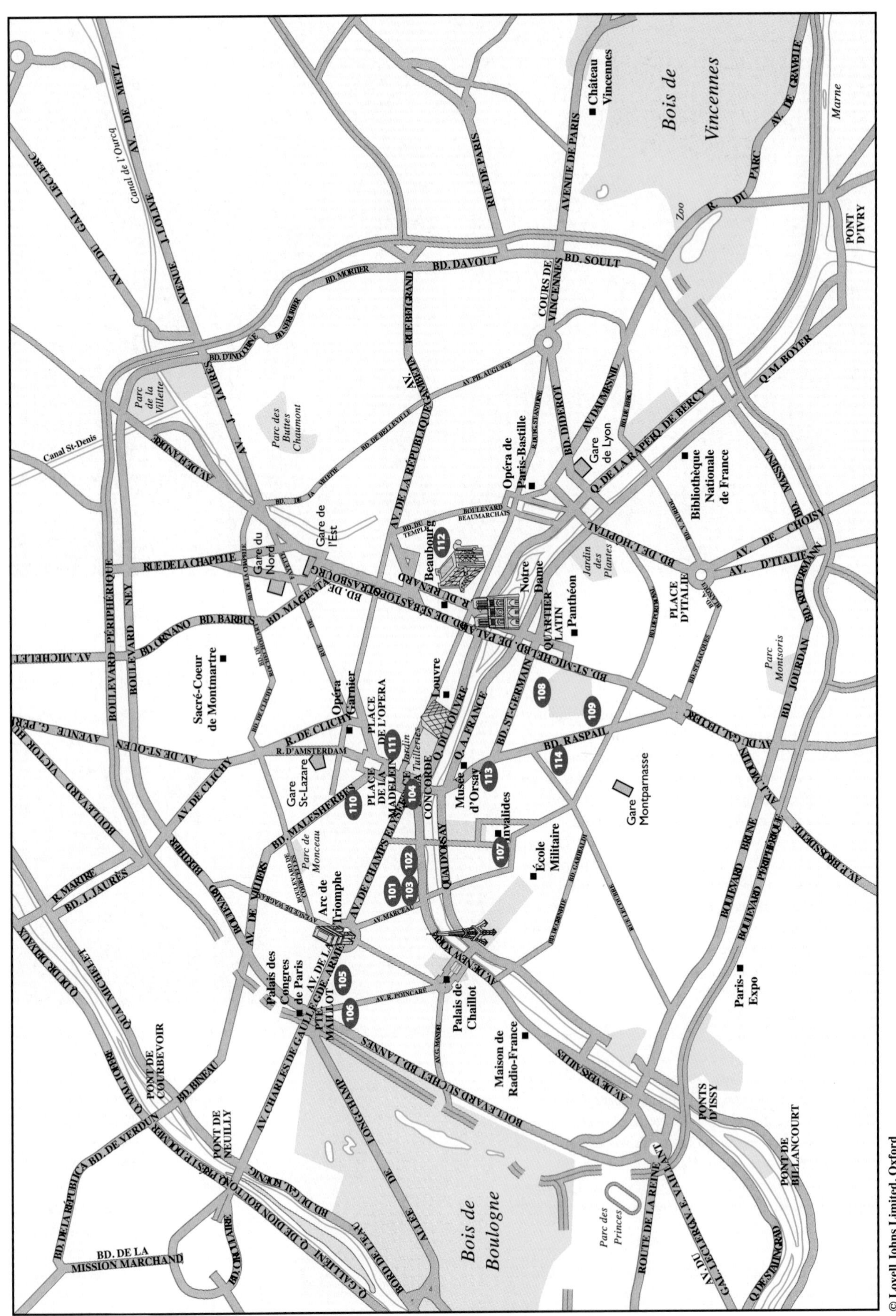

Hôtel de Sers

41, AVENUE PIERRE 1ER DE SERBIE, 75008 PARIS, FRANCE

This new hotel, in the heart of Paris, is in walking distance of the Champs-Elysées. The owner and architect have created an amazing building where classic Parisian architecture is combined with cutting-edge design, and includes a monumental staircase leading to the former salons of the Marquis de Sers. Bedrooms are bright with specially designed furniture and bathrooms are breathtaking. The restaurant overlooks a private courtyard where meals and drinks can be enjoyed.

Ce nouvel hôtel, au cœur de paris, est à quelques minutes à pied des Champs-Elysées. Le propriétaire et l'architecte ont créé un étonnant établissement où l'architecture Parisienne classique se mélange à la pointe du design et comprend notamment un escalier monumental menant aux anciens salons du Marquis de Sers. Les chambres sont claires et équipées de mobilier spécialement dessiné et les salles de bains sont superbes. Le restaurant donne sur une cour privée où repas et boissons sont servis.

Este hotel nuevo, sito en el corazón de París se encuentra a corta distancia a pie de los Campos Elíseos. El propietario y el arquitecto han creado un asombroso edificio en el que se combina la arquitectura clásica parisina con el diseño vanguardista; incluye una monumental escalera que sube hasta los antiguos salones del Marqués de Sers. Las habitaciones resultan impecables con muebles especialmente diseñados e impresionantes cuartos de baño. El restaurante da a un patio privado en el que se puede disfrutar de la comida o de una copa.

Our inspector loved: *The clever and delicate combination of the very modern with the history of the building.*

Directions: Avenue Pierre 1er de Serbie is off Avenue George V.

Web: www.johansens.com/hoteldesers
E-mail: contact@hoteldesers.com
Tel: +33 1 53 23 75 75
Fax: +33 1 53 23 75 76

Price Guide: (room only, excluding VAT)
double €450-600
suite €700-2,100

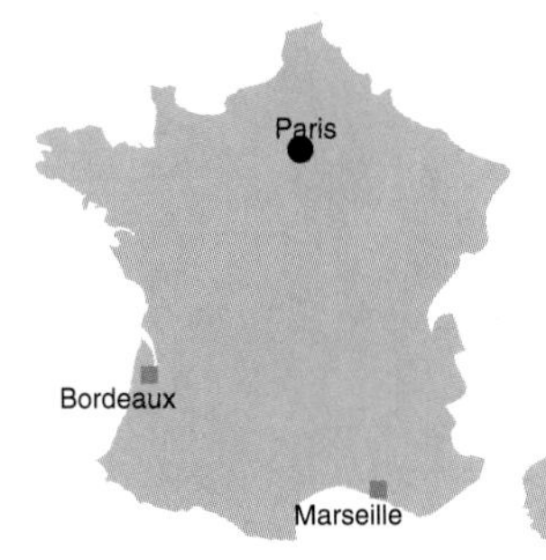

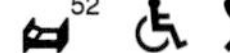

Hôtel San Régis

12 RUE JEAN GOUJON, 75008 PARIS, FRANCE

Directions: Rue Jean Goujon is off the Champs-Elysées and Avenue Montaigne.

Web: www.johansens.com/sanregis
E-mail: message@hotel-sanregis.fr
Tel: +33 1 44 95 16 16
Fax: +33 1 45 61 05 48

Price Guide: (room only)
single €330
double/twin €435-595
suite €655-1,050

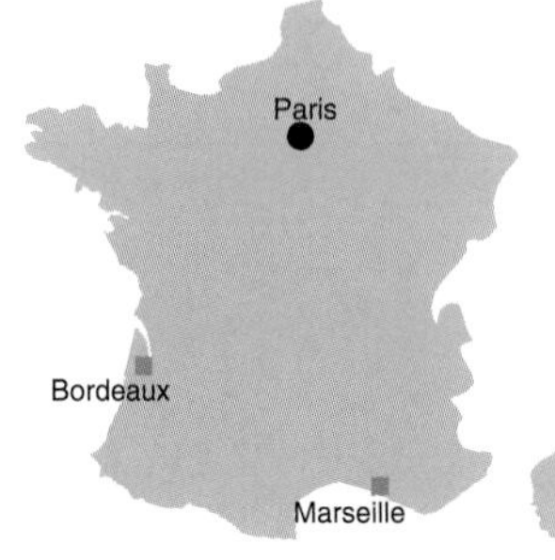

Deep in the heart of Paris's fashion district lies this small, intimate and beautifully appointed hotel. Built in 1857, the interior charmingly combines modern comforts with 19th-century furniture and antiques. Each of the 44 bedrooms has been individually decorated and boasts a marble bathroom as well as all modern conveniences. The restaurant, decorated in the style of an old library, is a haven of tranquillity and serves simply impeccable fare.

Ce luxueux petit hôtel parisien à l'atmosphère intime jouit d'une situation privilégiée au coeur du quartier de la mode. Construit en 1857, le San Régis marie à merveille des meubles et des objets d'art du XIXe siècle avec un confort des plus modernes. Chacune des 44 chambres a son propre charme et dispose d'une salle de bains en marbre et des dernières commodités. Le restaurant, aménagé dans le décor d'une bibliothèque est un havre de paix propice à la dégustation de mets exquis.

Este pequeño, íntimo y precioso hotel está situado en el corazón mismo del distrito de moda de París, construido en 1857, en su interior combina deliciosamente su moderno confort con el mobiliario y antigüedades del siglo XIX. Cada una de sus 44 habitaciones ha sido individualmente decorada y ostenta cuartos de baño de mármol además de todas las modernas instalaciones. El restaurante, decorado al estilo de una antigua biblioteca, es un refugio de tranquilidad donde se sirve sencillamente una comida impecable.

Our inspector loved: *The intimate atmosphere and sense of seclusion, set apart from the rest of the world, even though the buzz of Paris is only metres away.*

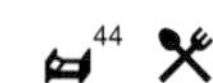

La Trémoille

14 RUE DE LA TRÉMOILLE, 75008 PARIS, FRANCE

This boutique-style hotel is now the epitome of 21st-century elegance. The bedrooms are beautifully designed in muted tones with inspiring use of fabric and equipped to a high standard (Internet access, CD and DVD players). The public rooms house a superb collection of Parisian photographic artwork. The restaurant and bar Senso offers superb French cuisine in an original setting designed by Sir Terence Conran. There is a new health and beauty centre with sauna, fitness facilities and superb treatment and massage rooms.

Ce boutique hôtel est l'exemple même de l'élégance du XXIe siècle. Les chambres sont décorées dans des tons doux avec une utilisation inhabituelle des tissus et offrent un équipement très haut de gamme (accès internet, lecteur CD & DVD). Les pièces communes abritent une collection d'oeuvres photographiques sur Paris. Le restaurant et bar Senso offre le meilleur de la cuisine française dans un décor original imaginé par Sir Terence Conran. Nouveau centre de remise en forme avec sauna et des salons de beauté et de massage.

Este hotel de estilo boutique se ha convertido en símbolo de la elegancia del siglo XXI. Sus habitaciones han sido magníficamente diseñadas en suaves tonos gracias a la inspirada utilización de la tela. También están equipadas al más alto nivel (acceso a internet y equipos de CD y DVD). Sus salones selet albergan una excepcional colección de fotografías artísticas de París. El restaurante y bar Senso proporciona fantástica cocina francesa en un original entorno diseñado por Sir Terence Conran. Dispone de un nuevo centro de salud con sauna, instalaciones de fitness y de excelentes salones de belleza y masaje.

Our inspector loved: *The décor in the bedrooms.*

Directions: Metro stations: Alma-Marceau or Franklin Roosevelt.

Web: www.johansens.com/tremoille
E-mail: reservation@hotel-tremoille.com
Tel: +33 1 56 52 14 00
Fax: +33 1 40 70 01 08

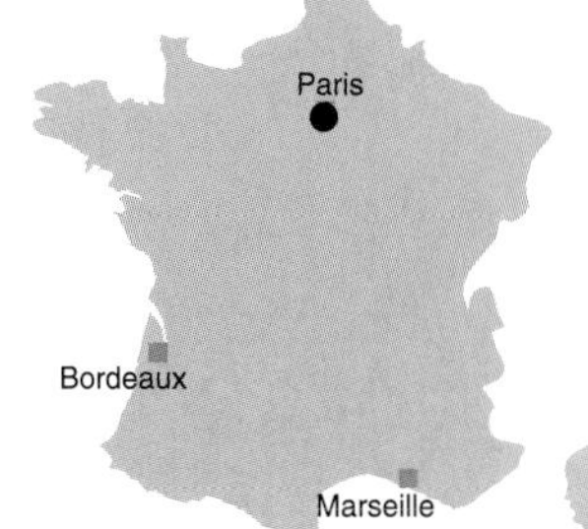

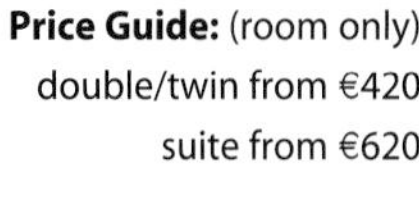

Price Guide: (room only)
double/twin from €420
suite from €620

Hôtel de Crillon

10, PLACE DE LA CONCORDE, 75008 PARIS, FRANCE

This renowned hotel stands proudly on Place de la Concorde, fronted by a Corinthian colonnade. Service is truly outstanding: professional staff look after guests' every need, and special touches such as fresh flowers, beautiful fabrics and thoughtful décor are found throughout the hotel. Furnished in a true 18th-century style, all of the bedrooms and suites are individual and some offer stunning city views. The gastronomic Les Ambassadeurs restaurant is located in a sumptuous listed room.

Ce palace de renom, avec sa façade de colonnes corinthiennes, se dresse fièrement Place de la Concorde. Le service est véritablement remarquable : le personnel professionnel est attentif au moindre désir des clients et des attentions particulières telles que fleurs fraîches, superbes étoffes et décoration raffinée se retrouvent à travers tout l'hôtel. Meublé dans un superbe style du XVIIIe siècle, toutes les chambres et suites sont différentes et certaines offrent de magnifiques vues sur la ville. Le restaurant gastronomique "Les Ambassadeurs" est situé dans une somptueuse salle classée.

Este famoso hotel provisto de columnas corintias a la entrada se enorgullece de estar en plena Place de la Concorde. El servicio es verdaderamente extraordinario: su personal de profesionales atiende puntualmente todas y cada una de las necesidades de los clientes. Pequeños detalles como flores naturales, hermosas telas o una esmerada decoración están presentes en todo el hotel. Amueblado al más auténtico estilo del siglo XVIII, todas las habitaciones y suites son individuales y algunas de ellas ofrecen espectaculares vistas a la ciudad. El restaurante gastronómico Les Ambassadeurs ocupa una suntuosa habitación catalogada de interés histórico.

Our inspector loved: *The superb restaurant, Les Ambassadeurs.*

Directions: The hotel overlooks Place de la Concorde.

Web: www.johansens.com/crillon
E-mail: crillon@crillon.com
Tel: +33 1 44 71 15 00
Fax: +33 1 44 71 15 02

Price Guide: (room only)
single €615
double/twin €695-890
suite €1,160-8,200

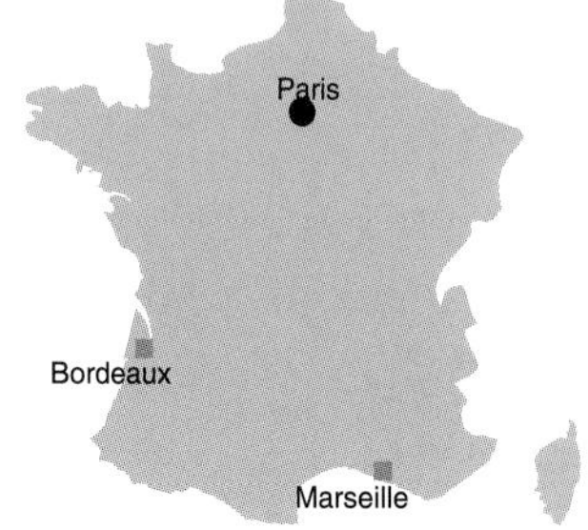

Hôtel Duret

30 RUE DURET, 75116 PARIS, FRANCE

Moments from Champs-Elysées, 2 minutes from the Arc de Triumph and within walking distance of Place de l'Etoile and Porte Maillot, this refined Parisian hotel prides itself on its extraordinary service and welcoming ambience. Inviting warm tones, complemented by bold splashes of colour adorn each room. Guest rooms have been decorated in different colour schemes and furnished with striking dark wood in cutting edge styles. A gourmet buffet breakfast is available and the lounge bar serves cocktails. Relax in the lobby bar or private salon with plasma TV.

Proche des Champs-Elysées et à 2 minutes de l'Arc de Triomphe, de la Place de l'Etoile et de la Porte Maillot, cet hôtel parisien raffiné peut s'enorgueillir de son service et de son atmosphère chaleureuse. Des tons chauds et attrayants accompagnés de touches de couleurs vives décorent chaque pièce. Les chambres sont décorées selon différents thèmes de couleurs et ont des meubles de style moderne en bois foncé. Un superbe buffet est proposé au petit-déjeuner et le bar lounge sert des cocktails. Les hôtes peuvent se relaxer au bar ou dans le salon privé équipé d'un écran plasma.

A unos minutos de los Champs-Elysées, a 2 minutos del Arco del Triunfo y a una distancia a pie de la Place de L'Etoile y Porte Maillot, este elegante hotel parisino se enorgullece por su extraordinario servicio y ambiente acogedor. Cada habitación está decorada en atractivos tonos cálidos complementados por salpicaduras de colores atrevidos, esquemas en diferentes colores y amuebladas con impresionantes maderas oscuras en estilo vanguardista. Hay desayuno buffet gourmet y el salón-bar sirve cócteles. Relájese en el bar del hall o en un salón privado equipado con televisor de plasma.

Directions: 16th arrondissement near Place de l'Etoile and Porte Maillot.

Web: www.johansens.com/duret
E-mail: reservation@hotelduret.com
Tel: +33 1 45 00 42 60
Fax: +33 1 45 00 55 89

Price Guide: (breakfast €15)
single €210-280
double €210-280
suite €410

Our inspector loved: *The superb, stylish designer furniture.*

  27  8    

LA VILLA MAILLOT

143 AVENUE DE MALAKOFF, 75116 PARIS, FRANCE

A short walk from the Champs-Elysées, the Villa Maillot is a charming, elegant and discreet haven in the centre of Paris. Behind the façade of this unique historic residence lies a friendly, modern interior, with pastel colours, fireplace and wooden floors creating creating an atmosphere of warmth and hospitality. The bedrooms are all well appointed and have rose-coloured marble bathrooms. Breakfast, selected from the enticing buffet, may be enjoyed in the newly redesigned garden conservatory.

A deux pas des Champs-Elysées, la Villa Maillot est un havre de charme, élégant et discret au coeur de la capitale. La façade de cet ancien hôtel particulier cache un hôtel moderne et amical, avec de subtiles nuances de pastels, une cheminée et des sols de bois créant une atmosphère chaleureuse et conviviale. Les chambres sont toutes bien équipées et offrent des salles de bains en marbre rose. Un superbe buffet petit déjeuner dressé dans les salons est servi dans la verrière complètement reconçue, nichée dans un jardin.

A corta distancia a pie de los Campos Elíseos, la Villa Maillot es un encantador, elegante y discreto remanso de paz en pleno centro de París. Tras la fachada de esta singular residencia histórica se encuentra un placentero y moderno interior decorado con colores en tonos pastel, con chimenea y suelos de madera que le proporcionan un acogedor y hospitalario ambiente. Sus habitaciones están todas bien acondicionadas y cuentan con cuartos de baño de mármol color rosa. Puede disfrutarse del desayuno, seleccionado de su sugerente buffet, en su jardín de invierno, recientemente rediseñado.

Our inspector loved: *The intimate and welcoming spa with steam bath, sauna and massage.*

Directions: Close to Porte Maillot and the Champs-Elysées.

Web: www.johansens.com/lavillamaillot
E-mail: resa@lavillamaillot.fr
Tel: +33 1 53 64 52 52
Fax: +33 1 45 00 60 61

Price Guide: (room only)
double/twin €250–390
suite €350–600

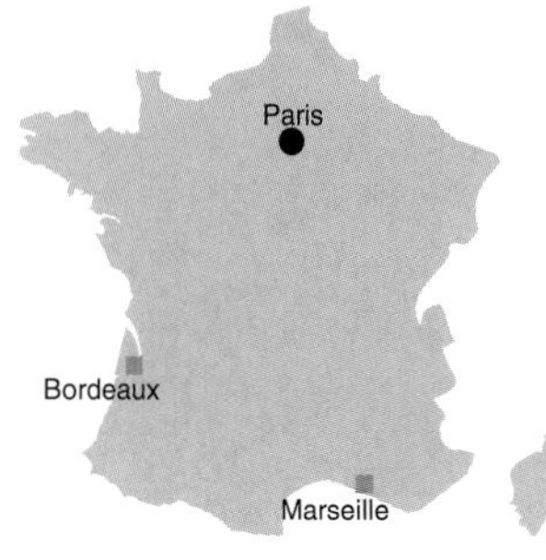

HÔTEL LE TOURVILLE

16 AVENUE DE TOURVILLE, 75007 PARIS, FRANCE

Though located in the heart of Paris, close to the Eiffel Tower, this neo-classical hotel enjoys a unique atmosphere of refined tranquillity. Soft pastel colours form a warm ambience and ideal background for the wealth of antique furniture and paintings that grace its salons and bedrooms. Guests are cosseted by the fine breakfasts served in the vaulted cellar room and the large range of toiletries that are thoughtfully provided in the marble bathrooms. WiFi access is available.

Bien qu'il se situe au coeur de Paris, à deux pas de la Tour Eiffel, cet hôtel néoclassique jouit d'une tranquillité raffinée. Les couleurs pastel créent une ambiance chaleureuse et soulignent à merveille la beauté des nombreux meubles et objets d'art anciens qui ornent les salons et les chambres. Les visiteurs choyés dégustent d'excellents petits déjeuners dans la cave voûtée et profitent du vaste choix d'articles de toilette gracieusement mis à leur disposition dans les salles de bains en marbre. Accès WiFi disponible.

A pesar de estar en pleno corazón de París, muy cerca de la Torre Eiffel, este hotel neoclásico goza de un singular toque de refinada tranquilidad. Sus suaves tonos pastel crean un cálido ambiente y un entorno ideal en pro de la exuberancia tanto de su mobiliario antiguo como de los lienzos que adornan los salones y habitaciones. Los clientes son agasajados con los excelentes desayunos servidos en el sótano abovedado así como con una amplia gama de artículos de tocador puestos a su disposición en los cuartos de baño de mármol. Acceso WiFi disponible.

Our inspector loved: *The superb paintings in the bedrooms.*

Directions: Between the Eiffel Tower and Les Invalides.

Web: www.johansens.com/tourville
E-mail: hotel@tourville.com
Tel: +33 1 47 05 62 62
Fax: +33 1 47 05 43 90

Price Guide: (breakfast €12)
double/twin €170–250
junior suite €310-330

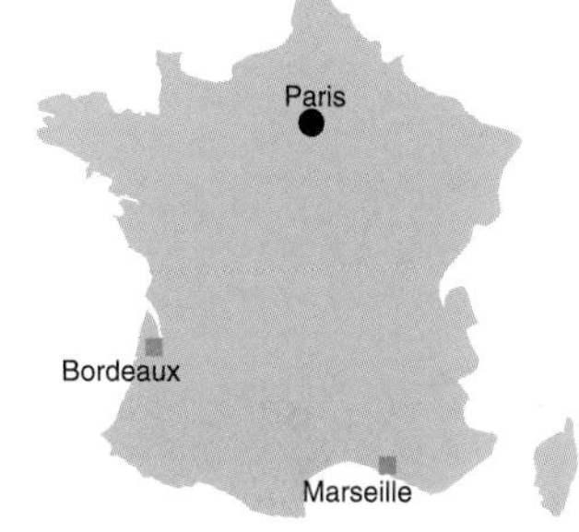

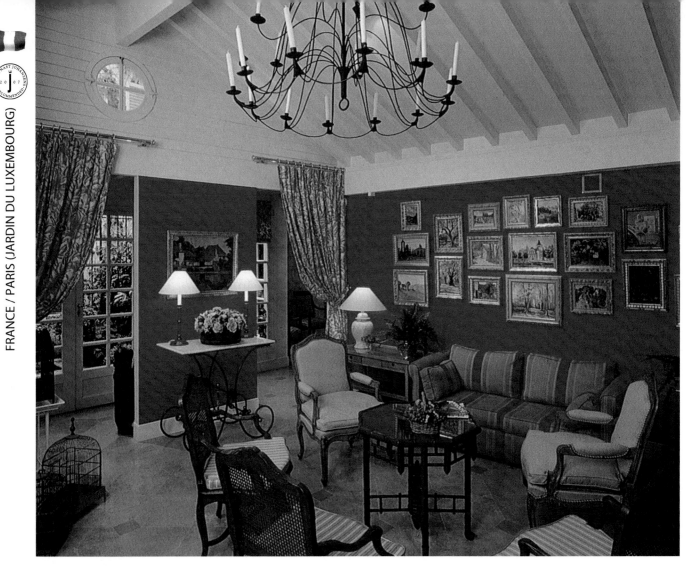

Le Relais Médicis

23 RUE RACINE, 75006 PARIS, FRANCE

Directions: The hotel is a few yards from Place de l'Odéon and a few minutes from Boulevard Saint-Germain.

Web: www.johansens.com/medicis
E-mail: reservation@relaismedicis.com
Tel: +33 1 43 26 00 60
Fax: +33 1 40 46 83 39

Price Guide:
single €138-188
double/twin €168-239
double de luxe €215-258

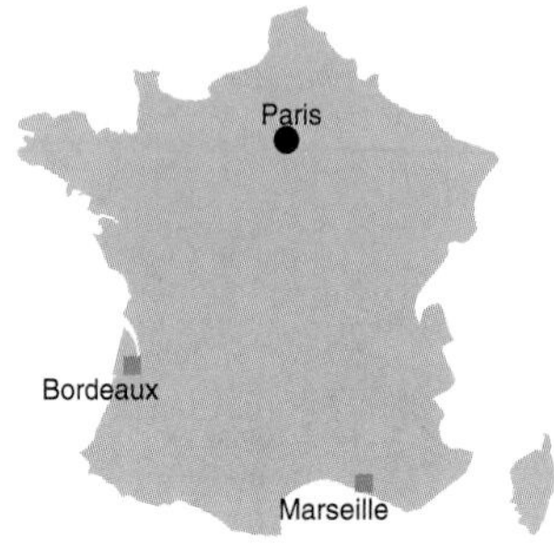

Tucked away just a few minutes from l'Odéon, the Jardin du Luxembourg and the Boulevard St Germain, this delightful hotel is arranged around a charming patio that is lavishly planted between April and September. Antique pieces, painted woodwork, Impressionist-style printed curtains and vintage photographs create a warm atmosphere. The 16 cosy bedrooms are surprisingly spacious and decorated with cheerful colours reminiscent of Provence and Italy; all have marble bathrooms and air conditioning. Numerous sights and attractions are within easy reach.

Situé à quelques minutes de l'Odéon du Jardin du Luxembourg et du Boulevard St. Germain, cet hôtel de charme est construit autour d'une fontaine et d'un joli patio très fleuri des mois d'Avril à Septembre. Des meubles antiques, des boiseries peintes, des rideaux "impressionnistes" et des photos très anciennes créent une ambiance chaleureuse. Les 16 chambres sont à la fois intimes et spacieuses et sont décorées de couleurs qui rappellent celles de Provence et de l'Italie. Elles disposent toutes de salles de bain en marbre et sont climatisées. De nombreuses attractions sont d'accès facile.

A tan sólo unos minutos de l´Odéon, de Jardin du Luxembourg y del Boulevard St. Germain, aunque escondido encontramos este encantador hotel rodeado por un delicioso patio rebosante de plantas desde abril a septiembre. Piezas antiguas, carpintería pintada, cortinas estampadas en estilo impresionista y fotografías de época le otorgan un ambiente muy acogedor. Sus 16 cómodas y sorprendentemente espaciosas habitaciones, decoradas con alegres colores, reminiscencia de Provenza e Italia, poseen mármol en los cuartos de baño y aire acondicionado. Se puede disfrutar de numerosos puntos de interés y atracciones de fácil acceso.

Our inspector loved: *The lounge with its homely ambience.*

LE SAINTE~BEUVE

9 RUE SAINTE~BEUVE, 75006 PARIS, FRANCE

Situated on a quiet street, this superbly renovated hotel is excellently positioned near to Saint-Germain-des-Prés, Saint-Sulpice and the Jardin du Luxembourg. The charming Le Sainte-Beuve has the atmosphere of a chic Parisian home, complemented by friendly and welcoming service. The bedrooms are attractively decorated with pastel colours and antique furnishings, whilst the suite is simply beautiful. The fashionable shops and cultural attractions of central Paris are all within easy reach.

Dans une rue calme et idéalement situé près de Saint-Germain-des-Prés, Saint-Sulpice et les Jardins du Luxembourg, l'hôtel Sainte-Beuve a l'atmosphère d'une maison chic parisienne, complétée par un service amical et accueillant. Toutes les chambres sont agréablement décorées avec des couleurs pastel et un mobilier ancien, alors que la suite est tout simplement superbe. Les magasins en vogue et attractions culturelles du centre de Paris sont tous d'accès facile.

Situado en una calle tranquila, este hotel magníficamente renovado goza de una posición excelente, cerca de Saint-Germain-des-Prés, Saint-Sulpice y el Jardin du Luxembourg. El ambiente del encantador Le Sainte-Beuve, es el de un elegante hogar parisino y se completa con un servicio cordial y acogedor. Las habitaciones están decoradas con gusto en colores pastel y muebles antiguos, mientras que la suite es sencillamente maravillosa. Las tiendas de moda y las atracciones culturales del centro de Paris están al alcance de la mano.

Our inspector loved: *The very welcoming lounge area.*

Directions: Between Saint-Germain-des-Prés and Jardin du Luxembourg.

Web: www.johansens.com/saintebeuve
E-mail: saintebeuve@wanadoo.fr
Tel: +33 1 45 48 20 07
Fax: +33 1 45 48 67 52

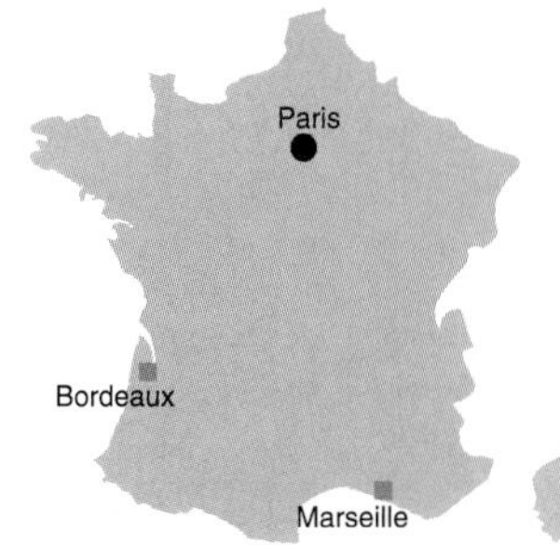

Price Guide: (breakfast €14.50)
room €135–338

Hôtel le Lavoisier

21 RUE LAVOISIER, 75008 PARIS, FRANCE

One of the most chic hotels in Paris, Hôtel le Lavoisier is mere minutes away from Place de la Concorde and the famous shops of the Boulevard Haussman. Well-chosen antique furniture and warm, elegant colour schemes compose a refinement that makes this hotel an ideal retreat from the busy streets of Paris. The intimacy of communal areas such as the cellar breakfast room, and the attentive service of the staff are suggestive of comforts from outside the city.

L'Hôtel Le Lavoisier, l'un des plus chics de Paris, n'est qu'à quelques minutes de la place de la Concorde et des célèbres magasins du boulevard Haussmann. Les meubles anciens choisis avec soin et les couleurs élégantes et chaleureuses du décor créent une ambiance raffinée qui fait de cet hôtel un refuge idéal pour échapper à la fébrilité des rues parisiennes. L'intimité des salles communes, telles que la petite salle à manger occupant la cave, et la prévenance du personnel évoquent le charme des hôtels provinciaux.

El Hôtel Le Lavoisier, uno de los hoteles más elegantes de París, se encuentra a tan sólo unos minutos de la Place de la Concorde y de las famosas tiendas de Boulevard Haussman. El mobiliario antiguo selecto así como las elegantes y cálidas combinaciones de color dan esa finura que hace de este hotel un lugar ideal en el que descansar del bullicio de las calles parisinas. La intimidad de sus espacios comunes como su sótano-salón de desayunos y el atento servicio de su personal evocan todas las comodidades que ofrece el exterior de la ciudad.

Our inspector loved: *Its ideal location in the heart of Paris, and the very friendly staff.*

Directions: Near Place Saint-Augustin.

Web: www.johansens.com/lelavoisier
E-mail: info@hotellavoisier.com
Tel: +33 1 53 30 06 06
Fax: +33 1 53 30 23 00

Price Guide: (room only, excluding VAT)
double/twin €230-261
suite €289–321

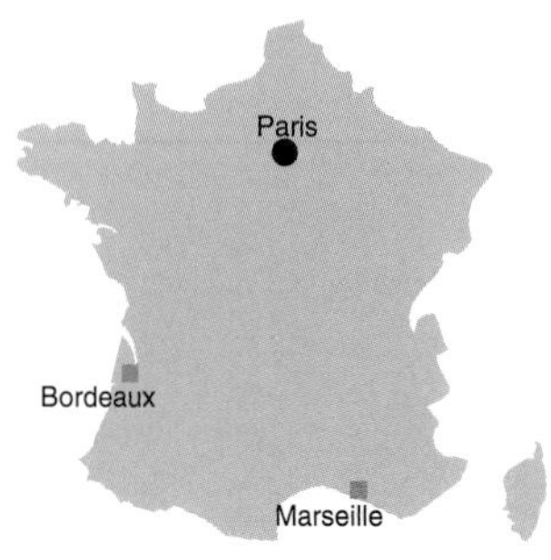

Hôtel Opéra Richepanse

14 RUE DU CHEVALIER DE SAINT~GEORGE, 75001 PARIS, FRANCE

This art deco hotel, which is located in the heart of historic Paris, next to rue Saint-Honoré and Place de la Madeleine, and between rue Royale and Place Vendôme, exudes a typically Parisian elegance. 3 suites and some of the rooms are particularly generously sized, perfect for families or businessmen who wish to hold their meetings in a welcoming setting. The hotel is ideally located for exploring the city on foot: luxury boutiques and shopping centres, museums, monuments, restaurants and events can be found nearby. A friendly and competent team helps organise your stay.

Au cœur du Paris historique, cet hôtel art déco à côté de la rue Saint-Honoré et de la Place de la Madeleine, entre la rue Royale et la Place Vendôme, est d'une élégance très parisienne. Les 3 suites et certaines chambres sont particulièrement grandes, pouvant accueillir des familles ou des hommes d'affaires à la recherche d'un espace convivial pour leurs rendez-vous professionnels. C'est le lieu idéal pour se rendre partout à pied: boutiques de luxe, grands magasins, musées, monuments, restaurants et spectacles. Une équipe accueillante et compétente vous aidera à organiser votre séjour.

Este hotel representativo del art deco ubicado en el corazón del París histórico, entre la rue Royale y la Place Vendôme y junto a la rue Saint-Honoré y la Place de la Madeleine, emana típica elegancia parisina. Las 3 suites de que dispone y algunas habitaciones son especialmente amplias, perfectas para familias o para hombres de negocios que deseen celebrar reuniones en un ambiente acogedor. El hotel se encuentra en el lugar ideal para quienes deseen explorar la ciudad a pie. En los alrededores podrá encontrar lujosas boutiques, centros comerciales, museos, monumentos, restaurantes y eventos. Un personal cualificado y atento le ayudará a planificar su estancia.

Our inspector loved: *The top floor bedrooms overlooking Place de la Madeleine.*

38

Directions: Centrally located, near to la Madeleine and Place de la Concorde.

Web: www.johansens.com/richepanse
E-mail: hotel@richepanse.com
Tel: +33 1 42 60 36 00
Fax: +33 1 42 60 13 03

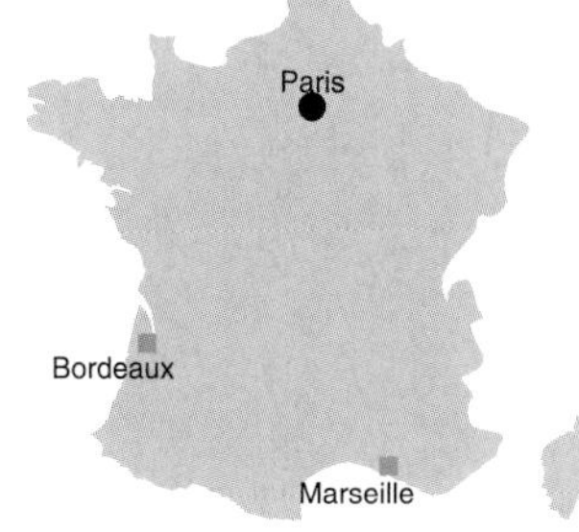

Price Guide: (room only)
double €240-350
suite €450-590

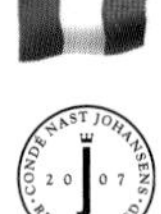

FRANCE / PARIS (MARAIS)

Hôtel du Petit Moulin

29-31 RUE DE POITU, 75003 PARIS, FRANCE

Directions: The hotel is situated between Bastille and République, close to the Hôtel de Ville and Place des Voges.

Web: www.johansens.com/petitmoulin
E-mail: contact@hoteldupetitmoulin.com
Tel: +33 1 42 74 10 10
Fax: +33 1 42 74 10 97

Price Guide: (2 private car parks available, free of charge)
comfort €180
superior €250
executive €280
de luxe €350

Hidden in a quiet street in the Marais district, this former bakery has been converted into a great example of inspirational design and imagination by Christian Lacroix. Using vibrant colours, each bedroom depicts a different theme reflecting the surrounding cultures and trends of the neighbourhood. Upon entering the Venetian-style reception guests may take the 17th-century wooden staircase to one of the ambient rooms. The typically French café filled with Edwardian furnishings and 1960s seating serves breakfast and beverages.

Cachée au coin de rues tranquilles du quartier du Marais, cette ancienne boulangerie, a été transformée en un exemple spectaculaire d'inspiration, de design et d'imagination par le couturier français Christian Lacroix. Utilisant des couleurs vives, chaque chambre dépeint un univers différent qui reflète les cultures et tendances du quartier. Après avoir été accueilli à la réception de style Vénitien, les hôtes peuvent emprunter l'escalier en bois du XVIIe siècle pour accéder aux chambres. Petit-déjeuner et boissons sont servis dans le café, typiquement français et meublé en style Belle Epoque avec des sièges des années 1960.

La que fuera una panadería, oculta en la esquina de una tranquila calle del barrio de Marais, se ha convertido en un espectacular hotel, muestra del inspirador diseño e imaginación del diseñador francés Christian Lacroix. Cada una de las habitaciones muestra, en una combinación de colores vivos, un tema diferente reflejo de las culturas circundantes y las modas del lugar. Entre al recibidor de estilo veneciano y puede subir las escaleras de madera del siglo XVII hasta llegar a una de sus espacios ambientales. En su típica cafetería francesa con asientos de los años 60 y repleta de muebles y elementos decorativos edwardianos, los clientes pueden tomar el desayuno y bebidas.

Our inspector loved: *The Pink Room.*

Hôtel Duc de Saint~Simon

14 RUE DE SAINT~SIMON, 75007 PARIS, FRANCE

This haven of tranquillity in the centre of Paris is hidden in a quiet street; only a plaque indicates its existence. Minutes from exclusive shops and restaurants, this elegant home-from-home has been frequented by celebrities and Nobel Prize winners. Individually styled, with the focus placed on guests' wellbeing, most bedrooms are fitted with the hotel's bespoke fabric and some have private terraces. An original stone staircase leads to the basement bar, a 17th-century coal and wine cellar; light meals are available.

Situé au centre de Paris, cet havre de paix est caché au détour d'une petite rue tranquille et seul un plaque indique son existence. A quelques pas de magasins et de restaurants de renommé, les hôtes sont accueillis dans cette élégante maison où l'on se sent comme chez soi, fréquentée par des célébrités et des Prix Nobel. Décorées de manière individuelle mais toujours avec l'objectif du bien-être du client, la plupart des chambres sont pourvues du tissu maison de l'hôtel et certaines ont des terrasses privées. Un escalier en pierre d'origine conduit au bar en sous-sol, ancienne cave à charbon à vins du XVIIe siècle. Des repas légers y sont servis.

Situado en el centro de París, este refugio de tranquilidad está escondido en una calle tranquila, solamente una placa nos dice que está ahí. A unos minutos de exclusivas tiendas y restaurantes los huéspedes se reciben en este elegante hotel frecuentado por famosos y premios Nobel para que se sienta como en su casa. Con un estilo muy individual y enfocado al bienestar de los clientes, la mayoría de las habitaciones están equipadas con telas propias del hotel y algunas tienen terrazas privadas. Una escalera en piedra le lleva al bar situado en la bodega, lugar donde se almacenaba el carbón y el vino en el siglo XVII. Comidas ligeras disponibles.

Our inspector loved: *The bedrooms with their own private sunny terraces.*

  34    

Directions: In the centre of Paris on Left Bank between Assemblé Nationale and Boulevard Saint-Germain.

Paris

Bordeaux

Marseille

Web: www.johansens.com/saintsimon
E-mail: duc.de.saint.simon@wanadoo.fr
Tel: +33 1 44 39 20 20
Fax: +33 1 45 48 68 25

Price Guide: (room only, including service charge)
double €220-280
suite €350-375

Hôtel le Saint~Grégoire

43 RUE DE L'ABBÉ GRÉGOIRE, 75006 PARIS, FRANCE

Set at the heart of the Rive Gauche, this small 18th-century hotel offers guests refined elegance in a tranquil environment. Overlooking the interior garden, the charming lobby with an open fire becomes a cosy retreat during winter. 20 unique bedrooms are adorned with period paintings and antiques and offer every modern amenity. Guests enjoy an imaginative breakfast in the stonewall cellar before exploring the Saint-Germain quarter.

Situé en plein coeur de la Rive Gauche, cet hôtel du XVIIIe siècle offre à ses visiteurs une élégance raffinée dans un environnement tranquille. Surplombant le jardin intérieur, le charmant hall de réception est encore plus attrayant en hiver avec son feu de cheminée. Les 20 chambres, toutes uniques, sont décorées de peintures d'époques et d'antiquités et offrent tout le confort moderne. Les hôtes peuvent déguster un petit déjeuner imaginatif dans la salle voutée aux murs de pierre, avant d'explorer le quartier Saint-Germain.

Situado en el corazón del rio Gauche, este pequeño hotel del siglo XVIII ofrece una elegancia refinada en un ambiente tranquilo. Desde su encantador hall se divisa el jardín interior y se puede disfrutar de una acogedora chimenea, refugio ideal en invierno. Cuenta con 20 habitaciones únicas, decoradas con pinturas de época, antigüedades y dotadas de todas las comodidades modernas. Los huéspedes pueden degustar un desayuno imaginativo en la bodega con paredes de piedra antes de salir a explorar el barrio St-Germain.

Our inspector loved: *The manager's warm welcome, and the feeling of entering a private home.*

Directions: Near rue du Bac St Placide and Rennes are the closest metro stations.

Web: www.johansens.com/saintgregoire
E-mail: hotel@saintgregoire.com
Tel: +33 1 45 48 23 23
Fax: +33 1 45 48 33 95

Price Guide: (breakfast €14, excluding VAT)
single €175
double/twin €185-230
junior suite €260

Paris
Bordeaux
Marseille

Château d'Augerville

PLACE DU CHÂTEAU, 45330 AUGERVILLE LA RIVIERE, FRANCE

This new and stunning hotel lies midway between Paris and beautiful Loire Valley and has its own fully mature 18-hole golf course. Comprising 3 buildings around a dramatic quad, the setting is most impressive and complemented by an extremely high standard of interior décor. The elegant public rooms pay homage to the stately château era, whilst the bedrooms and bathrooms are equipped to incorporate every modern luxury. The cuisine is refined, and during the summer months guests may sip apéritifs on the terrace overlooking the 9th hole.

Ce nouvel et superbe hôtel se situe à mi-chemin entre Paris et la magnifique Vallée de la Loire et possède son propre parcours de golf de 18 trous. Composé de 3 bâtiments entourant une cour spectaculaire, le cadre impressionnant est complété par une décoration intérieure du plus haut niveau. Les pièces communes rendent hommage à la grandeur de l'époque du château alors que les chambres et suites sont équipées pour accueillir tout le luxe moderne. La cuisine est raffinée et pendant les mois d'été, les clients peuvent boire l'apéritif sur la terrasse surplombant le trou numéro 9.

Este nuevo y espléndido hotel está ubicado entre París y el bello Valle del Loira. Posee su propio campo de golf de 18 hoyos perfectamente acondicionado. Además de constar de 3 edificios que rodean a un patio interior, su entorno es sumamente impresionante y se complementa con una decoración interior al más alto nivel. Sus elegantes salas comunes rinden homenaje a la época de los châteaux-mansiones, a la vez que sus dormitorios y cuartos de baño están preparados para acoger todo tipo de lujos modernos. Su cocina es refinada y durante los meses de verano puede verse a clientes saboreando aperitivos en la terraza con vistas al hoyo 9.

Directions: A6 > exit 14 > Malesherbes > towards Puiseaux and Golf > right to Augerville > left in the village.

Web: www.johansens.com/augerville
E-mail: reservation@chateau-augerville.com
Tel: +33 2 38 32 12 07
Fax: +33 2 38 32 12 15

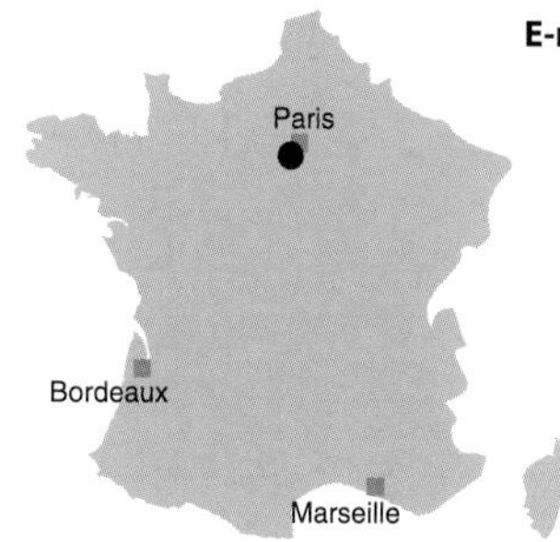

Price Guide:
single €160-380
double €160-380
suite €450-800

Our inspector loved: *The refined simplicity of the welcome.*

FRANCE / PARIS REGION (BARBIZON)

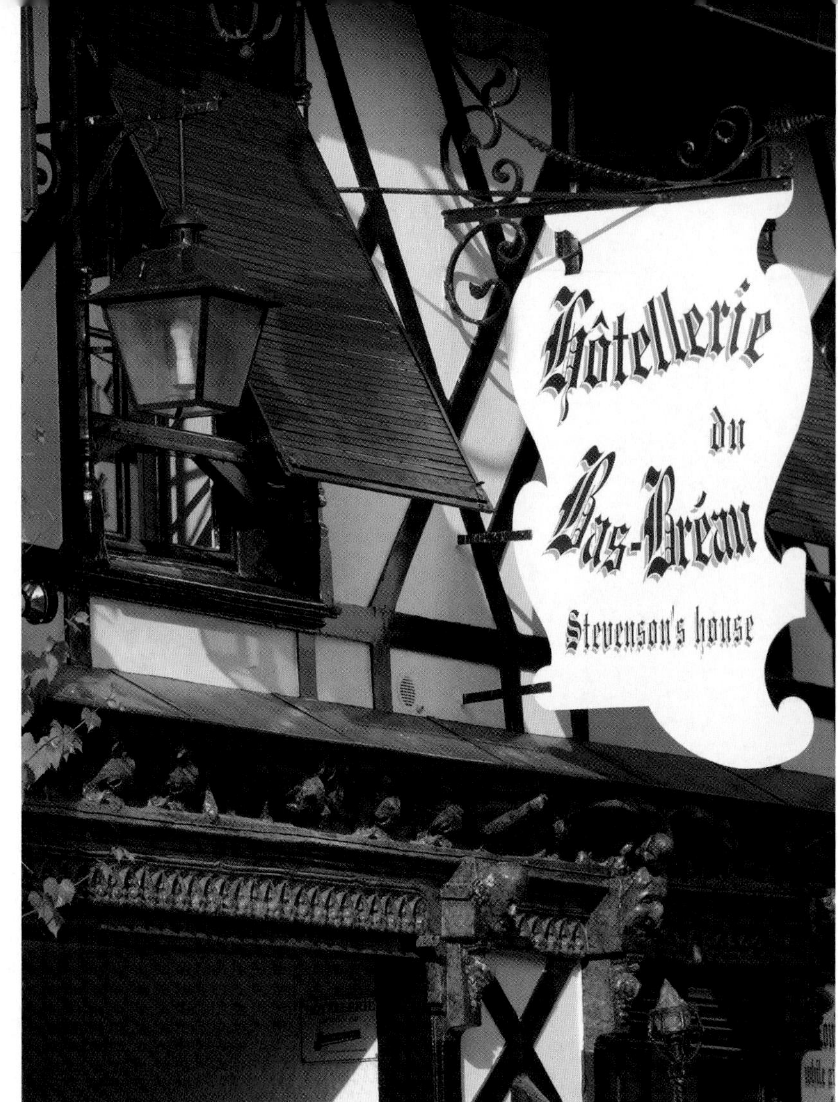

HOSTELLERIE DU BAS-BREAU

22 RUE GRANDE, 77630 BARBIZON, FRANCE

This former coaching inn is filled with memories of 19th-century European artists, poets and writers who gathered here and gained inspiration from the magnificent surroundings. Accommodation is available in the main timbered house but most rooms are located in the 2-storey building overlooking the garden. Romantic and spacious, each en-suite bedroom is individually decorated. The exceptional restaurant is very popular and offers an outstanding wine list. Take drinks in the bar, relax by the pool or enjoy the Fontainebleau forest.

Cet ancien relais de chasse était le lieu de prédilection d'artistes européen du XIXe siècle qui se retrouvaient et s'inspiraient des magnifiques paysages environnants. Quelques chambres sont situées dans la maison principale en bois mais la plupart sont dans le bâtiment surplombant le jardin. Romantiques et spacieuses, chacune des chambres est décorée de manière différente. L'excellent restaurant est très réputé et propose une impressionnante carte des vins. Les clients peuvent boire un verre au bar, se prélasser au bord de la piscine ou profiter de la forêt de Fontainebleau.

Esta antigua posada de postas está repleta de recuerdos de pintores, poetas y escritores europeos del siglo XIX que se reunían aquí y se inspiraban con su magnífico entorno. Puede alojarse en la casa de madera principal, pero la mayoría de las habitaciones se encuentran en el edificio de 2 plantas con vistas al jardín. Románticas y cada de espaciosos, las habitaciones tienen una decoración exclusiva. Su excepcional restaurante goza de gran popularidad y ofrece una excelente lista de vinos. Tómese una copa en su bar, relájese junto a la piscina o disfrute del bosque de Fontainebleau.

Our inspector loved: *The excellent gastronomic fare.*

Directions: Airport > Paris Orly > A6 > exit Fontainebleau > towards Barbizon.

Web: www.johansens.com/basbreau
E-mail: basbreau@relaischateaux.com
Tel: +33 1 60 66 40 05
Fax: +33 1 60 69 22 89

Price Guide: (room only)
single €145-385
double €245-385
suite €415-950

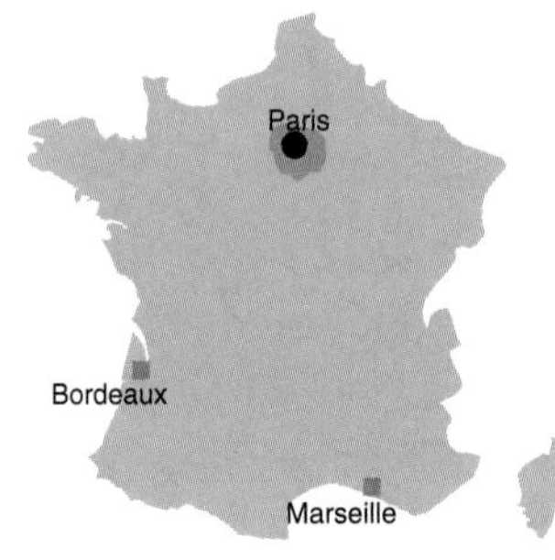

Château de Berchères

18 RUE DE CHÂTEAU, 28260 BERCHÈRES~SUR~VESGRES, FRANCE

Guests in search of an organic experience will be impressed with the innovative Château de Berchères, just 35 minutes west of Paris. This unique property has been decorated with a fruit and vegetable theme and the 21 rooms are named after produce such as aubergine, apple, olive and lychees. The painstaking attention to detail is evident by the themed sheets, doormats and even the bathroom tiles. Conserved fruit and vegetables and patterned curtains further reinforce the design in the public rooms.

Ceux en quête d'une expérience biologique seront impressionnés par l'innovant Château de Berchères, situé juste à 35 minutes à l'ouest de Paris. Cet établissement unique est décoré sur le thème des fruits et légumes et les 21 chambres ont des noms de produits tels qu'aubergine, pomme, olive et lychees. L'extrême attention au détail se traduit notamment par les draps, le paillasson et même les carreaux de salle de bain en harmonie avec le thème de la chambre. Des fruits et légumes en conserves et les rideaux ornés de motifs renforcent le design des pièces communes.

Los huéspedes que deseen vivir una experiencia ecológica quedarán impresionados con el innovador Château de Berchères, a sólo 35 minutos al oeste de París. Este singular edificio ha sido decorado con motivos frutales y horteses y sus 21 habitaciones reciben nombres de productos tales como la berenjena, la manzana, la aceituna y los lichis. Resulta evidente el esmero por cuidar el detalle en las sábanas, las alfombras e incluso en los azulejos de los cuartos de baño, decorados con motivos temáticos. La presencia de frutas y verduras en conserva así como el estampado de las cortinas refuerzan aún más el diseño de las zonas interiores comunes.

Our inspector loved: *The fruit and vegetable theme throughout the hotel.*

Directions: N112 from Paris to Houdan > exit through town > D933 towards Anet > pass through Anet > the château is 3km away.

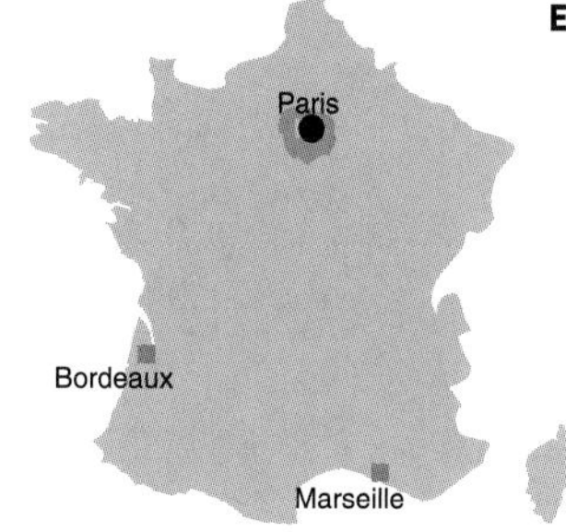

Web: www.johansens.com/bercheres
E-mail: chateau-de-bercheres@wanadoo.fr
Tel: +33 2 37 82 28 22
Fax: +33 2 37 82 28 23

Price Guide: (room only)
single €130-255
double €130-255
suite €410

LE MANOIR DE GRESSY

77410 GRESSY~EN~FRANCE, CHANTILLY, NEAR ROISSY, CHARLES DE GAULLE AIRPORT, PARIS, FRANCE

Built on the site of a 17th-century fortified farmhouse, Le Manoir de Gressy is a restful country retreat that recreates the cosy atmosphere of an old-fashioned inn. Whether relaxing by the pool or cycling through the countryside, Le Manoir's tranquil surroundings offer respite from the bustle of everyday life. On the terrace, a selection of the very best fresh produce form the market is served. The luxuriously appointed bedrooms are charmingly decorated and look out over the pool and landscaped courtyard garden.

Sur le site d'une ferme fortifiée du XVIIe siècle, le Manoir vous offre un cadre reposant à la campagne. Redécouvrez l'atmosphère feutrée d'une étape d'autrefois. A bicyclette le long des chemins de halage ou bien autour de la piscine, le Manoir de Gressy offre un cadre privilégié à tous ceux qui désirent oublier leur vie trépidante. Dans une ambiance chaleureuse, dégustez une sélection des meilleurs produits du marché sur la terrasse. Les chambres raffinées, d'un charme et d'un luxe discret, s'ouvrent toutes sur la piscine et le jardin intérieur paysager.

Construido en el recinto de una granja fortificada del siglo XVII, Le Manoir de Gressy es un pacífico refugio rural que recrea el acogedor ambiente de las antiguas posadas. Tanto si decide relajarse junto a la piscina como si desea montar en bicicleta por el campo, los tranquilos alrededores de Le Manoir ofrecen el necesario respiro al bullicio de la vida diaria. En su terraza se sirve una selección de los mejores productos frescos del mercado. Sus lujosas habitaciones están decoradas con todo encanto, tienen vistas a la piscina y al pintoresco jardín del patio.

Our inspector loved: *The spacious bedrooms.*

Directions: Paris > A1 or A3 > A104, N2 > D212 > Gressy.

Web: www.johansens.com/manoirdegressy
E-mail: information@manoirdegressy.com
Tel: +33 1 60 26 68 00
Fax: +33 1 60 26 45 46

Price Guide: (room only,
closed 27th July - 20th August)
luxury single/double €149-200
terrace single/double €149-230
suite single/double €260
special weekend offers are available

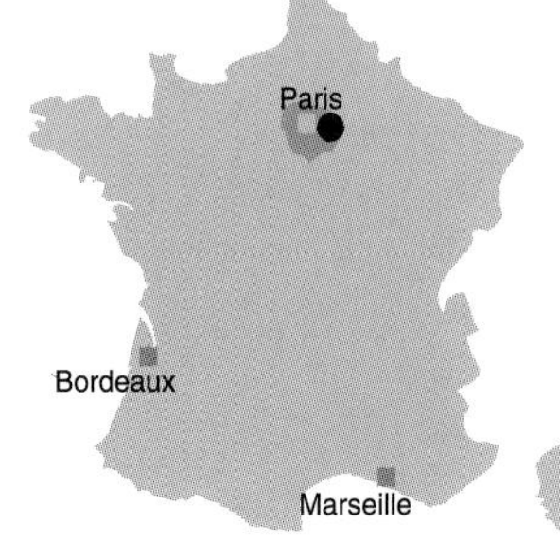

CHÂTEAU D'ESCLIMONT

28700 SAINT~SYMPHORIEN~LE~CHÂTEAU, FRANCE

Formerly the home of the the Rochefoucauld family, Le Château d'Esclimont is a fabulous example of 16th century architecture, nestled in the heart of a 60-hectare wooded park. Located just 1 hour from Paris, between Versailles and Chartres, guests may truly relax in this magnificent stately home with its 52 individually and tastefully decorated bedrooms. Dinner in the period-style restaurant is also a true gastronomic experience.

Ancienne résidence de la famille de La Rochefoucauld, Le Château d'Esclimont est un bel exemple d'architecture du XVIe siècle, niché au coeur d'un immense parc boisé de 60 ha. A 1h de Paris, entre Versailles et Chartres, les hôtes peuvent profiter du calme de cette magnifique demeure qui compte 52 chambres, toutes décorées différement avec gôut. Le diner dans la salle à manger d'époque est une expérience incontournable.

Antigua residencia de la familia de La Rochefoucauld, "Château d'Esclimont" es un ejemplo maravilloso de arquitectura del siglo XVI, localizada en el centro de un inmenso parque del bosque de 60 ha. A 1 hora de París, entre Versalles y Chartres, los clientes del hotel pueden aprovecharse de la calma de esta espléndida residencia que cuenta con 52 habitaciones, cada una de ellas se ha diseñado individualmente y con buen gusto. La cena en el comedor del mismo período es una experiencia una experiencia fantástica.

Our inspector loved: *Going for a picnic by the river.*

Directions: A11 > exit 1 > Ablis > direction of Chartres.

Web: www.johansens.com/esclimont
E-mail: esclimont@grandesetapes.fr
Tel: +33 2 37 31 15 15
Fax: +33 2 37 31 57 91

Price Guide: (room only)
room €160–390
double €160–390
suite €590–890

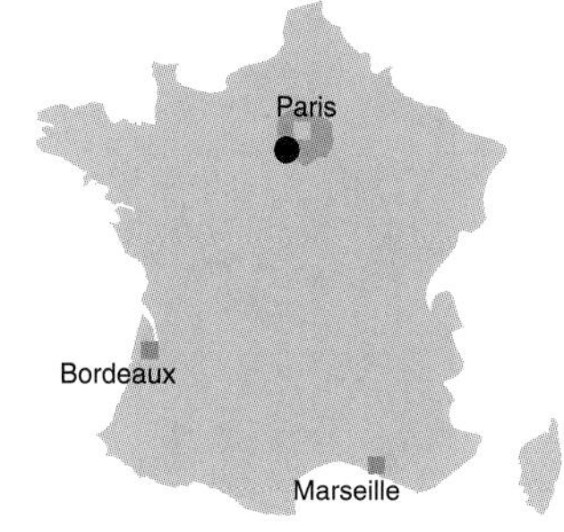

Cazaudehore la Forestière

1 AVENUE DU PRÉSIDENT KENNEDY, 78100 SAINT~GERMAIN~EN~LAYE, FRANCE

This charming family-run property boasts 30 individually decorated and themed bedrooms with contemporary bathrooms. Enjoy lazy afternoons with a book in the pretty lounge or simply recline and watch the world go by. The restaurant, housed in a separate building, is the hotel's true highlight. Inside the elegant surrounds, a team of professional staff serves excellent traditional yet innovative dishes. The hotel grounds are enhanced by modern sculptures and woodlands whilst the nearby tennis club can be enjoyed by guests.

Ce charmant hôtel, géré en famille, offre 30 chambres individuellement décorées et personnalisées avec des salles de bains contemporaines. Les hôtes peuvent apprécier des moments de détente dans le ravissant salon. Le restaurant, situé dans un bâtiment voisin, est la pièce maîtresse de l'établissement. Dans un cadre élégant, une équipe professionnelle sert une excellente cuisine entre tradition et invention. Le parc de l'hôtel est mis en valeur par des sculptures modernes et des bois et les clients peuvent profiter du club de tennis à proximité.

Este encantador hotel familiar ofrece 30 habitaciones con decorados y temas individualmente elegidos provistas de modernos cuartos de baño. Disfrute de las tardes de ocio con un libro en su bello salón o simplemente reclínese para ver el mundo pasar. El restaurante, emplazado en un edificio aparte, es la verdadera joya del hotel. En el interior de sus elegantes aledaños un equipo de profesionales le servirá excelentes platos tradicionales y innovadores. El entorno del hotel está realzado por esculturas modernas y zonas arboladas así como por un club de tenis cercano a disposición de los clientes.

Our inspector loved: *The discreet efficiency and genuine friendliness of the staff.*

Directions: Airport > head towards Paris > A13 to/from Paris > exit 6 > Rn 186 towards Saint-Germain > N184 towards Pontoise > just after the junction for Poissy turn right towards le Camp des Loges.

Web: www.johansens.com/cazaudehore
E-mail: cazaudehore@relaischateaux.com
Tel: +33 1 30 61 64 64
Fax: +33 1 30 73 73 83

Price Guide: (breakfast €18)
single €150-165
double €190-205
suite €250-275

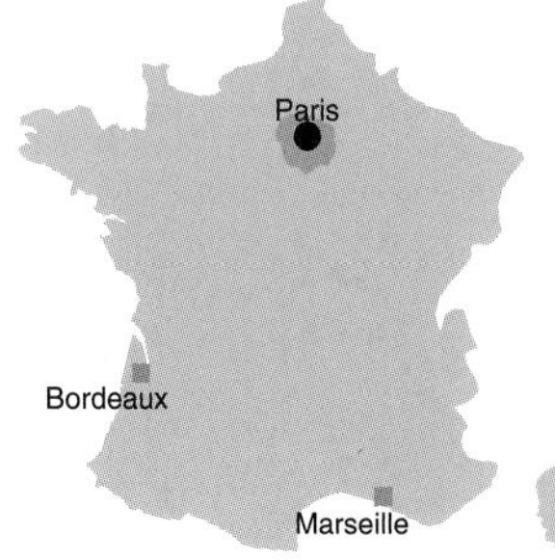

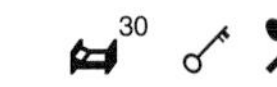

CHÂTEAU DE L'YEUSE

65 RUE DE BELLEVUE, QUARTIER DE L'ECHASSIER, 16100 CHÂTEAUBERNARD, FRANCE

Perfectly enlarged and restored with tasteful interiors, the château's superb décor includes wonderful furnishings and fabrics. Beautiful suites have stunning views across the park, the river Charente and surrounding countryside and are adjoined by spacious, well-equipped bathrooms. In the elegant high-ceilinged dining room attentive staff serve inventive local cuisine. There is an outdoor pool and indoor Jacuzzi and sauna, and guests can choose to relax on the large sun terrace, beneath the shade of the ancient oak trees or "Yeuses."

Agrandie et restaurée parfaitement avec goût, le superbe décor du Château inclut un fantastique ameublement et tissus. Les suites superbes, avec salle de bain contiguë spacieuse et parfaitement équipée, ont une vue imprenable sur le parc, la Charente et la campagne environnante. Dans l'élégante salle à manger à hauts plafonds, un personnel attentif sert une cuisine locale inventive. Les hôtes peuvent choisir d'utiliser la piscine extérieure ou le jacuzzi en salle, ou encore de se détendre sur la grande terrasse ensoleillée ou à l'ombre des vieux chênes appelés Yeuses.

Este château, perfectamente restaurado y ampliado con elegantes interiores, dispone de un maravilloso mobiliario y telas como parte de su excelente decoración. Sus bellas suites, que proporcionan espectaculares vistas al parque, al río Charente y a los terrenos colindantes, tienen espaciosos baños contiguos totalmente acondicionados. En su elegante comedor de techos altos su atento personal se encarga de servir los platos de cocina creativa de la zona. Hay asimismo una piscina al aire libre y jacuzzi y sauna interiores. Los clientes pueden optar entre relajarse al sol en la gran terraza o a la sombra de los ancestrales robles o "Yeuses".

Our inspector loved: *The cognac library.*

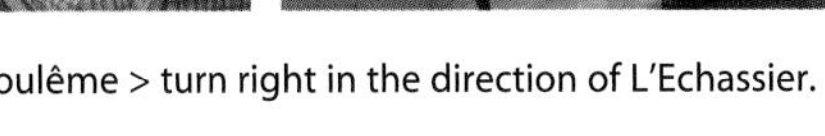

Directions: N141 from Angoulême > turn right in the direction of L'Echassier.

Web: www.johansens.com/chateaudelyeuse
E-mail: reservations.yeuse@wanadoo.fr
Tel: +33 5 45 36 82 60
Fax: +33 5 45 35 06 32

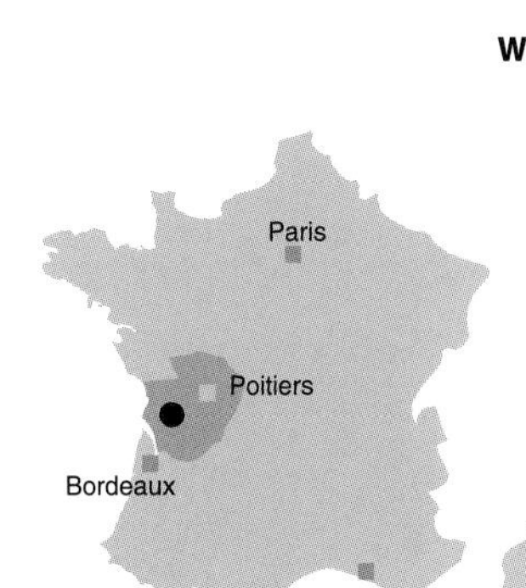

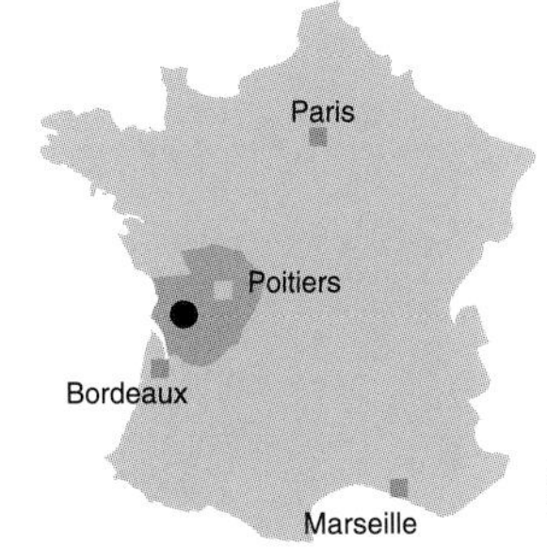

Price Guide: (room only, closed 18th December - 12th February)
single €98–167
double €98–167
suite €211–333

Hotel "Residence de France"

43 RUE MINAGE, 17000 LA ROCHELLE, FRANCE

Nestling in the heart of La Rochelle, this 16th-century stone building has been converted into a comfortable retreat set around a courtyard with rooms in one building and a bar, lounge and elegant formal dining room in the other. Evocative of an art gallery, the property is adorned with sculptures, paintings and contemporary furnishings, and spacious bedrooms are the essence of comfort. An easel in the restaurant displays the choice of classic, affordable dishes and after dinner, a stroll along the harbour with its famous 3 towers is a must.

Nichée au cœur de la Rochelle, cette bâtisse en pierre de XVIe siècle a été transformée en une adresse confortable organisée autour d'une cour intérieure avec les chambres d'un côté et le bar, salon et l'élégante salle à manger de l'autre. Evocateur d'une galerie d'art, l'établissement est rempli de sculptures, de tableaux et de mobilier contemporains et les chambres spacieuses sont l'essence même du confort. Un chevalet au restaurant présente un choix de plats classiques et abordables. Après le repas, la promenade sur le port avec ses fameuses 3 tours est un must.

Enclavado en el corazón de La Rochelle, este edificio de piedra del siglo XVI ha sido convertido en un cómodo refugio, ubicado alrededor de un patio, con las habitaciones en una nave y el bar, salón y elegante comedor en la otra. La propiedad esta adornada con esculturas, cuadros y muebles contemporáneos, evocando una galería de arte, y las habitaciones amplias son la esencia del confort. Un caballete situado en el restaurante muestra la oferta de platos clásicos, de poco precio, y después de cenar, es imprescindible darse un paseo por el puerto y contemplar las 3 famosas torres.

Our inspector loved: *The sculptures and paintings, which adorn the corridors.*

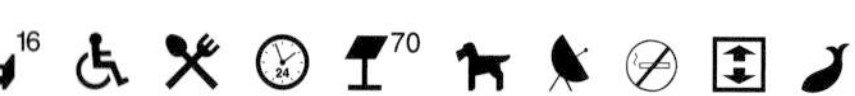

Directions: The nearest airport is La Rochelle. The hotel will supply detailed directions upon request.

Web: www.johansens.com/residencedefrance
E-mail: info@hotel-larochelle.com
Tel: +33 5 46 28 06 00
Fax: +33 5 46 28 06 03

Price Guide: (room only)
single €95-190
double €95-190
suite €155-290

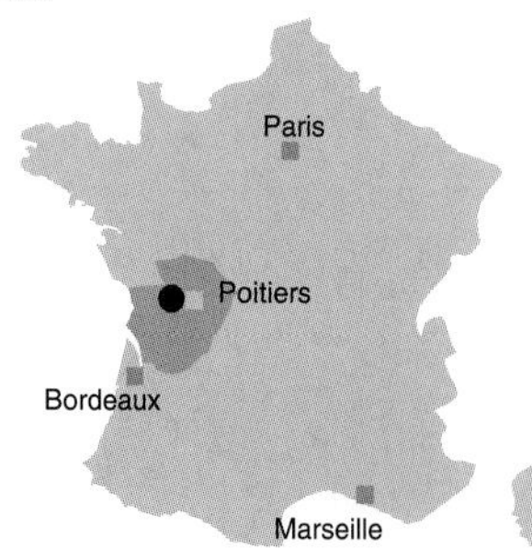

Château de la Couronne

16380 MARTHON, FRANCE

Château de la Couronne is a delightful oasis that has been completely refurbished and is surrounded by 5 acres of beautiful grounds. Handsome traditional architecture fuses effortlessly with ultra modern interior design whilst outstanding attention to detail can be discovered in every nook and cranny. The friendly proprietors ensure that guests feel completely at home whilst attentive service provides a carefree ambience that is the true secret of this remarkable château.

Château de la Couronne est un ravissant oasis complètement rénové et entouré de 2 ha de terres. La belle architecture traditionnelle se marie parfaitement avec le design intérieur ultra moderne et une attention au détail hors du commun peut-être appréciée dans tous les coins et recoins. Les propriétaires sympathiques veillent à ce que leurs hôtes se sentent chez eux et le service attentif contribue à l'atmosphère agréable et sans soucis, qui est le véritable secret de ce magnifique château.

Château de la Couronne es un lindo oasis totalmente renovado y rodeado de 2 ha de bella zona verde. La elegante arquitectura tradicional se combina de forma natural con el ultra moderno diseño interior al tiempo que se aprecia un gran esmero por el detalle hasta en los rincones más pequeños. Sus afables propietarios le harán sentirse como en casa a la vez que el atento servicio le proporcionará un ambiente relajado que constituye el verdadero secreto de este magnífico château.

Our inspector loved: *The exceptionally innovative decoration of the whole château.*

Directions: The nearest airports are Limoges and Bergerac. From Angoulême D939 > Brantôme > D4 > Marthon > turn left in the village centre towards Montbron > turn left at the war memorial.

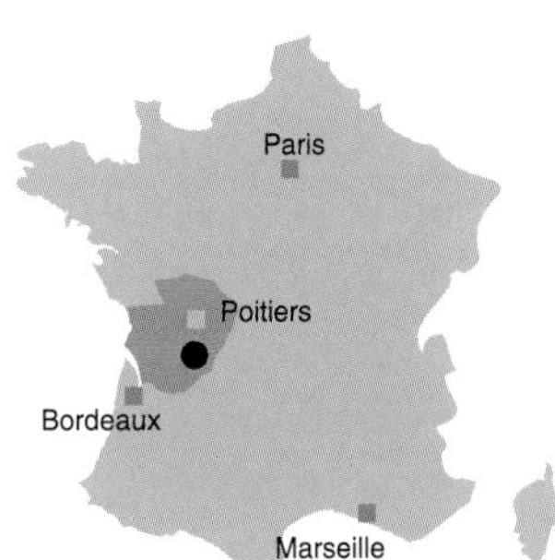

Web: www.johansens.com/couronne
E-mail: info@chateaudelacouronne.com
Tel: +33 5 45 62 29 96

Price Guide: (room only)
suite from €130

Domaine des Etangs

16310 MASSIGNAC, FRANCE

Directions: Nearest airport: Limoges. Nearest station: Angoulême. Angoulême > Limoges road N141 > at La Rochefoucauld, head to Montemboeuf (D13).

Web: www.johansens.com/etangs
E-mail: info@domainedesetangs.fr
Tel: +33 5 45 61 85 00
Fax: +33 5 45 61 85 01

Price Guide: (room only, closed 1st January - 19th March)
single €130-210
double €130-210
suite €230-260
duplex €315-550

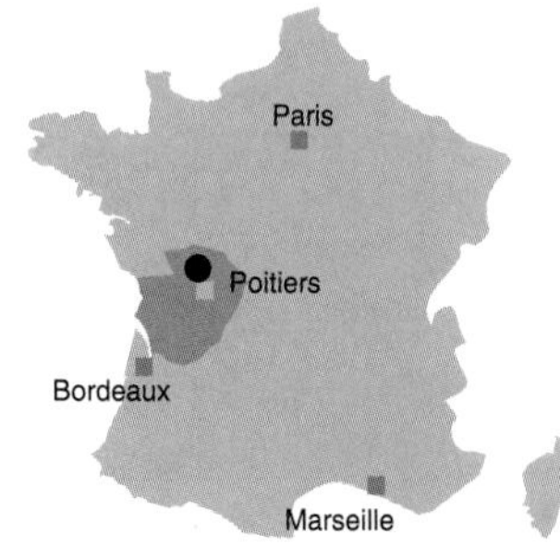

The Domaine is a vast, partially wooded property of over 2,000 acres including 76 acres of ponds and over 25km of private roads. Dotted around this immaculately kept piece of nature are an elegant château and 7 hamlets, housing 17 4-star guest rooms and suites. Most of the rooms, which are charmingly decorated with stone, glass, wood and copper, have impressive fireplaces, which can also be found in the salons and the Les Tournelles restaurant, where guests can enjoy delicious seasonal cuisine. Activities include tennis, swimming in the pool, boating on the lake and much more.

Le Domaine est une vaste propriété partiellement boisée de 850 ha, ponctués de 31 ha d'étangs et 25 km de routes privées. Dans une nature soigneusement préservée, se dressent un élégant château et 7 hameaux dans lesquels sont aménagées 17 chambres et suites 4 étoiles. La plupart des pièces, décorées en pierre, verre, bois et cuivre, possède une imposante cheminée a l'instar des salons et du restaurant Les Tournelles, qui sert une délicieuse cuisine de saison. Pour la détente, le domaine propose le court de tennis, la piscine chauffée, le canotage et toutes sortes de loisirs.

El Domaine es una vasta propiedad parcialmente arbolada de más de 850 ha, con 31 ha de estanques y más de 25 km de caminos de acceso privado. Un elegante château y 7 aldeas que albergan 17 habitaciones y suites de 4 estrellas salpican un paraje natural primorosamente cuidado. La mayoría de las habitaciones, decoradas a base de piedra, cristal, madera y cobre, disponen, al igual que los salones y el restaurante Les Tournelles, de impresionantes chimeneas. En el restaurante los clientes pueden disfrutar de la deliciosa cocina de temporada. Las actividades incluyen el tenis, la natación en la piscina, navegación en bote y mucho más.

Our inspector loved: *The feeling of total freedom, peace and quiet.*

Relais de Saint~Preuil

LIEU-DIT CHEZ RIVIERE, 16130 SAINT~PREUIL, FRANCE

With views of the vineyards of the Grande Champagne Cognac region, this former coaching inn has been completely renovated to provide luxurious accommodation in a welcoming yet unobtrusive environment. The 5 immaculate guest rooms have been individually decorated and offer magnificent bathrooms and every modern comfort. Guests may dine at the convivial table d'hôte, venture out to a local restaurant, use the outdoor barbecue or the fully fitted modern kitchen at all guests' disposal. Mountain bikes are available, and there is a tennis court and secluded swimming pool.

Avec une magnifique vue sur le vignoble de cognac en Grande Champagne, cet ancien relais de poste a été complètement rénové afin de proposer un hébergement luxueux dans un environnement accueillant mais discret. Les 5 chambres impeccables ont été individuellement décorées et offrent de somptueuse salles de bains et tout le confort moderne. Les hôtes peuvent choisir de dîner à la table d'hôtes conviviale ou peuvent utiliser le barbecue ou la cuisine entièrement équipée à disposition. Des VTT sont disponibles ainsi qu'un court de tennis et une piscine isolée.

Con vistas a los d viñedos de la región de la Grande Champagne Cognac, esta antigua venta de postas ha sido totalmente renovada para proporcionar alojamiento de lujo en un ambiente acogedor, mas discreto. Sus 5 impecables habitaciones han sido individualmente decorados y ofrecen magníficos cuartos de baño y todas las comodidades modernas. Los clientes podrán cenar en su cordial table d'hôte, dirigirse a un restaurante de la zona, hacer uso de la barbacoa al aire libre, o utilizar la moderna cocina totalmente equipada que esta a disposición de todos los huéspedes del hotel. El establecimiento dispone de bicicletas de montaña, así como una pista de tenis y una piscina aislada.

***Our inspector loved:** The simplicity and conviviality of the welcome.*

Directions: The nearest airport is Bordeaux. From Cognac take D24 to Ségonzac then D1 towards Barbézieux. Turn left towards Saint-Preuil. On arriving in the village, turn left towards Bouteville. 1km up this road is Chez Rivière. Turn right and go to the building on the hill.

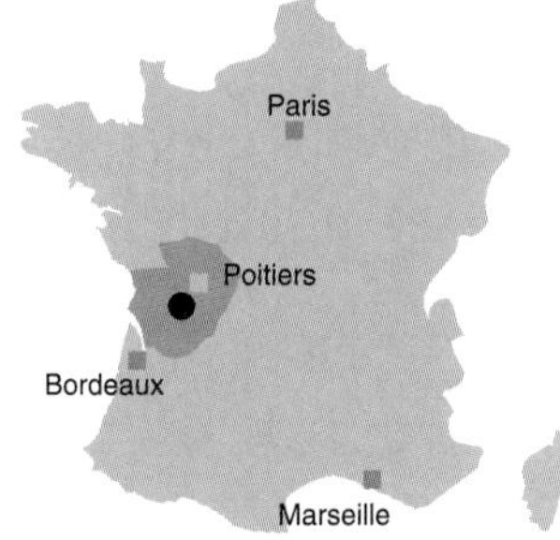

Web: www.johansens.com/saintpreuil
E-mail: relais.saint.preuil@wanadoo.fr
Tel: +33 5 45 80 80 08
Fax: +33 5 45 80 80 09

Price Guide:
single €80-120
double €95-135

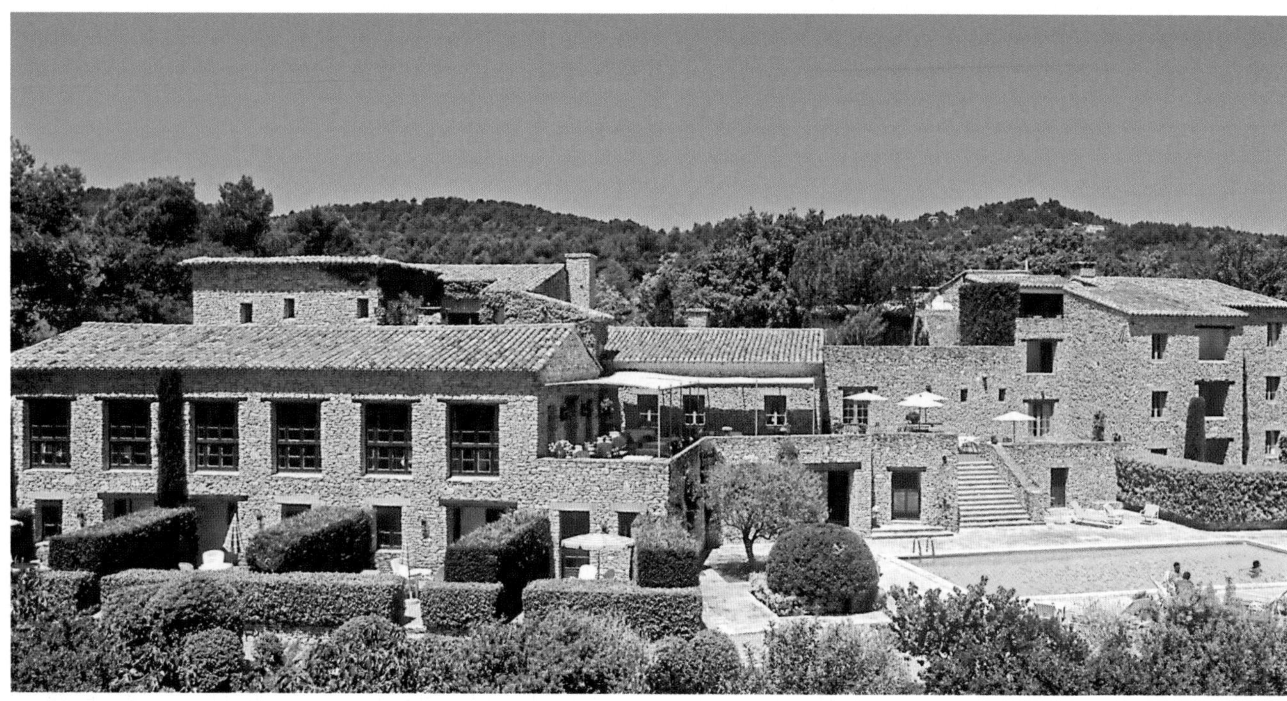

Les Mas des Herbes Blanches

JOUCAS, 84220 GORDES, FRANCE

Directions: A7 > exit Cavaillon towards Apt. at Coustellet > follow Gordes > Joucas.

Web: www.johansens.com/herbesblanches
E-mail: reservation@herbesblanches.com
Tel: +33 4 90 05 79 79
Fax: +33 4 90 05 71 96

Price Guide: (room only, excluding VAT, closed 2nd January - 9th March)
double €149-330
suite €320-685

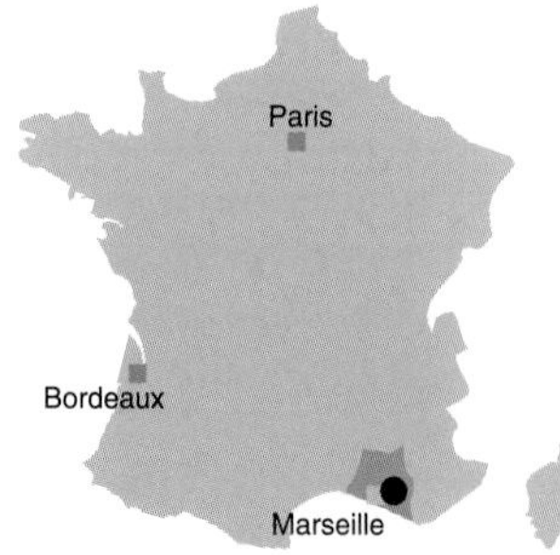

Nestled in the heart of Provence, this beautiful stone farmhouse overlooks the hills and farmlands of Luberon. Cool interiors feature rich ochre and bright colours typical of the region to create a feeling of space and relaxation. Bedrooms have terraces with amazing views and bathrooms are light and airy. Deliciously inventive Mediterranean cuisine is freshly prepared, served either on the terrace or in the restaurant, which is reminiscent of a winter garden. A heated swimming pool is located in the hotel's gardens.

Niché au cœur de la Provence, ce mas en pierres sèches surplombe les collines et terres du Luberon. La décoration intérieure utilise des ocres riches et des couleurs vives typiques de la région, créant ainsi un sentiment d'espace et de relaxation. Les chambres ont des terrasses avec de superbes vues et les salles de bains sont claires et spacieuses. Une cuisine Méditerranéenne délicieusement inventive est fraîchement préparée et servie soit sur la terrasse ou dans le restaurant, évoquant un jardin d'hiver. Une piscine chauffée se trouve dans les jardins de l'hôtel.

Enclavada en el corazón de la Provenza, esta bella granja de piedra tiene vistas a las colinas y terrenos de cultivo de Luberon. Sus refrescantes interiores de suntuosos colores llamativos y ocres característicos de la región logran aportar una sensación de amplitud y descanso. Las habitaciones disponen de terrazas con sorprendentes paisajes y sus cuartos de baño son luminosos y aireados. Su deliciosa y creativa cocina mediterránea se prepara cada día y se sirve tanto en la terraza como en el restaurante, el cual recuerda a un jardín invernal. Una piscina climatizada se encuentra situada en los jardines del hotel.

Our inspector loved: *The architecture of the houses, and sunny bedrooms.*

Domaine le Hameau des Baux

CHEMIN DE BOURGEAC, 13520 LE PARADOU, FRANCE

Tucked away in the Alpilles Mountains, minutes from the village of Les Baux de Provence, is this quintessential Provençal hamlet, designed by its Swiss owners. It comprises a farmhouse, barn, cottage, chapel, dovecote and mill built from local stone by local artisans, each separated by lawns and small courtyards. Most of the spacious guest rooms have private terraces leading out to the garden and all display carefully chosen antique furnishings complemented by fine fabrics and a modern touch creating a family home ambience.

Ce hameau typiquement provençal, conçu par ses propriétaires suisses, est caché au cœur des Alpilles, à quelques minutes des Baux de Provence. Il comprend un mas, un grange, un cabanon, une chapelle, un pigeonnier et un moulin construits en pierres traditionnelles par des artisans locaux, tous séparés par des pelouses et des petites cours. La plupart des chambres spacieuses ont une terrasse privée conduisant au jardin et toutes ont un mobilier ancien soigneusement choisi et complémenté par de beaux tissus, avec une touche moderne qui recrée une ambiance familiale.

Escondido entre las Montañas Alpilles a unos minutos de la aldea de Les Baux de Provenza se encuentra este caserío provenzal quintaesencial diseñado por sus propietarios suizos. Consta de finca, granero, cabaña, capilla, palomar y molino construidos con piedra local por artesanos locales y separados por césped y patios pequeños. La mayoría de las amplias habitaciones disponen de terrazas privadas que dan al jardín y todas ellas exhiben un mobiliario antiguo cuidadosamente elegido y complementado con finas telas y un toque moderno para crear un ambiente familiar hogareño.

Our inspector loved: *The amazing La Chapelle Suite, ideal for a special occasion.*

Directions: Join the D17 crossing Fontivielle/Maussane, then turn onto the D78D towards Les Baux.

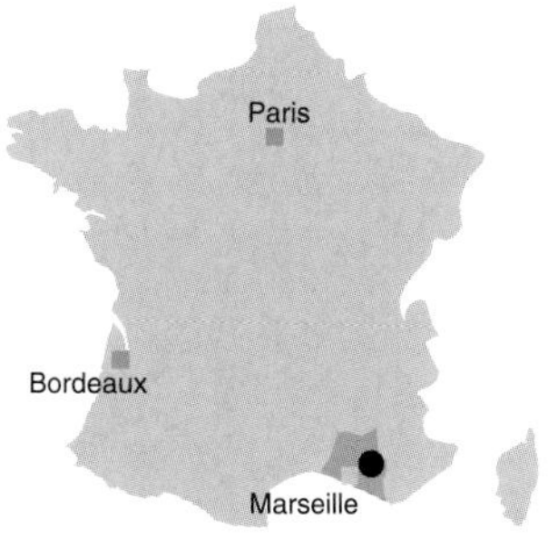

Web: www.johansens.com/hameaudesbaux
E-mail: contact@hameaudesbaux.com
Tel: +33 4 90 54 10 30
Fax: +33 4 90 54 45 30

Paris
Bordeaux
Marseille

Price Guide: (room only)
double €185-245
suite €255-480

Oustau de Baumanière

13520 LES BAUX~DE~PROVENCE, FRANCE

Directions: A7 > exit Cavaillon > Saint-Remy-de-Provence > Les Baux-de-Provence.

Web: www.johansens.com/oustadebaumaniere
E-mail: contact@oustaudebaumaniere.com
Tel: +33 4 90 54 33 07
Fax: +33 4 90 54 40 46

Price Guide: (room only, excluding VAT)
double €225-310
suite €360-490

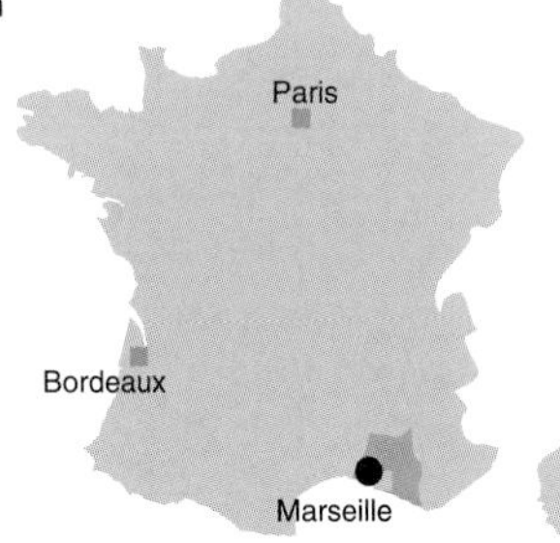

This simply stunning hotel has become internationally renowned as a place where refinement and style unite. The current chef patron continues the legacy left by his grandfather, and this little gem is characterised by the fragranced herbs that scent the delightful gardens, and prominently feature in the wonderful 2 Michelin-starred cuisine. Each of the suites and guest rooms is immaculately decorated in an individual style; some are contemporary whilst others are more Provençal in nature. The service is impeccably attentive yet discreet.

Cet hôtel tout simplement époustouflant est devenu, au niveau international, le symbole de l'union du style et du raffinement. Le chef et patron actuel continue dans la tradition familiale et ce petit joyau se caractérise par les différents parfums des herbes émanant du jardin qui tiennent une place primordiale dans la succulente cuisine 2 étoiles au Michelin. Chaque suite et chambre est décorée de façon immaculée dans un style individuel, certaines sont contemporaines, d'autres plus provençales par nature. Le service est impeccable, attentif et discret.

Este hotel realmente estupendo ha llegado a ser internacionalmente conocido como un lugar donde la elegancia y el estilo se unen. El actual patrón chef continúa el legado de su abuelo y esta pequeña joya se caracteriza por las hierbas aromáticas que perfuman los preciosos jardines y destaca su cocina con el maravilloso galardón de 2 estrellas Michelín. Cada suite y habitación está decorada en un estilo individual inmaculado, unas en estilo contemporáneo mientras que otras en uno más provenzal. El servicio es impecablemente atento pero discreto.

Our inspector loved: *The superb contemporary and original décor of the bedrooms in the main house.*

LE SPINAKER

POINTE DE LA PRESQU'ÎLE, PORT CAMARGUE, 30240 LE GRAU~DU~ROI, FRANCE

Set in the heart of the marina, this idyllic retreat is an oasis of greenery, palm trees and pines in an impressive peninsula location. 21 stylish guest rooms and suites lie scattered around a central swimming pool, each individually decorated and with its own private terrace overlooking the garden or harbour. The restaurant, Le Carré des Gourmets, is blissful, offering an invitation to enjoy the flavours of the south and the sea and sample a fantastic wine list with more than 250 independent wine makers within the region.

Situé à la pointe d'une presqu'île, le Spinaker est un oasis de verdure, de palmiers et de pins au coeur du port de plaisance. 21 chambres chics et individuellement décorées sont reparties autour de la piscine centrale, chacune avec sa propre terrasse avec vue sur le jardin ou le port. Le restaurant, le Carré des Gourmets, est un enchantement, et une invitation à apprécier les saveurs du Sud et de la meret déguster une carte des vins comprenant plus de 250 vins des viticulteurs indépendants de la région.

Situado en el corazón del puerto deportivo, este refugio idílico es un oasis de vegetación, palmeras y pinos que forma parte de una impresionante península. Las 21 elegantes habitaciones y suites, cada una con su terraza privada con vistas al mar o el puerto, se reparten alrededor de una piscina central. El restaurante, Le Carre des Gourmets, es encantador e invita a disfrutar de los sabores del sur y del mar, así como degustar de una increíble lista de vinos con mas de 250 viñedos independientes de la región.

Our inspector loved: *The feeling of being remote from the rest of the world, surrounded by the sea.*

Directions: From Nîmes > exit Gallargues. From Montpellier > exit airport. 16km from Montpellier Airport. 45km from Nîmes Airport.

Web: www.johansens.com/spinaker
E-mail: spinaker@wanadoo.fr
Tel: +33 4 66 53 36 37
Fax: +33 4 66 53 17 47

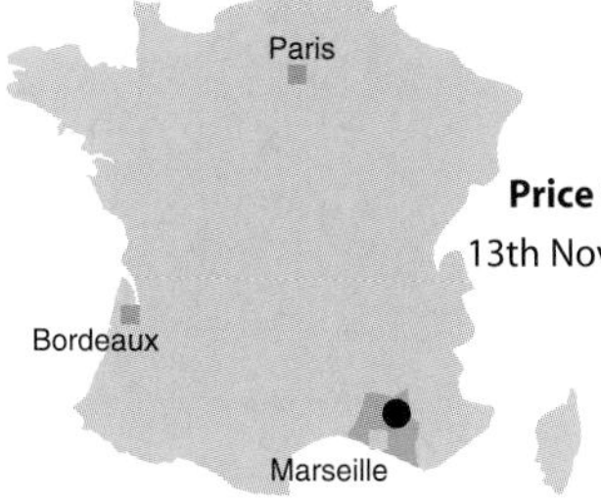

Paris
Bordeaux
Marseille

Price Guide: (breakfast €12, restaurant closed 13th Nov - 14th Feb, during this period the hotel is open Thurs - Sun only)
single/double €79-129
room with living room €99-159
suite €119-289

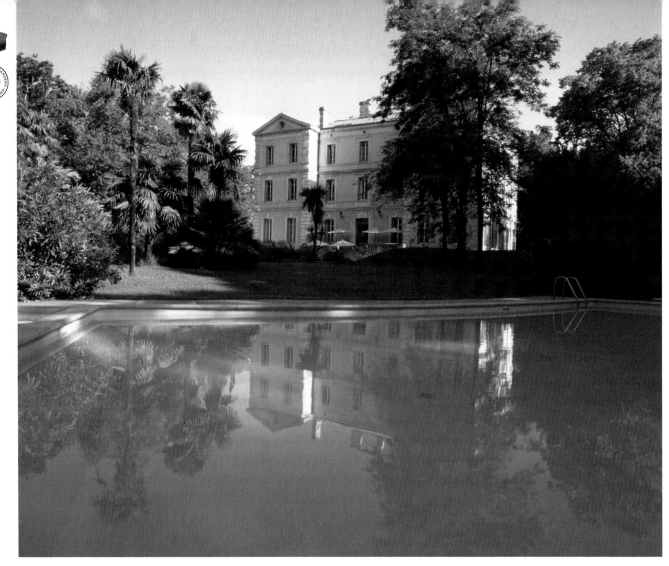

Château de Montcaud

COMBE, BAGNOLS~SUR~CÈZE, 30200 SABRAN, NEAR AVIGNON, FRANCE

Set amidst glorious private parkland in Provence, this château is an oasis of tranquillity. Guests are made to feel at home by welcoming staff and the friendly atmosphere. Spacious bedrooms are individually decorated and stylish with large windows that overlook the grounds. Tasty local specialities feature on the menu and summer lunches enjoyed under the large, old trees in the garden are a delight. There is a swimming pool and tennis court as well as a sauna and hammam.

Situé au cœur d'un magnifique parc privé en Provence, ce château est un oasis de paix. Grâce au personnel accueillant et à l'atmosphère amicale, les clients se sentent comme à la maison. Les chambres spacieuses sont élégantes, individuellement décorées et ont de grandes fenêtres donnant sur le parc. De délicieuses spécialités locales sont au menu et les déjeuners en été dans le jardin à l'ombre des grands arbres est un pur bonheur. L'hôtel possède une piscine, un tennis, un sauna et un hammam.

Ubicado entre espectaculares parques privados de la Provenza, este château es un verdadero oasis de paz. Los clientes logran sentirse como en casa gracias a su acogedora plantilla y afable ambiente. Sus amplias habitaciones están decoradas individualmente y con estilo, así como provistas de grandes ventanales con vistas a sus terrenos. Su carta incluye sabrosas especialidades locales y los almuerzos durante el verano que se pueden disfrutar a la sombra de sus grandes y ancestrales árboles del jardín son todo una delicia. Dispone de piscina y pista de tenis así como un sauna y un baño turco.

Our inspector loved: *The "jazz lunches" in the garden on Sundays.*

Directions: From the north A7 > exit Bollène. From the south A7 > exit Avignon Sud. From the south A9 > exit Remoulins > Bagnols-sur-Cèze > continue for 4km on D6 towards Alès.

Web: www.johansens.com/montcaud
E-mail: montcaud@relaischateaux.com
Tel: +33 4 66 89 60 60
Fax: +33 4 66 89 45 04

Price Guide: (room only, closed 1st January - 3rd April and 28th October - 31st December)
single €165-280
double €180-480
suite €360-750

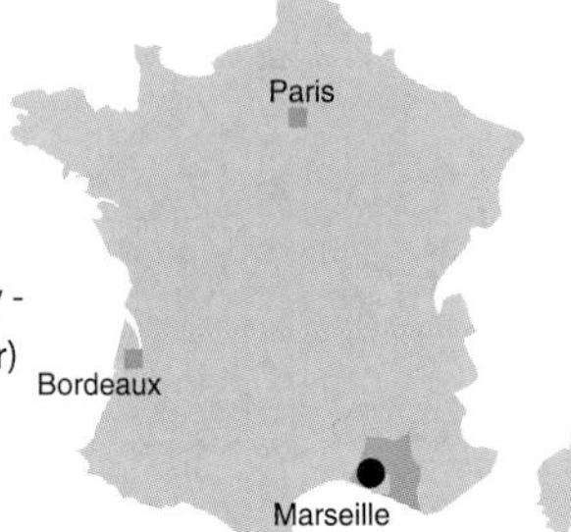

Château des Alpilles

ROUTE DÉPARTEMENTALE 31, ANCIENNE ROUTE DU GRÈS, 13210 SAINT~RÉMY~DE~PROVENCE, FRANCE

Dating from the 19th century, this elegant château is set within shady grounds where guests can relax under 100-year-old trees whilst the delicious scent of magnolia drifts by on the breeze. Tastefully decorated to the highest standard within an authentic period style, rooms are comfortable and spacious whilst suites are contemporary in design. Cuisine is refined and delicious, offering tempting regional treats.

Datant du XIXe siècle, cet élégant château se dresse dans un parc ombragé où les hôtes peuvent se relaxer sous des arbres centenaires entourés de délicieuses senteurs de magnolias. Elégamment et luxueusement décorées dans un style d'époque authentique, les chambres sont confortables et spacieuses et les suites ont une décoration contemporaine. La cuisine est raffinée et délicieuse, proposant des délices régionaux alléchants.

Este elegante château que data del siglo XIX se encuentra situado en medio de terrenos de bosques. Los clientes podrán relajarse a la sombra de centenarios árboles y sentir el delicioso aroma de magnolias impregnado en la brisa que fluye. Decoradas con sumo gusto al más alto nivel con auténtico estilo de época, sus habitaciones son cómodas y amplias y las suites de diseño contemporáneo. Su cocina es refinada y deliciosa y ofrece tentadoras delicias de la gastronomía regional.

Our inspector loved: *The superb park surrounding the château, with its swimming pool and tennis courts.*

Directions: D31 > Tarascon.

Web: www.johansens.com/chateaudesalpilles
E-mail: chateau.alpilles@wanadoo.fr
Tel: +33 4 90 92 03 33
Fax: +33 4 90 92 45 17

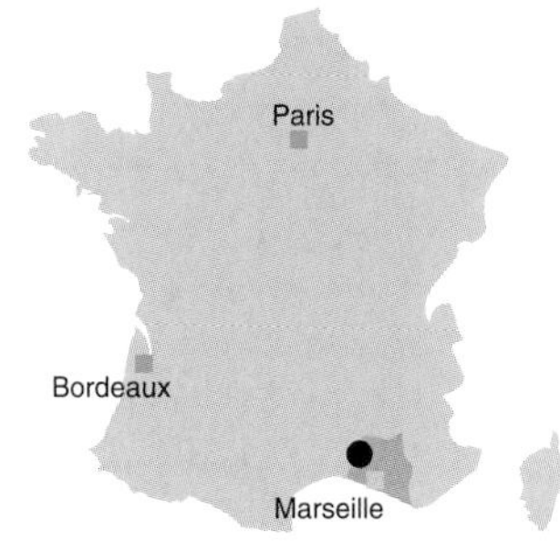

Price Guide:
single €175-192
double/twin €195–280
suite €252–390

20 40

Domaine des Andéols

84490 SAINT~SATURNIN~LÈS~APT, FRANCE

One of Alain Ducasse's 5 hotels, Domaine de Andéols is perched on a hill surrounded by olive groves and lavender fields. This beautiful hotel is an oasis of peace and tranquillity with views over the Luberon countryside which are stunning. The 18 modern, yet luxurious bedrooms in 9 individually designed houses, are elegantly furnished and adorned with unique works of art. Dining in the romantic restaurant is a delight where Chef Albert Boronat uses the finest local produce for his Provençal cuisine.

Un des 5 hôtels d'Alain Ducasse, le Domaine des Andéols est situé au sommet d'une colline, entouré d'oliviers et de champs de lavande, cet hôtel de charme est une oasis de calme et de tranquillité. Les vues sur la campagne du Luberon sont superbes. Les 18 chambres modernes et luxueuses sont réparties sur 9 maisons au design individual qui sont élégamment meublées et parées d'oeuvres d'arts uniques. Dîner dans le romantique restaurant est un ravissement et le chef Albert Boronat utilise les meilleurs produits locaux pour sa cuisine provençale.

Uno de los 5 hoteles de Alain Ducasse, Domaine de Andéols esta encaramado sobre una colina rodeada de olivares y campos de lavanda, este hotel magnífico constituye todo un oasis de paz y tranquilidad. Sus vistas al campo de Luberon son son espectaculares y las 18 lujosas y modernas habitaciones en 9 casas de diseño elegante están primorosamente amuebladas y adornadas de únicas obras de arte. Cenar en el restaurante romántico es una delicia, pues el chef Albert Boronat emplea los mejores productos de la zona para sus platos provenzales.

Our inspector loved: *The amazing terraces and views over the Luberon.*

Directions: Avignon > N100 > Coustellet > D2 > signs to Gordes > Saint-Saturnin-lès-Apt. 45 mins from Avignon Airport. 1 hr from Marseilles Airport. Nimes Airport is also close by. TGV from Avignon-Aix-en-Provence is 30 mins.

Web: www.johansens.com/domainedesandeols
E-mail: info@domaine-des-andeols.com
Tel: +33 4 90 75 50 63
Fax: +33 4 90 75 43 22

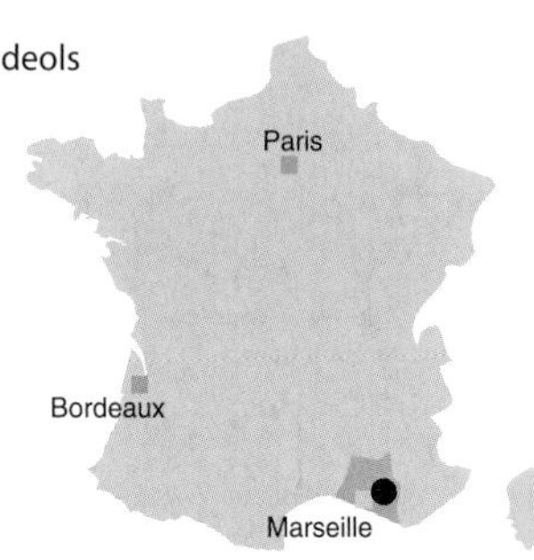

Price Guide:
junior suite €210-290
suite standard privilège €280-370
suite supérieure €420-520
suite prestige €550-650

Le Beau Rivage

2 RUE DU BEAU-RIVAGE, 69420 CONDRIEU, FRANCE

On the banks of the Rhône, close to the vineyards of Condrieu and the hills of Côtes Roties, this former fishermen's house has been magnificently renovated and extended. Each guest room, some with private terraces, is individually furnished and decorated with fresh flowers. Lyonnaise-style cuisine, created from local produce, is accompanied by the finest wines of the Rhône Valley in the spacious restaurant. Al fresco dining is available during the summer months. Explore the garden or relax in the bar, lounge or terrace whilst admiring the serene surroundings.

Sur les rives du Rhône, proche des vignobles de Condrieu et collines des Côtes Roties, cette ancienne maison de pêcheurs a été magnifiquement rénovée et agrandie. Chaque chambre, dont certaines avec terrasses privées, est individuellement meublée et décorée de fleurs fraîches. Une cuisine de style lyonnaise conçue à partir de produits frais et accompagnée de vins de premier choix est servie dans le spacieux restaurant. Il est possible de dîner à l'extérieur pendant les mois d'été. Les hôtes peuvent se promener dans le jardin ou se relaxer au bar, au salon ou sur la terrasse en admirant les alentours.

A orillas del río Ródano y próximo a los viñedos de Condrieu y a las colinas de Côtes Roties, esta antigua casa de pescadores ha sido espléndidamente renovada y ampliada. Cada una de las habitaciones, algunas de las cuales tienen terraza propia, está amueblada de forma diferente y decorada con flores naturales. La cocina, al estilo de Lyon y elaborada a partir de productos locales, se acompaña de los mejores vinos del Valle del Ródano en el amplio restaurante. Durante los meses de verano puede disfrutarse de la cena al aire libre. Pasee por el jardín o relájese en el bar, en el salón o en la terraza mientras admira y disfruta de la paz de los alrededores.

Our inspector loved: *The newly renovated suites with views of the river.*

 28

 20

Directions: A7 > exit Condrieu > follow signs.

Web: www.johansens.com/beaurivage
E-mail: infos@hotel-beaurivage.com
Tel: +33 4 74 56 82 82
Fax: +33 4 74 59 59 36

Price Guide: (room only)
double €110-150
suite €160-225

Château de Divonne

01220 DIVONNE~LES~BAINS, FRANCE

Located just 15km from Geneva, between the Alps and Jura, Château de Divonne is surrounded by lush parkland and offers spectacular views over Mont Blanc. This 18th to 19th-century stately home delightfully fuses the traditional and modern and its bedrooms are furnished and decorated to the highest standard. Guests may savour the fresh and flavoursome cuisine created by the hotel's chef whilst dining in the elegant restaurant or on the terrace overlooking the mountains.

A seulement 15 km de Genève, situé dans un écrin de verdure, entre Alpes et Jura, le Château de Divonne offre une vue spectaculaire sur le Mont Blanc. Gentilhommiere du XVIII et XIXe siècles, où se mélangement subtilement tradition et modernisme, toutes les chambres sont décorées selon les plus hauts standarts. Les hôtes peuvent déguster une cuisine fraîche et savoureuse préparer par le Chef en dinnant dans l'élegante salle à manger ou sur la terrace surplombant les montagnes.

A solamente 15km de Ginebra, y situada en un parque verdant entre los Alpes y el Jura, el Château de Divonne ofrece vistas espectaculares sobre el Mont Blanc. Este casa de señorío de los siglos XVIII a XIX deliciosamente se fusionan lo tradicional y lo moderno, y las habitaciones decoradas elegantemente del más alto nivel. Los clientes pueden apreciar la cocina fresca y sabrosa creada por el cocinero del hotel mientras que cenan en el restaurante o en la terraza que pasa por alto las montañas.

Our inspector loved: *The amazing views over the lake of Geneva and the Mont-Blanc.*

Directions: A6 > A40 > exit Bellegarde > Gex/Divonne.

Web: www.johansens.com/chateaudedivonne
E-mail: divonne@grandesetapes.fr
Tel: +33 4 50 20 00 32
Fax: +33 4 50 20 03 73

Price Guide: (room only, exlcuding VAT)
single €145–330
double €145–330
suite €380–440

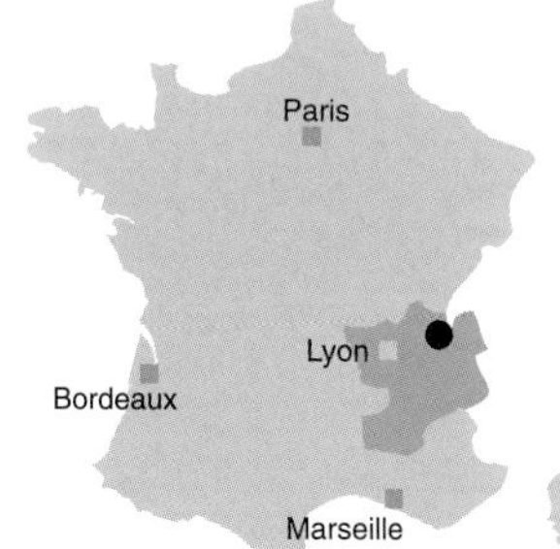

Domaine de Divonne

AVENUE DES THERMES, 01220 DIVONNE~LES~BAINS, FRANCE

The Domaine de Divonne is one of the most exclusive French resorts, the nearest to Geneva and the Swiss border. The magnificent estate consists of a 1930 art deco residence, the Grand Hotel, an 18-hole golf course and a casino. The elegant guest rooms offer balconies overlooking the Alps or Jura mountains and state-of-the-art technology. 5 restaurants, including the 1 Michelin star La Terrasse, offer a diversity of cuisine. The Atelier de Beauté Anne Sémonin and the health centre offer a wide range of relaxing treatments.

Le Domaine de Divonne est un resort unique en France. C'est également le plus proche de Genève et de la frontière suisse. Cet établissement de grand luxe, dans un style art déco des années 30, réunit Le Grand Hôtel, un golf 18 trous et un casino. Les chambres luxueuses disposent de balcons avec vue sur les Alpes et le Jura et un équipement technique trés complet. Il y a 5 restaurants, dont La Terrasse 1 étoile Michelin. L'Atelier de Beauté Anne Sémonin offre des soins personnalisés et relaxants.

El Domaine de Divonne es uno de los centros turísticos más exclusivos de Francia, el más cercano a Ginebra y la frontera suiza. Esta magnífica propiedad la constituyen una residencia art deco de 1930, el Gran Hotel, un campo de golf de 18 hoyos y un casino. Las elegantes habitaciones disponen de balcones con vistas a los Alpes o a los montes Jura y la más moderna tecnología. 5 restaurantes entre los que se incluye La Terrasse, de 1 estrella Michelín, ofrecen gran diversidad de platos. El salón de belleza Anne Sémonin ofrece una amplia gama de tratamientos.

Our inspector loved: *The views of the French Alps and Mont-Blanc.*

Directions: N1 from Geneva > Coppet/Divonne exit.

Web: www.johansens.com/domainededivonne
E-mail: info@domaine-de-divonne.com
Tel: +33 4 50 40 34 34
Fax: +33 4 50 40 34 24

Paris
Lyon
Bordeaux
Marseille

Price Guide: (half board, excluding VAT, per person)
double/twin €140-235
single occupancy supplement €75-170
suite €370-750
single occupancy supplement €300-680

  133    260       

Chalet Hôtel La Marmotte

61 RUE DU CHÊNE, 74260 LES GETS, FRANCE

Situated amidst the beautiful alpine trails and ski slopes of the French Alps, the very family-orientated La Marmotte is friendly and cosy and the perfect base from which to explore this exciting region. Guests of all ages will appreciate the range of activities, including on-site gym and indoor swimming pool and the recently opened spa, which features a hammam, sauna, and 8 treatment rooms. Exhilarating ski slopes, golf courses and Lac de Baignade are nearby, and lively Les Gets is within easy reach. The green fee for Golf des Gets is €15.

Au pied des pistes de ski et des sentiers pédestres des Alpes, vous attend un grand chalet convivial et confortable, la base parfaite pour explorer une région fascinante. Idéal pour les familles, cet hôtel offre des activités aux visiteurs de tout âge, qui peuvent profiter notamment du gymnase sur site, de la piscine couverte et du spa récemment ouvert avec hammam, sauna et 8 salles dévouées aux traitements. Pistes grisantes, golfs et lac de baignade ne sont qu'à deux pas, et l'animation des Gets, avec ses restaurants et ses magasins, n'est pas loin. Les frais pour le Golf des Gets sont €15.

Situado entre los bellos senderos alpinos y las pistas de esquí de los Alpes franceses, el Chalet Hôtel La Marmotte, ideal para las familias, es agradable y acogedor, y la base perfecta de la cual para explorar esta apasionante región. Todos los clientes, pequeños y mayores, podrán disfrutar de las distintas actividades e instalaciones, dentro de las cuales se encuentra un gimnasio, una piscina cubierta y un recién inaugurado spa con hammam, sauna y 8 salas para tratamientos curativos. En sus proximidades encontrará pistas de esquí, campos de golf así como el lago Baignade y el animado Les Gets. Se pagan €15 para el Golf des Gets.

***Our inspector loved:** The superb new spa and its amazing treatments.*

Directions: Leave the A40 and exit at Cluses.

Web: www.johansens.com/chaletlamarmotte
E-mail: info@hotel-marmotte.com
Tel: +33 4 50 75 80 33
Fax: +33 4 50 75 83 26

Price Guide: (half-board, excluding VAT, closed October - November and April - June) double/twin €139–216

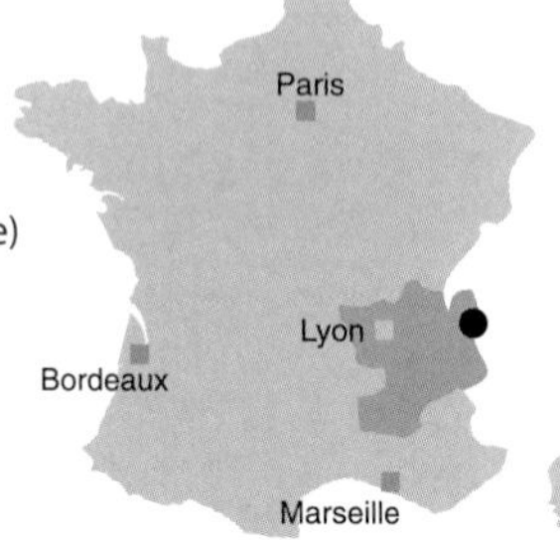

Le Fer à Cheval

36 Route du Crêt d'Arbois, 74120 Megève, France

This stunning hotel is composed of 4 traditional chalets that form a tiny village within the heart of Megève Ski Resort. The warm timber interior, with magnificent beams and roaring fireplaces, creates a cosy haven after a day on the slopes. Friendly staff, who are dedicated to the well-being of their guests, give a hearty welcome from the moment guests step in the door, and 2 superb restaurants offer a fantastic gastronomic experience featuring local dishes and sophisticated flavours.

Ce superbe hôtel, au cœur de la station de Megève, est composé de 4 chalets traditionnels formant un petit village. L'intérieur tout en bois est chaleureux, de magnifiques poutres et de beaux feux de bois créent un refuge confortable après une journée sur les pistes. Un personnel aimable et attentif au bien être des clients accueille chaleureusement les hôtes dés leur arrivée. Les 2 superbes restaurants proposent une réelle expérience gastronomique à partir de mets locaux et de saveurs raffinées.

Este impactante hotel esta compuesto de 4 chalets tradicionales que constituyen una pequeña aldea en pleno corazón de Megève Ski Resort. El acogedor interior en madera, con magnificas vigas y estrepitosos fuegos de chimenea, proporcionan a los clientes un recogido remanso tras un día de esquí. Su amable personal, asiduamente entregado al bienestar de sus clientes, les da una efusiva bienvenida desde el momento en que pisan el hotel, y 2 esplendidos restaurantes proporcionan una fantástica experiencia gastronómica que incluye platos locales y sabores sofisticados.

Our inspector loved: *The particularly warm décor in the bedrooms.*

Directions: Take the A40 or A43 to Megève.

Web: www.johansens.com/cheval
E-mail: fer-a-cheval@wanadoo.fr
Tel: +33 4 50 21 30 39
Fax: +33 4 50 93 07 60

Price Guide: (including dinner)
single €218-260
double €309-537
suite upon request

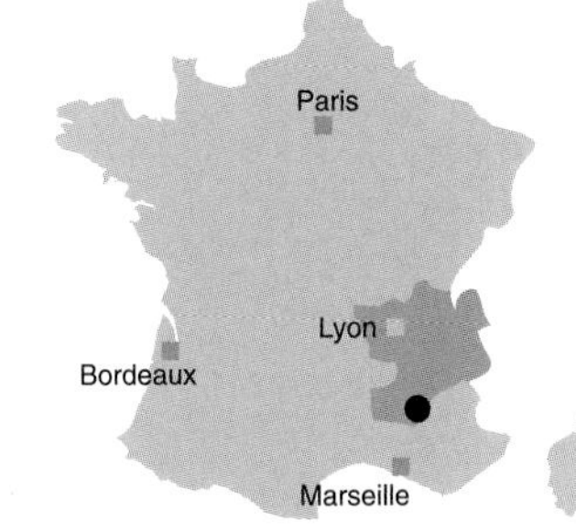

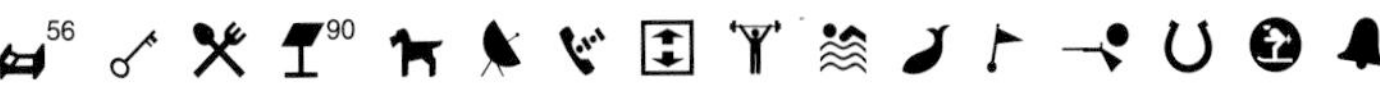

Château de Coudrée

DOMAINE DE COUDRÉE, BONNATRAIT, 74140 SCIEZ~SUR~LÉMAN, FRANCE

Perched on the edge of Lake Geneva, this 12th-century château with its turrets and pinnacles offers a truly fairy tale experience. With a mere 19 guest rooms, all furnished with antiques, this is an elite hotel. Exquisite salons, and a big terrace overlooking the pool and gardens down to the water's edge all contribute to the visitors' overall pleasure. A memorable gastronomic experience is also guaranteed.

Niché sur les bords du Lac de Genève, ce château du XIIe siècle avec ses 19 chambres meublées d'antiquités, offre une vision de conte de fée, avec ses tourelles et ses donjons. Des salons raffinés, un bar accueillant, une grande terrasse avec vue sur la piscine et le jardin descendant jusqu'au bord du lac rendent les séjours encore plus agréables. Une expérience gastronomique mémorable est également garantie.

Enclavado al norte del Lago Geneva, este château del siglo XII con sus torreones y pináculos proporciona una experiencia verdaderamente propia de de un cuento de hadas. Con solo 19 habitaciones, todas amuebladas con antigüedades, este es un verdadero hotel de élite. Tanto sus exquisito salones, su terraza con vistas a la piscina como sus jardines que llegan hasta la misma orilla contribuyen a proporcionarle a los visitantes un placer total. Queda garantizada también una experiencia gastronómica inolvidable.

Our inspector loved: *Its fantastic location on the shore of Lake Geneva, with its private boating stage and amazing views.*

Directions: A40 > Annemasse/Thonon/Evian > Sciez Bonnatrait.

Web: www.johansens.com/decoudree
E-mail: chcoudree@coudree.com
Tel: +33 4 50 72 62 33
Fax: +33 4 50 72 57 28

Price Guide: (closed during November)
single/double/twin €174-382
apartment €298–382

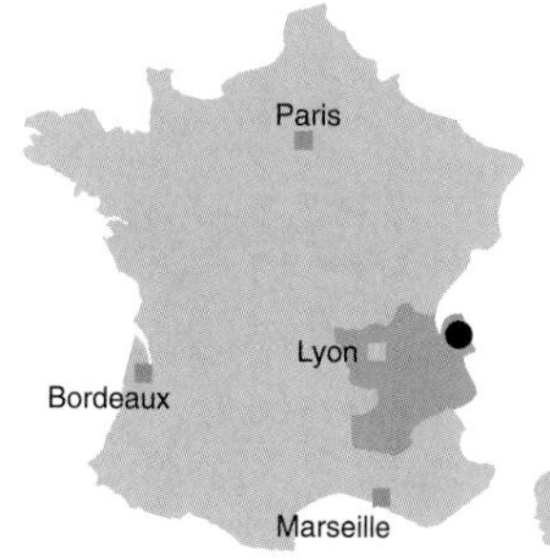

Hôtel du Palais

1 Avenue de l'Impératrice, 64200 Biarritz, France

The auspicious history of this 19th-century residence echoes proudly today. Marble pillars and chandeliers adorn its palatial foyer and exquisite antique furniture is found in the chic bars and luxurious bedrooms. The elegance of the 1 Michelin Star restaurant is worthy of the many notable guests who have chosen this magnificent hotel as their summer retreat. The recently opened Spa Impérial, in association with Guerlain, provides cutting-edge therapies, an indoor pool, 2 saunas, 2 hammams, a fitness centre and beauty parlour.

L'histoire prometteuse de cette résidence du XIXe siècle se répète fièrement aujourd'hui. Des colonnes de marbre et des lustres scintillants ornent le hall grandiose, et des meubles anciens raffinés agrémentent les bars élégants et les chambres luxueuses. Quant à l'élégant restaurant 1 étoile Michelin, il est digne des nombreux hôtes prestigieux qui ont fait de ce palais leur résidence d'été. Ouvert récemment, Spa Imperial offre, en association avec Guerlain, des thérapies d'avant-garde, une piscine intérieure, 2 saunas, 2 hammams, un centre de remise en forme et un salon de beauté.

Aun hoy suena con orgullo el eco de la auspiciosa historia de esta residencia del siglo XIX situada al borde del mar. Columnas de mármol y arañas relucientes adornan su palaciego hall y en los sofisticados bares y lujosas habitaciones se encuentran muebles antiguos exquisitos. El elegante restaurante, dotado con una estrella Michelín, es digno de los muchos huéspedes notables que han elegido este fabuloso hotel como su refugio veraniego. El Spa Imperial, de reciente construcción, ofrece terapias a lo ultimo en asociación con Guerlain, y consta de piscina interior, 2 saunas, 2 hammams, un gimnasio y peluquería.

Our inspector loved: *The grandeur of this palatial hotel.*

Directions: The hotel is situated in the centre of Biarritz. The nearest airport is Biarritz. Biarritz TGV station and Bordeaux Airport are 2 hours away. Bilbao, Spain is 2 hours away. San Sebastian is 30 minutes away.

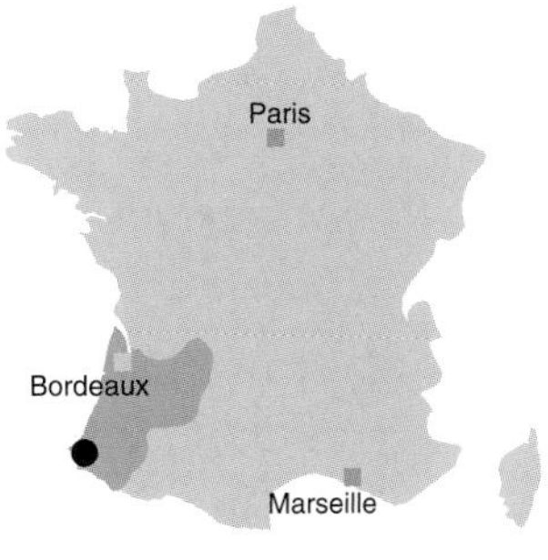

Web: www.johansens.com/palais
E-mail: manager@hotel-du-palais.com
Tel: +33 5 59 41 64 00
Fax: +33 5 59 41 67 99

Price Guide: (room only, excluding VAT)
single €260–475
double/twin €370–550
suite €600–1,550
royal suite upon request

           SPA

Château le Mas de Montet

PETIT-BERSAC, 24600 RIBÉRAC, DORDOGNE, FRANCE

This superbly restored Renaissance-style château, where President François Mitterrand was a regular visitor, is situated in the heart of 130 acres of quiet and peaceful parkland. English owners, Richard and John Ridley, offer the most welcoming hospitality and service. The attractive château has been completely refurbished, is stylishly decorated, and furnished throughout with a combination of lovely French and English pieces, and the comfortable en-suite guest rooms offer four-poster beds, modern facilities and panoramic views.

Ce château de style renaissance magnifiquement restauré, qui accueillait régulièrement le Président François Mitterrand, est situé au cœur de plus de 50 ha de terres tranquilles. Les propriétaires anglais Richard et John Ridley offrent un accueil et un service des plus chaleureux. Cet attrayant château complètement rénové est décoré avec style et est équipé d'un mélange de ravissants meubles français et anglais. Les chambres confortables ont des lits à baldaquins, tout l'équipement moderne et des vues panoramiques.

Este château de estilo renacentista admirablemente restaurado, regularmente visitado en su día por el Presidente François Mitterrand, se encuentra en pleno corazón de un tranquilo y apacible parque de 50 ha. Sus propietarios ingleses Richard y John Ridley, que ponen a disposición del cliente el más alto nivel de hospitalidad y servicio. Este atractivo château ha sido totalmente reformado, decorado con gusto y estilo y amueblado en su totalidad mediante una exquisita combinación de encantadoras piezas francesas e inglesas. Sus cómodos habitaciones en-suite disponen de camas con baldaquín, modernas instalaciones y vistas panorámicas.

Our inspector loved: *The beautifully decorated bedrooms and elegant bathrooms.*

Directions: Bergerac Airport > Roumaniere > 50km. Bordeaux Airport > Merignac >110km. Limoges Airport > Bellegarde > 100km.

Web: www.johansens.com/lemasdemontet
E-mail: reception@lemasdemontet.com
Tel: +33 5 53 90 08 71
Fax: +33 5 53 90 66 92

Price Guide: (room only)
room €132-250
suite €189-550

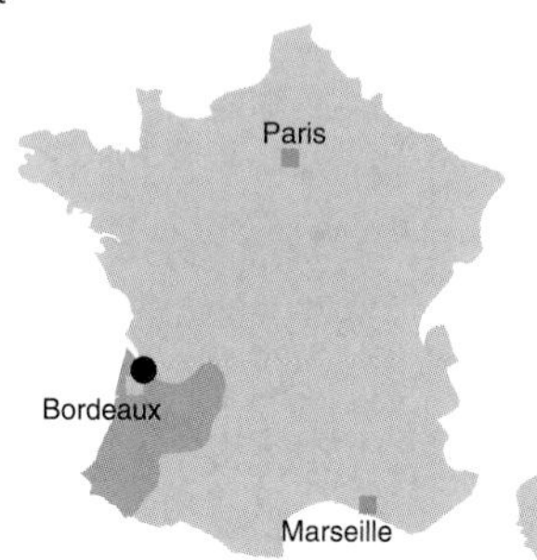

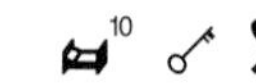

Château de Sanse

33350 SAINTE~RADEGONDE, FRANCE

This charming château, with its perfect combination of historical features and modern convenience, is set within beautifully tranquil surroundings amidst woodland, meadow and pretty gardens. The excellent staff are friendly and attentive, and ensure a memorable experience. Individually styled rooms are newly decorated in bright colours, giving an airy and cheerful relaxed atmosphere, and the restaurant, which overlooks rolling hills, offers superb international cuisine.

Ce charmant château qui allie parfaitement le confort moderne au décor historique est situé dans un cadre superbe et tranquille au sein des bois, prés et jolis jardins. Le personnel est remarquablement amical et attentif, et vous assure une expérience mémorable. Les chambres ont été individuellement décorées dans des couleurs vives, dégageant ainsi un sentiment d'espace et une atmosphère gaie et détendue. Le restaurant, qui offre une vue dégagée sur les collines, sert une succulente cuisine internationale.

Este encantador château, con su perfecta combinación de carácter histórico y modernas instalaciones, se encuentra ubicado en un bello y tranquilo entorno formado por bosques, prados y lindos jardines. Su excelente personal es afable y atento y hace lo posible por hacer las estancias memorables. Sus habitaciones de estilo individual han sido recientemente decoradas con colores vivos para proporcionar un ambiente jovial e informal, y el restaurante, con vistas a las onduladas colinas, ofrece una magnífica carta internacional.

Our inspector loved: *The very pretty restaurant and terrace overlooking beautiful surroundings.*

Directions: Bordeaux > N89 > Libourne > D936 > Castillon La Bataille > D17 > Pujols > D18 > Gensac.

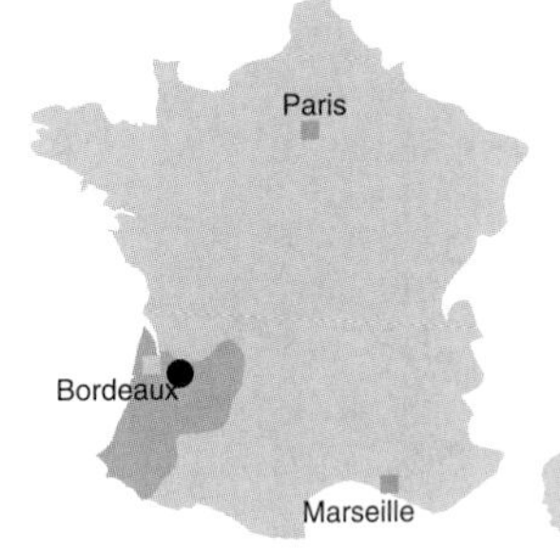

Web: www.johansens.com/chateaudesanse
E-mail: contact@chateaudesanse.com
Tel: +33 5 57 56 41 10
Fax: +33 5 57 56 41 29

Price Guide: (breakfast €12)
double/twin €100-135
suite €165-195

  16 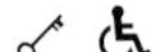   45    

Le Chaufourg~en~Périgord

24400 SOURZAC, PÉRIGORD, DORDOGNE, FRANCE

Directions: The nearest airport is Bergerac (25km). Bordeaux Airport is 90km away.

Web: www.johansens.com/chaufourg
E-mail: info@lechaufourg.com
Tel: +33 5 53 81 01 56
Fax: +33 5 53 82 94 87

Price Guide: (breakfast €16)
single €160
suite €325

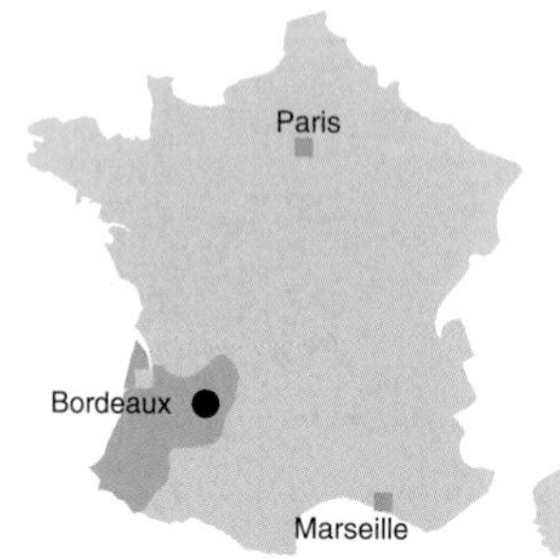

Tucked away between a park, meadows and gardens next to a pretty, meandering river, this charming, elegant 17th-century manor house is more a family home than a hotel. Owners Georges and Agnes Dambier, a well-known former fashion photographer has created a beautifully refined interior, and the comfortable, luxurious bedrooms offer every modern convenience. Excellent quality food is served inside or in the beautifully kept romantic garden. The region abounds with cultural and culinary attractions, and Georges is happy to help arrange trips and activities.

Caché derrière un parc, des prairies et des jardins près d'une ravissante rivière, cet élégant et ravissant manoir du XVIIe est plus une maison de famille qu'un hôtel. Les propriétaire Georges et Agnes Dambier, ancien photographe de mode réputé, a su créer un superbe intérieur raffiné et les chambres confortables et luxueuses offrent tout le confort moderne. Une cuisine d'une excellente qualité est servie à l'intérieur ou dans les magnifiques et romantiques jardins. La région abonde d'attractions culturelles et culinaires et Georges est toujours prêt à organiser des itinéraires et des activités

Enclavado entre un parque, arroyos y jardines junto a un precioso y sinuoso río, esta encantadora y elegante casa solariega del siglo XVII, es más un hogar que un hotel. Su propietarios, Georges y Agnes Dambier, un famoso exfotógrafo de modas, ha creado para éste un bello y refinado interior, a la vez que sus cómodas y lujosas habitaciones proporcionan todo tipo de comodidades modernas. Su excelente carta de calidad se sirve dentro o en su romántico, bello y primoroso jardín. La región dispone de abundantes atractivos culturales y gastronómicos, y Georges está encantado de poder colaborar en la organización de excursiones y otras actividades.

Our inspector loved: *The warm, natural welcome in this romantic environment.*

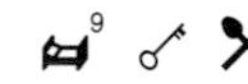     

CHÂTEAU DE CHALLAIN

49440 CHALLAIN~LA~POTHERIE, FRANCE

Built during the 19th-century for Duke de Rochefoucauld as the largest château in France, Château de Challain has been sensitively converted to provide 4 sumptuous suites. The authentic 19th-century atmosphere is wonderful and the interior is aptly adorned with stunning antiques and luxurious furnishings. Delicious Loire Valley treats are offered in the dining room or in the winter months, guests may relax by the fireside in the original château kitchen.

Construit au XIXe siècle par le Duc de Rochefoucauld comme le plus grand château de France, Château de Challain a été amoureusement transformé pour proposer 4 suites somptueuses. L'atmosphère authentique du XIXe siècle est impressionnante et l'intérieur est orné de magnifiques antiquités et de superbes ameublements. Des délicieuses spécialités de la Vallée de la Loire sont proposées dans la salle à manger et en hiver les hôtes peuvent se prélasser près du feu dans la cuisine d'origine du château.

Construido en el siglo XIX como el château más grande de Francia para el duque de Rochefoucauld, Château de Challain ha sido sensatamente convertido en 4 suites suntuosas. Se respira un ambiente autentico del siglo XIX y el interior esta decorado de forma idónea con antigüedades impresionantes y muebles lujosos. En el comedor se sirven delicias de valle del Loire y en los meses de invierno se puede descansar al lado del fuego en la cocina primitiva del Château.

Our inspector loved: *Being welcomed by the owner, and feeling so at home.*

Directions: A11 > exit 18 > D923 towards Candé > head towards Pouancé on D6. The nearest airport is Nantes.

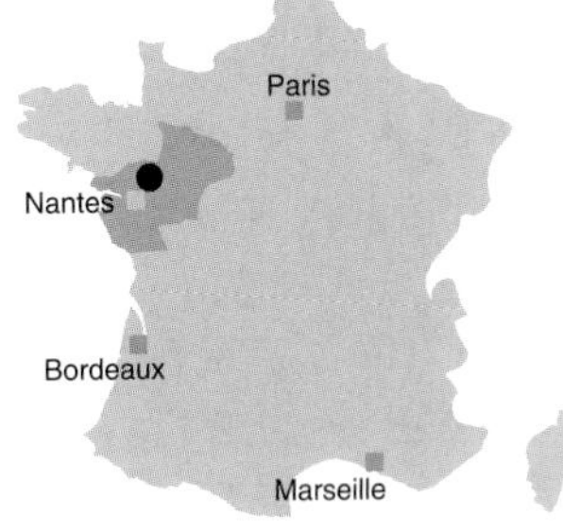

Web: www.johansens.com/challain
E-mail: chateauchallain@aol.com
Tel: +33 2 41 92 74 26
Fax: +33 2 41 61 54 25

Price Guide: (room only)
suite €200-350

Château des Briottières

49330 CHAMPIGNÉ, FRANCE

Surrounded by 360 acres of parkland "à l'anglaise", this magnificent family-owned stately home is set in the heart of peaceful Anjou. The luxurious interior, with its pervading air of serenity, features Louis XV antiques and quirky memorabilia. The immaculately presented bedrooms have windows overlooking the estate, inviting the rich perfumes of herbs and flowers. Traditional Anjou meals are served in the impressive period dining room.

Entouré d'un jardin anglais de 150ha, cette magnifique maison familiale est en plein coeur de la paisible région d'Anjou. L'intérieur luxueux dégage une ambiance sereine et présente des pièces Louis XV et des objets de collection. Les chambres immaculées donnent sur le domaine et laissent entrer le doux parfum des herbes aromatiques et des fleurs. Les repas traditionnels d'Anjou sont servis dans l'ancienne salle à manger impressionnante.

Rodeada de 150 ha de parque "à l'anglaise", esta magnífica mansión de regencia familiar se encuentra ubicada en el corazón de la tranquila región de Anjou. Su lujoso interior, provisto de antigüedades de la época de Luis XV y peculiares objetos de colección, emana una sensación de serenidad que todo lo invade. Sus habitaciones de inmaculada presentación disponen de ventanales con vistas a la propiedad que permiten la entrada a sus sugerentes aromas de hierbas y flores. Se sirven tradicionales platos de Anjou en su impresionante comedor de época.

Our inspector loved: *The secluded swimming pool in the hotel's grounds.*

Directions: A11 > exit 11 > D859 > Champigné > 4km.

Web: www.johansens.com/chateaudesbriottieres
E-mail: briottieres@wanadoo.fr
Tel: +33 2 41 42 00 02
Fax: +33 2 41 42 01 55

Price Guide: (room only)
single €150–250
double/twin €180–250
suites €280–320

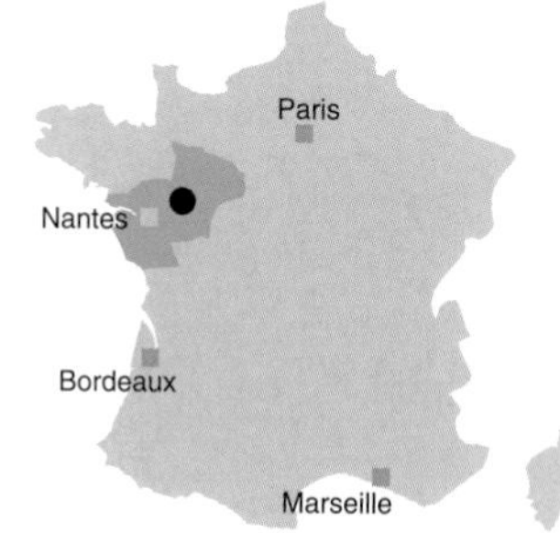

14 200

Great Britain

Hotel location shown in red (hotel) or purple (spa hotel) with page number

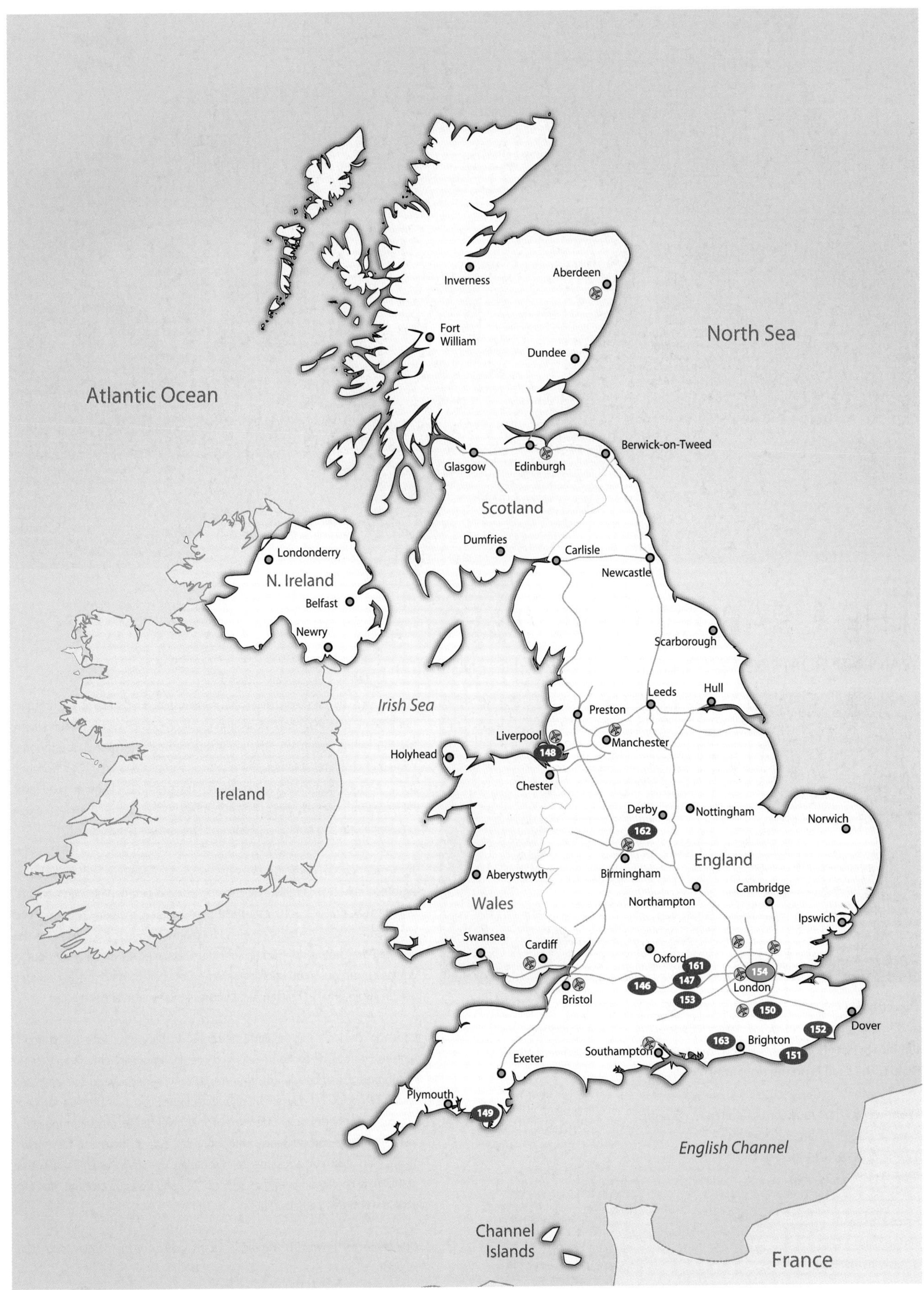

THE CRAB AT CHIEVELEY

WANTAGE ROAD, NEWBURY, BERKSHIRE RG20 8UE, ENGLAND

Surrounded by stunning Berkshire countryside, this superb, picturesque, traditionally thatched hotel has an impressive reputation with an AA and Remy award-winning restaurant that serves sublime seafood cuisine. Guest rooms, named after the most famous hotels of the world, are outstanding, featuring décor, furnishings, facilities and comforts chosen with the finest of good taste. All have been carefully designed, with those on the ground floor featuring a private garden and hot tub. London and Bath are within easy reach.

Au coeur de la magnifique campagne du Berkshire, ce superbe et pittoresque hôtel à la toiture de chaume, a une réputation impressionnante, notamment grâce à son restaurant primé au AA et Remy, qui sert une succulente cuisine de fruits de mer. Les chambres qui portent les noms des plus célèbres hôtels du monde, sont décorées avec un mobilier de gôut et équipés pour fournir un confort extrême. Les chambres du rez-de chaussée ont un jardin privé et bain chaud. Londres et Bath sont faciles d'accès.

Rodeado de los espectaculares terrenos de Berkshire, este magnífico y pintoresco hotel de techo de paja goza de una impresionante fama y de un restaurante galardonado con una AA y Remy, especializado en servir una exquisita cocina de mariscos. Sus habitaciones, con nombres de famosos hoteles del mundo, gozan de excepcional nivel de decoración, mobiliario, instalaciones y comodidades, seleccionadas con el mejor de los gustos. Todas han sido cuidadosamente diseñadas, contando además las de la planta baja con jardín privado y servicio de baño de agua caliente. Hay fácil acceso a Londres y a Bath.

Our inspector loved: *The amazing rooms, energy of the owners, and super location.*

Directions: Leave the M4, junction 13 (taking care not to join the A34 north) and follow signs to Chieveley. Turn left onto Graces Lane and after 1/3 mile turn left into School Road. Turn right at the top of the hill then right onto the B4494. The Crab is on the right after 1/2 mile.

Web: www.johansens.com/crabatchieveleyeuro
E-mail: info@crabatchieveley.com
Tel: +44 1635 247550
Fax: +44 1635 247440

Price Guide:
single from £120
double from £150

The French Horn

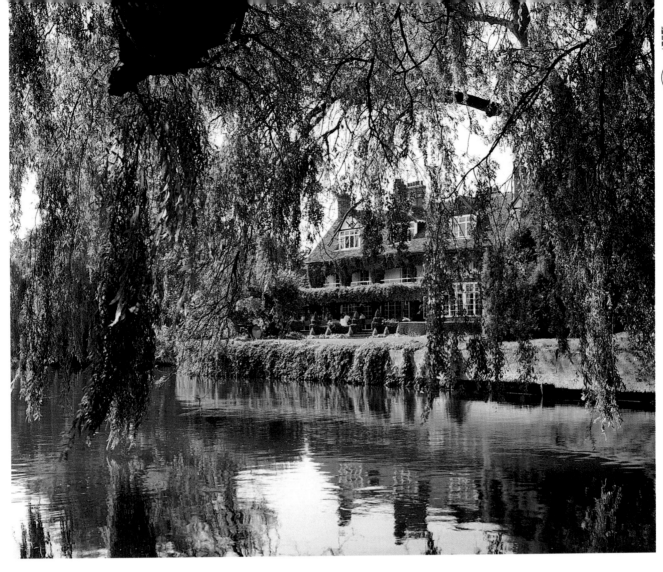

SONNING ON THAMES, BERKSHIRE, RG4 6TN, ENGLAND

This comfortable, charming hotel and gourmet restaurant is the epitome of the quaint, quintessential English riverside village retreat. Set near Windsor and the historic village of Sonning, there are 4 riverside cottages, alongside 4 riverside rooms, and 12 suites and en-suite double rooms to choose from. The family-run restaurant looks out onto the Thames and serves classic French cuisine alongside traditional English dishes, and the wine list is reputed to be amongst the finest in Europe. Meeting facilities for up to 16 delegates are available.

Cet hôtel confortable et luxueux avec son restaurant gastronome est la quintessence d'un village retrait au charme vieillot au bord de la rivière. Situé près de Windsor et le village historique de Sonning, l'hôtel propose 4 petites maisons et 4 chambres près de la rivière, ainsi que 12 suites et chambres attenantes. Le restaurant familial donne sur le Thames et sert une cuisine française classique ainsi que des plats traditionnels anglais et les vins sont réputés être parmi les meilleurs en Europe. Des facilités de conférence pour jusqu'à 16 personnes sont disponibles.

Este lujoso y confortable hotel con restaurante gourmet es un compendio de un refugio rural pintoresco a la orilla del río y con rasgos quintaesenciales ingleses. Ubicado cerca de Windsor y de la histórica aldea de Sonning. Tiene 4 casitas rurales ribereñas junto a 4 habitaciones que dan al río, y 12 suites y en-suite dobles donde poder elegir. El restaurante que da al Támesis, dirigido por una familia, sirve cocina francesa clásica junto con platos tradicionales ingleses y su lista de vinos goza de una gran fama en Europa por su exquisitez. Dispone de salones para celebrar congresos con capacidad para 16 personas.

Our inspector loved: *This lovely traditional hotel with its exceptional restaurant and attentive staff.*

Directions: M4 > exit junction 8/9 > follow A404 > at Thickets roundabout turn left > A4 towards Reading for 8 miles > Sonning > cross Thames on B478 > hotel is on the right.

Web: www.johansens.com/frenchhorneuro
E-mail: info@thefrenchhorn.com
Tel: +44 1189 692 204
Fax: +44 1189 442 210

Edinburgh
Dublin
Cardiff
London

Price Guide:
single £125–170
double/twin £160–215

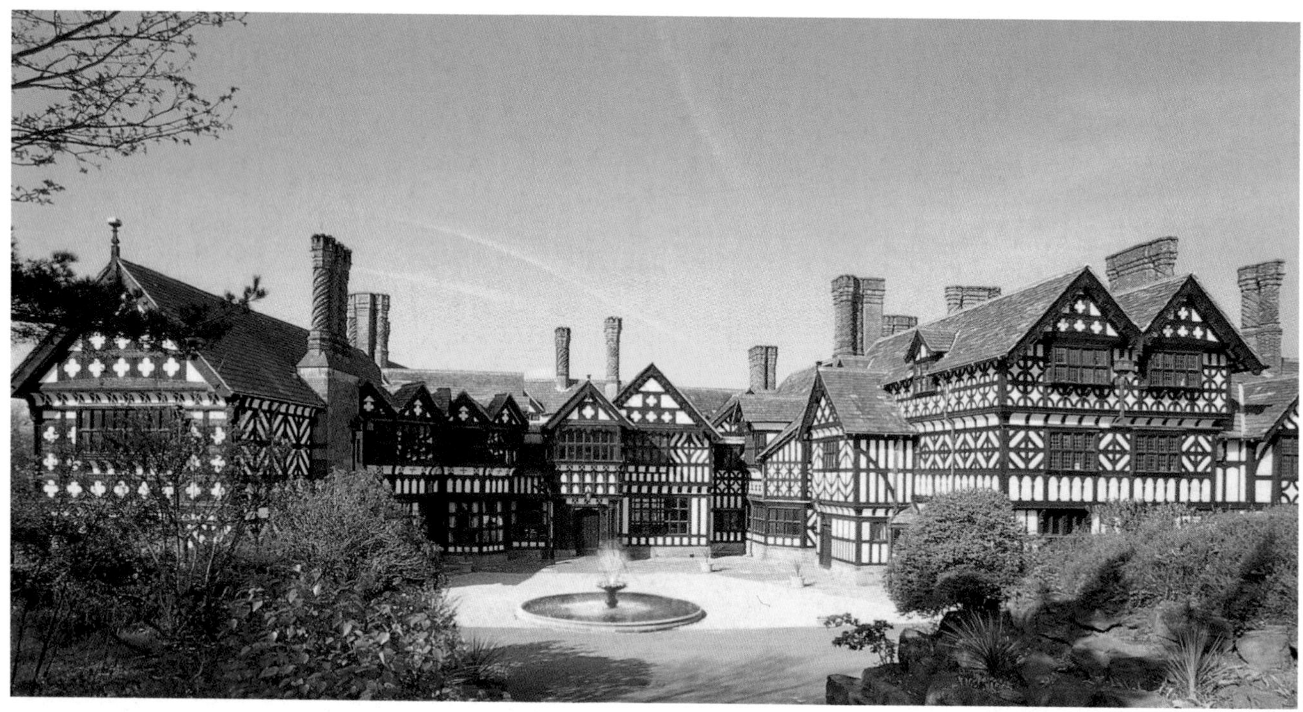

Hillbark Hotel

ROYDEN PARK, FRANKBY, WIRRAL, CH48 1NP, ENGLAND

Directions: Take M53, jct 3 for A552. Bear right on A551 towards Upton. After the hospital turn left onto Arrowe Brook Road then left onto Arrowe Brook Lane. Straight on at roundabout for ½ mile and Hillbark is on the left.

Web: www.johansens.com/hillbarkeuro
E-mail: enquiries@hillbarkhotel.co.uk
Tel: +44 151 625 2400
Fax: +44 151 625 4040

Price Guide:
single from £175
double/twin £175–250
suite £250–500

Nestling in the Wirral Peninsula, this magnificent Grade II listed hotel provides the finest luxury coupled with discreet and friendly service. It is surrounded by parkland and has marvellous views over the Dee Estuary across to the hills of North Wales. Suites and rooms are lavishly furnished and the house contains many historical features. Imaginative haute cuisine is served in the opulent restaurant together with an extensive selection of fine wines.

Niché sur la péninsule du Wirral, ce magnifique hôtel classé offre le meilleur du luxe associé à un service discret et accueillant. L'hôtel est entouré d'espaces verts et offre de superbes vues sur l'estuaire du Dee jusqu'aux montagnes du Nord du Pays de Galles. Les chambres et suites sont somptueusement décorées et l'hôtel contient de nombreuses caractéristiques historiques. Une haute cuisine imaginative accompagnée d'une sélection de délicieux vins est servi dans l'opulent restaurant.

Situado en la Wirral Peninsular, este magnífico hotel clasificado de Categoría II proporciona el más alto nivel de lujo a la par que un servicio discreto y afable. Se encuentra rodeado de parques y dispone de maravillosas vistas al estuario de Dee y a las colinas del norte de Gales en la lejanía. Las suites y las habitaciones son suntuosamente amuebladas y el edificio cuenta con numerosas antigüedades. Una creativa haute cuisine se sirve en su lujoso restaurante junto a una amplia selección de vinos de calidad.

Our inspector loved: *The peace and tranquillity in this magnificent Elizabethan-style house.*

19 500

Soar Mill Cove Hotel

SOAR MILL COVE, SALCOMBE, SOUTH DEVON, TQ7 3DS, ENGLAND

With 2,000 acres of coastline to explore and an enclosed beach a stroll away, this hotel is the perfect antidote to everyday stresses. Situated in 10 acres of grounds on Devon's southernmost coastal headland between Dartmouth and Plymouth, Soar Mill Cove Hotel is a paragon of tasteful décor and furnishings. Bedrooms and suites have every comfort, patios and panoramic outlooks. Award-winning cuisine is served in a classically elegant restaurant. A spa, 2 heated swimming pools and a range of leisure facilities are available.

Avec plus de 800 ha de littoral à explorer et une plage recluse située à quelques pas, cet hôtel représente le parfait antidote au stress de la vie de tous les jours. Au cœur d'un domaine de 4 ha sur le cap côtier le plus au sud du Devon entre Dartmouth et Plymouth, Soar Mill Cove Hotel est un modèle de goût et de décoration. Les chambres et suites ont patios, vues panoramiques ainsi que tout le confort possible. Une cuisine de qualité et reconnue est servie dans l'élégant restaurant. Un spa, 2 piscines chauffées et un choix d'équipements de loisirs sont disponibles.

Con 800 ha de línea costera por explorar y una playa cercada sólo a un paseo, este hotel es el perfecto antídoto para las tensiones de todos los días. Situado en medio de 4 ha de terreno propio sobre el cabo más meridional de la costa de Devon, entre Dartmouth y Plymouth, el hotel Soar Mill Cove Hotel es modelo por su gusto en decoración y mobiliario. Las habitaciones y suites disponen de todo tipo de comodidades, patios y panorámicos paisajes. Su galardonada carta se sirve en un elegante restaurante con decoración clásica. El hotel cuenta asimismo con spa, 2 piscinas climatizadas y gran variedad de instalaciones destinadas al ocio.

Our inspector loved: *The superb rooms with striking sensual fabrics and presentation; not forgetting the breathtaking location!*

Directions: Exeter Airport > A30 > A387 > A381 Totnes/Kingsbridge > signs to Salcombe. At Malborough signposted Soar follow signs for 2 miles.

Web: www.johansens.com/soarmillcoveeuro
E-mail: info@soarmillcove.co.uk
Tel: +44 1548 561566
Fax: +44 1548 561223

Price Guide:
single £94–180
double £180–240
suite from £216

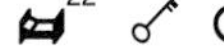

SPA

Ashdown Park Hotel

WYCH CROSS, FOREST ROW, EAST SUSSEX, RH18 5JR, ENGLAND

Amidst 186 acres of beautiful landscaped gardens, this grand 19th-century mansion has charm, character, luxurious comfort and attentive service. There is a relaxed, informal atmosphere, and delightfully decorated guest rooms. Some have elegant four-poster beds whilst each has every modern amenity. Enjoy carefully compiled menus of imaginative cuisine in the attractive Anderida restaurant, and the extensive wine list. Leisure facilities include an 18-hole par 3 golf course, indoor driving nets, spa and fitness amenities.

Situé au cœur de 75 ha de jardins paysagers, Ashdown Park Hotel est un imposant manoir du XIXe siècle rempli de charme, de caractère, de confort luxueux et de service attentif. L'hôtel possède une atmosphère décontractée, informelle et chambres délicieusement décorées. Certaines ont d'élégants lits à baldaquins et toutes offrent tout le confort moderne. Des menus habilement créés d'une cuisine imaginative accompagnés d'une superbe liste de vins sont servis dans le séduisant restaurant Anderida. Les activités de loisirs comprennent un parcours 18 trous de golf, pair-3, des filets de practice intérieur, spa et équipements de fitness.

Enclavado entre 75 ha de bellos y panorámicos jardines, Ashdown Park Hotel es una grandiosa mansión del siglo XIX con encanto, carácter, confort de lujo y servicio atento. Posee un ambiente relajado y desenfadado y habitaciones decoradas con sumo encanto. Algunas tienen elegantes camas con baldaquín si bien todas cuentan con todo tipo de instalaciones modernas. En el atractivo restaurante Anderida se ofrecen menus de cocina imaginativa compilados con esmero, junto a una extensa lista de vinos. Las instalaciones de ocio incluyen un campo de golf de 18 hoyos, par-3, redes de practica interiores, spa e instalaciones de fitness.

Our inspector loved: *The impressive and consistent standards.*

Directions: Take junction 10 of the M23 and join the A264 to East Grinstead, then the A22 to Eastbourne. The hotel is located east of the A22 at the Wych Cross traffic lights on the road signposted to Hartfield.

Web: www.johansens.com/ashdownparkeuro
E-mail: reservations@ashdownpark.com
Tel: +44 1342 824988
Fax: +44 1342 826206

Price Guide:
single £140–345
double/twin £170–235
suite £300–375

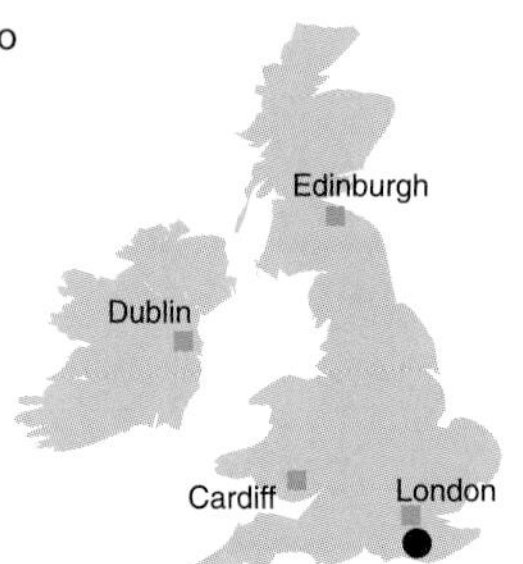

The Grand Hotel

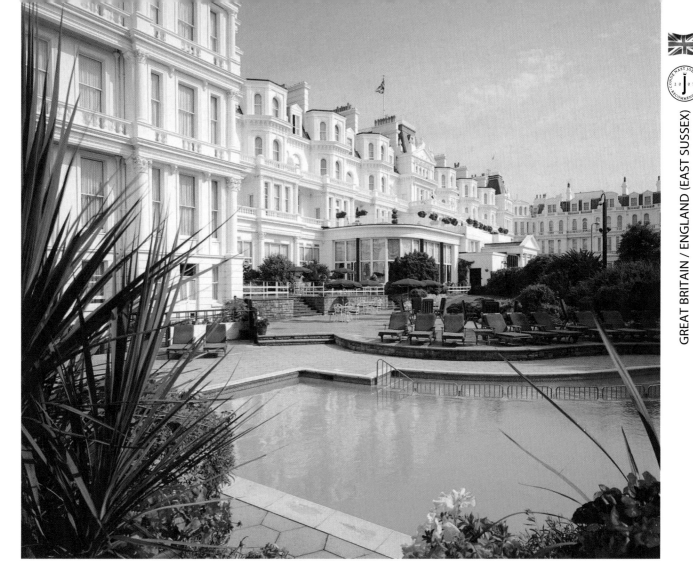

KING EDWARD'S PARADE, EASTBOURNE, EAST SUSSEX, BN21 4EQ, ENGLAND

On a superb promenade location with panoramic sea views, this hotel offers the utmost in luxury, style and service. The impressive white façade reflects the style and glories of the Victorian era and is complemented by an elegant interior with beautifully appointed reception rooms. Many of the 152 guest rooms and suites are opulently large; all are beautifully decorated and have every comfort. First-class cuisine in the Mirabelle and Garden restaurants have won numerous awards. Facilities include indoor and outdoor pools.

Bénéficiant d'un emplacement privilégié en front de mer avec des vues panoramiques, The Grand Hotel offre le meilleur du luxe, de style et de service. L'impressionnante façade blanche reflète le style et la splendeur de l'ère Victorienne et est parfaitement complétée par l'élégant intérieur et ses magnifiques salles de réceptions. La plupart des 152 chambres et suites sont très spacieuses, toutes sont superbement bien décorées et possèdent tout le confort moderne. Une cuisine de premier ordre dans les restaurants Mirabelle et Garden ont valu à l'hôtel de nombreuses récompenses. Les activités de loisirs comprennent piscines intérieure et extérieure.

The Grand Hotel goza de una privilegiada posición en el paseo marítimo y de panorámicas vistas al mar. Ofrece lo más avanzado en lujo, estilo y servicio. Su impresionante fachada blanca es reflejo del estilo y los tiempos gloriosos de la época victoriana y se combina con suma perfección con su elegante interior y bellas salas de recepción. Muchas de las 152 habitaciones y suites son generosamente grandes; todas están magníficamente decoradas y disponen de todo tipo de comodidades. La carta de primera clase de los restaurantes Mirabelle y Garden le ha proporcionado al hotel numerosos premias. Las instalaciones de ocio incluyen piscinas interior y exterior.

Our inspector loved: *The outstanding levels of service and comfort.*

Directions: From London > A22 to south coast. > follow signs to Eastbourne. Alternatively take M25 > join M23 towards Brighton > A27 to Lewes > Eastbourne. The hotel is at the western end of the seafront.

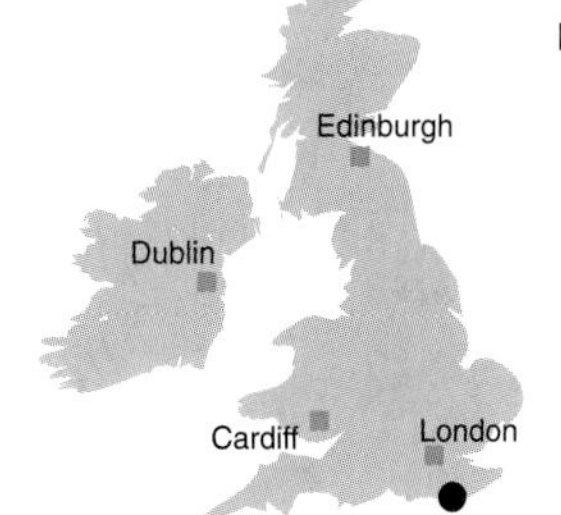

Web: www.johansens.com/grandeastbourneeuro
E-mail: reservations@grandeastbourne.com
Tel: +44 1323 412345
Fax: +44 1323 412233

Price Guide:
single £140-430
double/twin £170-460
suite £300-460

SPA

Rye Lodge

HILDER'S CLIFF, RYE, EAST SUSSEX, TN31 7LD, ENGLAND

Directions: A259 or A268 > Rye > follow Town Centre signs > travel through Landgate Arch > hotel is 100 yards on right.

Web: www.johansens.com/ryelodgeeuro
E-mail: info@ryelodge.co.uk
Tel: +44 1797 223838
Fax: +44 1797 223585

Price Guide:
single from £85
double £140–200

Rye Lodge is a delightful small hotel in the historic town of Rye with its quaint shops, tea rooms, pubs and restaurants, and boasts stunning views across the Estuary and Romney Marshes. The interior features relaxing colour schemes and the comfortable bedrooms are spacious with every modern convenience. The romantic Terrace Restaurant, with its high ceilings and Regency-style furniture, has large windows that look out to the lovely views. The Venetian Leisure Centre offers an aromatherapy steam cabinet, sauna and heated indoor pool.

Rye Lodge est un ravissant petit hôtel situé dans la ville historique de Rye avec ses boutiques pittoresques, salons de thé, pubs et restaurants, qui bénéficie de vues superbes sur l'Estuaire et les marécages de Romney. L'intérieur est décoré dans des tons doux et les chambres sont confortables et spacieuses avec toutes les commodités modernes. Le romantique Terrace Restaurant, avec ses hauts plafonds et ses meubles Régence, a de grandes fenêtres qui donnent sur de belles vues. Le centre de loisirs Venetian offre une cabine de soins-vapeur aromathérapiques, un sauna et une piscine intérieure chauffée.

Rye Lodge es un hotel pequeño histórico encantador en la localidad histórica de Rye, bordeada de pintorescas tiendas, teterías, tabernas y restaurantes. El hotel ofrece impresionantes vistas a las zonas pantanosas de Estuario y Romney. El interior se caracteriza por combinaciones de colores relajantes y sus habitaciones son confortables y espaciosas y cuentan con todas las comodidades modernas de hoy día. Su romántico restaurante terraza, de altos techos y detalles al estilo del periodo de la Regencia, dispone de grandes ventanas con vistas preciosas. El Centro Veneciano de Tiempo Libre dispone de una cabina de aromaterapia a vapor, sauna y piscina cubierta climatizada.

***Our inspector loved:** The thoughtful little touches, and the service.*

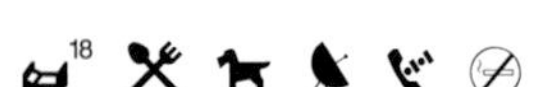

Tylney Hall

ROTHERWICK, HOOK, HAMPSHIRE, RG27 9AZ, ENGLAND

Surrounded by manicured, historic gardens, woodlands and the surrounding rolling countryside, Tylney Hall is an idyllic retreat that exudes elegance and tranquillity. Wood panelled interiors create a cosy atmosphere enhanced by crackling open fires and stunning antiques. Award-winning dining is a treat and opulent bedrooms are the ultimate in comfort. There are a wide variety of indoor and outdoor activities to choose from.

Entouré par des jardins historiques soignés, des bois et des paysages vallonés, Tylney Hall est un refuge idéal qui respire l'élégance et la tranquillité. L'intérieur en boiseries crée une atmosphère douillette, rehaussée par des feux de cheminées crépitants et de superbes antiquités. La cuisine, primée, est un plaisir et les chambres opulentes offrent le confort ultime. Il y a un grand choix d'activités intérieures et extérieures.

Rodeado de cuidadísimos jardines que emanan historia, de bosques y del ondulado paisaje de los alrededores, Tylney Hall es un lugar de descanso idílico que rezuma elegancia y tranquilidad. Los interiores recubiertos de paneles de madera ofrecen un ambiente acogedor, realzado por crepitantes lumbres de chimenea y sorprendentes antigüedades. La cena, merecedora de varios premios, es un verdadero festín y las espléndidas habitaciones ofrecen lo último en confort. Los clientes pueden elegir entre una amplia variedad de actividades en zona cubierta o al aire libre.

Our inspector loved: *The spacious and elegant drawing room where afternoon tea is a delight.*

Directions: M4, jct 11 towards Hook and Rotherwick > follow signs to the hotel > M3, jct 5 > A287 towards Newnham > over A30 into Old School Road > left for Newnham > right onto Ridge Lane > hotel is on the left after 1 mile.

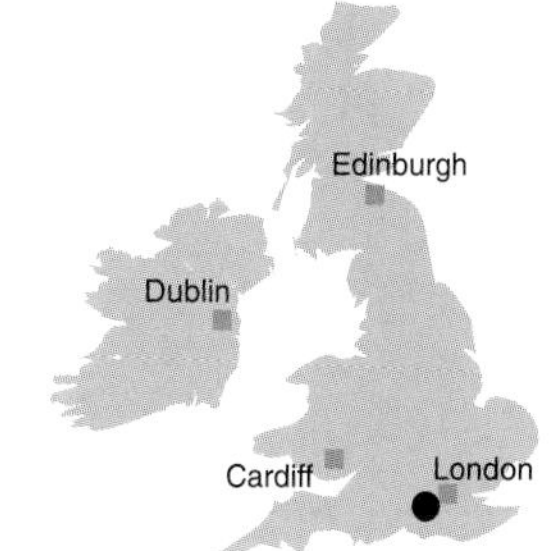

Web: www.johansens.com/tylneyhalleuro
E-mail: reservations@tylneyhall.com
Tel: +44 1256 764881
Fax: +44 1256 768141

Price Guide:
single £140–430
double/twin £170–235
suite £300–460

LONDON

Hotel location shown in red (hotel) or purple (spa hotel) with page number

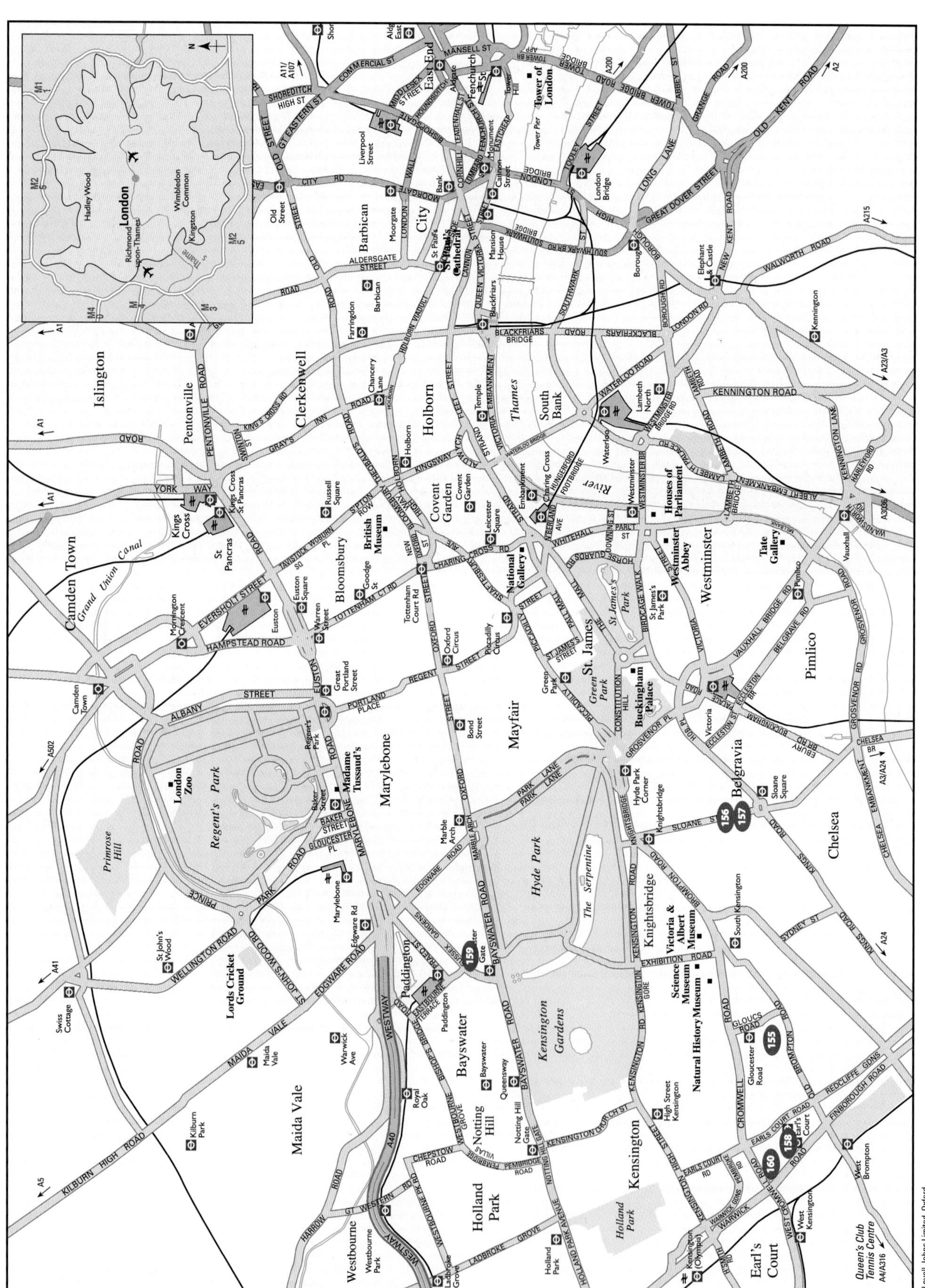

THE CRANLEY

10 BINA GARDENS, SOUTH KENSINGTON, LONDON, SW5 0LA, ENGLAND

Standing in the heart of Kensington, this charming and sophisticated town house blends traditional style and service with 21st-century technology. Beautiful antiques, hand-embroidered fabrics, striking colour combinations and stone are used throughout. Some of the delightful bedrooms feature four-poster beds and all benefit from luxurious bathrooms. Copious continental breakfasts, English afternoon tea and evening apéritifs are served. Many of London's restaurants and attractions are within walking distance.

Charmant et raffiné, cet hôtel particulier au coeur de Kensington allie un style et un service traditionnels à un confort moderne. L'intérieur est rehaussé par de belles antiquités, des tissus brodés à la main, des combinaisons de couleurs remarquables et l'usage de la pierre. Des lits à baldaquin trônent dans certaines des chambres, toutes équipées de salles de bains luxueuses. L'hôtel sert de copieux petits déjeuners continentaux, le thé de cinq heures et l'apéritif avant le dîner. Nombre des restaurants et des attractions de la capitale ne sont qu'à deux pas.

Sito en el corazón de Kensington, esta encantadora y sofisticada mansión combina el estilo y servicio tradicionales con la tecnología del siglo XXI. Cuenta por doquier con bellas antigüedades, telas bordadas a mano, sorprendentes combinaciones de colores y piedra. Algunas de sus encantadoras habitaciones disponen de camas con baldaquino y todas se benefician de tener lujosos cuartos de baño. Se sirven abundantes desayunos continentales, té inglés a las cinco y aperitivos por la noche. Muchos de los restaurantes o lugares de interés de Londres se encuentran a corta distancia a pie.

Our inspector loved: *The beautifully designed rooms and four-posters.*

Directions: The nearest underground stations are Gloucester Road and South Kensington.

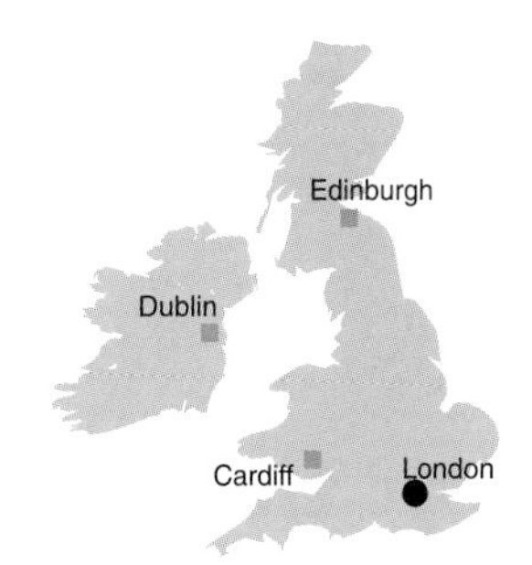

Web: www.johansens.com/cranleyeuro
E-mail: info@thecranley.com
Tel: +44 20 7373 0123
Fax: +44 20 7373 9497

Price Guide: (excluding 17.5% VAT)
double £155-200
executive £165-210
four poster £200-230
penthouse suite £265-305

 39

GREAT BRITAIN / ENGLAND (LONDON)

JUMEIRAH CARLTON TOWER

ON CADOGAN PLACE, LONDON, SW1X 9PY, ENGLAND

Directions: A 3-minute walk from Knightsbridge tube station (Piccadilly Line). Take Sloane Street/Brompton Road station exit, turn right down Sloane Street then left into Cadogan Place. Heathrow Airport is 25km away.

Web: www.johansens.com/carltontowereuro
E-mail: JCTinfo@jumeirah.com
Tel: +44 20 7235 1234
Fax: +44 20 7235 9129

Price Guide: (excluding VAT)
double from £325
suite from £525

Situated within easy reach of London's major attractions, this famously luxurious hotel offers 220 rooms, including 58 suites and a stunning Presidential Suite. There are several refined dining and bar venues to choose from including the renowned Rib Room & Oyster Bar and the exclusive Gilt Champagne Lounge. The Peak Health Club & Spa boasts one of the best views over London and offers a range of spa treatments, sauna, steam room, Jacuzzi and a 20m indoor pool. Extensive meeting space is available, including the sumptuous Ballroom and the contemporary Garden Rooms.

Situé à proximité des principales attractions touristiques de Londres, cet hôtel luxueux de renom propose 220 chambres élégantes et remises à neuf, dont 58 suites et la somptueuse Suite Présidentielle. Il y a plusieurs bars et restaurants raffinés, dont le célèbre Rib Room & Oyster Bar et l'exclusif salon à champagne Gilt. Le club de remise en forme "The Peak" offre l'une des plus belle vue sur Londres et propose une gamme de soins spa, un sauna, un hammam, un jacuzzi et une piscine intérieur de 20 m. Des équipements pour les réunions sont disponibles, dont une magnifique salle de bal et des Garden Rooms au style contemporain.

Situado a corta distancia de los principales lugares de interés de Londres, este famoso hotel de lujo dispone de 220 habitaciones, entre las que se incluyen 58 suites y la impresionante Presidential Suite. Tiene varios refinados comedores y bares, inclusive el afamado Rib Room & Oyster Bar y el exclusivo Gilt Champagne Lounge. El Peak Health Club y Spa ofrece unas de las mejores vistas de Londres así como tratamientos de spa, sauna, sala de vapor, jacuzzi y una piscina cubierta de 20 m. Hay instalaciones para reuniones, que incluyen un suntuoso salón de baile y Garden Rooms de estilo contemporáneo.

***Our inspector loved:** The health club and spa with the best views over London.*

 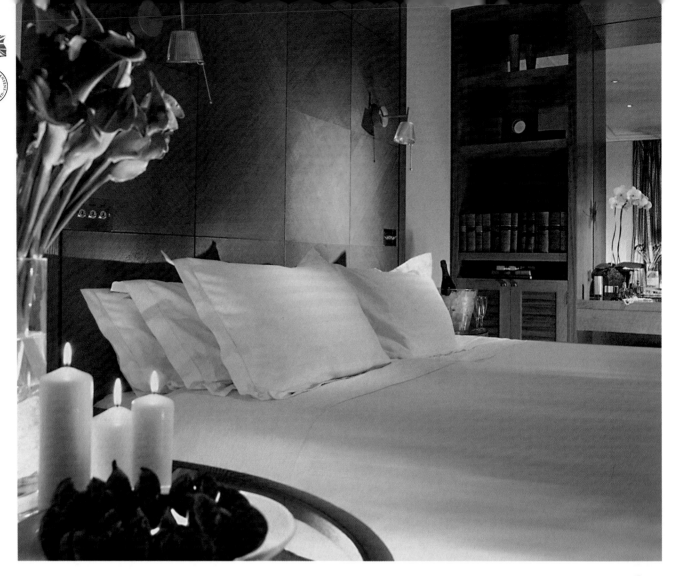

Jumeirah Lowndes Hotel

21 LOWNDES STREET, KNIGHTSBRIDGE, LONDON, SW1X 9ES, ENGLAND

Following a recent £8 million refurbishment, this chic boutique hotel is located in London's exclusive Belgravia Village. The stylish décor maximises light and space to create a sense of tranquillity and harmony, and the remodelled lobby area offers flowing public areas with an art deco influence complemented by vignettes and sculptures. The Mimosa Bar & Restaurant serves Mediterranean cuisine with al fresco dining on the terrace overlooking Lowndes Square preceded by cocktails in the welcoming bar.

Suite à une rénovation d'un montant de £8 millions, cet élégant boutique hôtel est situé dans le renommé Village de Belgravia. Le décor élégant maximise la luminosité et l'espace pour créer un sentiment de tranquillité et d'harmonie. La réception offre un espace public fluide à l'influence art déco complété par des vignettes et des sculptures. Le Bar Restaurant Mimosa sert une cuisine méditerranéenne et propose de dîner sur la terrasse surplombant Lowndes Square, après avoir siroté un cocktail dans le bar animé.

Después de haber gastado £8 millones en remodelarlo, este hotel boutique chic se encuentra en la exclusiva Village Belgravia. La elegante decoración maximiza la luz y el espacio para crear una sensación de tranquilidad y armonía. El área transformada del lobby ofrece zonas de descanso fluidas con influencia de arte deco complementado por las vignettes y las esculturas. En el Bar y Restaurante Mimosa se sirve cocina mediterránea también, hay la posibiliadad cenar al aire libre en la terraza que domina Lowndes Square, precedida por cócteles que se pueden degustar en el acogedor bar.

Our inspector loved: *The extensive refurbishment.*

Directions: The hotel is a short taxi ride from the West End, and the nearest tube stations are Knightsbridge, Hyde Park Corner and Sloane Square.

Web: www.johansens.com/lowndeseuro
E-mail: JLHinfo@jumeirah.com
Tel: +44 20 7823 1234
Fax: +44 20 7235 1154

Price Guide: (room only, excluding VAT)
double from £225
suite from £425

           SPA

The Mayflower Hotel

26-28 TREBOVIR ROAD, LONDON, SW5 9NJ, ENGLAND

Directions: Situated between Earls Court Road and Warwick Road. The nearest underground station is Earls Court.

Web: www.johansens.com/mayflowereuro
E-mail: info@mayflower-group.co.uk
Tel: +44 20 7370 0991
Fax: +44 20 7370 0994

Price Guide:
single £79
double £109
family room £130

This recently renovated hotel offers an intriguing blend of eastern influences and modern luxury. Vibrant fabrics and Indian and oriental antiques abound in the individually decorated bedrooms, 4 of which have balconies. High ceilings and hand-carved wardrobes and bedside tables are complemented by stylish bathrooms and state-of-the-art technology with Internet access and wide-screen televisions. Knightsbridge and Chelsea, the V&A and the Natural History and Science Museum are close by, whilst Earls Court Exhibition Centre is on the doorstep.

Cet hôtel récemment remis à neuf offre un mélange fascinant d'influences de l'Est et de luxe moderne. Des tissus vifs et objets d'art de l'Orient et de l'Inde ornent les chambres décorées de façon individuelle, dont 4 ont des balcons. Des plafonds hauts, armoires et tables de chevet sculptées à la main sont complétés par des salles de bains élégantes et équipements du dernier cri, comprenant accès Internet et des grands télévisions. Knightsbridge et Chelsea, les musées V&A et Natural History and Science sont tout proches, alors que le centre d'expositions Earls Court n'est pas loin.

Este hotel de reciente renovación ofrece una singular combinación de influencias orientales y lujo moderno. Espectaculares telas y antigüedades hindúes y orientales abundan en sus habitaciones de decoración individual, 4 de las cuales poseen balcones. Sus altos techos, sus armarios y mesitas de noche labradas a mano se combinan perfectamente con sus elegantes cuartos de baño y con la más moderna tecnología de acceso a internet y de televisiones de pantalla panorámica. En las cercanías se encuentran Knightsbridge, Chelsea, el V & A y el Museo de Historia Natural y Ciencia, estando el Centro de Exhibición Earls Court en la misma puerta del hotel.

Our inspector loved: *The cool Colonial reception and juice bar.*

The Royal Park

3 Westbourne Terrace, Lancaster Gate, Hyde Park, London, W2 3UL, England

Three stately Georgian town houses have been gracefully combined to create this little gem of a hotel. Beautifully designed, the style is very sympathetic to the building's heritage, combining deep colours, Regency stripes and rich furnishings. The delightful bedrooms exude timeless elegance, with magnificent beds and handmade mattresses. The hotel is ideally situated on the doorstep of Hyde Park and Kensington Palace Gardens and is within walking distance of Oxford Street and Notting Hill.

Trois majestueuses maisons datant du règne de George V ont été réunies afin de créer ce petit joyau hôtelier. Magnifiquement conçu, le style reflète l'histoire du bâtiment associant des couleurs sombres, des tissus Régence et de somptueux meubles. Les ravissantes chambres respirent l'élégance intemporelle avec leurs superbes lits et les matelas faits main. L'hôtel est idéalement situé aux portes de Hyde Park, des jardins de Kensington Palace et n'est qu'à quelques minutes à pied d'Oxford Street et de Notting Hill.

Tres majestuosas casas georgianas han sido elegantemente combinadas para crear esta pequeña joya de hotel. Con un diseño perfecto el estilo ha sido muy comprensivo con la herencia del edificio, combinando colores profundos, rayas Regency y muebles preciosos. Las encantadoras habitaciones rezuman elegancia eterna con camas magníficas y colchones artesanales. El hotel está situado idealmente a la entrada de Hyde Park y Kensington Palace Gardens y a un corto paseo de Oxford Street y Notting Hill.

***Our inspector loved:** The pretty, light bedrooms and fine antique furniture.*

Directions: The nearest underground station is Lancaster Gate. The hotel is a 2-minute walk from the Heathrow Express at Paddington Station.

Web: www.johansens.com/royalparkeuro
E-mail: info@theroyalpark.com
Tel: +44 20 7479 6600
Fax: +44 20 7479 6601

Price Guide: (excluding 17.5% VAT)
double £155-200
executive £165-210
four poster £200-230
suite £215-305

Twenty Nevern Square

20 NEVERN SQUARE, LONDON, SW5 9PD, ENGLAND

This elegant town house has been sumptuously restored with an emphasis on natural materials - linen, cotton and silks - and beautiful hand-carved beds and furniture. Each of the 23 intimate bedrooms is individually designed echoing both Asian and European influences. The hotel overlooks a tranquil garden square and has its own delightful restaurant, Café Twenty, serving modern European food. Guests are a mere 10 minutes from London's most fashionable shopping areas, restaurants, theatres and cultural attractions.

Restauré avec faste, cet élégant hôtel particulier privilégie aujourd'hui les matières naturelles – lin, coton et soie – et les beaux lits et autres meubles artisanaux. Chacune des 23 chambres intimes est décorée dans un style individuel aux influences asiatiques et européennes. L'hôtel donne sur un square paisible et dispose d'un restaurant raffiné, le Café Twenty, qui sert une cuisine européenne moderne. Les restaurants, les théâtres, les attractions culturelles et les rues commerçantes les plus chics de Londres ne sont qu'à 10 minutes.

Esta elegante casa ha sido suntuosamente restaurada poniendo énfasis en telas naturales: lino, algodón y sedas; y sus bonitas camas y mobiliario están tallados a mano. Cada una de sus 23 íntimas habitaciones ha sido diseñada individualmente mostrando influencias de Asia y de Europa. El hotel da a una tranquila plaza con jardín y posee su propio restaurante, Café Twenty, que sirve comida moderna europea. Los huéspedes pueden disfrutar de las zonas comerciales más de moda de Londres, a tan sólo 10 minutos, así como de restaurantes, teatros y atracciones culturales.

Our inspector loved: *The Easter furniture and colourful fabrics.*

Directions: 2 minutes from Earl's Court underground station.

Web: www.johansens.com/twentynevernsquareeuro
E-mail: hotel@twentynevernsquare.co.uk
Tel: +44 20 7565 9555
Fax: +44 20 7565 9444

Price Guide:
single £99-130
double £130–165
suite £275

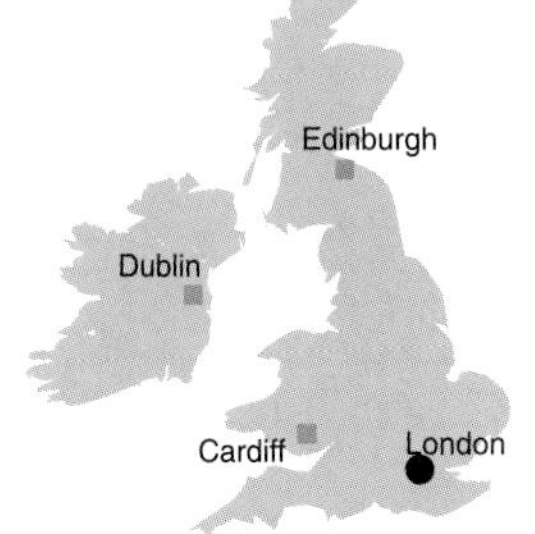

Phyllis Court Club

MARLOW ROAD, HENLEY-ON-THAMES, OXFORDSHIRE, RG9 2HT, ENGLAND

With an unrivalled position on the bank of the Thames overlooking the Henley Royal Regatta course, this illustrious historic hotel and club boasts elegant Georgian Architecture that is seamlessly complimented by extremely high standards of hospitality. Comfortable bedrooms have stunning traditional British décor with sweeping views of the lawns and gardens that reach towards the river.

Avec un emplacement hors pair sur les rives de la Tamise surplombant la ligne d'arrivée de la Régate Henley Royal, ce célèbre hôtel et club historique possède une élégante architecture Georgienne complétée par un hébergement du plus haut niveau. Les chambres confortables sont décorées dans un style Britannique traditionnel avec de superbes vues sur les pelouses et jardins amenant à la rivière.

Con una posición sin par, a la orilla del río Támesis y mirando hacia el curso done se celebran las regatas de Royal Henley, este ilustre e histórico hotel y club presume de una elegante arquitectura georgiana que se complementa exquisitamente con un altísimo estándar de hospitalidad. Las confortables habitaciones, con suntuosa decoración tradicional británica, tienen magnificas vistas hacia el césped y jardines que llegan hasta el río.

Our inspector loved: *The bright and airy Orangery, which adds to the splendour of Phyllis Court Club.*

Directions: M40, junction 4 to Marlow or M4, junction 8/9 > follow signs to Henley-on-Thames. Phyllis Court Club is on the A4155 between Henley and Marlow.

Web: www.johansens.com/phylliscourteuro
E-mail: enquiries@phylliscourt.co.uk
Tel: +44 1491 570 500
Fax: +44 1491 570 528

Price Guide:
single £90
twin/double £136

Hoar Cross Hall Spa Resort

HOAR CROSS, NEAR YOXALL, STAFFORDSHIRE, DE13 8QS, ENGLAND

The only spa resort in a stately home in England, Hoar Cross Hall is situated in over 100 acres of glorious Staffordshire countryside. Apart from the captivating surroundings, guests can enjoy up-to-the-minute water-based health treatments. With more than 80 trained therapists, the resort offers over 80 separate treatments ranging from hydro-therapy baths and blitz jets to floatation therapy and steam room treatments. Naturally, visitors may also partake of the excellent sporting facilities.

Le seul spa resort au sein d'un château en Angleterre, le Hoar Cross Hall est situé dans plus de 40 ha de campagne glorieuse de Staffordshire et dâte du XIXe siècle. Outre son superbe cadre, le visiteur peut également profiter des traitements de santé à base d'eau tout à fait avant-gardistes. Avec plus de 80 thérapistes spécialisés, le complexe propose plus de 80 traitements différents allant de l'hydrothérapie, aux jets, aux cabines de flottement et au hamman. Bien évidemment, les hôtes peuvent également utiliser les excellents aménagements sportifs.

El único spa resort ubicado en una casa solariega de Inglaterra, el Hoar Cross Hall está situado en una finca de 40 ha en la gloriosa campiña de Staffordshire. Además del cautivador entorno, los clientes pueden disfrutar de los últimos tratamientos curativos del agua. Con una plantilla de más de 80 expertos terapeutas, este lugar pone a su disposición más de 80 tratamientos distintos: desde los baños de hidroterapia, a la terapia por medio de chorros de agua, pasando por los tratamientos en salas de vapor. Naturalmente, los clientes tambien pueden beneficiarse de las excelentes instalaciones deportivas.

Our inspector loved: *The balance of excellent meals and welcoming restaurant combined with extensive facilities. Relaxed but so professional.*

Directions: Lichfield > A51 > A515 towards Ashbourne.

Web: www.johansens.com/hoarcrosshalleuro
E-mail: info@hoarcross.co.uk
Tel: +44 1283 575671
Fax: +44 1283 575652

Price Guide: (fully inclusive of spa treatments, breakfast and lunch)
single £168-218
double/twin £320-364
suite £384-494

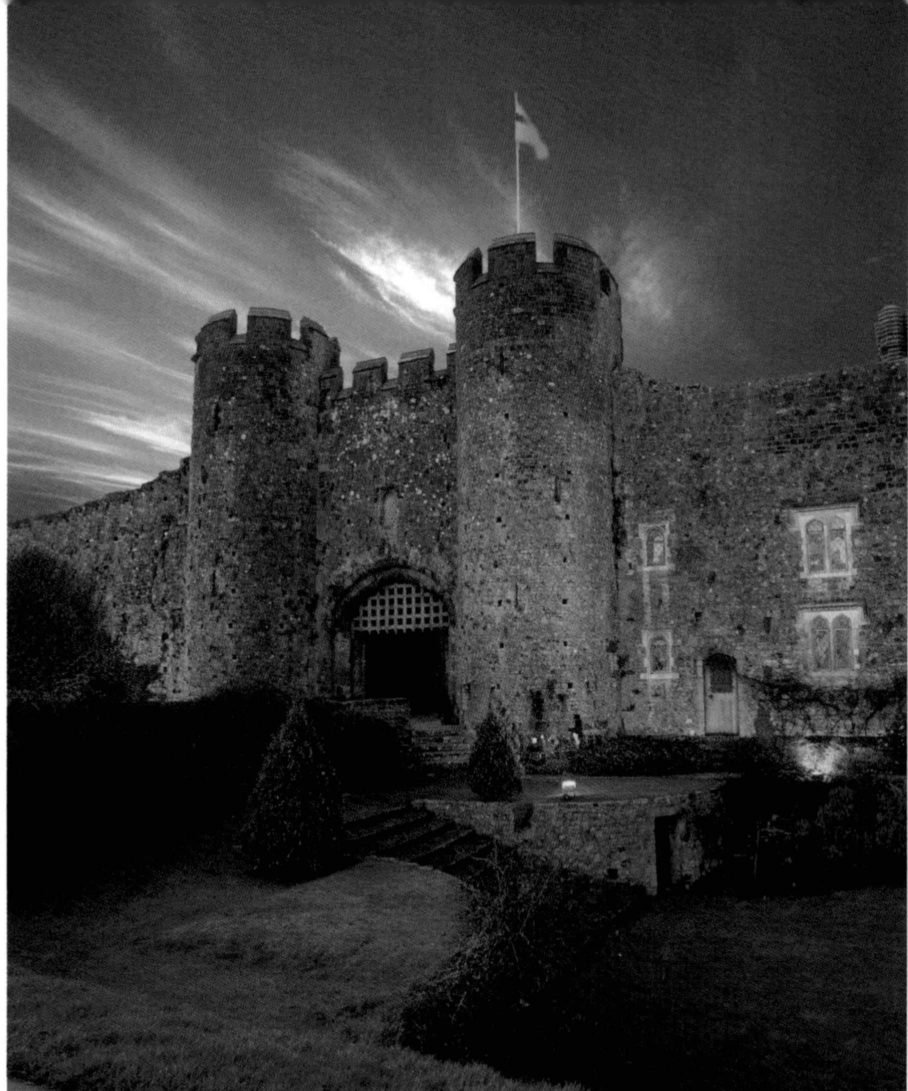

AMBERLEY CASTLE

AMBERLEY, NEAR ARUNDEL, WEST SUSSEX, BN18 9LT, ENGLAND

Winner of the Condé Nast Johansens Award for Outstanding Excellence and Innovation 2003, this medieval fortress is over 900 years old and boasts a fascinating history. Today it offers a warm welcome and the ultimate in contemporary yet timeless luxury. Distinctive new suites have been added, and each room is individually designed with its own whirlpool bath. The exquisite 12th-century Queen's Room makes the perfect setting for the hotel's creative cuisine, whilst nearby, Roman ruins, antiques, horse-racing and stately homes are found in abundance.

Le gagnant du prix Condé Nast Johansens Award for Outstanding Excellence and Innovation en 2003 a plus de 900 ans et un passé fascinant. Aujourd'hui, il réserve un accueil chaleureux à ses visiteurs qui y découvrent un luxe à la fois moderne et hors du temps. L'hôtel comprend de nouvelles suites et des chambres avec un bain à remous décorées de manière individuelle. Datant du XIIe siècle, la ravissante chambre de la reine forme un cadre parfait pour la cuisine de l'hôtel, situé dans une région où abondent les ruines romaines, les antiquaires, les champs de courses et les demeures ancestrales.

Ganador del premio Condé Nast Johansens Award for Outstanding Excellence and Innovation 2003, este castillo medieval cuenta con más de 900 años y ostenta una fascinante historia. Hoy día ofrece una cálida acogida dentro de su eterno lujo contemporáneo. Características nuevas suites se le han agregado y cada habitación ha sido diseñada individualmente con su propia baño con efectos de remolino. Merece la pena resaltar el Salón de la Reina del siglo XII donde se puede disfrutar la cocina creativa del hôtel, al mismo tiempo que encontrará en abundancia: ruinas romanas, antigüedades, carreras de caballos y casas solariegas.

Our inspector loved: *The countryside setting, and unusual treehouse and moat.*

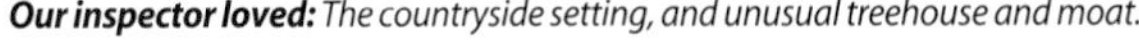

Directions: A29 - B2139 between Bury and Storrington.

Web: www.johansens.com/amberleycastleeuro
E-mail: info@amberleycastle.co.uk
Tel: +44 1798 831 992
Fax: +44 1798 831 998

Price Guide: (room only)
double/twin £155–385
suite £250–385

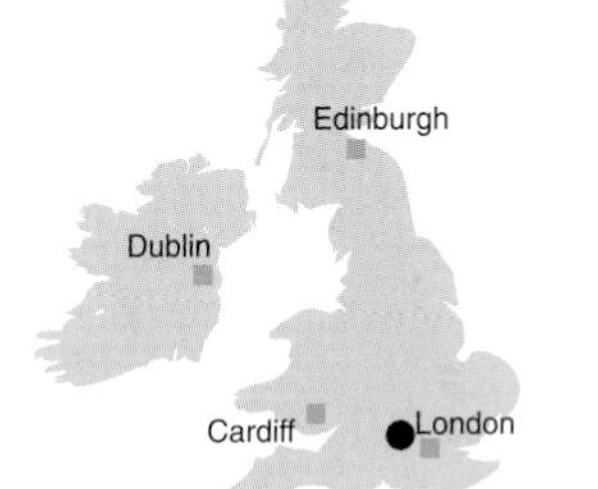

GREECE

Hotel location shown in red (hotel) or purple (spa hotel) with page number

Astir Palace Vouliagmeni

40 Apollonos Street, 166 71 Vouliagmeni, Athens, Greece

This impressive luxury resort has recently completed an extensive refurbishment. Comprising 3 exclusive hotels across an 80-acre, private peninsula, it is only a 40-minute drive from Athens, surrounded by pine forests and colourful gardens spectacularly set with panoramic sea views towards neighbouring isles. The hotels offer 420 spacious, comfortably furnished guest rooms, 30 suites, stylish restaurants, outdoor swimming pools and private beaches. There are also 75 bungalows, as well as extensive leisure and meeting facilities.

Cet impressionnant resort de luxe récemment réaménagé de manière considérable s'étend sur une péninsule privée de plus de 32 ha à 40 minutes en voiture d'Athènes. 3 hôtels uniques, entourés de forêts de pins et de jardins colorés sont situés de façon spectaculaire avec des vues panoramiques sur les îles voisines. Les hôtels offrent 420 chambres spacieuses et confortablement meublées, 30 suites, des restaurants de style, piscines extérieures et plages privées. Le resort offre également 75 bungalows ainsi que des équipements pour les loisirs et les affaires.

Este impresionante resort de lujo, que se ha beneficiado recientemente de una amplia remodelación, se encuentra a sólo 40 minutos en coche de Atenas. Está formado por 3 exclusivos hoteles, que se extienden a lo largo de una península privada de 32 ha, y rodeado de pinares y jardines llenos de colorido en un emplazamiento de espectaculares y panorámicas vistas al mar en dirección a las islas vecinas. Los hoteles disponen de 420 habitaciones amplias y de cómodo mobiliario, 30 suites, elegantes restaurantes, piscinas exteriores y playas privadas. Hay también 75 bungalows así como gran número de instalaciones para el ocio y para reuniones.

Directions: E Venizelos Airport is 25km away.

Web: www.johansens.com/astirpalace
E-mail: marketing-sales@astir.gr
Tel: +30 210 890 2000
Fax: +30 210 896 2582

Price Guide:
single €230-620
double €270-670
suite €700-6,000

Our inspector loved: *The luxury, and great views.*

Hotel Pentelikon

66 Diligianni Street, 14562 Athens, Greece

Directions: Set in the suburb of Kifissia. Venizelos Airport is 30 minutes away.

Web: www.johansens.com/pentelikon
E-mail: sales@pentelikon.gr
Tel: +30 2 10 62 30 650
Fax: +30 210 62 81 400

Price Guide:
single €270-360
double/twin €295-440
suite €560-2,500

Having undergone extensive refurbishment, this 5-star de luxe hotel is the epitome of style, offering state-of-the-art amenities, whilst retaining its historical charm. The luxurious bedrooms, new executive suites and penthouse are individually decorated and provide an intimate atmosphere. The gourmet Vardis restaurant is the only restaurant in Greece awarded a Michelin star for 7 consecutive years, and the new barBar is a fashionable and popular venue. Guest may relax by the stunning swimming pool, located in the tranquil gardens.

Après avoir subi une rénovation complète, cet hôtel de luxe 5* est un parfait exemple de style, offrant des équipements de pointe tout en gardant son charme historique. Les chambres luxueuses, les nouvelles suites exécutives et la suite penthouse sont décorées individuellement et offrent une atmosphère intime. Le restaurant gastronomique le Vardis est le seul restaurant en Grèce à avoir obtenu une étoile Michelin pendant 7 années consécutives. Le nouveau barBar est un endroit populaire et à la mode. Les hôtes peuvent aussi se détendre à côté de la superbe piscine située dans les jardins tranquilles.

Después de una renovación completa, este hotel de lujo de 5 estrellas es la pura esencia del estilo y ofrece modernas instalaciones sin perder su encanto histórico. Sus lujosas habitaciones, sus nuevas executive suites y el ático-penthouse están decoradas individualmente y ofrecen una atmósfera íntima. El restaurante gastronomico Vardis es el único de Grecia que ha sido galardonado con una estrella Michelín durante 7 años consecutivos. El nuevo barBar es un lugar de buen tono y muy de moda. Los clientes pueden relajarse al lado de la nueva piscina, situada en los tranquilos jardines.

***Our inspector loved:** The award-winning Michelin-starred Vardis restaurant.*

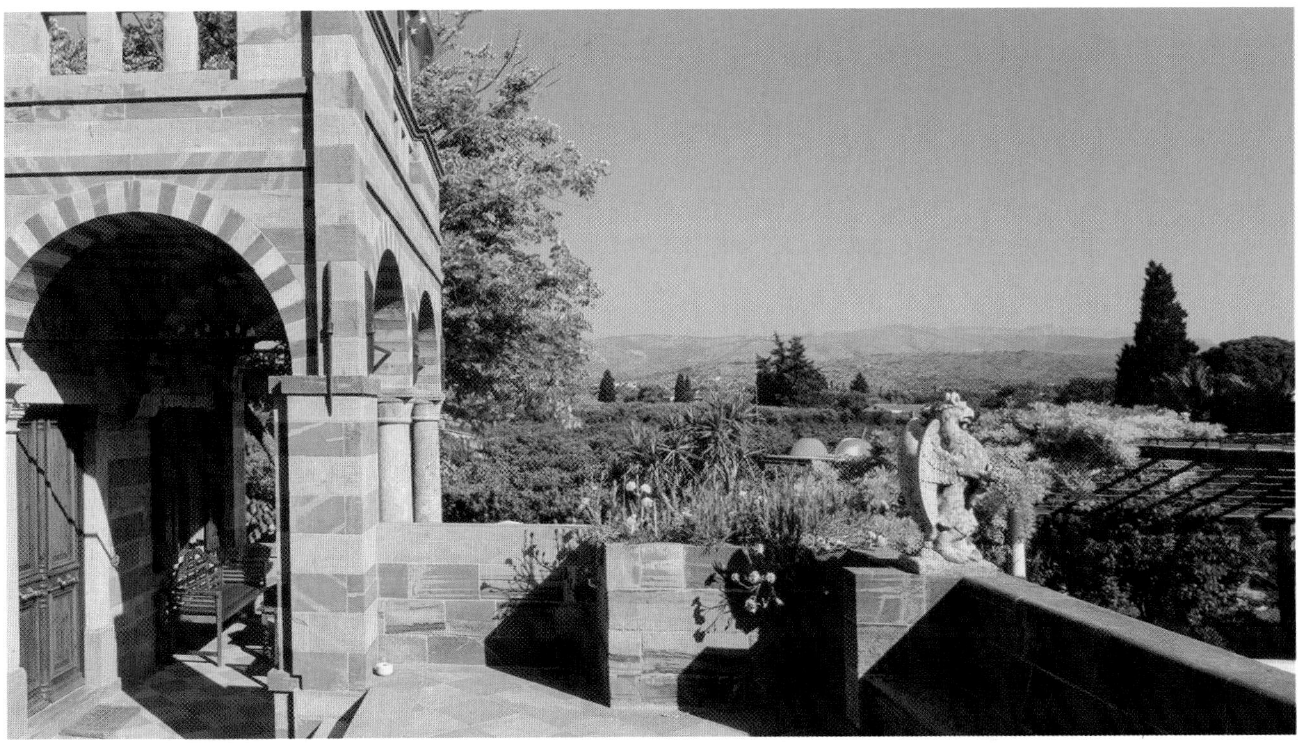

ARGENTIKON

KAMBOS, 82100 CHIOS, GREECE

Constructed during the 16th century, Argentikon comprises 5 buildings located in a flat plain surrounded by citrus trees. Originally the residence of nobility, today, the individually-styled suites reflect the grandeur of a bygone era with period furniture, chandeliers and beautiful fireplaces. The hotel's restaurant serves gourmet cuisine, prepared from the finest ingredients. Flower-filled walking paths lead guests through the surrounding gardens, orange grove and rose bushes. Explore the island's medieval villages and nearby beaches.

Construit au XVIe siècle, Argentikon est composé de 5 bâtiments situés sur une plaine et entourés d'arbres à agrumes. Anciennement une résidence de nobles, les suites individuellement décorées reflètent aujourd'hui la splendeur d'autrefois au travers de meubles d'époques, de chandeliers et de superbes cheminées. Le restaurant de l'hôtel sert une cuisine gastronomique préparée à partir des meilleurs ingrédients. Des allées fleuries guident les hôtes dans le jardin remplis d'orangers, et de rosiers. La plage voisine et les villages médiévaux de l'île sont à visiter.

Construido durante el siglo XVI, Argentikon comprende 5 edificios situados en una llanura rodeada de limoneros y naranjos. Fue originalmente residencia de la nobleza, de ahí que hoy las suites, cada una de estilo propio, reflejen la grandeza de tiempos pasados gracias a su mobiliario de época, lámparas de araña y bellas chimeneas. El restaurante del hotel sirve cocina gourmet preparada con los mejores ingredientes. Sus senderos cubiertos de flores llevan a los clientes al jardín circundante,que cuenta con naranjos y rosales Podrá explorar las localidades medievales de la isla y la playa cercana.

Our inspector loved: *The charming atmopshere of romance and history.*

Directions: Chios Airport is 15 minutes away. A transfer to and from the estate is free of charge.

Web: www.johansens.com/argentikon
E-mail: argentikon@yadeshotels.gr
Tel: +30 227 10 33 111
Fax: +30 227 10 31 465

Price Guide:
suite €550-2,500

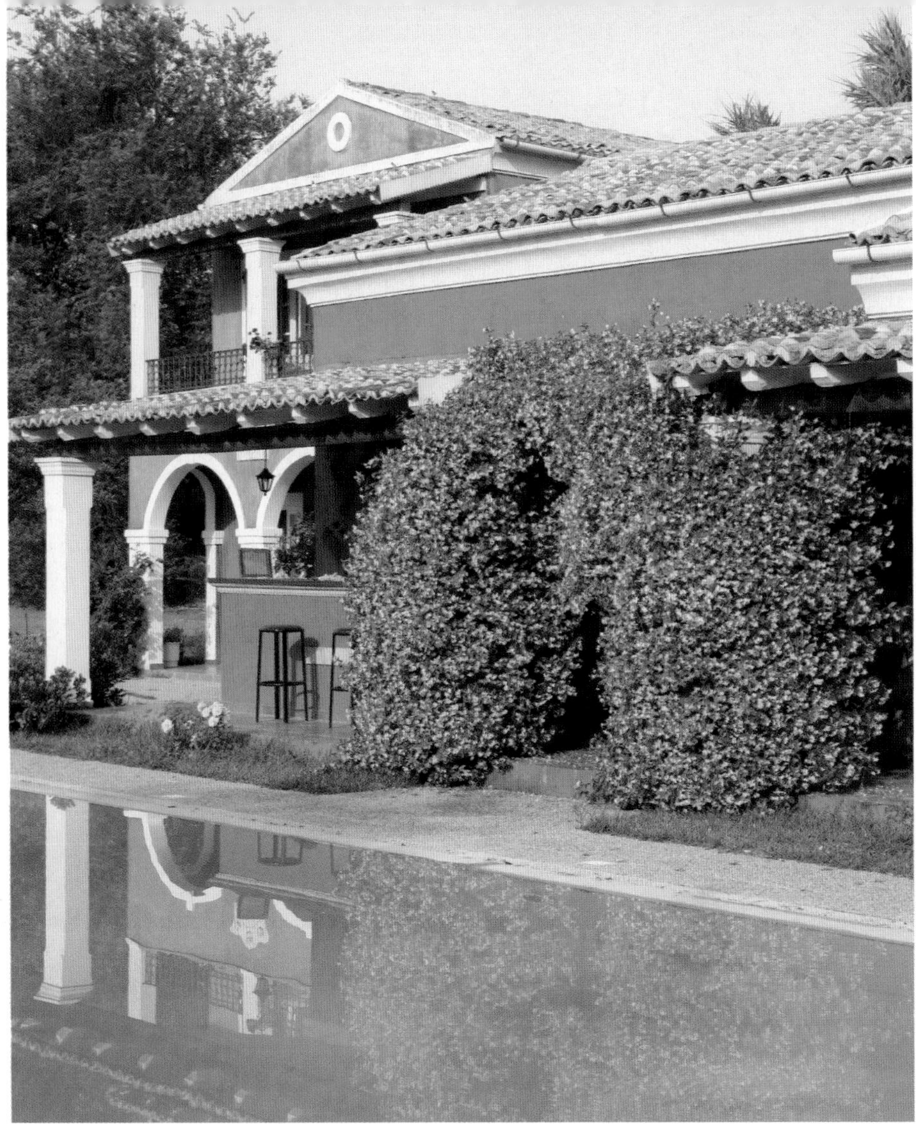

Villa de Loulia

PEROULADES, CORFU, GREECE

Directions: Corfu Airport is 35km away. The port is 30km away. A transfer to and from the hotel can be arranged.

Web: www.johansens.com/villadeloulia
E-mail: info@villadeloulia.gr
Tel: +30 266 30 95 394
Fax: +30 266 30 95 145

Price Guide: (closed November - February)
double from €180
suite €230

Athens
Rhodes
Iráklion - *Crete*

Located in one of the most beautiful corners of Corfu, surrounded by greenery and beaches, this mansion dates back to 1800 and today, proudly stands restored to its original splendour. The individually styled guest rooms with period furniture and tiles, exposed beams and polished floors, capture the hotel's noble heritage, whilst providing every modern amenity. Authentic Greek flavours are prepared for dinner from the freshest local ingredients and a delicious selection of local and homemade products are served at breakfast.

Situé dans l'un des plus beaux recoins de Corfu, entouré de verdures et de plages, cette demeure de 1800 à été restaurée à sa splendeur d'origine. Les chambres individuellement décorées de meubles d'époques, de poutres et de carrelage polis mettent l'accent sur l'héritage noble de l'hôtel tout en offrant un confort moderne. Les saveurs grecques traditionnelles sont preparées pour le dîner à partir d'ingrédients locaux et une délicieuse sélection de produits frais et fait maison sont servis au petit-déjeuner.

Situada en una de las esquinas más hermosas de Corfu, rodeada de vegetación y playas, esta mansión se remonta al 1800 y hoy día, se enorgullece de su restauración a su esplendor original. Sus 9 habitaciones de estilo propio gracias a su mobiliario de época, vigas visibles y suelos pulimentados, capturan la herencia noble del hotel, mientras que disponen de todas las instalaciones modernas. Los sabores griegos auténticos están preparados para la cena de los ingredientes locales más frescos, y una selección deliciosa de productos locales y de la casa se sirve en el desayuno.

Our inspector loved: *The sincere welcome and relaxed atmosphere.*

Athina Luxury Villas

KSAMOUDOCHORI, PLATANIAS, 73014 CHANIA, CRETE, GREECE

Nestling in 8 acres of pure Mediterranean landscape, Athina Luxury Villas is a complex of luxurious villas, located surprisingly close to the beach and resort town of Platanias. Each villa accommodates up to 6 people and offers spacious living rooms, fully equipped kitchens and Jacuzzis in the bathrooms. Private swimming pools, expensive pieces of locally crafted furniture and home cooked local delicacies create a feeling of character mixed with luxury that makes these villas a haven for the discerning guest.

Niché dans 4 ha d'un paysage typiquement méditerranéen, Athina Luxury Villas est un complexe de villas luxueuses, situées incroyablement près de la plage et de la station balnéaire de Platanias. Chaque villa peut loger 6 personnes et bénéficie d'un salon spacieux, d'une cuisine toute équipée et d'un jacuzzi dans la salle de bain. Piscines privées, mobilier artisanal local luxueux et mets délicats fait maison créent une atmosphère de caractère et de luxe qui fait de ces villas un havre pour les hôtes les plus exigeants.

Sobre un enclave de 4 ha de paisaje auténticamente mediterráneo, Athina Luxury Villas es un complejo formado por villas de lujo increíblemente cercano a la playa y a la localidad turística de Platanias. Cada villa puede alojar hasta 6 personas y cuenta con amplias salas de estar, cocinas totalmente equipadas y jacuzzis en sus cuartos de baño. Sus piscinas privadas, sus valiosos muebles de fabricación artesanal local y sus especialidades culinarias caseras típicas del lugar consiguen dar un toque de personalidad y lujo capaz de convertir estas villas en un verdadero paraíso para los clientes más exigentes.

Our inspector loved: *The total privacy.*

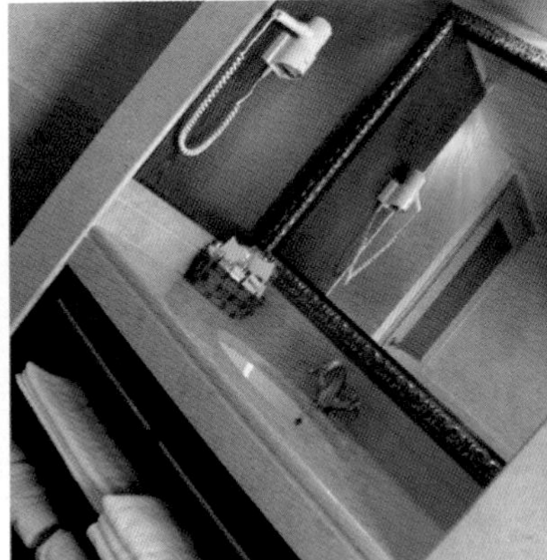

Directions: National Road > exit Platanias > left onto Ksamoudochori > follow signs. The nearest airport is Chania.

Athens
Rhodes
Iráklion - *Crete*

Web: www.johansens.com/athinaluxuryvillas
E-mail: info@athinavillas.gr
Tel: +30 28210 20960
Fax: +30 28210 20970

Price Guide: (room only)
villa €300-460

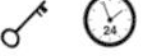

ELOUNDA GULF VILLAS & SUITES

ELOUNDA, 72053 CRETE, GREECE

Superbly located overlooking Mirabello Bay, this stunning collection of 18 villas and 10 suites offers privacy and luxury. Elegant, spacious and chic, all the villas have private pools with Jacuzzi, state-of-the-art kitchens, private terraces and luxurious bathrooms. Carefully and individually designed with different fabrics and styles, some have their own sauna, hammam and gym. The suites are located close to the seasonally heated large pool. There is a cosy and welcoming bar, and an à la carte restaurant in a delightful setting for romantic candle-lit dinners.

Superbement située surplombant la baie de Mirabello, cette magnifique collection de 18 villas et 10 suites offre intimité et luxe pour chaque client. Elégantes, spacieuses et chic, toutes les villas possèdent des piscines privées, des cuisines à la pointe, des terrasses et des salles de bain luxueuses. Chacune est décorée avec attention, de manière individuelle avec des tissus et des styles différents. Certaines ont leur propre sauna, hammam et gym. Les suites sont situées près de la grande piscine chauffée durante l'hiver. Il y a un confortable et acceuillant bar et le restaurant à la carte est le décor idéal pour un dîner aux chandelles.

Este sorprendente complejo de 18 villas y 10 suites de excelente ubicación y con vistas a la Bahía de Mirabello proporciona a todos sus clientes lujo e intimidad. Elegantes, amplias y modernas, todas las villas tienen piscinas propias, cocinas de último modelo, terrazas y lujosos cuartos de baños. Cada una de ellas muestra un cuidado diseño individualizado a base de diferentes telas y estilos. Algunas de ellas tienen su propia sauna, hamman y gimnasio. Las suites estan situadas cerca de la piscina grande que se calienta durante el invierno. Un bar cordial y acogedor y su restaurante a la carte constituye un entorno encantador para una cena romántica a la luz de las velas.

Our inspector loved: *The 4 new Superior Spa Villas.*

Directions: Heraklion Airport is 65km away. From airport > turn left towards Ag. Nikolaos > Elounda > after 6km turn right downhill > signposted.

Web: www.johansens.com/eloundagulf
E-mail: info@eloundavillas.com
Tel: +30 28410 90300
Fax: +30 28410 42274

Price Guide:
double €240-480
villa €575-3,375

Elounda Peninsula All Suite Hotel

72053 ELOUNDA, CRETE, GREECE

Located on a peninsula, this hotel boasts spectacular views over the bay of Mirabello. Large, airy suites have access to private heated seawater pools. There is a private beach, tennis, 9-hole par-3 golf course with academy, water sports, wellness spa, indoor pool, gym, a home cinema and a children's club. A wine cellar, a gourmet restaurant, a bar above the sea water, the "Playiada" square with its boutiques, jeweller, an art gallery and an orthodox chapel complete the hotel. The hotel's brand new luxury spa is operated by the famous Six Senses Spas.

Situé sur une péninsule, cet hôtel s'enorgueillit de vues spectaculaires sur la baie Mirabello. Les grandes suites ont accès à des piscines d'eau de mer chauffées privées. Le resort dispose de sa plage privée, tennis, golf à 9 trous par-3 avec école, sports nautiques, centre de bien-être, piscine couverte, centre de remise en forme, cinéma, club pour les enfants, une cave à vins et un restaurant gastronomique, un bar sur la mer ainsi que d'une place centrale "Playiada" avec boutiques, bijouterie, galérie d'art et une chapelle orthodoxe. Le nouveau et luxueux spa de l'hotel est géré par les célèbres Six Senses Spas.

Situado en una península, este hotel dispone de unas vistas espectaculares a la bahía de Mirabello. Sus amplias habitaciones tienen acceso a unas piscinas privadas de agua marina climatizada. El hotel ofrece una playa privada, tenis, campo de golf de 9 hoyos par-3 y clases, deportes acuáticos, centro deportivo, piscina cubierta, gimnasio, sala de cine y club infantil. Completan este resort una bodega, un restaurante gastronómico, un bar encima del mar, la "Playiada" con sus boutiques, joyería, una galería de arte y una capilla griego-ortodoxa. El nuevo spa lujoso está manejado por les célebres Six Senses Spas.

Our inspector loved: _The new Six Senses Spas, which is truly exceptional._

Directions: Available on request. The Heraklion Airport is 65km away.

Web: www.johansens.com/peninsulacrete
E-mail: eloundapeninsula@elounda-sa.com
Tel: +30 28410 68012
Fax: +30 28410 41889

Athens
Rhodes
Iráklion - *Crete*

Price Guide:
(closed 5th October 2006 - 28th April 2007)
suite €475–8,500

Pleiades Luxurious Villas

PLAKES, 72100 AGHIOS NIKOLAOS, CRETE, GREECE

Directions: Heraklion Airport > Elounda. The villas are located before Aghios Nikolaos on the left.

Web: www.johansens.com/pleiades
E-mail: pleia@otenet.gr
Tel: +30 28410 90450
Fax: +30 28410 90479

Price Guide: (self-catering)
2-bedroom villa €260-610
2-bedroom superior €350-770
3-bedroom villa €355-860

Set in a quiet location with beautiful views over the Mirabello gulf, just 2km on the way to Elounda from Aghios Nikolaos, this new complex consists of 9 individually designed villas sleeping 4-6 persons. Each villa has a spacious living area, fireplace, fully equipped kitchen and dining room as well as its own swimming pool and offers all modern amenities. Upon arrival, guests receive a complimentary bottle of wine and a fruit basket. A daily maid service is included and cook available upon request. Activities include water skiing, windsurfing, diving, golf and tennis.

Situé dans une position tranquille avec de vues sur le golfe de Mirabello et à 2 km sur la route à Elounda d'Aghios Nikolaos, ce nouveau complexe comprend 9 villas décorées de façon individuelle pour 4-6 personnes. Chaque villa a un espace vital spacieux, une cheminée, une cuisine et salle à manger bien équipées, ainsi que sa propre piscine et offrent toute facilité moderne. En arrivant, les hôtes sont offerts une bouteille de vin et une corbeille de fruits. Femme de ménage est inclus et chef de cuisine disponible sur demande. Loisirs: ski nautique, planche à voile, plongée, golf et tennis.

Situado en un lugar tranquilo, a tan sólo 2 km en el camino a Elounda de Aghios Nikolaos y con vistas al golfo de Mirabello, este nuevo complejo consta de 9 villas de diseño individual preparadas para alojar de 4 a 6 personas. Todas cuentan con un amplio espacio habitable, chimenea, cocina y comedor totalmente equipados así como piscina propia y toda clase de modernas comodidades. A su llegada, se les obsequia a los clientes con una botella de vino y una cesta de fruta. Servicio diario de habitaciones es incluida y cocinero disponible a pedido. Actividades del ocio: esquí acuático, windsurf, submarinismo, golf y tenis.

Our inspector loved: *The private swimming pools per villa.*

St Nicolas Bay Resort Hotel & Villas

PO BOX 47, 72100 AGHIOS NIKOLAOS, CRETE, GREECE

Flower-filled gardens with olive, lemon and orange trees surround this totally private, elegant hotel, which is a member of Small Luxury Hotels of the World. Located on a quiet seafront, with its own sandy beach, the hotel provides every comfort, mouth-watering cuisine and superb yet unobtrusive service. All rooms and suites have been fully renovated and enjoy stunning views, whilst suites have marble bathrooms with Jacuzzi; some boast a private heated pool. Facilities include water sports and the exquisite Poseidon Spa by Elemis.

Des jardins remplis de fleurs et d'oliviers, de citronniers et d'orangers entourent cet hôtel élégant, totalement privé, membre de Small Luxury Hotels of the World. Situé sur un bord de mer tranquille avec sa propre plage de sable, l'hôtel offre tous les conforts; une table savoureuse et un service impeccable et discret. Les chambres et suites qui ont été totalement renové offrent des vues imprenables. Les suites, certaines avec piscine privée chauffée, ont des salles de bain en marbre avec jacuzzi. Les loisirs comprennent sports nautiques et le superbe Spa Poseidon par Elemis.

Este hotel elegante y totalmente privado, miembro de Small Luxury Hotels of the World, se encuentra rodeado de jardines repletos de flores, olivos, limoneros y naranjos. Tranquilamente situado al lado del mar y con su propia playa arenosa, el hotel ofrece todas las comodidades, una sabrosa cocina y un servicio impecable y discreto. Todas las habitaciones se han restaurado totalmente y benefician magnifcas vistas. Las suites tienen además cuartos de baño de mármol con jacuzzi y algunas cuentan con piscina privada climatizada. Actividades: deportes acuáticos y el magnífico Spa Poseidon por Elemis.

Our inspector loved: *Taking breakfast by the pool.*

Directions: 65km from Heraklion > Aghios Nikolaos on the right-hand side on the road out of A. N. towards Elounda.

Web: www.johansens.com/stnicolasbay
E-mail: stnicolas@otenet.gr
Tel: +30 2841 025041
Fax: +30 2841 024556

Price Guide:
single €130-380
double/twin €170–430
suite €230–600
suite with private pool €600–1,500

IMARET

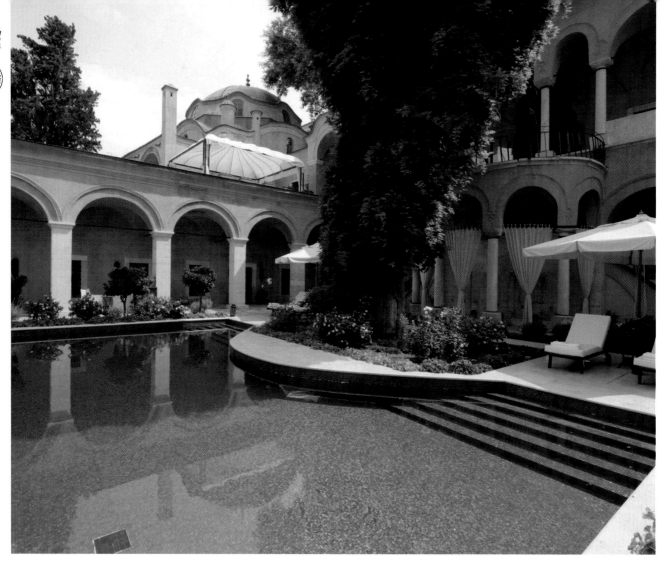

30-32 POULIDOU STREET, 65110 KAVALA, GREECE

Directions: Kavala's Airport is 20 minutes away. A transfer to and from the hotel can be arranged.

Web: www.johansens.com/imaret
E-mail: info@imaret.com
Tel: +30 2510 620 151-55
Fax: +30 2510 620 156

Price Guide: (breakfast €25)
single €220
double €290
suite €500-1,500

This Ottoman monument has been transformed into an intimate, luxury hotel set on a hilltop overlooking Kavala's harbour and Thassos Island. Built by Mohammed Ali Pasha of Egypt, almost 200 years ago, each bedroom and suite is a relaxing haven decorated with fine materials. Step back in time and take a walk in the fragrant gardens or enjoy an apéritif in the Lounge Bar before adjourning to the fine dining terrace restaurant for gourmet Mediterranean cuisine. Oriental treatment rooms and hammam are available.

Ce monument Ottoman a été transformé en hôtel luxueux et intime, qui se dresse au sommet d'une colline surplombant le port de Kavala et l'île de Thassos. Construit par Mohammed Ali Pasha de l'Egypte il y a presque 200 ans, les chambres et suites sont des paradis de relaxation décorées avec les meilleurs matériaux. Les hôtes peuvent revenir dans le passé en se promenant dans les jardins parfumés ou siroter un apéritif au lounge bar avant d'aller savourer une cuisine méditerranéenne gastronomique sur la terrasse. Des soins orientaux et un hammam sont disponibles.

Este monumento otomano ha sido transformado en hotel intimo y lujoso que se erige en la cima de una colina con vistas al puerto de Kavala y a la isla de Thassos. Construido por Mohammed Ali Pasha de Egipto hace casi 200 años, cada habitación y suite, decorada con exquisitos materiales, es un paraíso de descanso. Vuelva al pasado y pasee por los fragrantes jardines o disfrute de un aperitivo en el Lounge Bar antes de pasar a el exquisito restaurante-terraza y saborear su cocina gourmet mediterránea. Salas de tratamientos orientales y hammam son disponibles para los clientes.

Our inspector loved: *The careful blend of history and luxury.*

Pavezzo Country Retreat

KATOUNA, LEFKADA, GREECE

Pavezzo, meaning "home of the good life," comprises 9 Venetian houses and a honeymoon villa with private pool. Each house has either a private or shared pool. Nove Cento restaurant provides a variety of gourmet meals prepared by chef Mrs Evi Voutsina. Relax by the pool, browse through the book and DVD library or visit the boutique spa. Walk to the island of Lefkada, with its beautiful beaches, and admire the lake of Maradohori, old town and marketplace. Ideal for a romantic break or private getaway.

Pavezzo, qui veut dire 'maison de la bonne vie', se compose de 9 maisons vénitiennes et d'une maison pour les voyages de noces avec piscine privée. Chacune des maisons possède soit une piscine privée ou une piscine à partager. Le restaurant Nove Cento propose une variété de plats gastronomiques préparés par le chef Madame Evi Voutsina. Les hôtes peuvent se relaxer au bord de la piscine, jeter un coup d'œil sur la bibliothèque de livres et de DVD ou visiter la boutique du spa. Ils peuvent également aller sur l'île de Lefkada, avec ses superbes plages, et admirer le lac de Maradohori, la vieille ville et la place du marché. Pavezzo est l'endroit idéal pour un séjour romantique ou privé.

Pavezzo, que significa 'hogar de la buena vida' dispone de 9 casas venecianas y una villa para lunas de miel con piscina privada. Cada una de las casas cuenta con una piscina privada o compartida. El restaurante Nove Centro ofrece variados menús de gourmet preparados por la chef Sra. Evi Voutsina. Podrá relajarse junto a la piscina, consultar nuestra biblioteca de libros y DVDs o visitar el spa boutique. Podrá pasear hasta la isla de Lefkada, con sus bellas playas, o admirar el lago de Maradohori, el casco antiguo y el mercado. Es ideal para una estancia romántica o privada y discreta.

Our inspector loved: *The country retreat atmosphere.*

  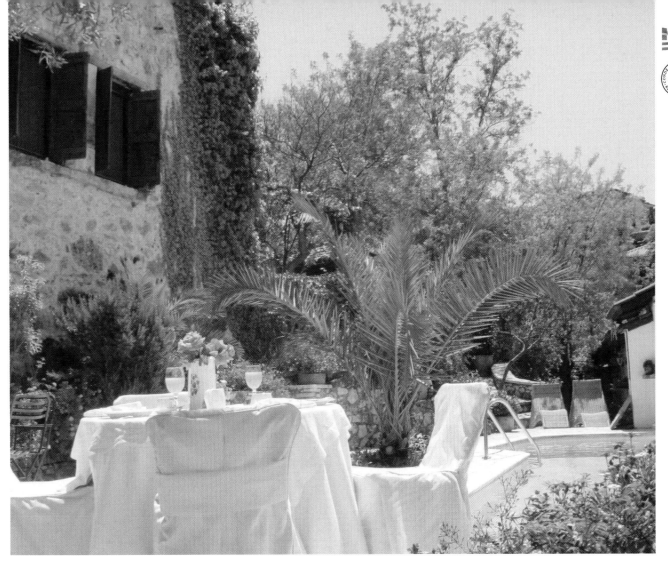       

Directions: Aktio Airport is 20 minutes away. The port is 15 minutes away.

Web: www.johansens.com/pavezzo
E-mail: info@pavezzo.gr
Tel: +30 26450 71782
Fax: +30 69450 71800

Price Guide:
suite €105-380

Athens
Rhodes
Iráklion - *Crete*

APANEMA

TAGOO, MYKONOS, GREECE

This elegant boutique hotel is set on the waterfront, just a 10-minute walk from Mykonos town. Built in 2000, the hotel has only 17 large rooms with balcony or terrace, providing a cosy and relaxed retreat from the island's vibrant lifestyle. Offering all the amenities of a large hotel, it is particularly suited for those who wish to relax and enjoy a private environment, with a choice between a soft or hard mattress, Hermès or Molton Brown bath products and breakfast until 2pm. Johansens guests are welcomed with fruit salad and a bottle of Chablis.

Cet élégant boutique hôtel est situé au bord de la mer, à 10 minutes à pied de la ville de Mykonos. Construit en 2000, l'hôtel ne dispose que de 17 grandes chambres avec balcon ou terrasse offrant un refuge intime pour échapper la vie trépidante de l'île. Offrant toutes les facilités d'un grand hôtel, il est idéal pour ceux qui veulent se relaxer dans un environnement privé. Il offre un choix de matelas forts et doux et des produits de bains Hermès ou Molton Brown. Le petit déjeuner est servi jusqu'à 14 h. En arrivant, les clients de Johansens reçoivent une salade de fruits et une bouteille de Chablis.

Este elegante hotel boutique se encuentra en primera línea de playa, a tan solo 10 minutos a pie desde la localidad de Mykonos. Construido en 2000, el hotel dispone únicamente de 17 habitaciones con balcón o terraza que lo convierten en un acogedor retiro ajeno al animado ambiente de la isla. Dotado de todas las facilidades de un gran hotel, es especialmente apropiado para quienes desean descansar y disfrutar de un ambiente íntimo, pudiendo elegir entre un colchón blando o duro, productos de baño Hermès o Molton Brown y desayuno hasta las 2 de la tarde. A los clientes de Johansens se les da la bienvenida con una ensalada de frutas y una botella de Chablis.

Our inspector loved: *The elegance in a relaxed atmosphere.*

Directions: Mykonos Airport > across the main sea port > 800m towards Tagoo on the right.

Web: www.johansens.com/apanema
E-mail: mail@apanemaresort.com
Tel: +30 22890 28590
Fax: +30 22890 79250

Price Guide: (closed April and November)
single €135-240
double €170-330
suite €260-385

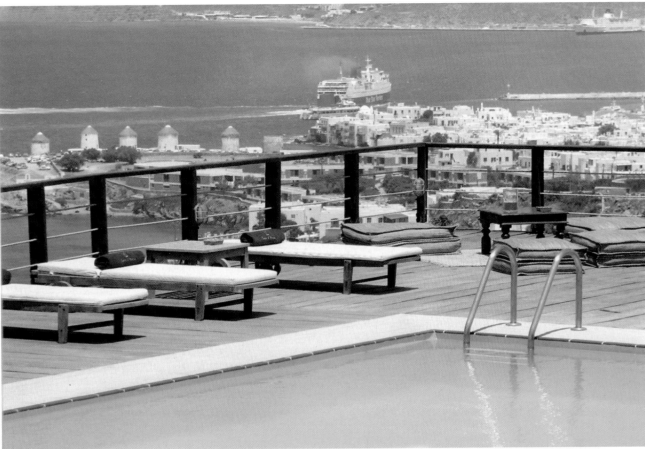

Tharroe of Mykonos

MYKONOS TOWN, ANGELICA, 84600 MYKONOS, GREECE

This hilltop location enjoys breathtaking sunsets and views over the Aegean Sea. Mykonos town centre is 5 minutes away and Ornos Bay is within walking distance. The modern décor features local artefacts and antiques, and the redecorated, luxurious en-suite bedrooms have a balcony or terrace. Traditional Greek and Mediterranean cuisine, organic and vegetarian menus are served in Barbarossa restaurant, whilst Colors of the Sunset Bar serves organic beers and cocktails. Princess Shanhaz Ayurvedic Natural Herbal Centre offers hair, body and spa treatments.

Sa location au sommet d'une colline offre des couchers de soleil à couper le souffle sur la mer Egée. Le centre de la ville de Mykonos n'est qu'à 5 minutes et la plage Ornos est accessible à pied. Le décor est moderne avec des artefacts locaux et des antiquités, et les chambres refaites luxueuses avec salle de bain ont balcon ou terrasse. Une cuisine grecque et méditerranéenne et des menus biologiques et végétariens sont servis au restaurant Barbarossa; des bières biologiques et des cocktails sont servis au Colors of the Sunset Bar. Le Princess Shanhaz centre ayurvédique offre des soins de beauté.

Su alta situación en una colina le proporcionará sobrecogedoras puestas de sol sobre el mar Egeo. El centro de Mykonos está a 5 minutos y la Bahía de Ornos está a corta distancia a pie. Su moderna decoración incluye objetos y antigüedades locales y sus lujosas habitaciones en-suite, recientemente redecoradas, tienen balcón o terraza. La cocina tradicional griega y mediterránea, así como menús orgánicos y vegetarianos, se sirven en el restaurante Barbarossa y podrá a su vez adquirir cerveza orgánica y cócteles en el Colors of the Sunset Bar. El herbolario ayurvédico natural Princess Shahaz ofrece tratamientos capilares, corporales y de salud.

***Our inspector loved:** The breathtaking sunsets.*

Directions: The hotel is 800m from Mykonos town centre.

Web: www.johansens.com/tharroe
E-mail: tharroe@myk.forthnet.gr
Tel: +30 22890 27370
Fax: +30 22890 27375

Price Guide:
single €115-315
double €125-375
suite €195-1,100

 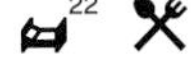        

Fashion Hotel

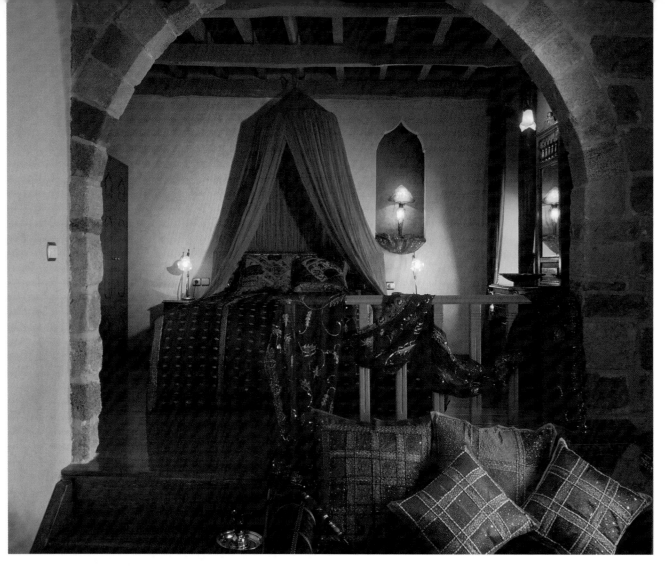

MEDIEVAL CITY, 26 PANETIOU AVENUE, 85100 RHODES, GREECE

Reached via cobblestone streets, this brand new hotel is a testament to creative design of the highest calibre thanks to renowned designers, Nikos and Takis. Influenced by the Orient, the interior is flooded with bright colours, silk fabrics and hand-embroidered pieces, and each suite provides totally unique accommodation with luxurious bathrooms containing large Jacuzzis, ethnic-style sitting areas and king-size beds. A la carte breakfast may be taken in the garden or in guests' suites, and cocktails enjoyed whilst admiring the view.

Cet hôtel tout neuf, auquel on accède au gré des rues pavés, est le témoignage d'un décor des plus créative, que l'on doit aux designers renommés Nikos et Takis. Influencé par l'Orient, l'intérieur est inondé de couleurs vives, de soieries et de pièces brodées main. Chaque suite offre un logement unique avec des salles de bain de luxe aux larges jacuzzis, des salons de style ethnique et de grands lits doubles. Le petit-déjeuner à la carte peut être pris dans le jardin ou dans les suites d'hôtes, et des cocktails peuvent être dégustés en admirant la vue.

Este hotel de reciente creación al que se llega a través de calles de adoquines constituye todo un tratado de diseño creativo del más alto nivel gracias a los reconocidos diseñadores Nikos y Takis. Por influencia oriental, su interior está cargado de brillantes colores, telas de seda y piezas de artesanales bordados a mano. Asimismo cada una de sus suites garantizan un inigualable confort gracias a sus lujosos cuartos de baño provistos de amplios jacuzzis, espacio para el relax de estilo étnico y camas de tamaño superior. Puede tomarse el desayuno a la carta en el jardín o en las propias suites así como disfrutar de sus cócteles mientras se admira el paisaje.

Our inspector loved: *The floor tiles in the bathrooms.*

Directions: Airport > Rhodes town > Old City > the hotel is opposite the old harbour Master's House.

Web: www.johansens.com/fashionhotel
E-mail: info@nikostakishotel.com
Tel: +30 22410 70773/4
Fax: +30 22410 24643

Price Guide:
double €100-180
suite €200-400

Melenos Lindos

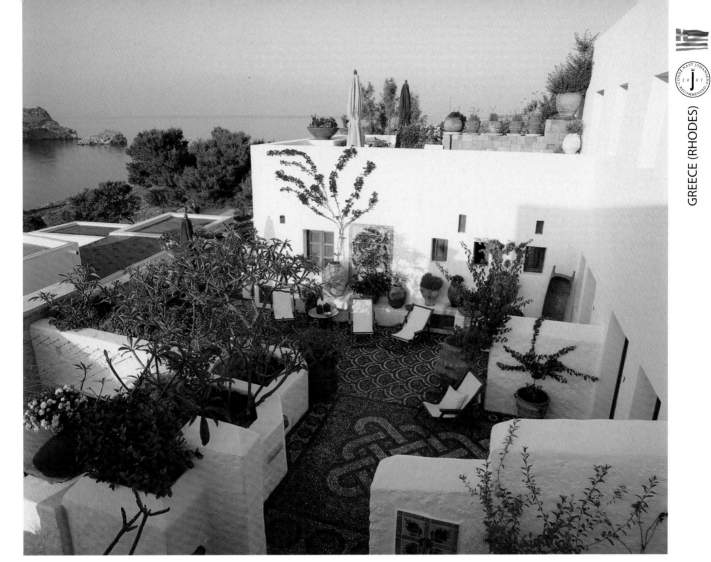

LINDOS, 85107 RHODES, GREECE

This truly exceptional small hotel is surrounded by fine examples of traditional architecture and small winding streets. Personal attention, magnificent sea views, quiet corners, superb food and the historical backdrop of the Lindian Acropolis makes this the perfect place to unwind and relax. Rooms are very spacious and filled with artefacts from Turkey and Greece with Ottoman and Venetian influences. Private terraces, cobblestone Rhodian flooring, small gardens, a good collection of books and cheerful personnel add to the special ambience.

Ce petit hôtel réellement exceptionnel est entouré de beaux exemples d'architecture traditionnelle et de petites rues tortueuses. Une attention personnelle, de magnifiques vues sur la mer, des coins calmes, une cuisine succulente et l'Acropolis lindienne en toile de fond en font l'endroit idéal pour se détendre complètement. Les chambres sont très spacieuses et décorées d'objets turcs et grecs aux influences ottomanes et vénitiennes. Terrasses privées, sols pavés rhodiens, petits jardins, une bonne collection de livres et un personnel enjoué participent à l'ambiance très spéciale.

Este excepcional hotelito esta rodeado de arquitectura clásica y pequeñas calles tortuosas. Atención personal, vistas magnificas al mar, rincones tranquilos, comida estupenda y, como telón de fondo, el histórico acrópolis de Lindos, hacen que este lugar sea perfecto para espaciarse y relajarse. Las habitaciones son muy espaciosas y están llenas de adornos provenientes de Turquía y de Grecia con influencias otomanas y venecianas. Terrazas privadas, suelos de piedra de Rodhes, pequeños jardines, una estupenda colección de libros y un personal alegre y amable forman parte del ambiente tan especial que tiene este hotel.

Our inspector loved: *The presentation of the great food.*

Directions: Lindos village is 45km from Rhodes International Airport. Airport > exit first left > turn right to Lindos > arrive at Lindos village > call the hotel.

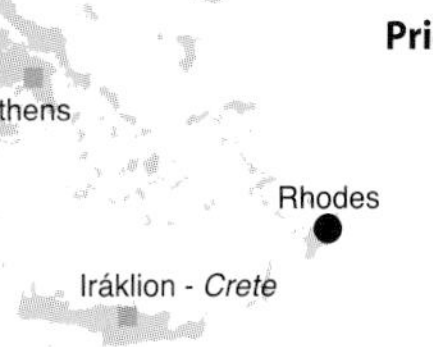

Web: www.johansens.com/melenoslindos
E-mail: info@melenoslindos.com
Tel: +30 224 40 32 222
Fax: +30 22 440 31 720

Price Guide: (closed November - March)
suite €180-490

GREECE (SANTORINI)

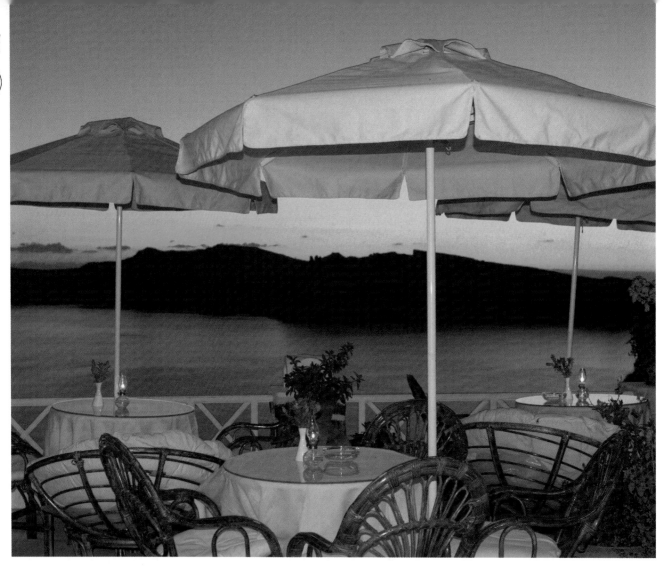

ALEXANDER'S BOUTIQUE HOTEL OF OIA

84702 OIA, SANTORINI, GREECE

A collection of 8 suites and 7 guest rooms comprise this little gem of a hotel conveniently located in stunning and tranquil Oia away from the bustling Fira bars and nightlife. The owner and manager have created a delightful haven replete with antiques, handmade artefacts and other special touches that complement the carefully designed and stylish bedrooms.

7 chambres et 8 suites composent ce petit joyau d'hôtel idéalement situé pour la beauté et la tranquillité de Oia, loin des bars et tavernas de Fira. Les propriétaires et gérants ont créé un ravissant paradis où une abondance d'antiquités, objets fait mains et autres touches complètent les chambres décorées avec goût.

Un conjunto de 8 suites y 7 habitaciones componen esta pequeña joya de hotel, convenientemente emplazado en la belleza y la tranquilidad de Oia, lejos del bullicio de los bares de Fira. El propietario y el director han creado un delicioso remanso donde las antigüedades, los objetos hechos a mano y otros toques personales contribuyen a adornar las elegantes habitaciones de esmerado y elegante diseño.

Our inspector loved: *The homely, cosy, private and friendly atmosphere.*

Directions: 20km from the harbour of Athinios and Santorini Airport.

Web: www.johansens.com/alexanders
E-mail: only@alexandershotel.com
Tel: +30 22860 71818
Fax: +30 22860 72375

Price Guide:
double €100-200
suite €250-600

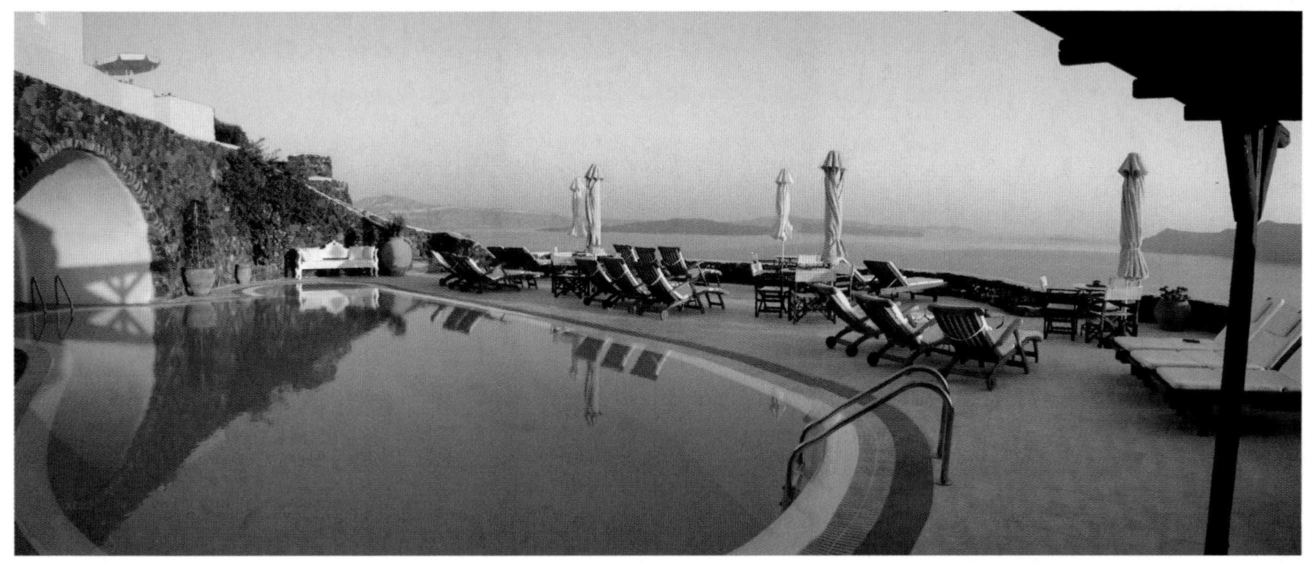

CANAVES OIA

OIA, 87402 SANTORINI, GREECE

Uniquely situated on the north-west tip of Santorini Island, this stunning luxury resort comprises 2 buildings, the hotel and suites, and offers guests every comfort together with panoramic views over the Caldera and Aegean Sea. Ancient caves and houses have been fashioned into tastefully elegant guest rooms with the most superior of facilities, amenities and objets d'art. All rooms have a private terrace, and some have a pool and Jacuzzi. The restaurant serves gourmet cuisine, and island tours on Canaves' luxury yacht can be arranged.

Exceptionnellement situé à la pointe nord-ouest de l'île de Santorini, ce sublime établissement d'un blanc étincelant, comprand un hôtel et des suites, et offre à ses hôtes tout le confort ainsi que des vues panoramiques sur Caldera et la mer Egée. D'anciennes caves et maisons ont été transformées avec goût en chambres élégantes, avec les structures et équipements de qualité et des objets d'art. Toutes les chambres ont une terrasse privée et certaines sont équipées d'une piscine et d'un jacuzzi. Le restaurant sert une cuisine gastronomique. Des excursions sur le yacht privé de Canaves peuvent être organisées.

De excepcional emplazamiento en la punta noroeste de la isla Santorini, este espléndido y lujoso establecimiento de resplandeciente blanco consta de 2 edificios, el hotel y las suites, proporciona a sus clientes todo tipo de confort así como panorámicas vistas a la Caldera y al mar Egeo. Sus antiguas cuevas y casas han sido convertidas en habitaciones y suites de elegante gusto provistas de instalaciones, comodidades y objetos de arte de calidad superior. Todas habitaciones disponen de terraza privada y algunas tienen piscina y jacuzzi. Su restaurante sirve comida gourmet. Pueden concertarse visitas turísticas por la isla en el yate de lujo Canaves.

Our inspector loved: *Watching the sunset by the pool area.*

Directions: Oia Airport > in the centre of Santorini.

Web: www.johansens.com/canavesoia
E-mail: canaves@otenet.gr
Tel: +30 22860 71453/71128
Fax: +30 22860 71195

Price Guide: (closed November - March)
double €310-370
suite €420-1,150

FANARI VILLAS

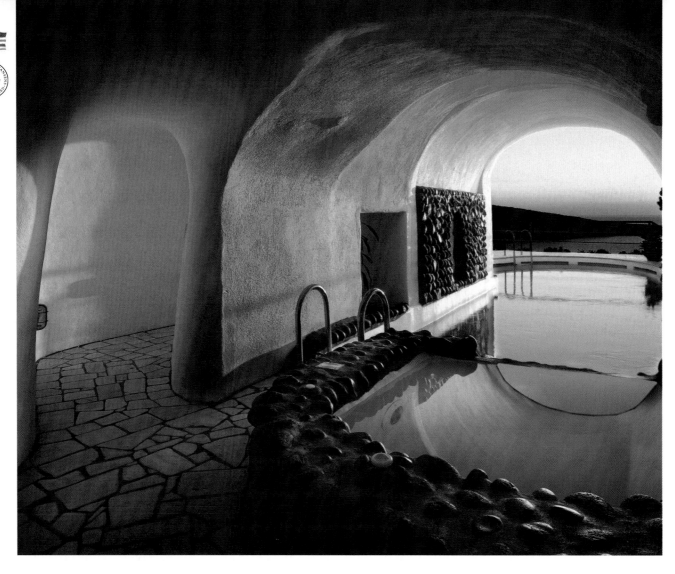

OIA, 84702 SANTORINI, GREECE

Directions: From the port or airport > Fira > Oia > at the end of Oia, Fanari Villas is on the left by the windmill.

Web: www.johansens.com/fanarivillas
E-mail: fanari@otenet.gr
Tel: +30 22860 71007
Fax: +30 22860 71235

Price Guide:
villa €290-340
suite €340-400

This delightful hotel lies tucked away at the end of Oia and has been carefully carved out of the rocks to create a collection of charming villas with fantastic Santorini views. Volcanic rock and local textiles create a quirky yet stylish ambience, whilst the pool area, with adjoining under-cave Jacuzzi, is particularly romantic. Fine dining on the terrace watching the sun set over the volcano is a must for any guest!

Ce ravissant hôtel se cache au bout du village de Oia et a été taillé dans la roche avec la plus grande attention afin de créer une ravissante collection de villas de charme avec de magnifiques vues sur Santorini. La roche volcanique et les tissus locaux créent une atmosphère particulière mais de style. Le coin piscine avec son jacuzzi attenant dans une cave, est particulièrement romantique. Un délicieux dîner sur la terrasse en regardant le coucher du soleil sur le volcan est un must pour tous les clients.

Este lindo hotel escondido en un rincón al otro extremo de Oia ha sido cuidadosamente excavado en roca para ofrecer un conjunto de villas encantadoras con fantásticas vistas a Santorini. La roca volcánica y los tejidos típicos locales consiguen crear un ambiente caprichoso y elegante al mismo tiempo. La zona de la piscina que cuenta con un jacuzzi contiguo inserto en una cueva resulta especialmente romántica. No se pierda las puestas de sol sobre el volcán desde la terraza mientras disfruta de una excelente cena.

Our inspector loved: *The cosy, friendly, refined and relaxed environment.*

Orloff Resort

SPETSES ISLAND, OLD HARBOUR, 18050 SPETSES, GREECE

Set on the Old Port of Spetses Island, Orloff Resort dates back to 1865; a mansion home to the historically eminent Greek family of Orloff. A refurbishment has transformed it into a modern retreat with 19 rooms in traditional surrounds. Local foremen have used natural materials such as rock, wood, pebbles, marble and limestone to create a representative of its region and this harmony is evident throughout the resort. This sense of local tradition is also evident in the gourmet kitchen where flavours and ingredients derive from Greek dishes.

Situé sur le vieux port de l'île de Spetses, Orloff Resort date de 1865 lorsque la demeure était la résidence de l'éminente famille grecque d'Orloff. Une remise à neuf l'a transformé en un refuge moderne de 19 chambres dans un environnement traditionnel. Les constructeurs locaux ont utilisé des matériaux naturels tels que la pierre, le bois, les galets, le marbre et le calcaire afin de créer un bâtiment typique de la région et cette harmonie se retrouve partout dans l'hôtel. L'esprit de tradition locale se retrouve également dans la cuisine gastronomique où les saveurs et les ingrédients dérivent des plats grecs.

Sito en el Viejo Puerto de la isla de Spetses, el Orloff Resort se remonta a 1865, cuando la mansión era la residencia de la familia griega históricamente eminente de Orloff. Una remodelación la ha transformado en un moderno lugar de retiro y descanso con 19 habitaciones en un entorno tradicional. Los constructores locales utilizaron materiales naturales tales como roca, madera, piedras, mármol y caliza para crear una propiedad representativa de la región, siendo tal armonía evidente por doquier. Esta sensación de tradición local se hace también evidente en la cocina gastronómica, donde los sabores y los ingredientes derivan de los platos griegos.

Our inspector loved: *The elegance of the courtyard.*

Directions: Athens > Pireus > fast ferry to Spetses Island. 1km from Spetses port. The nearest airport is Athens.

Web: www.johansens.com/orloffresort
E-mail: info@orloffresort.com
Tel: +30 229 807 5444/5
Fax: +30 229 807 4470

Price Guide:
single €90-195
double €90-195
suite €190-350
residence €450-840

Ireland

Hotel location shown in red (hotel) or purple (spa hotel) with page number

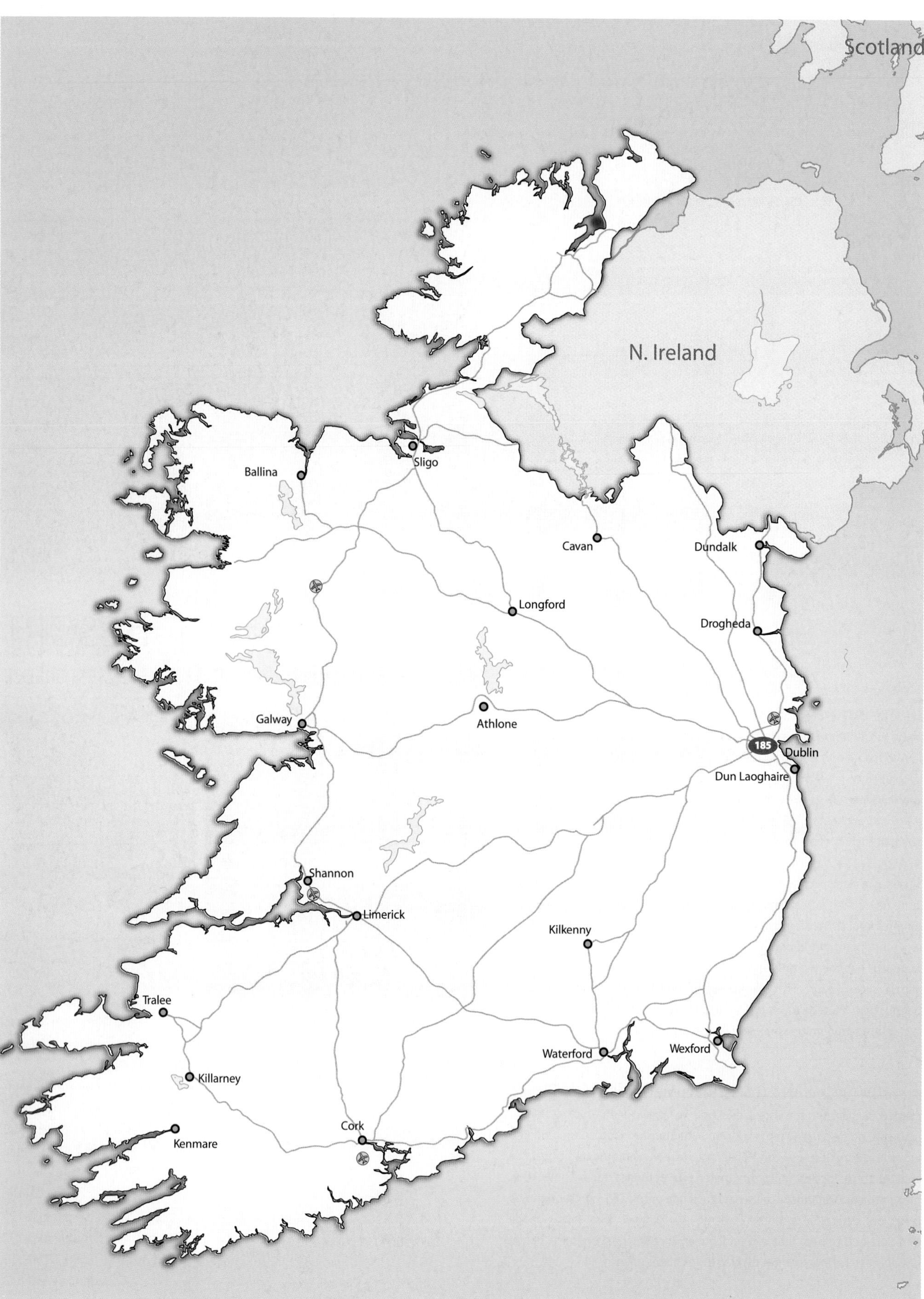

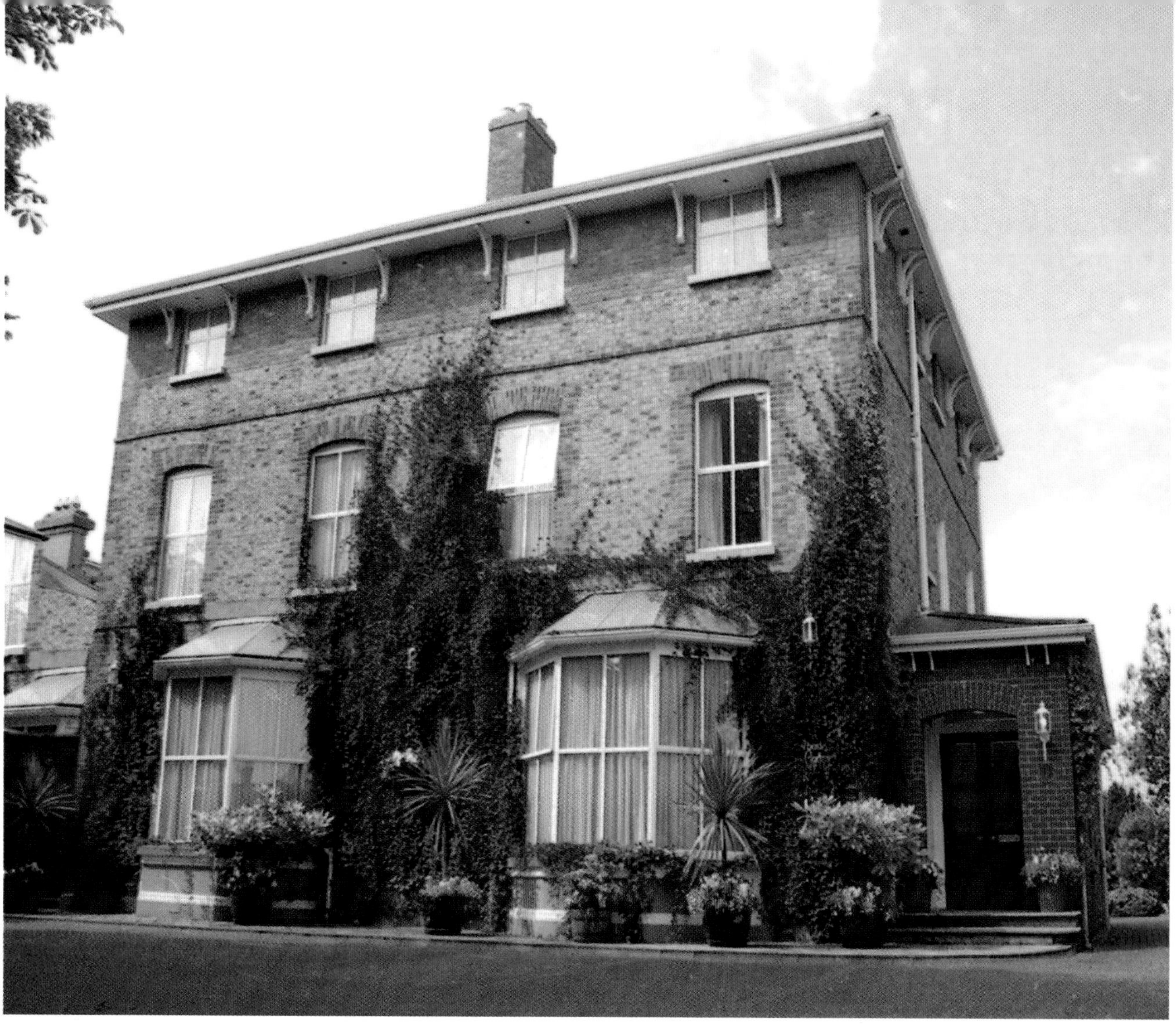

IRELAND (DUBLIN)

Aberdeen Lodge

53-55 Park Avenue, Ballsbridge, Dublin 4, Ireland

Located in the south city centre, set within formal gardens on a serene tree-lined avenue, this classic example of Edwardian architecture prides itself on ensuring that the needs of its guests are met wholeheartedly. Elegant bedrooms are furnished in complete harmony with the house, spacious suites feature Jacuzzis and period furniture, whilst the award-winning intimate dining room serves a special menu and good selection of fine wines. The hotel provides an ideal base from which to enjoy Dublin's sights and shopping in the famous Grafton Street. Private car park.

Situé au centre sud de la ville, ce bel exemple d'architecture édouardienne se dresse au milieu d'un jardin à la française, dans une paisible avenue bordée d'arbres, et met un point d'honneur à satisfaire tous les besoins des visiteurs. Les chambres élégantes sont en harmonie avec le reste de l'hôtel et les suites spacieuses comportent des jacuzzis et des meubles d'époque. La petite salle à manger primée propose un menu exceptionnel et un excellent choix de vins fins. L'hôtel est idéal pour visiter Dublin et faire du shopping dans la célèbre Grafton Street. Parking privé.

Al sur del centro de la ciudad emplazado dentro de los jardines formales en una tranquila avenida llena de árboles, este clásico ejemplo de arquitectura eduardina se jacta al asegurar que las necesidades de sus huéspedes están satisfechas incondicionalmente. Sus elegantes habitaciones están amuebladas en completa armonía con el edificio, en sus espaciosas suites destacan los jacuzzis y mobiliario de época, a la vez que en el comedor, íntimo y galardonado se sirve un menú especial y una buena selección de vinos. El hotel constituye una base ideal desde donde poder disfrutar los puntos de interés de Dublín y la famosa calle Grafton para ir de compras.También dispone de aparcamiento.

Our inspector loved: *The quiet seclusion so close to the city centre.*

Directions: Off Ailesbury Road, 7 minutes from the city centre by D.A.R.T.

Web: www.johansens.com/aberdeenlodge
E-mail: aberdeen@iol.ie
Tel: +353 1 283 8155
Fax: +353 1 283 7877

Edinburgh
Dublin
Cardiff
London

Price Guide:
single €106–139
double/twin €139–189
four poster €169-229
suite €190–299

ITALY

Hotel location shown in red (hotel) or purple (spa hotel) with page number

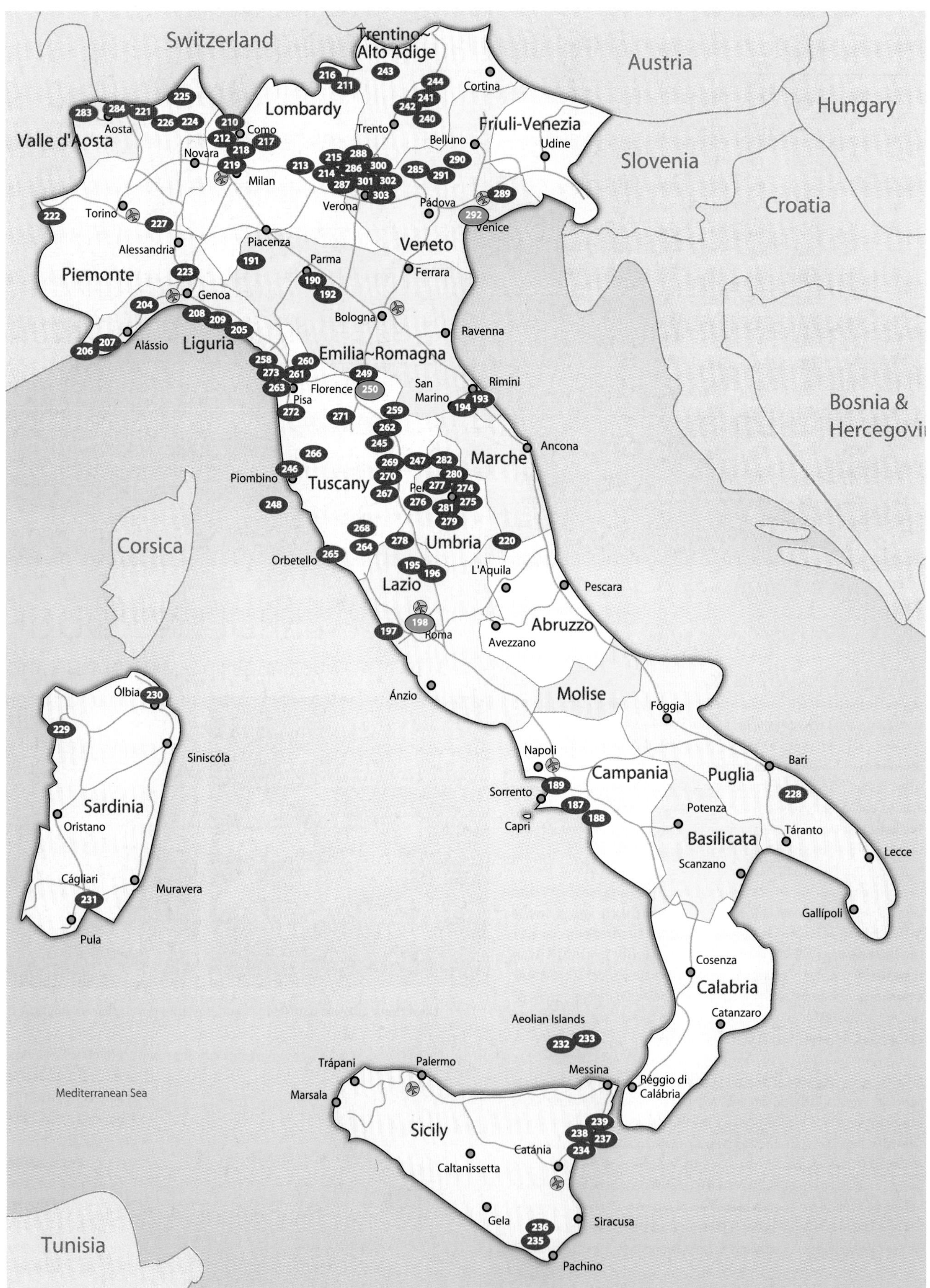

Furore Inn Resort & Spa

VIA DELL'AMORE, 84010 FURORE, AMALFI COAST, ITALY

Guests arriving at this beautiful stretch of Italy's coastline are in for an exceptional treat. Welcomed by an apéritif, and served by attentive and friendly staff, an instant sense of well-being is achieved. 3 stunning swimming pools and an elegant spa are complemented by some of the very best Italian wines and cuisine. The wine tasting tours and cookery lessons reflect the pride in the work taken by all the staff in this truly exemplary hotel.

Les hôtes arrivant sur cette magnifique partie de la côte Italienne pourront profiter d'un traitement exceptionnel. Accueillis avec un apéritif servi par un personnel cordial et attentif, un sentiment immédiat de bien-être est atteint. 3 magnifiques piscines et un élégant spa sont complétés par le meilleur du vin et de la cuisine Italienne. Les circuits de dégustation de vins et les cours de cuisine reflètent parfaitement le goût du travail bien fait pour tout le personnel de cet hôtel exemplaire.

Los clientes que lleguen a este bello paraje de la costa italiana se llevarán una bonita sorpresa. Al dárseles la bienvenida con un aperitivo, servido por su atento y cordial personal, se consigue transmitir una rápida sensación de bienestar. 3 sorprendentes piscinas y un elegante spa se complementan a la perfección con algunos de los mejores caldos italianos y con su carta. Los recorridos de degustación de vinos y las lecciones de cocina que se imparten son fiel reflejo del orgullo por el trabajo realizado que demuestra todo el personal de tan ejemplar hotel.

Our inspector loved: *The bar and restaurant staff who are so professional and friendly.*

Directions: The nearest train stations are Naples and Salerno. The nearest airport is Naples, and regular ferry services run from Naples and Sorrento to the Amalfi Coast.

Web: www.johansens.com/furoreinn
E-mail: information@furoreinn.it
Tel: +39 089 830 4711
Fax: +39 089 830 4777

Price Guide:
single €160-316
double €230-460
junior suite €350-550
duplex suite €460-750

ITALY / CAMPANIA (RAVELLO)

Hotel Villa Maria

VIA S. CHIARA 2, 84010 RAVELLO (SA), ITALY

Situated with a unique and breathtaking view of the Amalfi coast and the hills that gently slope down to it lies this family-owned hotel, which has a romantic and intimate ambience, as if staying in a private villa. The rooms are large and spacious overlooking the orchard that provides ingredients for the elegant dinner table. Guests also have use of the swimming pool at the nearby sister hotel, Hotel Giordano.

Cet hôtel familial à l'ambiance romantique et intime comme celle d'une villa privée, a des vues uniques et à couper le souffle sur la côte d'Amalfi et sur les collines qui descendent doucement vers celle-ci. Les chambres sont grandes et spacieuses et s'ouvrent sur les vergers d'où viennent certains ingrédients utilisés pour l'élégante table du dîner. Les hôtes peuvent également utiliser la piscine de l'hôtel partenaire tout proche, l'hôtel Giordano.

Este hotel de regencia familiar se distingue por sus singulares e imponentes vistas a la costa de Amalfi así como a las colinas que suavemente se deslizan hacia ella. Su ambiente romántico e íntimista proporciona al cliente la sensación de estar alojándose en una villa privada. Las habitaciones, grandes y espaciosas, dan todas al huerto del que se obtienen todos los ingredientes de su elegante mesa. Los clientes pueden asimismo disfrutar de la piscina en su hotel hermano, el Hotel Giordano.

Our inspector loved: *The amenities, and Giardino Ristorante with its stunning sea view.*

Directions: A3 (Naples – Salerno) > exit Angri > Costa Amalfitana > Ravello.

Web: www.johansens.com/villamaria
Email: villamaria@villamaria.it
Tel: +39 089 857255
Fax: +39 089 857071

Price Guide:
single €155–185
double €185–225
junior suite €405–445

17 100

Grand Hotel Cocumella

VIA COCUMELLA 7, 80065 SANT'AGNELLO, SORRENTO, ITALY

This former Jesuit monastery was transformed into a hotel in 1822. Traces of the past remain: the elegant hall was once the cloisters and the chapel is still used for weddings and concerts. Many of the guest rooms have antique furnishings and the bridal suite has an exquisite painted ceiling. Guests feast on aromatic Mediterranean dishes, and in summer, light buffet lunches are enjoyed by the pool. There is a fitness centre with Jacuzzi, sauna and steam bath, whilst massage and beauty treatments are available upon request.

Cet ancien monastère jésuite a été transformé en hôtel en 1822. Les traces du passé sont encore présentes, l'élégant hall occupe l'ancien cloître et la chapelle continue d'être utilisée pour des mariages ou des concerts. De magnifiques meubles anciens agrémentent les chambres et une peinture raffinée orne le plafond de la suite nuptiale. Les visiteurs dégustent des plats méditerranéens aux saveurs aromatiques l'été et des buffets légers sont proposés au bord de la piscine. Le centre de remise en forme offre jacuzzi, sauna et hammam, alors que des massages et des soins de beauté peuvent être appréciés sur demande.

Este antiguo monasterio jesuita se transformó en un hotel en 1822. Perduran muestras de su pasado: el elegante vestíbulo fue antaño el claustro y la capilla aún se usa para bodas y conciertos. Numerosas habitaciones tienen mobiliario antiguo y la suite nupcial posee un refinado techo pintado. Los clientes celebran sus aromáticos platos mediterráneos y en verano los ligeros almuerzos buffet se disfrutan junto a la piscina. Dispone de un centro fitness con jacuzzi, sauna y baños de vapor a la vez que puede el cliente, si lo solicita, recibir tratamientos de masaje y belleza.

Our inspector loved: *The relaxed barbecue lunch under the shade of orange trees by the pool, in teh agrumeto.*

Directions: Naples > Castellamare di Stabia > Sorrento.

Web: www.johansens.com/grandcocumella
E-mail: info@cocumella.com
Tel: +39 081 878 2933
Fax: +39 081 878 3712

Price Guide: (closed November-March)
single €230–330
double/twin €360–400
suite €500–910

Palazzo Dalla Rosa Prati

STRADA AL DUOMO 7, 43100 PARMA, ITALY

Directions: Located in the centre of Parma by the Duomo.

Web: www.johansens.com/palazzodallarosaprati
E-mail: info@palazzodallarosaprati.it
Tel: +39 0521 386 429
Fax: +39 0521 502 204

Price Guide: (room only)
suite €150-220

Bought by the Prati family in the 15th century, and currently home to the Marquis Dalla Rosa Prati and his family, this extraordinary palace dates back to 1220 and today provides 7 exclusive suite apartments with kitchenettes. Modern comforts cleverly integrate within the original architectural style, and each suite looks out to magnificent views of the main city monuments. La Forchetta restaurant serves flavoursome Italian cuisine, and the ancient, frescoed hall can accommodate meetings.

Acquis par la famille Prati au XVe siècle, actuellement la demeure du Marquis Dalla Rosa Prati et de sa famille, cet extraordinaire palace date de 1220 et offre aujourd'hui 7 suites-appartements de luxe avec kitchenettes. Le confort moderne est intégré dans l'architecture originale et chaque suite a une vue magnifique sur les monuments principaux de la ville. Le restaurant La Forchetta sert une succulente cuisine italienne, et des réunions peuvent être organisées dans l'ancien hall orné de fresques.

Este extraordinario palacio que data de 1220 fue comprado por la familia Prati en el siglo XV y hoy es la residencia del Marqués dalla Rosa y su familia, ofrece 7 exclusivos apartamentos suites con pequeña cocina. Conservando su estilo arquitectónico han incorporado el confort moderno sabiamente y cada suite disfruta de magníficas vistas a los principales monumentos locales. El restaurante La Forchetta sirve sabrosa cocina italiana y el antiguo hall con sus frescos puede acoger reuniones.

Our inspector loved: *The beauty centre.*

Torre di San Martino - Historical Residence

Loc. Borgo di Rivalta, 29010 Gazzola, Piacenza, Italy

Amidst the verdant hills of Piacenza, overlooking a magnificent castle rising from the banks of Trebbia River, stands this stylish, elegant bed and breakfast. Friendly staff welcome guests to their individually designed and extremely comfortable guest rooms, fitted with modern conveniences and antique furnishings, velvet upholstery, four posters and beamed ceilings. Traditional local cuisine is savoured in the nearby restaurants, and guided excursions to the castle can be organised.

Cette élégante et chic maison d'hôtes se tient au cœur de collines verdoyantes de Piacenza donnant sur un magnifique château qui s'élève sur les rives de la Trebbia. Le charmant personnel accueille les hôtes dans leurs chambres extrêmement confortables avec poutres au plafond ; celles-ci ont été individuellement décorées avec un mobilier ancien dont un lit à baldaquin, des tissus de velours et équipées de tout le confort moderne. Une cuisine traditionnelle locale peut être dégustée dans les restaurants tous proches, et des excursions guidées au château peuvent être organisées.

Con vistas a un magnifico castillo que se levanta a la ladera del río Trebbia, esta elegante casa de huéspedes se ubica entre las verdes colinas de Piacenza. El amable personal del hotel acomoda a los huéspedes en sus muy confortables habitaciones, de diseño individual y equipadas con instalaciones modernos y muebles antiguos, tapizados de terciopelo, camas con dosel y techos de vigas. Saboree la cocina tradicional local en los restaurantes cercanos, y se pueden organizar excursiones al castillo.

Our inspector loved: *The perfect blend of history and modernity.*

Directions: A1 > exit Piacenza Sud > follow directions to Castello di Rivalta and Gossolengo. The nearest airport is Milan Malpensa.

Web: www.johansens.com/torredisanmartino
E-mail: info@torredisanmartino.it
Tel: +39 0523 972002
Fax: +39 0523 972030

Price Guide: (closed 1 week in January)
single €200
double €280
suite €400

Hotel Posta (Historical Residence)

PIAZZA DEL MONTE, 2, 42100 REGGIO EMILIA, ITALY

Directions: A1 (Milano/Roma) > exit at Reggio Emilia > town centre.

Web: www.johansens.com/posta
E-mail: info@hotelposta.re.it
Tel: +39 05 22 43 29 44
Fax: +39 05 22 45 26 02

Price Guide: (closed 2 weeks in August and 1 week for Christmas)
single €135-155
double €190-210
suite €230-270

In the town's historic centre, this imposing medieval building has a long tradition of hospitality. The influence of the different centuries is reflected in the blend of styles throughout. The bar, with refined and unusual atmosphere, is delightful, whilst the splendid Salone del Capitano is available for meetings and banquets. Food enthusiasts will appreciate pre-arranged excursions in and out of town to visit a cheese factory, where the famous Parmigiano Reggiano (Parmesan cheese) is produced, and the owner's very own traditional balsamic vinegar.

Situé au cœur de la ville historique, cette maison médiévale imposante possède une longue tradition d'hospitalité. L'influence des siècles passés se révèle dans le mélange de styles. Le bar possède une atmosphère élégante et insolite, et le Salone del Capitano est l'endroit idéal pour des conférences ou des banquets. Les gourmets apprécieront les excursions organisées dans et à l'extérieur de la ville, comprenant une visite à une fromagerie fabriquant le célèbre Parmigiano Reggiano (Parmesan), et le traditionnel vinaigre balsamique produit par le propriétaire.

Situado en el centro histórico de la ciudad, este imponente edificio medieval goza de una hospitalidad con una larga tradición. La huella que han dejado los siglos puede apreciarse en la deliciosa combinación de estilos que hay por todo el hotel. El bar, con un ambiente refinado e insólito, resulta particularmente encantador, mientras que el espléndido Salone del Capitano está disponible para reuniones y banquetes. Los gourmets apreciaran las excursiones dentro y fuera de la ciudad, incluida la visita a la fabrica de queso donde se hace el legendario Parmigiano Reggiano (queso parmesano), y el vinagre balsamico de produccion propia.

Our inspector loved: *The magnificent medieval-style façade.*

Hotel des Nations

LUNGOMARE COSTITUZIONE 2, 47838 RICCIONE (RN), ITALY

Situated on the beach, this quiet, charming hotel was conceived according to the wellness philosophy. Sea views and antique furniture enhance the elegant bedrooms. Organic food and local delicacies are served in the harmoniously decorated breakfast room, and guests can make reservations at the adjacent restaurant. This is the first hotel in the country to have a flower-farm and offers flower therapies alongside health treatments such as massage, reflexology and mud therapy. Some of Italy's major experts in pre-hypnosis therapy for relaxation are also available.

Situé sur la plage, ce charmant hôtel a été conçu suivant les principes du bien-être. Une vue sur la mer et de meubles anciens mettent en valeur les chambres élégantes. Une nourriture biologique et des spécialités locales sont servies dans la salle du petit-déjeuner. Les repas peuvent être pris dans le restaurant adjacent. C'est le premier hôtel qui possède une ferme de fleurs et offre des soins aux fleurs ainsi que des traitements tels que massage, réflexologie et bains de boue. Parmis les plus grands experts Italiens en traitement pré-hypnotique relaxant sont également à disposition.

Situado en la playa, este tranquilo y encantador hotel fue concebido de acuerdo a la filosofía del bienestar. Las vistas al mar y las piezas de mobiliario antiguo dan realce a sus elegantes habitaciones. En el salón de desayunos de armoniosa decoración pueden degustarse productos orgánicos así como otros manjares del lugar. Los clientes pueden asimismo hacer sus reservas en el restaurante adyacente. Este es el primer hotel de este país en forma de flor y ofrece terapias con flores así como otros tratamientos para la salud tales como masajes, reflexología y terapias con barro. Para la relajación, el hotel también cuenta con algunos de los expertos en terapia pre- hipnótica más importantes de Italia.

Our inspector loved: *The owner's knowledge of Chinese medicine.*

Directions: A14 > exit Riccione > follow directions to Riccione Mare.

Web: www.johansens.com/hoteldesnations
E-mail: info@desnations.it
Tel: +39 0541 647878
Fax: +39 0541 645154

Price Guide: (closed 10th - 25th December)
single €95–175
double €150–270
suite €320–550

HOTEL TITANO

CONTRADA DEL COLLEGIO 31, 47890 SAN MARINO (RSM), SAN MARINO REPUBLIC

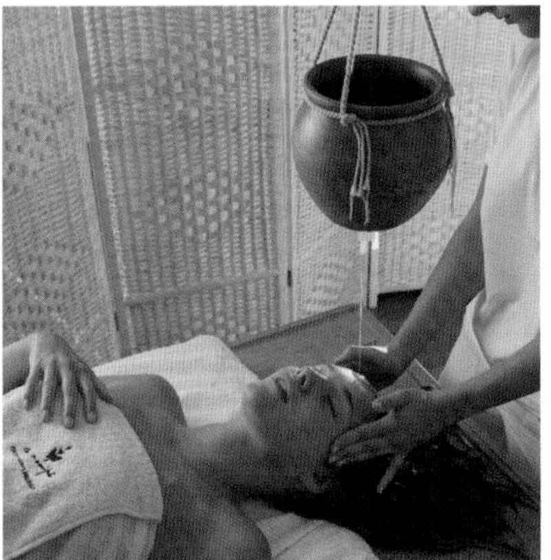

Within the heart of the ancient Republic of San Marino, amidst the winding, cobbled streets, stands the 19th-century Hotel Titano. With views of the surrounding countryside, each bedroom is unique and represents the hotel's history. Light meals, cocktails and homemade cakes are savoured in Il Terrazzino, which looks out to Contrada, whilst local dishes are served in La Terrazza where magnificent views of the Apennines are enjoyed. Maurice Messegue Beauty Centre provides diet and herbal consultations as well as body treatments.

Au cœur de l'ancienne République de San Marino, dans les tortueuses rues pavées se tient l'hôtel Titano. Avec vues sur la campagne environnante, chaque chambre est unique et représente l'histoire de l'hôtel. Des repas légers, cocktails et gâteaux maisons peuvent être savourés à l'Il Terrazzino, qui donne sur le Contrada, et des mets locaux sont servis à la Terrazza d'où l'on profite d'une vue sur les Apennins. Le centre de beauté Maurice Mességué offre des conseils de diététique et de phytothérapie ainsi que des traitements pour le corps.

El hotel Titano del siglo XIX, se encuentra en el corazón de la antigua República de San Marino entre calles adoquinadas y pintorescas. Con vistas al paisaje colindante, cada habitación es única y representa la historia del hotel. Dando a Contrada se encuentra Il Terrazzino donde podrá saborear tapas, cócteles y pasteles caseros; los platos locales se sirven en La Terrazza con magníficas vistas de los Apeninos. En el centro de belleza Maurice Messegue se proporcionan dietas, consultas herbales y tratamientos corporales.

Our inspector loved: *The dominating location of the oldest hotel in the world's oldest republic.*

Directions: A14 > exit Rimini Sud > signs to San Marino.

Web: www.johansens.com/hoteltitano
E-mail: info@hoteltitano.com
Tel: +378 99 10 07
Fax: +378 99 13 75

Price Guide: (closed November - mid-March)
double €90-190
suite €310-390

Relais Falisco

VIA DON MINZONI 19, 01033 CIVITA CASTELLANA (VT), ITALY

Thanks to a careful restoration this historical palace, dating back to Civita Castellana's 17th century, offers guests an authentic insight into its past splendour. Elegantly furnished rooms and suites display a variety of architectural styles, whilst the watchtower provides wonderful views and added appeal. The bar and lounge, complete with piano and fireplace, overlook the little garden and fountain, and the old cellar and Etruscan cave house a well-equipped gym, Jacuzzi and sauna.

Grâce à une magnifique restauration, ce palais historique datant du XVIIe siècle, offre aux hôtes un témoignage authentique des splendeurs de l'époque. Meublées élégamment, les chambres et suites proposent une grande variété de styles d'architectures et la tour offre de superbes vues et un attrait supplémentaire. Le bar et lounge, avec notamment piano et cheminée, donnent sur le petit jardin et la fontaine. La salle de gym très équipée, le sauna et le jacuzzi se cachent dans les anciennes caves et la grotte étrusque.

Este histórico palacio gracias a una cuidada restauración ofrece a sus huéspedes una visión genuina de su esplendoroso antepasado que data del siglo XVII de la Civita Castellana. Habitaciones y suites amuebladas elegantemente muestran una variedad de estilos arquitectónicos como el atalaya que proporciona maravillosas vistas y una atracción más. El bar y el salón equipados con piano y chimenea tienen vistas a pequeño jardíne con fuente. Una antigua bodega junto a una cueva etrusca albergan un gimnasio bien equipado, jacuzzi y sauna.

***Our inspector loved:** Spending the perfect evening in the "cave pool" with candles and champagne.*

Directions: Fiumicino or Ciampino Airport > GRA > Florence (A1) > exit Magliano Sabina > the hotel is in the old centre.

Milan
Venice
Rome

Web: www.johansens.com/falisco
E-mail: relaisfalisco@relaisfalisco.it
Tel: +39 0761 54 98
Fax: +39 0761 59 84 32

Price Guide:
single €90-100
double €140-150
suite €150-200

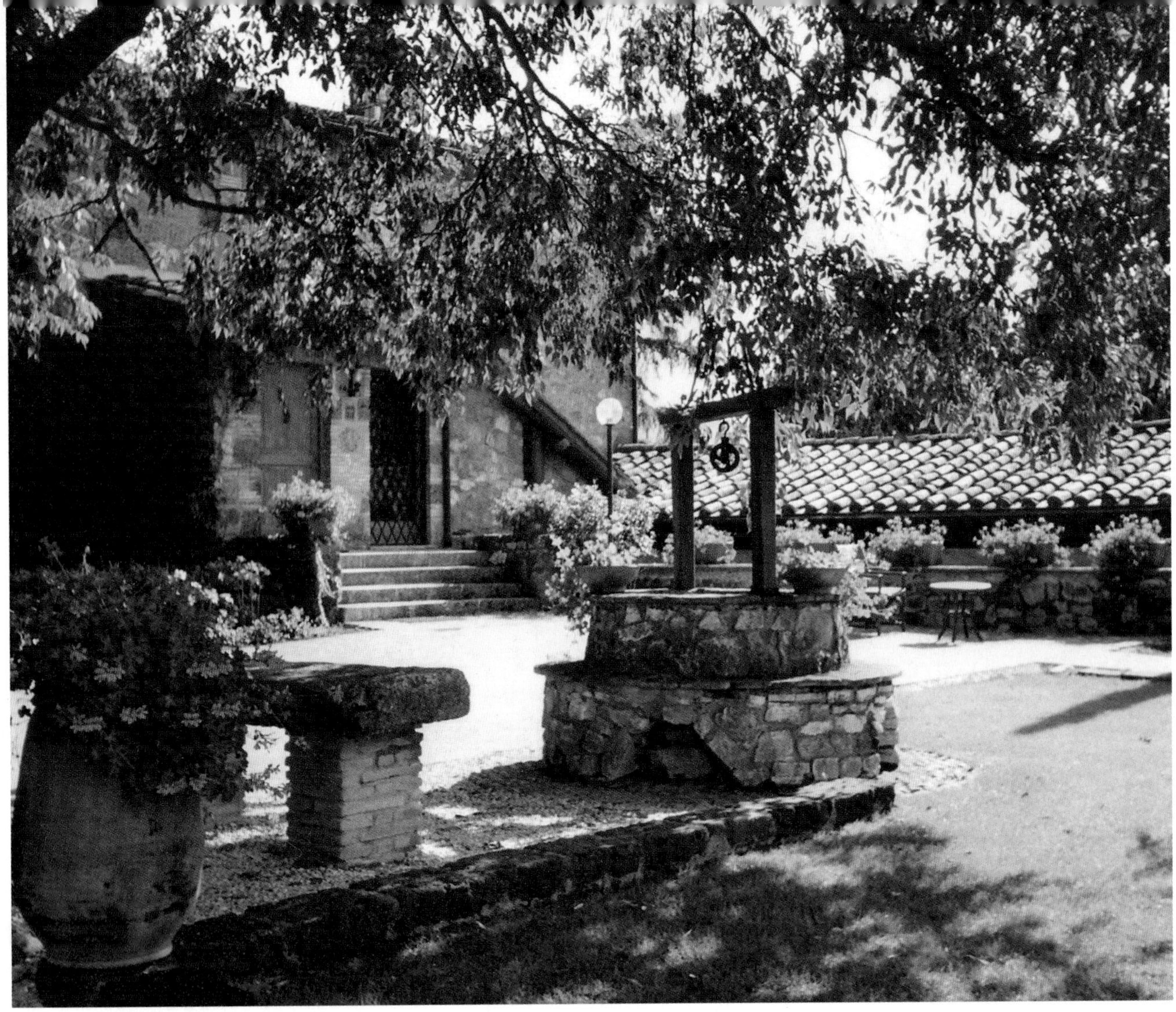

La Locanda della Chiocciola

LOC. SERIPOLA SNC, 01028 ORTE, ITALY

This sumptuous 15th-century farmhouse, set by the Tiber River Valley, is enveloped by 50 acres of Italian landscape. The 8 bedrooms are enhanced by antique furnishings and en-suite bathrooms. A 17th-century fireplace dominates the spacious dining room, and local produce is used to create traditional dishes. The swimming pool and new wellness lounge, with its Jacuzzi, steam bath, sauna and Kneipp-style showers, are ideal places to relax.

Cette somptueuse ferme du XVe siècle, située dans la vallée du Tibre, est entourée par 20 ha de paysages Italiens. Les 8 chambres sont mises en valeur par du mobilier ancien et des salles de bain en-suite. Une cheminée du XVIIe siècle trône dans la spacieuse salle à manger et des produits locaux sont utilisés pour créer les plats traditionnels. La piscine et le nouveau centre de bien être avec son jacuzzi, hammam, sauna et douches Kneipp sont les endroits parfaits pour se relaxer.

Esta exuberante casa de granja del siglo XV sita junto al valle del río Tíber se encuentra resguardada por 20 ha de paisaje italiano. Las 8 habitaciones aumentan su atractivo gracias a su mobiliario de antigüedades y cuartos de baño en-suite. El espacioso comedor esta presidido por una chimenea del siglo XVII. Los platos tradicionales se preparan con productos de la zona. La piscina y el nuevo salón de wellness, con su jacuzzi, baño de vapor, sauna y duchas al estilo Kneipp son lugares ideales para el relax.

Our inspector loved: *The Tiber Valley setting; the best starting point to explore the Etruscan area.*

Directions: The nearest airport is Rome Fiumicino. A1 > exit Orte > turn immediately left towards Orte town > follow signs for Penna on Teverina > located 7km from the exit of the Autostrada.

Web: www.johansens.com/lalocanda
E-mail: info@lachiocciola.net
Tel: +39 0761 402 734
Fax: +39 0761 490 254

Price Guide: (closed 1st - 26th December and 6th January - 28th February)
single €70-75
double €100-120
suite €115-135

LA POSTA VECCHIA HOTEL SPA

PALO LAZIALE, 00055 LADISPOLI, ROME, ITALY

Overlooking the sea, La Posta Vecchia, built on ancient Roman foundations, has a quiet luxuriousness. Many of the original structures such as stone doorways and fireplaces are preserved whilst stunning mosaics and antiques have been restored and displayed in the hotel's museum. Exquisite décor and warm colour schemes create a welcoming atmosphere and the Italian cooking is simply delicious. There is a private beach and excellent leisure facilities including a beauty salon. The hotel provides a shuttle service to and from Rome.

Surplombant la mer, le Posta Vecchia, construit sur d'anciennes fondations romaines, bénéficie d'un luxe tranquille. La plupart des installations originelles telles qu'encadrements de porte en pierre et cheminées a été préservée alors que d'étonnantes mosaïques et antiquités ont été restaurées et sont présentées dans le musée de l'hôtel. Le décor raffiné et les couleurs chaudes créent une atmosphère accueillante; la cuisine italienne est tout simplement délicieuse. L'hôtel dispose d'une plage privée et d'excellentes installations de loisirs, incluant un salon de beauté. Un service de navette à et de Rome est disponible.

El Posta Vecchia, construido sobre cimientos romanos, goza de vistas al mar y está un lujo discreto. Muchas de las estructuras originales como las entradas de piedra y las chimeneas se han conservado, mientras que maravillosos mosaicos y antigüedades han sido restaurados y están en exposición en el museo del hotel. Su décor exquisito y sus esquemas de cálidos colores crean un ambiente acogedor; la cocina italiana, es simplemente deliciosa. Está dotado de una playa privada y de excelentes instalaciones de ocio, inclusive de un salón de belleza. Servicio de lanzadera a y desde Roma está disponible.

Our inspector loved: *The indulgent experience in the spa.*

Directions: A12 > Cerveteri > Ladispoli > SSI Aurelia > exit Palo Laziale. The nearest airport is Fiumicino.

Web: www.johansens.com/postavecchia
E-mail: info@lapostavecchia.com
Tel: +39 0699 49501
Fax: +39 0699 49507

Price Guide: (double occupancy, closed November - March)
superior room €590
junior suite €950
master suite €1,550

          SPA

Rome

Hotel location shown in red (hotel) or purple (spa hotel) with page number

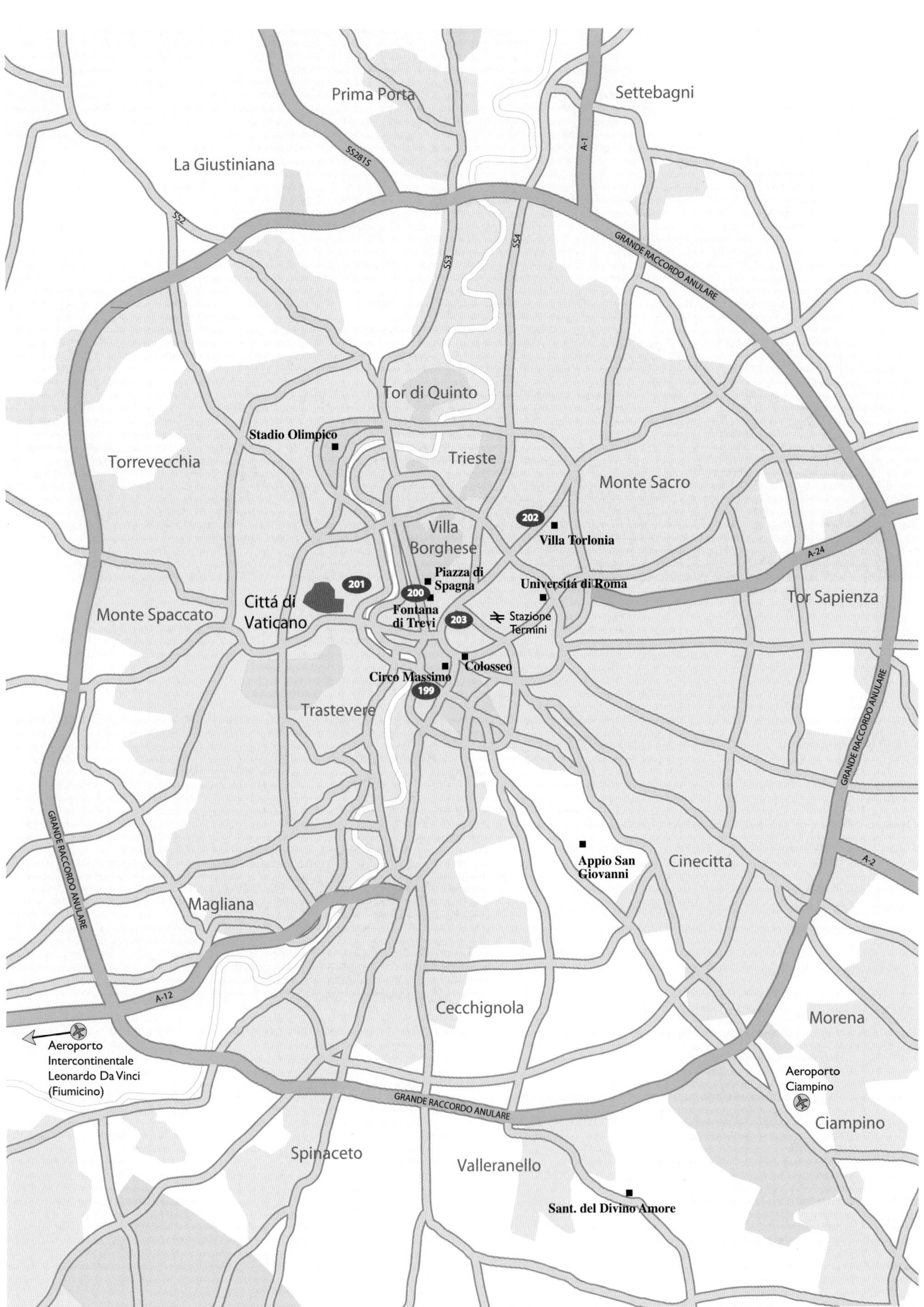

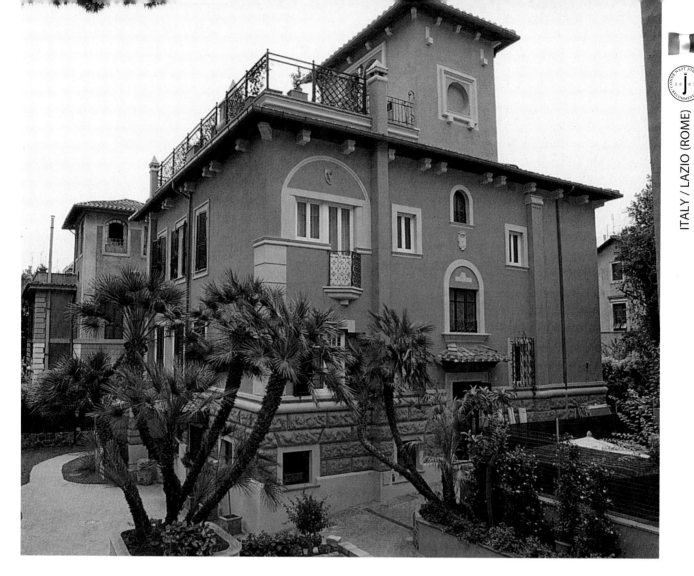

Hotel Aventino

VIA SAN DOMENICO 10, 00153 ROME, ITALY

Newly restored with care and respect for the district's historic past this charming city centre hotel enjoys an atmosphere of refined and innovative tranquillity. Décor and furnishings evoke a world of genteel and traditional relaxation, which radiates out from elegant public rooms and spacious guest rooms with all modern facilities to the attractive shady garden. The lounge boasts an antique fireplace, which during the colder months creates a very romantic and charming atmosphere. An ideal base for exploring Rome's treasures.

Récemment restauré avec soin et respect de l'histoire du quartier, cet hôtel charmant du centre ville bénéficie d'une atmosphère tranquille et raffinée. Le décor et le mobilier évoquent un monde de distinction associé à une détente traditionnelle, qui irradient des élégantes salles communes et des chambres spacieuses disposant de tout le confort moderne, jusqu'au beau jardin ombragé. Le salon a une cheminée antique, qui pendant des moins plus froids, crée une atmosphére romantique et charmante. Une base idéale pour explorer les trésors de Rome.

Recientemente restaurado con esmero y al mismo tiempo respetando el pasado histórico de la zona, este encantador, urbano y céntrico hotel disfruta de un ambiente refinado y una tranquilidad innovativa. El décor y el mobiliario evocan un mundo de relajación refinada y tradicional que se irradia desde las elegantes zonas comunes y las espaciosas habitaciones con todas las comunidades modernas hasta el atractivo y sombreado jardín. El salón ostenta una chimenea antigua que durante los meses fríos crea un ambiente muy romántico y acogedor. Es el lugar ideal para explorar los tesoros de Roma.

Our inspector loved: *The "jazz apéritif" at the nearby sister Hotel S. Anselmo.*

21

Directions: Located in the heart of the city.

Web: www.johansens.com/aventino
E-mail: info@aventinohotels.com
Tel: +39 06 57 00 57
Fax: +39 06 5783 604

Milan
Venice
Rome

Price Guide:
double (single occupancy) €165
double €157

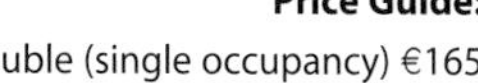

ITALY / LAZIO (ROME)

Hotel dei Borgognoni

VIA DEL BUFALO 126 (PIAZZA DI SPAGNA), 00187 ROME, ITALY

Hidden in a "vicolo", within the surrounding area of the Trevi Fountain, one of the loveliest corners of the city, stands this quiet, chic hotel. Elegant and exclusive, the exquisite hall and common area have been furnished to reflect the refined style and ambience throughout. Ideally located, the hotel is a short walk from the Trevi Fountain and the Spanish Steps as well as many cultural delights. Each of the en-suite bedrooms overlooks the enclosed garden with its abundance of flowers; some have a spacious terrace. The solarium provides an welcome respite, and conference rooms are available.

En los alrededores de la Fuente de Trevi, pero escondido en un "vicolo", se encuentra este tranquilo y chic hotel. Elegante y exclusivo, el mobiliario del exquisito hall y de las zonas publicas refleja el estilo y el ambiente refinado de todo el hotel. Debido a su ideal ubicación, el hotel está a pocos pasos de la Fuente de Trevi y de la Plaza de España así como de otras delicias culturales que ofrece esta ciudad. Todas las habitación en-suite, algunas con amplia terraza, dan al jardín cercado del hotel, con su profusión de flores. El solarium ofrece un lugar de descanso, y el hotel también dispone de salas para congresos.

Ubicado en la zona próxima a la Fuente de Trevi pero escondido en un "vicolo" se encuentra este encantador hotel. Recientemente renovado, el hall y las zonas comunes han sido realzados para reflejar la exquisita elegancia de su ambiente. Debido a su emplazamiento el hotel está a un corto paseo a pie de la Fuente de Trevi y de los "Spanish Steps" además de muchos otros encantos culturales. Cada habitación en-suite da al jardín cercado del hotel, destacando en él la profusión de flores. El elegante salón ofrece un lugar relajante para disfrutar de una bebida. El hotel también tiene disponible salas para congresos.

Our inspector loved: *The location: discreet and secluded.*

Directions: The hotel is a short walk from Piazza di Spagna metro station, directly behind Trevi Fountain. Private parking is available.

Web: www.johansens.com/borgognoni
E-mail: info@hotelborgognoni.it
Tel: +39 06 6994 1505
Fax: +39 06 6994 1501

Price Guide:
single €225-247
double €290-325
suite upon request

Hotel dei Consoli

VIA VARRONE 2/D, 00193 ROMA, ITALY

In the heart of town, near the Tiber river and the Vatican, this charming hotel welcomes guests into a peaceful retreat. Its history dates back to the 19th century and ornate public rooms feature soaring stucco decorations, Murano chandeliers, antique furniture, fresh flowers and excellent paintings. Guest rooms, many of which overlook St Peter's dome, are beautifully appointed with period style furniture, rich fabrics, objets d'art and spacious bathrooms. The hotel boasts a superb location for the business and leisure traveller alike.

Situé en plein centre ville, près du fleuve de Tibre et du Vatican, cet hôtel charmant offre à ses hôtes un refuge de paix. L'hôtel date du XIXe siècle et les salles publiques fleuries sont ornées de grandes décorations de stuc, lustres de Murano, des meubles antiques, des belles peintures et des fleurs. Les chambres, dont plusieurs donnent sur le Dôme Saint Pierre, sont meublées dans le style de l'époque et décorées avec des tissus de luxe et des objets d'art. Les salles de bains sont toutes spacieuses. L'hôtel revendique un endroit superbe pour le voyageur d'affaires ainsi que pour le voyageur de loisirs.

En el corazón de la ciudad, cerca del río Tíber y Vaticano, este encantador hotel acoge a clientes que buscan un lugar de descanso. Su historia se remonta al siglo XIX y sus preciosos salones comunes disponen de elevados motivos decorativos en estuco, lámparas de Murano, mobiliario antiguo, flores recién cortadas y excelentes obras pictóricas. Las habitaciones unas con vistas de la cúpula de San Pedro, están acondicionadas con gusto con muebles de estilo de época, suntuosas telas, objetos de arte y amplios cuartos de baño. El hotel se enorgullece de su excelente localización tanto para el viajero de negocios como para el turista.

Our inspector loved: *The brand new top-roof terrace with its marvellous view above St Peter's Dome!*

 28

 20

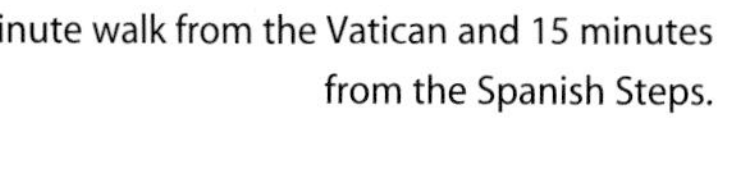

Directions: The hotel is a 2-minute walk from the Vatican and 15 minutes from the Spanish Steps.

Web: www.johansens.com/deiconsoli
E-mail: info@hoteldeiconsoli.com
Tel: +39 0668 892 972
Fax: +39 0668 212 274

Price Guide:
single €100-220
double €150-300
junior suite €200-480

Hotel Fenix

VIALE GORIZIA 5/7, 00198 ROME, ITALY

Directions: The hotel is situated in the city centre. 40 minutes from Fiumicino and Ciampino Airports.

Web: www.johansens.com/fenix
E-mail: info@fenixhotel.it
Tel: +39 06 8540 741
Fax: +39 06 8543 632

Price Guide:
single €140
double €150-190

Opened in 1960, this elegant hotel is situated in Rome's Trieste district, 20 minutes from the famous shopping area around Via Veneto and close to many historical and cultural attractions. Some of the comfortable bedrooms and suites are furnished in neo-classical style; many have private terraces, and the suites offer Jacuzzi bathtubs. Traditional Mediterranean and Roman dishes are served in the subtly lit restaurant or in the bedrooms (Mon-Fri). The meeting room can cater up to 25 people. Guided tours can be arranged by the hotel.

Ouvert en 1960, cet élégant hôtel est situé dans le quartier Trieste de Rome, à seulement 20 minutes des boutiques autour de Via Veneto et proche de nombreuses attractions culturelles et historiques. Certaines des chambres et suites confortables sont meublées dans un style néoclassique, beaucoup ont des terrasses privées et les suites possèdent un jacuzzi. Des plats traditionnels, méditerranéens et romains sont servis dans le restaurant à l'éclairage subtil ou dans les chambres (du lundi au vendredi). Les salles de réunion accueillent jusqu'à 25 personnes. Des visites guidées peuvent être organisées par l'hôtel.

Este hotel en el distrito Trieste de Roma abrió sus puertas al público en el 1960, y se encuentra a tan sólo 20 minutos de la famosa zona comercial Via Veneto y también muy cercano a numerosas atracciones culturales e históricas. Algunas de sus cómodas habitaciones y suites están amuebladas en estilo neoclásico, muchas tienes terrazas privadas y las suites baños con jacuzzi. En el restaurante sutilmente iluminado se pueden disfrutar tanto platos mediterráneos tradicionales como romanos, también hay servicio de habitaciones (de lunes a viernes). El salón para reuniones tiene capacidad hasta para 25 personas. El hotel puede organizar tours dirigidos si se requieren.

Our inspector loved: *The guided visits to the recently restored Villa Torlonia.*

73

25

VILLA SPALLETTI TRIVELLI

VIA PIACENZA 4, 00184 ROME, ITALY

This magnificent example of a 20th-century "urban villa" stands on the Quirinale Hill and offers total peace and seclusion. Its character has been maintained with magnificent antiques and a Liberty wrought iron staircase with flower-designed balcony made by Edoardo Gioja and beautiful Italian gardens. The Cultural Heritage Bond-awarded library is filled with beautiful bookcases with valuable, ancient books. Enjoy breakfast in the dining room; dinner is prepared by prior arrangement. A Wellness Centre is also available.

Ce splendide exemple du XXe siècle de "villa urbaine" se dresse sur le Quirinale et offre une intimité et un isolement total. Le caractère de la maison a été parfaitement respecté grâce à de magnifiques antiquités, un escalier circulaire en fer forgé avec un entresol au décor floral par Edoardo Gioja et de beaux jardins italiens. La magnifique bibliothèque reconnue comme Héritage Culturel est remplie de livres anciens de valeur. Dans la salle à manger, les hôtes peuvent déguster un petit-déjeuner. Dîner est préparé sur demande préalable uniquement. Un Wellness Centre est disponible.

Este magnifico ejemplo de villa urbana del siglo XX se erige en la Colina Quirinale y ofrece una absoluta paz y total aislamiento. La personalidad de la mansión se ha respetado totalmente mediante magníficas antigüedades, una escalera de hierro forjado estilo Liberty con descansillo de diseño floreal, creación de Edoardo Gioja y espléndidos jardines al estilo italiano. Unas librerías bellísimas, repletas de valiosos libros antiguos, se encuentran en la biblioteca, premiada como Patrimonio Cultural. Los clientes pueden tomar el desayuno en el comedor, mientras que la cena se prepara por encargo. Un centro wellness también esta a disposición de los clientes.

***Our inspector loved:** This oasis of charm and refinement in the heart of the city.*

Directions: Located in the city centre, a 20-minute walk from Central Station. Trains to Fiumicino and Ciampino Airports (shuttle bus from Ciampino railway station to airport) run every 15 minutes.

Milan
Venice
Rome

Web: www.johansens.com/villaspallettitrivelli
E-mail: info@villaspallettitrivelli.com
Tel: +39 06 48907934
Fax: +39 06 4871409

Price Guide:
romantic room €600
de luxe room €800
junior suite €1,000
de luxe suite €1,200

 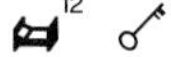      

Hotel Punta Est

VIA AURELIA 1, 17024 FINALE LIGURE (SV), ITALY

Directions: Genoa > Autostrada > A10 Savona > Finale Ligure.

Web: www.johansens.com/puntaest
E-mail: info@puntaest.com
Tel: +39 019 600611
Fax: +39 019 600611

Price Guide:
(closed mid-April - mid-October)
single €120-160
double/twin €220-280
suite €270–480

This elegant 18th-century villa was once a private summer residence. Today, it is a unique hotel, nestled in its own park with shaded pathways and olive groves, and fabulous panoramic views over the Ligurian Sea. Relaxation is guaranteed both by the swimming pool and the private beach. The hotel's unique natural grotto, with its stalagmites and stalactites, is like a magical Aladdin's Cave, where guests may relax in the water or attend memorable musical events, weddings and parties.

Cette élégante villa du XVIIIe siècle fût un temps une résidence privée d'été. Aujourd'hui, c'est un hôtel unique, niché dans son parc privé aux allées ombragées et oliveraies qui offrent des vues panoramiques fabuleuses sur la Mer Ligurienne. La détente est garantie au bord de la piscine et sur les plages privées. Dans sa grotte originale ornée de stalactites et stalagmites qui rappelle la cave magique d'Aladin, les hôtes peuvent se détendre dans l'eau ou assister à des évènements musicaux mémorables, mariages et fêtes diverses.

Esta elegante villa del siglo XVIII fue antaño una residencia de verano privada. Hoy día es un singular hotel enclavado en su propio parque con senderos protegidos del sol y olivares, así como con fabulosas vistas al Mar de Liguria. El relax está garantizado tanto en la piscina como en su playa privada. La cueva natural que posee el hotel, con sus estalagmitas y estalactitas, es única y proporciona un lugar para descansar en el agua o, como una mágica cueva de Aladino, se convierte en un entorno irrepetible para eventos musicales, bodas y fiestas.

Our inspector loved: *The amazing view, and the magnificent Aladdin's Cave.*

Abbadia San Giorgio - Historical Residence

PIAZZALE SAN GIORGIO, 16030 MONEGLIA (GE), ITALY

This 15th-century Franciscan complex is situated midway between Portofino and Cinque Terre, in historic Moneglia. The guest rooms are peaceful and relaxing and stylishly decorated with antique objet d'arts. Organic breakfast is taken in the Refectory, and wines and spirits may be enjoyed by the ancient fireplace before dining at the nearby Villa Edera Hotel. A pool, sauna and gym are also at guests' disposal at the Villa. Seminars, cooking demonstrations and personalised excursions on foot, bike or boat can be organised.

Cet ensemble franciscain datant du XVe siècle se trouve à Moneglia à mi-chemin entre Portofino et Cinque Terre. Les chambres paisibles et relaxantes sont décorées avec d'antiquités. Un pain d'agriculture biologique est servi au Réfectoire et les hôtes peuvent déguster vins et alcools forts auprès de la cheminée avant le diner à l'hôtel voisin Villa Edera. Egalement à disposition à la Villa, piscine, sauna et gym. Séminaires, cours de cuisine et excursions personnalisées pédestres, cyclistes ou en bateau peuvent être organisées.

Este complejo franciscano del siglo XV se encuentra a medio camino entre Portofino y Cinque Terre, en la histórica Moneglia. Las habitaciones son tranquilas y cómodas y están decoradas con gusto a base de objetos de arte antiguos. El desayuno orgánico puede tomarse en el Refectorio. Antes de cenar en el cercano hotel Villa Edera los clientes pueden disfrutar de los vinos y licores junto a la antigua chimenea. La Villa pone asimismo a disposición de los clientes una piscina, una sauna y un gimnasio, así como la posibilidad de organizar seminarios, demostraciones culinarias y excursiones personalizadas a pie, en bicicleta o en barco.

Our inspector loved: *The unusual setting, and the cloister.*

Directions: A12 Genova - Livorno > exit Sestri Levante > follow signs to Moneglia.

Web: www.johansens.com/abbadiasangiorgio
E-mail: info@abbadiasangiorgio.com
Tel: +39 0185 491119
Fax: +39 0185 49470

Price Guide: (closed November - 20th December)
double €150-170
junior suite €175-250
suite €210-300

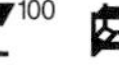

Hotel San Giorgio - Portofino House

VIA DEL FONDACO, 11, 16034 PORTOFINO (GENOVA), ITALY

This charming hotel is situated in a quiet location a few steps from the main square and harbour of Portofino and offers guests an elegant alternative to the usual type of accommodation in this area. The hotel's greatest treasure is its wonderful garden, where guests can relax and take breakfast. Local traditional décor abounds throughout; local "Ardesia" slate has been used for the floors and bathrooms. A meeting room can accommodate up to 15, and there is a small wellness centre.

Cet hôtel de charme, situé dans un endroit tranquille à quelques mètres de la place principale et du port de Portofino, offre à ses hôtes une alternative élégante au type d'hébergement généralement proposé dans cette région. Le plus grand trésor de l'hôtel est son magnifique jardin, où les hôtes peuvent se détendre et prendre leur petit-déjeuner. Une décoration traditionnelle régionale se retrouve à travers tout l'hôtel; des feuilles d'ardoise locale ont été utilisées pour les sols et les salles de bains. La salle de réunion peut accueillir jusqu'à 15 personnes et l'hôtel possède un petit centre de remise en forme.

Este encantador hotel, situado en una zona tranquila a un paso de la plaza principal y el puerto de Portofino, ofrece a sus clientes una elegante alternativa al típico alojamiento de la zona. El mayor tesoro de este hotel lo constituye su espléndido jardín donde los huéspedes pueden descansar y donde se puede también desayunar.Todo el lugar está decorado a la manera tradicional propia del lugar. Para los baños y los suelos se ha empleado la pizarra Ardesia de la zona. El hotel dispone asimismo de una sala de reuniones con un aforo de hasta 15 personas, así como de un pequeño centro wellness.

Directions: A12 > exit Rapallo > follow signs to Santa Margherita > Portofino.

Web: www.johansens.com/portofinohouse
E-mail: info@portofinohsg.it
Tel: +39 0185 26991
Fax: +39 0185 267139

Price Guide:
(closed during the winter season)
double €245-425
suite €425-710

Our inspector loved: *The perfect combination of local materials and design.*

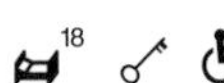        

Grand Hotel Diana Majestic

VIA OLEANDRI 15, 18013 DIANO MARINA (IM), ITALY

This small resort hotel has a great position just by the sea with its own private sandy beach, and is set in delightful ancient olive groves. The comfortable bedrooms all have a balcony and sea view, whilst the new suites have the added temptation of a large terrace with outdoor Jacuzzi. Excellent Mediterranean cuisine is served nightly, whilst the terrace by the sea provides a stunning backdrop for candle-lit dining. The hotel's bar boasts 60 brands of whisky and 100 bottles of the finest liqueurs and spirits from the 1920s.

Cette petite station de vacances se trouve tout près de la mer avec sa propre plage de sable et parmi des anciennes oliveraies merveilleuses. Toutes les chambres confortables ont un balcon avec vue sur la mer, et les nouvelles suites offrent une grande terrasse avec Jacuzzi en plein air. Une cuisine excellente méditerranéenne est servie chaque soir, alors que la terrasse près de la mer est l'endroit parfait pour des dîners aux chandelles. Le bar offre 60 marques de whisky ainsi que 100 bouteilles de liqueurs et de spiritueux des années 1920.

Este pequeño hotel de costa, de privilegiada posición de cercanía al mar con su propia y arenosa playa privada, está situado entre encantadores y ancestrales olivares. Sus cómodas habitaciones tienen todas balcones y vistas al mar. Una inmensa terraza y un jacuzzi al aire libre les aportan a las nuevas suites un toque de atractivo adicional. Se sirve excelente cocina mediterránea por la noche a la vez que la terraza junto al mar proporciona un impresionante telón de fondo para las cenas a la luz de las velas. El bar dispone de 60 marcas de whisky y 100 botellas de los más refinados licores de la década de los veinte.

Our inspector loved: *The romantic terrace overlooking the sea.*

Directions: Exit A10 at San Bartolomeo Al Mare, then follow signs for Diano Marina. Easy access from Genoa and Nice Airports.

Web: www.johansens.com/dianamajestic
E-mail: grandhotel@dianamajestic.com
Tel: +39 0183 402 727
Fax: +39 0183 403 040

Price Guide:
(closed mid-October - 23rd December)
single €100-230
double €120-240
suite €220-450
superior suite €350-1,500

  80   50     

GRAND HOTEL MIRAMARE

VIA MILITE IGNOTO, 30, 16038 SANTA MARGHERITA LIGURE - GENOVA, LIGURIA, ITALY

This historic hotel stands between lush green hills and deep blue sea in the heart of the Italian Riviera. Overlooking the promenade to the beautiful village of Portofino, this 100-year-old, family-owned hotel is one of the region's most exclusive venues. Its elegant ambience, impeccable service and culinary delights attract an international clientele who appreciate a comfortable blend of traditional style and modern amenities. Enjoy the wellness centre, eSPAce - Sense of Beauty. Guests are entitled to complimentary use of the fully-equipped public beach Miramare.

Cet hôtel chargé d'histoire est idéalement situé au cœur de la Riviera italienne entre les collines verdoyantes et le bleu profond de la mer. Surplombant le front de mer menant au village de Portofino, cette demeure centenaire familiale est l'un des sites les plus exclusifs de la région. Son atmosphère élégante, son service impeccable et ses délices culinaires attirent une clientèle internationale qui apprécie le mariage du style traditionnel et des techniques modernes. On se détend au centre de bien-être eSPAce – Sense of Beauty. L'entrée à la plage publique Miramare bien approvisionnée est gratuite.

Este histórico hotel goza de una idílica situación entre las verdes laderas y el azulado mar en el corazón de la Riviera italiana. Con vistas al paseo marítimo de la aldea de Portofino, el hotel, de centenaria regencia familiar, es uno de los establecimientos más exclusivos de la región. Su ambiente elegante, su servicio impecable y sus delicias gastronómicas de gourmet atraen a una clientela internacional que sabe apreciar la combinación de estilo tradicional y modernas instalaciones. Se puede relajar en el centro de salud: eSPAce – Sense of Beauty. Acceso a la playa pública Miramare totalmente equipada está gratuito.

Our inspector loved: *The blue sea facing the hotel and the tropical garden at the rear.*

Directions: A12 Genoa-Livorno road > turn off towards Rapallo and Santa Margherita (approximately a 40-minute drive from Genoa International Airport). Transport to and from the airport can be arranged.

Web: www.johansens.com/grandmiramare
E-mail: miramare@grandhotelmiramare.it
Tel: +39 0185 287013
Fax: +39 0185 284651

Price Guide:
single €155-235
double/twin €245-385
junior suite €380-600
suite €520-780

Hotel Vis à Vis

VIA DELLA CHIUSA 28, 16039 SESTRI LEVANTE (GE), ITALY

Set on an idyllic hillside overlooking Sestri Levante and 2 spectacular bays, this family-run hotel is surrounded by olive trees and is an enchanting place to stay. Guests will be mesmerised by the breathtaking view from the hotel's elegant restaurant Olimpo, which serves delicious food complemented by the finest regional wines. There is an open-air barbecue on the terrace and a magnificent roof garden, Ponte Zeus. An outside lift links the hotel to the centre of town.

Situé sur les flancs idylliques d'une colline avec vue sur le Sestri Levante et 2 baies superbes, cet hôtel familial entouré d'oliviers est un endroit enchanteur où séjourner. Les hôtes seront ébahis par la vue à couper le souffle qu'ils auront à partir de l'élégant restaurant Olimpo, qui sert une cuisine délicieuse accompagnée des meilleurs vins régionaux. Il y a un barbecue en plein air sur la terrasse et un jardin sur le toit magnifique, Ponte Zeus. Un ascenseur extérieur relie l'hôtel au centre-ville.

Ubicada en la ladera de una idílica colina con vistas a Sestri Levante y a 2 espectaculares bahías, este hotel familiar rodeado de olivos es un lugar encantador donde hospedarse. Los clientes quedarán hipnotizados por el sobrecogedor paisaje desde su elegante restaurante, Olimpo, que sirve una deliciosa carta acompañada de los mejores vinos de la región. Dispone también de barbacoa al aire libre en su terraza y de un magnífico jardín en la azotea, Ponte Zeus. Un ascensor exterior conecta el hotel con el centro urbano.

Our inspector loved: *The spectacular view of the 2 bays from the restaurant and terrace, and exquisite cuisine.*

Directions: A12 > Genoa > Livorno > Sestri Levante > follow the signs to Centro > the hotel is signposted.

Web: www.johansens.com/visavis
E-mail: visavis@hotelvisavis.com
Tel: +39 0185 42661
Fax: +39 0185 480853

Price Guide:
(closed 10th January - 10th February)
single €120–150

double €170–260
suite €290–380

Grand Hotel Villa Serbelloni

VIA ROMA 1, 22021 BELLAGIO, LAKE COMO, ITALY

Directions: A9 > exit Como Sud > follow directions to Bellagio.

Web: www.johansens.com/serbelloni
E-mail: inforequest@villaserbelloni.com
Tel: +39 031 950 216 or +39 031 956 450
Fax: +39 031 951 529

Price Guide: (closed mid-November - March)
single €225-260
double €355-560
suite €715-980

Built in the early 19th century, this majestic villa stands in a beautiful and sunny position on a promontory between the two halves of Lake Como, and has an air of grandeur and luxury that few can rival. Elegantly frescoed ceilings, stunning crystal chandeliers and lush carpeting are complemented by stylish antique pieces, whilst 2 restaurants serve the very best in international cuisine. 2 swimming pools, a private beach and a luxury health spa complete the feeling of total relaxation.

Cette villa majestueuse fut construite au début du XIXe siècle et se trouve dans un endroit ensoleillé sur un promontoire entre les deux parties du lac Como. Son air de grandeur et de luxe est incomparable. L'hôtel est pourvu de plafonds ornés de fresques élégantes, de lustres magnifiques de cristal, de tapis somptueux et de pièces antiques raffinées. Les 2 restaurants servent des plats délicieux internationaux, alors que les 2 piscines, une plage privée et un centre de remise en forme luxueux créent une ambiance de détente absolue.

Construida a principios del siglo XIX, esta majestuosa villa se erige en un bello y soleado promontorio sito en medio del Lago de Como. Muy pocos pueden igualar su grandioso y lujoso aspecto. Sus elegantes techos de frescos, sus impresionantes lámparas-araña de cristal y su suntuoso alfombrado se complementan con el estilo de sus antigüedades. Sus 2 restaurantes sirven lo mejor de la cocina internacional. 2 piscinas, una playa privada y un lujoso centro de salud-spa terminan de proporcionar la sensación de relax absoluto.

***Our inspector loved:** The unique, incomparable atmosphere.*

Bagni di Bormio Spa Resort

LOCALITÀ BAGNI NUOVI, 23038 VALDIDENTRO (SONDRIO), ITALY

Dating back to 1836, this is a stunning example of the architectural splendour of the Belle Epoque. The spacious public rooms are bedecked with period furnishings, beautiful frescoes and Murano glass chandeliers. The bedrooms are classically appointed while the white Carrara marble bathrooms, with thermal water Jacuzzi baths, add a touch of opulence. The opportunies to pamper oneself are endless and include 7 outdoor thermal water pools, Roman baths, caves with thermal springs and over 30 types of treatments.

Datant de 1836, cet hôtel est un magnifique exemple de la splendeur architecturale de la Belle Epoque. Les pièces communes, spacieuses, sont ornées de meubles d'époque, de superbes fresques et de chandeliers en verre de Murano. Les chambres sont dans un style classique et le marbre blanc de Carrare des salles de bains apporte une touche d'opulence. Les occasions de se faire dorloter sont infinies avec 7 piscines extérieures d'eau thermale, des bains Romains, des caves de sources thermales et plus de 30 soins différents.

Este es un ejemplo impactante del esplendor arquitectónico de la belle époque remontándose a 1836. Las espaciosas habitaciones comunes están decoradas con muebles de época, bonitos frescos y candelabros de cristal de Murano. Las habitaciones están amuebladas en estilo clásico y los cuartos de baño con mármol blanco de Carrara, los baños jacuzzi con agua termal añaden al conjunto un toque de opulencia. Hay un sinfín de oportunidades para darse un capricho que incluyen 7 piscinas exteriores de aguas termales, baños romanos, cuevas con manantiales termales y más de 30 clases de tratamientos.

Our inspector loved: *The splendid ballroom overlooking the valley, and the huge spa with hot spring water from 9 mountain sources.*

Directions: Milan > Lecco > E36 to Colico > E38 to Sondrio - Bormio (Valtellina).

Web: www.johansens.com/bagnidibormio
E-mail: info@bagnidibormio.it
Tel: +39 0342 901890
Fax: +39 0342 913511

Price Guide:
single €134-196
standard double (Oro) €180-270
standard double (Platino) €230-334
junior suite €230-334
suite €272-378

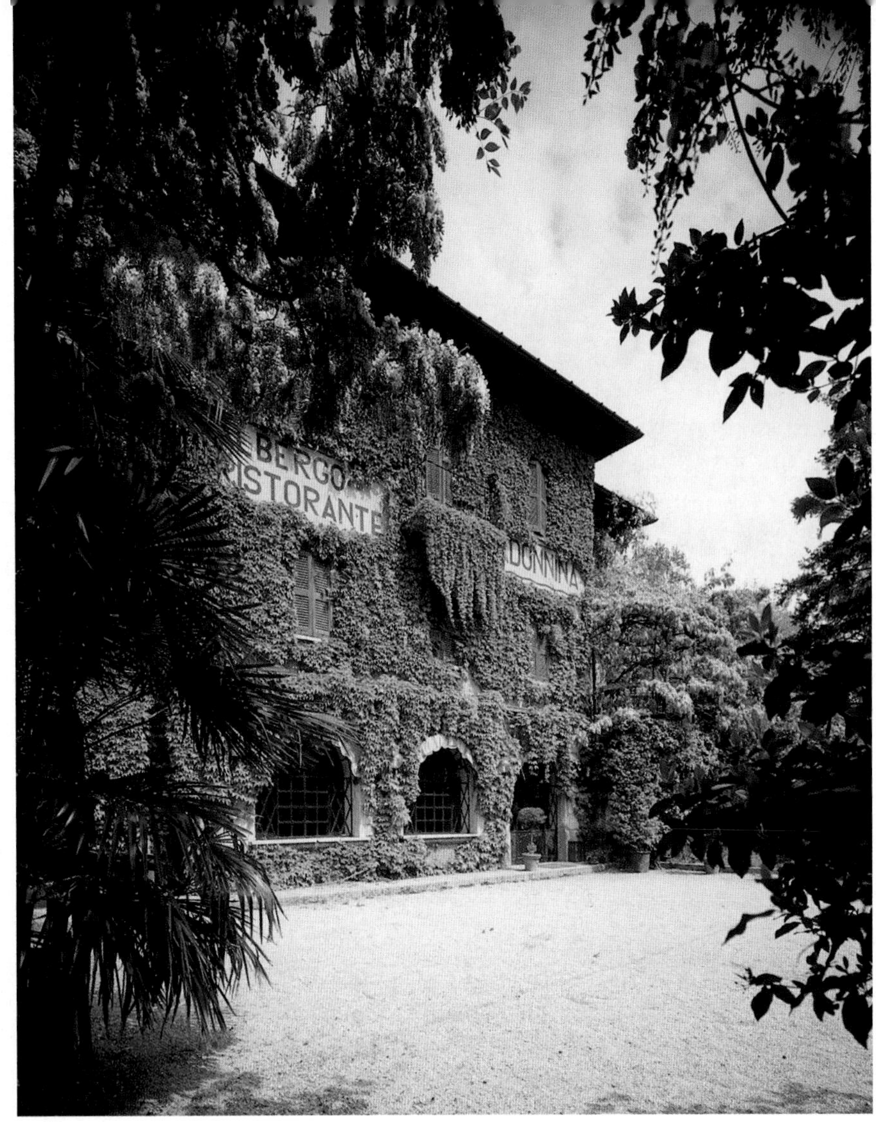

ALBERGO MADONNINA

LARGO LANFRANCO DA LIGURNO 1, 21050 CANTELLO - VARESE, ITALY

Directions: A8 (Auostrada dei Laghi) from Milan towards Varese > exit Gazzada > Tangenziale Varese Est towards Gaggiolo.

Web: www.johansens.com/madonnina
E-mail: info@madonnina.it
Tel: +39 0332 417 731
Fax: +39 0332 418 402

Price Guide: (breakfast €8, closed in January)
single €70
double €100
suite €200-250

Close to the Italian-Swiss border and Malpensa Airport this is a relaxing retreat for those wishing to enjoy tranquil country life and inhale the freshest of air or for a 1-2 night stopover ideally located on the way from Switzerland to Tuscany, Umbria and the south of Italy. This is also an ideal base for touring the region featuring Lugano and the lakes of Como and Maggiore. The colourful wisteria on the exterior contrasts to the simple yet elegant interior décor and furnishings. Guest rooms are comfortable, and the candle-lit cuisine is a delight.

Ce charmant hôtel situé proche de la frontière italo-suisse et de l'aéroport de Malpensa, est refuge parfait pour ceux qui souhaitent profiter de la vie à la campagne et respirer un air plus pur ou pour ceux qui souhaitent faire une halte de 1 ou 2 nuits entre la Suisse, la Toscane, l'Ombrie et le sud de l'Italie. C'est également une base parfaite pour visiter la région qui comprend Lugano et les lacs Majeur et de Côme. L'extérieur coloré par la glycine est en contraste avec la décoration et l'ameublement intérieur simple mais élégant. Les chambres sont confortables et les repas aux chandelles ravissants.

Cerca de la frontera entre Italia y Suiza y del aeropuerto de Malpensa, este hotel es un lugar de descanso y relax para aquellos que desean disfrutar de la tranquila vida campestre y respirar un aire más fresco, o para pasar 1 o 2 noches camino de Toscana, Umbría y el sur de Italia proveniente de Suiza. También es la base ideal para visitar la región en la que se encuentra Lugano y los lagos de Como y Maggiore. La vistosa glicina de color contrasta con el sencillo y al mismo tiempo elegante mobiliario y decoración interior. Las habitaciones son confortables y la cocina, servida a la luz de las velas, es una delicia.

Our inspector loved: *The hotel's charm of a bygone era, and exquisite cuisine.*

10 200

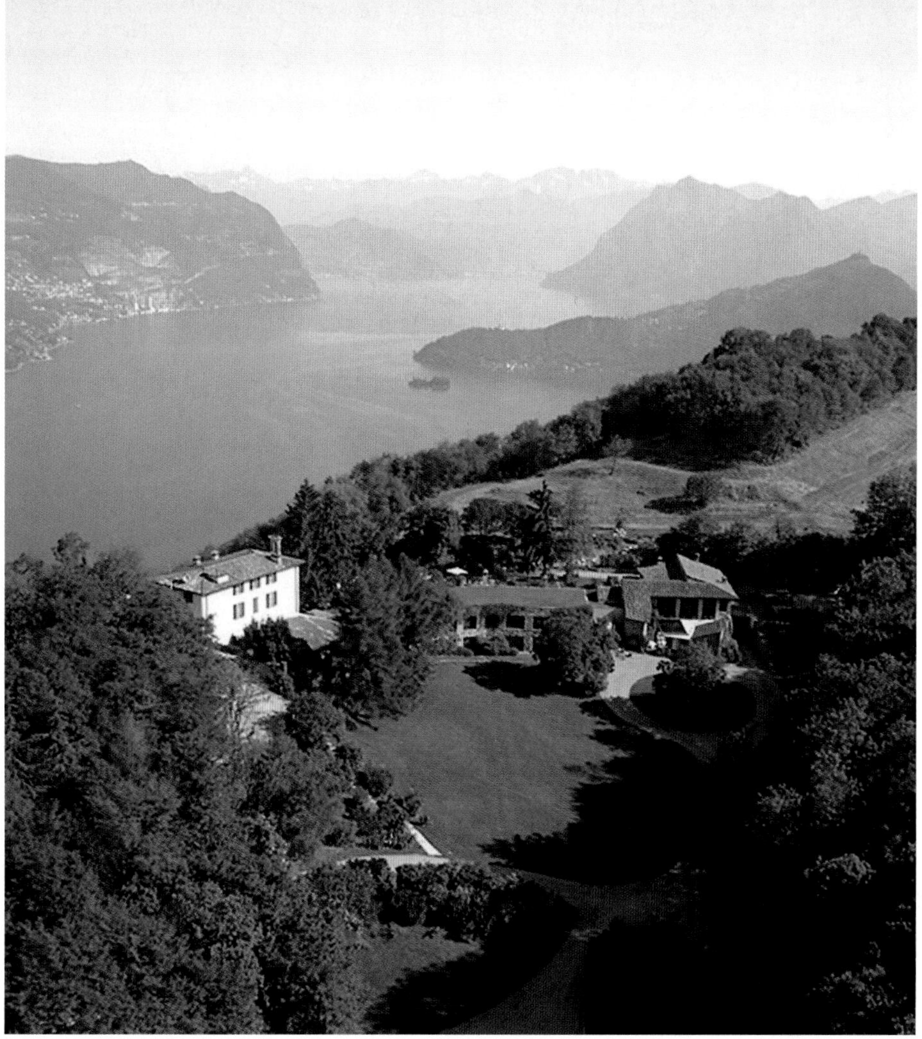

I Due Roccoli Relais

VIA SILVIO BONOMELLI, STRADA PER POLAVENO, 25049 ISEO (BRESCIA), ITALY

From the Iseo Hills amidst verdant private parkland, I Due Roccoli Relais looks down to the magnificent Lake Iseo and the Franciacorta wine region. Formerly an 18th-century aristocratic residence with annexes, this elegant hotel provides 16 bedrooms and 3 suites. Most have balconies or terraces that take advantage of the spectacular views. Romantic, refined and enchanting, the hotel is decorated with period furnishings and adorned with beautiful works of art. Delicious cuisine may be enjoyed by candlelight in the courtyard during the summer months.

Au sein de son parc verdoyant, le Relais I Due Roccoli surplombe des Collines d'Iseo, le magnifique lac du même nom et la région viticole de Franciacorta. Cet élégant hôtel propose 16 chambres et 3 suites dans une ancienne résidence aristocratique du XVIIIe siècle avec dépendances. La plupart des chambers ouvre sur un balcon ou une terrasse offrant des vues spectaculaires. Romantique, raffiné et enchanteur, cet hôtel est décoré avec un mobilier d'époque et orné d'œuvres d'art. Une cuisine délicieuse peut être dégustée aux chandelles dans la cour pendant des mois d'été.

I Due Roccoli Relais mira, desde los Montes de Iseo y rodeado de un verde parque privado, al espléndido Lago Iseo y a la región vinícola de Franciacorta. Este elegante hotel, antigua residencia aristocrática del siglo XVIII y dotada de anejos, dispone de 16 habitaciones y 3 suites. La mayoría tienen balcones o terrazas desde las cuales se puede disfrutar de unas espectaculares vistas. El hotel, romántico, refinado y encantador, está decorado con muebles de época y adornado con bellas obras de arte. En los meses de verano los clientes podrán disfrutar en el patio de su deliciosa carta a la luz de las velas.

Our inspector loved: *The romantic setting.*

Directions: A4 > exit Rovato > follow signs to Iseo > follow signs to Polaveno.

Web: www.johansens.com/idueroccoli
E-mail: relais@idueroccoli.com
Tel: +39 030 9822 977/8
Fax: +39 030 9822980

Price Guide: (room only, closed 1st November - mid-March)
single €97
double €130-150
suite €175

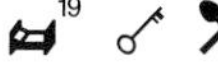

ITALY / LOMBARDY (LAKE GARDA - GARDONE RIVIERA)

Grand Hotel Gardone Riviera

VIA ZANARDELLI 84, 25083 GARDONE RIVIERA (BS), LAKE GARDA, ITALY

Directions: A4 (Milano - Venezia) > exit Desenzano > follow signs to Salò - Gardone.

Web: www.johansens.com/gardoneriviera
E-mail: ghg@grangardone.it
Tel: +39 0365 20261
Fax: +39 0365 22695

Price Guide: (closed November - March)
single €106-134
double €179-237
junior suite €227-285

Built in 1884, a refined atmosphere of a bygone era pervades the hotel. The elegantly decorated guest rooms and suites boast beautiful lakeside views. During summer a lunch buffet is served on the garden terrace and a romantic dinner, complete with stunning backdrop, can be enjoyed at the Veranda Restaurant. Winnies Bar has a relaxed ambience with live music and dancing. Facilites include a private lake promenade and beach, swimming pool, whirlpool, sauna, steam bath and tennis club nearby. 3 golf courses are within a 20-minute drive.

De cet hôtel magnifique construit en 1884, émane une atmosphère raffinée des temps passés. Les chambres et suites élégamment décorées s'enorgueillissent de vues splendides sur le lac. L'été, un buffet est servi pour le déjeuner dans le jardin en terrasse et un dîner romantique, sur une toile de fond superbe, peut être dégusté au restaurant Véranda. Le Bar Winnies offre une ambiance détendue, avec orchestre et piste de danse. Les hôtes ont accès à la promenade et à la plage privée au bord du lac, à la piscine, aux bains à remous et à vapeur, au sauna et au club de tennis tous proche. 3 cours de golf sont accessible en moins de 20 minutes de voiture.

Este magnífico hotel construido en 1884 rezuma un refinado estilo característico de épocas pasadas. Sus habitaciones y suites de elegante decoración alardean bellas vistas al lago. Durante el verano se sirve almuerzo-buffet en la terraza-jardín, y la romántica cena puede disfrutarse en el Veranda Restaurant en un inigualable entorno. El Winnies Bar le ofrece un ambiente relajado con música en directo y baile. Las instalaciones incluyen un paseo al borde del lago con playa privada, piscina, whirlpool, sauna y un club de tenis muy cerca del hotel. También hay 3 campos de golf a 20 minutos en coche.

***Our inspector loved:** The enchanting position and landscape.*

Hotel Bellerive

VIA PIETRO DA SALÒ 11, 25087 SALÒ (BS), ITALY

Located on the shores of glistening Lake Garda, this beautiful venue offers professional service and an inviting ambience that reflects the mesmerising colours of the lake and lights of the charming harbour nearby. The stylish bedrooms have been carefully decorated with fresh tones and comfortable furnishings. The hotel's 100km restaurant serves delicious Gardenese delicacies, whose ingredients are locally sourced and always fresh. The historical Salò quarter is nearby, where guests will delight in exploring the atmospheric narrow streets and gardens.

Situé sur les bords du miroitant lac de Garde, ce magnifique hôtel propose un service professionnel dans une ambiance accueillante qui reflète les fascinantes couleurs du lac et des lumières du port voisin. Les chambres stylées ont été soigneusement décorées de tons frais et de mobilier confortable. Le restaurant 100 km de l'hôtel sert de délicieux plats de la région de Garde à partir d'ingrédients frais et locaux. Le quartier historique Salò est proche et les hôtes prendront plaisir à en parcourir les rues étroites et les jardins.

Situado a orillas del deslumbrante lago de Garda, este bello lugar proporciona un servicio profesional y un cálido ambiente reflejo de los fascinantes colores del lago y las luces del encantador puerto cercano. Sus elegantes habitaciones han sido cuidadosamente decoradas con tonos frescos y cómodos muebles. El restaurante del hotel, 100 km, sirve deliciosas especialidades de la zona de Garda con ingredientes locales y siempre naturales. El histórico barrio Salò se encuentra cerca; allí los clientes podrán deleitarse explorando sus pintorescas callejuelas y jardines.

Our inspector loved: *The soothing colour scheme, and beautiful lamps.*

Directions: A4 > exit Desenzano or Brescia est > follow directions to Salò.

Web: www.johansens.com/bellerive
E-mail: info@hotelbellerive.it
Tel: +39 0365 520 410
Fax: +39 0365 290 709

Milan
Venice
Rome

Price Guide: (closed 15th December - 20th January)
single €120-185
double €160-235
suite €235-345

Hotel Marzia

VIA PEDRANA 388, 23030 LIVIGNO (SO), ITALY

Directions: From Milan > signs to Lecco > A36 to Colico > A38 to Sondrio - Bornio (Valtellina) > signs to Livigno. A bus to the town centre operates every 15 minutes.

Web: www.johansens.com/marziahotel
E-mail: info@marziahotel.it
Tel: +39 0342 996 020
Fax: +39 0342 971 070

Price Guide:
single €55-112
double €90-164
suite €130-220

This exuberant, welcoming hotel is situated within walking distance of the village centre in one of the most popular ski resorts of northern Italy. Built in 2002, a modern classic style pervades throughout and each well-equipped, vibrant bedroom and suite reflects the bright colour of a precious stone. Some have balconies and views over the snow-capped mountains and Lake Livigno. Relax in the cosy bar lounge or in the small wellness centre. Alternatively, enjoy cross-country runs, cycling or nearby skiing.

Cet accueillant et exubérant hôtel est situé à quelques minutes à pied du centre du village d'une des stations de ski les plus populaires de l'Italie du nord. Construit en 2002, un style moderne classique règne et chaque chambre et suites éclatante et bien équipée revêt la couleur vive d'une pierre précieuse. Certaines possèdent des balcons et ont vue sur les sommets enneigés et le Lac Livigno. Les hôtes peuvent se relaxer dans l'accueillant et confortable bar lounge ou le petit centre de bien-être. Alternativement, cross country, cyclisme ou ski tout proche sont possibles.

Este exuberante y acogedor hotel esta situado a pocos pasos del centro de la localidad, en una de las estaciones de esquí más conocidas del norte de Italia. Construido en 2002, el interior es de estilo clásico moderno y cada alegre habitación o suite, excelentemente acondicionada, refleja el vivo color de una piedra preciosa. Algunas disponen de balcones con vistas a las montañas nevadas y al lago Livigno. Los clientes podrán relajarse en el acogedor salón-bar o en el pequeño centro wellness. Por otra parte, pueden disfrutar de los senderos de esquí de fondo, hacer ciclismo, o aprovecharse de las cercanas pistas de esquí.

Our inspector loved: *The joyful atmosphere and the unusual display of precious stones by each bedroom door.*

L'Albereta

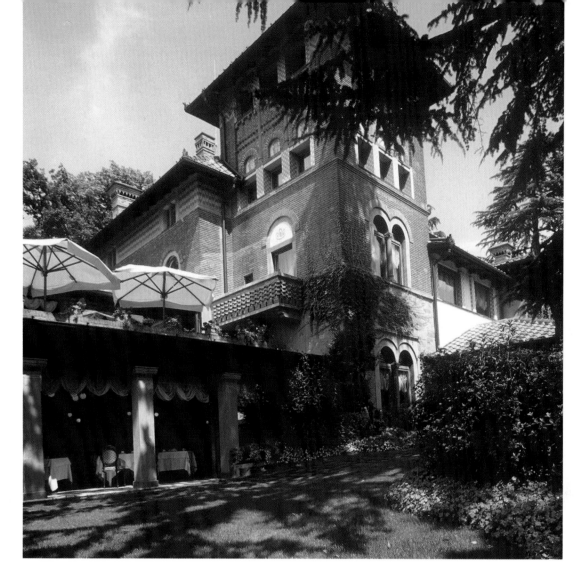

VIA VITTORIO EMANUELE II, NO 23, 25030 ERBUSCO (BS), ITALY

L'Albereta is a sumptuous hideaway set in the renowned wine region of Franciacorta with spectacular views of Lake Iseo and the Alps. Each bedroom is exquisitely decorated with period furnishings and decadent fabrics, and the most discerning palate will be impressed by the sublime dishes created by Gualtiero Marchesi. For those wishing to be pampered, The Henri Chenot Espace Vitalité is ideal. Nearby activities include an 18-hole golf course, shopping in Milan or a wine-tasting tour of the Moretti cellars.

L'Albereta est une superbe adresse située dans la très réputée région de Franciacorta avec des vues spectaculaires sur le lac Iseo et sur les Alpes. Chaque chambre est décorée avec raffinement avec des meubles d'époque et de magnifiques tissus et les palais les plus expérimentés seront impressionnés par les plats sublimes créés par Gualtiero Marchesi. Pour ceux voulant se faire dorloter, l'Espace Vitalité Henri Chenot est idéal. A proximité de l'hôtel se trouvent un parcours de golf 18 trous, Milan pour le shopping ou les caves de Moretti pour des dégustations de vins.

L'Albereta es un suntuoso escondite donde descansar situado en la celebrada región vinícola de Franciacorta con vistas espectaculares al Lago Iseo y a los Alpes. Cada habitación está decorada con exquisitez gracias al mobiliario de época y a sus decadentes telas. Hasta el más delicado de los paladares quedará impresionado por los sublimes platos creados por Gualtiero Marchesi. Para aquellos que deseen una estancia regalada, el Henri Chenot Espace Vitalité resulta ideal. Las actividades que se pueden realizar en las cercanías incluyen jugar en un campo de golf de 18 hoyos, hacer compras en Milán o un tour de cata de vinos de las bodegas de Moretti.

Our inspector loved: *The helpful staff who will gladly organise a variety of events for their guests.*

Directions: A4 Milano – Venezia road > exit Rovato.

Web: www.johansens.com/albereta
E-mail: info@albereta.it
Tel: +39 030 7760 550
Fax: +39 030 7760 573

Price Guide: (room only)
double (single occupancy) €190-430
double €230-580
suite €590-930

Hotel de la Ville

VIALE REGINA MARGHERITA 15, 20052 MONZA (MI), ITALY

Within a quiet residential town, a short distance from Milan and the Formula One race track, Hotel de la Ville stands opposite the former summer palace of the Royal House of Savoy. Warm hospitality, exquisitely furnished public rooms and attentive staff ensure a stress-free stay. Each bedroom is individually decorated and La Villa, originally an aristocratic home, offers 7 exclusively private bedrooms and suites. Guests may enjoy an apéritif in the American Bar before savouring the regional specialities served in the highly regarded Derby Grill, one of the finest restaurants in Italy.

Au coeur d'une ville résidentielle tranquille, proche de Milan et du circuit de Formule 1, Hôtel de la Ville fait face à l'ancienne résidence d'été de la famille Royale de Savoy. Accueil chaleureux, décoration extrêmement soignée et personnel attentif sont les garants d'un séjour sans stress. Chaque chambre est décorée de manière individuelle et La Villa, une ancienne maison de maître, offre 7 chambres et suites exclusives. On prend l'apéritif à l'American Bar avant de déguster les spécialités régionales au fameux Derby Grill, l'un des meilleurs restaurant d'Italie.

En una tranquila ciudad residencial, a corta distancia de Milán y de la pista de Fórmula 1, el Hotel de la Ville está situado frente al palacio de verano de la Casa Real de Saboya. Una acogedora hospitalidad junto con la exquisitez en el mobiliario de las zonas comunes y el atento servicio del personal le asegura una estancia relajada. Cada habitación está decorada individualmente y la Villa, originariamente un hogar aristocrático, ofrece 7 habitaciones y suites exclusivamente privadas. Los huéspedes pueden disfrutar el aperitivo en el Bar Americano antes de degustar las especialidades regionales que se sirven en el reputado Derby Grill, uno de los mejores restaurantes de Italia.

Our inspector loved: *The private collections of antiques and objets d'art.*

Directions: A4 > exit Sesto San Giovanni Cinisello Balsamo.

Web: www.johansens.com/hoteldelaville
E-mail: info@hoteldelaville.com
Tel: +39 039 3942 1
Fax: +39 039 367 647

Milan
Venice
Rome

Price Guide: (breakfast €25, closed 1st - 25th August and 24th December - 6th January)
single €187-207
double (single occupancy)€237
double €267-307
suite €417-467
villa €347-517

Petit Palais maison de charme

VIA MOLINO DELLE ARMI 1, 20123 MILAN, ITALY

Lovingly restored to its former splendour as a "Résidence de Charme", Petit Palais is an elegant and refined hotel in a central location from which to explore the heart of Milan. Attention to detail such as stucco works, curtain drapes, antique furnishings and expensive pieces of art create a lavish yet cosy ambience. Each of the 18 suites is delectably furnished and equipped with kitchenette and all modern facilities. Relax inside the lobby or "salotto" with its magnificent fireplace or outdoors on the roof garden terrace.

Amoureusement restauré à sa splendeur d'antan, comme "Résidence de Charme", Petit Palais est un hôtel élégant et raffiné, idéalement situé pour découvrir la ville de Milan. Une attention au détail telle que le stucage, les drapés de rideaux, les meubles anciens et les coûteuses œuvres d'arts créent une atmosphère somptueuse et douillette à la fois. Chacune des 18 suites est délicieusement meublée et équipée d'une kitchenette et de tout le confort moderne. Les hôtes peuvent se relaxer dans le lobby ou 'salotto' avec sa magnifique cheminée ou sur la terrasse sur le toit.

Restaurado con sumo cuidado para devolverle su antiguo esplendor como "Résidence de Charme", el Petit Palais se presenta como un hotel elegante, refinado y céntrico para quienes deseen explorar el corazón de Milán. El esmero puesto en los pequeños detalles tales como las obras realizadas en estuco, las cortinas, los muebles antiguos y las valiosas piezas de arte crean un ambiente fastuoso y al mismo tiempo acogedor. Cada una de las 18 suites está amueblada con gran exquisitez y equipada de una pequeña cocina y de todas las comodidades modernas. Los clientes pueden relajarse en el vestíbulo o "salotto" con su espléndida chimenea, o al aire libre en su terraza con jardín situada en el ático.

Our inspector loved: *The cosy ambience.*

Directions: Located in the centre of Milan.

Web: www.johansens.com/petitpalais
E-mail: info@petitpalais.it
Tel: +39 02 584 891
Fax: +39 02 584 40732

Price Guide: (room only)
suite (single occupancy) €209-330
suite €231-360
royal suite (single occupancy) €275-440
royal suite €302-480

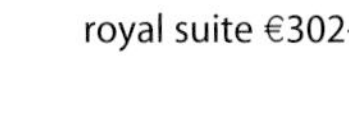

Castel di Luco

ACQUASANTA TERME, FRAZIONE CASTEL DI LUCO, 63041 (AP), ITALY

Directions: The nearest airports are Rome, Ancona (Falcunara) and Pescara. The nearest train station is S Benedetto del Tronto.

Web: www.johansens.com/casteldiluco
E-mail: casteldiluco@tiscali.it
Tel: +39 0736 802319
Fax: +39 0736 802319

Price Guide:
double €155

Over a thousand years of history pervade Castel di Luco, which has previously served as a private residence, a prison, a shelter for knights and a granary. Today, the young owners Laura and Francesco offer a warm welcome to their guests. 4 suites are located in the tiny hamlet which encircles the fortress. Each has original brick paving stones, travertine walls, wooden beamed ceilings and views of the surrounding countryside. The elegant restaurant, housed in the formerly frescoed hallways, serves authentic local cuisine.

Plus de mille ans d'Histoire imprègnent l'atmosphère de Castel di Luco, qui fût une résidence privée, une prison, un refuge pour chevaliers et un silo. Aujourd'hui, les jeunes propriétaires Laura et Francesco acceuillent chaleureusement leurs hôtes. Les 4 suites sont situées dans le petit hameau au pied de la forteresse. Chacune a un carrelage en briques, des murs en pierre de travertin, des poutres au plafond et embrasse une vue sur la campagne environnante. L'élégant restaurant, situé dans le vestibule orné de fresques, sert une authentique cuisine locale.

En sus más de mil años de historia Castel di Luco ha sido residencia privada, cárcel, refugio de nobles caballeros y granero. Hoy sus jóvenes propietarios, Laura y Francesco, ofrecen una calurosa bienvenida a sus clientes. Sus 4 suites se encuentran situadas en una pequeña aldea que rodea la fortaleza. Todas conservan sus adoquines originales en ladrillo, muros de travertino, techos de vigas de madera y ofrecen vistas al paisaje circundante. Su elegante restaurante, ubicado en las antiguas salas adornadas con frescos, sirve auténticos platos de cocina local.

Our inspector loved: *Wining and dining in the restaurant with its frescoed walls and vaulted ceilings.*

Hotel Cristallo

PIAZZA DEGLI ALBERGHI, 13021 ALAGNA (VC), ITALY

Nestled within the village of Alagna at the foot of majestic Monte Rosa, one of the highest mountains in Europe, world famous for heli-ski and its trekking routes, Hotel Cristallo is simply charming. Its inspirational interior creates a breathtaking balance between local ancient culture and modern design, enhanced by warm colour schemes and a cosy ambience. The hotel's gourmet restaurant is superb and offers a wide choice of excellent Piedmontese wines. The Grand Tour of the Alps passes the hotel.

Au cœur du village d'Alagna, au pied du majestueux Mont Rose, l'une des plus hautes montagnes d'Europe à la renommée mondiale pour l'héliski et l'alpinisme, l'hôtel Cristallo est simplement charmant. Sa décoration intérieure inspirée est un mélange original entre la culture locale ancienne et le design moderne, le tout relevé par des combinaisons de couleurs chaudes et une ambiance douillette. Le restaurant gastronomique de l'hôtel est magnifique et propose un large choix de vins piedmontais. Le Grand Tour des Alpes passe par l'hôtel.

Este encantador hotel está ubicado en el pueblo de Alagna a los pies del majestuoso Monte Rosa, una de las montañas más altas de Europa y famosa en el mundo entero por sus rutas de trekking y lugar donde practicar heli-eski. Su decoración interior muestra un sorprendente equilibrio entre la cultura local antigua y el diseño moderno, que se acentúa con colores cálidos y ambiente acogedor. Dispone de un magnífico restaurante gourmet que ofrece una amplia selección de excelentes vinos del Piemonte. El Gran Tour de los Alpes pasa por delante del hotel.

Our inspector loved: *The soothing colours, and the artistic décor in the bedrooms.*

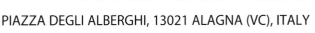

Directions: Milano Airport > A26 Genova/Alessandria > exit Romagnano-Ghemme > signs to Alagna Valsesia.

Web: www.johansens.com/cristallo
E-mail: info@hotelcristalloalagna.com
Tel: +39 0163 922 822/23
Fax: +39 0163 922 821

Price Guide: (closed during May and November)
double €160-230
junior suite €200-350
suite €300-500

Hotel Bes

VIA NAZIONALE 18, 10050 CLAVIÈRE (TO), ITALY

Directions: A32 > Torino > Bardonecchia > Frejus > exit Oulx > SS24 Monginevro. The nearest airpot is Torino Caselle.

Web: www.johansens.com/hotelbes
E-mail: hotelbes@hotelbes.com
Tel: +39 0122 878735
Fax: +39 0122 444502

Price Guide: (closed during May and October)
single €89-170
double €79-230
suite €109-290

Hotel Bes is located directly in front of the ski slopes in Clavière, on the border with France. Surrounded by peaks of 3,000 metres, guests are only 30 metres from the Vialattea and French tracks. Each guest room is well appointed and fitted with beautiful wooden furniture; 4 executive rooms have canopy beds and the suites boast Jacuzzis. Public rooms display original masterpieces by Picasso and Giacomo Balla. Traditional local dishes and superb Italian meals are complemented by a vast selection of wines available from the cellar.

L'hôtel est situé à l'orée des pistes de ski de Clavière à la frontière française. Entouré de sommets de 3000m, les hôtes ne sont qu'à 30m des domaines de Vialattea et des domaines français. Chaque chambre est équipée d'un beau mobilier en bois. 4 chambres de catégorie exécutive ont des lits à baldaquins et les suites disposent de jacuzzi. Les salles communes sont ornées d'originaux de Picasso et Giacomo Balla. Les plats locaux traditionnels et une cuisine italienne succulente sont accompagnés d'une vaste sélection de vins disponibles au cellier.

El hotel Bes se encuentra justo delante de las pistas de ski de Clavière, en la frontera con Francia. Rodeados de picos de 3000 metros, los clientes se encuentran a sólo 30 metros de las pistas de nieve de Vialattea y de Francia. Todas las habitaciones tienen un excelente acabado y un bello mobiliario de madera. 4 habitaciones de ejecutivos poseen camas con baldaquino y las suites incluyen jacuzzi. Los salones comunes muestran obras maestras originales de Picasso y Giacomo Balla. Tanto los platos locales tradicionales como la estupenda comida italiana van acompañados de una amplia selección de vinos de la bodega.

Our inspector loved: *Its ideal location for skiers and the vicinity to Turin as well as its enchanting surroundings.*

Albergo L'Ostelliere

FRAZIONE MONTEROTONDO 56, 15065 GAVI (AL), PIEMONTE, ITALY

This former farmhouse has been rebuilt, extended and refurbished into a 21st-century luxury 4-star hotel resort surrounded by well-stocked vineyards in the beautiful Piemontese hills, 50km from Genoa. Its peaceful and tranquil setting is complemented by antique furnishings, attractive wall art as well as refined and comfortable en-suite accommodation. A prestigious gourmet restaurant serves exquisite local and national cuisine and an excellent selection of wines from an 18th-century cellar.

Cette ancienne ferme a été reconstruite, agrandie et transformée en un luxueux resort hôtel 4 étoiles du XXIe siècle, et est entourée de vignes sur les magnifiques pentes du Piemont, à 50 kms de Gêne. En plus de son emplacement calme et tranquille, l'hôtel est décoré de meubles antiques, de superbes tableaux modernes et offre un hébergement confortable et raffiné. Un restaurant gastronomique prestigieux sert une délicieuse cuisine régionale et nationale ainsi qu'une excellente sélection de vins gardée dans une cave du XVIIIe siècle.

Esta antigua granja ha sido reconstruida, expandida y reamueblada para convertirla en un lujoso complejo hotelero de 4 estrellas propio del siglo XXI. Está rodeado de generosos viñedos en las bellas colinas del Piemonte, a 50 kms de Génova. Su tranquilo y apacible emplazamiento se complementa con mobiliario de anticuario, atractivo arte mural así como refinado y cómodo alojamiento en-suite. Un prestigioso restaurante gourmet sirve una exquisita carta de platos locales y nacionales y una excelente selección de vinos procedentes de una bodega del siglo XVIII.

***Our inspector loved:** The spectacular view of the vineyards, and the enchanting 18th-century cellars.*

Directions: A7 (Milan – Genoa) > exit Serravalle Scrivia.

Web: www.johansens.com/ostelliere
E-mail: info@ostelliere.it
Tel: +39 0143 607 801
Fax: +39 0143 607 811

Price Guide:
double €145–€185
suite €200–€630

Villa dal Pozzo d'Annone

STRADA STATALE DEL SEMPIONE 5, 28832 BELGIRATE (VB), LAKE MAGGIORE, ITALY

Idyllically located on the shores of Lake Maggiore, this exclusive villa stands within beautiful gardens and park. Reminiscent of a Victorian stately home, featuring original 15th-19th-century furnishings, guests may stay in one of 6 suites within the main villa or one of 12 luxurious rooms located in Borgo Ottocentesco, the restored former homes of gardeners and naval men. Enjoy an apéritif by the pool or in the cosy bar before dinner in the Bistrot-Wine Bar, accompanied by fine Italian wines. Sailing and water skiing can be arranged.

Idéalement situé sur les rives du Lac Majeur, cette villa prestigieuse se dresse au milieu de superbes jardins dans un parc. Evoquant toute sa splendeur de l'époque victorienne et agrémentée de meubles originaux du XVe au XIXe siècle, la villa accueille ses hôtes dans l'une des 6 suites du bâtiment principal ou l'une des 12 chambres luxueuses dans l'annexe située à Borgo Ottocentesco, anciennes maisons rénovées du personnel. L'apéritif pourra être apprécié près de la piscine ou au bar confortable avant de dîner au Bistrot-Bar à Vins en dégustant de délicieux vins italiens. Voile et ski nautique peuvent être organisés.

Idealmente ubicada en las orillas del lago Maggiore, este exclusiva villa se alza entre atractivos jardines y parques. Evocadora de una casa solariega victoriana, destacan en ella su mobiliario original de los siglos XV al XIX. Los huéspedes pueden elegir su estancia entre una de las 6 suites en la villa principal o en una de las 12 lujosas habitaciones situadas en Borgo Ottocentesco, las antiguas casas restauradas de los jardineros y de los hombres de la marina. Disfrute el aperitivo junto a la piscina o en el acogedor bar antes de cenar en la vinoteca Bistro, acompañado de los deliciosos vinos italianos. Navegación y esquí acuático pueden ser organizados.

Directions: A26 > exit Arona. 35km from Malpensa Airport.

Web: www.johansens.com/dalpozzodannone
E-mail: info@villadalpozzodannone.com
Tel: +39 0322 7255
Fax: +39 0322 772021

Price Guide:
(the villa is open from Easter - October and Borgo Ottocentesco is open all year)
suite €250-620

Milan
Venice
Turin
Rome

Our inspector loved: *The amazingly spacious bathrooms in the main villa.*

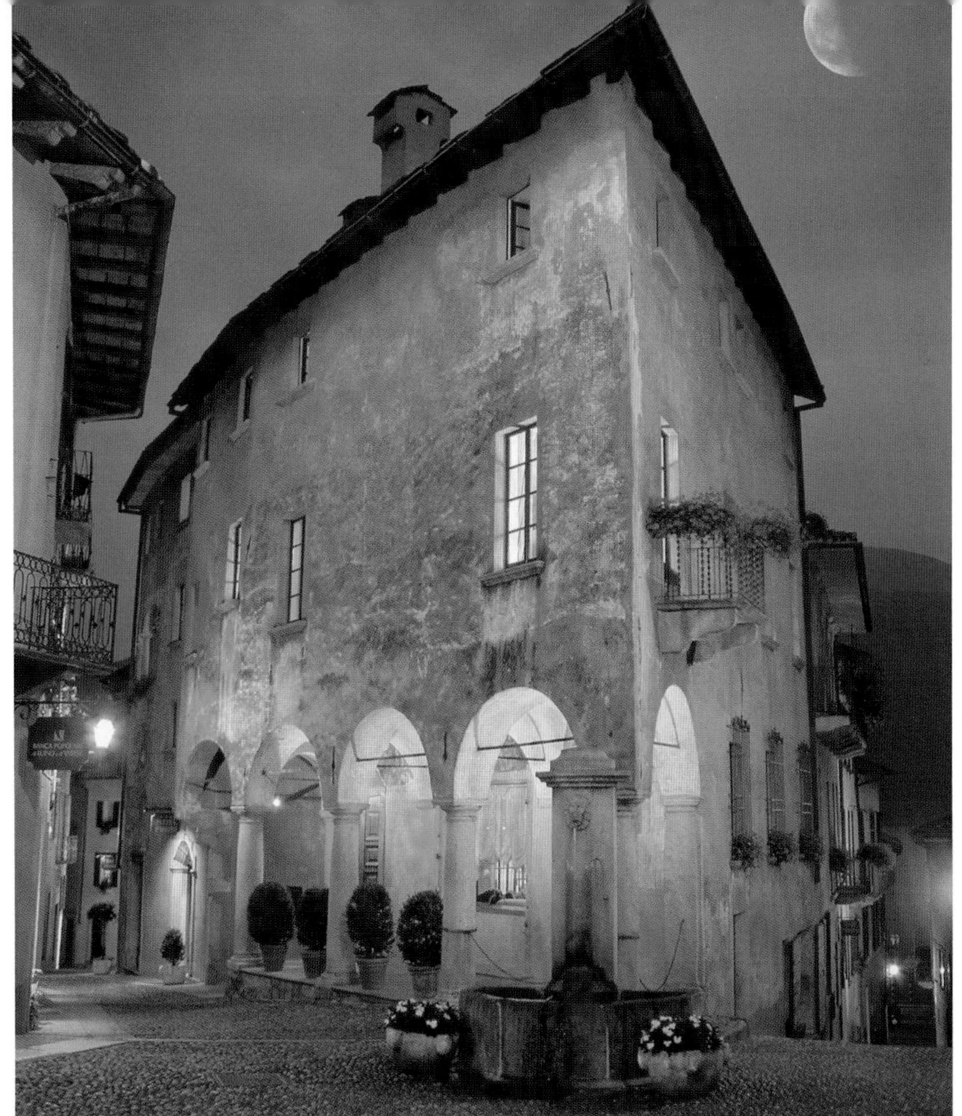

HOTEL PIRONI

VIA MARCONI 35, 28822 CANNOBIO, LAKE MAGGIORE (VB), ITALY

This small hotel stands on the shore of Lake Maggiore, near Italy's border with Switzerland and the medieval village of Cannobio. Housed in a 15th-century building that was originally a Franciscan monastery, this hotel has a magical atmosphere, largely due to a skilful restoration combining romantic, cosy rooms, original frescoes, antiques, vaulted ceilings, stone columns and a gentle touch of modern design. Guests have access to a private swimming pool and may wish to visit the 15,000m^2 park nearby.

Ce petit hôtel se situe sur les rives du Lac Majeur, près de la frontière suisse et du village médiéval de Cannobio. L'hôtel était à l'origine un monastère Franciscain du XVe siècle. Il y règne aujourd'hui une atmosphère magique grâce à l'habile restauration qui allie des chambres romantiques et confortables, des fresques originales, des antiquités, des plafonds voûtés, des colonnes en pierre et une subtile touche moderne. Les hôtes ont accès à la piscine privée et peuvent visiter le parc tout proche, qui s'étend sur 15000m^2.

Este pequeño hotel está situado a orillas del lago Maggiore, cerca de la frontera de Italia con Suiza y de la aldea medieval de Cannobio. Instalado en un edificio del siglo XV que fuera originariamente un monasterio franciscano, el hotel proporciona un ambiente mágico gracias en buena parte a su eficiente restauración, en la que se combinan las habitaciones acogedoras y románticas, los frescos originales, las antigüedades, los techos abovedados, las columnas de piedra y un suave toque de modernidad en el diseño. Los huéspedes tienen acceso a una piscina privada y pueden disfrutar del parque de 15.000 m^2 cuadrados que esta cerca del hotel.

Our inspector loved: *The breakfast room with frescoed ceiling and walls, and the terracotta floor.*

Directions: A26 Genova - Gravellona > exit Baveno/Stresa > follow signs to Locarno (Switzerland).

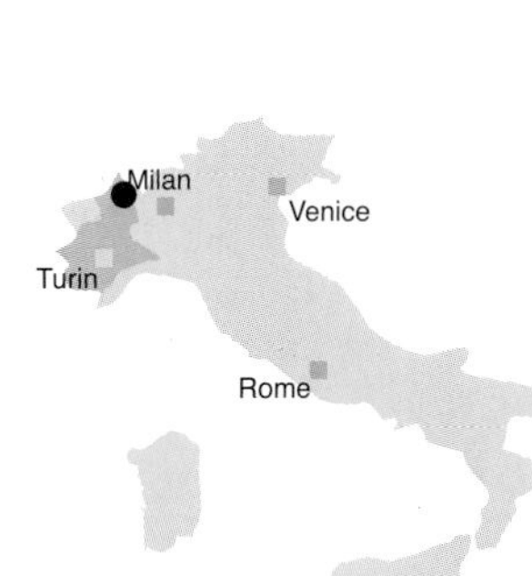

Web: www.johansens.com/hotelpironi
E-mail: info@pironihotel.it
Tel: +39 0323 70624
Fax: +39 0323 72184

Price Guide:
(closed 12th November - 17th March)
single €110
double €135-160

HOTEL VILLA AMINTA

VIA SEMPIONE NORD 123, 28838 STRESA (VB), ITALY

Directions: A8 motorway from Milan towards Lago Maggiore > exit Carpugnino > follow signs to Stresa.

Web: www.johansens.com/aminta
E-mail: booking@villa-aminta.it
Tel: +39 0323 933 818
Fax: +39 0323 933 955

Price Guide: (room only,
closed November - beginning of March)
double €204.60-354.20
junior suite €528
suite €528-752.40

Milan
Venice
Turin
Rome

This recently renovated 5-star de luxe hotel is a charming villa situated on the shores of Lake Maggiore, one of the most enchanting lakes in Italy. All bedrooms have a romantic décor, stucco works, precious furniture and look out over the gorgeous lake. Gastronomic delights are served in the elegant Il Mori and Mediterranean cuisine is available in the lake-facing Le Isole restaurant. Sightseeing tours, lake cruises and water-skiing are just some of the activities guests may enjoy, whilst nearby places of interest include Isola Bella, Villa Pallavicino and Locarno.

Ce charmant et luxueux hôtel 5 étoiles rénové récemment, est situé sur les bords du Lac Majeur, l'un des lacs les plus enchanteurs d'Italie. Les chambres s'ouvrent sur de merveilleuses vues sur le lac et ont toutes un décor romantique: ornements en stuc et meubles de valeur. Des plaisirs gastronomiques sont servis à l'élégant Il Mori et une cuisine méditerranéenne est proposée au restaurant Le Isole qui fait face au lac. De nombreuses activités sont disponibles, telles que des excursions, des croisières sur le lac et du ski nautique. Parmi les sites proches à visiter, on compte Isola Bella, Villa Pallavicino et Locarno.

Este hotel de lujo 5 estrellas recientemente renovado es una encantadora villa a la orilla del lago Maggiore, uno de los lagos más fantásticos de Italia. Todas las habitaciones poseen un décor romántico, trabajos en estuco, mobiliario precioso y vistas al maravilloso lago. Delicias de la gastronomía se sirven en el elegante Il Mori, y el restaurante Le Isole, con vistas al lago, ofrece cocina mediterránea. Visitas turísticas, cruceros por el lago y esquí acuático son algunas de las actividades que se pueden llevar a cabo, y hay lugares interesantes en los alrededores, como Isola Bella, Villa Pallavicino y Locarno.

45 110

Relais Il Borgo

VIA BILETTA 60, 14030 PENANGO (AT), ITALY

Amidst the Monferrato Hills in Cioccaro village, stands the enchanting Relais Il Borgo. Originally a cluster of farms, the Firato family have successfully restored and converted the buildings into a charming 8-bedroomed hotel. A relaxed, away-from-it-all atmosphere pervades the property, which is enhanced by warm hospitality. All of the bedrooms overlook the pool and vineyards, and gourmet food is served in the restaurant alongside a good regional wine list.

Au cœur des collines de Monferrato dans le village de Cioccaro se trouve l'enchanteur Relais Il Borgo. La famille Firato a restauré et converti avec succès ce groupe de fermes en un ravissant hôtel de 8 chambres. Une atmosphère de détente et d'isolement, renforcée par un accueil chaleureux, règne sur la propriété. Toutes les chambres surplombent la piscine et les vignes, et une cuisine gastronomique est servie au restaurant accompagnée d'une excellente carte de vins régionaux.

El encantador Relais Il Borgo se encuentra en la aldea de Cioccaro, entre los Montes de Monferrato. La familia Firato ha restaurado magníficamente lo que originariamente era un conjunto de granjas, convirtiendo tales edificios en un precioso hotel de 8 habitaciones. Un ambiente tranquilo y relajado inunda todo el inmueble, acrecentado por una calurosa hospitalidad. Todas las habitaciones dan a la piscina y a los viñedos. El restaurante ofrece una cocina gourmet junto a una buena carta de vinos regionales.

Our inspector loved: *The cosy atmosphere, and the convenient location.*

Directions: A21 > Toriso-Piacenza > exit Asti east > follow signs to Calliano-Moncalvo. A26 Genova-Gravellona > exit Casale Monferrato > follow signs to Moncalvo.

Milan
Venice
Turin
Rome

Web: www.johansens.com/relaisilborgo
E-mail: ilborgodicioccaro@virgilio.it
Tel: +39 0141 921272
Fax: +39 0141 923067

Price Guide:
(closed mid-December - end January)
single €100
double €120

Relais Villa San Martino

VIA TARANTO, ZONA G - 59, 74015 MARTINA FRANCA (TA), ITALY

Idyllically set in a natural park surrounded by oak, eucalyptus, pine and olive trees, Villa San Martino was built on the site of a 19th-century villa. From the grandest to the smallest, all rooms are elegant, inviting and comfortable with a warm, unpretentious atmosphere. The restaurant, Duca di Martina, serves exquisite Mediterranean cuisine featuring local seafood. To enhance the perfect balance of care and pleasure visit the luxurious hammam-style Oasis spa, which offers multisensorial treatments for the face and body.

Situé dans un parc naturel entouré de chênes, d'eucalyptus, de pins et d'oliviers, Villa San Martino fut construite au site d'une villa du XIXe siècle. De la plus grande à la plus petite, toutes les pièces sont élégantes, accueillantes et confortables et l'atmosphère est chaleureuse et sans prétentions. Le restaurant, Duca di Martina, sert une délicieuse cuisine méditerranéenne à base de fruits de mer locaux. Offrant une combinaison parfaite de soins et de plaisir, le Spa luxueux Oasis au style d'un hammam offre des traitements de visage et corps multisensoriels.

Idílicamente enclavada en el seno de un parque natural rodeado de olmos, eucaliptos, pinos y olivos, Villa San Martino fue construida en el lugar que ocupaba una villa del siglo XIX. Todas las habitaciones, desde las más grandiosas a las más pequeñas, son elegantes, acogedoras y cómodas y su ambiente cálido y sencillo. El restaurante, Duca di Martina, sirve excelente comida mediterránea que incluye marisco de la zona. Para conseguir el equilibrio perfecto entre placer y esmero, no deje de visitar el spa "Oasis", diseñado al estilo de un lujoso hammam y el en cual podrá recibir diversos tratamientos multisensoriales faciales y corporales.

Our inspector loved: *The relaxing ambience, art, culture, and good food.*

Directions: Bari Airport is 75km away. Brindisi Airport is 60km away.

Web: www.johansens.com/martino
E-mail: info@relaisvillasanmartino.com
Tel: +39 080 480 5152
Fax: +39 080 485 77 19

Price Guide:
single €200-240
double €240-280
suite €350-430

Villa Las Tronas

LUNGOMARE VALENCIA 1, 07041 ALGHERO (SS), ITALY

Until the 1940s this 5-star hotel was the residence of Italian royalty during their holidays in Sardinia, and today it retains a tranquil, aristocratic ambience. A short distance from the centre of Alghero, the villa is an exclusive retreat, and all of the distinct, classically furnished rooms and suites have either sea or garden views. The panoramic restaurant serves refined Mediterranean cuisine by candlelight while piano and flute music is played in the background. Tea and cocktails can be enjoyed in the bar. There is also a wellness centre and meditation room.

Jusque dans les années 1940 cet hôtel 5 étoiles était la résidence de la famille Royale d'Italie lors de ses séjours en Sardaigne. Villa Las Tronas a gardé aujourd'hui sa tranquillité et son atmosphère aristocratique. A deux pas du centre de Alghero, la villa est une oasis exclusive et toutes les chambres différentes et meublées dans un style classique ont vues sur la mer ou sur la jardin. Le restaurant panoramique sert une cuisine Méditerranéenne aux chandelles avec piano et flûte joués en musique de fond. Des cocktails ou du thé sont proposés au bar. Egalement disponibles un centre de remise en forme et une salle de méditation.

Hasta los años 40, este hotel de 5 estrellas fue la residencia estival de la realeza italiana en Cerdeña, y aún hoy mantiene ese mismo ambiente tranquilo y aristocrático. Situada a corta distancia del centro de Alghero, la villa ofrece un descanso exclusivo. Todas las habitaciones y suites, distintas y decoradas con muebles clásicos, tienen vistas al mar o al jardín. El restaurante panorámico sirve cocina refinada mediterránea a la luz de las velas y con musica de piano y flauta al fondo. El té de la tarde y cocteles se pueden tomar en el bar. Tambien hay un centro wellness y una sala de meditacion.

Our inspector loved: *The fascinating atmosphere.*

Directions: The nearest airport is Alghero. The hotel will provide guests with detailed directions.

Web: www.johansens.com/lastronas
E-mail: info@hvlt.com
Tel: +39 079 981 818
Fax: +39 079 981 044

Price Guide:
single €180-215
double €210-350
suite €450-520

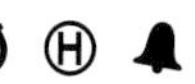

Grand Hotel in Porto Cervo

LOCALITÀ CALA GRANU, 07020 PORTO CERVO (SS), ITALY

Directions: Olbia > Porto Cervo / Costa Smeralda > main road to Porto Cervo Marina sign > Cala Granu / Cala del Faro > 800m > hotel is on right-hand side.

Web: www.johansens.com/portocervo
E-mail: hotelinportocervo@tiscali.it
Tel: +39 0789 91533
Fax: +39 0789 91508

Price Guide: (closed 10th October - April)
standard €72-195
superior €102-250
half board:
standard €92-220
superior €124-295

In the charming bay of Cala Granu, and just 2 kilometres from the famous town square, stands this new luxury hotel. Most of the rooms and suites have sea views, furnished balconies or terraces and modern amenities. There are 2 restaurants, including the recently opened Orange, which serves dinner by reservation only. The hotel is proud of its panoramic swimming pool and the fitness centre, illuminated tennis courts and fully-equipped sunbathing area at the beach.

Ce nouvel hôtel de luxe se trouve dans la ravissante baie de Cala Granu et à seulement 2 kilomètres de la fameuse place de la ville. La majorité des chambres et suites ont vues mer, des balcons ou terrasses équipées et tout l'équipement moderne. Il y a 2 restaurants, dont celui récemment ouvert "Orange" qui est sur réservation uniquement. La piscine panoramique, le centre de remise en forme, les courts de tennis illuminés et la plage équipée pour les bains de soleil font la fierté de l'hôtel.

En la encantadora bahía de Cala Granu y a sólo 2 kilómetros de la famosa plaza de la localidad, se levanta este nuevo hotel de lujo. La mayoría de las habitaciones y suites disponen de vistas al mar, balcones o terrazas amuebladas y modernas instalaciones. Tiene 2 restaurantes, uno de los cuales, el recientemente abierto Orange, sirve cenas unicamente haciendo reserva previa. El hotel se siente orgulloso de su panorámica piscina y centro de fitness, sus pistas de tenis iluminadas y su zona totalmente equipada para tomar el sol en la playa.

Our inspector loved: *The sea views.*

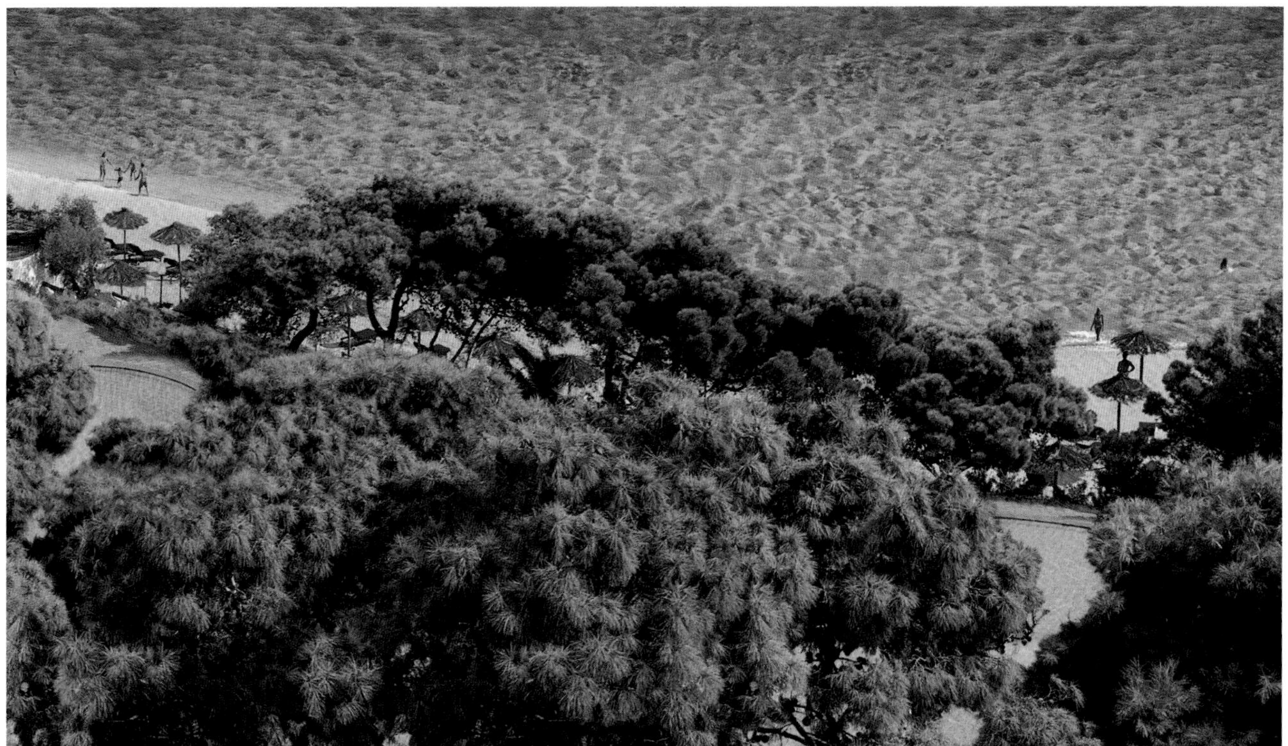

Villa del Parco and Spa at Forte Village

SS 195, KM 39.600, SANTA MARGHERITA DI PULA, 09010 CAGLIARI, ITALY

Lush surroundings and 5-star service are hallmarks of Villa del Parco and Spa, one of 7 sophisticated hotels and 25 suites that comprise the Forte Village, recognised as a leader among Italy's most luxurious resorts. Bedrooms are spacious, delightfully decorated and furnished, have a large terrace or garden and marble bathrooms with whirlpool. The top-floor outdoor restaurant, Belvedere, serves excellent Italian cuisine. Set within a botanical garden, Thermae del Forte offers a variety of treatments, has 6 open-air thalassotherapy pools, Turkish bath and gym.

Environnement luxuriant et service 5étoiles sont les distinctions de Villa del Parco et Spa, l'un des 7 hôtels et 25 suites sophistiqués que comporte le Forte Village, reconnu comme le meilleur des complexe de luxe italiens. Les chambres sont spacieuses, délicieusement décorées, ont une grande terrasse ou un jardin et des salles de bains en marbre avec bain bouillonnant. Le restaurant Belvedere, en plein air au dernier étage sert une excellente cuisine italienne. Situé dans un jardin botanique, Thermae del Forte offre une variété de soins, 6 piscines de thalassothérapie en plein air, un bain turc et une salle de remise en forme.

Sus suntuosos alrededores y un servicio de 5* son las señas de identidad de Villa del Parco y Spa, uno de los 7 exquisitos hoteles y 25 suites que componen la Forte Village, considerada como la principal de entre los centros turísticos de lujo de Italia. Las habitaciones son amplias, están magníficamente decoradas y disponen de una gran terraza o jardín y cuartos de baño de mármol con remolinos. El restaurante exterior del último piso, Belvedere, sirve una cocina italiana excelente. Ubicado en un jardín botánico, los Thermae del Forte ofrecen tratamientos, 6 piscinas de talassoterapia al aire libre, baño de vapor y gimnasio.

Our inspector loved: *The exclusive ambience, impeccable service, and abundance of facilities.*

Directions: A 40-minute drive from Cagliari Airport.

Web: www.johansens.com/villadelparco
E-mail: forte.village@fortevillage.com
Tel: +39 070 92171
Fax: +39 070 921246

Price Guide:
(half-board, closed 1st October - 12th May)
double €700-1,210

GRAND HOTEL ARCIDUCA

VIA G FRANZA, 98055 LIPARI (ME), ISOLE EOLIE, ITALY

Lipari is the largest island of the Aeolian archipelago, and the hotel was named for and inspired by the Archduke Luigi Salvatore of Austria, once a frequent visitor to these shores. Built with a noble elegance, this hamlet of 3 buildings is located in a quiet, yet central part of the old village and is close to Lipari's Castle, the main street and the small beach of Portinente. Bedrooms offer a wide range of amenities, and guests can dine on the terrace overlooking the pool.

Lipari est la plus grande île de l'archipel des îles Eolienne et l'hôtel fut inspiré et nommé d'après l'Archiduc Luigi Salvatore d'Autriche, fréquent visiteur de ces côtes. Construit avec une élégance majestueuse, ce hameau de 3 bâtiments est situé dans une partie calme et pourtant centrale du vieux village, près du château de Lipari, de la rue principale et de la petite plage de Portinente. Les chambres sont très bien équipées et les hôtes peuvent dîner sur la terrasse surplombant la piscine.

Lipari es la isla más grande del archipiélago de Eolio. El nombre del hotel es homenaje e inspiración del que fuera un día un asiduo visitante de este lugar, el Archiduque Luigi Salvatore de Austria. Construida con refinada elegancia, esta aldea de tan solo 3 edificios se encuentra en un lugar tranquilo y al mismo tiempo céntrico del antiguo pueblo y muy cerca del castillo de Lipari, de la calle principal, así como de la pequeña playa de Portinente. Las habitaciones proporcionan una amplia gama de servicios y los clientes pueden disfrutar de la cena en la terraza con vistas a la piscina.

Our inspector loved: *The home-from-home ambience.*

Directions: The nearest airports are Catania, Reggio Calabria and Palermo. The nearest harbours are Milazzo, Messina, Reggio Calabria, Neaples and Palermo.

Web: www.johansens.com/arciduca
E-mail: info@arciduca.it
Tel: +39 090 9812 136
Fax: +39 090 9811 387

Price Guide:
single €70-220
double €90-300
suite €235-420

Hotel Signum

VIA SCALO 15, 98050 SALINA~MALFA, ITALY

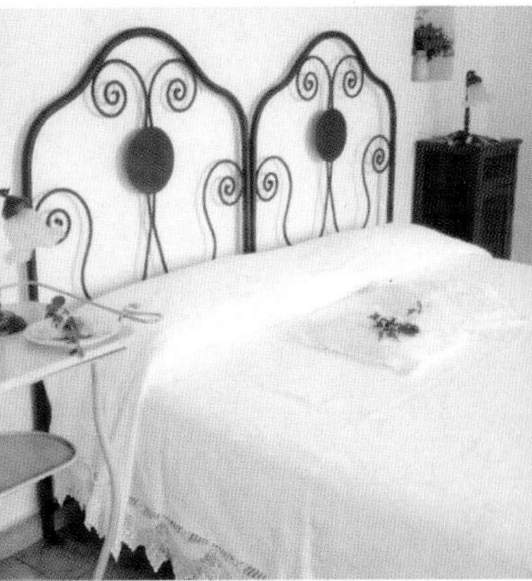

In the shadow of 2 volcanoes and surrounded by lemon trees and jasmin, this hotel is truly unique. Family-run with an "open house" style, guests are taken care of yet given the privacy and freedom to "live" the island. The ambience is quaint and charming, and the interior décor retains traditional features such as wrought iron, embroidered bed linen and period furniture. Guests may enjoy panoramic views of Stromboli and Panarea from the pool and terraces whilst the restaurant serves creative, local specialities.

À l'ombre de 2 volcans, cet hôtel plongé dans les citronniers et les jasmin, est véritablement unique. Géré en famille dans un style très convivial, les hôtes reçoivent toutes les attentions mais peuvent à leur guise explorer l'île. L'ambiance est pittoresque et charmante et la décoration intérieure a conservé des caractéristiques traditionnelles telles que le fer forgé, les draps brodés et le mobilier d'époque. De la piscine et de les terrasses, les hôtes peuvent apprécier des vues panoramiques de Stromboli et de Panarea, tandis que le restaurant sert les specialités locales et créatifs.

A la sombra de 2 volcanes, este hotel rodeado por los limoneros y el jazmín, es verdaderamente singular . La familia que lo regenta aplican la política de "puertas abiertas": se ocupan del cuidado de los clientes sin coartarles la libertad e intimidad para "vivir" la isla. El ambiente es pintoresco a la vez que encantador y la decoración interior conserva elementos tradicionales como el hierro forjado, la ropa de cama bordada y el mobiliario de época. Los clientes pueden gozar de vistas panorámicas de Stromboli y de Panarea de la piscina y de las terrazas, mientras que el restaurante sirve las especialidades culinarias de la zona.

Our inspector loved: *The exclusivity of the hotel.*

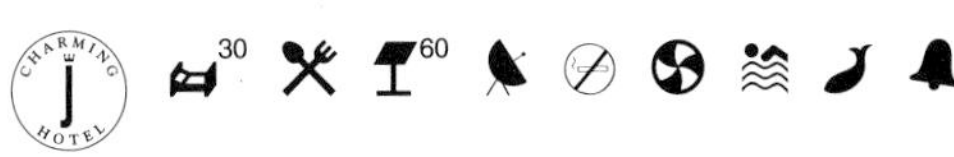

Directions: Naples, Catania or Palermo > Milazzo > speed ferry to Salina.

Web: www.johansens.com/signum
E-mail: salina@hotelsignum.it
Tel: +39 090 9844 222
Fax: +39 090 9844 102

Price Guide:
double €110-260
de luxe double €180-300

Castello di San Marco

VIA SAN MARCO 40, 95011 CALATABIANO, TAORMINA (CT), ITALY

Castello di San Marco stands between the romantic town of Taormina and Mount Etna. Its splendid ancient towers, small church and surrounding walls are magnificent testaments to a bygone era, as are the opulent chandeliers, lava rock arches and fireplaces of the interior. Each with their own terrace, the 14 double rooms, 14 junior suites and 2 suites are situated in the park surrounding the castle, while restaurants, a Moresque lounge, meeting and private dining rooms and romantic garden pool are located within the castle walls.

Castello di San Marco se dresse entre la romantique ville de Taormina et le Mont Etna. Ses superbes vieilles tours, petite église et murs sont un magnifique testament de l'histoire de même que les opulents chandeliers, les arches de pierre de lave et les cheminées intérieures. Chacune avec leur terrace privée, les 14 chambres doubles, les 14 junior suites et les 2 suites sont situées dans le parc entourant le château tandis que les restaurants, le salon Moresque, la salle de conférence, les salles à manger et le romantique jardin avec piscine sont à l'intérieur du mur d'enceinte.

Castello di San Marco se eleva entre la romántica ciudad de Taormina y el monte Etna. Sus espléndidos torreones antiguos, su pequeña iglesia y las murallas que lo rodean son un magnífico testimonio de una época ya pasada así como las majestuosas lámparas araña, los arcos de piedra de lava y las chimeneas del interior. Cada una con su propia terraza, las 14 habitaciones dobles, 14 junior-suites y 2 suites, se localizan en el parque que rodea el castillo, mientras que varios restaurantes, un salón de estilo árabe, salas de juntas y comedores privados, y un romántico jardín con piscina están situados en el interior de las murallas.

Our inspector loved: *The charming Sicilian atmosphere.*

Directions: Catania Airport is 40km away. Taormina Railway Station is 7km away. A18 > Giardini - Naxos.

Web: www.johansens.com/castellodisanmarco
E-mail: info@castellosanmarco.it
Tel: +39 095 641 181
Fax: +39 095 642 635

Price Guide:
double (single occupancy) €105-120
double €140-200
junior suite €215-315
suite €225-330
grand suite €240-350

Palazzo Failla Hotel

VIA BLANDINI 5, 97010 MODICA (RG), ITALY

This hotel used to be home to the aristocratic Failla family, from Modica, and retains many characteristics of a noble Sicilian building such as handmade tiles, frescoed walls and ceilings and antique furniture. Each room is elegantly furnished, and those seeking a particularly romantic stay should reserve the Green Room. Promising young Chef Accursio Craparo, from the 3 Michelin-starred Le Calandre, offers an innovative menu in La Gazza Ladra restaurant. Modica's spectacular churches and Baroque monuments are not to be missed.

Cet hôtel fut la résidence de l'aristocratique Famille Failla de Modica et garde de nombreuses caractéristiques des somptueux bâtiments Siciliens tels que les carrelages faits main, les fresques murales et les meubles antiques. Chacune des chambres est élégamment meublée et ceux à la recherche d'un séjour romantique devront réserver la Chambre Verte. Le nouveau Chef prometteur Accursio Craparo, venant du restaurant 3 étoiles Michelin "Le Calandre", sert un menu raffiné et innovant au restaurant La Gazza Ladra. Les spectaculaires églises et monuments baroque de Modica sont à visiter.

Este hotel fue en el pasado hogar de la aristocrática familia Failla, de Módica y conserva aún muchos de los rasgos propios de un edificio siciliano tales como las tejas artesanas, los frescos murales y su mobiliario antiguo. Cada habitación está amueblada con elegancia. Todos los que busquen disfrutar especialmente de una estancia romántica deberían reservar la Habitación Verde. Un joven chef de prometedor futuro, Accursio Crapano, procedente de Le Calandre, galardonado con 3 estrellas Michelín, prepara una refinada e innovadora carta en el restaurante La Gazza Ladra. Las espectaculares iglesias y los monumentos barrocos de Módica son de obligada visita.

***Our inspector loved:** The attractive ceramic tiled floor in the de luxe Blue Room.*

Directions: Airport > Catania > SS 194 to Modica.

Web: www.johansens.com/plalazzopfailla
E-mail: info@palazzofailla.it
Tel: +39 0932 941 059
Fax: +39 0932 941 059

Price Guide:
single €110
de luxe double €195
classic double €150
superior double €170
junior suite €210

LOCANDA DON SERAFINO

VIA XI FEBBRAIO, 15 RAGUSA IBLA, ITALY

This tastefully renovated 19th-century mansion sits in the heart of the beautiful Baroque city of Ragusa Ibla and offers 10 comfortable and elegant air-conditioned rooms with handmade wooden furniture, luxurious mattresses and a choice of pillows. The charming cellar restaurant, within easy walking distance, serves traditional cuisine by candlelight and boasts a wine list of over 700 labels. The hotel's private, fully-equipped beach and additional family-run restaurant is 20km away in Marina di Ragusa.

Ce manoir du XIXe siècle, rénové avec goût, se trouve au cœur de la superbe ville baroque de Ragusa Ibla. Il offre 10 chambres élégantes et confortables, équipées d'air conditionné, de meubles en bois faits main, de somptueux matelas et d'un choix d'oreillers. Le charmant restaurant, situé à quelques minutes à pied, sert une cuisine traditionnelle à la chandelle et propose une carte de plus de 700 vins. A 20 kms, à Marina di Ragusa se trouve la plage de l'hôtel entièrement équipée ainsi qu'un autre restaurant tenu par la famille.

Esta mansión del siglo XIX renovada con sumo gusto se encuentra en el corazón de la bella ciudad barroca de Ragusa Ibla. Dispone de 10 cómodas y elegantes habitaciones con aire acondicionado y mobiliario artesano de madera, lujosos colchones y gran variedad de almohadas. Su encantador restaurante-bodega, de fácil acceso a pie, sirve una tradicional carta a la luz de las velas y tiene motivos para enorgullecerse de su lista de vinos de más de 700 marcas. El hotel cuenta con una playa privada plenamente equipada así como un restaurante adicional de gerencia familiar a 20 kms, en Marina di Ragusa.

Our inspector loved: *Ibla & Don Serafino: an experience for the senses.*

Directions: The nearest airport is Catania.

Web: www.johansens.com/serafino
E-mail: info@locandadonserafino.it
Tel: +39 0932 220 065
Fax: +39 0932 663 186

Price Guide:
single €120-145
double €140-180
junior suite €200

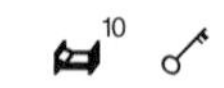

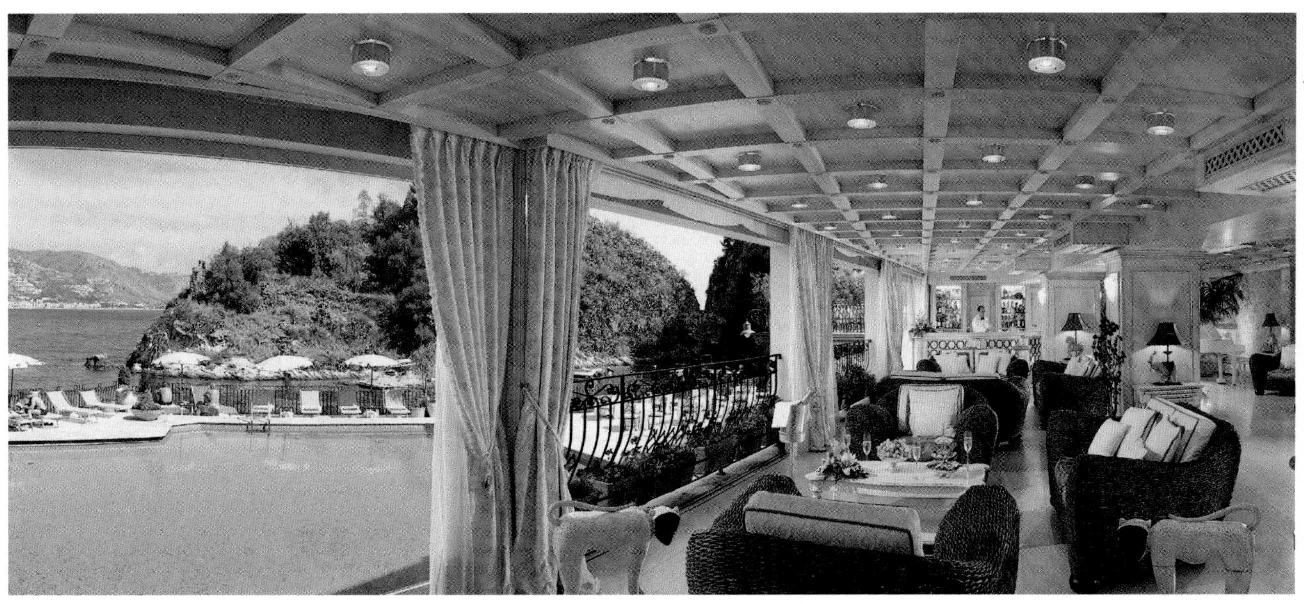

Grand Hotel Atlantis Bay

VIA NAZIONALE 161, TAORMINA MARE (ME), ITALY

The toast of Taormina Sea, this newly opened hotel has already become home to many celebrities and international guests. Entering the hotel is like walking into an enchanted cave and its lavishly decorated stone walls, carved out of the stone of the bay, hold a huge aquarium of colourful tropical fish. Guest rooms are decorated with cool white washed walls and simple, delicate fabrics. From the candle-lit restaurant to the terraces and panoramic views, it is impossible not to be swept away by the hotel's exotic ambience.

La coqueluche de la mer de Taormina, cet hôtel récemment ouvert est déjà devenu la nouvelle base de nombreuses célébrités et hôtes internationaux. Entrer dans cet hôtel est comme pénétrer dans une cave enchantée et sur ses murs de pierre somptueusement décorés, sculptés dans le roc de la baie, se tient un immense aquarium de poissons tropicaux. Les chambres sont décorées de murs lessivés blancs et d'étoffes simples et délicates. Du restaurant éclairé aux chandelles, aux terrasses et vues panoramiques, il est impossible de ne pas être ensorcelé par l'ambiance exotique de l'hôtel.

Este recién inaugurado hotel ya se ha convertido en el hogar de muchos famosos y clientes internacionales y es la estrella de Taormina Mar. Entrar al hotel es como introducirse en una cueva encantada y sus profusamente decoradas paredes de piedra, talladas en la piedra de la bahía albergan un enorme acuario de peces tropicales multicolores. Las habitaciones con paredes encaladas en blanco están decoradas con telas sencillas y delicadas. Desde el restaurante con velas hasta las terrazas con vistas panorámicas resulta imposible no entusiasmarse por el ambiente exótico del hotel.

Our inspector loved: *The truly extraordinary panoramic view.*

Directions: Highway Catania - Messina > exit Taormina > follow signs to Taormina > the hotel is located on Taormina's seafront. Catania Airport is 50km away.

Web: www.johansens.com/atlantis
E-mail: info@atlantisbay.it
Tel: +39 0942 618 011
Fax: +39 0942 23 194

Price Guide:
single €212-424
double €322-508
suite €534-762

 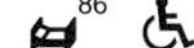 86    220 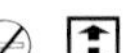   

Grand Hotel Mazzarò Sea Palace

VIA NAZIONALE 147, 98030 TAORMINA (ME), ITALY

Directions: Highway Catania - Messina > exit Taormina > follow signs to Taormina. Catania Airport is 50km away.

Web: www.johansens.com/mazzaroseapalace
E-mail: info@mazzaroseapalace.it
Tel: +39 0942 612 111
Fax: +39 0942 626 237

Milan
Venice
Rome
Palermo

Price Guide:
single €212-424
double €322-508
suite €534-826

The Grand Hotel stands in one of Taormina's most enchanting spots right on the beach of a small bay and offers breathtaking views. The bedrooms are exquisitely furnished and have amazing terraces; some even boast private pools. Large windows look out onto the pool terrace and beyond to the sea. Guests can enjoy the private beach and the attention of exclusive and outstanding service provided by the extremely friendly staff. Taormina is easily reached by cable car.

L'hôtel se trouve dans un des endroits les plus enchanteurs de Taormina, sur la plage d'une petite baie, offrant des vues à couper le souffle. Les chambres meublées avec beaucoup de goût, ont des terrasses incroyables, et certaines ont des piscines privées. De grandes fenêtres ouvrent sur la terrasse autour de la piscine et le golfe. Les hôtes peuvent profiter de la plage privée et d'un service exclusif et impeccable d'un personal amical. Taormina est facilement accessible par téléphérique.

El Gran Hotel se encuentra en unos de los lugares más encantadores de Taormina, justo en la playa en una pequeña bahía, ofreciendo vistas espectaculares. Las habitaciones están amuebladas con exquisitez y ofrecen sorprendentes terrazas, algunas incluso ostentan piscinas privadas. Grandes ventanales dan a la terraza de la piscina, y más allá, al mar. Los clientes pueden disfrutar de playa privada y de una exclusiva atención y un excepcional servicio ofrecido por el acogedor personal. A Taormina se puede acceder muy fácilmente por teleférico.

Our inspector loved: *The hotel's cardinal rule: exclusivity.*

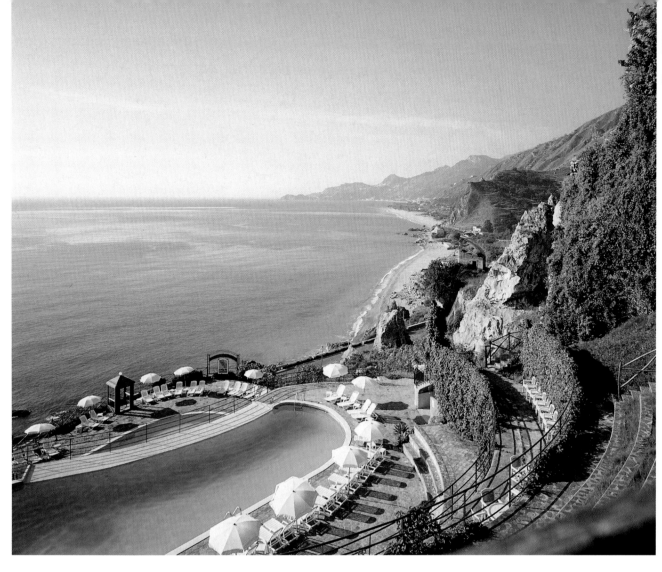

Baia Taormina Hotel - Resort & Spa

STATALE DELLO IONIO, KM 39, 98030 MARINA D'AGRO, TAORMINA RIVIERA (ME), ITALY

The recent inauguration of the Grand Palace wing, next to the existing hotel, blends perfectly into the natural surroundings due to the use of native stone, Sicilian and traditional Caltagirone ceramics. Beautiful views of the Ionian Sea are enjoyed from several open terraces, whilst the spacious yet cosy interior reflects local style with a designer's touch. The wellness centre offers guests a wide range of beauty and massage treatments. To reserve a room in the new wing please quote Condé Nast Johansens.

L'inauguration récente de l'aile Grand Palace juste à côte de l'actuel hôtel, se fond parfaitement dans son environnement naturel grâce à l'utilisation de pierres locales et de céramiques siciliennes et traditionnelles de Caltagirone. De belles vues sur la mer Ionienne peuvent être appréciées de plusieurs terrasses ouvertes alors que l'intérieur spacieux quoique douillet reflète le style local avec la touche particulière d'un designer. Le centre Wellness offre un grand choix de traitements de beauté et de massages. Pour réserver une chambre dans la nouvelle aile, merci de mentionner Condé Nast Johansens.

La reciente inauguración del ala Grand Palace, armoniza perfectamente con su entorno gracias a la utilización de la piedra del lugar y de la típica cerámica de Sicilia y Caltagirone. Desde las amplias terrazas abiertas se disfrutan bellas vistas del mar Ionico, mientras que el interior, espacioso y al mismo tiempo acogedor, refleja el estilo local con un toque de diseño. La zona wellness ofrece a clientes una amplia variedad de tratamientos de belleza y de masajes. Para reservar una de las habitaciones del nuevo ala, por favor mencionen a Condé Nast Johansens.

Our inspector loved: *The extremely kind and helpful staff.*

Directions: Catania > A18 towards Catania-Messina > exit Taormina > SS114 > Km 39. Catania Airport is 50km away.

Web: www.johansens.com/baiataormina
E-mail: hotel@baiataormina.com
Tel: +39 0942 756 292
Fax: +39 0942 756 603

Price Guide:
standard €85-150
de luxe €95-160
single (standard) €125-220
executive €120-185
junior suite €140-205

  122  250    

Romantik Hotel Turm

PIAZZA DELLA CHIESA 9, 39050 FIÈ ALLO SCILIAR (BZ), ITALY

Located high up in the centre of a natural park, this stylish hotel is set in a tower dating back to the 13th century. The family are collectors of art, and many works, including paintings by Picasso and De Chirico, can be admired throughout the hotel. The charming bedrooms are decorated with local fabrics and old carved wood furniture. Exquisite dishes and excellent wines are served in the gourmet restaurant, whilst the hotel's breathtaking, newly opened wellness centre offers a wide range of hay, wine and herb treatments and baths.

Situé en haut au centre d'un parc naturel, cet hôtel élégant se trouve dans un tour datant du XIIIe siècle. La famille collectionne des tableaux, et de nombreux œuvres d'art, comprenant des tableaux de Picasso et De Chirico, peuvent être admirés dans tout l'hôtel. Les chambres charmantes sont ornées avec des tissus de la région et des meubles en bois sculpté. Des plats exquis et excellents vins sont servis dans le restaurant gourmet, alors que le nouveau centre de beauté sensationnel offre des traitements et bains de foin, de vin et d'herbes.

Este hotel, una torre del siglo XIII, se encuentra en un monte al centro de un parque natural. Los propietarios son coleccionistas de arte, y en varias estancias del hotel se pueden contemplar cuadros de Picasso y De Chirico. Las encantadoras habitaciones están decoradas con telas de la región y muebles artesanales antiguos. Platos exquisitos y vinos excelentes se sirven en el restaurante gourmet, y el fabuloso centro de salud, recientemente inaugurado, ofrece una gran variedad de tratamientos y baños a las hierbas, vino y paja.

Our inspector loved: *The exceptional, very romantic restaurant.*

Directions: A22 > exit Bolzano Nord > follow signs to Altopiano dello Sciliar > Alpe di Siusi > Fiè allo Sciliar.

Web: www.johansens.com/turm
E-mail: info@hotelturm.it
Tel: +39 0471 725014
Fax: +39 0471 725474

Price Guide: (closed mid-November - 20th December and 8th January - 31st January)
single €88–147
double/twin €144–318
suite €220–370

Posthotel Cavallino Bianco

VIA CAREZZA 30, 39056 NOVA LEVANTE (BZ), DOLOMITES, ITALY

Situated in Val d'Ega, at the heart of the Dolomites, close to Verona and Venice, lies this former staging post, owned by the Wiedenhofer family since 1865. First-class comfort is offered in an elegant setting; the cuisine and cellar are a refined blend of Mediterranean and Alpine flavours. The fantastic wellness centre has indoor/outdoor pools, Jacuzzi, saunas, relax areas, fitness room, beauty and spa treatments. Activities: tennis, skiing, cross-country skiing, horse riding (own stables), walking and climbing amidst stunning mountain scenery. The hotel's little chapel is an idyllic location for weddings.

Situé au Val d'Ega au cœur des Dolomites, près de Vérone et de Venise, cet ancien relais est géré par la famille Wiedenhofer depuis 1865. L'hôtel offre tout le confort moderne dans un cadre élégant. La cuisine et la cave proposent une combinaison de saveurs méditerranéennes et alpines. Le centre de bien-être fantastique offre piscine couverte, jacuzzi, saunas, zones de détente, piscine en plein air, salle de remise en forme, traitements de beauté, massages et bains. Activités: tennis, ski, ski de randonné, équitation (propre écurie), golf, randonnés et l'alpinisme en plein coeur d'une région magnifique. La petite chapelle de l'hôtel est l'endroit idéal pour des mariages.

Situado en el Val d'Ega, al pie de los Dolomitas y cerca de Verona y Venecia, este hotel, antigua venta, está en manos de la familia Wiedenhofer desde 1865. Ofrece confort de primera en un ambiente elegante. La cocina y la bodega ofrecen una refinada mezcla de sabores mediterráneos y alpinos. El fantástico centro de salud tiene piscina interior y exterior, jacuzzi, saunas, zonas de relax, gimnasio y tratamientos de belleza y masajes. Para los más activos hay tenis, esquí, esquí de fondo, equitación (el hotel tiene cuadra), paseos y montañismo. La pequeña capilla del hotel es un lugar idílico para la celebración de bodas.

Our inspector loved: *The aroma of the unique pine sauna in the panoramic spa.*

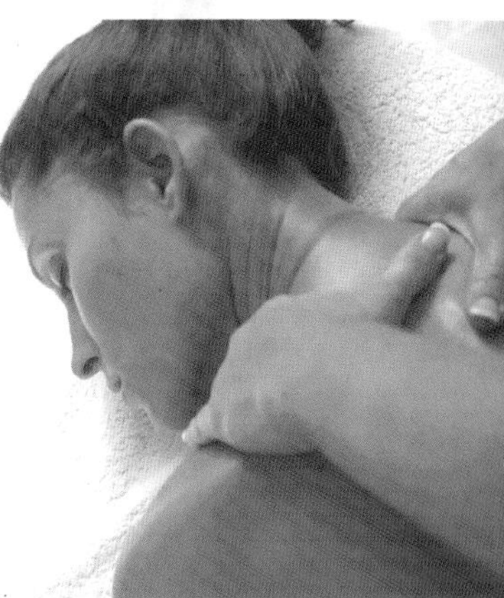

Directions: A22 > Bolzano North > Nova Levante > Val d'Ega-Lago di Carezza.

Web: www.johansens.com/weissesrossl
E-mail: posthotel@postcavallino.com
Tel: +39 0471 613113
Fax: +39 0471 613390

Trento
Milan
Venice
Rome

Price Guide: (closed 2nd November - 7th December and 20th March - 1st June)
single €85–155
double/twin €150–290
suite €200–350

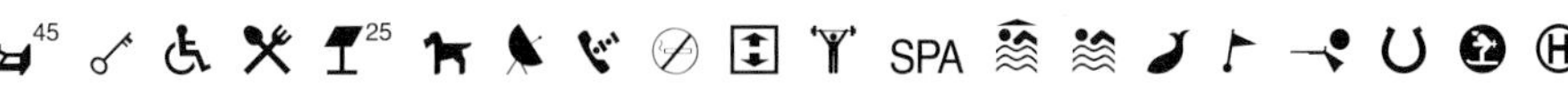

Romantik Hotel Art Hotel Cappella

STR. PECEI 17, ALTA BADIA - DOLOMITES, 39030 COLFOSCO - CORVARA (BZ), ITALY

Dating back to 1912, this hotel has a long tradition of hospitality. The owner, an artist and photographer, has utilised her extensive cultural knowledge and travel experiences to create a warm and inviting atmosphere, carefully blending modern art, rare ethnic pieces and hand-crafted furnishings. 2 restaurants provide casual dining. Many sports activities make for an action packed holiday, whilst there is a spa for those in search of a more relaxed break. Starting right at the doorstep, guests are connected to the ski slopes of Sella Ronda and Alta Badia. An elegant designer Smokers' Lounge is now available.

Datant de 1912, cet hôtel a une longue tradition d'hospitalité. La propriétaire, artiste et photographe, a utilisé ses connaissances artistiques et ses expériences de voyages pour créer une atmosphère chaleureuse, mélangeant art moderne, pièces ethniques et mobilier fait main. 2 restaurants offrent des dîners simples. On peut choisir parmi de nombreuses activités sportives alors que ceux qui sont à la recherche d'un séjour plus reposant peuvent profiter du spa. Depuis la porte les hôtes ont accès aux pistes de Sella Ronda et Alta Badia. Une salle à fumer est maintenant disponible.

Desde 1912, este hotel tiene una larga tradición de hospitalidad. La propietaria, artista y fotógrafa, ha utilizado su extensiva cultura y experiencia obtenida viajando, para crear un ambiente cálido y atractivo con la acertada mezcla de arte moderno, piezas étnicas y muebles de artesanía. Hay 2 restaurantes para cenas informales, muchas actividades deportivas para los que quieren moverse y un spa para aquellos que buscan unas vacaciones mas relajadas. Las pistas de ski de Sella Ronda y Alta Badia empiezan prácticamente a la puerta del hotel. Un salon para fumadores esta disponible ahora.

Our inspector loved: *The entire experience; feeding the mind, body and soul.*

Directions: Please enquire at hotel; ask for Renata Kostner.

Web: www.johansens.com/cappella
E-mail: info@hotelcappella.com
Tel: +39 0471 836183
Fax: +39 0471 836561

Trento
Milan
Venice
Rome

Price Guide: (closed 10th April - 16th June and 23rd September - 7th December)
single €93-215
double €136-430
suite €238-490

Castel Fragsburg

VIA FRAGSBURG 3, 39012 MERANO, ITALY

A member of Relais & Châteaux, this stunning hotel was originally built for participants of noble shooting parties and guests of local feudal lords. Rich in Teutonic trappings, character and charm it stands midway on the side of a sun-flooded mountain high above Merano. Views of the surrounding mountains and the township below are enjoyed from verandas, decks and beautifully furnished rooms. Excellent accommodation, an award-winning restaurant serving gourmet dinners, attentive service and a well-equipped health spa.

Construit à l'origine pour les participants de nobles parties de chasse et pour les invités des seigneurs féodaux locaux, ce superbe hôtel membre du guide Relais & Châteaux, est riche en caractère, charme et signes extérieurs de Teutons. Il se dresse au milieu d'une montagne ensoleillée, en altitude au dessus de Merano. De magnifiques vues sur les montagnes avoisinantes et sur la vallée peuvent être observées depuis les vérandas, les terrasses et les chambres délicieusement meublées. Cet établissement offre un excellent hébergement, un restaurant renommé, un service attentif et un spa très bien équipé.

Un miembro de la guía Relais & Châteaux este magnífico hotel, originalmente construido para alojar a los participantes de las aristocráticas partidas de caza y a los invitados de los señores feudales de la zona, está repleto de teutónico boato, personalidad y encanto. Se erige sobre el centro de una ladera de generosa exposición solar con vistas a la ciudad de Merano. El espléndido paisaje de las montañas circundantes y de la localidad al fondo se pueden disfrutar desde diversas galerías, miradores y habitaciones de bello acabado. Dispone de un excelente servicio de alojamiento, un galardonado restaurante que sirve cenas de gourmet, pone a disposición del cliente un atento servicio así como las espléndidas instalaciones de un spa.

Our inspector loved: *The breathtaking views, and impeccable hospitality.*

Directions: From the A22 Modena-Brennero > exit Bolzano Sud > head towards Merano > exit Merano Sud > Merano > at the second roundabout take the first right for Dorf Tirol > after 2.5km turn right > Labers > travel 5km.

Web: www.johansens.com/fragsburg
E-mail: info@fragsburg.com
Tel: +39 0473 244071
Fax: +39 0473 244493

Price Guide: (half-board, including 7-course gourmet dinner)
single €150-160
double €280-340
suite €320-380

HOTEL GARDENA GRÖDNERHOF

STR. VIDALONG 3, 39046 ORTISEI, ITALY

Directions: From the north or south via Brennero motorway A22 > exit Chiusa/Klausen - Val Gardena/Gröden > signs to Val Gardena > once in Ortisei follow orange arrows to hotel. The nearest airports are Bolzano, Verona, Innsbruck and Munich.

Web: www.johansens.com/gardena
E-mail: info@gardena.com
Tel: +39 0471 796 315
Fax: +39 0471 796 513

Trento
Milan
Venice
Rome

Price Guide:
double €160-486
suite €234-626

Hotel Gardena Grödnerhof has been family-owned for 3 generations. The open and airy style in the lobby extends into the large bedrooms and suites; all have balconies overlooking the grounds. The award-winning restaurant is housed in a number of cosy, wood-panelled areas, and the spa is truly unique, with various saunas and steam baths located in an alpine village of wooden huts. Facilities include a heated pool and a splendid beauty farm and a fitness centre. Excursions to nearby places of interest can be arranged.

L'hôtel Gardena Grödnerhof appartient à la même famille depuis 3 générations. Le style ouvert et aéré de la réception se retrouve dans les chambres spacieuses et les suites, un balcon surplombant le parc. Le restaurant primé est constitué de petits recoins confortables avec lambris muraux. Le spa est vraiment unique, avec des saunas et bains situées dans des huttes en bois au sein d'un village alpin. Aussi disponibles une piscine couverte chauffée, une splendide centre de beauté et un centre de fitness. Des excursions aux centres d'intérêt proches peuvent être organisées.

El Hotel Gardena Grödnerhof, ha sido poseído por una familia durante 3 generaciones. El estilo abierto y desenfadado que distingue su vestíbulo se extiende de igual manera a sus amplias habitaciones, y suites; todas con sus balcones propias con vistas a zonas ajardinadas. Su galardonado restaurante se encuentra ubicado en distintas zonas sumamente acogedoras paneladas en madera. Su spa, con varias salas dedicadas a tratamientos de salud, sito en un pueblecito alpino de cabañas de madera, es realmente único. Entre sus instalaciones destacan una piscina interior a climatizada, un centre de belleza espléndido y un gimnasio. También pueden concertarse excursiones a lugares de interés en los alrededores.

***Our inspector loved:** The exclusive wine cellar and one-of-a-kind spa.*

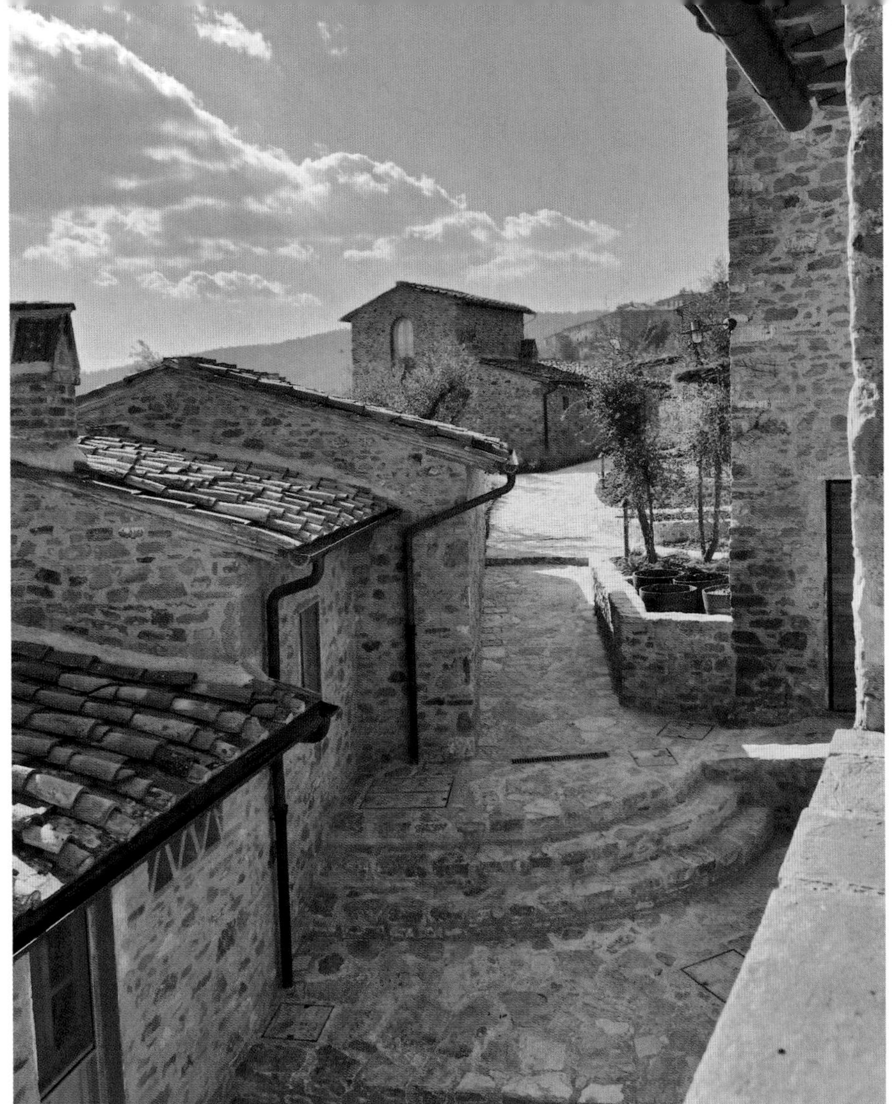

Le Case Del Borgo - Tuscan Luxury Living

LOC. DUDDOVA, 52020 AMBRA (AREZZO), ITALY

Set on top of a hill overlooking the Ambra Valley and the rolling hills of the Chianti area, this ancient hamlet comprises 9 skilfully restored buildings that are a showcase of traditional Tuscan style with the finest local materials such as wood, stone, terracotta and stucco. Each apartment has been harmoniously decorated and furnished, reflecting the perfect integration of luxurious contemporary pieces and original antiques. A 400m² swimming area is set amidst an oasis of olive trees, whilst the pièce de résistance will be the stunning private Wellness Suite, which will be opening soon.

Situé au sommet d'une colline surplombant la vallée Ambra et les paysages vallonnés du Chianti, cet ancien hameau est composé de 9 bâtiments habilement restaurés dans le plus pur style traditionnel Toscan avec les meilleurs matériaux locaux tels que le bois, la pierre, le stuc et la terracotta. Chacun des appartements a été soigneusement décoré et meublé, mêlant harmonieusement de superbes pièces contemporaines à des antiquités. La piscine de 400 m² est cachée au milieu d'un oasis d'oliviers et la pièce de résistance sera la Suite privée Wellness, qui s'ouvrira bientôt.

Situada en la cima de un cerro con vistas al valle Ambra y a las colinas de la comarca de Chianti, esta antigua aldea cuenta con 9 edificios magistralmente restaurados y representativos del estilo tradicional toscano a base de materiales de primera calidad como madera, piedra, terracota y estuco. Cada apartamento se ha decorado de manera que puede verse la perfecta armonía que guardan entre sí los lujosos elementos contemporáneos con las piezas de anticuario originales. En medio de un oasis de olivos se encuentra la piscina de 400 m², si bien la guinda la pone la Wellness Suite privada, que se abrirá pronto.

Our inspector loved: *The "Tuscan mammas" cooking specifically for each guest.*

Directions: From A1 > exit Arezzo > follow directions to Civitella > Siena > Ambra > Duddova.

Milan
Venice
Florence
Rome

Web: www.johansens.com/lecasedelborgo
E-mail: info@lecasedelborgo.com
Tel: +39 055 991 871
Fax: +39 055 991 872/87

Price Guide: (closed 7th January - 7th February)
room €190-280
suite €325-660
(per week)
house €1,838-4,950

  14   30      

Tombolo Talasso Resort

VIA DEL CORALLO 3, 57024 MARINA DI CASTAGNETO CARDUCCI (LI), ITALY

Located in the heart of the Etruscan Riviera Coast near the medieval towns of Castagneto Carducci and Bolgheri, this resort is a paradise of wellbeing and relaxation. Its uniquely furnished facilities boast a Wellness and Thalassotherapy Centre, where sea water is heated at various temperatures and combined with marine elements to offer a wide selection of treatments. Other features of the resort include a superb restaurant and wine bar, an outdoor pool, private beach and well-equipped conference facility.

Situé au cœur de la côte étrusque, près des villes médiévales de Castagneto Carducci et Bolgheri, ce resort est le paradis du bien-être et de la relaxation. Ses équipements uniques offrent un Centre de Thalassothérapie où l'eau de mer est chauffée à différentes températures et mélangée à des produits marins afin d'obtenir une gamme complète de soins. Le resort propose également un magnifique restaurant et bar à vins, une piscine extérieure et une plage privée et d'un centre d'affaires très bien équipé.

Localizado en el corazón de la Costa Riviera etrusca próximo a los pueblos medievales de Castagneto Carducci y Bolgheri, este destino es un paraíso de bienestar y relajación. Sus prestaciones amuebladas exclusivamente cuentan con un Centro Wellness y Talasoterapia donde el agua de mar se calienta a varias temperaturas y se combina con elementos marinos para ofrecer una amplia selección de tratamientos. También dispone de un estupendo restaurante y vinoteca, piscina exterior, playa privada y facilidades para celebrar conferencias.

Our inspector loved: *The immeasurable pleasure of relaxing in the Talasso grotto and its pools.*

Directions: Motorway to Livorno > exit Donoratico.

Web: www.johansens.com/tombolo
E-mail: info@tombolotalasso.it
Tel: +39 0565 74530
Fax: +39 0565 744052

Price Guide:
double (single occupancy) €224-390
double €298-520
suite €468-940

Villa Marsili

VIALE CESARE BATTISTI 13, 52044 CORTONA (AREZZO), ITALY

The breathtaking views of Valdichiana, Mount Amiata, Lake Trasimeno and the medieval village of Cortona make this historic house a truly unique destination. With a history dating back to the 14th century, the villa was restored in 1786 to become an elegant mansion, which now provides 27 guest rooms with spacious bathrooms and impressive frescoes, including 3 suites and 6 de luxe bedrooms with private Jacuzzis. A relaxed, refined ambience pervades throughout and into the delightful garden that looks out to the village and wooded valley.

Les vues à couper le souffle de Valdichiana, Mount Amiata, Lake Trasimeno et du village médiéval de Cortona font de cette maison historique une destination vraiment unique. Avec une histoire qui remonte au XIVe siècle, la villa a été restaurée en 1786 pour devenir une demeure élégante, qui offre maintenant 27 chambres d'hôtes avec des salles de bain spacieuses et des fresques impressionnantes, y compris 3 suites et 6 chambres de catégorie luxe avec jacuzzis privés. Une ambiance détendue et raffinée règne dans la maison et dans le jardin charmant qui donne sur le village et la vallée boisée.

Esta histórica casa en el pueblo medieval de Cortona con vistas espectaculares a Valdichiana, Monte Amiata y el Lago Trasimeno es un auténtico destino único. Con una historia que se remonta al siglo XIV, el pueblo fue restaurado en 1786 para convertirse en una mansión elegante con 27 habitaciones, amplios cuartos de baño y frescos impresionantes, incluyendo 3 suites y 6 cuartos de baño con jacuzzi privado. Un ambiente relajado y refinado se difunde por todas partes y hasta por el jardín encantador que da al pueblo y al valle con bosques.

Our inspector loved: *The view of the gentle, colourful hills of Valdichiana.*

Directions: A1 > exit Valdichiana > E45 > exit Cortona.

Web: www.johansens.com/villamarsili
E-mail: info@villamarsili.net
Tel: +39 0575 605 252
Fax: +39 0575 605 618

Price Guide:
single €90-110
double €140-230
suite €250-310

  27       

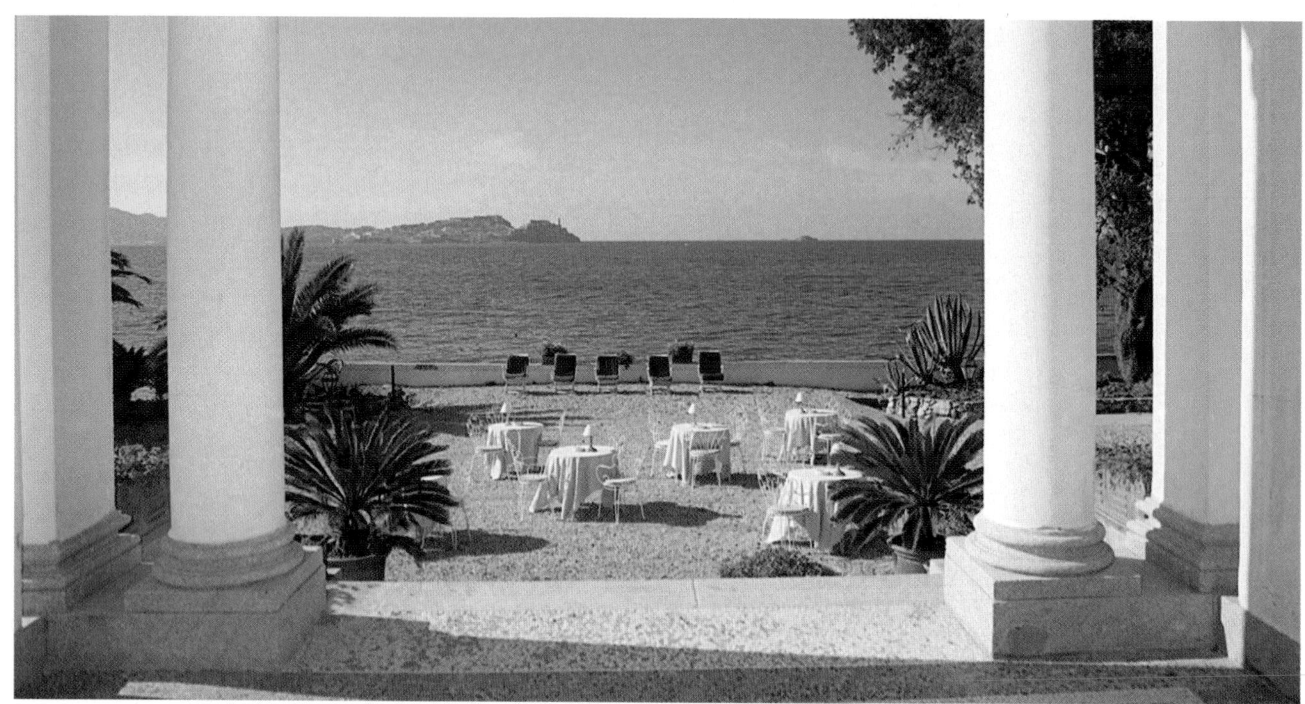

Hotel Villa Ottone

LOC. OTTONE, 57037 PORTOFERRAIO (LI), ISOLA D'ELBA, ITALY

Directions: Take a ferry from Piomino to Elba/Portoferraio > head towards Porto Azzurro - Bagnaia. A transfer from Campo Nell'Elba can be arranged.

Web: www.johansens.com/ottone
E-mail: hotel@villaottone.com
Tel: +39 0565 933 042
Fax: +39 0565 933 257

Price Guide: (per person, including lunch or dinner, closed mid-October - end March)
classic room €87-163
de luxe €142-232
superior €127-203
suite €200-315

2 km from the Golf Club, this historic villa, renowned for its authentic frescos, is surrounded by magnificent gardens, which overlook the private beach. The hotel's new suites, with 40m² sea-view terraces, and the 5 cottages blend attractively into the quiet gardens. The restaurants offer exquisite specialities, accompanied by fine Italian wines, and guests may enjoy an apéritif at sunset whilst musicians play beautiful harmonies. Not far from the Chianti wineries, the island of Elba offers a fascinating variety of history, from Etruscan and Roman traces to evidence of Napoleon's exile.

A 2 km du Golf, cette villa historique, célèbre pour ses fresques d'origine, est entourée d'un merveilleux parc qui domine la plage privée. Les nouvelles suites de l'hôtel, dotées de terrasses de 40 m² avec vue sur la mer, et les 5 cottages sont parfaitement intégrés au cœur du parc. Les restaurants proposent des spécialités raffinées et les meilleurs vins italiens, alors que d'excellents musiciens accompagnent l'apéritif au coucher du soleil. Non loin des vignobles du Chianti, l'île d'Elbe offre une variété de documents historiques, des civilisations étrusques et romaines aux traces de l'exil de Napoléon.

A 2 km del Golf, esta villa de época, famosa por sus frescos originales, está rodeada por un parque maravilloso que se abre a la playa privada. Los apartamentos del nuevo hotel con terrazas de 40 m² con vistas al mar y los 5 cottage están perfectamente integrados en el parque. Los restaurantes proponen especialidades refinadas, acompañadas por los mejores vinos italianos, y los músicos acompañan el aperitivo del atardecer. No muy lejos de los viñedos del Chianti, la isla de Elba ofrece una variedad de documentos históricos, desde la dominación etrusca y romana hasta los vestigios del exilio de Napoleón.

Our inspector loved: *The theatrical setting of the villa.*

31 50

Monsignor Della Casa Country Resort

VIA DI MUCCIANO 16, 50032 BORGO SAN LORENZO, FLORENCE, ITALY

Located in the stunning Mugello area near Florence, this country resort is simply charming. The farmhouses, barns and stables of the ancient hamlet next to the 16th-century Villa of Monsignor della Casa have been converted into beautiful villas and suites, decorated in an elegant country style with trussed ceilings, cotto floors, fireplaces and wrought-iron canopied beds. Tuscan dishes and wines are served in the welcoming wine bar and restaurant. Guests can enjoy a small wellness centre, 2 swimming pools, a tennis court, children's playground and a nearby golf course.

Situé dans la magnifique Mugello, près de Florence, ce country resort est tout à fait charmant. Les fermes, granges et écuries de l'ancien hameau près de la villa du XVIe siècle de Monseigneur della Casa ont été transformées en superbes villas et suites décorées dans un style champêtre élégant avec des plafonds aux poutres apparentes, des sols en terracotta, des cheminées et des lits à baldaquin en fer forgé. Des plats et vins toscans sont servis dans le bar à vins et restaurant. Il y a un petit centre de remise en forme, 2 piscines, un court de tennis, un espace de jeux pour les enfants et un parcours de golf à proximité.

Situado en la impresionante zona Mugello próxima a Florencia, este resort rural es simplemente encantador. Las granjas, graneros y establos de este antiguo caserío junto a la Villa de Monsignor della Casa del siglo XVI han sido convertidos en hermosos chalets y suites, todos ellos decorados en un estilo rural elegante con techos entramados, suelos cottos, chimeneas y camas de hierro forjado con dosel. Se sirven vinos y platos de la región toscana en la vinoteca y el restaurante. Los huéspedes también pueden disfrutar de un pequeño centro wellness, 2 piscinas, una pista de tenis, un campo de juego para niños y un campo de golf cercano.

Our inspector loved: *The refined style.*

Directions: A1 > exit Barberino del Mugello > follow signs to San Piero a Sieve and Borgo San Lorenzo. 27km from Florence.

Web: www.johansens.com/monsignor
E-mail: booking@monsignore.com
Tel: +39 055 840 821
Fax: +39 055 840 8240

Milan
Venice
Florence
Rome

Price Guide: (closed from 10th January - mid-March)
single from €130
double €145-195
suite €195-290

FLORENCE

Hotel location shown in red (hotel) or purple (spa hotel) with page number

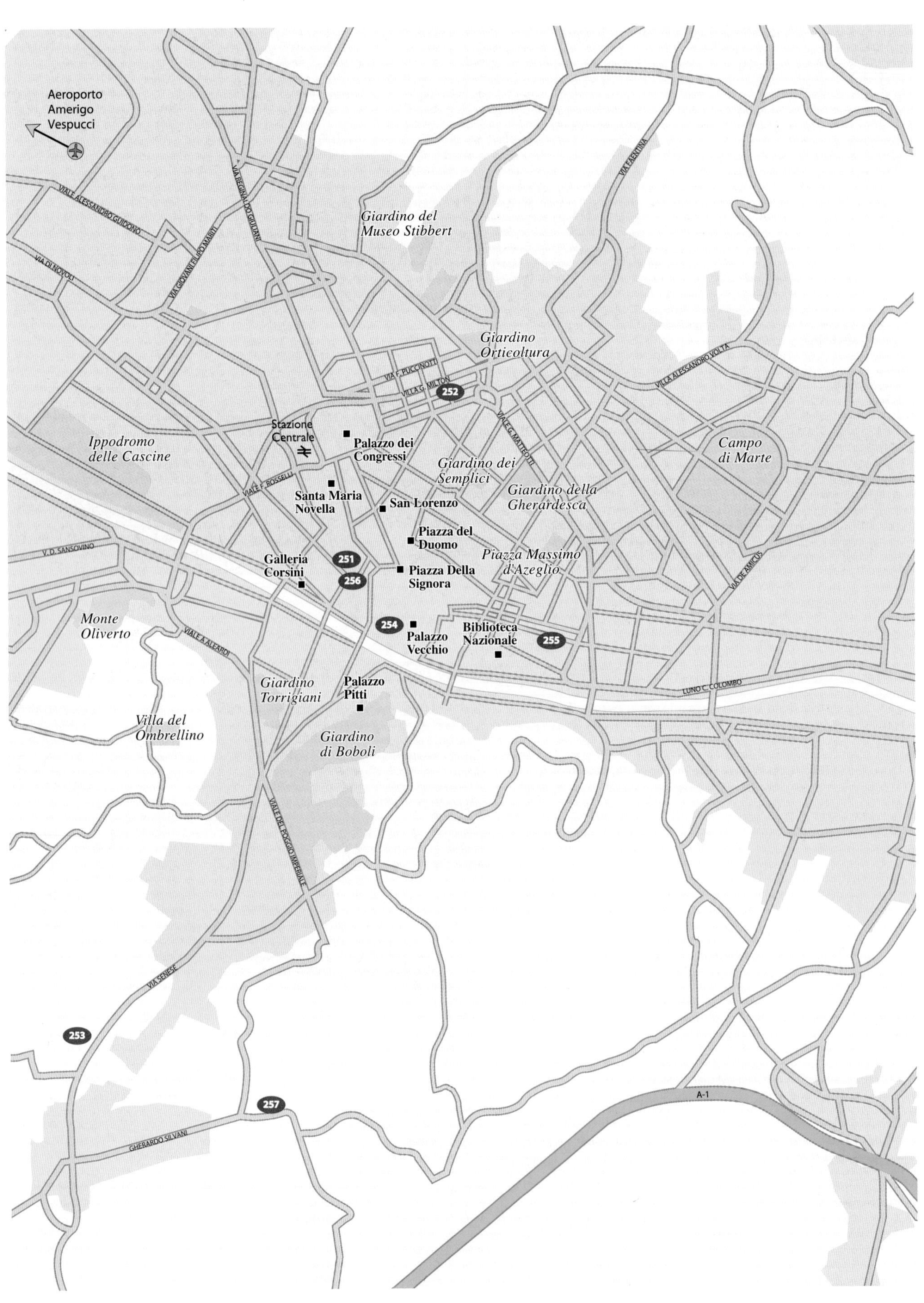

Casa Howard

18 Via della Scala, Piazza Santa Maria Novella, Florence, Italy

The homely Casa Howard is an intimate and elegant mansion within walking distance of the Uffizi, the Duomo and Via Tornabuoni. The themed guest rooms, including 2 suites, and 1 small apartment creatively mix antique furnishings with modern style and are adorned with special touches such as fresh flowers and family portraits. Breakfast includes homemade jams and honey, whilst dinner reservations can be arranged by the helpful housekeepers. The house has a large Turkish hammam.

La simple Casa Howard est une demeure élégante et discrète proche de l'Uffizi, le Duomo et la Via Tornabuoni. Les chambres à thème, ainsi que les 2 suites et le petit appartement, mélangent de manière créative ameublement ancien et style moderne et sont agrémentés de petites touches spéciales telles que fleurs fraiches et portraits de famille. Confitures et miel faits maison sont servis au petit déjeuner, et les réservations pour le diner peuvent être prises par les gouvernantes très serviables. La maison dispose d'un grand hammam turc.

La hogareña mansión Casa Howard es íntima y elegante y se encuentra muy próxima andando al Uffizi, al Duomo y a la Vía Tornabuoni. Las habitaciones temáticas de los huéspedes incluyen 2 suites y un pequeño apartamento, donde se mezclan con creatividad muebles antiguos y estilos modernos, a la vez que están decorados con detalles especiales como flores frescas y retratos familiares. El desayuno incluye mermelada y miel caseras, las amables gobernantas pueden hacerles la reserva para la cena. En la mansión hay un gran hammam turco.

Our inspector loved: *The children's room with special climbing wall.*

Directions: Located in the city centre, very close to Piazza Santa Maria Novella.

Web: www.johansens.com/casahoward
E-mail: info@casahoward.it
Tel: +39 066 992 4555
Fax: +39 066 794 644

Price Guide: (breakfast €15)
single €100-230
double €170-270
suite €500-600

 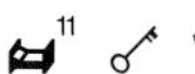      

Hotel Lorenzo Il Magnifico

VIA LORENZO IL MAGNIFICO 25, 50129 FLORENCE, ITALY

This amazing villa, located in the heart of Florence, is the epitome of refined, simple elegance. The emphasis is on comfort and exceptional hospitality, provided by the wonderful staff. Each room is equipped with Jacuzzi bath or shower, whilst particular care has been taken in the selection of the superb bath and bed linens. A pretty garden and private meeting room for up to 30 delegates complete the villa's amenities. Guests' cats and dogs are welcome.

Cette magnifique villa située au cœur de Florence est la quintessence d'élégance raffinée et simple. Une importance particulière est accordée au confort et à l'hospitalité offerte par le personnel d'exception. Chaque chambre dispose d'un bain ou douche jacuzzi, et d'une superbe sélection de linge. La villa dispose aussi d'un beau jardin et d'une salle de conférences privée pouvant accueillir jusqu'à 30 délégués. Les chats et les chiens des hôtes sont les bienvenus.

Esta villa maravillosa se encuentra a unos pasos del centro de Florencia y es la epitomía de una elegancia refinada. El maravilloso personal proporciona una hospitalidad excepcional y se concede gran énfasis al confort. Cada habitación está equipada con baño jacuzzi o ducha, al mismo tiempo que se ha seleccionado con esmero la ropa de baño y de cama. Un bonito jardín, y sala privada de reuniones para hasta 30 delegados completan la oferta de la villa. Se admiten perros y gatos.

Our inspector loved: *The simple elegance demonstrated by the fresh flowers and beautiful linens.*

Directions: A1 > any exit to Florence > follow directions to Viali di Circonvallazione and Piazza della Libertà.

Web: www.johansens.com/lorenzomagnifico
E-mail: booking@lorenzoilmagnifico.net or info@lorenzoilmagnifico.net
Tel: +39 055 463 0878
Fax: +39 055 486 168

Price Guide: (a parking area is at guests' disposal)
double (single occupancy) €110-260
double €120-300
suite €250-500

Marignolle Relais & Charme

VIA DI S QUIRICHINO A MARIGNOLLE 16, 50124 FLORENCE, ITALY

Situated in the Certosa Convent area, a short distance from the historical centre of Florence this little gem of a hotel overlooks the beautiful hillside countryside around the city. The 9 spacious rooms are immaculately styled reflecting the owners' impeccable taste and attention to detail. The panoramic terrace and quiet gardens are the perfect locations for a drink, and light meals can be prepared upon request. Ideally positioned for exploring the historical city centre as well as enjoying some great golf courses and numerous Tuscan attractions in the vicinity. Wine testing can be arranged.

Situé dans le quartier du couvent de Certosa, proche du centre historique, ce petit joyau d'hôtel offre des vues sur la magnifique campagne entourant Florence. Les 9 chambres spacieuses meublées avec soin reflètent le goût impeccable du propriétaire ainsi que son attention au détail. La terrasse panoramique et les jardins sont des lieux parfaits pour boire un verre. Des plats légers peuvent être préparés sur demande. Idéalement situé pour visiter le centre ville historique, les attractions de la région ou pour découvrir de superbes terrains de golf. Des dégustations de vin peuvent être arrangées.

Situado cerca del Convento de Certosa, a corta distancia del centro historico, esta pequeña joya de hotel tiene vistas al bello entorno de colinas que rodea a Florencia. Sus 9 amplias habitaciones están diseñadas con inmaculado estilo, reflejo del gusto impecable y esmero por el detalle de su propietario, siendo su panorámica terraza y tranquilos jardines los lugares perfectos para tomar una copa. Pueden prepararse comidas ligeras a petición del cliente. Una posición ideal para explorar el histórico centro urbano así como para disfrutar de algunos de los campos de golf y de los numerosos atractivos de la región de la Toscana. Pueden organizarse catas de vino.

Our inspector loved: *Enjoying breakfast or a snack in the glass-walled gazebo.*

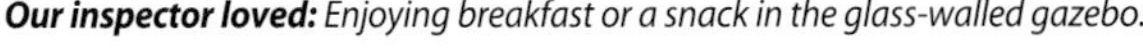

Directions: A1 > exit Firenze Certosa > Via Senese > Via Delle Bagnese.

Milan
Venice
Florence
Rome

Web: www.johansens.com/marignolle
E-mail: info@marignolle.com
Tel: +39 055 228 6910
Fax: +39 055 204 7396

Price Guide:
double (single occupancy) €165-225
double €195-255
suite €255-375

Relais Piazza Signoria

VIA VACCHERECCIA 3, 50122 FLORENCE, ITALY

This enchanting guest house stands in the exclusive Piazza Signoria, home to Palazzo Vecchio, the Uffizi and loggia with numerous famous statues, in the heart of Florence. Each of the private, newly opened suite-apartments has been furnished in a refined, modern style and is equipped with every comfort including a cooking area. Fabulous views of the renowned square are enjoyed from each suite and some have terraces, which are an ideal location for a romantic evening meal.

Cette ravissante maison d'hôtes se situe sur la très chic Piazza Signoria au cœur de Florence où se tiennent le Palazzo Vecchio et l' Uffizi. Chacune des suites-appartements récemment ouvertes a été meublée avec raffinement dans un style contemporain et est équipée de tout le confort moderne y compris un coin cuisine. Les suites bénéficient de vues fabuleuses sur la célèbre place; certaines ont des terrasses, lieu idéal pour des diners romantiques.

Este encantador hostal se encuentra en la exclusiva Piazza Signoria junto al Palacio Vecchio y a Uffizi, en el corazón de Florencia. Cada apartamento-suite recién estrenado ha sido amueblado con un estilo moderno y refinado a la vez que equipados con todo el confort incluyendo la zona de la cocina. Desde cada suite se disfruta de fabulosas vistas a la famosa plaza, algunas de ellas disponen de terrazas, marcos ideales para degustar románticas cenas.

***Our inspector loved:** The exclusivity, and location.*

Directions: Located in the centre of Florence, at the corner of Via Vacchereccia and Piazza Signoria.

Web: www.johansens.com/piazzasignoria
E-mail: info@relaispiazzasignoria.com
Tel: +39 055 3987239
Fax: +39 055 286306

Price Guide: (room only)
double €130-190
suite €250-290

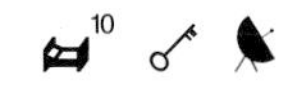

RELAIS SANTA CROCE

VIA GHIBELLINA 15, 50122 FLORENCE, ITALY

With its stunning central location in a splendid 18th-century palace, this hotel offers the ultimate in luxury and an atmosphere of charming refinement. Beautiful frescoes adorn the high ceilings whilst original architectural elements and period furniture blend harmoniously with discreet modern touches. Bedrooms are extremely elegant with all amenities and a high-quality service. Delicious international cuisine is prepared using fresh seasonal ingredients.

Doté d'un parfait emplacement central, cet hôtel situé dans un somptueux palais du XVIIIe siècle offre le summum du luxe et une atmosphère de charme raffinée. De magnifiques fresques ornent les hauts plafonds et les éléments d'architecture originaux ainsi que les meubles d'époque se mélangent parfaitement aux discrètes touches modernes. Les chambres, d'une rare élégance, possède tout l'équipement moderne ainsi qu'un service de tout premier ordre. Une délicieuse cuisine internationale est préparée utilisant des produits frais de saison.

Situado magníficamente en la parte central de un espléndido castillo del siglo XVIII, este hotel ofrece lo último en lujo así como un ambiente refinado y encantador. Los altos techos están adornados con bellos frescos a la vez que los elementos arquitectónicos originales y el mobiliario de época se combinan armoniosamente con discretos detalles modernos. Las habitaciones, dotadas de todas las comodidades y un servicio de alta calidad, son sumamente elegantes. Su deliciosa cocina internacional utiliza ingredientes naturales de temporada.

Our inspector loved: *The charming music room with its small stage and splendid architectural details.*

Directions: Follow directions to the centre towards Piazza Santa Croce.

Web: www.johansens.com/santacroce
E-mail: info@relaisantacroce.com
Tel: +39 055 2342230
Fax: +39 055 2341195

Price Guide:
double (single occupancy) €300-510
double €350-560
suite €710-1800

Residenza del Moro

VIA DEL MORO 15, 50123 FLORENCE, ITALY

Directions: Follow directions to the centre and Piazza Santa Maria Novella.

Web: www.johansens.com/delmoro
E-mail: info@residenzadelmoro.com
Tel: +39 055 290884
Fax: +39 055 2648494

Price Guide: (Continental breakfast and service included, excluding tax)
double €490
suite €1,550

Residenza del Moro is a 11-suite luxury hotel situated on the noble floor of a 16th-century aristocratic palace within the heart of Florence. Sumptuous furnishings, stunning contemporary artworks and precious ornaments span across the centuries and are thoughtfully placed throughout the hotel. Each suite boasts original period details, stucco and frescoes, and has been individually decorated with refined brocades, silks and antiques. An excellent breakfast is enjoyed in each room or the private roof garden.

Residenza del Moro est un hôtel de luxe de 11 suites situé à l'étage majestueux d'un palais aristocratique du XVIe siècle, en plein cœur de Florence. Un mobilier somptueux, de superbes œuvres d'art contemporaines et des ornements précieux couvrant plusieurs siècles sont délicatement exposés à travers tout l'hôtel. Chaque suite possède des détails d'origine, des décorations en stuc et des fresques, et à été décorée avec des meubles antiques, des soies et des brocarts raffinés. Un délicieux petit-déjeuner est servi en chambre ou dans le jardin privé aménagé sur le toit.

Residenza del Moro es un hotel de lujo con 11 suites construido sobre la noble planta de un palacio aristocrático del siglo XVI en pleno corazón de Florencia. El suntuoso mobiliario, las impresionantes obras de arte contemporáneas y los preciosos ornamentos dan muestra de diversidad de siglos y se encuentran cuidadosamente colocados por todo el hotel. Cada suite contiene detalles originales de la época, estuco y frescos y ha sido individualmente diseñada a base de elegantes brocadas, sedas y piezas de anticuario. Los clientes podrán disfrutar de un excelente desayuno bien en su habitación o en la terraza ajardinada privada.

Our inspector loved: *The stage-like setting of the bathing area in the Alcova Suite*

11 20

VILLA MONTARTINO

VIA GHERARDO SILVANI 151, 50125 FLORENCE, ITALY

Set 3km from the heart of Florence, above the beautiful Ema Valley and surrounded by stone walls, olive trees and vineyards, Villa Montartino and Residence Le Piazzole offer quality service in a peaceful setting. The luxurious, spacious rooms have views of the hills and contain original antiques and modern conveniences. Dinner can be arranged in the beautiful Loggia; wine and extra virgin olive oil produced here, can be tasted in the old cellars, with prior notice. Private chapel and meeting room for or up to 30 guests, 2 heated swimming pools, Jacuzzi, steam bath, 2 private car parks.

S'élevant au dessus de la belle vallée de l'Ema, à 3 km du centre de Florence et entourée de murs de pierre, d'oliviers et de vignobles, la paisible Villa Montartino et Residence Le Piazzole offrent un service irréprochable. Les chambres luxueuses ont vue sur les collines et sont spacieuses, contenant des antiquités originales et tout le confort moderne. Le dîner peut être servi dans la belle loggia, et on peut déguster des vins et l'huile d'olives faite à la maison aux vieilles caves. Chapelle et salle de réunions pour 30 personnes, 2 piscines chauffées, jacuzzi, bain turc, 2 parkings privés.

Ubicada a 3 kilometros del centro de Florencia, por encima del bonito Valle Ema y rodeada de murallas de piedra, olivares y viñedos, este hotel ofrece un servicio de calidad en un marco muy tranquilo. Las lujosas y espaciosas habitaciones disfrutan de magníficas vistas a las colinas, decoradas con antigüedades originales y comodidades modernas. En el hermoso Loggia se pueden tomar cenas. Como en esta zona se produce vino y aceite de oliva virgen extra es una aliciente añadido poder degustarlos con cita previa. También cuenta con una capilla privada y un salón de reuniones para 30 invitados, 2 piscinas climatizadas, jacuzzi, baño de vapor y 2 aparcamientos.

Our inspector loved: *The splendid location on the Florentine hills.*

Directions: A1 > exit Firenze-Certosa > SS2 to Galluzzo > Via Gherardo Silvani.

Web: www.johansens.com/villamontartino
E-mail: info@montartino.com
Tel: +39 055 223520
Fax: +39 055 223495

Price Guide: (closed during December)
double/twin €260
suite €335
weekly rate: apartment €1,000–1,800

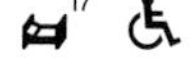

Hotel Byron

VIALE A MORIN 46, 55042 FORTE DEI MARMI (LU), ITALY

Comprising 2 Liberty-style villas overlooking the seafront, Hotel Byron is situated in one of the most exclusive areas on the Versilian coast. Recent renovations have restored the house to its original elegance, and it is now a refined hotel with the ambience of a private residence. Interior decorations have been personally chosen by the owners and give the hotel a fresh, crisp style, with a profusion of plants and flowers. The restaurant, La Magnolia, has an excellent reputation for its fine cuisine and wine selection.

Composé de 2 villas dans le style Liberty surplombant le bord de mer, Hôtel Byron est situé sur l'une des plus belles parties de la côte de Versilia. De récentes rénovations ont rendues à la maison son élégance d'origine et c'est maintenant un hôtel raffiné avec l'atmosphère d'une résidence privée. La décoration d'intérieure à été choisie par les propriétaires et donne à l'hôtel un style frais et croustillant avec une profusion de plantes et de fleurs. Le restaurant La Magnolia à une excellente réputation pour sa délicieuse cuisine et sa sélection de vins.

Consistente en 2 villas al estilo Liberty con vistas a la playa, el Hotel Byron esta situado en una de las zonas mas exclusivas de las costa versiliana. Recientes innovaciones le han devuelto a la casa su elegancia original y ahora resulta ser un refinado hotel con ambiente propio de una residencia privada. Su decoración interior ha sido escogida personalmente por sus propietarios, la cual le confiere al hotel un estilo fresco, impecable y generoso de plantas y flores. El restaurante, La Magnolia, tiene una reputada fama por su excelente carta y selección de vinos.

Our inspector loved: *The sparkling white walls and shining marble floor.*

Directions: A12 > exit Versilia.

Web: www.johansens.com/byron
E-mail: info@hotelbyron.net
Tel: +39 0584 787 052
Fax: +39 0584 787 152

Price Guide:
single €196-273
double €265-573
apartment €394-834
suite €428-1,207

Relais Villa Belpoggio (Historical House)

VIA SETTEPONTI PONENTE 40, 52024 LORO CIUFFENNA, AREZZO, ITALY

Standing on the slopes of the Pratomagno Mountains, this classic, 17th-century aristocratic country residence offers spectacular views of the Arno Valley and Chianti Mountains. Warm Tuscan hospitality and genuine country living await guests in this home away from home. Locally carved furnishings adorn the individually decorated guest rooms and the 2 self-catering apartments, and a flavoursome buffet breakfast of local, fresh specialities is available in the old cellars. The villa's private and idyllic 18th-century chapel can hold wedding ceremonies.

Sur les pentes des montagnes de Pratomagno, cette aristocratique demeure de campagne datant du XVII e siècle, offre des vues spectaculaires sur la vallée de l'Arno et les montagnes de Chianti. La chaleureuse hospitalité toscane et la véritable vie campagnarde attendent les hôtes dans ce « second chez-soi ». Des meubles sculptés à la main ornent les chambres et les 2 gîtes individuellement décorés ; un savoureux petit déjeuner-buffet de produits frais et locaux est servi dans les vieux celliers. Dans l'idyllique chapelle privée du XVIIIe siècle, des mariages peuvent être célébrés.

Esta clásica residencia aristocrática del siglo XVII se ubica en las laderas de las Montañas Pratomagno y ofrece vistas espectaculares del Valle Arno y de las Montañas Chianti.Se caracteriza por su cálida hospitalidad Toscana y por su ambiente rural genuino para que se sienta como en su propia casa. Sus habitaciones están decoradas individualmente con mobiliario tallado por artesanos locales al igual que 2 apartamentos self-catering. Un desayuno buffet lleno de especialidades suculentas, locales y frescas está disponible en las antiguas bodegas. La villa privada también posee una idílica capilla del siglo XVIII donde se pueden celebrar bodas.

Our inspector loved: *The romantic ambience, and convenience to major towns.*

Directions: A1 (Firenze - Roma) > exit Valdarino > follow signs to Loro Ciuffenna and Castelfranco.

Web: www.johansens.com/villabelpoggio
E-mail: info@villabelpoggio.it
Tel: +39 055 9694411
Fax: +39 055 9694411

Price Guide: (closed 8th January - 31st March)
double (single occupancy) €100-120
double €120-210
suite €150-210

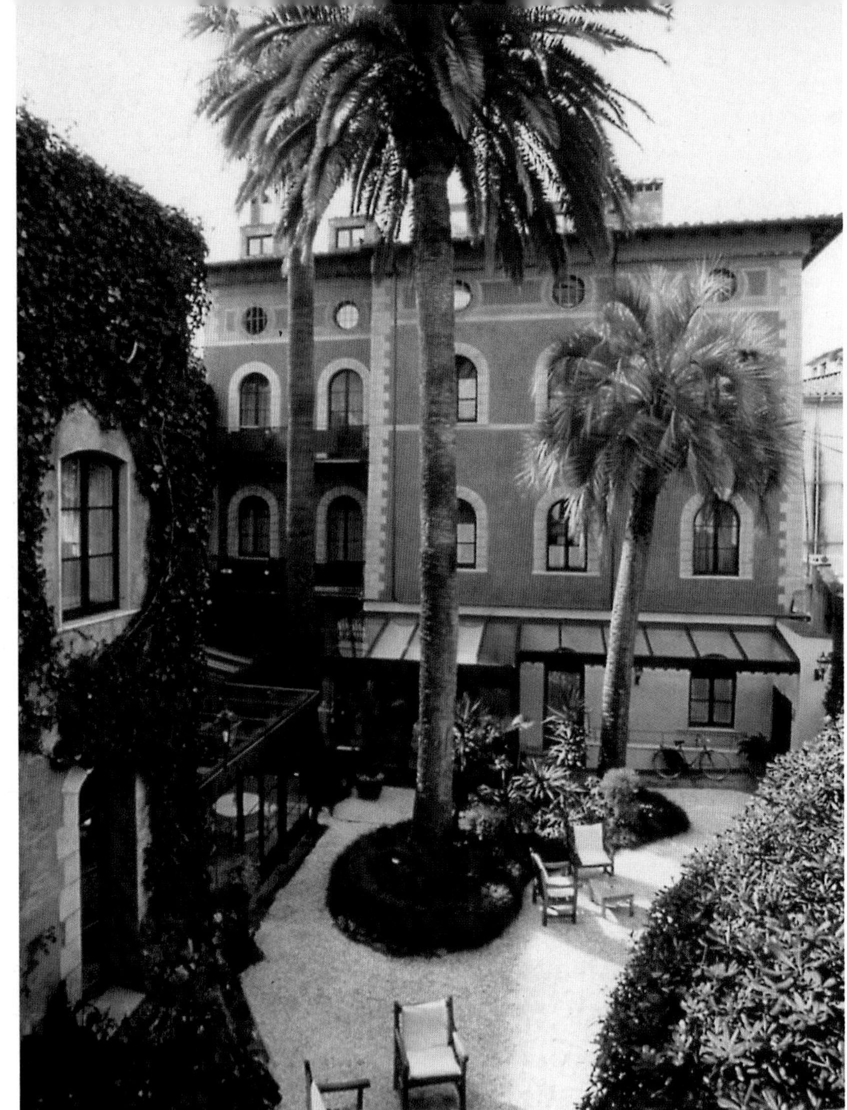

Albergo Pietrasanta - Palazzo Barsanti Bonetti

VIA GARIBALDI 35, 55045 PIETRASANTA (LUCCA), ITALY

Directions: A12 (Genova-Livorno) > exit at Versilia > Pietrasanta > Viale Apua > historical centre > Vicolo Lavatoi. Only a 10-minute drive from Forte dei Marmi.

Web: www.johansens.com/pietrasanta
E-mail: info@albergopietrasanta.com
Tel: +39 0584 793 727
Fax: +39 0584 793 728

Price Guide: (closed during the winter season)
double €270-380
junior suite €360-700
suite €550-800

This authentic 17th-century palace, in true Renaissance style, has been uniquely restored. Its main hall combines contemporary paintings with antique furniture, marble tile floors and beautiful moulded stucco and fresco ceilings. The covered courtyard has been transformed into a breakfast area, and the waterfall completes its evocative charm. Spacious bedrooms combine attractive fabrics with antique décor and beautiful paintings. Some of the most renowned restaurants in the region are in walking distance.

Cet authentique palais du XVIIe siècle, de style Renaissance, a été restauré de manière unique. Sa salle principale marie à merveille peintures contemporaines à des meubles anciens, un sol carrelé en marbre et des plafonds couronnés de stuc et ornés de fresques. La cour couverte a été spécialement aménagée pour le petit-déjeuner et la cascade complète son charme au pouvoir évocateur. Les chambres spacieuses mélangent d'attrayants tissus à un décor antique et de jolies peintures. Les plus fameux restaurants de la région sont à quelques minutes à pieds.

Este auténtico palacio del siglo XVII, de verdadero estilo renacentista, ha sido restaurado con singular estilo. Su vestíbulo principal combina cuadros contemporáneos con muebles antiguos, solería de azulejos en mármol y bellos techos de estuco moldeado y frescos. El patio cubierto ha sido convertido en zona para el desayuno, y la cascada del rincón completa su evocador encanto. Las habitaciones espaciosas combinan elegantes telas con sabor a antiguo y pinturas magníficas. Existen en las cercanías algunos de los restaurantes más renombrados.

Our inspector loved: *The outstanding collection of contemporary artwork.*

Albergo Villa Marta

VIA DEL PONTE GUASPERINI 873, SAN LORENZO A VACCOLI, 55100 LUCCA, ITALY

This 19th-century hunting lodge is situated amongst hills and olive groves at the foot of the renowned Monti Pisani, near the historical town of Lucca. Its style is that of a refined country residence and the utmost attention has been paid to its décor. All 11 rooms are light and spacious, and some have frescoed ceilings whilst others enjoy great views of the surrounding countryside. Art exhibitions and classes and wine tastings are also on offer at the hotel.

Ce pavillon de chasse du XIXe siècle se trouve au milieu des collines et oliveraies au pied du célèbre Monti Pisani, près de la ville historique de Lucca. Son style est celui d'une résidence secondaire raffinée et la plus grande attention a été apportée à la décoration. Les 11 chambres sont claires et spacieuses, certaines ont des fresques au plafond alors que d'autres ont de superbes vues sur la campagne avoisinante. Expositions d'art, cours et dégustations de vins sont également disponibles à l'hôtel.

Próximo a la histórica ciudad de Lucca y a los pies del conocido Monti Pisani se encuentra este refugio de caza del siglo XIX rodeado de colinas y olivares. Su décor ofrece un exquisito estilo acorde con su entorno rural. Sus 11 habitaciones son luminosas y espaciosas, algunas lucen techos con frescos y otras disponen de maravillosas vistas de su paisaje circundante. También en el hotel podrá disfrutar de exposiciones de arte, clases y degustaciones de vino.

Our inspector loved: *The fresh country style combined with exquisite refinement.*

Directions: A11/A12 Firenze-Mare motorway > Lucca est > Pisa > SS12.

Web: www.johansens.com/villamarta
E-mail: info@albergovillamarta.it
Tel: +39 0583 37 01 01
Fax: +39 0583 37 99 99

Price Guide: (closed during January)
classic double €160
superior double €180
double de luxe €200

Country House Casa Cornacchi

LOC. MONTEBENICHI, 52021 AREZZO, TUSCANY, ITALY

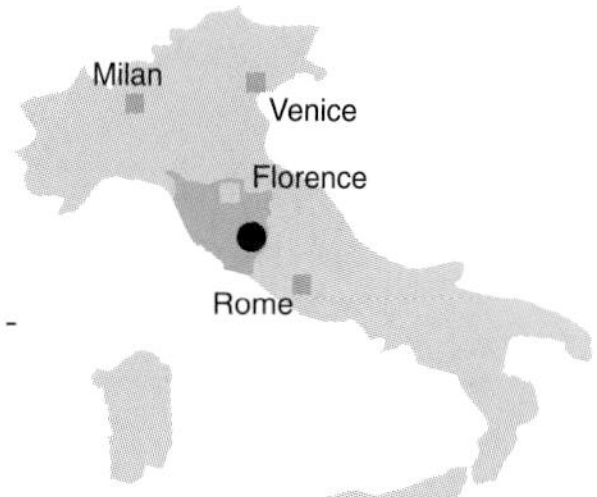

After an exhilarating drive through the breathtaking countryside between Siena and Arezzo, guests receive a warm welcome at this relaxing and tranquil country residence. Casa Cornacchi consists of fully restored stone buildings dating back to the 16th century and offers exquisitely furnished bedrooms, a panoramic swimming pool and Jacuzzi as well as some fine Tuscan wines. Guests can explore this enchanting Chianti region with its wonderful treasures of art, history and nature.

Après une promenade en voiture vivifiante à travers la belle campagne de Siena et Arezzo, les hôtes reçoivent le bon accueil à cette résidence de campagne tranquille et relaxante. Les bâtiments en pierre datant du XVIe siècle ont été restaurés et offrent des chambres exquisément ornées, une piscine panoramique et jacuzzi ainsi que de fins vins toscans. La région enchanteresse de Chianti avec son art, son histoire et sa nature fascinants, est à découvrir.

Después de un vigoroso viaje por el campo contemplando el espectacular paisaje entre Siena y Arezzo se llega a esta tranquila y serena casa de campo. Casa Cornacchi consiste en unos edificios restaurados de piedra del siglo XVI, que hoy ofrecen habitaciones amuebladas con gusto exquisito, una piscina panorámica y jacuzzi, así como unos vinos toscanos buenísimos. Desde aquí se puede visitar la encantadora región de Chianti con sus fabulosos tesoros de arte, historia y naturaleza.

Our inspector loved: *The hotel's fantastic location in the heart of Tuscany.*

Directions: From Rome: take A1 > exit at Valdichiana > Siena exit at Colonna del Grillo > Bucine Montebenichi > exit at Montebenichi. From Florence: take A1 > eixit at Valdarno > Siena > Bucine > Ambra > Montebenichi.

Web: www.johansens.com/cornacchi
E-mail: info@cornacchi.com
Tel: +39 055 998229
Fax: +39 055 9983863

Price Guide: (closed beginning of January - end of March)
suite €140-200
apartment €180-250
villa from €250

Hotel Relais Dell'Orologio

VIA DELLA FAGGIOLA 12/14, 56126 PISA, ITALY

In the centre of Pisa, a short distance from Piazza dei Miracoli and Piazza dei Cavalieri, stands this carefully restored 14th-century tower house. Soothing colour schemes and period pieces furnish the spacious guest rooms that feature exposed beams and provide every modern comfort; each has Internet and PC connections. The Hallet's Bar restaurant oozes romance, and breakfast may be enjoyed in the Italian garden whilst drinks are served on the veranda. Nearby sites include the local church, monastery and Natural Reserve of San Rossore, which leads down to the sea.

Au centre de Pise, tout près de la Piazza dei Miracoli et de la Piazza dei Cavalieri, se tient cette tour soigneusement restaurée datant du XIVe siècle. Des couleurs apaisantes et des meubles d'époque habillent les chambres spacieuses aux poutres apparentes et au confort le plus moderne ; toutes ont des prises ordinateur et connexion internet. Le restaurant Hallet's Bar invite à la romance, le petit-déjeuner peut être pris dans le jardin italien, et des boissons dégustées sur la véranda. A visiter tout proche l'église locale, le monastère et la Réserve Naturelle de San Rossore qui mène tout droit à la mer.

En el centro de Pisa, a corta distancia de Piazza dei Miracoli y Piazza di Cavalieri, se encuentra esta cuidadosamente restaurada casa-torre del siglo XIV. Colores relajantes y piezas de época amueblan las amplias habitaciones con sus vigas de madera, sin olvidar los detalles modernos como conexiones para ordenador e Internet. Se puede cenar en el romántico restaurante, Hallet's, desayunar en el jardín italiano y tomar un aperitivo en la veranda del hotel. La iglesia local, el monasterio y la Reserva Natural de San Rossore, que desciende hacia el mar, se encuentran a pocos pasos del hotel.

Our inspector loved: *The romantic, intimate atmosphere.*

Directions: A12 > exit Pisa Centro > Piazza Duomo > hotel.

Web: www.johansens.com/relaisorologio
E-mail: info@hotelrelaisorologio.com
Tel: +39 050 830 361
Fax: +39 050 551 869

Price Guide:
single €200-260
double €270-380
suite €550-760

CASTELLO DI VICARELLO

LOC. VICARELLO, 58044 POGGI DEL SASSO (GR), ITALY

This Tuscan retreat is an untouched paradise and ideal for those wishing to escape the trappings of modern-day life and unwind. Its setting in Maremma offers a seductive Italian landscape with olive groves, vineyards and forests facing the Siena and Grosseto countryside. The property dates back to 1100 and has been tastefully restored using antique stone, wood, terracotta whilst the rooms are a delight to explore with antique furnishings and collections reflecting the owners' passion for global cultures and traditions. Meals are available upon request.

Cette adresse Toscane est un paradis intact, idéal pour ceux qui souhaitent échapper aux inconvénients de la vie moderne et se relaxer. Son emplacement a Maremma offre une séduisante vue des paysages Italiens avec des oliveraies, des vignobles et des forêts faisant face à la campagne de Sienne et de Grosseto. La demeure date de 1100 et a été restaurée avec goût et attention en utilisant des vieilles pierres, du bois, de la terracotta. Les chambres sont un pur ravissement et meublées d'antiquités et de collections, reflétant ainsi la passion des propriétaires pour toutes les cultures et traditions. Les repas sont servis sur demande.

Este refugio de la Toscana, un paraíso natural, es el lugar ideal para aquellos que deseen relajarse y escapar del estrés de la vida moderna. Su ubicación, en Maremma, ofrece un paisaje Italiano seductor, con olivares, viñedos y bosques frente a los campos de Siena y Grosseto. La propieda data del año 1100 y ha sido restaurada con gusto, utilizando piedra, madera y terracota. Es un placer recorrer las habitaciones con sus muebles antiguos y colecciones que reflejan la pasión del propietario por culturas y tradiciones de otras partes del mundo. Se pueden servir comidas si los huéspedes lo desean.

Directions: SS223 Siena-Grosseto > exit Paganico > follow directions to Sasso d'Ombrone and Poggi del Sasso.

Web: www.johansens.com/vicarello
E-mail: info@vicarello.it
Tel: +39 0564 990 718
Fax: +39 0564 990 718

Price Guide: (excluding 5% service charge)
de luxe €300
suite €380-500
villa €700-980

Our inspector loved: *The unusual mix of cultures and design of the interiors.*

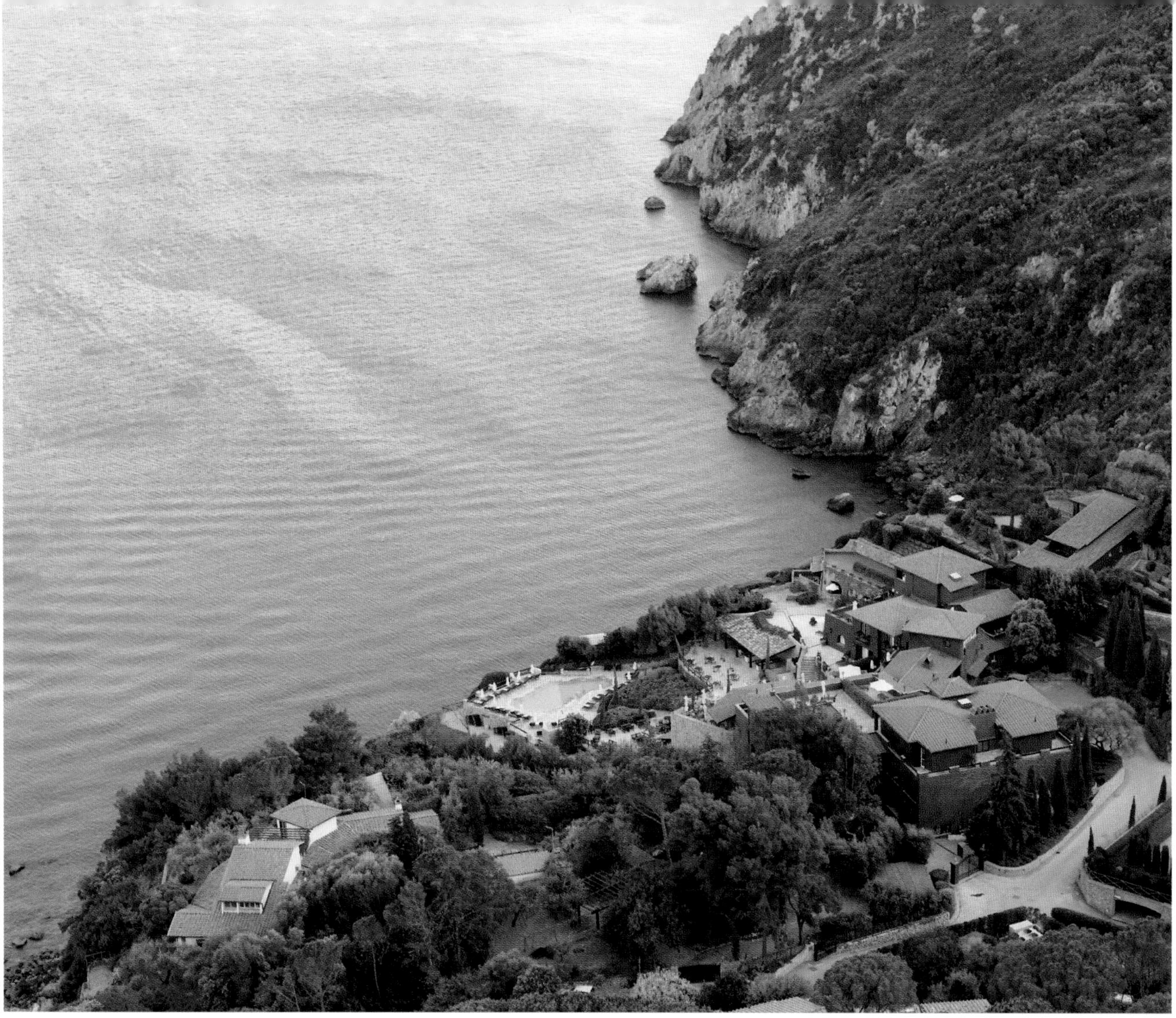

Il Pellicano Hotel & Spa

LOC. SBARCATELLO, 58018 PORTO ERCOLE (GR), TUSCANY, ITALY

This stunning villa, set amongst old olive trees in a spectacular setting, is located on the breathtaking Argentario Peninsula. Each room is uniquely decorated, bright, and offers either a view of the park or magnificent sea. The Michelin-star rated restaurant serves international cuisine and wine at Il Pelican restaurant or al fresco at La Terrace Barbecue. After a day of water skiing, tennis or swimming in the heated seawater pool guests can take advantage of the Paradise Spa and relax with a massage. The hotel boasts its very own private cove.

Cette villa superbe est située parmi de vieux oliviers dans un cadre spectaculaire sur la péninsule magnifique d'Argentario. Chacune des chambres est claire et décorée de manière unique, avec des vues sur le parc ou la mer. Le restaurant à 1 étoile Michelin sert une cuisine internationale et des vins au restaurant Il Pellicano ou à l'extérieur à La Terrazza. Après une journée de ski nautique, de tennis ou au bord de la piscine d'eau de mer chauffée, les clients peuvent se rendre au Paradise Spa et apprécier un massage. L'hôtel possède sa propre anse.

Este villa hermosa se encuentra rodeada de unos ancestrales olivos en un sitio espectacular en la península de Argentario. Cada habitación está clara y decorada individualmente, con vistas del parque o el mar. Los clientes pueden disfrutar de su carta internacional calificada con 1 estrella Michelín así como de sus vinos en el restaurante Il Pellicano o al aire libre en La Terrazza. Tras pasas el día praticando el esquí acuático, el tenis o la natación en la piscina climatizada de agua marina, los clientes pueden hacer uso del Paradise Spa y relajarse con un masaje. El hotel tiene su propia cala privada.

Our inspector loved: *This magical place where life is a dream from which you never want to wake.*

Directions: Rome > A12 > Civitavecchia > Orbetello > Porto Ercole.

Milan
Venice
Florence
Rome

Web: www.johansens.com/ilpellicano
E-mail: info@pellicanohotel.com
Tel: +39 0564 858111
Fax: +39 0564 833418

Price Guide: (closed from November to beginning of April)
double €354-774
suite €850-1,393
half board compulsory during high season:
double €489-892
suite €966-1,488

ITALY / TUSCANY (ROCCATEDERIGHI - GROSSETO)

PIEVE DI CAMININO (HISTORICAL RESIDENCE) 

VIA PROV. DI PERUZZO, 58028 ROCCATEDERIGHI - GROSSETO, ITALY

Directions: Aurelia Road towards Livorno and Grosseto > exit Braccagni > follow directions to Montemassi - Sassofortino. Or Siena - Grosseto freeway > exit Civitella Marittima > Follonica > Montemassi > Sassofortino.

Web: www.johansens.com/caminino
E-mail: caminino@caminino.com
Tel: +39 0564 569 736/7 or +39 3933 356 605
Fax: +39 0564 568 756

Price Guide: (excluding breakfast)
suite 2 people (per night) €120-150
apartment 2 people (per week) €750-950
apartment 4-5 people (per night) €220-240
apartment 4-5 people (per week) €1,300-1,450

This ancient 1,235-acre farm has been brought back to life whilst respecting its 11th-century origin by a family of architects. A small hamlet set within the walls of a historical Romanesque monastery, Pieve di Caminino stands in a large olive grove amphitheatre with stunning views of the sea and hills featuring fortresses and castles. Each accommodation has a fireplace and terrace and is decorated with family antique furniture. The fragrant garden is filled with English and Tuscan roses, lavender and jasmin; the ideal place for a siesta.

Cette ancienne ferme de plus de 500 ha a été "ressuscitée" par une famille d'architectes, qui a su conservrer le caractère d'origine du XIe siècle. Un petit hameau situé dans les murs d'un monastère roman historique, Pieve di Caminino s'élève dans une grande oliveraie en forme d'amphithéâtre avec des vues splendides sur la mer et sur les collines aux châteaux et forteresses. Décoré avec des meubles anciens appartenant à la famille, chaque logement a une cheminée et une terrasse. Le jardin parfumé est planté de roses anglaises et toscanes, de lavande et de jasmin; l'endroit idéal pour la sieste.

Propiedad de una familia de arquitectos, este antigua granja de 500 ha a sido devuelta a la vida respetando sus origines del siglo XI. Un pequeño poblado, ubicado dentro de los muros de un histórico monasterio romanesco, Pieve di Caminino se sitúa dentro de un anfiteatro de olivares con impresionantes vistas al mar y a las colinas salpicadas de castillos y fuertes medievales. Cada habitaciones tiene chimenea y terraza propia, y está amueblado con antigüedades y muebles de la familia. En el fragrante jardín abundan las rosas inglesas y toscanas, la lavanda y el jazmín: el lugar ideal para una siesta.

Our inspector loved: *The panoramic swimming pool.*

HOTEL BORGO CASABIANCA

LOCALITÀ CASABIANCA, 53041 ASCIANO (SI), ITALY

This carefully restored, ancient villa is a very comfortable 4-star hotel. The original noble rooms are now bedrooms and suites; some are decorated with 18th and 19th-century frescoes. There are also simple country cottages and some have original working fireplaces. The refined La Tinaia restaurant serves traditional Tuscan dishes alongside fine Italian wines. Enjoy fishing on the hotel's lake, and sampling the organic farm's extra-virgin olive oil DOP Terre di Siena. Tastings of Tuscan produce and wines can be arranged.

Cette ancienne villa habillement restaurée est un confortable hôtel 4 étoiles. Les pièces nobles d'origine sont dorénavant les chambres et suites, dont certaines décorées avec des fresques du XVIIIe et XIXe siècle. Il y a également de simples petits cottages campagnards, quelques-uns avec leur cheminée d'origine. Le restaurant raffiné "La Tinaia" sert des plats toscans traditionnels accompagnés de vins fins d'Italie. Les hôtes peuvent pêcher dans le lac de l'hôtel ou déguster l'huile d'olive extra-vierge organique DOP Terre di Siena de la ferme. La dégustation de produits et de vins toscans peut-être organisée.

Esta antigua villa cuidadosamente restaurada es un confortable hotel de 4 estrellas. Las habitaciones aristocráticas originales son en la actualidad dormitorios y suites. Algunas de ellas están decoradas con frescos de los siglos XVIII y XIX. Hay también casas de campo rústicas simples. Algunas conservan sus chimeneas originales en funcionamiento. El elegante restaurante La Tinaia sirve la tradicional cocina toscana acompañada de excelentes vinos italianos. Disfrutará pescando en el lago del hotel o degustando el aceite orgánico extra-virgen Terre di Siena con DOP. Asimismo pueden concertarse degustaciones de productos y vinos toscanos.

Directions: Set on the hills, on the Val di Chiana and Crete Senesi border. A1 > exit Val di Chiana > follow directions to Sinalunga and Asciano.

Milan
Venice
Florence
Rome

Web: www.johansens.com/casabianca
E-mail: casabianca@casabianca.it
Tel: +39 0577 704 362
Fax: +39 0577 704 622

Price Guide: (closed January - March)
double €170-198
suite €240-360

Our inspector loved: *The breathtaking views of the amazing landscape.*

Borgo La Bagnaia Resort, Spa and Events Venue

STRADA STATALE 223 KM 12, 53016 LOCALITA BAGNAIA - SIENA, ITALY

Directions: 12km south of Siena on the Siena - Grosseto freeway.

Web: www.johansens.com/labagnaia
E-mail: info@labagnaia.it
Tel: +39 0577 813000
Fax: +39 0577 817464

Price Guide: (closed from beginning of November - beginning of March)
single €200-300
double €300-450
suite €450-1,500

Wildlife including fawn, deer, leverets and pheasants wander freely in Borgo La Bagnaia Resort's surrounding 2,700 acres of magnificent countryside, which features a beautiful medieval church and Buddha Spa. This ancient borgo is the perfect hideaway for a relaxing break with exclusively designed spacious rooms displaying interesting collections of Chinese and Indian antiques complemented by unique, eye-catching fabrics. The enticing spa offers various treatments aimed at restoring the balance of mind, body and spirit.

Des animaux tels que faons, cerfs, levrauts et faisans se promènent en liberté dans les 1,000 ha de superbes campagnes qui entourent le resort de Borgo La Bagnaia et qui comptent une superbe église médiévale et un Spa Buddha. Cet ancien borgo est le refuge idéal pour un séjour relaxant dans l'une des chambres spacieuses, exclusivement conçues et exposant d'intéréssantes collections d'antiquités Chinoises et Indiennes en complément de superbes tissus. Le séduisant spa offre de nombreux soins destinés à restaurer l'équilibre entre le corps et l'esprit.

Entre la fauna salvaje que merodea en plena libertad por las 1,000 ha de magníficos terrenos rurales del Borgo La Bagnaia Resort se incluye a cervatillos, ciervos, lebratos y faisanes. Dispone asimismo de una bella iglesia medieval así como de un spa budista. Este antiguo borgo es el retiro ideal para un relajado descanso gracias a sus amplias habitaciones de exclusivo diseño provistas de interesantes colecciones de antigüedades chinas e hindúes que se complementan con sus irrepetibles y llamativas telas. Su atractivo spa ofrece variados tratamientos destinados a devolver al cliente su equilibrio mental, corporal y espiritual.

Our inspector loved: *The vastness of the estate, and the feeling of being in the Garden of Eden.*

Relais Dionora

VIA VICINALE DI POGGIANO, 53040 MONTEPULCIANO (SIENA), ITALY

Dionora is an enchanting pearl amidst the magical scenery of Tuscany, immersed within nature and the scent of flowers and herbs. Cool interiors have stunning timber beams and rich, luxurious furnishings that are extremely stylish and captivate the traditional elegance of the area. All the bedrooms have a private Jacuzzi, sauna and fireplace. Breakfast is served in the Lemon House by the swimming pool, which offers gorgeous views over the surrounding countryside.

Dionora est une véritable perle plongée dans la nature et les senteurs d'herbes et de fleurs, au cœur des paysages magnifiques de Toscane. A l'intérieur, de magnifiques poutres en bois et un ameublement luxueux et très stylé reflètent l'élégance traditionnelle de la région. Toutes les chambres possèdent en plus d'une cheminée, un sauna et un jacuzzi privés. Le petit-déjeuner est servi près de la piscine dans la "Lemon House", qui offre de superbes vues sur la campagne avoisinante.

Dionora es una joya encantadora dentro del mágico paisaje de la Toscaza, inmersa en plena naturaleza y aroma a flores y hierbas. Sus frescos interiores, cautivadores de la tradicional elegancia de la zona, poseen deslumbrantes vigas de madera y un mobiliario suntuoso y lujoso de un gran estilo. Cada habitacion tiene su propio jacuzzi, sauna y chimenea. El desayuno se sirve en el Lemon House junto a la piscina, la cual ofrece unas vistas preciosas al paisaje de los alrededores.

Our inspector loved: *The enchanting surroundings.*

Directions: From the north: A1 > exit Bettolle/Valdichiana > follow signs to Montepulciano. From the south: A1 > Chiusi/Chianciano Terme > follow signs to Montepulciano.

Web: www.johansens.com/dionora
E-mail: info@dionora.it
Tel: +39 0578 717 496
Fax: +39 0578 717 498

Price Guide:
(closed 10th December - 14th February)
double €280
suite €360

Villa di Poggiano

VIA DI POGGIANO 7, 53045 MONTEPULCIANO (SIENA), TUSCANY, ITALY

Built as a summer retreat by an aristocratic family in the 18th century, this elegant and exclusive villa nestles in 15 acres of parkland on a hilltop with views of endless vineyards and olive groves of the Orcia Valley, close to the historic town of Montepulciano. Furnishings of the 3 bedrooms and 6 suites, which overlook either a splendid marble swimming pool or the valley, reflect the refined style of the villa with its fine antique furniture and paintings.

Construite comme résidence d'été par une famille aristocratique du XVIIIe siècle, cette villa chic et élégante se niche au cœur de plus de 6 ha de parcs au sommet d'une colline avec des vues sans fin sur les vignobles et oliveraies de la vallée d'Orcia, près de la ville historique de Montepulciano. L'ameublement des 3 chambres et 6 suites, qui surplombent soit la splendide piscine de marbre, soit la vallée, reflète le style raffiné de la villa avec son mobilier ancien et ses peintures.

Construida como lugar de retiro estival por una familia aristócrata en el siglo XVIII, esta elegante y noble villa se encuentra situada en la cima de una colina, en una zona verde de 6 ha, desde la que se puede contemplar los innumerables viñedos y olivares del Valle de Orcia, muy cerca de la histórica ciudad de Montepulciano. El mobiliario y la decoración de sus 3 habitaciones y 6 suites, con vistas bien a una magnífica piscina de mármol o al valle, reflejan el refinado estilo de esta villa gracias a sus elegantes muebles antiguos y lienzos.

Our inspector loved: *The neo-classic swimming pool in the huge park.*

Directions: A1 > exit Chiusi - Chianciano > follow signs to Montepulciano.

Web: www.johansens.com/villadipoggiano
E-mail: info@villapoggiano.com
Tel: +39 0578 758292
Fax: +39 0578 715635

Price Guide:
(closed 3rd November - 31st March)
double €195-210
suite €230-300

Castel Pietraio

STRADA DI STROVE 33, 53035 MONTERIGGIONI, ITALY

Castel Pietraio is steeped in local history and today is the centre of a strong wine-growing estate. Whilst marble bathrooms and Jacuzzi baths have been added to ensure every comfort, there is still an enchanting medieval ambience. Considerately planned to accommodate guests' every requirement, there is a swimming pool, playground and walking paths on site, whilst the tower is lit by torches for grand banquets and special occasions in the Capacci hall. There are 2 golf courses nearby.

Ce château imprégné d'histoire est aujourd'hui le noyau d'un important domaine viticole. L'installation de salles de bains en marbre et de jacuzzis pour le plus grand confort du visiteur n'a rien ôté au charme médiéval de l'endroit. Conçu de manière à satisfaire tous les besoins des visiteurs, cet hôtel dispose d'une élégante piscine, d'un terrain de jeu et un chemin de randonnée. La tour est illuminée par des torches lors des grands banquets et des occasions speciales organisés dans la salle Capacci. 2 parcours de golf se situent à proximité.

Castel Pietraio está impregnada de historia del lugar y es hoy en día el centro de una importante propiedad vinícola. Aunque se le han añadido cuartos de baño de mármol y jacuzzi para garantizar todo el confort posible, perduran en el un encantador ambiente medieval. Preparado a conciencia para acomodarse a todas las exigencias de los clientes, dispone de una elegante piscina, recinto de recreo y una trayectoria para caminar, en sus instalaciones, siendo su torreón iluminado con antorchas para los grandiosos banquetes y las ocasiones especiales que se celebran en la sala Capacee. Hay 2 campos de golf en las cercanías.

Our inspector loved: *The central location between Florence and Siena.*

Directions: A1 Florence – Siena road, exit at Monteriggioni > SS541 towards Badia Isola.

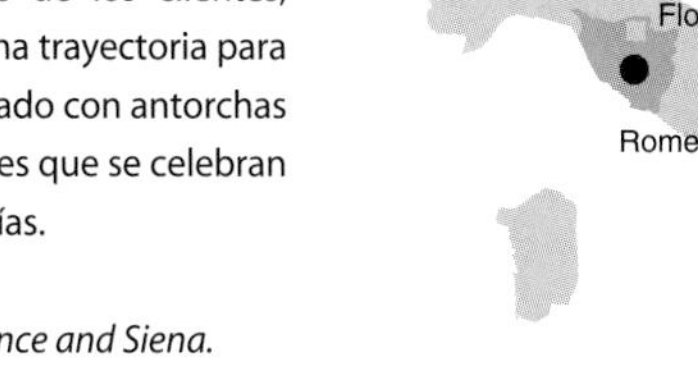

Web: www.johansens.com/castelpietraio
E-mail: monteriggioni@interfree.it
Tel: +39 0577 300020
Fax: +39 0577 300977

Price Guide: (closed 19th - 25th January)
single €100-130
double/twin €120–150
junior suite €150-180

Relais La Suvera (Dimora Storica)

53030 PIEVESCOLA – SIENA, ITALY

In 1989 the Marchess Ricci and his wife Principessa Eleonora Massimo created this elite and luxurious hotel composed of 4 beautifully restored houses surrounding a courtyard. The elegant reception has a welcoming ambience, enhanced by a display of wines from their own vineyard. The exquisite salons are bedecked with antiques and the family art collection. Guests feast on Tuscan dishes served in the hotel's restaurant.

C'est en 1989 que le marquis Ricci et son épouse la princesse Eleonora Massimo ont créé cet hôtel luxueux de grand standing formé de 4 maisons superbement restaurées autour d'une cour. L'élégante réception se caractérise par une ambiance chaleureuse, accentuée par une série de bouteilles de vins provenant du vignoble du Relais. Les salons ravissants sont agrémentés de belles pièces anciennes et d'une collection d'oeuvres d'art de la famille. Les hôtes se régalent de succulents plats toscans servis au restaurant de l'hôtel.

En 1989, el marqués Ricci y su esposa, la princesa Eleonora Massimo, crearon este lujoso hotel de elite, compuesto por 4 casas bellamente restauradas que rodean un patio central. La elegante zona de recepción tiene ambiente acogedor que se realza con una estupenda muestra de vinos procedentes del propio viñedo. Los exquisítos salones están repletos de antigüedades y la colección de arte de los propietarios. En el restaurante se sirve una verdadera fiesta de platos toscanos.

Our inspector loved: *The family's collection of antiques, and the hotel's cultural heritage.*

Directions: Superstrada Siena-Florence > Colle Val d'Elsa > Grosseto.

Web: www.johansens.com/relaislasuvera
E-mail: lasuvera@lasuvera.it
Tel: +39 0577 960 300
Fax: +39 0577 960 220

Price Guide:
(closed 5th November - 20th April)
double/twin €385–680
suite €600–1,200

32 50

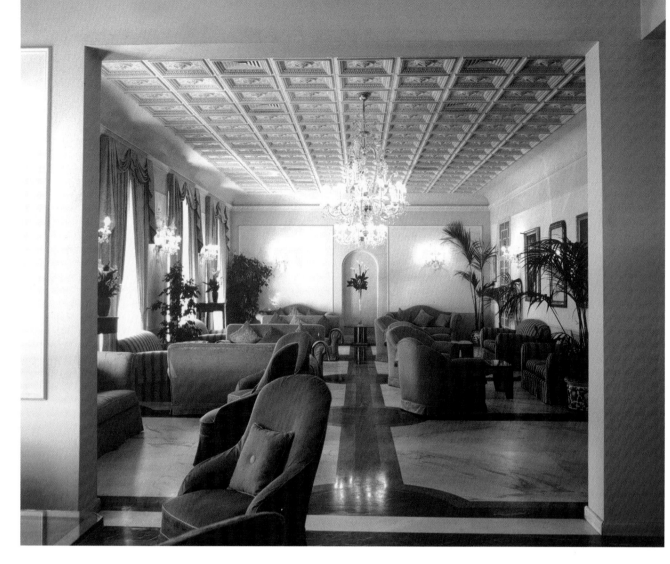

Hotel Plaza e de Russie

PIAZZA D'AZEGLIO 1, 55049 VIAREGGIO (LU), ITALY

This splendid hotel was the first built in Viareggio in 1871 and retains a stately magnificence that is today combined with modern comfort and luxury. Tall and elegantly proportioned rooms are all individually decorated with rich antiques, Italian marble and classic Murano chandeliers. The gourmet restaurant, La Terrazza, offers Mediterranean inspired high cuisine and the terrace has outstanding views of the Versilia coast climbing up towards the Apuan Alps and is a stunning place to enjoy some spectacular sunsets.

Ce splendide hôtel fut le premier construit à Viareggio en 1871 et garde une imposante magnificence qui est aujourd'hui combinée au luxe et au confort moderne. Les chambres, grandes et en élégante harmonie sont individuellement décorées avec de somptueuses antiquités, du marbre italien et des chandeliers de Murano. Le restaurant gastronomique La Terrazza sert une délicate cuisine d'inspiration méditerranéenne et la terrasse offre non seulement de superbes vues sur la côte de Versilia jusqu'aux Alpes Apuanes mais est également l'endroit idéal pour admirer de magnifiques couchers de soleil.

Este espléndido hotel fue el primero que se construyó en Viareggio en 1871 y conserva una majestuosidad que hoy día se combina con el confort moderno y el lujo. Sus altas habitaciones de elegantes proporciones están decoradas individualmente con valiosas antigüedades, mármol italiano y clásicas lámparas de araña de Murano. Su restaurante gourmet, La Terrazza, ofrece alta cocina de inspiración mediterránea y su terraza inigualables vistas a la costa Versilia y a las laderas de los Alpes Apuanos. Es también un lugar inmejorable para disfrutar de espectaculares puestas de sol.

Our inspector loved: *The roof terrace with its splendid view of the Versilia Riviera.*

Directions: A12 > exit Viareggio - Camaiore.

Web: www.johansens.com/russie
E-mail: info@plazaederussie.com
Tel: +39 0584 44449
Fax: +39 0584 44031

Price Guide:
single €132-192
double €183-283
junior suite €291-343

ROMANTIK HOTEL LE SILVE DI ARMENZANO

06081 LOC. ARMENZANO, ASSISI (PG), ITALY

Directions: Perugia > Assisi> S 75 > Armenzano.

Web: www.johansens.com/silvediarmenzano
E-mail: info@lesilve.it
Tel: +39 075 801 9000
Fax: +39 075 801 9005

Price Guide: (closed from 5th November - 30th March)
single €100–150
double/twin €165–220
suite €400-500

This small hotel dates back to before the birth of St Francis of Assisi, the patron saint of animals. Le Silve is 700 metres above sea level, built on a plateau at the foot of the Subasio mountains. The air is scented by olive groves, and deer and horses ramble through the beautiful countryside. Umbrian cooking is delicious and here, the bread is baked traditionally in the fireplace. A charming sense of unspoilt rural simplicity is created by touches such as al fresco dining and country furniture.

Ce petit hôtel dâte d'avant la naissance de Saint-François d'Assise, le saint patron des animaux. Le Silve se situe à 700 mètres au-dessus du niveau de la mer. Il a été construit sur un plateau, au pied des montagnes du Subasio. L'air y est parfumé par les oliveraies et des biches et des chevaux gambadent dans le magnifique parc. La cuisine ombrienne est délicieuse et le pain proposé est cuit de façon traditionnelle dans la cheminée. Le diner servi à l'extérieur et le mobilier de style campagnard dégagent un agréable sentiment de simplicité rurale.

Este pequeño hotel data de épocas anteriores al nacimiento de San Francisco de Asís, patrón de los animales. Le Silve se encuentra a 700 metros sobre el nivel del mar sobre una meseta a los pies de los montes de Subasio. El aire esta perfumado por los olivares, y los ciervos y los caballos se mueven a sus anchas por sus bellos campos. La cocina de Umbría es deliciosa y aquí el pan se hace al estilo tradicional, al fuego de chimenea. Su encantador ambiente de virginal simplicidad campestre se consigue gracias a detalles tales como la cena al aire libre y el mobiliario rural.

Our inspector loved: *The elegance of this charming retreat, which offers traditional dishes and homemade delicacies.*

San Crispino Resort & Spa

LOC TORDANDREA - ASSISI, TORDANDREA (PG), ITALY

This elegant country resort is ideal for a relaxing holiday with a difference enriched by the treatments offered in its sublime spa. Tastefully furnished bedrooms are decorated with refined rustic style inspired by the abundance of beautiful plants and flowers surrounding the hotel. Delicious Umbrian cuisine is served in the delightful resort restaurant and guests can unwind in the reading room or by the pool, which benefits from spectacular views over Assisi.

Cet élégant resort de campagne est idéal pour des vacances relaxantes avec en plus les traitement proposés dans le sublime spa. Les chambres, meublées avec goût, sont décorées dans un style rustique raffiné inspiré par l'abondance de superbes fleurs et plantes entourant l'hôtel. Une délicieuse cuisine Ombrienne est servie dans le ravissant restaurant du resort. Les hôtes peuvent se détendre dans la salle de lecture ou au bord de la piscine qui offre des vues spectaculaires sur Assisi.

Este elegante Resort rural es ideal para pasar unas vacaciones de relax diferentes y enriquecidos por todo lo que pueda ofrecerle su magnífico spa. Las habitaciones están decoradas elegantemente con un estilo rústico refinado, inspirado por la abundancia de bonitas plantas y flores que circundan el hotel. En el encantador restaurante se sirve sabrosa cocina local. Los huéspedes pueden relajarse en la sala de lectura o en la zona de piscina desde donde se disfrutan fantásticas vistas de Asís.

Our inspector loved: *The refined ambience, décor, and the sweet welcome.*

Directions: 4km from Assisi towards Tordandrea.

Web: www.johansens.com/sancrispinoresortspa
E-mail: booking@assisibenessere.it and info@assisiwellness.com.
Tel: +39 075 804 3257
Fax: +39 075 804 3257

Price Guide: (per person, including access to wellness centre)
single €97
double €75-85
suite €95

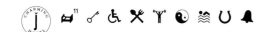

Relais Alla Corte del Sole

LOC. I GIORGI, 06061 PETRIGNANO DEL LAGO (PG), ITALY

This delightful, 15th-century monastic village with its renovated, rebuilt and refurbished accommodation stands near Lake Trasimeno, midway between Cortona and Montepulciano. It is the ideal retreat for anyone seeking to be pampered and enjoy the region's cultural centres. Each guest room is charmingly elegant, air-conditioned and has every home comfort. The new restaurant serves a menu that combines tradition with innovation, has a wonderful view of the landscape and an enchanting atmosphere. The beautifully maintained grounds feature a large swimming pool.

Ce charmant village monastique datant du XVe siècle avec des logements rénovés, reconstruit et remis à neuf, est situé près du lac Trasimeno, entre Cortona et Montepulciano. Il est l'endroit parfait pour des personnes cherchant à se dorloter et profiter des centres culturels de la région. Chaque chambre est élégante, climatisée et dispose de tout le confort moderne. Le nouveau restaurant d'une atmosphère enchanteresse sert un menu traditionnel et innovateur et offre des vues splendides sur les environs. Il y a une grande piscine dans le parc superbement entretenu.

Esta encantadora aldea monástica del siglo XV con su alojamiento renovado, reconstruido y reamueblado se encuentra cerca del lago Trasimeno, a mitad de camino entre Cortona y Montepulciano. Es el lugar ideal para el que desea regalarse comodidad y disfrutar de los centros culturales de la región. Cada una de las habitaciones tiene un elegante encanto y aire acondicionado así como confort casero. El nuevo restaurante sirve un menu tradicional y innovador en un ambiente encantador y con vistas maravillosas. Sus terrenos, excelentemente cuidados, incluyen también una gran piscina.

Our inspector loved: *The mouthwatering breakfast, superb attention to detail, and exclusivity.*

Directions: A1 > exit Valdichiana/Bettolle > take Superstrada to Perugia > second exit for Cortona > follow signs for Montepulciano.

Web: www.johansens.com/cortedelsole
E-mail: info@cortedelsole.com
Tel: +39 075 9689008
Fax: +39 075 9689070

Price Guide: (closed in 10th - 30th January)
double €166-265
suite €243-340

Castello di Petroia

LOCALITÀ SCRITTO DI GUBBIO, PETROIA, 06020 GUBBIO (PG), ITALY

Steeped in Italian history and the birthplace of Count Federico da Montefeltro, Duke of Urbino, Castello di Petroia is a beautiful collection of buildings housed within castle walls. The duke played a key part in the Italian Renaissance and the castle has been restored today in complete sympathy with its origins. Guests at the castle are assured of a quite unique experience. The common rooms are beautiful, and the swimming pool a truly relaxing haven overlooking the peaceful woods and grounds that surround the estate.

Imprégné d'histoire italienne, et le lieu de naissance du Comte Federico da Montefeltro, Duc d'Urbino, Castello di Petroia est un ensemble de bâtiments situés au sein des murs du château. Le Duc joua un rôle important pendant la renaissance italienne et le château a maintenant été restauré en accord avec ses particularités d'origine; ses hôtes peuvent donc jouir d'une expérience unique. Les pièces communes sont superbes et la piscine, avec sa vue sur les bois et le parc entourant la propriété, est l'endroit idéal pour se détendre.

Inmerso en la historia de Italia y lugar de nacimiento del Conde Federico da Montefeltro, Duque de Urbino, Castello de Petroia es un bello conjunto de edificios ubicado entre los muros de un castillo. El duque tuvo un papel decisivo en el Renacimiento italiano y el castillo ha sido restaurado en la actualidad respetando al máximo sus orígenes. Los clientes tendrán la oportunidad de disfrutar aquí de una experiencia única. Las estancias comunes son hermosas. Su piscina, un verdadero remanso en el que relajarse, da a las apacibles zonas arboladas y ajardinadas que rodean el lugar.

Our inspector loved: *The fascinating history behind this authentic castle.*

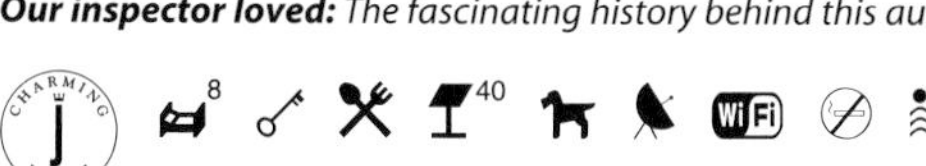

Directions: E45 (Orte–Cesena) > exit at Bosco > the castle is on the SS298.

Web: www.johansens.com/castellodipetroia
E-mail: info@castellodipetroia.com
Tel: +39 075 92 02 87
Fax: +39 075 92 01 08

Price Guide:
(closed in January - end of March)
tower €120–140
double/twin €125–145
suite €160–200

I Casali di Monticchio

VOCABOLO MONTICCHIO 34, 05011 ALLERONA, ORVIETO (TR), ITALY

This pastoral hideaway, in the rolling foothills of the Appenines offers luxurious farmhouse living in peaceful countryside with amenities expected from a first-class hotel. The careful restoration has ensured that the charming original style has been maintained; the former stables are now the restaurant where delicious Umbrian cuisine is served. Above the restaurant is the grand vaulted salon that leads to the suites, whilst guest rooms are located in converted outhouses fitted with fine Italian furnishings and an interior design that reflects the farmhouse's heritage.

Cette petite cache campagnarde, aux pieds de l'Apennin, offre un séjour dans un luxueux corps de ferme avec l'équipement qu'on attend d'un hôtel de 1ère catégorie. La restauration soigneuse a permis de conserver le charmant style original ; les anciennes étables sont maintenant le restaurant où est servie une délicieuse cuisine ombrienne. Au-dessus du restaurant se tient le grand salon voûté qui conduit aux suites. Les chambres d'hôtes sont situées dans les remises qui ont été converties et aménagés de manière raffiné grâce à l'ameublement italien qui reflète l'héritage de la ferme.

Este refugio pastoril, a los pies de los Apeninos, ofrece una vida de lujo en casa de labranza rodeada de campo y tranquilo, con todas las conveniencias de un hotel de primera. La cuidada rehabilitación del edificio ha respetado el encanto original de esta casa de campo: los antiguos establos se han convertido en un restaurante donde se sirve la deliciosa cocina de Umbría. Encima del restaurante hay un gran salón abovedado que conduce a las suites, mientras que las habitaciones normales se encuentran en lo que antiguamente eran dependencias, hoy decoradas con buenos muebles italianos reflejando el patrimonio de la casa.

Our inspector loved: *The complete peacefulness.*

Directions: A1 > exit Fabro > turn left and pass through Fabio > continue straight on for 6km > Allesiona Scolo > up the hill for 7km.

Web: www.johansens.com/monticchio
E-mail: info@monticchio.com
Tel: +39 0763 62 83 65
Fax: +39 0763 62 83 65

Price Guide:
double €240
suite €300

L'Antico Forziere

VIA DELLA ROCCA 2, 06051 CASALINA DERUTA (PG), ITALY

Set in a prime location to enjoy the pleasures of Umbria, this charming country house hotel is located near Deruta, famous for its artworks and majolica. The inviting ambience, created by the owners, lead guests into this antique rural building where each guest room is well appointed and exudes a typical Umbrian country atmosphere; the 3 suites have private access. The proprietor's twin sons create traditional cuisine and serve Italian wines in the classic dining room or on the terrace.

Idéalement situé pour profiter des plaisirs de l'Ombrie, ce charmant hôtel de campagne se trouve près de Deruta, réputé pour ses illustrations et ses céramiques. L'ambiance accueillante, créée par les propriétaires, conduit les clients dans cet ancien bâtiment rural où toutes les chambres sont bien agencées et respirent l'atmosphère typique de la campagne de l'Ombrie. Les 3 suites ont un accès privé. Les fils jumeaux du propriétaire proposent une cuisine traditionnelle et servent des vins Italiens dans la salle à manger classique ou sur la terrasse.

Situada en una situacion privilegiada para disfrutar de los placeres de la Umbría, este encantador hotel rural se encuentra cerca de la localidad de Deruta, famosa por su artesanía y majórica. Su acogedor ambiente creado por los propietarios atraen a los clientes a este antiguo edificio rural donde cada habitación esta perfectamente acondicionada y emana un característico sabor a campo de la Umbría. Las 3 suites disponen de acceso privado. Los hijos mellizos del propietario crean platos de cocina tradicional y sirven vinos italianos en el clásico comedor o en la terraza.

Our inspector loved: *The sublime cuisine, and warm welcome.*

Directions: From north: A1 towards Roma > exit Valdichiana > E45 towards Perugia> exit Casalina. Or take A14 from Bologna to Ancona > exit for Cesena north > E45 towards Roma > exit Casalina. From south: A1 towards Firenze > exit Orte > E45 towards Perugia > exit Casalina. The nearest airport is S. Egidio.

Web: www.johansens.com/lanticoforziere
E-mail: info@anticoforziere.com
Tel: +39 075 972 4314
Fax: +39 075 972 9392

Price Guide: (closed 10th - 31st January)
single €65-75
double €85-100
suite €125-150

Le Torri di Bagnara (Medieval Historical Residences)

STRADA DELLA BRUNA 8, 06080 PIEVE SAN QUIRICO, PERUGIA, ITALY

Directions: E45 (Orte - Ravenna) > exit Resina > SS Tiberina (towards north) > turn left at Km89.7 > Pieve San Quirico - Bagnara.

Web: www.johansens.com/bagnara
E-mail: info@letorridibagnara.it
Tel: +39 075 579 2001 and +39 335 6408 549
Fax: +39 075 579 3001

Milan
Venice
Perugia
Rome

Price Guide: (room only, per week, closed 8th Jan - 1st Mar)
Tower apartments (2 beds) €380-750
Tower apartments (4-5 beds) €775-1,300
Abbey rooms (per room, per night)
double/twin €120-190
junior suite €140-230

Owned by the Tremi-Giunta family since 1901, descendants of Emperor Napoleon I, this historic complex offers guests a peaceful refuge high on a hill overlooking the Tiber Valley. Le Torri di Bagnara consists of 2 main buildings surrounded by a 1,300-acre estate, which includes tobacco and beet plantations, a nature reserve, swimming pool and botanical, organic and flower-filled gardens. A 12th-century Tower houses 4 superb apartments; the 11th-century Abbey Relais de Charme offers luxury bedrooms, junior suites, a meeting room and a church.

Propriété depuis 1901 de la famille Tremi-Giunta, descendants de Napoléon Bonaparte, ce complexe historique offre à ses hôtes un refuge tranquille haut perché sur une colline surplombant la vallée du Tibre. Le Torri di Bagnara historique est composé de 2 bâtiments principaux entourés d'un domaine de plus de 500 ha comprenant des plantations de tabac et de betteraves, une réserve naturelle, une piscine et des jardins fleuris biologiques. Une tour du XIIe siècle abrite 4 superbes appartements, l'abbaye du XIe siècle abrite un Relais de Charme avec de luxueuses chambers, suites juniors, une salle de réunion et une église.

Propiedad desde 1901 de la familia Tremi-Giunta, descendientes del Emperador Napoleón I, este histórico complejo ofrece a sus huéspedes un tranquilo refugio en lo alto de una colina con vistas al Valle de Tiber. Le Torri di Bagnara consta de 2 edificios principales enclavados dentro de una propiedad de 500 ha que incluye plantaciones de tabaco y remolacha, una reserva natural, una piscina, además de jardines botánicos y orgánicos repletos de flores. Una Torre del siglo XII alberga 4 magníficos apartamentos, la Abadía del siglo XI dispone de un Relais de Charme con de habitaciones de lujo y suites junior.

Our inspector loved: *The outstanding natural beauty.*

Alla Posta dei Donini

VIA DERUTA 43, 06079 SAN MARTINO IN CAMPO (PG), ITALY

This magnificent mansion dates back to 1600 and was once the summer residence of the Earl of Donini and his family. Restored in the 18th and 19th centuries, this Umbrian property is adorned with paintings and frescos by celebrated Perugian artists. The elegant interior is appointed in soft pale shades with striking chandeliers and rich rugs, and bedrooms furnished with warm and simple colour schemes. The Italian garden features a century-old botanic park, swimming pool and club house.

Cette magnifique demeure date de 1600 et fut la résidence d'été du Comte de Donini et de sa famille. Restaurée aux XVIIIe et XIXe siècles, cette propriété Ombrienne est ornée de peintures et de fresques d'artistes célèbres de Pérouse. L'élégant intérieur est décoré dans des tons doux avec de magnifiques chandeliers et de somptueux tapis, et les chambres sont dans des tons chauds et naturels. Le jardin à l'italienne se compose d'un parc botanique centenaire, d'une piscine et d'un pavillon.

Esta magnífica mansión data de 1600 y fue antaño la residencia veraniega del Conde de Donini y su familia. Restaurada en los siglos XVIII y XIX, esta propiedad de Umbría está adornada con lienzos y frescos, obra de famosos artistas de Perugia. Su elegante interior de suaves y pálidos tonos cuenta con impresionantes lámparas de araña y suntuosas alfombras, y sus dormitorios están amueblados con diseños de colores cálidos y simples. El jardín italiano dispone de un centenario parque botánico, piscina y club-bar.

Our inspector loved: *The elegant Italian décor, and the charming park.*

Directions: E45 (Cesena - Roma) > exit Torgiano San Martino in Campo.

Web: www.johansens.com/postadonini
E-mail: info@postadonini.it
Tel: +39 075 609 132
Fax: +39 075 609 132

Price Guide:
double (single occupancy) €140-212
double €140-242
junior suite €180-270

La Preghiera

VIA DEL REFARI, 06018 (PG), CALZOLARO, UMBERTIDE, ITALY

Directions: E45 > exit Promano. Near Città di Castello and only 40 minutes from Assisi, Perugia, Cortona and Lake Trasimeno.

Web: www.johansens.com/lapreghiera
E-mail: info@lapreghiera.com
Tel: +39 075 9302428
Fax: +39 075 9302428

Price Guide:
double (single occupancy) €135-285
double €150-300
suite €250-350

This converted 12th-century monastery is a romantic retreat ideally located for exploring the delights of Umbria and Tuscany. Standard luxuries include silk and cotton blended bed linen, en-suite marble bathrooms, under-floor heating and period furniture. Meals containing locally reared meat and fresh fruit and vegetables are prepared with prior notice, whilst buffet breakfast is available until late. In-house treatments can be arranged, and the private chapel is an idyllic setting for a wedding.

Ce monastère converti du XIIe siècle est une retraite romantique parfaitement située pour explorer les délices d'Ombrie et de Toscane. Le luxe standard consiste en draps de soie et coton mélangés, de salles de bain en marbre, chauffage au sol et mobilier d'époque. Préparés sur demande, les repas sont composés de fruits et légumes frais, et la viande provient d'élevages locaux. Le buffet du petit-déjeuner peut être servi jusqu'à tard. Il est possible d'organiser sur place des soins et des manucures. La chapelle privée est l'endroit idyllique pour une cérémonie de mariage.

Este romántico refugio emplazado en un monasterio convertido del siglo XII es el lugar ideal para explorar los encantos de Umbría y Toscana. Entre sus lujos Standard incluye ropa de cama de seda y algodón mezclados, cuartos de baño en suite de mármol, mobiliario de época y calefacción por suelo radiante. Las comidas se usa carne local, fuita fresca y verduras son preparadas sobre demanda anterior. El desayuno del buffet se sirve hasta tarde. Masajes y manicura se pueden organizar en el hotel y la capilla privada es un lugar idílico para celebrar una boda.

Our inspector loved: *The toy soldier museum with over 30,000 pieces.*

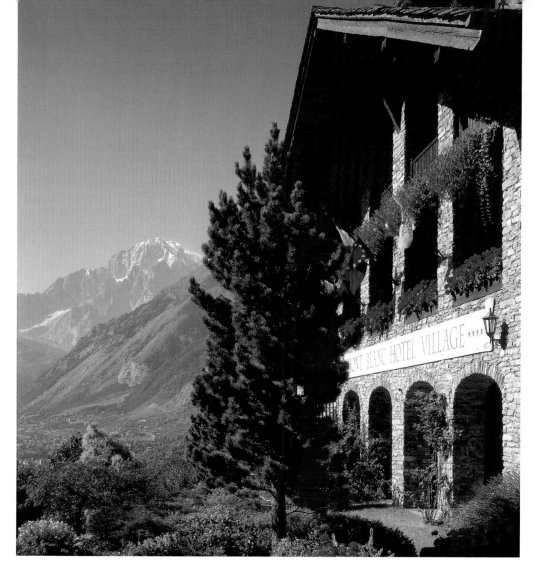

Mont Blanc Hotel Village

LOCALITA LA CROISETTE 36, 11015 LA SALLE (AO), VALLE D'AOSTA, ITALY

Described as a window looking onto Mont Blanc, this hotel is located in the heart of the Western Alps, amidst some of the most important skiing areas. Formed by a collection of wooden and stone chalets in the style of the Valle d'Aosta, public rooms and spacious bedrooms have cotto floors and elegant furniture. In the main building the hotel boasts one of the most prestigious restaurants in the area. Enjoy the spa, tennis courts and gym, and the hotel's special agreement with a local golf course.

Décrit comme une fenêtre sur le Mont-Blanc, cet hôtel est situé au cœur des Alpes Occidentales et au milieu des principaux domaines skiables. Formé d'un groupe de chalets en bois et en pierre dans le style traditionnel de la Vallée d'Aoste, les pièces commune et les chambres spacieuses ont des sols en terre cuite et un mobilier élégant. Dans le bâtiment principal, l'hôtel peut se vanter d'avoir un des restaurants plus prestigieux de la région. Les loisirs comprennent un centre de remise en forme, un spa et des courts de tennis ainsi que golf grâce à un accord spécial avec le club local.

Este hotel, calificado como la ventana al Mont Blanc, se encuentra en el corazón de los Alpes occidentales rodeado de algunas de las pistas más importantes del esquí. Formado por un conjunto de chalets de piedra y madera al estilo del Valle de Aosta, sus estancias comunes y sus amplias habitaciones cuentan con suelos de "cotto" y elegantes muebles. El hotel tiene en el edificio principal uno de los restaurantes de mayor prestigio de la zona. Los clientes pueden disfrutar del spa, pistas de tenis y el gimnasio, asi como de un acuerdo especial que tiene el hotel con un campo de golf cercano.

Directions: Take the A5 to Morgex.

Web: www.johansens.com/montblanc
E-mail: info@hotelmontblanc.it
Tel: +39 0165 864 111
Fax: +39 0165 864 119

Milan
Venice
Rome

Price Guide: (closed 15th October - 30th November)
single €75-200
double €150-350
suite €170-470

Our inspector loved: *The most fascinating mountain scenery.*

Hotel Jolanda Sport

LOC. EDELBODEN 31, GRESSONEY~LA~TRINITE, 11020 GRESSONEY LA TRINITA (AOSTA), ITALY

Nestling in the heart of the Monterosa ski resort, this recently refurbished alpine retreat will delight winter sport enthusiasts and those searching for a cosy bolthole for a relaxing break. Located in Gressoney-La-Trinité, just by the Punta Jolanda chair ski lift, guests can enjoy the 130km of ski runs in the morning and spend an afternoon unwinding in the spa. The restaurant offers a fine selection of traditional dishes and excellent wines to sate an appetite after a day on the slopes.

Niché au cœur du resort de Monterosa, cet hôtel alpin récemment restauré ravira les fanatiques de sports d'hiver ou ceux à la recherche d'un refuge pour un séjour relaxant. Situé à Gressoney-La-Trinité, au départ du télésiège de Punta Jolanda, les hôtes peuvent profiter des 130 kms de pistes le matin et passer l'après-midi à se détendre au spa. Le restaurant propose une délicieuse sélection de plats traditionnels et d'excellents vins qui rassasieront les appétits après une journée sur les pistes.

Este refugio alpino se encuentra en el corazón de la estación de esquí Monterosa, que ha sido reformado recientemente, encantará a los deportistas de invierno y a los que buscan un descanso relajante en un lugar acogedor. Ubicado en Gressoney-la-Trinité junto al telesilla de Punta Jolanda, los huéspedes pueden disfrutar de 130 kilómetros de pistas de esquí por la mañana y por la tarde relajarse en el spa. El restaurante ofrece una selección de exquisitos platos tradicionales y excelentes vinos para deleitar el apetito después de un día en las pistas.

Our inspector loved: *The charm of a mountain chalet, and the direct access to one of the most impressive ski resort on the Alps.*

Directions: A5 > exit Pont St Martin > road to Gressoney.

Web: www.johansens.com/jolandasport
E-mail: info@hoteljolandasport.com
Tel: +39 0125 366 140
Fax: +39 0125 366 202

Price Guide: (closed October - November)
standard €75-102
romantik €85-115
suite €90-125

Hotel Villa Ca' Sette

VIA CUNIZZA DA ROMANO 4, 36061 BASSANO DEL GRAPPA, ITALY

The Hotel Villa Ca' Sette takes its name from a Venetian family who built the villa as a summer residence in the 18th century and is a truly stylish home from home. An atmosphere of quiet elegance is created by immaculate style and harmonious use of space whilst original local furniture and antiques create an authentic feel. Delicious food can be enjoyed in the award-winning restaurant or in the lovely manicured Italian garden. Bassano has a rich cultural life, stunning Venetian architecture, museums and a number of frescoed palazzi.

L' hôtel Villa Ca' Sette tient son nom d'une famille vénitienne qui construit la villa comme résidence d'été au XVIIIe siècle. On se sent vraiment chez soi dans cet hôtel élégant. Une atmosphère d'élégance discrète est créée par le style immaculé et l'utilisation harmonieuse de l'espace, renforcée par un mobilier local original et des antiquités ajoutant au caractère authentique. Une cuisine délicieuse est servie dans le restaurant renommé ou le beau jardin dessiné au style italien. Bassano a une riche vie culturelle, une architecture vénitienne superbe, des musées et des palais ornés de fresques.

El Hotel Villa Ca' Sette toma el nombre de una familia veneciana que construyó la villa como residencia estival en el siglo XVIII, habiéndose convertido en una casa de sabor verdaderamente hogareño. Su ambiente de apacible elegancia lo proporciona su estilo impecable y su armonioso uso del espacio, a la par que su original mobiliario y antigüedades procedentes de la zona le confieren un toque de autenticidad. Podrá degustar su deliciosa carta en su galardonado restaurante o en su encantador y cuidadísimo jardín italiano. Bassano tiene una rica vida cultural, sorprendente arquitectura veneciana, museos y gran variedad de palazzi con frescos.

Our inspector loved: *This stylish home away from home, and excellent dining.*

Directions: A4 > A31 towards Valdastico > exit at Dueville > take the main road to Bassano del Grappa. 1 hour and 30 minutes from Venice Airport.

Milan
Venice
Rome

Web: www.johansens.com/ca-sette
E-mail: info@ca-sette.it
Tel: +39 0424 383 350
Fax: +39 0424 393 287

Price Guide:
single €115–130
double €180–210
suite €360–460

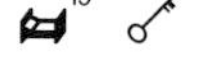

Color Hotel

VIA SANTA CRISTINA 5, 37011 BARDOLINO (VR), ITALY

This welcoming hotel takes its inspiration from colour, the essence of life and wellbeing. Chromatherapy transforms the interior into a relaxing and cheerful environment, featuring innovative furnishings and decorations. Guests will love the new pool, with its uniquely designed waterfall and trendy lounge area with tented gazebos. The stunning new suites are extremely spacious and have a lovely view of the pool. Bardolino is an ideal base to explore the beauties of Lake Garda and the surrounding area, famous for wine and oil production.

Cet hôtel accueillant prend son inspiration dans les couleurs, l'essence de la vie et le bien être. La chromothérapie transforme l'intérieur en un environnement gai et relaxant en présentant une décoration et un mobilier innovants. Les hôtes aimeront la nouvelle piscine avec sa cascade au design unique et son coin salon branché avec ses gazebos voilés. Les sublimes nouvelles suites sont très spacieuses et ont de belles vues sur la piscine. Bardolino est la base idéale pour explorer les beautés du Lac de Garde et de ses environs, connus pour sa production de vin et d'huile.

Este acogedor hotel se inspira en los colores, la esencia de la vida y el bienestar. La cromoterapia transforma su interior en un ambiente relajante y alegre, con decoración y mobiliario ultramodernos. Les encantara la nueva piscina con su cascada de diseño único y su modernísima zona de descanso con pabellones. Las estupendas nuevas suites son muy espaciosas, con bonitas vistas de la piscina. Bardolino es una base ideal desde donde explorar los encantos del Lago de Garda y sus alrededores, zona conocida por su producción de vinos y de aceites.

Our inspector loved: *The friendly staff and the colourful atmosphere.*

Directions: A22 > exit Affi > follow signs to Lago di Garda.

Web: www.johansens.com/color
E-mail: info@colorhotel.it
Tel: +39 045 621 0857
Fax: +39 045 621 2697

Price Guide:
single €70-165
double/twin €120-195
junior suite €160-305
suite €190-380

AI CAPITANI HOTEL

VIA CASTELLETTO 2/4, PESCHIERA DEL GARDA (VR), ITALY

Situated in the historical centre of town and looking out towards the port, this wonderful 5-star hotel offers the utmost luxury in an intimate environment. With 17 guest rooms, the style is one of modern luxury characterized by clean and simple lines and natural wooden floors. The service is attentive, yet discreet. The small spa situated on the second floor offers a massage area; an excellent place to de-stress and enjoy the views; alternatively take advantage of the hotel's private boat and limousine drivers to explore this beautiful area of Italy.

Situé dans le centre historique de la ville et tourné vers le port, ce merveilleux hôtel 5 étoiles offre le meilleur du luxe dans un environnement privé. Avec ses 17 chambres, il possède un style luxueux moderne caractérisé par ses lignes simples et nettes et ses parquets. Le service est attentionné et discret. Le petit spa situé au deuxième étage offre un coin massage ; un endroit parfait pour se relaxer et admirer les vues, alors que les plus aventureux peuvent utiliser le bateau privé de l'hôtel et les chauffeurs de limousine pour visiter cette belle région de l'Italie.

Ubicado en el centro histórico del pueblo y con vistas al puerto, este maravilloso hotel de 5 estrellas ofrece el lujo máximo en un ambiente íntimo. Consta de 17 habitaciones en estilo moderno de lujo caracterizado por líneas limpias y sencillas con suelos en madera natural. El servicio es atento pero discreto. El pequeño spa con zona para masajes se encuentra en la segunda planta y es un lugar excelente para relajarse y disfrutar de las vistas. Los más activos pueden aprovecharse del barco privado, o de los vehículos con chofer que posee el hotel, para explorar esta bellisima región de Italia.

Our inspector loved: *The luxury and intimacy in the centre of town.*

Directions: 20km from Verona. From Milan > A4 > exit Peschiera del Garda > follow signs to the centre.

Milan
Venice
Rome

Web: www.johansens.com/aicapitani
E-mail: reservation@aicapitani.com
Tel: +39 045 6400782 or 7553071
Fax: +39 045 6401571 or 7552885

Price Guide:
de luxe €390-650
junior suite €450-800
suite €550-950
luxury suite €790-1,200

Locanda San Vigilio

LOCALITÀ SAN VIGILIO, 37016 GARDA (VR), ITALY

Reached via a lane lined with age-old cypress and olive trees, this 16th-century villa overlooks the beautiful Lake Garda in the small port of San Vigilio. Awarded 4 stars, the villa offers 7 rooms in the main inn and another 4 in an adjacent building. 3 additional private suites benefit from their own access and exclusive gardens; Casa degli Archi comprises 3 levels, 2 bedrooms and lounge. Drinks may be enjoyed in the Bar Taverna overlooking the lake from its lawns and gardens.

Cette villa du XVIe siècle à laquelle on accède après avoir longé une allée bordée de cyprès, surplombe le superbe lac Garda dans le petit port de San Vigilo. La villa 4 étoiles, dispose de 7 chambres dans le bâtiment principal et de 4 autres dans l'annexe adjacente. 3 autres suites privées bénéficient de leur propre entrée et jardin luxueux ; Casa degli Archi a 3 étages, 2 chambres et un salon. Les hôtes peuvent prendre un verre au bar la Taverna qui, de ses pelouses et jardins, offre une très belle vue sur le lac.

A esta villa del siglo XVI con vistas al bonito Lago Garda en el pequeño puerto de San Vigilio se llega por un camino bordeado de viejos cipreses y olivos. Galardonado con 4 estrellas, la villa ofrece 7 habitaciones en el edificio principal y otras 4 en un edificio contiguo, 3 suites privados adicionales se benefician de su propio acceso y excelentes jardines. Casa degli Archi consta de 3 niveles, 2 habitaciones y un salón. Las bebidas se pueden disfrutar en el Bar Taverna con vistas al lago desde sus céspedes y jardines.

Our inspector loved: *The enchanting private verandas, and romantic dining room.*

Directions: A4 > exit Perschiera del Garda. From Peschiera to San Vigilio, 15km. From Peschiera to Verona Airport, 15km. From San Vigilio to Verona Airport, 35km. A22 > exit Affi - Lago di Garda Sud. From Affi to San Vigilio, 15km. From Affi to Verona Airport, 20km. From San Vigilio to Verona Airport, 35km.

Web: www.johansens.com/sanvigilio
E-mail: info@punta-sanvigilio.it
Tel: +39 045 725 66 88
Fax: +39 045 627 81 82

Milan
Venice
Rome

Price Guide: (room only)
double €245-325
suite €385-680

Park Hotel Brasilia

VIA LEVANTINA, 30017 LIDO DI JESOLO, ITALY

Located on the eastern side of the Lido di Jesolo across the lagoon from Venice, the hotel boasts a quiet position, a private sandy beach and 2 swimming pools. Recently refurbished in soft, elegant shades and fabrics, all bedrooms are comfortable and boast terraces and sea views. At the Ipanema Restaurant guests can enjoy candle-lit dinners of local and international cuisine and exquisite wines from the cellar. Lunch is served either on the veranda or alongside the pool.

Situé côté Est du Lido di Jesolo en face de Venise sur l'autre rive du lagon, l'hôtel bénéficie d'une position tranquille, d'une plage de sable privée et de 2 piscines. Récemment redécorées dans des tons et tissus doux et élégants, toutes les chambres sont confortables avec terrasses et vue sur la mer. Au restaurant Ipanema, les hôtes peuvent dîner aux chandelles une cuisine locale et internationale accompagnée de vins fins du cellier. Le déjeuner est servi soit sous la véranda soit au bord de la piscine.

Situado en la parte este del Lido di Jesolo al otro lado de la laguna de Venecia, este hotel presume de su localización tranquila, su playa arenosa privada y 2 piscinas. Tras su reciente acondicionamiento en suaves y elegantes tonos y telas, todas sus habitaciones son cómodas y presumen de poseer terrazas y vistas al mar. En el Ipanema Restaurant sus clientes pueden disfrutar de cenas a la luz de las velas con platos locales e internacionales así como exquisitos vinos de su bodega. El almuerzo se sirve tanto en su terraza o a la vera de la piscina.

Our inspector loved: *The unsurpassed care for their guests.*

Directions: A4 > Quarto D'Altino > Lido Di Jesolo > "Zona Est".

Web: www.johansens.com/parkhotelbrasilia
E-mail: info@parkhotelbrasilia.com
Tel: +39 0421 380851
Fax: +39 0421 92244

Price guide: (closed October - April)
double (single occupancy) €95–160
double €120–200
suite €200–260

Relais Duca di Dolle

VIA PIAI ORIENTALE 5, 31030 ROLLE DI CISON DI VALMARINO (TV), ITALY

Directions: Highway A27 > Vittorio Veneto Nord exit > follow signs to Follina > Pieve di Soligo > before Pieve di Soligo turn left for Rolle > Arfanta > signs for Podere Bisol.

Web: www.johansens.com/foresteriabisol
E-mail: foresteria@bisol.it
Tel: +39 0438 975 809
Fax: +39 0438 975 792

Price Guide: (room only, closed 1 week in January)
double €90-210

Opened a few years ago to cater for the Bisol winery's guests, the relais is located in an area of protected natural beauty and enjoys stunning uninterrupted views. The accommodation is housed in 2 buildings and comprises a double room and 6 apartments with high-tech Boffi kitchens and a stylish mixture of modern and country furnishings. 2 excellent restaurants are within walking distance, and snacks accompanied by Bisol wine are served by the pool.

Ouvert depuis quelques années pour loger les hôtes des vignobles de Bisol, la relais se trouve dans une zone naturelle protégée et profite des superbes vues sans fins. Les logements sont situés dans 2 bâtiments et comprennent une chambre double, et 6 appartements avec cuisine Boffi ultra moderne que mélange style moderne et traditionnel campagnard. Tout près, on trouve 2 excellents restaurants, et des snacks accompagnes de vin de Bisol peuvent être servis auprès de la piscine.

Inaugurada hace unos años para acomodar a los huéspedes de las bodegas Bisol, la relais esta ubicada en una zona protegida de belleza natural con vistas impresionantes ininterrumpidas. El alojamiento se encuentra en 2 edificios y se compone de una habitación doble y de 6 apartamentos amueblados con cocinas Boffi de alta tecnología, y una mezcla estilosa de piezas modernas y rústicas, Hay 2 restaurantes en los alrededores a los cuales se puede acudir a pie, y al lado de la piscina se sirven comidas ligeras acompañadas de vino de Bisol.

Our inspector loved: *The free-form pool, and stunning views.*

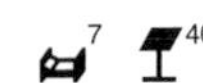

ALBERGO AL SOLE

VIA COLLEGIO 33, 31011 ASOLO, TREVISO, ITALY

Nestled in the heart of the medieval village of Asolo, in this fabulous area on an important wine route, this beautiful, timeless hotel has a warm atmosphere surrounded by a rich diversity of art and culture, close to some of the most beautiful examples of Palladian villas. Elegant bedrooms are luxuriously decorated with authentic furniture whilst antique-style baths live in harmony with Jacuzzi showers and modern comforts. La Terrazza Bar and Restaurant has breathtaking views and is the ideal place for delicious culinary treats.

Tapi au cœur du village médiéval d'Asolo, dans cette région magnifique sur une importante route de vin, cet hôtel intemporel à l'atmosphère chaleureuse est entouré d'une grande diversité culturelle et artistique, à proximité des plus beaux exemples de villas Palladiennes. Les chambres élégantes sont luxueusement décorées de meubles authentiques et les baignoires de style ancien se marient parfaitement avec les douches jacuzzis et autres équipements modernes. Le bar et restaurant La Terrazza offre des vues à couper le souffle et est l'endroit idéal pour déguster de véritables plaisirs culinaires.

Enclavado en el corazón de la aldea medieval de Asolo, dentro de esta región maravillosa en una ruta importante de vino, este bello e intemporal hotel de acogedor ambiente está rodeado de una rica variedad de arte y cultura así como de algunos de los mejores ejemplos de bellas villas palatinas. Sus elegantes habitaciones están lujosamente decoradas con auténtico mobiliario, a la par que sus cuartos de baño de estilo antiguo coexisten en perfecta armonía con sus duchas jacuzzi y otros adelantos modernos. La Terrazza Bar y Restaurante proporciona sobrecogedores paisajes y es el lugar ideal para el deleite gastronómico.

Our inspector loved: *The romantic cast-iron baths.*

Directions: In the historical centre of the medieval village of Asolo. From Milan > A4 Vicenza > A31 Dueville > s.s. 248 Bassano del Grappa > Asolo. From Venice > A27 Treviso > s.s. 348 Montebelluna > Asolo.

Web: www.johansens.com/alsole
E-mail: info@albergoalsole.com
Tel: +39 0423 951 332
Fax: +39 0423 951 007

Price Guide:
(closed 24th December - 8th January)
single €110-150
standard double €170-205
superior double/suite €205-255

        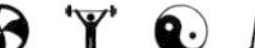

VENICE

Hotel location shown in red (hotel) or purple (spa hotel) with page number

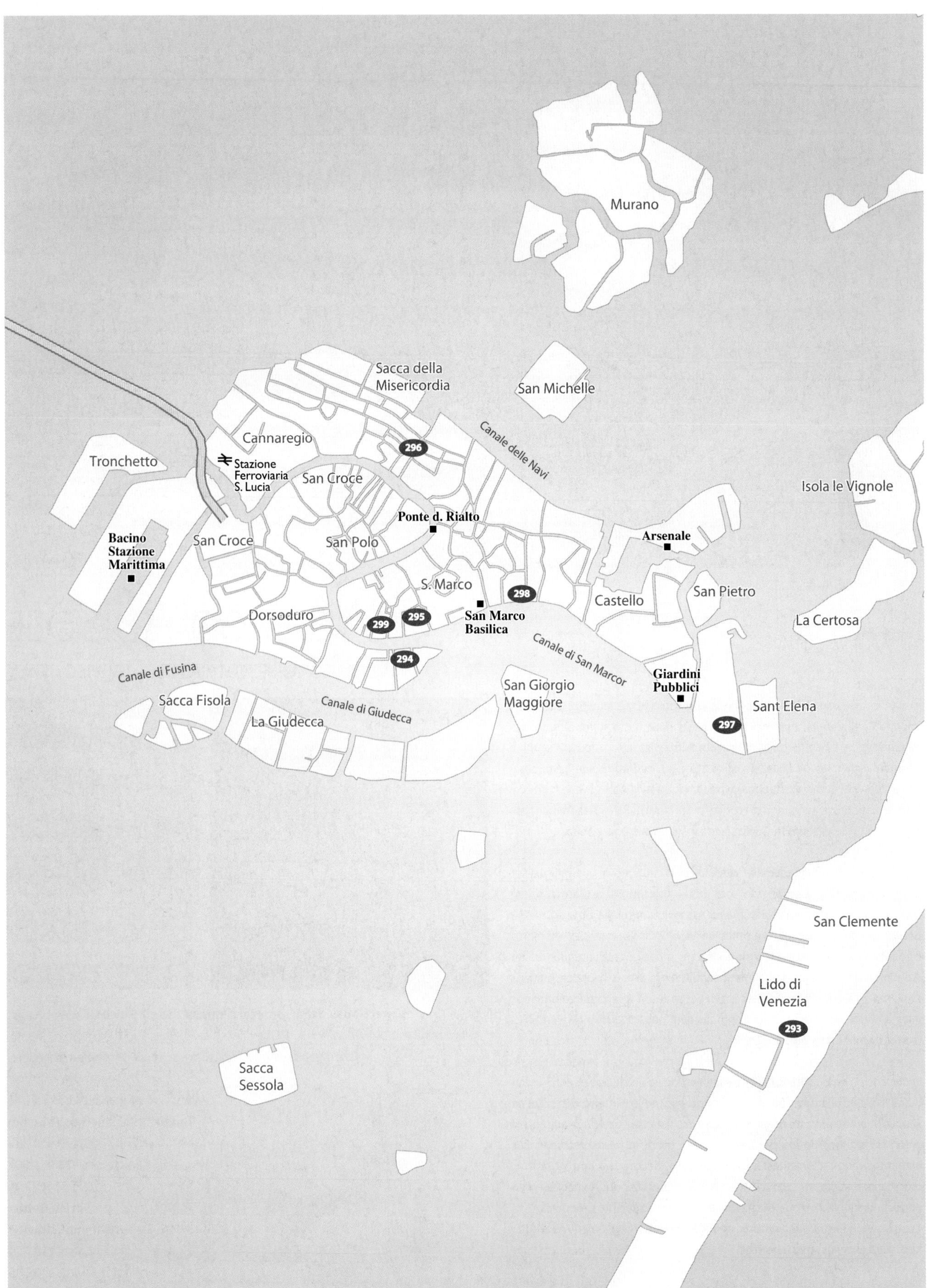

Albergo Quattro Fontane - Residenza d'Epoca

VIA QUATTRO FONTANE 16, 30126 LIDO DI VENEZIA, VENICE, ITALY

A distinctive country house set in an idyllic garden on the Lido amongst orchards and productive vineyards, away from the hustle and bustle of Venice, the Albergo is only 10 minutes by water-bus from St Mark's Square. Signore Bevilacqua, whose family has owned the property for over 50 years, has collected some very unusual antique furniture, art and artefacts from all over the world. Venetian specialities complement wine from local vineyards. Guests have access to a nearby beach.

Maison de campagne raffinée dans un jardin idyllique sur le Lido, l'Albergo, avec ses vergers et ses vignobles, est à seuleument 10 minutes en navette-bateau de la place Saint Marc. Le Signore Bevilacqua, dont la famille est propriétaire depuis 50 ans, a collectionné des meubles, de l'art et des objets façonnés originaux provenant du monde entier. Des spécialités vénitiennes complètent la carte de vins des producteurs locaux. Les hôtes ont accès à la plage voisine.

El Albergo es una singular casa rural ubicada en un idílico jardín en el Lido entre huertas y fértiles viñas, lejos del bullicio de Venecia. Está a sólo 10 minutos en barco-bus desde la Piazza San Marco. El Signore Bevilacqua, cuya familia lleva siendo dueña del establecimiento más de 50 años, ha recopilado algunos muebles antiguos, objetos de arte y utensilios realmente inusuales traídos de todo el mundo. Las especialidades venecianas son el adecuado complemento al vino procedente de los viñedos del lugar. Los clientes tienen acceso a la playa próxima.

Our inspector loved: *The unique colonial atmosphere, and eclectic furnishings.*

Directions: Lido via San Marco > Albergo.

Web: www.johansens.com/albergoquattrofontane
E-mail: info@quattrofontane.com
Tel: +39 041 526 0227
Fax: +39 041 526 0726

Price Guide: (closed 7th November - 12th April)
single €110–270
double/twin €170–420
apartment €300-600

Ca Maria Adele

DORSODURO 111, 30123 VENICE, ITALY

Within beautiful 16th-century surrounds, Ca Maria Adele is a short walk from St Mark's Square in an exclusive quarter of the city with views of the magnificent Santa Maria della Salute church. Rooms contain rich furnishings and offer discreet luxury designed to satisfy the most discerning guest. 5 unique themed guest rooms are particularly opulent, and the elegant, intimate Lounge Room is adorned with interesting objet d'arts and exciting fabrics. The romantic, Moroccan-inspired terrace is filled with glowing lanterns and colourful silk cushions.

Installé dans un magnifique environnement du XVIe siècle, Ca Maria Adele est situé à quelques minutes à pied de la Place St Marc et offre des vues sur la superbe église de Santa Maria della Salute. Les chambres et salons composés de somptueux meubles offrent un luxe discret destiné à satisfaire les plus exigeants. Les 5 chambres à thèmes sont particulièrement chics, opulentes et uniques. Le Lounge Room, élégant et intime, présente d'intéressants objets d'arts et de beaux tissus. La terrasse romantique d'inspiration Marocaine se compose de lanternes luisantes et de coussins colorés en soie.

Inserto en un bello entorno del siglo XVI, Ca Maria Adele está a un corto paseo a pie de la Piazza San Marco en una zona selecta de la ciudad, con vistas a la espléndida iglesia de Santa Maria della Salute. Las habitaciones y las salas, con mobiliario suntuoso, son discretamente lujosas para satisfacer a los clientes más perspicaces. 5 habitaciones con motivos temáticos resultan especialmente suntuosas y de un glamour inigualable, mientras que la elegante Lounge Room es intima, con espléndidas telas e interesantes objetos de arte. La romántica terraza, de inspiración marroquí esta decorada con faroles y coloridos cojines de seda.

Our inspector loved: *The romantic ambience, and passion for detail.*

Directions: Located opposite St Mark's Square. From Piazzele Roma take the waterbus to St Mark's Square and disembark at Salute. The hotel has a private landing stage for guests arriving by water-taxi.

Web: www.johansens.com/camariaadele
E-mail: info@camariaadele.it
Tel: +39 041 52 03 078
Fax: +39 041 52 89 013

Price Guide:
double €269.50-308
de luxe €308-467.50
themed €418-638
suite €462-693

  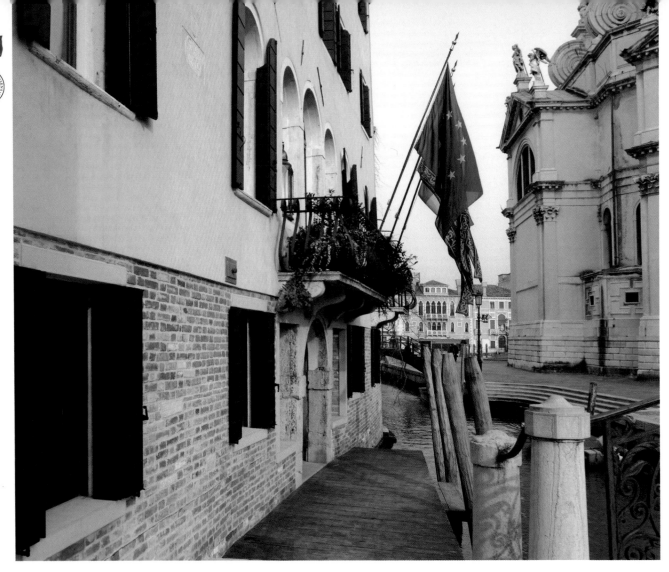      

Hotel Flora

SAN MARCO 2283/A, 30124 VENICE, ITALY

Built in the 17th century as a notable school for painting, Hotel Flora is located in the heart of Venice, steps from St Mark's Square. Renowned for its long tradition of hospitality, it has preserved the warmth and charm of an intimate and refined guest house. Elegant interiors reflect a passion for culture and rooms have beautiful Venetian-style period furniture. Guests may relax in the courtyard filled with greenery and flowers; a haven in the middle of the city. This is the sister property of Novecento.

Construit au XVIIe siècle en tant qu'école d'art picturale, Hôtel Flora est située au cœur de Venise, à quelques pas de la Place St Marc. Réputé depuis toujours pour son hospitalité, l'hôtel a su garder la chaleur et le charme d'une maison raffinée et intime. Les intérieurs élégants sont le reflet d'une passion pour la culture et les chambres ont de magnifiques meubles d'époque de style vénitien. Les hôtes peuvent se relaxer dans la cour intérieure remplie de plantes et de fleurs ; un paradis au milieu de la ville. Hotel Flora est associé à l'hôtel Novecento.

Construida en el siglo XVII como acreditada academia de pintura, el Hotel Flora se encuentra situado en el corazón de Venecia, a un paso de la Piazza San Marco. Famoso por su larga trayectoria hospitalaria, ha logrado conservar la afabilidad y el encanto propios de un "guest house" íntimo y refinado. Sus elegantes interiores reflejan pasión por la cultura. Además sus habitaciones disponen de bello mobiliario de época de estilo veneciano. Los clientes pueden relajarse en el patio interior repleto de flora y vegetación; es en definitiva una remanso en medio de la ciudad. Asociado al hotel Novecento.

Our inspector loved: *The lush garden, cosy rooms, and caring staff.*

  43  15     

Directions: Located behind St Mark's Square on Calle XXII Marzo.

Web: www.johansens.com/hotelflora
E-mail: info@hotelflora.it
Tel: +39 041 52 05 844
Fax: +39 041 52 28 217

Price Guide:
single €140-180
double €185-260
superior €185-290

Hotel Giorgione

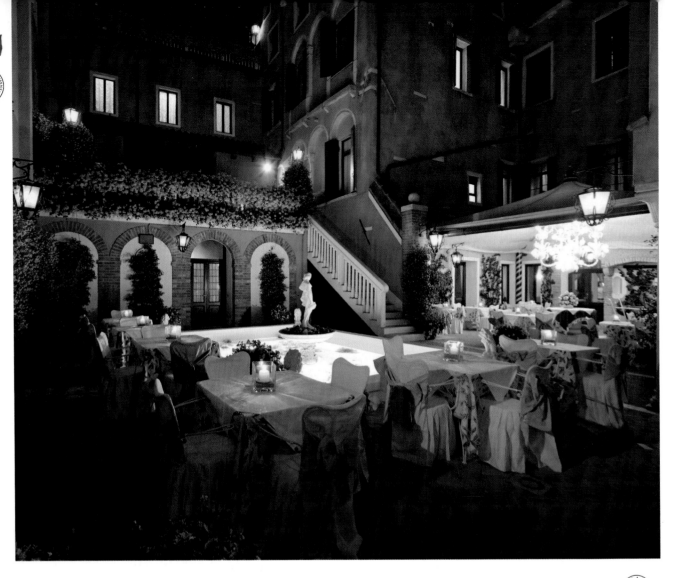

SS APOSTOLI 4587, 30131 VENICE, ITALY

A 15th-century building houses this charming hotel, which is set in a quiet location in the centre of the old town, close to the Rialto bridge and a few minutes from Piazza San Marco. The recently renovated hotel provides all modern comforts whilst retaining its original charm. All rooms are decorated in a romantic and refined style with antique Venetian pieces of furniture. Breakfast is served inside or outside in the beautiful garden. At the adjacent Osteria-Enoteca Giorgione guests can enjoy a great variety of wines and local dishes.

Un bâtiment du XVe siècle abrite ce charmant hôtel, situé dans un endroit calme au centre de la vieille ville, à proximité du pont Rialto et de la Piazza San Marco. Récemment rénové, l'hôtel est équipé de toutes les commodités modernes tout en conservant son charme d'origine. Les chambres sont décorées dans un style romantique et raffiné avec des meubles vénitiens antiques. Le petit-déjeuner est servi à l'intérieur ou à l'extérieur dans le jardin. Dans la Osteria-Enoteca Giorgione voisine, les clients peuvent goûter à une variété de vins et de plats locaux.

Un edificio del siglo XV acoge a este encantador hotel, sito en un lugar tranquilo del centro del casco antiguo, cerca del Puente de Rialto y a unos minutos de la Piazza San Marco. Este hotel, de reciente renovación, dispone de todas las comodidades a la vez que conserva su encanto original. Todas las habitaciones están decoradas al estilo romántico y refinado con antiguo mobiliario veneciano. El desayuno se sirve dentro o fuera, en su bello jardín. En la adyacente Osteria-Enoteca Giorgione los clientes pueden disfrutar de una gran variedad de vinos y platos de la gastronomía local.

Our inspector loved: *The warm welcome and the romantic Venetian courtyard with lovely fountain.*

Directions: Airport > bus to Piazzale Roma > Vaporetto to Cà d'Oro. Railway station > Vaporetto to Cà d'Oro.

Web: www.johansens.com/giorgione
E-mail: giorgione@hotelgiorgione.com
Tel: +39 041 522 5810
Fax: +39 041 523 9092

Price Guide:
rooms €105–400

Hotel Sant' Elena Venezia

Calle Buccari 10, Sant' Elena, 30132 Venice, Italy

A former convent, this attractively designed hotel is situated on an unspoilt island of serenity and greenery on the eastern shore of the city's lagoon adjacent to the gardens of the Biennale Art Exhibition and monastery of the Olivetani monks, a short walk from the centre of Venice. Bedrooms and suites are delightfully furnished and have every comfort from air conditioning to satellite television. There is also a private garden where guests may enjoy breakfast or simply relax.

Ancien couvent, ce séduisant hôtel design est situé sur une île calme, verdoyante et encore intacte, sur la côte Est de la lagune de la ville, attenante aux jardins de la Biennale d'Exposition d'Arts et du monastère des moines olivétains. Les chambres et suites sont élégamment meublées et possèdent tout le confort moderne, de la climatisation à la télévision par satellite. L'hôtel propose également à ses hôtes un jardin privé pour prendre le petit-déjeuner ou tout simplement se relaxer.

Este hotel de diseño sugestivo, antiguo convento, se encuentra en una isla de serenidad y vegetación a la orilla este de la laguna de Venecia, al lado de los jardines de la famosa exposición de arte La Biennale y del monasterio de los monjes Olivetani, y a un paseo del centro de Venecia. Las habitaciones están bellamente amuebladas y contienen todas las comodidades modernas como aire acondicionado y televisión por satélite. El hotel también posee un bonito jardín privado donde se puede desayunar o simplemente descansar.

Our inspector loved: *The refreshing modern décor, and the green garden area.*

Directions: A 15-minute walk from St Mark's Square. From Piazzale Roma the hotel is a 30-minute waterbus ride.

Milan
Venice
Rome

Web: www.johansens.com/santelena
E-mail: info@hotelsantelena.com
Tel: +39 041 27 17 811
Fax: +39 041 27 71 569

Price Guide:
double (single occupancy) €80-260
double €96-298
triple €150-310
junior suite €120-348

 75

Londra Palace

RIVA DEGLI SCHIAVONI, 4171, 30122 VENICE, ITALY

Just a few steps from the Piazza San Marco and the Grand Canal, this exclusive boutique hotel offers guests a feeling of unforgettable glamour and a romantic atmosphere. Each of the spacious, richly decorated bedrooms and suites, most of which afford stunning views of the lagoon, is a unique experience in itself, evoking a sense of discreet luxury. Guests can enjoy refined cuisine in a sophisticated setting at the hotel's restaurant, Do Leoni, and during the warmer months, lunch or drinks are served on the veranda.

A deux pas de la Place San Marco et le Grand Canal, cet hôtel exclusif propose aux visiteurs un sens de prestige inoubliable dans une atmosphère romantique. Chacune des chambres et suites spacieuses et somptueusement décorées, dont la plupart offrent une vue imprenable sur la lagune, est une expérience unique en soi, évoquant un sens de luxe discrète. Une cuisine raffinée est servie dans un cadre sophistiqué au restaurant Do Leoni, et pendant les mois plus chauds, les hôtes peuvent prendre un verre ou déjeuner sur la véranda.

Sólo a un paso de la Piazza San Marco y el Gran Canal, este exclusivo hotel boutique ofrece a sus clientes la posibilidad de sentir su inolvidable glamour y su romántico ambiente. Cada una de las amplias y profusamente decoradas habitaciones y suites, la mayoría de las cuales aportan sorprendentes vistas a la laguna, constituyen una experiencia única en sí misma, evocadora de una sensación de discreto lujo. Los huéspedes pueden disfrutar de su refinada cocina en un sofisticado entorno en el restaurante del hotel, Do Leoni. Durante los meses más cálidos, el almuerzo o las copas se sirven en la terraza.

Directions: Located in the city centre, near Piazza San Marco.

Web: www.johansens.com/londrapalace
E-mail: info@hotelondra.it
Tel: +39 041 5200533
Fax: +39 041 5225032

Price Guide:
double/twin (single occupancy) €265-475
double/twin €275-585
junior suite €490-790

Our inspector loved: *The views of the Grand Canal, and the charming staff.*

Novecento Boutique Hotel

San Marco 2684, 30124 Venice, Italy

Tucked away between St Mark's Square and the Accademia Galleries, this stylish boutique hotel offers a cosy and evocative ambience influenced by 1930s style and inspired by the works of artist and fashion designer Mariano Fortuny, who lived in Venice during the late 19th century. Furniture and tapestries from the Mediterranean and Far East give the guest rooms an exclusive and refined character and co-ordinate excellently with 21st-century facilities. Breakfast can be enjoyed in a small, pretty garden. This is the sister property of Hotel Flora.

Caché entre la Place St Marc et les Galeries de l'Académie, cet élégant boutique hôtel à l'atmosphère chaleureuse et évocatrice du style des années 30 fut inspiré par le travail de l'artiste et créateur de costumes Mariano Fortuny qui vécu à Venise à la fin du XIXe siècle. Mobilier et tapisseries originaires de Méditerranée et du Moyen-Orient donnent aux chambres un caractère raffiné et exclusif et se mélangent parfaitement aux équipements du XXIe siècle. Le petit-déjeuner est servie dans un ravissant petit jardin. Novecento est associé à l'Hotel Flora.

Escondido entre la plaza de San Marco y las galerías Accademia, este elegante hotel boutique ofrece un ambiente acogedor y evocativo de los años 30, inspirado por la obra del diseñador de moda Mariano Fortuny quien vivió en Venecia durante los últimos años del siglo XIX. Los muebles y tapices, provenientes de la zona del Mediterráneo y del lejano oriente, dan a las habitaciones un carácter exclusivo y refinado, combinando perfectamente con todas las comodidades del siglo XXI. El desayuno puede tomarse en el pequeño y encantador jardín. Este hotel está asociado al Hotel Flora.

Our inspector loved: *The Oriental influence, and warm welcome.*

   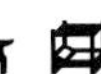     

Directions: Located in Calle del Dose, between St Mark's Square and the Accademia Galleries.

Web: www.johansens.com/novecento
E-mail: info@novecento.biz
Tel: +39 041 24 13 765
Fax: +39 041 52 12 145

Price Guide:
room €150-260

LOCANDA SAN VEROLO

LOCALITÀ SAN VEROLO, 37010 COSTERMANO (VR), ITALY

On a hillside, inland from Lake Garda, stands the elegantly restored Locanda San Verolo. Dating back to the late 16th century, this magnificent former farmhouse opened in 2001 to offer comfortable guest rooms equipped with every modern amenity. Antique furnishings, wooden beams and fine drapes adorn each room, decorated in yellow and warm colour schemes against red brick or wooden flooring with spacious, marble bathrooms. The intimate Antica Osteria serves delicious, unpretentious food with the best local wine.

Superbement restauré, Locanda San Verolo se tient sur les flancs de colline en retrait du lac Garda. Datant de la fin XVIe siècle, ce magnifique ancien corps de ferme a ouvert ses portes en 2001 pour offrir à ses hôtes des chambres confortables avec tout l'équipement moderne. Les sols en briques rouges et les planchers contrastent avec les tons jaunes et chaleureux qui habillent les chambres; celles-ci sont toutes décorées de meubles anciens, de poutres et de belles draperies, tandis que c'est le marbre qui a été choisi pour garnir les salles de bain. L'intime Antica Osteria sert une cuisine délicieuse et sans prétentions qui est accompagnée des meilleurs vins locaux.

Sobre una colina, cercano al Lago Garda, se encuentra Locanda San Verolo elegantemente restaurado. Fue una magnífica casa de campo desde finales del siglo XVI que abrió sus puertas el año 2001 para ofrecer habitaciones confortables equipadas con todas las facilidades modernas. Cada una de ellas posee muebles antiguos, vigas de madera y elegantes cortinas en tonos amarillos y de color cálido que contrastan con el ladrillo rojo o el suelo de madera y ofrece también espaciosos baños de mármol. Antica Osteria es íntima y sirve comida deliciosa y sencilla con su mejor vino local.

Directions: Please contact the property directly for directions.

Web: www.johansens.com/sanverolo
E-mail: info@sanverolo.it
Tel: +39 045 720 09 30
Fax: +39 045 620 11 66

Price Guide: (room only)
double €235-280
suite €300-350

Our inspector loved: *The tasteful interior design, and welcoming atmosphere.*

Villa Giona

VIA CENGIA 8, 37029 SAN PIETRO IN CARIANO (VR), ITALY

Surrounded by beautifully manicured lawns and acres of vineyards the approach to this delightful hotel is truly inspiring. Situated in the heart of the Valpolicella region the hotel boasts its own small wine production and has a wine bar that offers regular wine tastings. Distressed wooden floors and traditional Italian furrniture lend a rustic charm to this stylish hotel and guests' every care has been thought of with luxurious bathrooms offering chunky power showers, fluffy bathrobes and luxurious Bulgari toiletries.

L'approche de ce charmant hôtel entouré de pelouses parfaitement entretenues et d'hectares de vignes, est réellement exaltante. Situé au cœur de la région de Valpolicella, l'hôtel s'enorgueillit de sa petite production viticole et a de son propre bar à vins qui offre des dégustations régulièrement. Des parquets vieillis et un mobilier traditionnel italien prêtent un charme rustique à cet hôtel chic ; des salles de bain luxueuses avec de grosses douches puissantes, des peignoirs épais et des produits de toilette luxueux de chez Bulgari pourvoient aux besoins des hôtes.

La entrada a este encantador hotel es realmente admirable, rodeado de césped hermosamente cuidado y acres de viñedos. Sito en el corazón de la región de Valpolicella el hotel se jacta de poseer su pequeña producción vinícola y en su bar se ofrecen regularmente degustaciones de vinos. Suelos de madera y mobiliario tradicional italiano otorgan al hotel con gran estilo un encanto rústico donde se cuida con detalle los lujosos cuartos de baño que poseen duchas electrónicas de fácil manejo, albornoces de calidad y lujosos artículos de tocador Bulgari.

Our inspector loved: *The fantastic manicured grounds.*

 15
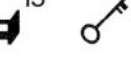
 80

Directions: 6km from central Verona. 17km from Verona Airport. 13km from Verona Nord exit, of the A22. Follow signs for Valpolicella > San Pietro in Cariano > Villa Giona.

Web: www.johansens.com/villagiona
E-mail: villagiona@villagiona.it
Tel: +39 045 685 50 11
Fax: +39 045 685 50 10

Price Guide: (closed November - March)
single €120-300
double €180-330
suite €250-400

Relais la Magioca

VIA MORON 3, 37024 NEGRAR - VALPOLICELLA (VR), ITALY

Directions: A4 > exit Verona Sud > Negrar–Valpolicella > A22 > exit Verona Nord > Valpolicella–Negrar.

Web: www.johansens.com/lamagioca
E-mail: info@magioca.it
Tel: +39 045 600 0167
Fax: +39 045 600 0840

Price Guide:
double/twin €190–250
suites €210–280

Set in an immaculate park, this charming relais offers breathtaking views, a romantic atmosphere and total peace and tranquillity. An ancient stone-built farmhouse, it has been furnished with refined taste and attention to detail. The 6 individually designed bedrooms are charming and comfortable, lounge and delightful breakfast room create a typical country house ambience. Sample local wines in the fabulous cellar and visit nearby attractions including Verona, the vineyards of Valpolicella and Soave and Lake Garda. Venice is also within easy reach.

Situé dans un parc splendide, ce relais charmant, havre de paix, offre une vue à couper le souffle et une atmosphère romantique. Un ancien corps de ferme en pierre, il a été restauré et meublé avec raffinement jusque dans ses moindres détails. Les 6 chambres, décorées différemment, sont charmantes et confortables, et avec le salon et la ravissante salle du petit déjeuner, créent une ambiance typique de maison de campagne. Des vins locaux peuvent être dégustés dans la cave excellente, et Vérone, les vignobles de Valpolicella et de Soave et le Lac Garda sont des attractions touristiques très proches. Venise est également facile d'accès.

Sito en un impecable parque, este encantador relais ofrece vistas espectaculares, y un ambiente romántico. Una antigua granja construida en piedra, que ha sido acondicionada con refinado gusto y esmero por el detalle. Sus 6 habitaciones, de diseño individualizado, son encantadoras y cómodas y el salón y su preciosa sala de desayunos les aportan un estilo propio de casa rural. Puede degustar los vinos de la zona en su fabulosa bodega, y Verona, los viñedos de Valpolicella y Soave y el lago Garda son lugares de interés cercanos. Venecia se encuentra también cerca.

Our inspector loved: *The romantic Jacuzzi in the bedroom.*

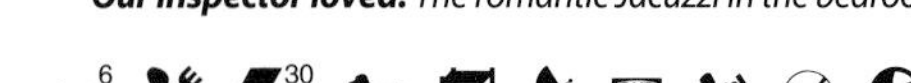

HOTEL GABBIA D'ORO (HISTORICAL RESIDENCE)

CORSO PORTA BORSARI 4A, 37121 VERONA, ITALY

Set in the historical centre of Verona, this very special small luxury hotel is housed in a 18th-century palazzo. Wooden ceilings, frescoes and precious paintings abound, whilst in the bedrooms antique furniture, oriental carpets, rich accessories, beautiful fabrics and lace create a romantic ambience. The Orangerie, a charming winter garden, is the perfect place to enjoy a cup of coffee or a light snack. The vineyards of Valpolicella and Lake Garda are all within easy reach, whilst Venice is a popular destination for a day trip.

Au cœur historique de Vérone, ce petit hôtel de luxe très spécial se situe au sein d'un palais du XVIIIe siècle. Les plafonds en bois, fresques et peintures précieuses, ainsi que le mobilier ancien des chambres, les tapis orientaux, les accessoires luxueux, les beaux tissus et dentelles créent une atmosphère particulièrement romantique. L'Orangerie, un charmant jardin d'hiver, est l'endroit idéal pour déguster une tasse de café ou un repas léger. Les vignobles de Valpolicella et le Lac Garda sont faciles d'accès et Venise est une destination populaire pour une journée de sortie.

Ubicado en el centro histórico de Verona, este pequeño hotel de lujo muy especial se alberga en un palazzo del siglo XVIII. Abundan en él los techos de madera, los frescos y las delicadas obras pictóricas. En sus habitaciones son el mobiliario antiguo, las alfombras orientales, los suntuosos accesorios, sus bellas telas y encajes lo que le aportan un ambiente romántico. El Orangerie, encantador jardín invernal, es el lugar ideal para disfrutar de una taza de café o un tentempié. Los viñedos de Valpolicella y el lago Garda se encuentran a escasa distancia, siendo Venecia destino favorito para una excursión de un día.

Our inspector loved: *The suite's secluded terrace with outdoor bathtub.*

Directions: In historical centre of Verona, near Piazza delle Erbe.

Web: www.johansens.com/gabbiadoro
E-mail: gabbiadoro@easyasp.it
Tel: +39 045 8003060
Fax: +39 045 590293

Price Guide:
single €160–290
double €220–380
suite €285–850

  27   10       

Latvia

Hotel location shown in red (hotel) or purple (spa hotel) with page number

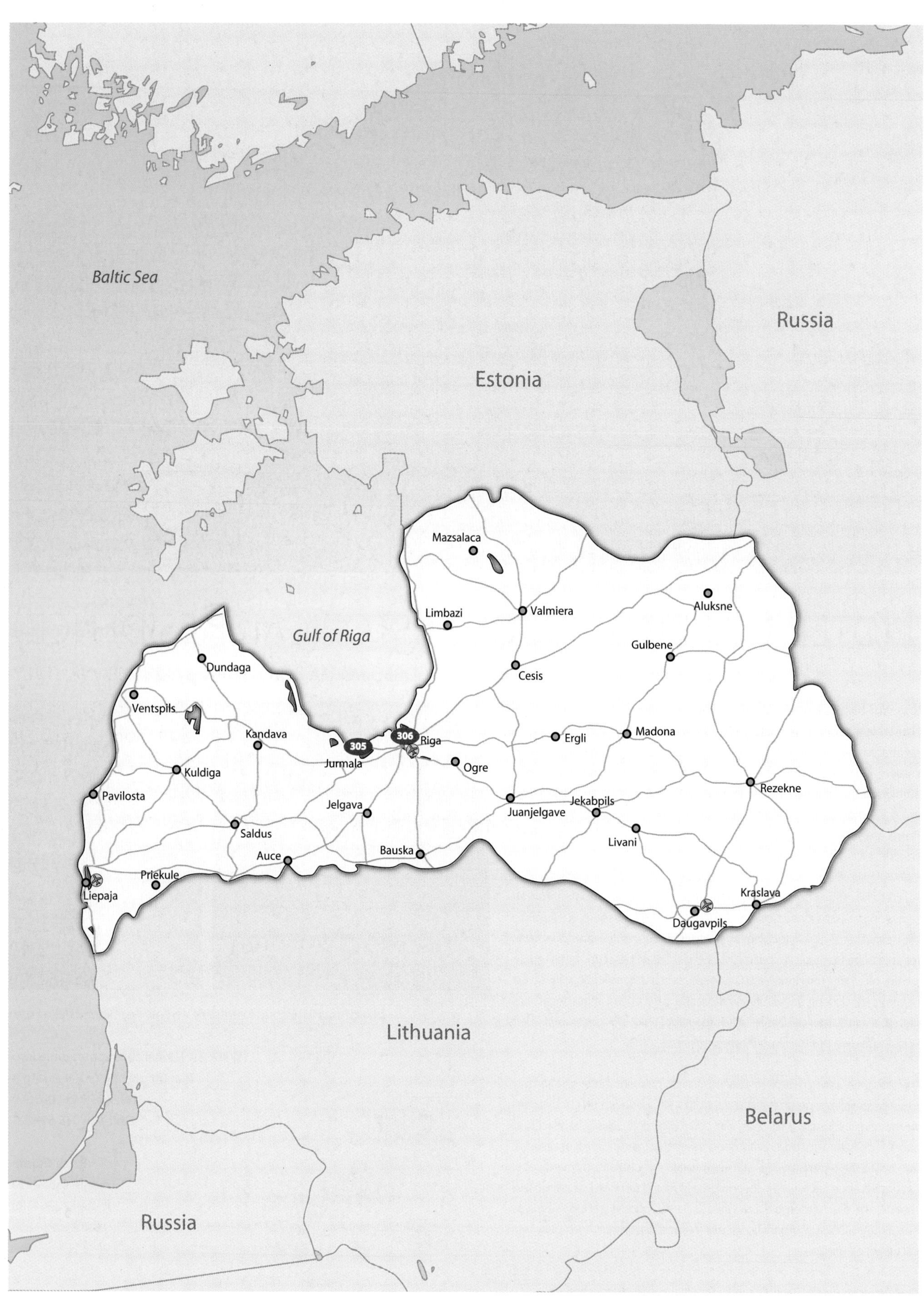

TB Palace Hotel & Spa

PILSONU STREET 8, JURMALA, LV-2015, LATVIA

With its soft sand beach, dunes, quaint wooden cottages and fresh pine scented air, Jurmala has been Latvia's most popular seaside resort since the 19th century. The prestigious TB Palace, formerly a bank and a hospital, is situated at its very centre, offering visitors a comfortable, classical interior, superb dining, excellent service, a Turkish spa with every amenity and conference room. There are only 4 guest rooms and each is individually opulent in style, furnishings and décor; 2 have private terraces.

Avec ses plages de sable fin, ses dunes, ses chalets pittoresques en bois et ses odeurs de pins frais, Jurmala est, depuis le XIXe siècle, la station balnéaire la plus populaire de Lettonie. Le prestigieux TB Palace, anciennement une banque et un hôspital, est situé au centre et offre aux visiteurs une décoration intérieure classique et confortable, une délicieuse cuisine, un excellent service et un spa turque avec tous les équipements et une salle de réunion. Il y a seulement 4 chambres d'hôtes et chacune d'entre elles est dans un style, un décor et un aménagement opulent. 2 d'entre elles ont des terrasses privées.

Jurmala, con su playa de arena fina, dunas, pintorescas casitas de madera y su fresco olor a pino, es el centro de verano costero más famoso de Letonia desde el siglo XIX. El prestigioso TB Palace, antiguo banco y hospital, está situado en el mismo centro para ofrecer a sus visitantes un interior clásico y confortable, una carta excelente, una magnífica atención así como un balneario turco con todos los servicios y un salón de reunión.. Hay sólo 4 habitaciones; cada una de ellas muestra un estilo opulento, mobiliario y decoración propios. 2 tienen terraza propia.

Our inspector loved: *The excellent service and marvellous food in the exquisite restaurant.*

Directions: Riga Airport is 15km away.

Web: www.johansens.com/tbpalace
E-mail: tbpalace@tbpalace.com
Tel: +371 714 7094
Fax: +371 714 7097

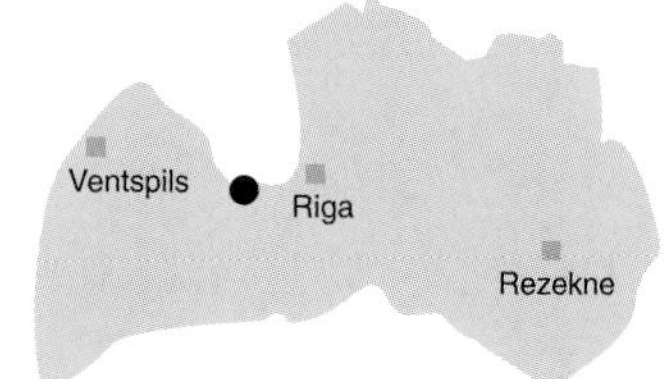

Price Guide:
winter €300-700
summer €400-800

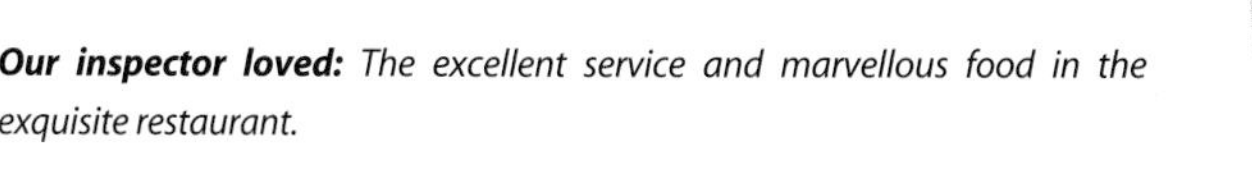

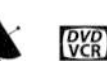

HOTEL BERGS

BERGS BAZAAR, ELIZABETES STREET 83/85, LV-1050, RIGA, LATVIA

This immaculate, modern hotel is located in the business area just outside the old city walls of Riga and has the reputation of being an oasis of tranquillity in the city centre. Hotel Bergs has the intimate ambience of an elegant private residence with a blend of contemporary and 19th-century architectural design and décor that incorporates fine examples of Latvian art. Suites have every facility, public lounges are extremely comfortable, and the restaurant serves gourmet cuisine.

Cet hôtel moderne, impeccable est situé dans le quartier d'affaires, juste derrière les murs de la vieille ville de Riga et a la réputation d'être un havre de tranquillité dans le centre ville. Hôtel Bergs possède l'ambiance intime d'une résidence privée avec une touche de contemporain, un design architectural du XIXe siècle et un décor qui intègre de beaux spécimens de l'art Letton. Les suites sont bien équipées, les salons sont très confortables et le restaurant sert une délicieuse cuisine.

Este moderno e impecable hotel, ubicado en la zona comercial justo al otro lado de las murallas del casco antiguo de Riga, tiene fama de ser todo un oasis de paz y tranquilidad en el centro de la ciudad. El Hotel Bergs ofrece el ambiente íntimo de una elegante residencia particular a base de combinar la decoración y el diseño arquitectónico contemporáneos con los del siglo XIX, dentro de los cuales se exhiben algunas muestras del arte letón. Las suites disponen de toda clase de instalaciones y los salones comunes son enormemente confortables. El restaurante del hotel hace gala de su cocina gourmet.

Our inspector loved: *The simplicity of the modern design giving so much comfort to guests, and the extension to the restaurant area, which now opens out to the summer terrace with its impressive sculpture.*

Directions: Riga Airport is 13km away.

Web: www.johansens.com/bergs
E-mail: hotelbergs@hotelbergs.com
Tel: +371 777 09 00
Fax: +371 777 09 40

Price Guide:
suite €175-350

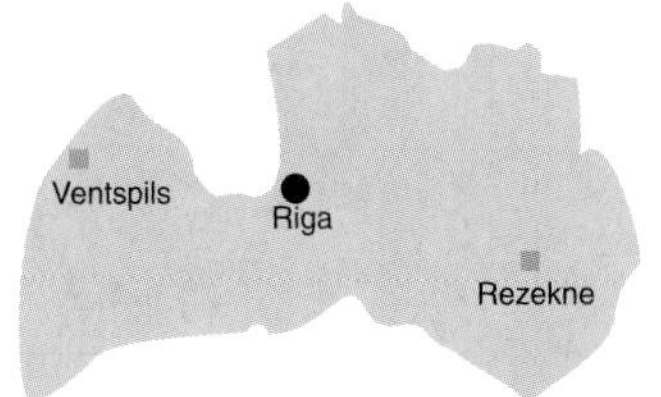

LITHUANIA

Hotel location shown in red (hotel) or purple (spa hotel) with page number

LITHUANIA (VILNIUS)

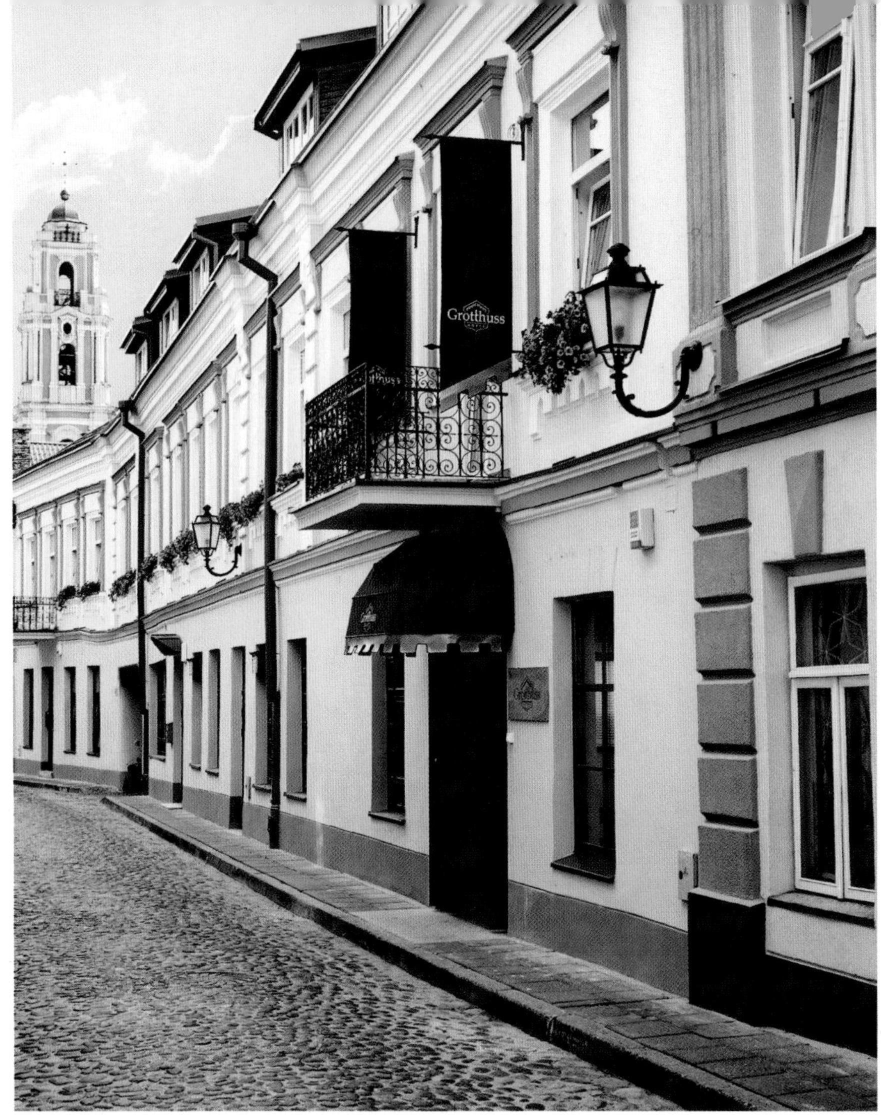

Grotthuss Hotel

LIGONINĖS 7, 01134 VILNIUS, LITHUANIA

Directions: Located in the centre of Vilnius's old town. The nearest airport is Vilnius.

Web: www.johansens.com/grotthusshotel
E-mail: info@grotthusshotel.com
Tel: +370 5 266 0322
Fax: +370 5 266 0323

Price Guide: (20% discounts available during weekends)
superior €128
business €180
suite €250

Formerly owned by aristocracy, this homely yet exclusive hotel stands in a quiet, cobbled street in the heart of Vilnius. The spacious, comfortable bedrooms and suites overlook the flower-filled courtyard and fountain or look out across the old town that boasts exquisite examples of European 13th-15th century architecture with Gothic, Renaissance and Baroque styles. First-class cuisine alongside French wines is served in La Pergola Restaurant, which faces the internal courtyard featuring Vilnius's 16th-century city walls.

Ancienne résidence d'un aristocrate, cet accueillant et exclusif hôtel se situe dans une rue pavée calme au cœur de Vilnius. Les chambres et suites confortables ont vues sur la cour intérieure fleurie et sa fontaine ou sur la vieille ville qui peut se vanter de posséder de superbes exemples d'architectures de styles Gothique, Renaissance et Baroque de l'Europe du XIIIe au XVe siècle. Une cuisine de premier ordre accompagnée de vins français est servie au restaurant La Pergola qui donne sur la cour intérieure bordée par les murs de la ville datant du XVIe siècle.

Este hogareño aunque lujoso hotel, antigua propiedad de la nobleza, se erige en una tranquila calle adoquinada del corazón de Vilnius. Sus amplias y cómodas habitaciones y suites dan al patio interior repleto de flores y fuente o al casco antiguo, que cuenta con excelente ejemplos de los estilos gótico, renacentista y barroco de la arquitectura europea de los siglos XIII-XV. Su cocina de primera categoría se sirve acompañada de vinos franceses en La Pergola Restaurant, situado frente al patio interno, provisto de muros de la ciudad de Vilnius del siglo XVI.

Our inspector loved: *My inviting, spacious room.*

The Narutis Hotel

24 PILIES STREET, 01123 VILNIUS, LITHUANIA

Beautifully restored and equipped with modern facilities, this elegant, family-owned hotel, the oldest in Vilnius, is situated in the heart of the Old Town in a 16th-century building, which was first recorded in the 1581 Book of World Cities as a place for an overnight stay. Its Gothic cellars house an acclaimed restaurant serving European, traditional Lithuanian and Mediterranean cuisine whilst original ancient wall paintings, alcoves and beams feature in many of the 50 unique and luxurious guest rooms.

Magnifiquement restauré et pourvu des équipements modernes, cet élégant hôtel géré en famille, le plus ancien à Vilnius, est situé au cœur de la vieille ville dans un bâtiment du XVIe siècle, qui fut enregistré en 1581 dans le livre des villes du monde comme un lieu de passage. Dans ses caves gothiques, l'hôtel abrite son restaurant primé qui sert une cuisine Européenne, Lithuanienne et Méditerranéenne. Les peintures, alcôves et poutres d'origine sont présentes dans la plupart des 50 chambres luxueuses.

Este elegante hotel de regencia familiar, el más antiguo de Vilnius, excelentemente restaurado y equipado de modernas instalaciones, esta situado en el corazón del casco antiguo en un edificio del siglo XVI. Se tiene constancia documental de el en el Libro de Ciudades del Mundo de 1581 como lugar donde pernoctar. Sus bodegas góticas dan cabida a un afamado restaurante que sirve platos europeos, lituanos tradicionales y mediterráneos mientras sus genuinas y antiguas pinturas murales, cámaras y vigas están presentes en muchas de sus 50 lujosas y extraordinarias habitaciones.

Our inspector loved: *The new ball/conference room, and the indoor swimming pool.*

Directions: The nearest airport is Vilnius.

Web: www.johansens.com/narutis
E-mail: info@narutis.com
Tel: +370 5 2122 894
Fax: +370 5 2622 882

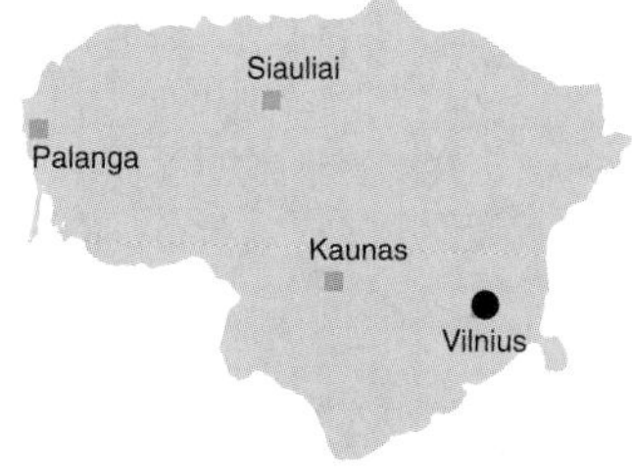

Price Guide:
single €160
double €200-260
suite €230-640

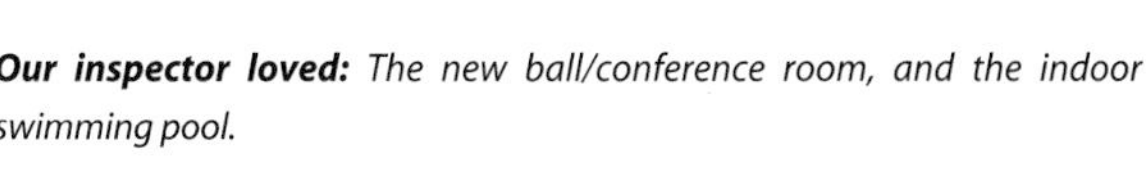

LUXEMBOURG

Hotel location shown in red (hotel) or purple (spa hotel) with page number

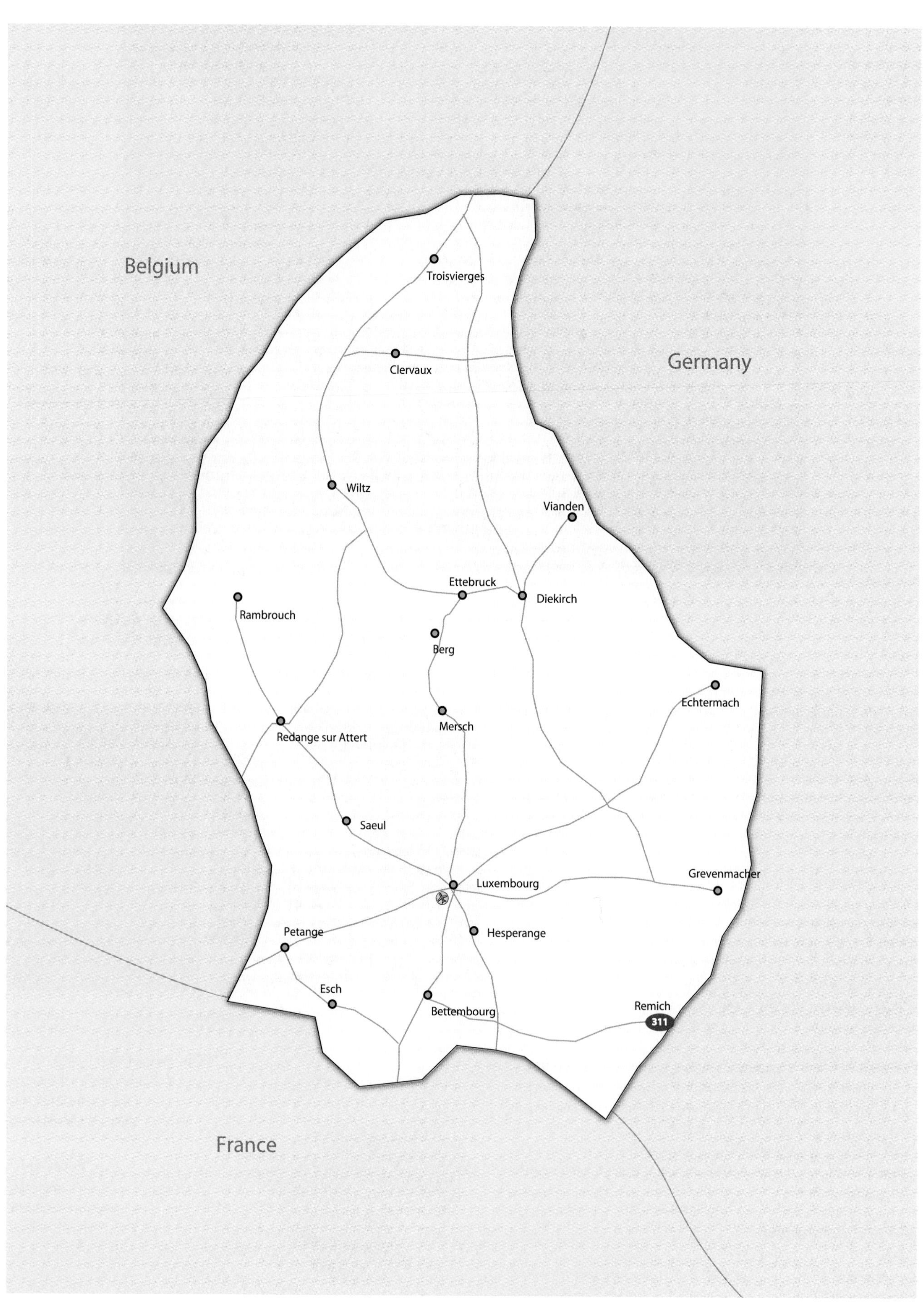

Hotel Saint~Nicolas

31 Esplanade, 5533 Remich, Luxembourg

Set in the picturesque town of Remich, this family-run hotel affords fantastic views across the esplanade and lush vineyards as it lies on the banks of the river Moselle. The eclectic hotel features unusual public rooms adorned with interesting paintings. The hotel's Lohengrin Restaurant serves traditional French cuisine; a true gastronomic delight. Complimentary broadband Internet access is available.

Situé dans la ville pittoresque de Remich, cet hôtel familial offre des vues fantastiques sur l'esplanande et les vignobles étant situé sur les berges de la rivière Moselle. Cet hôtel éclectique a des salles communes originales décorées de peintures uniques. Le restaurant de l'hôtel, le Lohengrin est un délice gastronomique proposant une cuisine traditionnelle française. Un service Internet ASDL gratuit est disponible.

Situado en la pintoresca ciudad de Remich, a orillas del río Moselle, este hotel de regencia familiar ofrece fantásticas vistas fluviales y a exuberantes viñedos. El carácter ecléctico del hotel ofrece insólitos espacios comunes adornados con lienzos de sumo interés. El Lohengrin Restaurant del hotel sirve platos tradicionales franceses: verdaderas delicias gastronómicas. Dispone de un servicio gratuito de banda ancha para acceso a internet.

Our inspector loved: *The idyllic location on the Mosel in this wine country, and the refined cuisine.*

Directions: Luxembourg > E29 > Remich or A13 > exit 13 Schengen.

Web: www.johansens.com/saintnicolas
E-mail: hotel@pt.lu
Tel: +35 226 663
Fax: +35 226 663 666

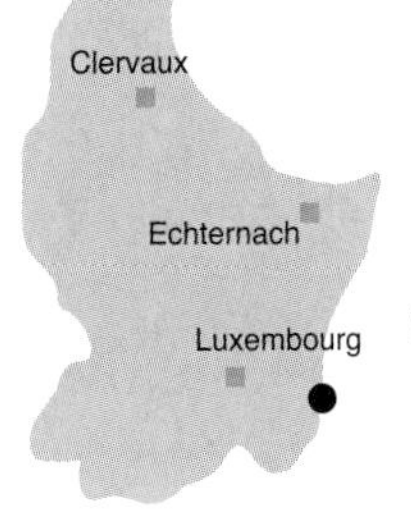

Price Guide:
single €81-106
double/twin €105-130
gastronomic offer (incl 2-night stay) €178–203

Montenegro

Hotel location shown in red (hotel) or purple (spa hotel) with page number

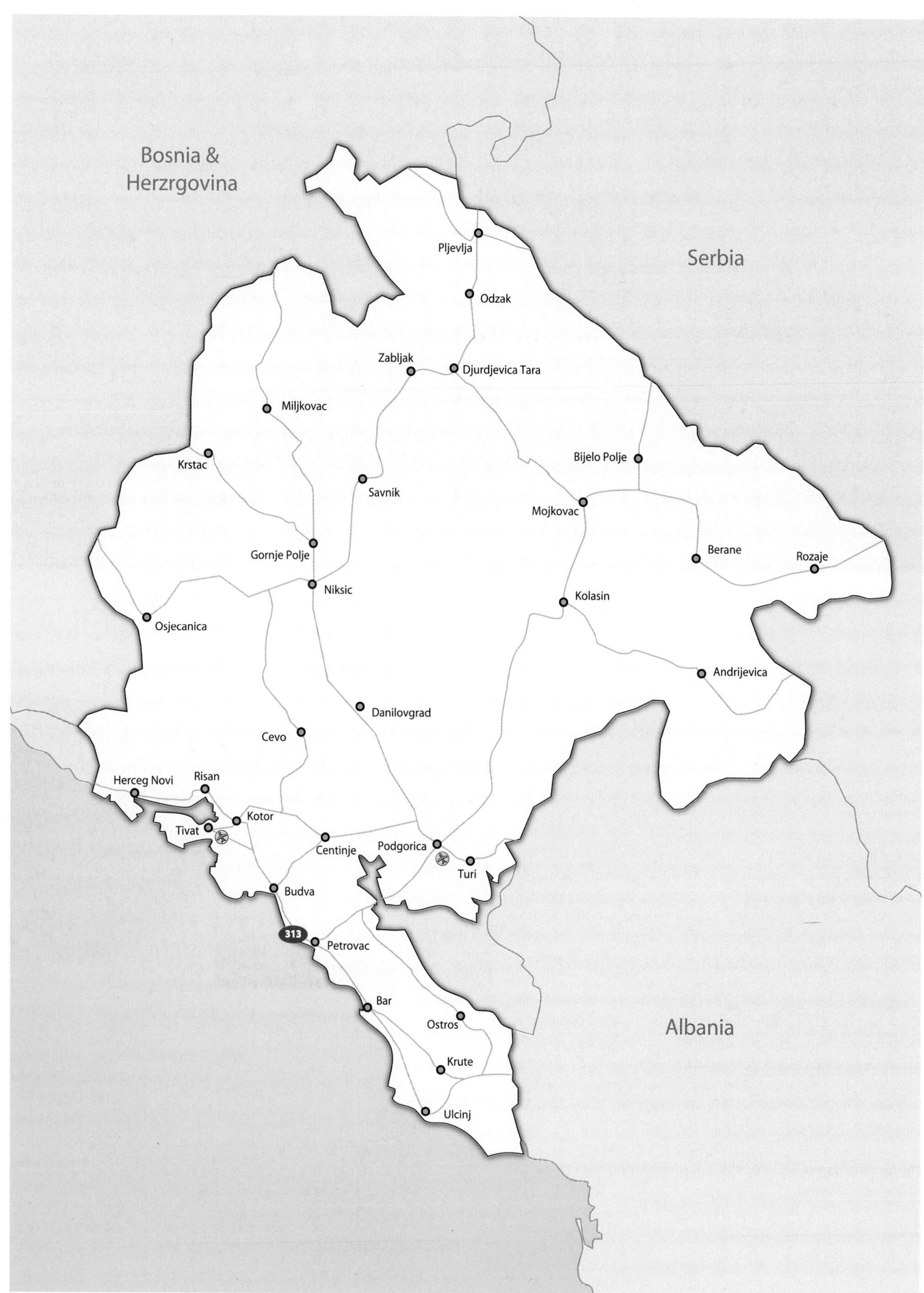

Villa Montenegro

2 VUKICE MITROVIC STR, 86312 ST. STEFAN, MONTENEGRO

Located on a beautiful stretch of Montenegrin coast opposite the "Hotel Island," popular with the stars, Villa Montenegro is the perfect retreat for those looking to explore this relatively unknown corner. Designed in a modern style, the hotel combines luxury accommodation with first-class amenities. The suites have private terraces as well as an in-house chef, and the restaurant offers an exceptional selection of Mediterranean and international cuisine.

Située sur une magnifique étendue de la côte Monténégrine, en face de l'Hotel Island," prisé par les stars, Villa Montenegro est un refuge idéal pour ceux souhaitant explorer ce coin encore peu connu. Créé dans un style moderne, l'hôtel propose un hébergement luxueux avec des équipements de tout premier ordre. Les suites ont des terrasses privées ainsi qu'un chef attitré. Le restaurant offre une cuisine d'inspiration méditerranéenne et internationale.

Situado en una bella zona de la costa montenegrina, enfrente del "Hotel Islan" sitio frecuentado por los famosos, Villa Montenegro es el refugio ideal para aquellos que desean explorar esta esquina del mundo relativamente desconocida. De diseño moderno, el hotel combina el lujo con instalaciones de primera. Las suites tienen terrazas y un chef particular, mientras que el restaurante ofrece una selección excepcional de platos mediterráneos e internacionales

***Our inspector loved:** The spicy Montenegro food, the Jacuzzis, the spacious bathrooms, and top security.*

Directions: Dubrovnik is 2 hours away and Podgorica is 1 hour. Tivat Airport is 30 minutes from the hotel.

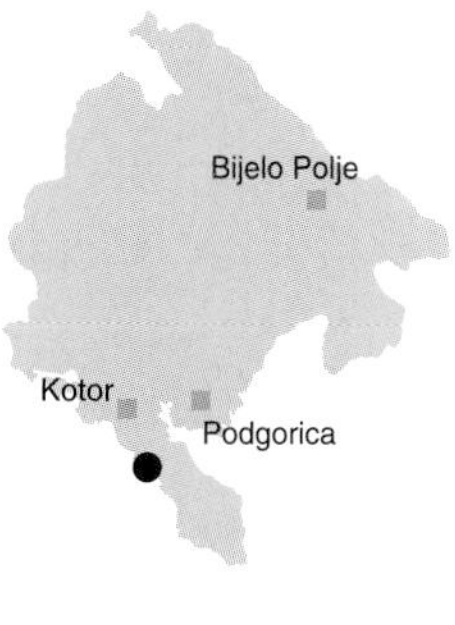

Web: www.johansens.com/villamontenegro
E-mail: info@villa-montenegro.com
Tel: +381 86 468 802
Fax: +381 86 468 809

Price Guide: (including airport transfer)
double €196-500
suite €420-1,500

Bijelo Polje
Kotor
Podgorica

The Netherlands

Hotel location shown in red (hotel) or purple (spa hotel) with page number

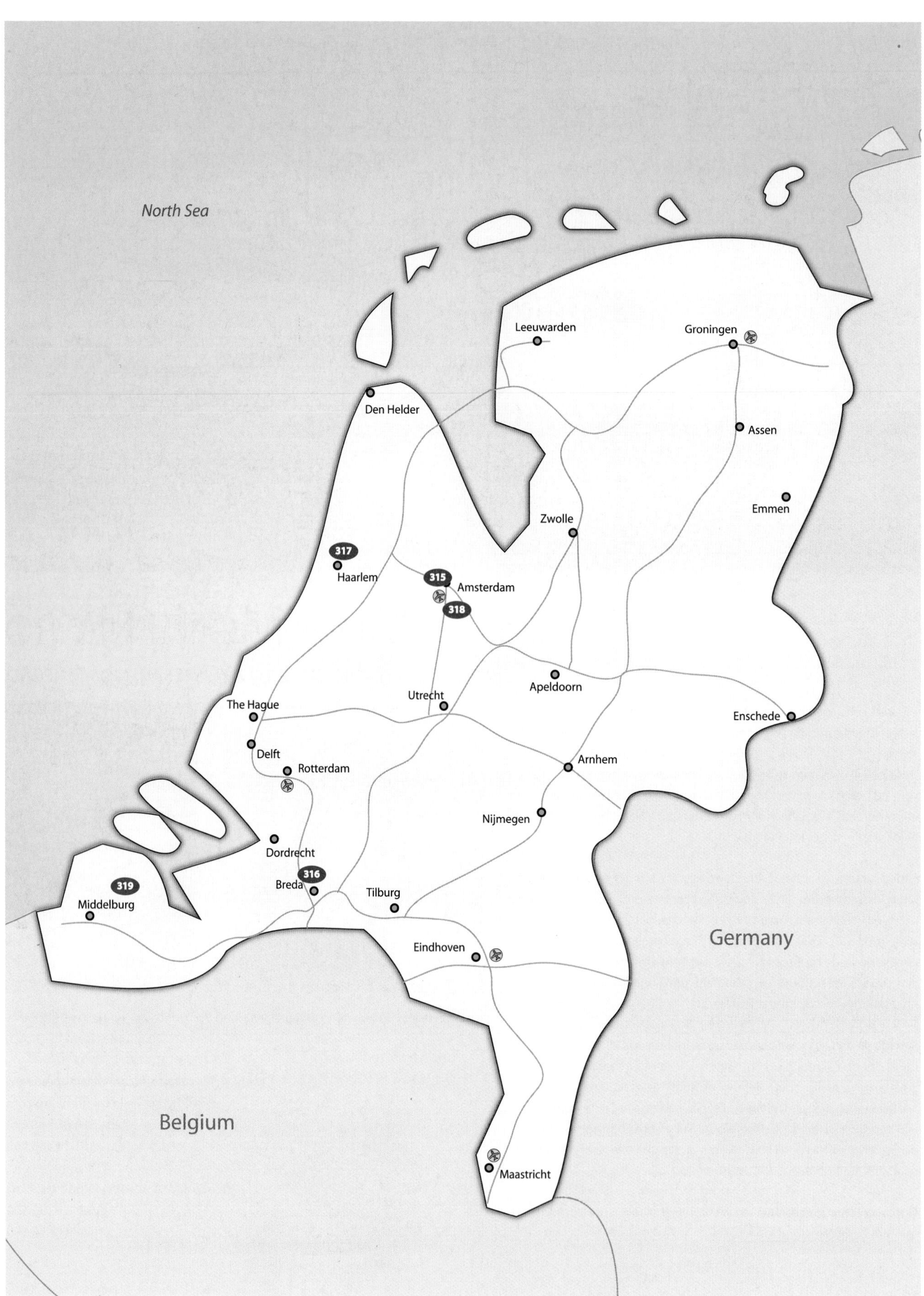

Ambassade Hotel

HERENGRACHT 341, 1016 AMSTERDAM, THE NETHERLANDS

The Ambassade is a most attractive hotel in the heart of Amsterdam. Originally 10 separate houses, each the home of a wealthy merchant on the Herengracht ("the Gentlemen's Canal"), the hotel has been converted into one building which retains all the erstwhile interior architecture and the external façades. Over the years, numerous authors have stayed at this hotel; an extensive collection of signed books can be found in the library. A special Internet office is available free of charge. The hotel's luxurious float and massage centre Koan Float, is situated further along the street.

L'Ambassade est un hôtel très attrayant dans le coeur d'Amsterdam. Originellement 10 maisons séparées, chacune étant la maison d'un riche marchand de Herengracht (Le "Canal des Messieurs"), l'hôtel a été converti en un bâtiment qui comprend toute l'architecture intérieure ancienne et les façades extérieures d'époque. De nombreux auteurs ont visité cet hôtel, et on peut admirer une collection de livres signés dans la bibliothèque. Un bureau avec service Internet gratuit est disponible. Le centre de massage luxueux Koan Float, appartenant à l'hôtel, est situé à proximité.

El Ambassade es uno de los hoteles más atractivos del corazón de Ámsterdam. Lo que originalmente eran 10 casas independientes, hogar cada una de ricos mercaderes en el Herengracht ("El Canal de los Caballeros"), se ha convertido en un hotel de un solo edificio que conserva toda su antigua arquitectura interior y sus fachadas exteriores. Con el paso de los años han residido entre sus muros numerosos escritores, y puede visitarse una extensa colección de libros firmados. Una sala de internet está a disposición gratuita. El lujoso centro de masajes, Koan Float, está situado en la misma calle.

Our inspector loved: *The hotel's love of the arts - especially the focus on the Cobra collection.*

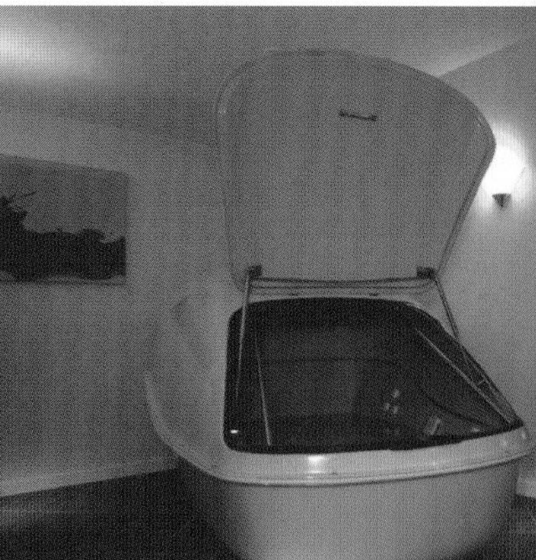

Directions: Schiphol Airport > take a taxi, train or car to the centre of the city.

Web: www.johansens.com/ambassade
E-mail: info@ambassade-hotel.nl
Tel: +31 20 5550222
Fax: +31 20 5550277

Price Guide: (breakfast €16, excluding 5% VAT)
single €185
double €185-225
suite €250-325

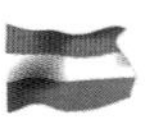

Bliss Hotel

TORENSTRAAT 9, 4811 XV BREDA, THE NETHERLANDS

Bliss Hotel is a wonderful testament to modern design that successfully balances contemporary comfort with timeless elegance reminiscent of the 1900s, when this house was originally built. It is located in the old part of town, and both business and leisure travellers alike stay in themed suites where the décor reflects the room's name such as Classic, Dickens and Jones and Long Island. Restaurant Chocolate opens out to a terrace during warmer months and serves an interesting French menu with Oriental influences.

Le Bliss Hotel est un exemple splendide d'art moderne qui a su allier parfaitement le confort contemporain à une élégance intemporelle rappelant le siècle passé, date de construction de la maison. Il est situé dans la vieille ville, et aussi bien les voyageurs d'affaires que les touristes aiment s'installer dans les suites dont le nom reflète le thème, tels que Classic, Dickens and Jones, et Long Island. Le restaurant Chocolat ouvre sur une terrasse pendant les mois les plus chauds et sert une cuisine française aux influences orientales intéressante.

El hotel Bliss es un testimonio ejemplar del diseño moderno que combina con éxito el confort actual con la eterna elegancia de principios del siglo pasado, cuando fue construido. Situado en el casco antiguo es ideal tanto para turistas como para hombres y mujeres de negocios, donde las suites temáticas reflejan en su décor nombres como Classic, Dickens y Jones y Long Island. En el restaurante Chocolate se sirve un interesante menú francés con influencias orientales y durante los meses cálidos se extiende a una terraza.

Our inspector loved: *The individually designed rooms, especially the wedding suite with terrace.*

Directions: Please contact the hotel for detailed directions.

Web: www.johansens.com/blisshotel
E-mail: info@blisshotel.nl
Tel: +31 076 533 5980
Fax: +31 076 533 5981

Price Guide:
suite €210-400

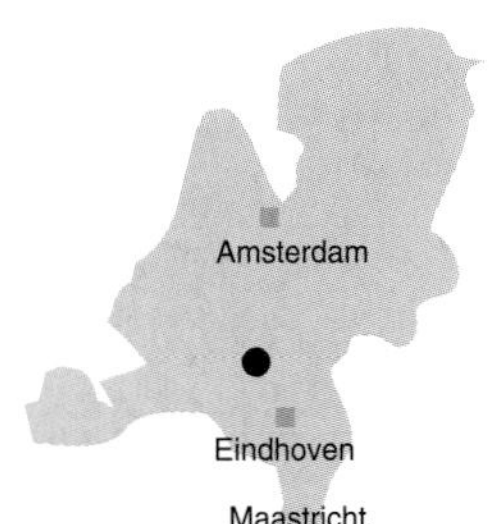

Duin & Kruidberg Country Estate

DUIN EN KRUIDBERGERWEG 60, 2071 SANTPOORT, AMSTERDAM, THE NETHERLANDS

This impressive old Dutch-style property, nestled within romantic landscaped grounds, features an eclectic mix of historic décor from the stately English hall to the stunning Rococo-style dining room. The bright, bold bedrooms boast individual character and modern conveniences. Ideal for corporate functions, there are 5 multipurpose conference rooms and a contemporary restaurant. For leisure, guests may enjoy the fitness and sauna area and the property is only a short distance from the cultural capital, Amsterdam and Schiphol Airport.

Cette impressionnante ancienne propriété de style Hollandais, nichée au cœur de paysages romantiques, propose un décor historique éclectique allant de l'imposant hall de style anglais à la magnifique salle à manger de style Rococo. Les chambres claires ont leur propre caractéristiques et tout l'équipement moderne. Idéal pour les sociétés, il y a 5 salles de conférences polyvalentes et un restaurant contemporain. Pour les loisirs, les clients peuvent profiter du fitness et du sauna et l'hôtel est proche de la capitale culturelle, Amsterdam et de l'aéroport, Schiphol.

Esta impresionante propiedad de estilo holandes antiguo, dentro de una romántica finca ajardinada, tiene una mezcla historica ecléctica en la decoración que va desde el hall típico inglés solariego, hasta el impresionante comedor de estilo Rococó. Las habitaciones, con colores vivos y atrevidos, ostentan carácter individual y comodidades modernas. Lugar ideal para reuniones de empresa, con sus 5 habitaciones multiusos y un restaurante contemporáneo. En los momentos de ocio, los clientes pueden disfrutar del centro de salud y sauna o ir a Amsterdam, la capital cultural, que se encuentra a corta distancia del hotel y del aeropuerto de Schiphol.

Our inspector loved: *The decorative fireplace and beautiful bronze urns in the elegant reception hall.*

Directions: Schiphol Airport > A9 to Santpoort.

Web: www.johansens.com/duinkruidberg
E-mail: info@duin-kruidberg.nl
Tel: +31 23 512 1800
Fax: +31 23 512 1888

Price Guide:
single €215
double €245-315
suite €365-415

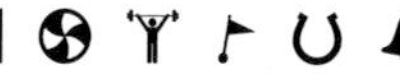

Hotel Restaurant de Nederlanden

DUINKERKEN 3, 3633 EM, VREELAND AAN DE VECHT, THE NETHERLANDS

Idyllically located on the River Vecht, this charming 9-bedroom property, including 2 junior suites, benefits from river views and a recent refurbishment. Guests may gather by the open hearth in the relaxing lounge before dining in the conservatory to savour the Michelin-starred, French seasonal menu, prepared by Chef Erik de Boer and his dedicated team. The Sommelier is on-hand to choose affordable, famous wines from around the world to accompany the meal.

Avec sa situation idyllique sur la Vecht, cette charmante propriété récemment re-décorée possède 9 chambres dont 2 suites juniors, et bénéficie de vues sur la rivière. Les hôtes peuvent s'assembler autour de l'âtre dans un salon à l'atmosphère détendue avant le dîner dans la véranda où ils savourent une cuisine Française de saison, primée au guide Michelin et préparée par le Chef Erik de Boer et son équipe dévouée. Le sommelier est disponible pour aider à choisir d'abordables grands crus du monde entier pour accompagner au mieux le repas.

Idealmente emplazado sobre el río Vecht, este encantador hotel de 9 habitaciones incluyendo 2 suites júnior, ofrece vistas al río y un reciente remodelado. Los huéspedes pueden reunirse junto a la chimenea para relajarse en el salón antes de cenar en el conservatorio, galardonado con una estrella Michelín, donde podrán degustar un menú francés de temporada preparado por el chef Eric de Boer y su equipo. El sommelier le aconsejará su elección de los famosos y razonables vinos de todas partes del mundo para acompañar su comida.

Our inspector loved: *The view of the "De Vecht" Canal from the elegant dining room and some of the bedrooms.*

Directions: The hotel is 20 minutes from Amsterdam Airport (Schiphol).

Web: www.johansens.com/denederlanden
E-mail: denederlanden@nederlanden.nl
Tel: +31 294 232 326
Fax: +31 294 231 407

Price Guide: (breakfast €19.50)
single €195-325
double €195-325
suite €225-325

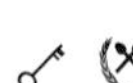

Auberge de Campveerse Toren

KAAI 2, 4351 AA VEERE, THE NETHERLANDS

This 600-year-old inn has been in the Van Cranenburgh family for over 60 years and has played host to many Royal visitors during its long and interesting history. Located on the Veerse Meer yacht harbour, this romantic retreat is close to the city of Middelburg with its museums, art galleries and beaches. Guest rooms are extremely comfortable and the de luxe apartments have magnificent views of the harbour and lake. The renowned restaurant specialises in fresh fish and seafood.

Cette auberge vieille de 600 ans est dans la famille Van Cranenburgh depuis plus de 60 ans et a hébergé de nombreux visiteurs royaux pendant sa longue et intéressante histoire. Située sur le port nautique de Veerse Meer, cette romantique retraite est proche de la ville de Middelburg et de ses musées, galeries d'art et des plages. Les chambres sont extrêmement confortables et les appartements de luxe ont des vues splendides sur le port et le lac. Le restaurant sont ses fermeuses spécialités de poissons et fruits de mer frais.

Esta posada con 600 años de antigüedad ha pertenecido a la familia Van Cranenburgh más de 60 años y ha sido visitada por muchos huéspedes de la Realeza durante su larga e interesante historia. Ubicada en el puerto deportivo Veerse Meer, este romántico refugio está próximo a la ciudad de Middelburg con sus museos, galerías de arte y playas. Las habitaciones son extremadamente cómodas y los apartamentos de lujo gozan de magníficas vistas al puerto y al lago. El afamado restaurante se especializa en pescados y mariscos frescos.

Our inspector loved: *The spectacular view over the Veerse Meer, which looks like a 17th-century Dutch painting!*

Directions: From Zavetem (Brussles) by train or car > Gent to Terneuzen (Holland) > through the tunnel to Middelburg > 6km to Veere.

Web: www.johansens.com/campveersetoren
E-mail: info@campveersetoren.nl
Tel: +31 0118 501 291
Fax: +31 0118 501 695

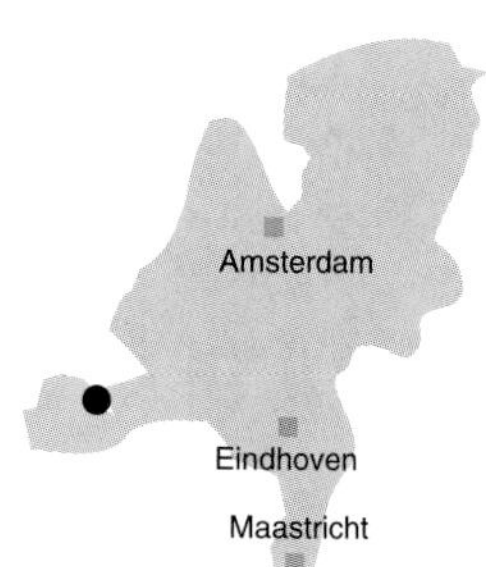

Price Guide:
(excluding €1 per person per night VAT)
single €100-150
double €120-165
suite €165

POLAND

Hotel location shown in red (hotel) or purple (spa hotel) with page number

Hotel Copernicus

UL. KANONICZA 16, 31-002 KRAKÓW, POLAND

Situated on the oldest street in Kraków, the Gothic façade stands out amidst the surrounding Renaissance buildings. The former home of Nicholas Copernicus, the astronomer, the building boasts an interesting history and is now a stunning hotel. Painstakingly restored, the hotel comprises 29 elegant guest rooms that are complemented by beautiful furnishings and bathrooms. From the dramatic pool, situated in the vaults, to the panoramic roof-top terrace, Hotel Copernicus has a magical atmosphere that combines comfort with tradition and modernity.

Situé dans la plus vieille rue de Cracovie, la façade gothique se détache au sein des bâtiments Renaissance environnants. Ancienne résidence de l'astronome Nicolas Copernic, le bâtiment qui s'enorgueillit d'une histoire intéressante, est maintenant un superbe hôtel. Méticuleusement restauré, l'hôtel comprend 29 chambres d'hôtes élégantes qui sont complétées par de beaux tissus d'ameublement et salles de bain. De la spectaculaire piscine situées dans les caves à la terrasse panoramique sur le toit, l'Hôtel Copernicus possède une atmosphère magique qui combine confort au traditionnel et moderne.

Situado en la calle más antigua de Kraków, su fachada gótica destaca entre los edificios renacentistas de los alrededores. Este edificio, antigua casa del astrónomo Nicolás Copérnico y en la actualidad magnífico hotel, puede presumir de su interesante historia. Tras una delicada restauración, este hotel dispone ahora de 29 elegantes habitaciones con bello mobiliario y cuartos de baño. Desde su espectacular piscina, situada en recogidas profundidades, hasta su panorámica terraza en techo, el Hotel Copernicus proporciona un mágico ambiente en el que se combina tradición y modernidad.

Our inspector loved: *The "Beet Carpaccio," the wonderful flower arrangment.*

Directions: The nearest airport is Kraków. Secure parking is available for €15 per day.

Web: www.johansens.com/copernicus
E-mail: copernicus@hotel.com.pl
Tel: +48 12 424 34 00/1/2
Fax: +48 12 424 34 05

Price Guide:
single €187
double €212-240
suite €300-375

PORTUGAL

Hotel location shown in red (hotel) or purple (spa hotel) with page number

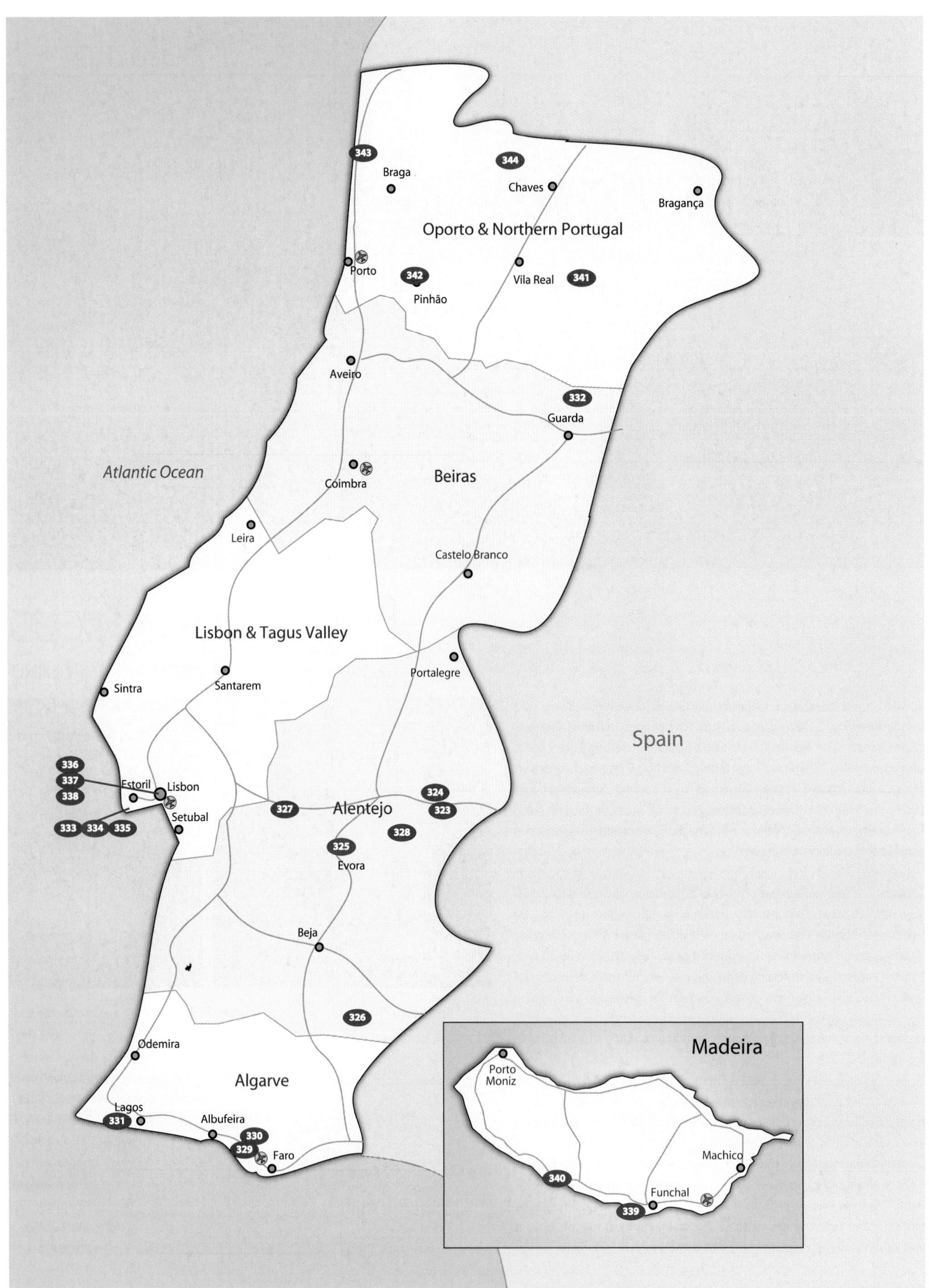

Casa do Terreiro do Poço

LARGO DOS COMBATENTES DA GRANDE GUERRA 12, 7150-152 BORBA, PORTUGAL

Linked by balconies and stairs, the 3 buildings that comprise Casa do Terreiro do Poço overlook a pretty citrus orchard in the tranquil village of Borba in Alentejo. The main house is home to the welcoming owners and ground, first and second floor apartments featuring beautiful frescoes and a private tower. Casas do Jardim have their own private entrances via the garden and provide relaxing living areas, kitchenettes and en-suite bedrooms. Bold splashes of colour cleverly complement the period furnishings and antiques.

Réunis par les balcons et escaliers, les 3 bâtiments que composent Casa do Terreiro do Poço surplombent une ravissante citronneraie dans le village tranquille de Borba en Alentejo. La maison principale est celle des accueillants propriétaires mais à chaque étage se trouvent des appartements pour les hôtes. Celui au dernier étage offre de superbes fresques et une tour privée. Les appartements de casas do Jardim ont leur entrées privées par le jardin et proposent des espaces de vie relaxants, des kitchenettes et des chambres. Des touches de couleurs vives complétent parfaitement les antiquités et le mobilier d'époque.

Conectados por balcones y escaleras, los 3 edificios de que consta Casa do Terreiro do Poço dan a un precioso huerto de cítricos de la tranquila aldea de Borba en Alentejo. El edificio principal es el hogar de sus hospitalarios propietarios y donde se encuentran los apartamentos de planta baja, de primer piso y de segundo piso con bellos frescos y una torre privada. Casas do Jardim tienen sus propias entradas por el jardín y se componen de relajantes zonas de estar, cocinitas y habitaciones con baño en-suite. Atrevidos brochazos de color se complementan ingeniosamente con el mobiliario de época y las antigüedades.

Our inspector loved: *The superb, individual décor in all the rooms.*

 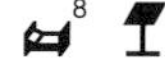       

Directions: Faro or Lisbon > A6 > Borba.

Web: www.johansens.com/casadoterreiro
E-mail: geral@casadoterreirodopoco.com
Tel: +351 917 256077
Fax: +351 268 083624

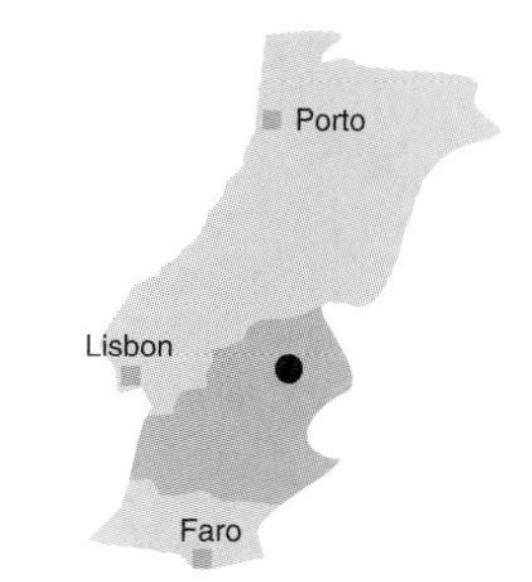

Price Guide:
single €65-75
double/twin €75-85
junior suite €90-100
royal suite €120-150

Monte da Fornalha

BORBA - ESTREMOZ, PORTUGAL

This small oasis of peace and tranquillity is located between the villages of Estremoz and Borba, close to Évora and Alentejo's wine routes. The spacious lounge, with large fireplace, dining area and bedrooms have been decorated with a rustic, warm design and great attention to detail. Homemade jams and local breads and cheeses are served each morning whilst dinner can be prepared upon request.

Cet intime oasis de paix est situé entre les villages d'Estremoz et de Borba, près des routes des vins d'Evora et d'Alejento. Le salon spacieux avec sa grande cheminée, la salle à manger et les chambres ont été décorés dans un style rustique et chaleureux où chaque détail compte. Confitures faites maison et pains et fromages locaux sont servis chaque matin tandis que les dîners sont préparés sur demande.

Este pequeño oasis de paz y tranquilidad se encuentra entre los pueblos de Estremoz y Borba, próximo a Evora y a la rutas vinícolas de Alentejo. En el espacioso salón hay una gran chimenea y el comedor y las habitaciones han sido decoradas en un diseño rústico y cálido con todo tipo de detalles. En el desayuno encontrará mermeladas caseras así como panes y quesos del lugar mientras que la cena se prepara con aviso previo.

Our inspector loved: *The rural peacefulness.*

Directions: Lisbon > Estremoz > signposted.

Web: www.johansens.com/montedafornalha
E-mail: montedafornalha@sapo.pt
Tel: +351 268 840 314
Fax: +351 268 891 885

Price Guide:
double €90-100
junior suite €100-130

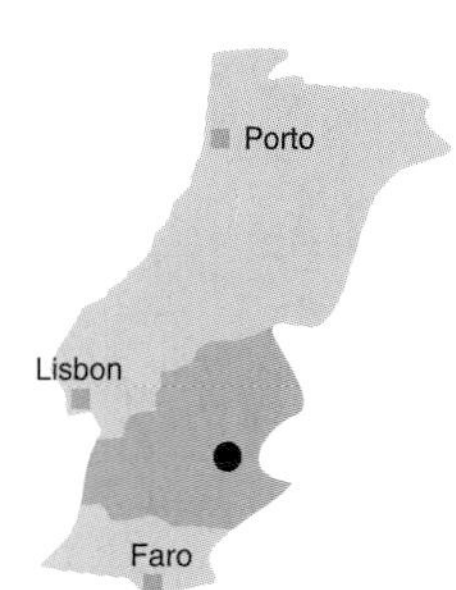

Convento do Espinheiro Heritage Hotel & Spa

CANAVIAIS, 7005-839 ÉVORA, PORTUGAL

A member of Starwood's Luxury Collection, this former convent, set in the World Heritage listed city of Évora, has been converted into a 59-bedroom hotel. Vestiges from the property's 15th-century past include an olive press and stunning chapel, which has been fully restored and is licenced for weddings. With the wine routes of Estremoz and the Alentejo nearby, sourcing vintages for the daily wine tastings is easy while the property's old cellar is now home to a gastronomic restaurant.

Membre de la Luxury Collection de Starwood, cet ancien couvent, situé dans la ville d'Évora, classée patrimoine mondial par l'UNESCO, a été transformé en hôtel de 59 chambres. Des vestiges de la propriété datant du XVe siècle comprennent une presse à olive et une superbe chapelle, qui a été complètement restaurée et accueille aujourd'hui les mariages. Avec la route des vins d'Estremoz et l'Alentejo, trouver des bons crus et déguster des bons vins est facile alors que l'ancienne cave du couvent est aujourd'hui devenu le restaurant gastronomique.

Miembro del Starwood's Luxury Collection, este antiguo convento ubicado en la ciudad de Évora, nombrada Patrimonio de la Humanidad, ha sido convertido en un hotel de 59 habitaciones. Entre los vestigios de su pasado, que se remontan al siglo XV, este hotel cuenta con una prensa de aceite y una impresionante capilla, totalmente restaurada y autorizada para celebrar matrimonios. Gracias a la cercanía de las rutas vinícolas de Estremoz y el Alentejo, los vinos de calidad aparecen con asiduidad en las catas diarias, siendo además la antigua bodega el emplazamiento de un restaurante gourmet en la actualidad.

Our inspector loved: *The lovely indoor swimming pool.*

Directions: Lisbon Airport > A6 > Évora on the road to Estremoz.

Web: www.johansens.com/espinheiro
E-mail: sales@conventodoespinheiro.com
Tel: +351 266 788 200
Fax: +351 266 788 229

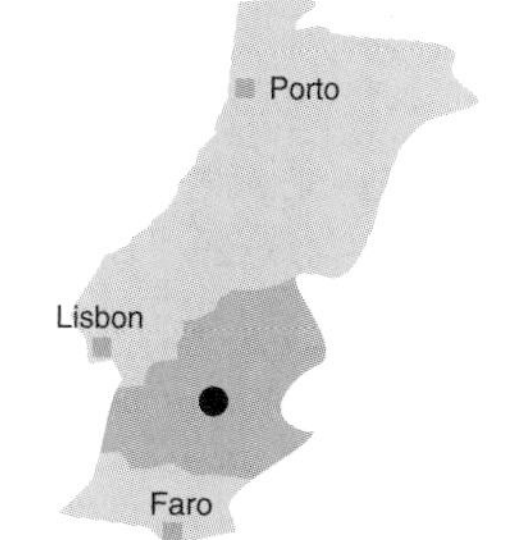

Price Guide:
double €240-280
suite €600-850

Estalagem São Domingos

RUA DR VARGAS, MINA DE SÃO DOMINGOS, 7750-171 MÉRTOLA, PORTUGAL

Set on the edge of Guadiana Valley's nature reserve, this former palace is surrounded by 4,940 acres of beautiful countryside. Decorated with a blend of Alentejo and late Victorian style, 6 guest rooms are situated within the old palace whilst 25 are located in the hotel's new area. Seppia Restaurant and Bar offers local cuisine; snacks are served in Sombra bar and drinks are available in Marbles bar. The hotel's astronomic observatory is a popular attraction, with regular astronomy nights.

Situé sur les bords de la réserve naturelle de la vallée du Guadiana, cet ancien palais est entouré de 2,000 ha de superbes paysages. Décorées dans un subtil mélange de traditionnel Alentejo et de la fin de l'ère Victorienne, 6 chambres sont situées dans l'ancien palais tandis que les 25 autres sont dans un nouveau bâtiment de l'hôtel. Le bar restaurant Seppia propose une cuisine locale, des collations sont servis au bar Sombra et les boissons au bar Marbles. L'observatoire astronomique de l'hôtel est une véritable attraction, avec de réguliès soirées d'astronomie.

Ubicado en el límite de la reserva natural del valle Guadiana, este antiguo palacio está rodeado de 2,000 ha de un paisaje maravilloso. La decoración ha fundido el estilo de Alentejo con el victoriano posterior, 6 de las habitaciones se encuentran en el antiguo palacio mientras que otras 25 están en la nueva zona del hotel. El restaurante Seppia y el bar ofrecen cocina local, las tapas se sirven en el bar Sombra y las bebidas en el Marbles. El hotel posee también como atracción popular un observatorio astronómico, con noches de astronomia regulares.

Our inspector loved: *Lying in the hammock next to the pool.*

Directions: The nearest airports are Lisbon and Faro. From Faro Airport head towards Spain > Castro Marim - Mértola. From Lisbon Airport > Beja > Mértola.

Web: www.johansens.com/saodomingos
E-mail: recepcao@hotelsaodomingos.com
Tel: +351 286 640 000
Fax: +351 286 640 009

Price Guide:
single €96-176
double €120-220

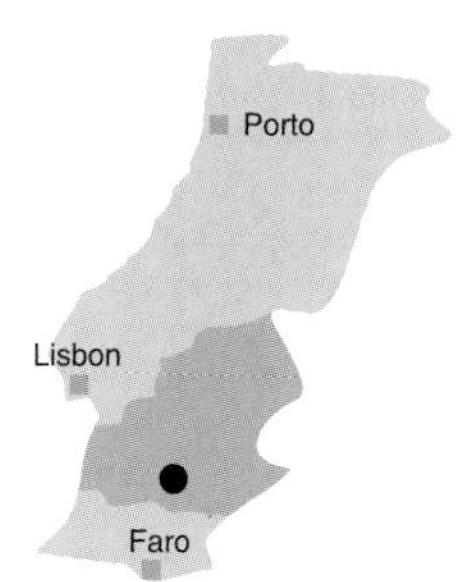

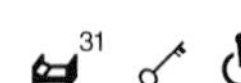

Monte do Chora Cascas

APT 296, 7050-013 MONTEMOR~O~NOVO, PORTUGAL

Situated close to Evora, this lovely 7-bedroom guest house offers every comfort and amenity. Owner Sónia Estima Marques is very involved with the running of the house and has a keen eye for detail. Flower displays and reading material abound, bedrooms are tastefully furnished and decorated, breakfasts are beautifully presented, superb dinners are served in a delightful setting and there is a large garden swimming pool with surrounding terrace overlooking the old town.

Située près d'Evora, cette adorable pension de famille offre tout le confort et équipements modernes. La méticuleuse propriétaire Sónia Estima Marques est énormément impliquée dans la gestion de la maison. Avec des fleurs dans les vases et de la lecture à foison, les chambres sont meublées et décorées avec gout; les petits-déjeuners sont joliment présentés; les délicieux dîners sont servis dans un endroit charmant et une grande piscine de jardin, entourée d 'une terrasse, surplombe la vieille ville.

Situada muy cerca de Évora, esta preciosa casa de huéspedes de 7 habitaciones ofrece todo tipo de servicios y comodidades. Su propietaria, Sónia Estima Marques, se dedica por completo a ella y cuida muy bien los pequeños detalles. Las exposiciones florales son abundantes y el material de lectura prolijo. Las habitaciones están decoradas y amuebladas con gusto. La presentación de los desayunos es estupenda y las excelentes cenas que ofrece se sirven en un entorno maravilloso. El lugar dispone también de un gran jardín-piscina con una terraza alrededor desde la que se puede contemplar la antigua ciudad.

Our inspector loved: *The excellent hospitality, and eye for detail.*

Directions: Lisbon > A6 > Evora.

Web: www.johansens.com/montechoracascas
E-mail: info@montechoracascas.com
Tel: +351 266 899 690
Fax: +351 266 899 690

Price Guide: (room only, excluding VAT)
double €115-150

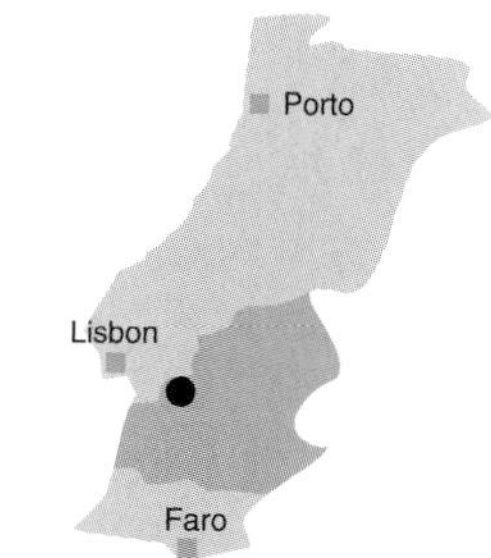

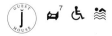

Convento de São Paulo

ALDEIA DA SERRA, 7170-120 REDONDO, PORTUGAL

Directions: Lisbon > A6 > Évora/Estremoz > Redondo > signposted.

Web: www.johansens.com/conventodesaopaulo
E-mail: hotelconvspaulo@mail.telepac.pt
Tel: +351 266 989 160
Fax: +351 266 989 167

Price Guide:
single €105–205
double/twin €120–220
suite €200–230

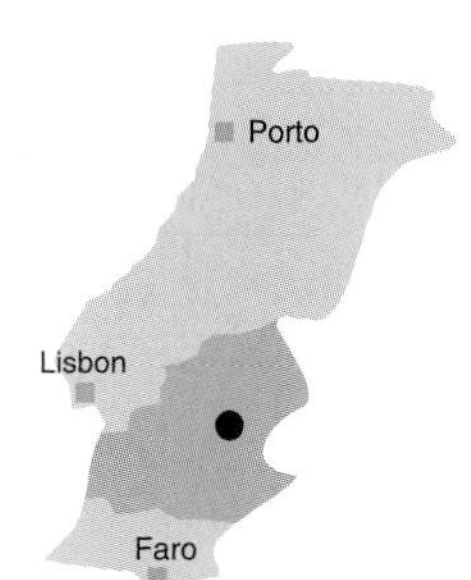

Situated between Estremoz and Redondo in the Alentejo, Convento de São Paulo, "the Monastery of Saint Paul", was constructed in 1182 by monks seeking a tranquil location to pray. Many vestiges of the 12th century have remained; the original chapel and church are popular venues for weddings and special events, whilst the bedrooms are the old chambers of the monks. Guests dine beneath the splendour of 18th-century fresco paintings in the stylish restaurant. The convent also has a collection of 50,000 tiles.

Situé dans l'Alentejo, entre Estremoz et Redondo, le Convento de São Paulo fût construit en 1182 par des moines en quête d'endroit tranquille pour prier. De nombreux vestiges du XIIe siècle ont été conservés; la chapelle et l'église originales sont des endroits populaires pour les mariages ou les occasions spéciales, et les anciennes cellules des moines servent aujourd'hui de chambres. Les hôtes dînent sous de somptueuses fresques du XVIIIe siècle, dans l'élégante salle à manger. Le couvent aussi dispose d'une collection de 50 000 carreaux.

Situado entre Estremoz y Redondo en el Alentejo, el Convento de São Paulo fue construido en 1182 por unos monjes que buscaban un lugar tranquilo en que rezar. Son muchos los vestigios del siglo XII que han perdurado, la capilla original y la iglesia son lugares preferidos para bodas y otros eventos especiales, mientras que las antiguas celdas de los monjes sirven hoy de habitaciones. Los clientes cenan al abrigo de la grandiosidad de los frescos del siglo XVIII del elegante restaurante. El convento dispone además de una colección de 50.000 azulejos.

Our inspector loved: *The lovely junior suite with open fireplace.*

32

130

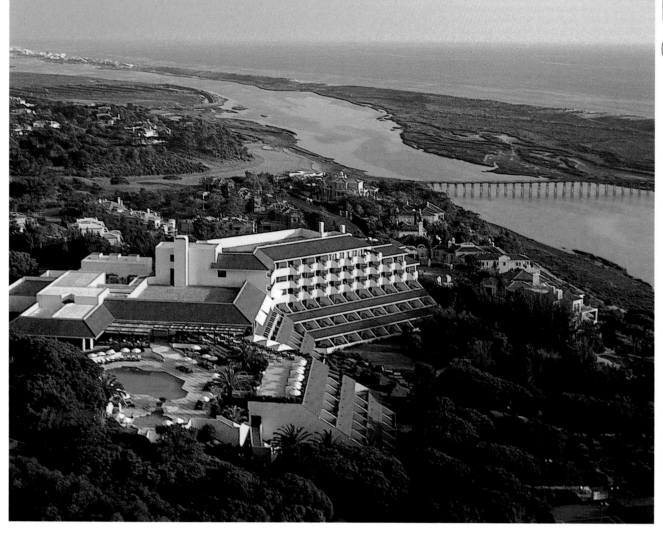

Hotel Quinta do Lago

8135-024 ALMANCIL, ALGARVE, PORTUGAL

Overlooking the tranquil estuary of the Ria Formosa, on the doorstep of the Algarve's most famous golf courses, this hotel has benefited from several renovations. All bedrooms have large terraces and are sea-facing, there is a small spa and indoor and outdoor pools with lovely views of the park and ocean. At night the upper-deck patio is candle-lit to create a romantic atmosphere for diners. Quita Do Lago beach is a short walk away.

Surplombant le calme estuaire du Ria Formosa, aux portes de plus prestigieux parcours de golf de l'Algarve, c et hôtel a subi plusieurs rénovations. Toutes les chambres ont de grandes terrasses et sont face à la mer. Il y a un petit spa ainsi que des piscines extérieure et intérieure offrant de charmante vues sur le parc et l'océan. Le soir, le patio supérieur est éclairé à la bougie afin de créer une atmosphère romantique pour le dîner. La plage de Quinta do Lago est à quelques mètres.

Con vistas al tranquilo estuario de la Ría Formosa, a las puertas de los campos de golf más famosos del Algarve, este hotel se ha beneficiado de varias renovaciones. Todas las habitaciones disponen de amplias terrazas con vistas al mar. Asimismo cuenta con un pequeño spa así como con piscinas cubiertas y al aire libre con maravillosas vistas al parque y al océano. Por la noche el patio de estructura elevada se ilumina con velas para crear un ambiente romántico durante las cenas. La playa Quita Do Lago se encuentra a corta distancia a pie.

Our inspector loved: *The unique setting of this luxury hotel.*

Directions: Faro > IPI > Almancil.

Web: www.johansens.com/quintadolago
E-mail: reservations@quintadolagohotel.com
Tel: +351 289 350 350
Fax: +351 289 396 393

Price Guide:
single €188-536
double €221-536
suite €536-3,090

Quinta Jacintina

GARRÂO DE CIMA, 8135-025 ALMANCIL, PORTUGAL

This charming brand new boutique hotel is a true gem, positioned close to the many renowned, fashionable beaches of the Algarve as well as superb golf courses, restaurants and shopping facilities. The restaurant is excellent and the comfortable bar offers the perfect meeting place for friends. Bedrooms are decorated in pretty pastel shades alongside elegant furnishings to provide the ultimate in luxury and comfort.

Ce charmant et tout nouvel hôtel boutique est un vrai joyau, situé près de la plupart des plages réputées et à la mode de l'Algarve, ainsi que des superbes parcours de golf, restaurants et boutiques. Le restaurant est délicieux et le bar confortable est l'endroit idéal pour se retrouver entre amis. Les chambres sont décorées dans de ravissants tons pastels avec un mobilier élégant qui procure ainsi le meilleur du luxe et confort.

Este nuevo y encantador hotel boutique es una verdadera joya situada en las cercanías de las numerosas y famosas playas de moda del Algarve así como de espléndidos campos de golf, restaurantes e centros comerciales. El restaurante es excelente y su cómodo bar es el lugar ideal para reunirse con los amigos. Los habitaciones están decorados en bonitas tonalidades de colores pastel, con elegante mobiliario y proporcionan el máximo en lujo y confort.

Our inspector loved: *The fantastic colour schemes.*

Directions: Faro > Almancil.

Web: www.johansens.com/jacintina
E-mail: info@algarvehotel.co.uk
Tel: +351 289 350 090
Fax: +351 289 350 099

Price Guide:
double €200-350

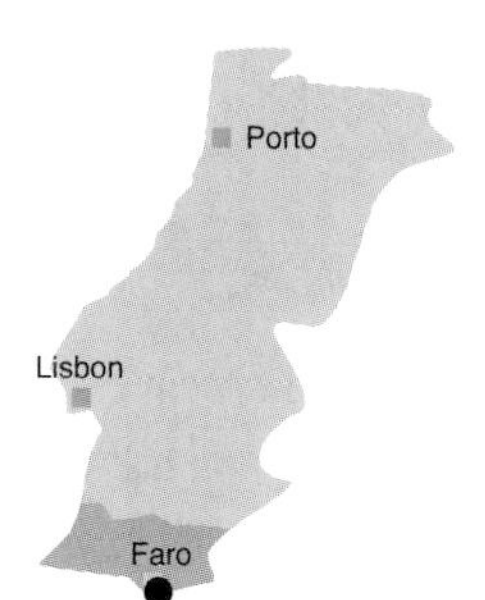

Villa Esmeralda

PORTO DE MÓS, 8600 LAGOS, PORTUGAL

This charming hotel stands within a subtropical palm garden above the bay of Porto de Mós, near the historical town of Lagos. A special home-from-home comfort features throughout the hotel and in the spacious guest rooms, which include 2 junior suites. Each room boasts views of the ocean, terrace or garden. Guests may take breakfast or tea on the terrace and savour the fresh fish of the day in the beach restaurant. The hotel has a private entrance to the beach.

Cette hôtel de charme se dresse au cœur d'un jardin subtropical de palmiers au-dessus de la baie de Porto de Mós, près de la ville historique de Lagos. Le sentiment particulier d'être comme à la maison se ressent à travers tout l'hôtel ainsi que dans les chambres spacieuses, qui comprennent 2 junior suites. Chaque chambre offre une vue sur l'océan, la terrasse ou le jardin. Les clients peuvent apprécier leur petit-déjeuner ou le thé sur la terrasse et déguster le poisson frais du jour au restaurant de la plage. L'hôtel à un accès privé à la plage.

Este encantador Hôtel está situado en un jardín de palmeras subtropicales, por encima de la Bahía de Porto de Mós, próximo al histórico pueblo de Lagos. Las habitaciones son espaciosas, 2 de ellas son Júnior Suites, todo el hotel disfruta de un confort que le hará sentirse como en casa. Cada habitación ofrece grandes vistas, bien del océano, de la terraza, o del jardín. Los huéspedes pueden desayunar o tomar el té en la terraza y saborear el pescado fresco del día en el restaurante de la playa. El hôtel también tiene acceso directo y privado a la playa.

Our inspector loved: *The unbeatable location.*

Directions: Faro Airport > IPI > Lagos > Porto de Mós.

Web: www.johansens.com/esmeralda
E-mail: villa.esmeralda@sapo.pt
Tel: +351 282 760 430
Fax: +351 282 760 433

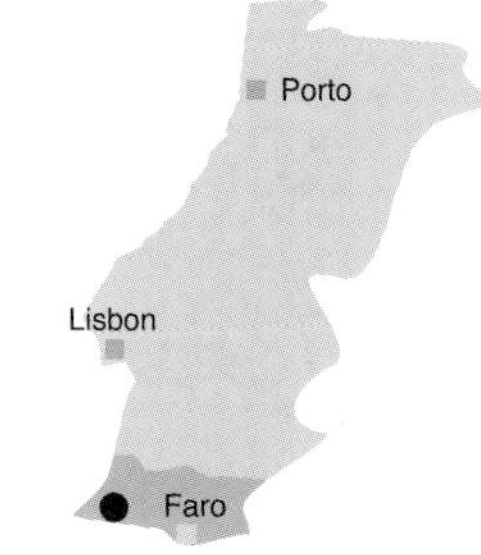

Price Guide:
double €112-186
junior suite €122-210

Casas do Côro

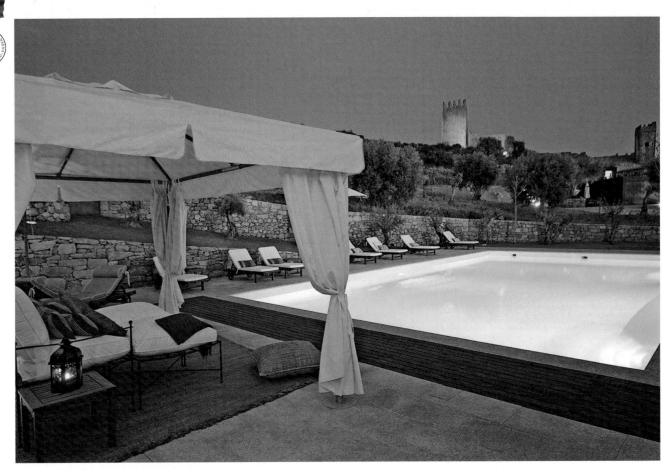

MARIALVAMED TURISMO HISTÓRICO E LAZER LDA, LARGO DO CÔRO, 6430-081 MARIALVA, MÊDA, PORTUGAL

Directions: From Porto take A25. From Lisbon take A1 > A23 > A25. From Madrid take A62 Marialva (Mêda).

Web: www.johansens.com/casasdocoro
E-mail: casa-do-coro@assec.pt
Tel: +351 91 755 2020
Fax: +351 27 159 0003

Price Guide:
single €108-133
double €120-145
suite €160-190

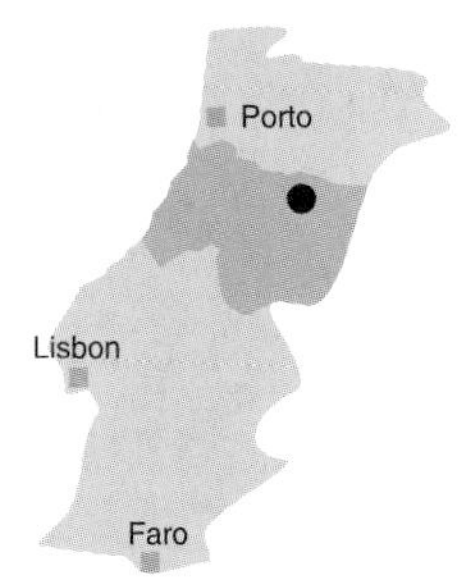

Step back in time in this rural retreat located in a picturesque medieval town in the Douro Valley. Beautifully restored stone houses offer 14 bedrooms with charming décor and every modern comfort. After a sumptuous breakfast, including homemade bread, jam and cakes, guests may relax on one of the pretty pastel deckchairs or soak in the Jacuzzi and enjoy the glorious views of the castle. Dinner is served in one of the inviting lounges boasting rich fabrics and comfortable furnishings.

Repartez dans la passé dans ce refuge campagnard situé dans une charmante ville médiévale de la vallée du Douro. Les maisons en pierre ont été magnifiquement restaurées et proposent 14 chambres au décor charmant et avec le confort moderne. Après un somptueux petit-déjeuner, composé de pain, de confitures et de gâteaux faits maisons, les hôtes peuvent se relaxer sur les ravissants transats pastels ou profiter du jacuzzi en admirant les superbes vues sur le château. Le dîner est servi dans l'un des accueillant salons équipé de superbes tissus et de meubles confortables.

Viaje en el túnel del tiempo a este lugar de descanso rural situado en una encantadora ciudad medieval en el Valle del Duero. Sus magníficas casas restauradas de piedra disponen de 14 habitaciones de primorosa decoración y provistas de todas las comodidades modernas. Tras un generoso desayuno que incluye pan, mermelada y pasteles, todo casero, los clientes pueden relajarse en un precioso sillón-hamaca o zambullirse en el jacuzzi y disfrutar de las espléndidas vistas al castillo. La cena se sirve en uno de sus acogedores salones provistos de suntuosas telas y cómodos muebles.

Our inspector loved: *The sheer magic of this wonderful place.*

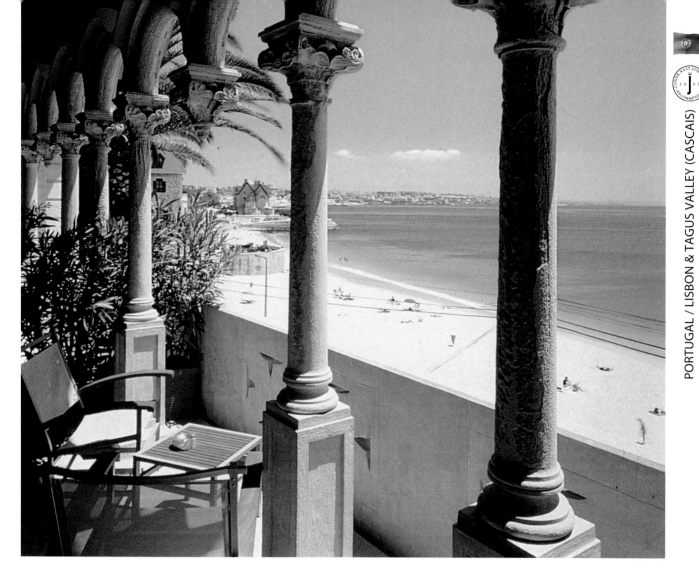

Albatroz Palace, Luxury Suites

RUA FREDERICO AROUCA 100, 2750-353 CASCAIS, LISBON, PORTUGAL

This carefully restored former royal summer retreat is situated on the cliffs above Conceição beach in the charming fishing village of Cascais. Sheer indulgence is reflected by the elegant décor featuring antique and modern furnishings. The 4 luxurious rooms and 2 suites boast sea views and with Albatroz Hotel a few metres away guests may dine in the locally renowned restaurant and swim in the hotel's pool with panoramic views of the bay below. Golf and sightseeing can be arranged. Guests can be picked up from the airport in a private taxi with English-speaking driver (€55).

Cet ancien retrait royal restauré est situé sur les falaises au-dessus de la plage de Conceição au village de Cascais. Une ambiance d'indulgence est reflétée dans le décor élégant avec des ameublements anciens et modernes exquis. Les 4 chambres et les 2 suites ont vues sur la mer, et Albatroz Hotel étant à quelques mètres, les hôtes peuvent passer des soirées dans son restaurant renommé et nager dans sa piscine avec des vues panoramiques. Excursions et golf peuvent être organisés. Un chauffeur qui parle l'anglais est disponible pour chercher les hôtes de l'aéroport (€55).

Anteriormente residencia real de verano, ha sido restaurada cuidadosamente y se encuentra sobre los acantilados de la playa Conceição en el atractivo pueblo de pescadores de Cascais. La indulgencia auténtica se refleja en el elegante décor donde destaca lo moderno y lo antiguo. 4 habitaciones súper lujo y 2 suites ofrecen vistas al mar. En el hotel Albatroz, a tan sólo unos metros, los clientes pueden cenar en el famoso restaurante local y nadar en la piscina con vistas panorámicas a la bahía. La práctica del golf y visitas turísticas pueden ser organizadas, así como el poder ser recogidos a su llegada al aeropuerto por un taxista que habla inglés (€55).

Our inspector loved: *The sheer luxury and beauty of the place.*

Directions: 24km from the centre of Lisbon. 15km from Sintra. 4km from Estoril. 24km from Lisbon. From the airport take the A5 towards Cascais.

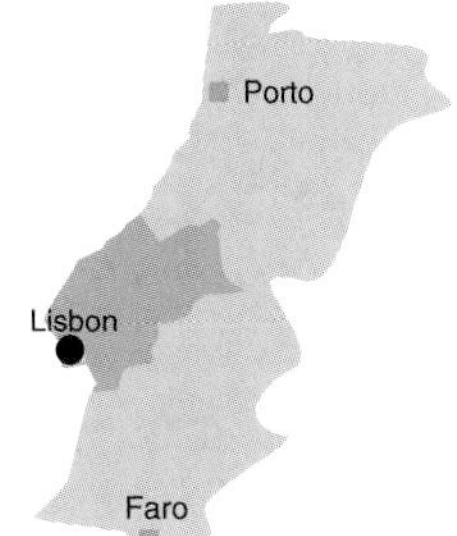

Web: www.johansens.com/albatroz
E-mail: albatroz@albatrozhotels.com
Tel: +351 21 484 73 80
Fax: +351 21 484 48 27

Price Guide:
single €150-322
double €180-355
suite €275-510

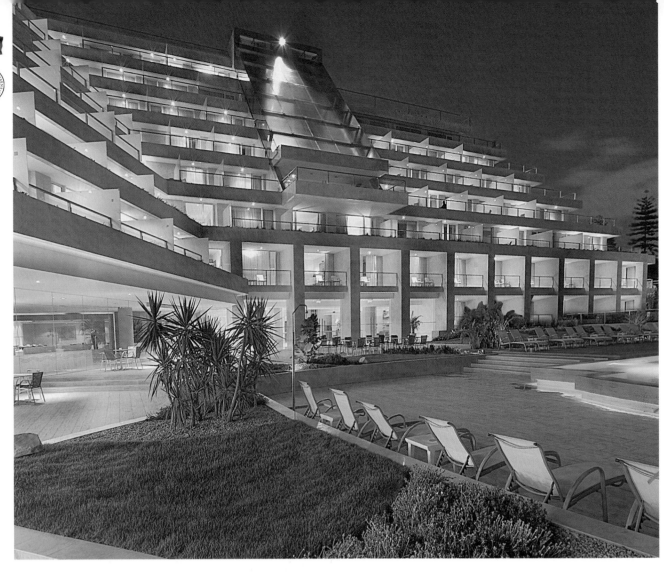

Hotel Cascais Mirage

AV. MARGINAL, NO 8554, 2754-536 CASCAIS, PORTUGAL

Situated between Cascais and Estoril, next to the ocean, this hotel is unique because it is the most modern in the area. The personal touch has not been lost however, and little surprises include rose petals in the bathroom, a chocolate on the pillow and tea in guests' rooms. Living areas are spacious, and there is an outstanding restaurant. The pool, with its ocean view, has an exquisite wooden deck for relaxing.

Situé entre Cascais et Estoril, à côté de l'océan, cet hôtel est unique par sa modernité dans la région. Les touches personnelles n'ont pas été oubliées et se traduisent par de petites surprises comme des pétales de rose dans la salle de bain, du chocolat sur l'oreiller et du thé dans les chambres. Les pièces à vivre sont spacieuses et le restaurant est exceptionnel. La piscine, outre sa vue sur la mer, a une plage en bois pour se relaxer.

Situado entre Cascais y Estoril, junto al océano, este hotel es único porque es el más moderno de la zona. No ha perdido sin embargo su toque personal y entre las pequeñas sorpresas se incluyen pétalos de rosa en el cuarto de baño, un bombón sobre la almohada y té en las habitaciones. Dispone de amplio espacio y un magnífico restaurante. La piscina, con vistas al océano, tiene una plataforma de madera para el relax de los clientes.

***Our inspector loved:** The sumptuous, fresh breakfast.*

Directions: Lisbon Airport > Cascais.

Web: www.johansens.com/cascaismirage
E-mail: geral@cascaismirage.com
Tel: +351 210 060 600
Fax: +351 210 060 601

Price Guide:
standard €260-355
junior suite €475
suite €700-2,500

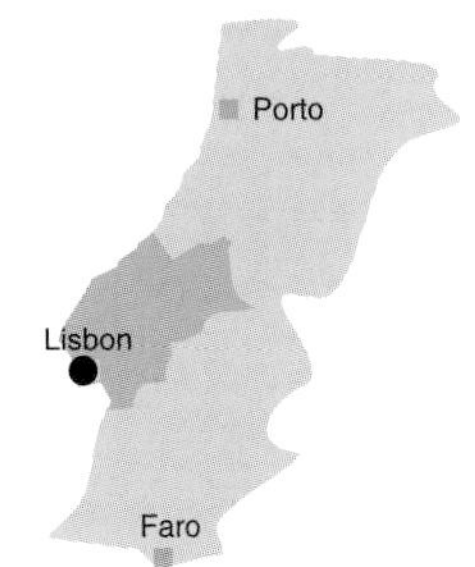

192 800 SPA

SENHORA DA GUIA

ESTRADA DO GUINCHO, 2750-642 CASCAIS, PORTUGAL

Surrounded by the sea, beautiful gardens and Sintra Natural Park, this 5-star hotel is situated 40 minutes from Lisbon on the Estoril Coast between Cascais and Guincho Beach. Filled with light and decorated in vibrant colours, the guest rooms are extremely comfortable; some have terraces and panoramic views. The Terrace Restaurant offers Portuguese meals with a Mediterranean influence, created from fresh, seasonal, local produce. The health and wellness centre includes a Jacuzzi, gym and sauna, and 5 golf courses are nearby.

Entouré par la mer, de beaux jardins et le Parc Naturel de Sintra, cet hôtel 5 étoiles est situé à 40 minutes de Lisbonne sur la côte Estoril entre les plages de Cascais et Guincho. Extrêmement lumineuses et décorées dans des couleurs vives, les chambres d'hôtes sont très confortables ; certaines ont une terrasse et des vues panoramiques. Le restaurant Terrace sert une cuisine portugaise avec une influence méditerranéenne, préparée à partir de produits frais locaux et de saison.

Este hotel de 5 estrellas, rodeado de mar, de bonitos jardines y del Parque Natural Sintra está a 40 minutos de Lisboa en la Costa de Estoril entre Cascais y Playa Guincho. Lleno de luz y decorado con colores vivos, las habitaciones son extremadamente cómodas, algunas con terrazas y vistas panorámicas. El Restaurante Terrace sirve comida portuguesa con influencia mediterránea y se hace con productos locales frescos y de temporada. El centro de salud y wellness incluye jacuzzi, gimnasio y sauna. Hay 5 campos de golf próximos.

Our inspector loved: *The lovely new restaurant with bright colours.*

Directions: Lisbon > Cascais.

Web: www.johansens.com/senhoradaguia
E-mail: reservas@senhoradaguia.com
Tel: +351 214 869 239
Fax: +351 214 869 227

Price Guide:
single €115-240
double €135-270
superior €180-300

As Janelas Verdes

RUA DAS JANELAS VERDES 47, 1200-690 LISBON, PORTUGAL

This small 18th-century palace offers a romantic atmosphere in the heart of Lisbon, next to the National Art Museum. The home-from-home ambience is enhanced by the friendly staff and inviting neo-classical décor fitted with objets d'art, paintings and mementoes of a bygone era. Bedrooms are individually decorated and the ivy-covered patio is a peaceful haven. Drinks may be taken on the panelled library's balcony overlooking the River Tagus, and breakfast savoured in the garden during warmer months.

Ce petit palais du XVIIIe siècle offre une atmosphère romantique au cœur de Lisbonne, à deux pas du Musée National d'Arts. Le personnel amical et l'attrayante décoration néoclassique avec ses objets d'art, peintures et souvenirs d'autrefois créent une atmosphère chaleureuse où l'on se sent comme chez soi. Les chambres sont décorées de manière individuelle et le patio couvert de lierre est un refuge tranquille. L'apéritif peut-être dégusté sur le balcon de la bibliothèque en bois surplombant le Tage et le petit-déjeuner peut-être pris dans le jardin pendant les mois les plus chauds.

Este pequeño palacio del siglo XVIII, situado junto al Museo de Arte Nacional, proporciona un romántico ambiente en pleno corazón de Lisboa. Su estilo hogareño queda realzado por su amable personal y por su acogedora decoración neoclásica complementada con objetos de arte, lienzos y recuerdos de tiempos pasados. Las habitaciones están individualmente decoradas y su patio recubierto de hiedra es un refugio de paz. Puede tomarse una copa en la terraza de la biblioteca de paneles con vistas al río Tajo y deleitarse con el desayuno en su jardín durante los meses más cálidos.

Our inspector loved: *The pretty garden.*

Directions: Lisbon Airport > taxi to As Janelas in the city.

Web: www.johansens.com/janelasverdes
E-mail: janelas.verdes@heritage.pt
Tel: +351 21 39 68 143
Fax: +351 21 39 68 144

Price Guide: (breakfast €14)
single €219-270
double €227-295

29

     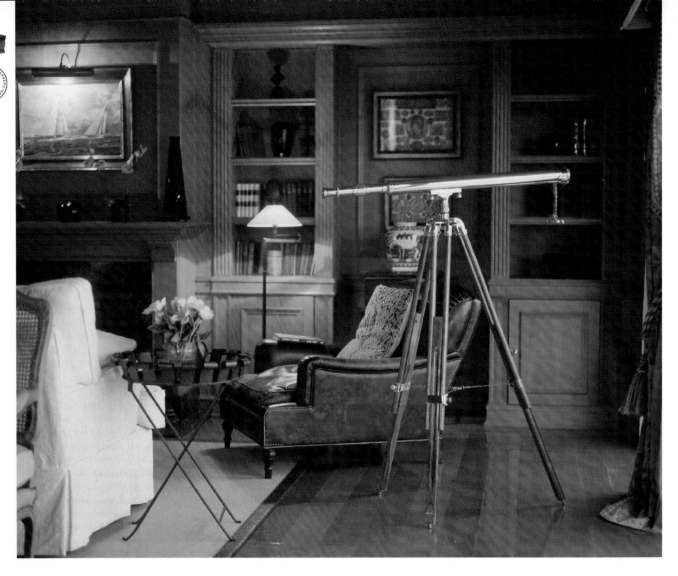   

Heritage Av Liberdade

AVENIDA DA LIBERDADE 28, 1250-145 LISBON, PORTUGAL

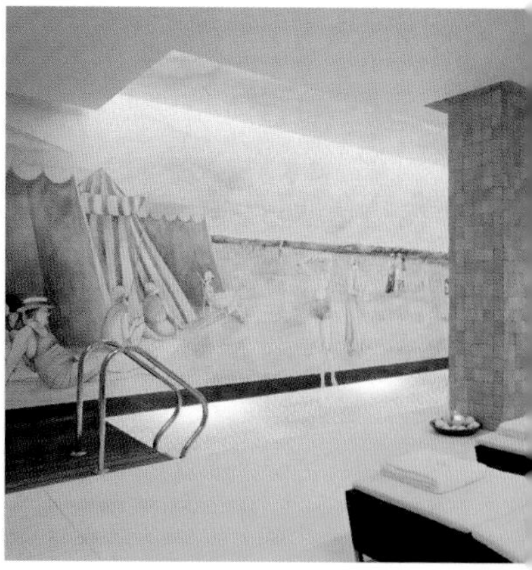

The architect Miguel Câncio Martins renovated this former palace to become a great example of Portuguese design. The 18th-century façade elements, masonry work, veranda railings, main wooden entrance, original ceramics and pieces of furniture remain, whilst a first-class Portuguese town-house interior welcomes guests. The modern and the traditional successfully combine in the 42 varied guest rooms. Ideally located to explore the historic centre of Lisbon.

L'architecte Miguel Câncio Martins a rénové cet ancien palais pour le transformer en un exemple magistral de design portugais. Les éléments de façade du XVIIIe siècle, le travail de maçonnerie, la véranda, l'entrée principale en bois, les céramiques originales et les pièces d'ameublement ont été conservés alors que les hôtes sont accueillis dans un intérieur d'hôtel particulier portugais de première catégorie. Le moderne et le traditionnel se marient parfaitement dans les 42 chambres d'hôtes au décor unique. C'est le lieu idéal pour explorer le centre historique de Lisbonne.

El arquitecto, Miguel Câncio Martins ha renovado este antiguo palacio para convertirlo un gran ejemplo de diseño portugués. La fachada del siglo XVIII, el trabajo en piedra, las barandillas de la veranda, la entrada principal en madera, la cerámica y algunas piezas del mobiliario se han conservado consiguiendo un interior digno de casa de ciudad Portuguesa de primera que da buena acogida sus huéspedes. Lo moderno y lo tradicional se combinan con éxito en las 42 variadas habitaciones. Idealmente situado para explorar el centro histórico de Lisboa.

Our inspector loved: *The creative design.*

Directions: The property is a taxi ride from Lisbon Airport.

Web: www.johansens.com/liberdade
E-mail: avliberdade@heritage.pt
Tel: +351 213 404 040
Fax: +351 213 404 044

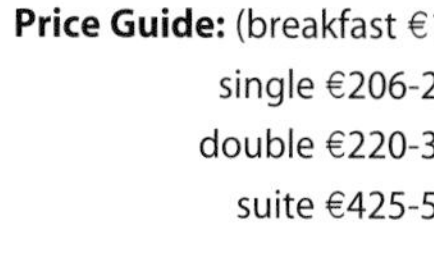

Price Guide: (breakfast €14)
single €206-293
double €220-320
suite €425-550

  42       

Hotel Britania

RUA RODRIGUES SAMPAIO 17, 1150-278 LISBON, PORTUGAL

Opened in 1944 and designed by the famous Portuguese modernist architect Cassiano Branco, this prestigious, family-run hotel is the only surviving original art deco hotel in Lisbon. It has been lovingly restored to regain its 1940's ambience and is now classified as a historic building. Service is simply outstanding. Beautiful photographs of Lisbon adorn the walls of the welcoming lounge with its fireplace and small library, and the 33 very spacious bedrooms feature a relaxing décor and marble bathrooms.

Ouvert en 1944 et conçu par le fameux architecte moderne portugais Cassiano Branco, ce prestigieux hôtel de famille est le seul hôtel art déco d'origine à Lisbonne. Il a été soigneusement restauré afin de garder son ambiance des années 1940 et c'est maintenant un monument classé. Le service est tout simplement parfait. De superbes photographies de Lisbonne décorent les murs ainsi que l'accueillant salon avec sa cheminée et petite bibliothèque. Les 33 chambres spacieuses ont une décoration relaxante et des salles de bain en marbre.

Inaugurado en 1944 y diseñado por el célebre arquitecto modernista portugués Cassiano Branco, este prestigioso hotel de regencia familiar es el único hotel Art Deco original que queda en la ciudad de Lisboa. Ha sido restaurado con sumo encanto para volver a proporcionarle su estilo característico de los anos 1940 y está hoy considerado como edificio histórico. El servicio es sencillamente extraordinario. Las paredes de su acogedor salón, provisto de chimenea y de una pequeña biblioteca, están adornadas de bellas fotografías de Lisboa. Sus 33 amplias y espaciosas habitaciones, todas con cuartos de baño de mármol, proporcionan un verdadero ambiente de relax.

Our inspector loved: *The old photographs in the lounge.*

Directions: Lisbon Airport > city centre.

Web: www.johansens.com/britania
E-mail: britania.hotel@heritage.pt
Tel: +351 21 31 55 016
Fax: +351 21 31 55 021

Price Guide: (breakfast €14)
single €196-225
double €210-245

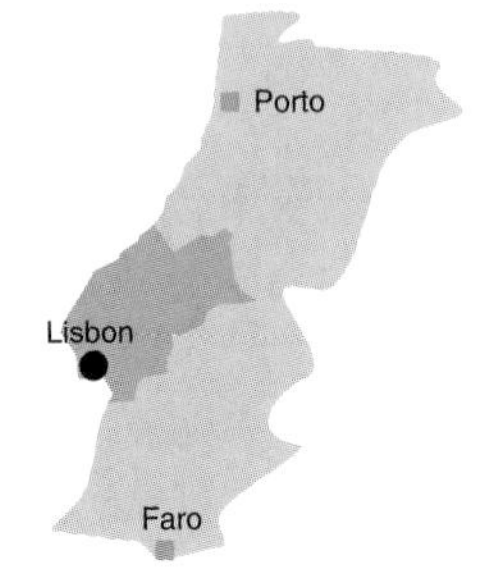

Quinta da Bela Vista

CAMINHO DO AVISTA NAVIOS 4, 9000 FUNCHAL, MADEIRA, PORTUGAL

It is a joy to stay in this traditional house, with its tall windows and green shutters, overlooking Funchal Bay and surrounded by 22,000m² of exotic gardens. The interiors are a blend of sophistication and rich, classical furnishings. Guests enjoy their apéritifs in the cheerful bar or on the sunny terraces before choosing between the elegant restaurant serving fine food and the best wines or the more informal dining room.

Surplombant la baie de Funchal et entourée de 22 000 m² de jardins exotiques, c'est un vrai plaisir de séjourner dans cette maison traditionnelle, avec ses grandes fenêtres et ses volets verts. L'intérieur est un mélange de sophistication et de richesse, avec des meubles classiques. Les visiteurs dégusteront leur apéritif dans le bar animé ou sur les terraces ensoleillées avant de se décider entre le restaurant élégant servant des plats fins et les meilleurs vins ou la salle à manger plus informelle.

Es un verdadero placer alojarse en esta casa tradicional de altos ventanales y verdes postigos, rodeada de 22.000 m² de jardines exóticos y con vistas a la Bahía Funchal. En sus interiores se mezcla la sofisticación con el lujoso mobiliario clásico. Los clientes podrán disfrutar del aperitivo tanto en su encantador bar como en las soleadas terrazas antes de decidirse por una excelente cocina acompañada de los mejores vinos servida en su elegante restaurante o por otra algo más informal en su comedor.

Our inspector loved: *The excellent cuisine.*

Directions: Main road > Rua do Dr Pita. Madeira International Airport is a 30-minute drive.

Web: www.johansens.com/quintadabelavista
E-mail: info@belavistamadeira.com
Tel: +351 291 706 400
Fax: +351 291 706 401

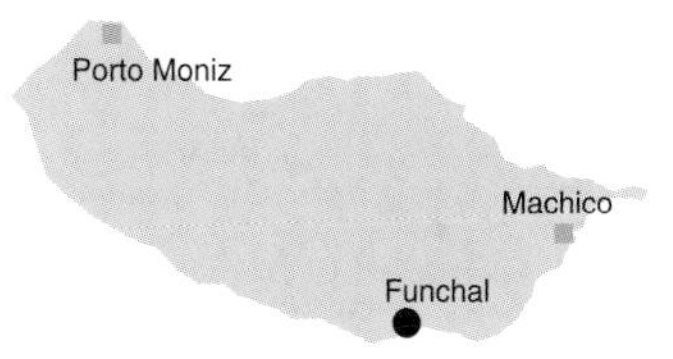

Price Guide:
single €137–260
double/twin €182–366
suite €360–440

Estalagem da Ponta do Sol

QUINTA DA ROCHINHA, 9360 PONTA DO SOL, MADEIRA, PORTUGAL

Directions: Take the hotel's complimentary 35-minute shuttle bus ride from Madeira Airport.

Web: www.johansens.com/pontadosol
E-mail: info@pontadosol.com
Tel: +351 291 970 200
Fax: +351 291 970 209

Price Guide:
single €75-95
twin €85-120

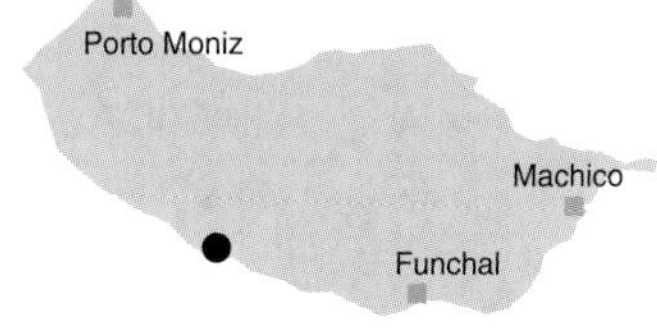

Simply stunning, this special hotel is built on the edge of a cliff overlooking the ocean and pretty town of Ponta do Sol. Modern architecture and unique style combine with the original buildings to create a relaxing, luxurious atmosphere that does not detract from its breathtaking natural surroundings. The walls are adorned with black and white photographs and furnishings are cool and comfortable. An awe-inspiring pool seems to melt into the sea. Good local food is served in the restaurant, which has huge windows and spectacular views.

Tout simplement spectaculaire, cet hôtel très spécial est construit au bord de la falaise et surplombe l'océan et la ravissante ville de Ponta do Sol. Une architecture moderne et un style unique s'allient aux bâtiments d'origine afin de créer une atmosphère luxueuse et relaxante, sans porter atteinte à son environnement naturel à vous couper le souffle. Les murs sont couverts de photographies en noir et blanc et l'ameublement est design et confortable. La piscine, impressionnante, semble se fondre dans l'océan. Le restaurant offre des vues spectaculaires à travers ses baies vitrées.

Sencillamente sorprendente. Este distinguido hotel está construido al borde de un acantilado desde el que se divisa el océano y la bella localidad de Ponta do Sol. Su moderna arquitectura y estilo único se combinan con los originales edificios para crear un ambiente de relax y lujo que no le resta valor al impresionante entorno natural. Las paredes están adornadas con fotografías en blanco y negro y su mobiliario es moderno y cómodo. Una imponente piscina parece fundirse con el mar. El restaurante, de enormes ventanales y espectaculares vistas, sirve la buena comida típica del lugar.

***Our inspector loved:** This simply special hotel.*

Quinta de San José

5130-123 ERVEDOSA DO DOURO, PORTUGAL

A handsome guest house in a stunning location. Quinta de San José stands regally at the foot of a hillside surrounded by terraced vines on the banks of the beautiful River Douro in the unspoilt valley which gives the tranquil waters its name. This is a World Heritage Site and magnificently blends into its environment. 4 stone-built fully-contained houses, each with 2 en-suite bedrooms and every modern facility, radiate from the main building with its elegant dining and sitting rooms. There is a pool and private pier.

Une charmante pension de famille dans un endroit sublime. Quinta de San José se dresse majestueusement au pied d'un côteau entouré de vignes en terrasses sur les rives de la superbe rivière Douro, portant le nom de la vallée intacte dans laquelle elle sinue. C'est un site du Patrimoine Mondial qui se marie parfaitement dans son environnement. 4 maisons en pierre entièrement équipées, chacune avec 2 chambres et tout l'équipement moderne, rayonnent autour de la maison principale et de ses élégants salon et salle à manger. L'hôtel dispose d'une piscine et d'une jetée privée.

Un bello quinta de espléndido emplazamiento. Quinta de San José se erige con majestad al pie de una colina rodeada de terrazas de viñedos a la orilla del bello río Douro a su paso por su virginal valle que da nombre a sus tranquilas aguas. Está considerado como Patrimonio de la Humanidad y goza de una magnífica fusión con el medio ambiente. Sus 4 edificios construidos en piedra y totalmente acondicionados cuentan cada uno de ellos de 2 habitaciones en-suite dotadas de todas las modernas instalaciones. Éstos se encuentran adyacentes al edificio principal, provisto de elegantes salones y comedores. Dispone asimismo de piscina y muelle privado.

Our inspector loved: *The spectacular location.*

Directions: Porto > A4 > A28 > N/222 > Ervedosa.

Web: www.johansens.com/quintasanjose
E-mail: sjose.douro@iol.pt
Tel: +351 254 420000 or +351 917 220450
Fax: +351 254 420009

Price Guide:
double €150

Vintage House

LUGAR DA PONTE, 5085-034 PINHÃO, PORTUGAL

Directions: Porto > A4 - IP4 > Vila Real > Viseu > A24 > Régua/Santa Marta de Penaguião > follow signs to Pinhão.

Web: www.johansens.com/vintagehouse
E-mail: vintagehouse@hotelvintagehouse.com
Tel: +351 254 730 230
Fax: +351 254 730 238

Price Guide:
single €106–170
double/twin €119–186
suite €152–339

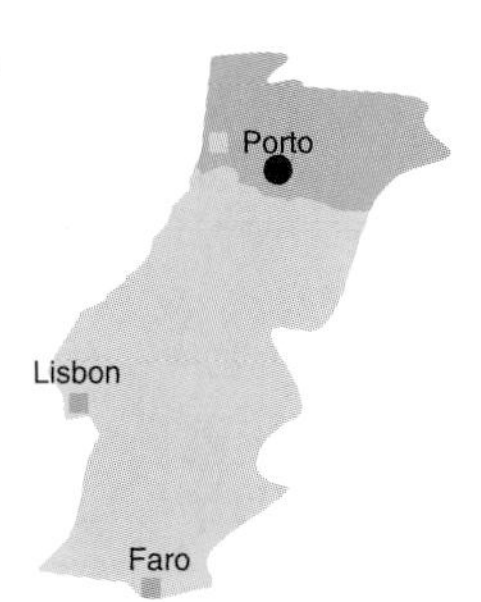

On the very edge of the River Douro this elegant hotel is surrounded by the famous port vineyards of the world's oldest demarcated wine region. A former wine estate, dating back to the 18th century, its name is derived from the surrounding vineyards. Today, the owners run specialist wine tasting courses for enthusiasts, and the bar is situated in the former Port wine lodge. The hotel has been refurbished to reflect the building's heritage and now manages to combine the character of a period property with modern comforts and facilities.

Situé au bord du Douro et entouré par les vignobles fameux de Porto, la plus vieille région viticole du monde, cet élégant hotel se trouve sur une ancienne exploitation viticole du XVIIIe siècle, et tient son nom des vignobles environnants. Aujourd'hui, les propriétaires organisent des cours de dégustation pour les passionnés, et le bar se trouve dans les anciennes "cuves". L'hôtel a été meublé pour refléter l'héritage du bâtiment et arrive maintenant à combiner le caractère de l'ancienne propriété avec le confort et facilités modernes.

Ubicado en la misma orilla del río Duero en la famosa región vinícola más antigua del mundo y rodeado de viñedos, se encuentra este elegante hotel que en el siglo XVIII fue una finca de viñedos de Oporto. Su nombre le viene dado por los viñedos circundantes. Hoy sus dueños organizan cursos especiales de cata de vinos para los entusiastas y el mismo bar se encuentra en el que fuera la antigua bodega del vino Oporto. Ha sido restaurado cuidadosamente reflejando la herencia del edificio y hoy logra combinar el carácter arquitectónico de la época con el confort de las instalaciones modernas.

Our inspector loved: *The fantastic location on the River Douro.*

 43   80       

Casa da Torre das Neves

LUGAR DE NEVES, VILA DE PUNHE 4905-653, VIANA DO CASTELO, PORTUGAL

Surrounded by beautiful gardens filled with orange trees and magnificent bougainvillaea, this charming Michelin Guide recommended guest house, exudes luxury within a comfortable and relaxed environment. Inviting interiors have warm woods and subtle colours to enhance the sunlight, whilst spacious suites are beautifully decorated with antique furnishings and elegant fabrics. Enjoy romantic dinners by candlelight and light lunches by the pool.

Entouré de somptueux jardins remplis d'orangers et de magnifiques bougainvilliers, cette maison d'hôte de charme également recommandée par le guide Michelin, respire le luxe dans un environnement confortable et détendu. Les intérieurs accueillants sont composés de bois chauds et de couleurs subtiles qui mettent en valeur la lumière du soleil tandis que les suites sont superbement décorés de meubles antiques et d'élégants tissus. Les hôtes peuvent profiter des dîners romantique aux chandelles et de déjeuners légers près de la piscine.

Rodeada de bellos jardines repletos de naranjos y magníficas buganvillas, esta encantadora casa de huéspedes recomendado también por la guia Michelin, rebosa lujo dentro de un entorno cómodo y distendido. Los sugerentes interiores son de tenues y cálidos tonos en madera para de esta forma realzar la luz natural solar. A su vez las espaciosas suites están elegantemente decoradas con muebles antiguos además de finas telas. Podrá disfrutar de románticas cenas a la luz de las velas o de ligeros almuerzos junto a la piscina.

Our inspector loved: *The lush gardens surrounding the classic pool area.*

Directions: A28 to Viana do Castelo > exit 21 > Zona Industrial I Chafé > 4km (right) > Barrozelas / Vila Verde > turn left at Neves.

Web: www.johansens.com/torredasneves
E-mail: torreneves@sapo.pt, torreneves@hotmail.com and jpaa@s-amorim.pt
Tel: +351 932 032 980 and +351 258 771 300
Fax: +351 226 178 854

Price Guide:
double €85-95
suite €100-125

Vidago Palace Hotel & Golf

PARQUE DE VIDAGO, 5425-307 VIDAGO, PORTUGAL

This well-renowned hotel will be closed in 2007, re-opening in 2008. The transformation into a 5-star de luxe spa, golf and conference hotel will result in a true palace. Guest rooms and golf villas overlooking 40 acres of centenary natural parkland will have every comfort, and excellent cuisine will be served in the elegant restaurant with a welcoming atmosphere of a bygone era: la Belle Epoque. There will be an E'SPA design spa, and golf enthusiasts will enjoy the 18-hole, par 72 mountain golf course inspired by McKenzie Ross design.

Ce fameux hôtel sera fermé en 2007 et re-ouvrira ses portes en 2008. La transformation en un luxeux spa 5-étoiles, golf et hôtel de conférence fera de ce lieu un véritable palace. Les chambres et les villas au bord du golf qui dominent les 16 ha du parc naturel centenaire disposeront de tout le confort et une délicieuse cuisine sera servi dans l'élegant restaurant à l'atmosphère d'antant : la belle époque. Il y aura un spa conçu par E'SPA et les amoureux du golf pourront profiter du terrains de 18 trous de golf, par-72 inspiré par McKenzie Ross.

Este bien conocido hotel se mantendrá cerrado durante el 2007 y abrirá sus puertas de nuevo en el 2008. Se transformará en un hotel de lujo de 5 estrellas con spa, golf y salas para conferencias resultando en un verdadero palacio. Las habitaciones y villas de golf con vistas a los 16 ha de parque natural centenario, serán de todo confort, y en el elegante restaurante con ambiente acogedor de la belle epoque, se servirá cocina creativa. Habrá un Spa diseñado por ESPA, y los amantes del golf podrán disfrutar del campo de golf de 18 hoyos par 72 de montaña inspirado en diseño por McKenzie Ross.

Our inspector loved: *The beautiful old trees surrounding the hotel.*

Directions: Porto > Vila Real > Chaves.

Web: www.johansens.com/vidago
E-mail: vidagopalace@unicer.pt
Tel: +351 276 990 900
Fax: +351 276 907 359

Price Guide:
Please contact the hotel for 2008 rates.

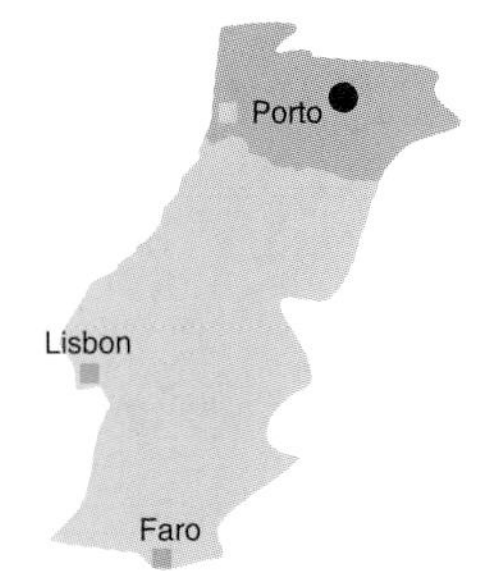

Slovakia

Hotel location shown in red (hotel) or purple (spa hotel) with page number

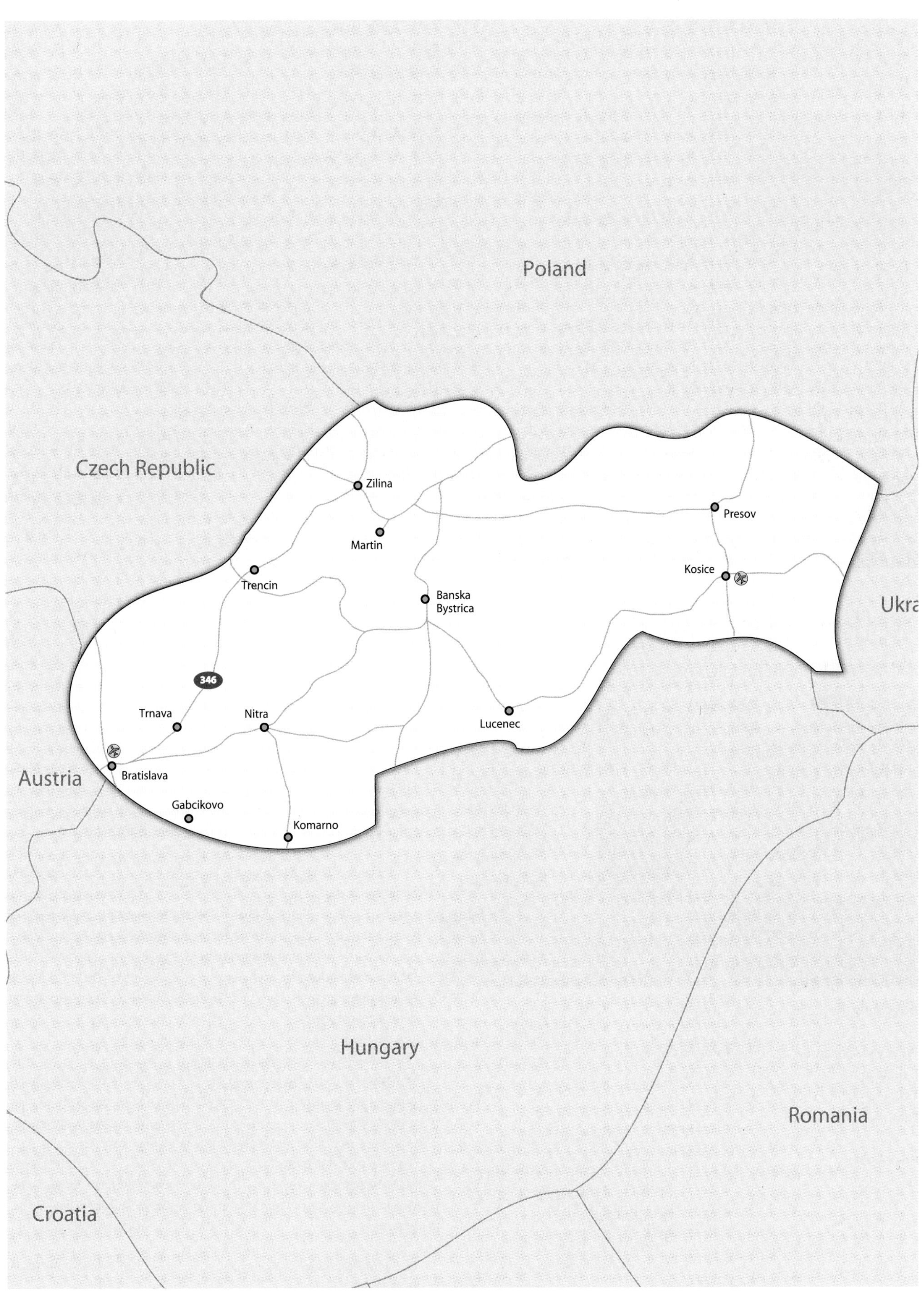

The Château

SALGOVCE 28, 95606 SLOVAKIA

Directions: The nearest airport is Bratislava.

Web: www.johansens.com/thechateausk
E-mail: info@thechateau.sk
Tel: +421 385 395 155
Fax: +44 7005 961 845

Price Guide:
single €99
double €135-260
suite €145-270

The delightful village of Salgovce is within easy access of the Slovakian capital Bratislava, and the spa town of Piestany. Built as a hunting lodge in the 18th century, The Château has been lovingly restored and transformed into luxurious accommodation and now offers excellent shooting opportunities as well as specialist Vino Vie Spa treatments. The new English owners extend the warmest of welcomes and the summer months see delightful concerts and opera singing taking place on the terrace.

Le délicieux village de Salgovce est proche de la capitale slovaque Bratislava, et de la station thermale de Piestany. A l'origine un pavillon de chasse du XVIIIe siècle, le Château a été amoureusement restauré et transformé en un hébergement de luxe qui offre dorénavant d'excellentes possibilités de s'entraîner au tir ainsi que des traitements spécialisés Vino Vie Spa. Les nouveaux propriétaires anglais offrent un accueil des plus chaleureux et les mois d'été, de charmants concerts et chants d'opéra se tiennent sur la terrasse.

La encantadora aldea de Salgovce tiene fácil acceso a la capital eslovaca de Bratislava y a la ciudad-balneario de Piestany. Este château, construido como refugio de cazadores en el siglo XVIII, ha sido restaurado con ternura y transformado en un alojamiento de lujo que actualmente ofrece excelentes oportunidades para la práctica de la caza así como para disfrutar de tratamientos en el especializado Vino Vie Spa. Sus nuevos propietarios ingleses dan su más cálida bienvenida y durante los meses de verano tienen lugar excepcionales conciertos y canto de ópera en su terraza.

Our inspector loved: *The friendly, happy host and smiling Hungarian "hussar" in its blue uniform.*

Slovenia

Hotel location shown in red (hotel) or purple (spa hotel) with page number

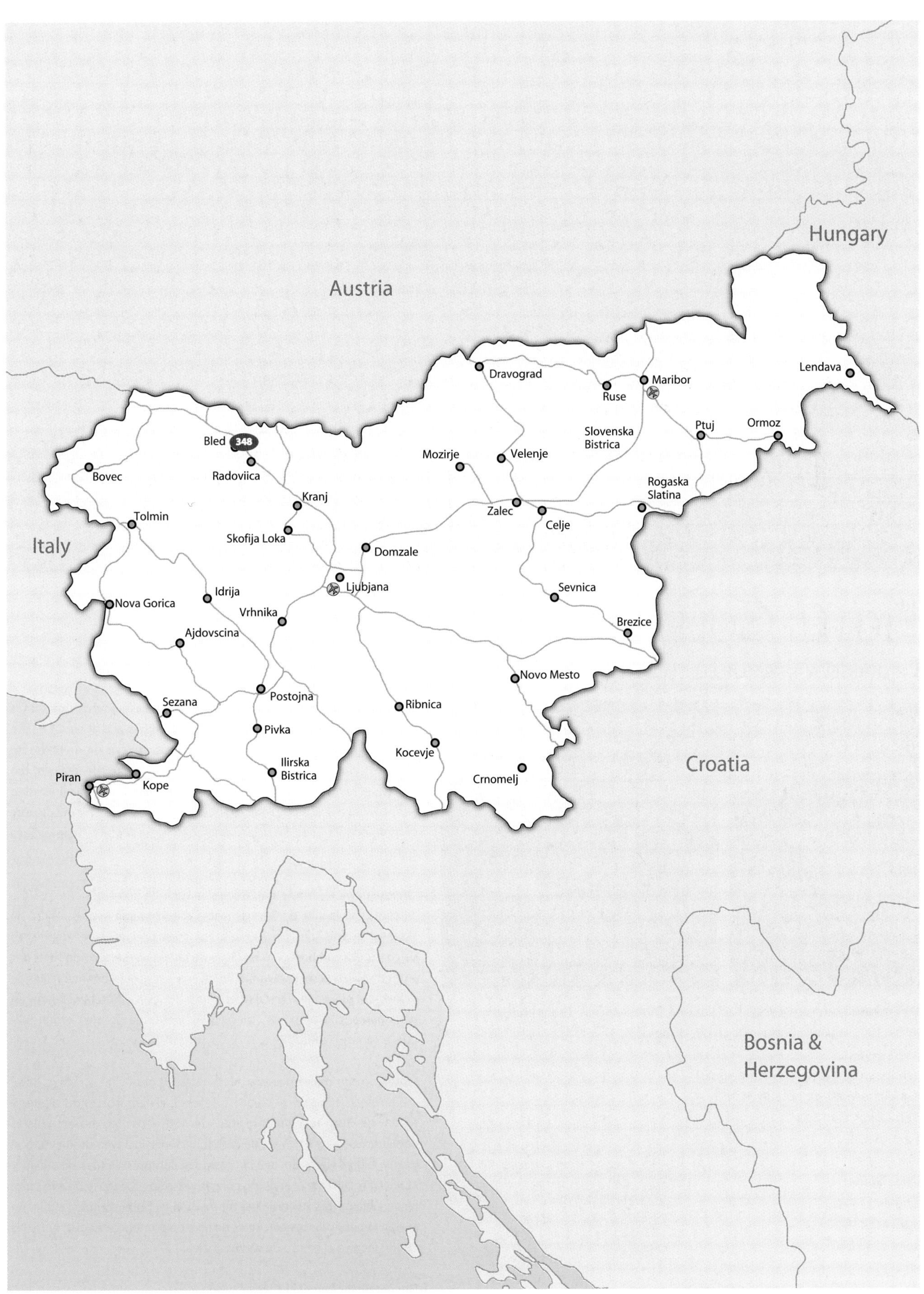

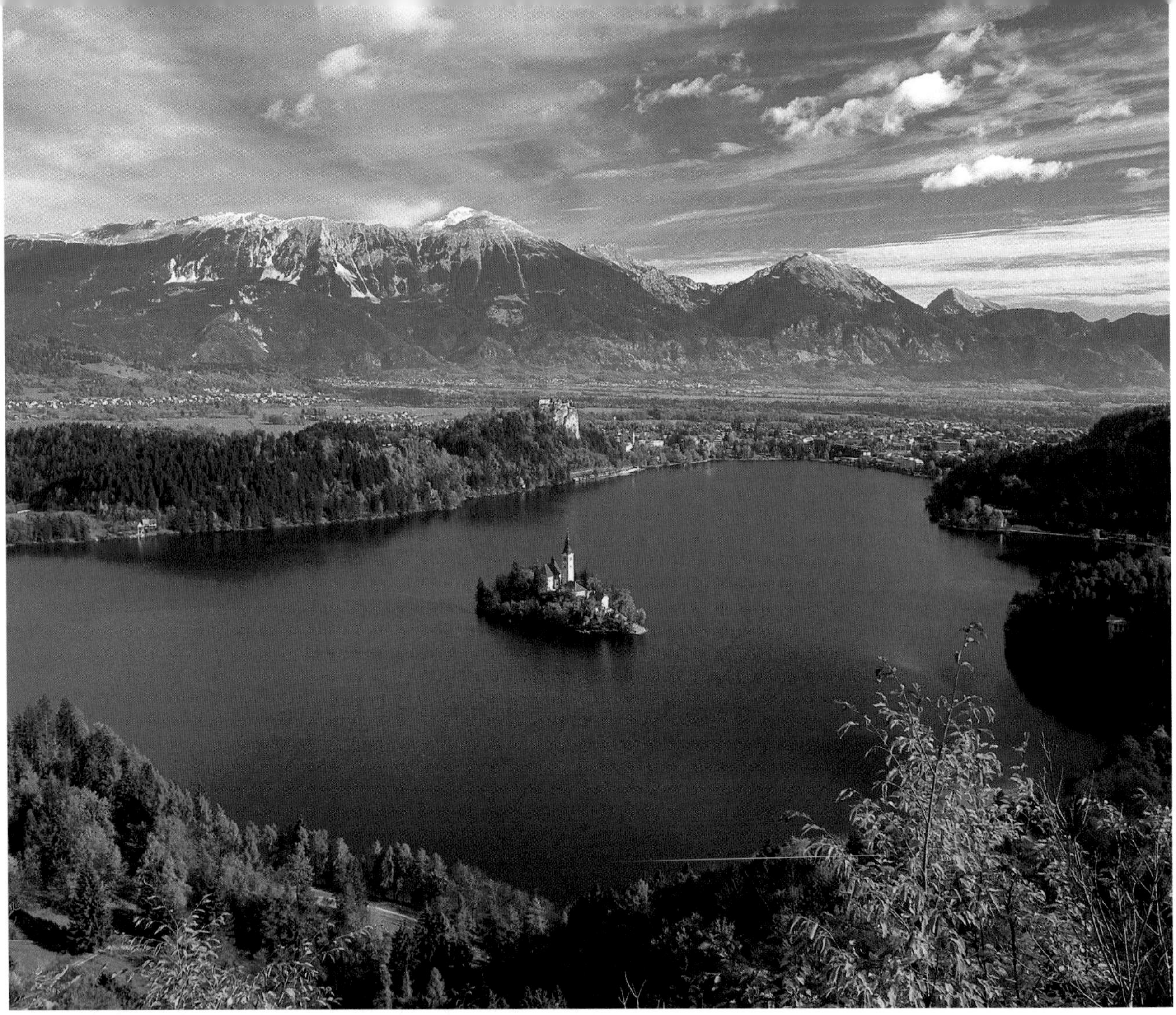

SLOVENIA (BLED)

HOTEL GOLF

CANKARJEVA 4, 4260 BLED, SLOVENIA

Directions: The nearest airport is Ljubljana, Brnik, which is a 30-minute drive away. 150 parking spaces are at guests' disposal.

Web: www.johansens.com/hotelgolfsi
E-mail: recgolf@gp-hotels-bled.si
Tel: +386 4579 1700
Fax: +386 45791701

Price Guide:
single €113-159
double €138-184
suite €238-258

Enclosed by majestic ancient trees, this attractive modern hotel stands in the heart of Bled, Slovenia's acclaimed alpine and thermal health resort for more than 100 years. Spectacular views from bedroom balconies look out to the lake and a clifftop castle to the peaks of the Julian and Karavanke Alps. In winter this is a wonderland of invigorating air, snow and ice. Completely renovated, the hotel combines luxury accommodation with first-class amenities, including the Wellness Ziva centre.

Entouré de vieux arbres majestueux, ce superbe hôtel moderne se situe au centre de la ville de Bled, le resort thermal alpin le plus réputé de Slovénie depuis plus de 100 ans. Les vues spectaculaires depuis les balcons des chambres vont du lac et du château à pic aux sommets des alpes de Julian et de Karavanke. En hiver, c'est le pays des merveilles de neige, de glace et d'air. Entièrement rénové, l'hôtel mélange un hébergement luxueux avec des équipements de premier ordre, tells que le centre Wellness Ziva.

Protegido por majestuosos y ancestrales árboles, este atractivo hotel moderno se erige en el corazón de Bled, el famoso centro alpino y termal de Eslovenia durante más de 100 años. Sus espectaculares paisajes desde los balcones de las habitaciones incluyen desde vistas al lago y a un escarpado castillo hasta las cumbres alpinas de Julian y Karavanke. Durante el invierno constituye todo un paraíso de aire puro, nieve y hielo. Tras su completa renovación, el hotel combina el lujo en el alojamiento y las instalaciones de ocio de primera categoría, entre las que se incluye el centro de wellness Ziva.

Our inspector loved: *The breathtaking scenery.*

SPAIN

Hotel location shown in red (hotel) or purple (spa hotel) with page number

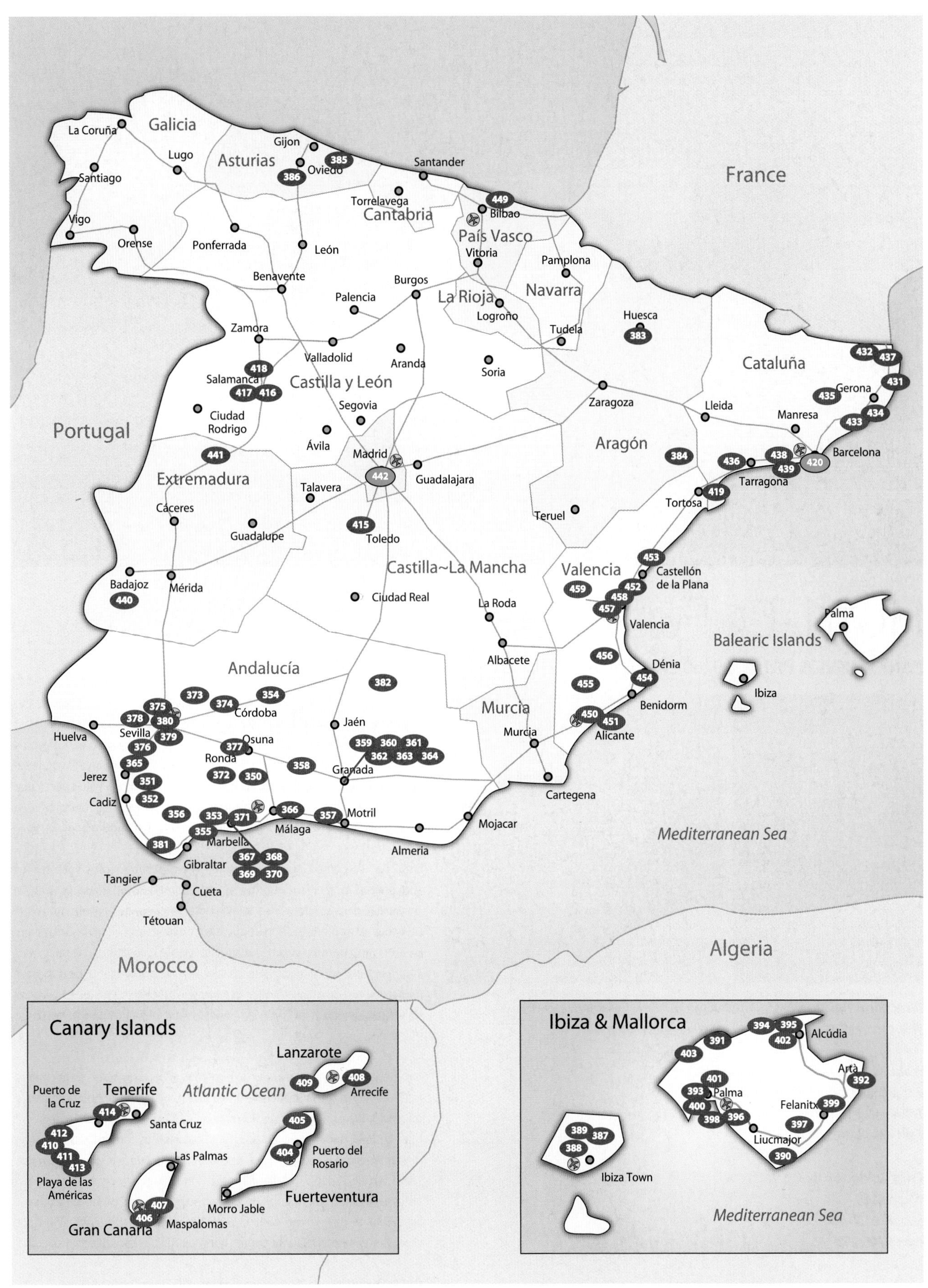

HOTEL LA FUENTE DEL SOL

PARAJE ROSAS BAJAS, 29260 LA JOYA, ANTEQUERA, SPAIN

Directions: Málaga > A45 > Antequera > exit 148, Casabermeja towards Villanueva de la Concepción and La Joya > hotel is signposted.

Web: www.johansens.com/fuentedelsol
E-mail: info@hotelfuentedelsol.com
Tel: +34 95 12 39 823
Fax: +34 95 12 32 090

Price Guide: (excluding VAT)
single €120
double €150-180
suite €200-250

Perched on a mountain slope with impressive panoramic views of the mountains and sea beyond, there is uninterrupted peace and tranquillity at this ideal getaway from the hustle and bustle of the city and coast. Décor is comfortable and rustic with modern, high beamed ceilings and a wonderful sense of space. Bedrooms have a cosy, warm atmosphere with spectacular views; some have a Jacuzzi and terrace. The excellent restaurant offers a superb menu and fine wines. For relaxation there is an indoor pool and spa.

Situé sur les pentes d'une montagne avec de somptueuses vues sur les sommets et la mer au loin, il y a un sentiment continu de paix et de tranquillité dans ce refuge idéal loin de l'effervescence de la ville et de la côte. Le décor est confortable et rustique avec de hauts plafonds modernes aux poutres apparentes et une impressionnante sensation d'espace. Les chambres ont une atmosphère chaleureuse et douillette et de superbes vues, certaines possèdent jacuzzi et terrasses. L'excellent restaurant propose un délicieux menu et de bons vins. Pour se relaxer, il y a une piscine intérieure et un spa.

Encaramado en la ladera de una montaña y con unas vistas panorámicas impresionantes a las montañas y al mar del horizonte, este hotel constituye un refugio ideal para disfrutar de una permanente paz y tranquilidad lejos del bullicio de la ciudad y de la costa. La decoración es cómoda y rústica y de modernos altos techos de viga, proporcionando con ello una maravillosa sensación de espacio. Las habitaciones son cálidas y acogedoras y tienen vistas espectaculares. Algunas de ellas disponen además de jacuzzi y terraza. Su excelente restaurante ofrece un menú magnífico y buenos vinos. Los clientes que deseen relajarse podrán hacerlo en la piscina cubierta o en el spa.

Our inspector loved: *The truly spectacular views - breathtaking.*

Hacienda El Santiscal

AVDA. EL SANTISCAL 129 (LAGO DE ARCOS), 11638 ARCOS DE LA FRONTERA, SPAIN

Surrounded by fields of sunflowers, this 15th-century manor house, exquisitely restored, offers glorious views of the lake and historic town of Arcos. A welcoming atmosphere envelopes the property as Señora Gallardo invites guests into her home to enjoy the ambience of a traditional Andalucían hacienda. All rooms have been newly decorated. Traditional home-cooked dishes feature vegetables, olives and oranges grown in the Hacienda's own groves and gardens. A mobile phone is provided for guests in each room.

Entouré de champs de tournesols, ce manoir du XVe siècle, restauré de façon exquise, offre des vues imprenables sur le lac et la ville historique d'Arcos. Une accueillante atmosphère caractérise la propriété, et Madame Gallardo invite les hôtes dans sa demeure afin de leur faire profiter de l'ambiance traditionnelle d'une Hacienda andalouse. Des plats traditionnels faits-maison sont composés des légumes, olives et oranges qui ont poussé dans le verger et le potager de la Hacienda. Un téléphone portable est mis à la disposition des clients dans chaque chambre.

Rodeada por campos de girasoles esta casa señorial del siglo XV, exquisitamente restaurada, ofrece magníficas vistas del lago y de la histórica y milenaria Arcos de la Frontera. Su ambiente acogedor envuelve la finca al tiempo que la señora Gallardo invita a los huéspedes a su casa para disfrutar del encanto de una tradicional hacienda andaluza. Todas las habitaciones han sido recientemente decoradas. Los tradicionales platos caseros disponen de verduras, aceitunas y naranjas cultivadas en los propios terrenos y jardines de la Hacienda. Cada habitación dispone de un teléfono móvil.

Our inspector loved: *Staying in a house that was inhabited during the time of America's discovery.*

Directions: Sevilla Cádiz motorway > exit Arcos - Circuito > follow signs to A-383 to Arcos de la Frontera > follow signs to Antequera > A372 towards El Bosque > follow signs to "El Santiscal".

Barcelona
Madrid
Málaga

Web: www.johansens.com/haciendaelsantiscal
E-mail: reservas@santiscal.com or haciendasantiscal@santiscal.com
Tel: +34 956 70 83 13
Fax: +34 956 70 82 68

Price Guide: (room only, excluding VAT)
single €48-72
double/twin €65-99
suite €84-137

Hotel Cortijo Faín

CARRETERA DE ALGAR KM 3, 11630 ARCOS DE LA FRONTERA, CÁDIZ, SPAIN

This pretty 17th-century building has been beautifully renovated and now represents the heart of one of the most elegant golf estates in southern Spain. The championship golf course is stunning and includes ancient olive trees and fabulous views of Arcos and the surrounding countryside. Today, the cortijo houses 9 individual, stylish and comfortable bedrooms; some with French windows and balconies. The ambience is one of informal luxury, ideally suited for this fascinating and much-loved area of southern Spain.

Ce joli bâtiment XVIIe siècle a été admirablement renové et incorporé dans l'un des plus élégants golfs du sud de l'Espagne. Le superbe terrain de golf est une orné de vieux oliviers et offre des vues magnifiques sur l'Arcos et la campagne environnantes. Aujourd'hui le cortijo héberge 9 chambres confortables, chacune decorée dans un style particulier; certaines ont des portes-fenêtres et balcons offrant ainsi les meilleures vues. L'ambiance est celle d'un luxe détendu, parfaite pour cette fascinante et tant-aimée région du sud de l'Espagne.

A este bonito edificio que data del siglo XVII, hábilmente renovado para mantener toda su belleza original, se le ha incorporado uno de los complejos de golf más elegantes del sur de España. Un acertado diseño y cuidado profesional conforman un campo de golf de alta competición adornado por miles de olivos centenarios y con vistas impresionantes de Arcos y la Sierra de Cádiz. Hoy el cortijo alberga 9 habitaciones diseñadas individualmente, con espaciosos cuartos de baño, y algunas, con amplias terrazas. El ambiente es de lujo informal y perfectamente adecuado para esta zona del sur de España tan apreciada.

Our inspector loved: *The space and light in the bedrooms and bathrooms.*

Directions: From Jerez > motorway to A-382 Arcos > follow signs to Arcos/Algar > hotel is signposted. From Seville > motorway to Cádiz/Jerez > follow signs to A-382 Arcos > signs to Algar > hotel is signposted.

Web: www.johansens.com/cortijofain
E-mail: hotelcortijofain@arcosgardens.com
Tel: +34 956 704 131
Fax: +34 956 717 932

Price Guide: (room only, excluding VAT)
single €110-140
double €140-180

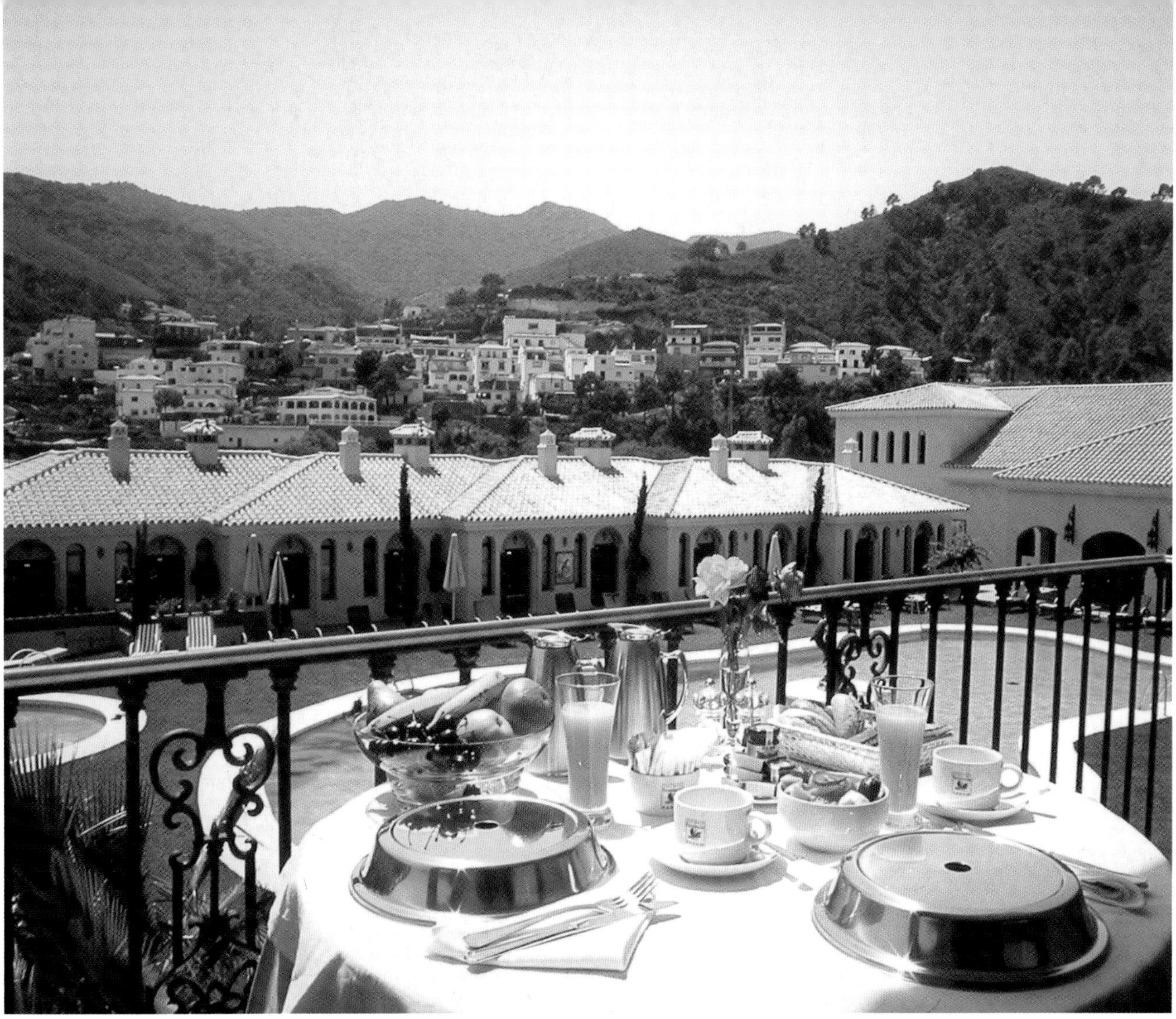

Gran Hotel Benahavís

HUERTA DE RUFINO S/N, 29679 BENAHAVÍS, MÁLAGA, SPAIN

Gran Hotel Benahavis is set at the foot of the mountains and surrounded by nature, yet is just 15 minutes from Marbella and its beaches. The 95 spacious rooms and suites combine elegance and luxury, and as well as 2 outdoor pools there is a spa with a small treatment covered pool with cascading water for neck and shoulder massages. Depending on the season, the hotel offers an indoor bar and restaurant or an outdoor pool bar restaurant, and provides excellent service and value for money.

Gran Hotel Benahavis est situé au pied de montagnes et est entouré de la nature tout en étant qu'à 15 minutes de Marbella et ses plages. Les 95 chambres et suites spacieuses allient l'élégance et le luxe, et en plus des 2 piscines extérieures, l'hôtel possède un spa avec une petite piscine couverte à l'eau tombant en cascade pour les massages des épaules et du cou. Dépendant de la saison, les hôtes peuvent dîner au bar ou au restaurant à l'intérieur, ou au restaurant avec bar près de la piscine. L'hôtel offre un excellent service et rapport qualité prix.

El Gran Hotel Benahavis se encuentra al pie de las montañas rodeado por la naturaleza, si bien sólo a 15 minutos Marbella y sus playas. Sus 95 espaciosas habitaciones y suites combinan el lujo y la elegancia. Además de 2 piscinas exteriores, el hotel tiene un spa y una pequeña piscina cubierta con agua cayendo en cascada para los masajes de los hombros y del cuello. Según la estación, hay un bar y un restaurante cubiertos o un restaurante con bar cerca de la piscina. El hotel ofrece un excelente servicio a buen precio.

Our inspector loved: *Being pampered in this healthy, peaceful environment.*

Directions: Málaga - Cádiz road (A7, formerly N340) > exit Benahavís or follow signs to Benhavís > hotel is signposted.

Web: www.johansens.com/hotelbenahavis
E-mail: info@granhotelbenahavis.com
Tel: +34 902 504 862
Fax: +34 902 504 861

Price Guide: (excluding VAT)
double (single occupancy) €105-140
double €120-170
suite €160-285

95 200 SPA

Hospes Palacio del Bailío

RAMIREZ DE LAS CASAS DEZA 10-12, 14001 CORDOBA, SPAIN

This magnificent hotel, mainly built between the 16th and 18th centuries, is situated in one of Cordoba's classic Moorish buildings. The original elements of the building have been carefully preserved, including the Roman ruins that now lie under the glass pavings of one of the patios. Modern design and innovation with rich textures and strong colours adorn the interior. The Senzone Gastronomic Restaurant & Tapas Bar serves local-inspired cuisine created from fresh natural produce. The stunning Bodyna Spa and wellness area affords views over the original Roman baths.

Ce magnifique hôtel, constuit entre le XVIe et XVIIIe siècle, est situé dans un bâtiment maure classique de Cordoba. Les éléments originaux ont été soigneusement préservés, y compris les ruines romaines qui se trouvent sous le carrelage en verre d'un des patios. Un design moderne et innovant aux textures riches et aux couleurs fortes orne l'intérieur. Le Senzone Restaurant Gastronomique & Tapas Bar sert une cuisine d'inspiration locale préparée à partir de produits naturels frais. Le splendide Bodyna Spa et zone de remise en forme ont des vues privilégiées sur les bains romains originaux.

Este magnífico hotel construido principalmente entre los siglos XVI y XVIII está ubicado en uno de los clásicos edificios árabes de Córdoba. Sus componentes originales han sido cuidadosamente respetados, incluyendo las ruinas romanas preservadas bajo el suelo de cristal de uno de los patios. Un diseño moderno, unas innovadores y generosas texturas y un vivo colorido adornan su interior. Su Senzone Restaurante Gastronómico & Tapas Bar sirve platos de inspiración local a partir de productos frescos y naturales, y su espléndido Bodyna Spa y centro de salud dispone asimismo de vistas a los baños romanos originales.

Directions: Seville Airport > AVE speed train > city centre.

E-mail: hospes@hospes.es
Web: www.johansens.com/hospesbailio
Tel: +34 957 498 993
Fax: +34 957 498 994

Price Guide: (room only, excluding VAT)
single €160-230
double €180-250
suite €210-600

Barcelona
Madrid
Málaga

Our inspector loved: *The perfect blend of elements, textures, colours and lighting that fuse to create a welcoming and peaceful atmosphere throughout.*

GRAN HOTEL ELBA ESTEPONA & THALASSO SPA

URB. ARENA BEACH, CTRA. ESTEPONA-CÁDIZ 151, 29680 ESTEPONA, SPAIN

Situated on a private beach, this magnificent hotel offers spacious guest rooms with breathtaking sea views. The traditional décor is interspersed with modern elements and the use of wooden furnishings, bathrooms, terraces and parquet floors creates a warm, cosy ambience. Dining is an unforgettable experience. The 3 restaurants, and 1 buffet restaurant for breakfast, offer a wide variety of gastronomic delights from traditional Spanish fare to exotic Asian cuisine. The largest thalasso spa in Andalucía, with over 60 treatments, is available and includes an ice room and log cabin sauna.

Situé sur une plage privée, cet hôtel offre de spacieux hébergements avec des vues sur la mer. Le décor traditionnel est parsemé d'éléments modernes et le présence de bois dans les salles de bains, sur le mobilier, les terrasses et les parquets crée une atmosphère chaleureuse. La table est superbe: 3 restaurants, plus 1 pour les buffets du petit-déjeuner, proposent un large choix de délices gastronomiques, de la cuisine traditionnelle espagnole aux saveurs exotiques asiatiques. Le plus grand Spa thalasso d'Andalucie a plus de 60 soins disponibles dont une cabine de glace et un sauna.

Ubicado en una playa privada, este magnífico hotel ofrece habitaciones espaciosas con vistas espectaculares al mar. La decoración tradicional entremezcla elementos modernos y el uso del mobiliario de madera, cuartos de baño, terrazas y suelos de parquet crean un ambiente cálido y acogedor. La cena es una experiencia inolvidable. Los 3 restaurantes y el del desayuno-buffet ofrecen una amplia variedad de delicias gastronómicas desde la tradicional comida española a la exótica asiática. El spa thalasso es el más grande de Andalucía, con más de 60 tratamientos y también incluye una sala de hielo y una cabina de sauna.

Our inspector loved: *The heated pool overlooking the Mediterranean.*

Directions: From Gibraltar > Cádiz - Málaga road > Málaga > Km 151. From Málaga > Málaga - Cádiz road > Cádiz > Km 151.

Web: www.johansens.com/elbaestepona
E-mail: elbaestepona@hoteleselba.com
Tel: +34 952 809 200
Fax: +34 952 809 201

Price Guide: (room only, excluding VAT)
double (single occupancy) €160-250
double €230-390
suite €265-1,050

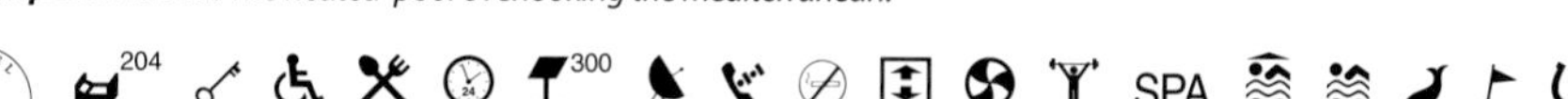

HOTEL CASABLANCA

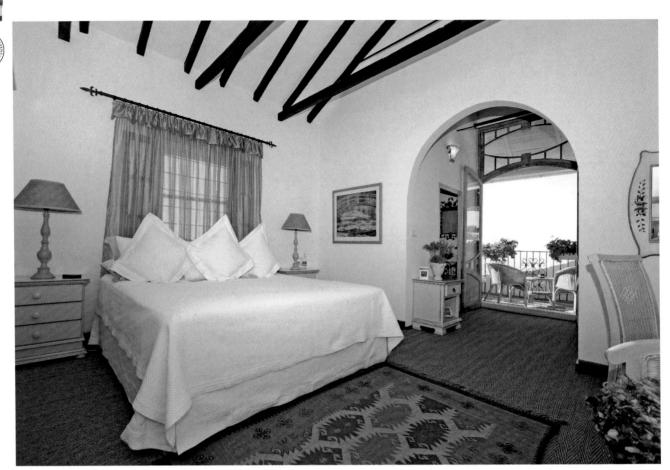

CALLA TEODORO DE MOLINA, NO 12, 29480 GAUCIN, MÁLAGA, SPAIN

Directions: Málaga > N340 towards Cádiz > Manilva > Gaucin > hotel is signposted.

Web: www.johansens.com/hotelcasablanca
E-mail: enquiries@casablanca-gaucin.com
Tel: +34 952 151 019
Fax: +34 952 151 495

Price Guide: (closed end of December - March)
double €140-200

Perched high on a mountain in this pretty Andalucían village, this stunning little gem of a hotel has the most wonderful views towards Africa and the rock of Gibraltar, yet is surprisingly just 30 minutes from the coast. Providing a winning combination of luxury and informality, there are just 9 rooms, each carefully designed to reflect rustic Spanish, Moorish and Colonial influences. The open-plan sitting room is a delightful place to relax, and outdoor dining is available on the exquisite terrace during the summer. WiFi is available throughout the hotel.

Haut perché au sommet d'une montagne dans un ravissant village Andalou, ce superbe joyau d'hôtel offre de magnifiques vues sur l'Afrique et le rocher de Gibraltar, tout en étant qu'à 30 minutes de la côte. Dans un style de luxe et de décontraction, l'hôtel propose 9 chambres, chacune décorée avec attention afin de refléter des influences Espagnoles rustiques, Marocaines et Coloniales. Le salon semi-extérieur est idéal pour se relaxer et l'on peut dîner sur la ravissante terrasse pendant l'été. Wifi disponible dans tout l'hôtel.

Encaramado en una montaña de un precioso pueblo andaluz, este imponente hotel es una pequeña joya y cuenta con la más maravillosa de las vistas a África y al Peñón de Gibraltar, a pesar de estar a sólo 30 minutos de la costa. Ofrece une acertada combinación de lujo y sencillez. Sólo dispone de 9 habitaciones, que han sido cuidadosamente diseñadas para mostrar las distintas influencias coloniales, árabe y de la España rústica. Su salón de estructura abierta es un lugar encantador para descansar y durante el verano se puede cenar al aire libre en su preciosa terraza. El WiFi está disponible en todo el hotel.

***Our inspector loved:** The many inviting shady areas on different levels - perfect for relaxing or taking in the wonderful views.*

Casa de los Bates

CARRETERA NACIONAL 340 MÁLAGA - ALMERIA, KM 329, 5 SALOBREÑA - MOTRIL, PROVINCIA DE GRANADA, SPAIN

This lovely 19th-century Italian-style villa, with romantic tropical garden, transports guests to a bygone era. The elegant, aristocratic interior blends comfort with exceptional style, family portraits and attention to detail that ensure a unique home away from home atmosphere. Breakfast is served al fresco on the terrace, which has amazing sea views. Beautiful bedrooms are spacious and light with pastel hues and pretty fabrics. Perfectly located for visits to the Alpujarra and Sierra Nevada.

Cette ravissante villa de style italien du XIXe siècle, avec son jardin tropical romantique, transporte ses hôtes dans le passé. L'intérieur élégant et aristocratique mélange confort avec style exceptionnel, portraits de famille et une attention au détail qui assure l'atmosphère unique d'une maison privée. Le petit-déjeuner est au frais servi sur la terrasse qui offre de somptueuses vues mer. Les superbes chambres sont claires et spacieuses avec des teintes pastels et de beaux tissus. L'hôtel est idéalement situé pour visiter l'Alpujarra et la Sierra Nevada.

Esta encantadora Casa del siglo XIX de estilo italiano provista de un romántico jardín tropical, transporta a los clientes a épocas pasadas. Sus elegantes y aristocráticos interiores conjugan el confort con el estilo excepcional, los retratos de familia y el cuidado hasta el último detalle. Todo ello proporciona un irrepetible ambiente de hospitalidad hogareña. El desayuno se sirve al aire libre en la terraza mirador, con magníficas vistas al mar. Sus bellas habitaciones son amplias y luminosas gracias a sus tonos de pastel y sus lindas telas. Tiene un emplazamiento ideal para los que deseen visitar la Alpujarra y Sierra Nevada.

Our inspector loved: *The huge, elegant terrace, and romantic centenary chandeliers.*

Directions: Málaga > motorway towards Motril and Almeria > CN340 > at km 329.5 turn left > hotel is signposted.

Web: www.johansens.com/casadelosbates
E-mail: info@casadelosbates.com
Tel: +34 958 349 495
Fax: +34 958 834 131

Price Guide:
single €102.89
double €141.48
suite €192.92-264

SPAIN / ANDALUCÍA (GRANADA)

BARCELÓ LA BOBADILLA ***** GL

FINCA LA BOBADILLA, APTO. 144, 18300 LOJA, GRANADA, SPAIN

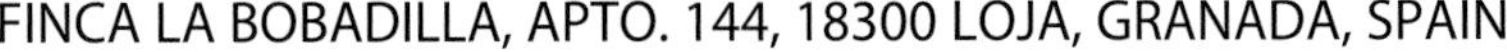

Directions: A92 Granada–Sevilla road > exit 175 Salinas. Granada and its airport are 45 minutes away. Málaga Airport is 1 hour away.

Web: www.johansens.com/bobadilla
E-mail: labobadilla.info@barcelo.com
Tel: +34 958 32 18 61
Fax: +34 958 32 18 10

Price Guide:
single €277–347
double/twin €388–457

Following a major extension the Andalucían-styled Barceló La Bobadilla offers 70 gorgeously appointed bedrooms, all with individual touches. El Cortijo restaurant has been refurbished and extended and the new event room caters for 160 delegates. The recently opened 700m² spa is an opulent addition to this magnificent Granada complex and the treatments on offer will delight guests wishing to be pampered. Horse-riding, cycling and quad biking are ideal ways to explore the surrounding area.

Grâce à une important extension, le Barceló La Bobadilla, de style andalou, comporte maintenant 70 chambres superbement équipées, toutes avec une touche particulière. Le restaurant El Cortijo a été remis à neuf et agrandit et la nouvelle salle de conférence peut accueillir 160 délégués. Le spa de 700m², récemment ouvert, est une riche addition à ce refuge de Grenade. Les traitements offerts feront la joie des hôtes souhaitant se faire choyer. Equitation, vélo et quad sont les moyens idéaux pour explorer les environs.

El hotel Barceló La Bobadilla de estilo andaluz tras una ampliación importante ofrece 70 magníficas habitaciones, todas ellas con detalles diferentes. El Restaurante El Cortijo también ha sido ampliado y reformado y el nuevo salón de actos acoge a 160 delegados. El Spa de 700m² recientemente. Abierto es una adición opulenta a este magnifico complejo granadino con una oferta de tratamientos que deleitarán a los huéspedes que deseen recibirlos. Equitación, ciclismo y práctica de quad son formas ideales de explorar los alrededores de la zona.

Our inspector loved: *The exceptional variety of individually decorated rooms.*

70 160 SPA

El Ladrón de Agua

CARRERA DEL DARRO 13, 18010 GRANADA, SPAIN

Ideally situated alongside the River Darro, beneath the Alhambra in the Albayzín quarter, this little 16th-century palace is not only perfectly located for exploring the city but also has a lively atmosphere that reflects life outside its walls. Elegantly and simply decorated to maximise the beautiful architecture, the public areas regularly play host to art exhibitions and music recitals. The bedrooms are stylish; and several, like the "suite torreón" have exceptional views of the Alhambra.

Idéalement situé le long de la rivière Darro, derrière l'Alhambra dans le quartier d'Albayzin, ce petit palais du XVI e siècle est non seulement idéalement situé pour explorer le coeur de la ville, mais possède également une atmosphère gaie qui reflète la vie derrière ses murs. Décorées simplement et élégamment afin de mettre en avant la magnifique architecture, sa cour centrale, bibliothèque et galeries sont régulièrement le théâtre d'expositions d'art et de récitals de musique. Les chambres sont élégantes; et plusieurs, comme "suite torreón", offrent des vues exceptionnelles sur l'Alhambra.

Privilegiadamente emplazada en el valle del río Darro, frente la Alhambra, en el barrio del Albayzin, este palacete del siglo XVI es el lugar ideal desde donde empezar a explorar el corazón de la ciudad. Además posee una atmósfera alegre que refleja la vida que existe fuera de sus paredes. Decorada de forma elegante y sencilla para maximizar la bella arquitectura, su patio central, biblioteca y galerías se utilizan a menudo para acoger exposiciones de arte y recitales de música. Las habitaciones tienen estilo y calidez; y varios de ellas, como la "suite torreón", gozan de vistas excepcionales de la Alhambra.

Our inspector loved: *The cultural focus whereby the hotel's public areas offer art exhibits, musical recitals and paintings to complement the ambience and bring the guests closer to Granada's heritage.*

Directions: The nearest airports are Granada (20 minutes) and Málaga (90 minutes).

Web: www.johansens.com/ladrondeagua
E-mail: info@ladrondeagua.com
Tel: +34 958 21 50 40
Fax: +34 958 22 43 45

Price Guide: (breakfast €9.50, excluding VAT)
single €79-172
standard double €105-109
superior double €134-139
superior extra €155-165
suite torreón €207-218

Hospes Palacio de los Patos

C/ Solarillo de Gracia 1, 18002 Granada, Andalucía, Spain

Directions: Direct flights are available to Granada. From Córdoba, Sevilla and Málaga take the A-92. From Madrid, Jaén, Almería and Murcia take N-323.

Web: www.johansens.com/lospatos
E-mail: palaciopatos@hospes.es
Tel: +34 958 535 790
Fax: +34 958 536 968

Price Guide: (room only, excluding VAT)
single €160-250
double €190-280
suite €350-900

The historic Palacio de Los Patos combines the grace and character of the 19th century with 21st-century décor and facilities. Situated within landscaped gardens in the heart of Granada, the hotel is within easy walking distance of many of the city's attractions. The main hotel is a former aristocratic home with superb period features that include a preponderance of white marble, painted ceilings and a spectacular staircase leading to luxurious bedrooms. An adjacent building houses Senzone restaurant, pool, Bodyna Spa & Sensations and some additional guest rooms.

L'historique Palacio de Los Patos allie la grâce et la caractère du XIXe siècle avec une décoration et des équipements du XXIe siècle. Situé parmi des jardins paysagers au cœur de Grenade, l'hôtel est proche d'un grand nombre d'attractions de la ville. Le bâtiment principal était une ancienne maison d'aristocrates avec de superbes particularités de l'époque qui comprennent une prépondérance de marbre blanc, des plafonds peints et un spectaculaire escalier menant aux chambres luxueuses. Un bâtiment adjacent accueille le restaurant Senzone, la piscine, le Bodyna Spa & Sensations et plus de chambres.

El histórico Palacio de los Patos combina la elegancia y personalidad propias del siglo XIX con la decoración e instalaciones del siglo XXI. Situado en una zona ajardina en pleno corazón de Granada, el hotel se encuentra a corta distancia a pie de muchos de los lugares de interés de la ciudad. El hotel principal es una antigua casa aristocrática provista de algunos magníficos detalles de época tales como la abundancia de mármol blanco, techos pintados y una espectacular escalera que conduce a los lujosos dormitorios. El restaurante Senzone, la piscina, el Bodyna Spa & Sensations y unas habitaciones adicionales se encuentran en un edificio adyacente.

Our inspector loved: *The magnificent ceiling frescos in the Royal Suite.*

SPA

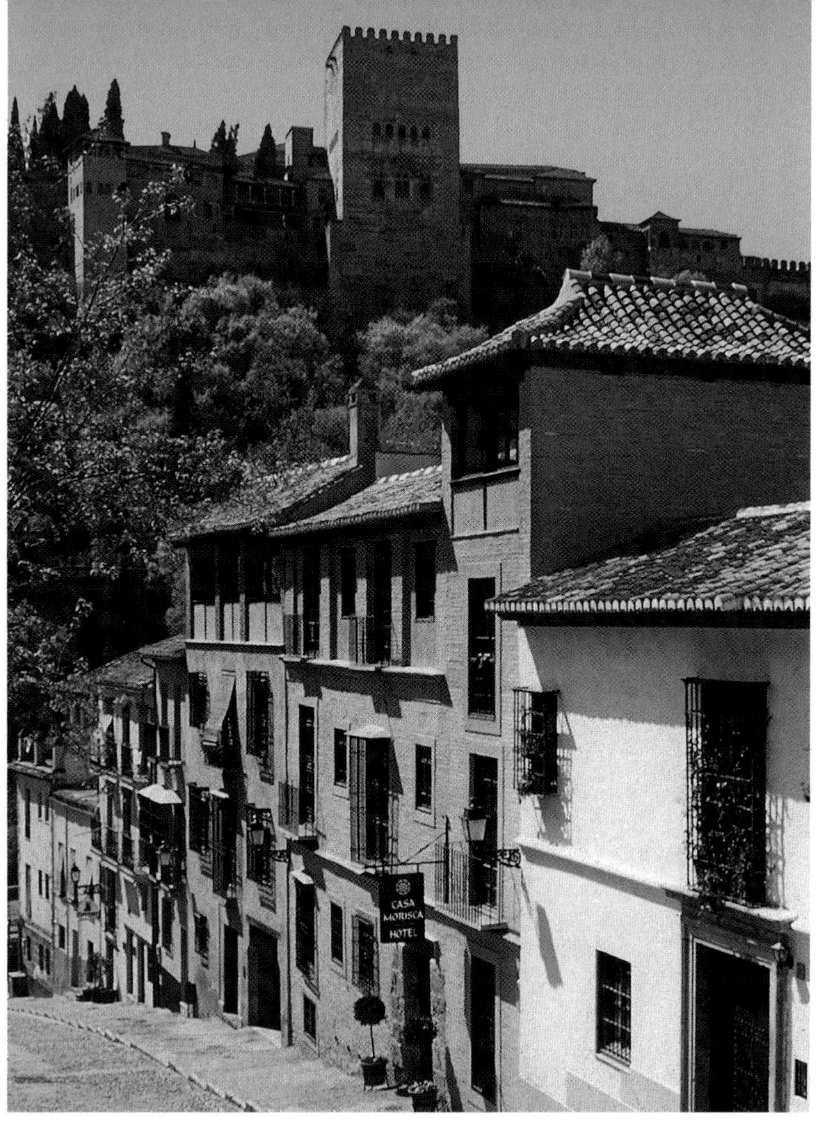

Hotel Casa Morisca

CUESTA DE LA VICTORIA 9, 18010 GRANADA, SPAIN

Situated in the historic "Albayzín" quarter with view of the Alhambra, this stunning, recently restored Moorish-style stately town house offers guests a true feel of this ancient city. The décor includes original features such as a Moorish brick façade, carved wooden ceilings dating from the 15th century, marble columns and old ceramic tiles. An interior open-air courtyard with fountains and small pool is surrounded by a 2-floor gallery, giving access to the 14 individually decorated bedrooms, some of which offer hydromassage baths.

Situé dans le quartier historique "Albayzín" avec vue sur l'Alhambra, cette magnifique résidence de style Mauresque, récemment restaurée, offre aux hôtes une excellente impression de cette ville ancienne. Le décor comprend des caractéristiques originelles, telles que la façade Mauresque en brique, des plafonds sculptés en bois datant du 15e siècle, des colonnes en marbre et des vieux carreaux en céramique. La cour intérieure à ciel ouvert, avec fontaines et petite piscine, est entourée par des galeries sur 2 niveaux, qui mènent aux 14 chambres décorées de façon individuelle, quelques-unes offrent des bains hydro-massage.

Situada en el histórico barrio del "Albayzín" y con vistas a la Alhambra, esta impresionante Casa Morisca, recientemente restaurada, proporciona el verdadero ambiente de esta antigua ciudad. La decoración incluye elementos originales tales como una fachada árabe de ladrillo, techos labrados en madera que datan del siglo XV, columnas de mármol y azulejos de cerámica antiguos. El patio interior descubierto, que cuenta con fuentes y un estanque, esta rodeado por galerías en 2 pisos que dan acceso a las 14 habitaciones. La decoración de cada habitación es individualizada, y algunas cuentan con bañeras de hidromasaje.

Our inspector loved: *The magnificent carved wooden ceiling in Room 8.*

  14    16      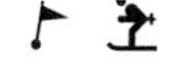

Directions: Near the Alhambra in the town centre. The nearest airport is Granada. From Granada Airport follow signs to the city centre.

Web: www.johansens.com/morisca
E-mail: info@hotelcasamorisca.com
Tel: +34 958 221 100
Fax: +34 958 215 796

Barcelona
Madrid
Granada

Price Guide: (room only, excluding VAT)
double €118-148
junior suite €198

HOTEL PALACIO DE SANTA INÉS

CUESTA DE SANTA INÉS 9, 18010 GRANADA, SPAIN

Directions: Located in the heart of Granada. From Granada Airport head into the historic quarters of the city. The hotel is 20 minutes by car.

Web: www.johansens.com/sanaines
E-mail: sinespal@teleline.es
Tel: +34 958 22 23 62
Fax: +34 958 22 24 65

Price Guide: (room only, excluding VAT)
single €85
double €110-160
suite €250

This restored 16th-century palace is located in a prime position from which to explore the magnificent sights of historic Granada. The impressive courtyard, with its fountain and magnificent paintings, leads guests into rooms decorated with a timeless elegance featuring original antique and contemporary furnishings. Some of the guest rooms look out to the Alhambra, and 3 conference rooms are available. Within walking distance of historical sites and convents, there are also bracing alpine walks in the surrounding Sierra Nevada to enjoy.

Ce palace restauré du XVIe siècle possède un emplacement unique pour explorer les magnifiques sites historiques de Grenade. De l'impressionnante cour intérieure avec sa fontaine et ses tableaux, les hôtes accèdent aux chambres à l'élégance intemporelle remplies d'antiquités et de meubles contemporains. Certaines des chambres ont vues sur l'Alhambra et 3 salles de conférences sont disponibles. Proches de sites historiques et de couvents à visiter, les hôtes peuvent également profiter des promenades vivifiantes dans la Sierra Nevada environnante.

Este palacio restaurado del siglo XVI goza de una situación excelente para explorar los esplendorosos lugares de interés de la Granada histórica. El impresionante patio con su fuente y espléndidos lienzos conduce a diversas habitaciones de eterna elegancia en las que pueden verse auténticos muebles antiguos y contemporáneos. Algunos de las habitaciones tienen vistas a la Alhambra. Hay además 3 salas de conferencia. A corta distancia a pie de los conventos y de los lugares de interés histórico, podrá disfrutar de tonificantes rutas alpinas por la vecina Sierra Nevada.

Our inspector loved: *The restored original frescoes adorning the walls in the interior patio and reception area.*

PALACIO DE LOS NAVAS

CALLE NAVAS 1, 18009 GRANADA, SPAIN

Originally built as an aristocratic town house, this charming hotel opened in May 2005, and is ideally located to explore the historic quarter of Granada. There are just 19 individually designed bedrooms and suites, all classic, simple and elegant. The use of wood, wrought iron, terracotta and locally produced tiles creates a stylish ambience that is evident throughout the hotel and perfectly complements the exceptionally high levels of service that are such a key part of this hotel's ethos.

Construit à l'origine en hôtel particulier, ce charmant hôtel, ouvert en mai 2005, est idéalement situé pour explorer le quartier historique de la ville de Grenade. Il y a seulement 19 chambres et suites toutes individuellement décorées dans un style classique, simple et élégant. L'utilisation de bois, de fer forgé, de terracotta et de carrelage fabriqué localement crée une ambiance chic qui se retrouve partout dans l'hôtel et qui complète parfaitement l'excellent niveau de service, qui est un des point clé de la philosophie de l'hôtel.

Originalmente construido como mansión nobiliaria, este encantador hotel abrió sus puertas en mayo de 2005. Se encuentra en el sitio ideal para explorar el barrio histórico de Granada. Sólo dispone de 19 habitaciones y suites de diseño individualizado, todas ellas de estilo clásico, sencillas y elegantes. El uso de la madera, el hierro forjado, la terracota y los azulejos típicos del lugar le proporcionan un ambiente y estilo que se hace evidente por todo el hotel y que complementa el altísimo nivel de servicio que forma parte fundamental de la filosofia de este hotel.

Our inspector loved: *The attentive service, and ideal location in the city centre.*

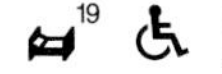

Directions: Fly direct to Granada and take the motorway to Granada city centre.

Web: www.johansens.com/palaciodelosnavas
E-mail: reservas@palaciodelosnavas.com
Tel: +34 958 21 57 60
Fax: +34 958 21 57 60

Barcelona
Madrid
Granada

Price Guide: (excluding VAT)
single €90
double €120-140
suite €175-199

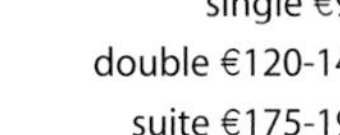

Santa Isabel la Real

SANTA ISABEL LA REAL 19, 18010 GRANADA, SPAIN

In a magnificent standpoint overlooking the entire city, this beautifully restored 16th-century town house offers 11 bedrooms located around a courtyard supported by stone columns with central patio. Period features, antiques, colourful fabrics and tapestries adorn the rooms alongside every modern comfort expected by today's traveller. The historic neighbourhood of Albayzín boasts many sites, monuments, parks and churches to explore, and many restaurants to sample. The breakfast salon can be converted into a meeting room.

Avec un magnifique point de vue surplombant la ville entière, cette demeure du XVIe siècle parfaitement restaurée dispose de 11 chambres agencées autour d'une cour à colonnades et d'un patio central. Des éléments d'architecture d'époque, un mobilier ancien, des étoffes et tapisseries bigarrées décorent les chambres en harmonie avec tout le confort moderne que le voyageur peut espérer. Le voisinage historique d'Albayzín regorge de nombreux sites, monuments, parcs et églises à explorer, ainsi que de nombreux restaurants à essayer. Le salon du petit-déjeuner peut être transformé en salle de réunion.

Situado en un magnífico mirador, con vistas a la ciudad entera, se encuentra esta maravillosa casa restaurada del siglo XVI que consta de 11 habitaciones distribuidas alrededor de un patio sostenido en su parte central por columnas de piedra. Rasgos de época, antigüedades, telas y tapicerías coloridas adornan las habitaciones junto con el confort moderno que el visitante actual espera. El barrio histórico del Albaicín se enorgullece de poseer muchos monumentos, parques, iglesias para explorar y restaurantes para probar. El salón del desayuno se puede convertir en una sala de reuniones.

Our inspector loved: *The quiet and peaceful ambience.*

Directions: 20 minutes from Granada Airport. Situated on the main street of the historical neighbourhood, Albayzín, a 5-minute walk from the city centre.

Web: www.johansens.com/santaisabel
E-mail: info@hotelsantaisabellareal.com
Tel: +34 958 294 658
Fax: +34 958 294 645

Price Guide: (breakfast €10, excluding VAT)
single €90-160
standard double €100
special double €120
superior double €140
torreon-mirador €170

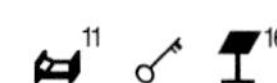

Casa Viña de Alcantara

CTRA. DE ARCOS KM 7.8, JEREZ (CÁDIZ), SPAIN

This charming, family-owned country house hotel nestles in a grand estate featuring a beautiful lawned garden shaded by cypress, bay and palm trees running into vineyards and to a lake. This is an ideal stopover on the Jerez to Arcos road for those touring the pueblos blancos or visiting the great sherry bodegas. The cool interior tastefully blends modern furnishings with fine antiques. Bedrooms are spacious, decorated in pale earth colours and are extremely comfortable.

Ce charmant petit hôtel de campagne familial est niché au sein d'un grand parc avec jardins ombragés par des cyprès, lauriers, et palmiers donnant sur les vignobles et le lac. C'est l'escale idéale sur la route de Jerez à Arcos pour ceux faisant le tour des Pueblos Blanco ou visitant les fantastiques bodegas (distilleries) de sherry. Dans la fraîcheur de l'intérieur se fondent avec goût ameublement moderne et antiquités. Les chambres spacieuses et extrêmement confortables sont décorées dans des couleurs pâles et naturelles.

Esta encantadora casa de campo de propiedad familiar se encuentra dentro de una gran extensión de bellos jardines de césped y zonas de sombra proporcionadas por cipreses, laureles y palmeras que se abren a viñedos y a un lago. Es lugar de parada ideal en la carretera de Jerez a Arcos para aquellos que deseen visitar los pueblos blancos o las excelentes bodegas de vino jerez. El fresco interior acoge una elegante combinación de moderno mobiliario y excelentes piezas de anticuario. Las habitaciones son espaciosas y sumamente cómodas y están decoradas en pálidos tonos de color tierra.

Our inspector loved: *The hand-painted decorations in the bathrooms combined with the large powerful shower heads - bliss!*

Directions: The nearest airport is Jerez. From the airport take N1V towards Jerez > third exit to Arcos de la Frontera > Areos on A382 > hotel is on the right at Km 7.8.

Web: www.johansens.com/vinadealcantara
E-mail: info@vinadealcantara.com
Tel: +34 956 393 010
Fax: +34 956 393 011

Price Guide: (excluding VAT)
double €150

El Molino de Santillán

CTRA. DE MACHARAVIAYA, KM 3, 29730 RINCÓN DE LA VICTORIA, MÁLAGA, SPAIN

Tucked away in a large tract of hills, this Andalucían farmhouse is a rare gem. Each individually designed, rustic-styled bedroom overlooks the gardens and some feature colour washed walls and CD players; the tower suite is exquisite. The sea is 5km away and Granada, Seville, Córdoba and Málaga are within easy driving distance. Enjoy the paddle tennis court and golf and horse riding nearby. The hotel's vegetable garden provides fresh ingredients in the restaurant. 2 large conservatories can be used as meeting space.

Nichée au creux de ses propres collines, cette ferme andalouse est une vraie merveille. Chacune des chambres décorées de façon individuelle jouit d'une vue sur le parc. Certaines chambres ont des murs badigeonnés en couleur et des lecteurs CD, et la suite dans la tour est superbe. La mer n'est qu'à 5 km, et Grenade, Séville, Cordoue et Málaga ne sont pas loin. Il y a un court de tennis paddle et le golf et l'équitation à proximité. Des légumes du jardin sont utilisés au restaurant de l'hôtel. 2 grands jardins d'hiver servent de salles de conférences.

Escondido entre montes, este cortijo andaluz es una verdadera joya. Las habitaciones estan decoradas individualmente en estilo rustico y tienen vistas a los jardines. Algunas, con paredes de color, tienen lector de CD, y la suite en la torre es exquisita. El mar esta a 5km y Málaga, Granada, Córdoba, y Sevilla se pueden visitar fácilmente en coche. Disfruten del paddle tennis o a pocos kilómetros los campos de golf y centro de equitación. El huerto del hotel, aporta ingredientes frescos para la cocina. 2 grandes invernaderos se pueden utilizar para reuniones.

Our inspector loved: *Its location: so close yet so far from the pace of the Costa.*

Directions: Málaga – Almería road > exit No 258 Macharaviaya > hotel is signposted.

Web: www.johansens.com/molinodesantillan
E-mail: informacion@molinodesantillan.es
Tel: +34 952 40 09 49
Fax: +34 952 40 09 50

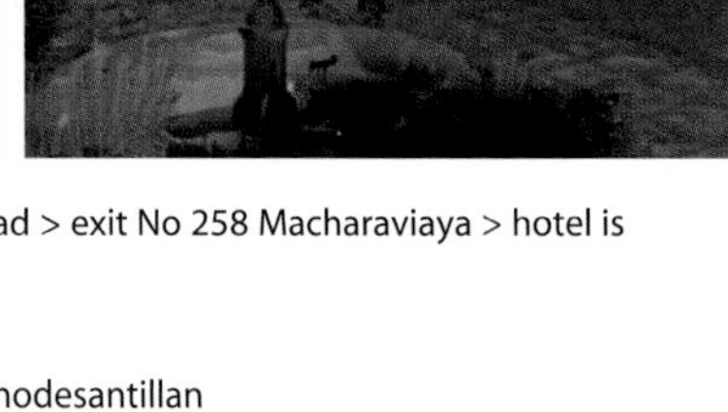

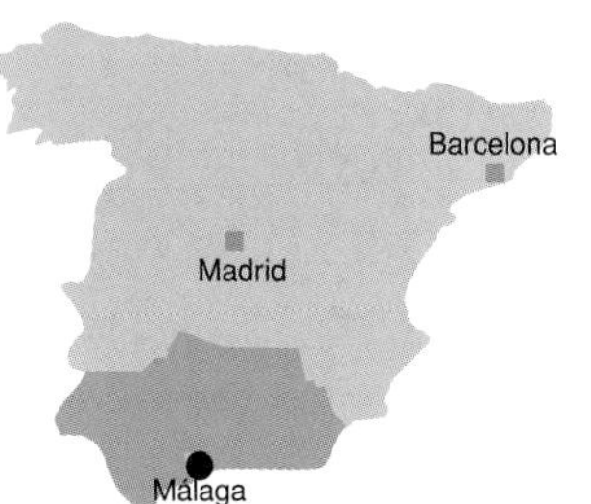

Price Guide: (breakfast €7, closed mid-January - mid-February)
single €69.90–95.90
double €91.90–149.90
suites €162.9–289.90

Hotel Molina Lario

MOLINA LARIO 22, 29015 MÁLAGA, SPAIN

This new hotel is superbly located in the centre of the cultural and shopping areas of historic Málaga, with stunning views over a lush park towards the sea. Its 19th-century architecture has been lovingly preserved to include many original features, high ceilings and huge windows. The roof terrace, which has a decked area and swimming pool, boasts excellent views of the bustling city port, where the docked ocean liners seem close enough to touch.

Ce nouvel hôtel est superbement situe dans le centre culturel et commercial du Málaga historique, avec de magnifiques vues sur un parc luxuriant vers la mer. Son architecture du XIXe siècle a été soigneusement préservée pour inclure de nombreux éléments originaux, de hauts-plafonds et d'immenses fenêtres. Le toit-terrasse, avec plancher et piscine, s'enorgueillit d'excellentes vues sur le port animé de la ville, où les paquebots amarrés semblent être à portée de main.

Este nuevo hotel se encuentra magníficamente situado en el centro de la zona cultural y comercial de la histórica ciudad de Málaga y cuenta con impresionantes vistas a un exuberante parque en dirección al mar. Su arquitectura del siglo XIX conserva con sumo esmero muchas de sus características originales, sus altos techos y sus grandes ventanales. La panorámica terraza-ático, provista de zona de relax y piscina, posee excelentes vistas al transitado puerto de la ciudad, en el que los transatlánticos atracados están tan cerca que parece que pueden tocarse con la mano.

Our inspector loved: *The open view from the roof terrace of the park and port.*

Directions: Málaga > follow signs to Málaga city centre > at Plaza de la Marina turn left into Calle Molina Lario > the cathedral entrance is a few steps further on this street.

Web: www.johansens.com/hotelmolina
E-mail: molinalario@galleryhoteles.com
Tel: +34 952 06 002
Fax: +34 952 06 001

Price Guide: (room only, excluding VAT)
single €95-230
double €95-230
suite €150-515

GRAN HOTEL GUADALPIN BANÚS

C/ EDGAR NEVILLE, S/N 29660 NUEVA ANDALUCÍA, MARBELLA, MÁLAGA, SPAIN

Twinned with sister property, Gran Hotel Guadalpin Marbella, this beachfront hotel offers 181 rooms and suites decorated in beautiful Colonial style with sea views, terraces with rattan sofas and divans, and a swimming pool overlooking the sea. Ideal for beach lovers, the hotel is situated on the shores of Puerto Banús. Its 4 restaurants, with terraces facing the seafront, serve rice dishes from around the world, seafood, Basque-Mediterranean cuisine and gourmet Italian cuisine.

A côté de l'établissement jumeau, Gran Hotel Guadalpin Marbella, cet hôtel en bord de mer offre 181 chambres et suites avec vue sur mer, décorées en style Colonial, des terrasses équipées de canapés en rotin et divans, et une piscine surplombant la mer. Idéal pour les amoureux de la plages, l'hôtel est situé sur le rivage de Puerto Banús. Ses 4 restaurants, dont les terrasses donnent sur le bord de mer, servent du riz venant des quatre coins du monde, des fruits de mer, une cuisine méditerranéenne aux notes basques et une cuisine italienne raffinée.

En línea con su establecimiento hermano, Gran Hotel Gvadalpin Marbella, este hotel en primera línea de playa y con decoración de marcado acento colonial, dispone de 181 habitaciones y suites con vistas al mar, terrazas con sofás y divanes de caña y una piscina desde la que se contempla el mar. Ideal para los amantes de la playa, el hotel está situado a orillas de Puerto Banús. Sus 4 restaurantes con terrazas frente al mar ofrecen arroces del mundo, marisco, cocina vasca- mediterránea y alta gastronomía italiana.

Our inspector loved: *The spacious private terraces: cosy, comfortable and cool, with dark wood and white cotton.*

Directions: For detailed directions please visit the hotel's website.

Web: www.johansens.com/granhotelguadalpinbanus
E-mail: info@guadalpin.com or reservas@guadalpin.com
Tel: +34 952 89 94 04 or +34 952 89 97 00
Fax: +34 952 86 81 72 or +34 952 89 97 01

Price Guide: (buffet breakfast €23, excluding VAT)
double superior (single occupancy) €130-320
double superior €130-320
junior suite superior €190-380

Barcelona
Madrid
Málaga

 181       

Gran Hotel Guadalpin Marbella

BLVD. PRÍNCIPE ALFONSO DE HOHENLOHE, 29600 MARBELLA, MÁLAGA, SPAIN

Excellence, exclusivity and luxury totally describe the 5-star Gran Hotel Guadalpin Marbella, a prestigious, leisure and business retreat, located on Marbella's main avenue, close to the Conference Centre and just a few minutes from the beach and city centre. This innovative and modern hotel is equipped with 127 bedrooms and suites with terraces, some with Jacuzzis as well as wonderful sea views. Award-winning gourmet, Japanese and Mediterrean cuisine is served in the 3 restaurants. There is also an excellent Spa.

Excellence, exclusivité et luxe décrivent les qualités du Gran Hotel Guadalpin, hôtel 5-étoiles, une retraite de loisirs et d'affaires prestigieuse, situé sur l'avenue principale de Marbella, près du Palais des Congrés, de la plage et du centre-ville. Cet hôtel moderne et innovant, compte 127 chambres et suites avec terrasses, certaines avec jacuzzi ; et offre une vue magnifique sur la mer. Les 3 restaurants de l'hôtel proposent une cuisine gastronomique, japonaise et méditerranéenne. L'hôtel dispose également d'un excellent Spa.

Excelencia, exclusividad y lujo describen a Gran Hotel Gvadalpin Marbella. Su ubicación en la avenida principal de Marbella, junto al Palacio de Congresos y a pocos minutos de la playa y del centro de la ciudad hacen de este hotel de 5 estrellas un lugar ideal para estancias de placer o de negocios. Edificio moderno e innovador, cuenta con 127 habitaciones y suites con terrazas, algunas de ellas con jacuzzi, que ofrecen maravillosas vistas al mar. Sus 3 restaurantes ofrecen cocina de autor, japonesa y cocina mediterránea. El hotel dispone también de un excelente Spa.

Our inspector loved: *Relaxing in the Jacuzzi on the terrace of the bedroom whilst enjoying a drink and gazing at the Mediterranean.*

Directions: Please visit the hotel's website for detailed directions.

Web: www.johansens.com/granhotelguadalpinmarbella
E-mail: reservas@guadalpin.com or info@guadalpin.com
Tel: +34 952 89 94 04 and +34 952 89 94 00
Fax: +34 952 86 81 72 and +34 952 89 94 01

Price Guide:
(buffet breakfast €23, excluding VAT)
double (single occupancy) €100-290
double €130-320
2-bedroom superior suite €270-540

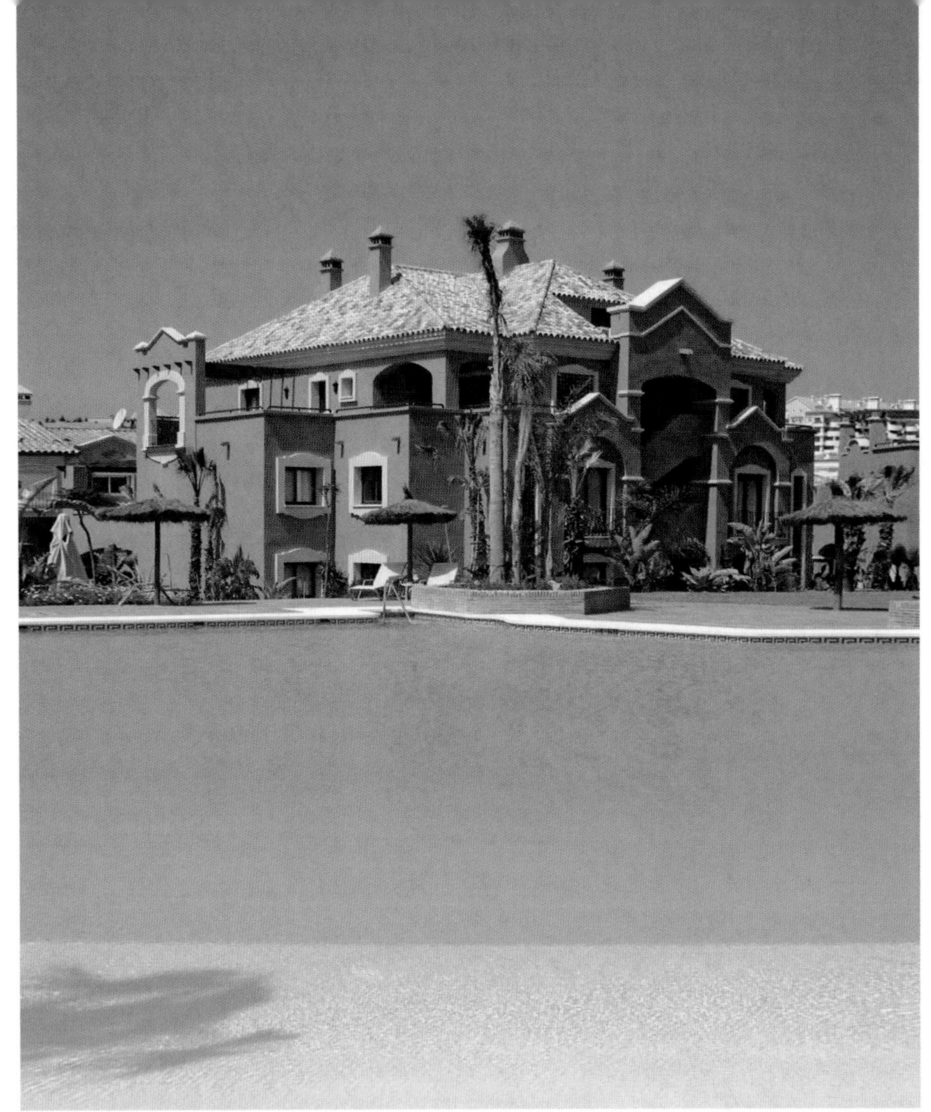

Vasari Resort & Spa

URB. LA ALZAMBRA, EDIF. VASARI CENTER, 29660 MARBELLA, MÁLAGA, SPAIN

Directions: Málaga motorway towards Cádiz > exit Marbella > go through town > Puerto Banus > Urb. Alzambra > Vasari Resort.

Web: www.johansens.com/vasari
E-mail: reservas@vasariresort.com
Tel: +34 952 907 806
Fax: +34 952 906 798

Price Guide: (room only, excluding VAT)
apartment for 1 or 2 persons €135-260
apartment for 4 persons €180-400
duplex penthouse for 4 persons €250-475

This is a new style of chic Vasari holiday resort. A family venue consisting of 1, 2 and 3-bedroom serviced apartments, each is surrounded by well-tended gardens, lush shady foliage, cooling swimming pools, and there is a well-stocked bar. Each apartment is tastefully decorated in pastel colours and equipped to a high quality, modern standard. Guests enjoy excellent cuisine in the elegant restaurant, and added relaxation or exercise can be relished in the well-equipped fitness and spa centre.

Ce très chic nouveau complexe de vacances de style Vasari acceuille des familles dans des appartements de 1, 2 ou 3 chambres. Tous sont entourés de beaux jardins ombragés par de luxuriants feuillages, et ont accès aux piscines et un bar bien achalandé. Ces appartements sont joliment décorés dans des couleurs pastelles avec un équipement moderne et de très haute qualité. Les hôtes peuvent déguster une cuisine excellente dans l'élégant restaurant. Et pour encore plus de détente, le centre thermal et de remise en forme bien équipé est à disposition.

He aquí un nuevo estilo chic de complejo hotelero de vacaciones Vasari, un centro familiar consistente en apartamentos de 1, 2 ó 3 habitaciones con servicio de habitaciones incluido. Cada uno de ellos está rodeado de jardines excelentemente cuidados, exuberante follaje de generosa sombra, refrescantes piscinas y un bar con gran variedad de bebidas. Todos los apartamentos están decorados con sumo gusto a base de colores de pastel y equipados con gran calidad y modernidad. Los clientes pueden disfrutar de su excelente carta en su elegante restaurante y gozar de un toque añadido de relax y ejercicio a sus estancias en su magníficamente equipado centro fitness y spa.

Our inspector loved: *The space and privacy with every convenience of a hotel.*

Gran Hotel Guadalpin Byblos

Urbanización Mijas Golf, 29650 Mijas, Málaga, Spain

This luxurious 5-star hotel is a golfer's paradise, offering glorious views of the surrounding gardens and golf courses. There are also 2 delightful restaurants: La Fuente, with its magnificent terrace by the swimming pool, serves Mediterranean dishes with little Andalucían touches; and the famous gastronomic restaurant, Le Nailhac. The Thalasso Spa by La Prairie, covers 2,500m^2 and is the ideal place for relaxing, pampering and enjoying treatments.

Ce luxueux hôtel 5-étoiles, paradis des golfeurs, offre de splendides vues sur les jardins et sur les terrains de golf. L'hôtel dispose également de 2 exquis restaurants : La Fuente, avec sa fabuleuse terrasse au bord de la piscine, sert une cuisine méditerranéenne agrémentée d'une note andalouse; et le fameux restaurant gastronomique, Le Nailhac. Le Thalasso Spa de La Prairie, couvre une surface de 2500 m^2; c'est l'endroit idéal pour se détendre, se faire choyer et profiter des traitements.

Este lujoso hotel de 5-estrellas ofrece espectaculares vistas a los jardines y campos de golf de los alrededores. Los amantes del golf encontrarán en este hotel el lugar ideal en el que practicar este deporte. El hotel dispone además de 2 exquisitos restaurantes: La Fuente, con una formidable terraza junto a la piscina, que ofrece cocina mediterránea con suaves toques de cocina andaluza; y el famoso restaurante gastronómico Le Nailhac. El Thalasso Spa por La Prairie, con una superficie de 2.500 m^2, es un espacio único en el que relajarse, mimarse y disfrutar de los tratamientos de belleza.

Our inspector loved: *The open spaces inside the hotel, and the relaxing scenery.*

Directions: Please visit the hotel's website for detailed directions.

Web: www.johansens.com/granhotelguadalpinbyblos
E-mail: reservas@guadalpin.com or info@guadalpin.com
Tel: +34 952 89 94 04 or +34 952 89 94 03
Fax: +34 952 86 81 72 or +34 952 89 94 01

Barcelona
Madrid
Málaga

Price Guide: (excluding VAT)
double €130-320
junior suite superior €190-380
2-bedroom suite €270-530

Hotel Molino del Arco

PARTIDO DE LOS FRONTONES S/N, 29400 RONDA, MÁLAGA, SPAIN

Nestled within the beautiful rural countryside and mountainous Serrania de Ronda, Hotel Molino del Arco is a secluded haven. Originally an 18th-century olive mill, it has been converted into a lovely hotel. Tasteful interior décor features an eclectic mix of modern and antique pieces whilst the unique bedrooms are stunning and surrounded by pretty gardens, terracotta patios and cool waterways. The hotel is located just 8km from Ronda with its many fabulous attractions.

Niché au cœur de la magnifique campagne montagneuse de Serrania de Ronda, l'Hôtel Molino del Arco est un havre de paix. Originellement un moulin à huile du XVIIle siècle, il a été transformé en un ravissant hôtel. L'intérieur élégant est un mélange éclectique de moderne et d'antiquités. Les chambres sont superbes et entourées d'adorables jardins, de patios en terracotta et de points d'eau. L'hôtel est situé à 8 km de Ronda et de ses fabuleuses attractions.

Situado en una bonita zona rural al abrigo de los montes de la Serranía de Ronda, el Hotel Molino del Arco es un pacifico refugio. Lo que en el siglo XVIII fue un molino de aceite y sus dependencias ha sido convertido en un encantador hotel. Esta amueblado con exquisito gusto usando una ecléctica mezcla de piezas modernas y antiguas, y todas las habitaciones son únicas, rodeadas de bonitos patios, jardines y fuentes. El hotel se encuentra a solo 8 km de Ronda y sus múltiples encantos.

Our inspector loved: *The lovely spacious rooms and bathrooms.*

Directions: Málaga Airport > Málaga > ring road > follow sings to Almeria/Motril > exit Campillos/Universidad > A357 > after Ardales turn left to Teba/Ronda > secondary road > A367 > turn left towards Ronda.

Web: www.johansens.com/molinodelarco
E-mail: info@hotelmolinodelarco.com
Tel: +34 952 114 017
Fax: +34 952 11 44 57

Price Guide: (room only, excluding VAT, closed January and February)
double (single occupancy) €96-120
double €120-200
suite €240-900

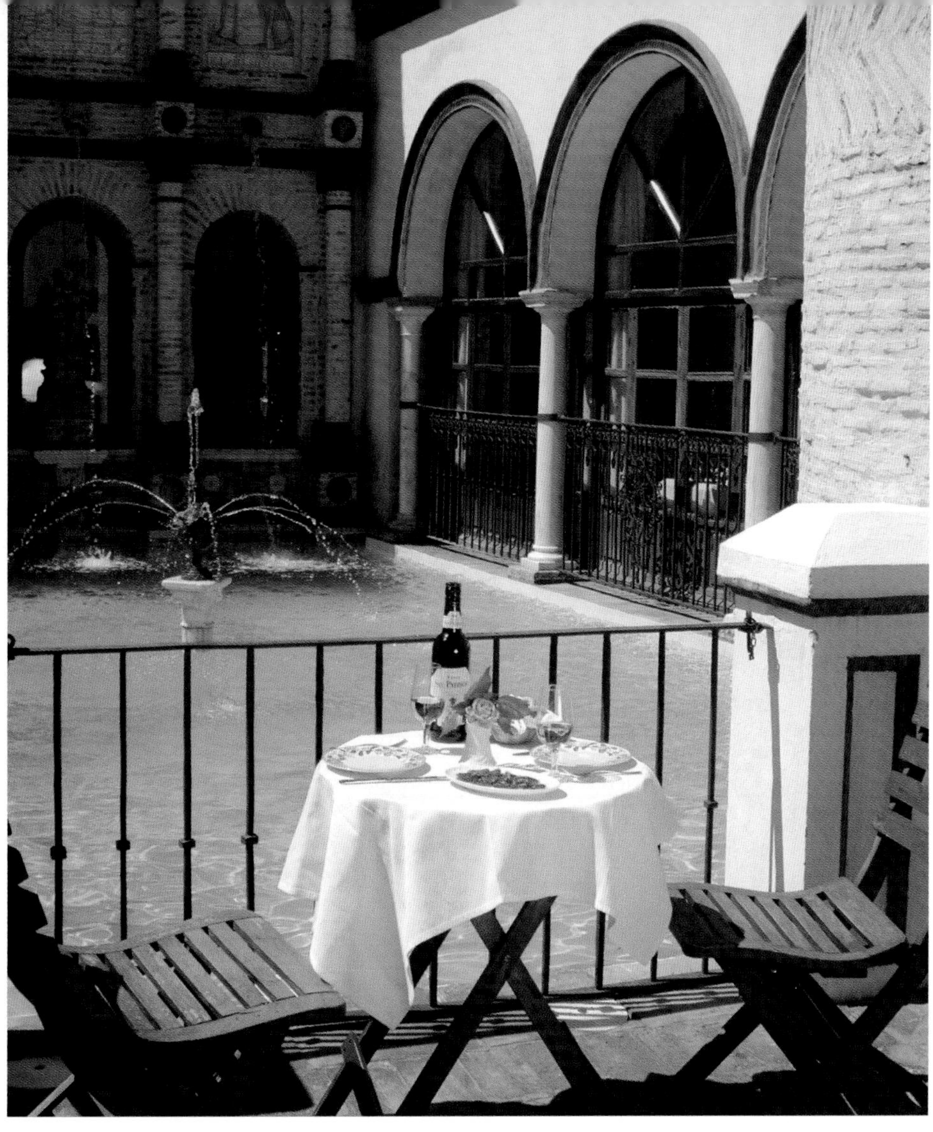

Palacio de San Benito

C/SAN BENITO S/N, 41370 CAZALLA DE LA SIERRA, SEVILLA, SPAIN

Originally a 15th-century church, the hotel was once a stopover for pilgrims and the present owner's family played host to Philip V, the first Bourbon king of Spain. Today its atmosphere is that of a cosy private hunting lodge, filled with exquisite portraits and heirlooms from that period. Unique bedrooms feature Liberty fabrics, fireplaces and tiny patio gardens and there is also a wonderful chapel, dining room and swimming pool that doubles as a fountain. The restaurant serves a traditional menu, complemented with local wine, in a unique setting.

A l'origine une église du XVe siècle, cet hôtel fut autrefois une étape pour les pèlerins et la famille du propriétaire actuel accueillit Philippe V, premier roi Bourbon d'Espagne. De nos jours, son atmosphère est douillette comme celle d'un pavillon de chasse privé, rempli de délicieux portraits et tableaux de famille d'époque. Les chambres uniques sont décorées en tissus Liberty, et bénéficient de cheminées et petits patios ou jardins; l'hôtel dispose également d'une adorable chapelle, d'une salle de restaurant et d'une piscine qui se présente aussi comme une fontaine. Le restaurant sert une cuisine traditionnelle, accompagnée de vins locaux dans un environnement exceptionnel.

Lo que originariamente fuese una iglesia del siglo XV y también una parada de peregrinos, es hoy este hotel en el que la familia de sus dueños hospedó al primer rey Borbón de España, Felipe V. Hoy posee el ambiente acogedor de un albergue privado de caza, lleno de retratos exquisitos y reliquias de esa época. En sus singulares habitaciones destacan telas Liberty, chimeneas y diminutos patios ajardinados. Tiene también una capilla maravillosa, un comedor y una piscina que además hace de fuente. En el restaurante se sirve un menu tradicional maridado con vinos de la tierra en un ambiente único.

Our inspector loved: *The small, individual patios in some of the rooms.*

Directions: Airport > N-IV for Seville > A431 to Alcala del Río > A431 to Villaverde del Río > A431 to Cantillana > A432 to El Pedroso > A432 to Cazalla de la Sierra > the hotel is on the right-hand side upon entering Cazalla on Paseo del Moro. 1 hour form Seville and 90 minutes from Cordoba.

Barcelona
Madrid
Seville

Web: www.johansens.com/palaciodesanbenito
E-mail: info@palaciodesanbenito.com
Tel: +34 954 88 33 36
Fax: +34 954 88 31 62

Price Guide: (excluding VAT)
room €130-220

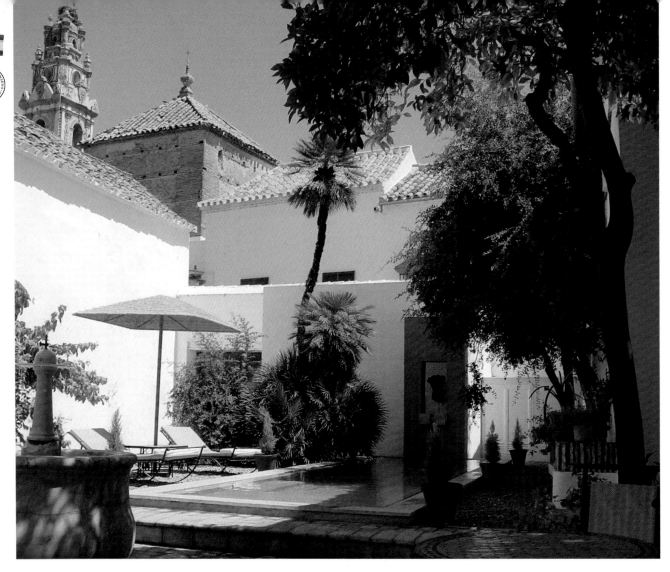

Hotel Palacio de Los Granados

EMILIO CASTELAR 42, 41400 ÉCIJA, SEVILLA, SPAIN

Directions: Sevilla - Córdoba motorway > exit Écija > hotel is signposted.

Web: www.johansens.com/granados
E-mail: info@palaciogranados.com
Tel: +34 955 905 344
Fax: +34 955 901 412

Price Guide: (excluding VAT)
double €120-150
suite €160-190

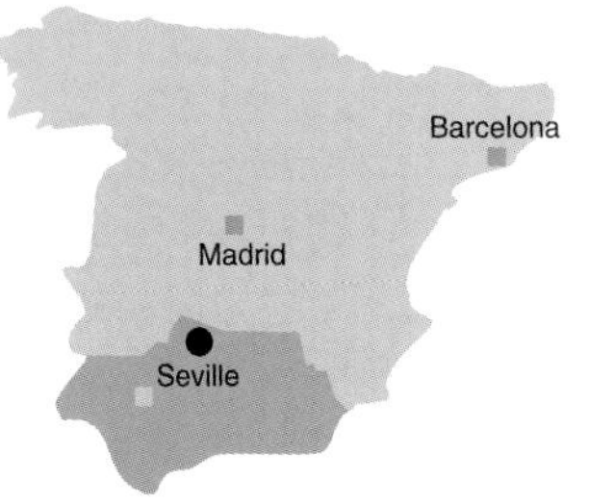

This stylish little "palacio" has recently been lovingly and painstakingly restored by its owners, who fell in love with the building and the town it lies in. Seville is steeped in history, and the hotel retains a distinctly Moorish character. Lofty cloisters lead to elegant and stylish rooms, and a delightful garden with wooden galleries and pretty fountain. The welcome is as warm and attentive as the restoration project itself; a real little gem.

Cet élégant petit "palacio" a récemment été rénové avec le plus grand soin par son propriétaire tombé amoureux du bâtiment et de la ville. Séville est imprégnée d'histoire et l'hôtel garde distinctement un caractère mauresque. Les cloîtres élevés mènent aux chambres élégantes et à un charmant jardin avec des galeries en bois et une jolie fontaine. L'accueil est aussi chaleureux et attentif que la restauration elle-même. Un véritable petit bijou.

Este pequeño elegante palacio ha sido recientemente restaurado con todo esmero y cariño por sus dueños que se enamoraron del edificio y del pueblo donde se encuentra. Sevilla está repleta de historia y el hotel mantiene un carácter distinguidamente árabe. Los claustros sublimes le conducen a las habitaciones elegantes y de gran estilo y al jardín encantador con galerías de madera y una bonita fuente. La bienvenida es tan cálida y atenta como lo es el mismo proyecto de restauración: una auténtica pequeña joya.

Our inspector loved: *The peaceful and colourful back garden with its orange trees, pomegranates and geraniums.*

Hotel Cortijo Águila Real

CTRA. GUILLENA–BURGUILLOS KM 4, 41210 GUILLENA, SEVILLA, SPAIN

This charming 4-star Andalucían country house was perfectly restored as a hotel in 1991 and features well-appointed bedrooms and junior suites. Each room has its own individual décor and name; hand-painted furniture and extravagant tapestries adorn the walls. Homemade dishes comprise fresh local produce as well as food grown on the hotel farm, and the new dining room, with removable glass panels, overlooks the peaceful, relaxing gardens and beyond. Various events can be held in the large sound-proof hall, formerly the old stables.

Cet élégant manoir andalou 4 étoiles a été superbement restauré en hôtel en 1991 et propose des chambres et des junior suites impeccables. Chaque chambre se distingue par son propre nom et sa décoration spécifique. Des meubles peints à la main et de somptueuses tapisseries ornent les murs. Les plats faits-maison sont élaborés à partir de produits régionaux frais ou de la ferme de l'hôtel, et la nouvelle salle à manger avec des vitres détachables s'ouvre sur les jardins paisibles et relaxants. Une grande salle insonorisée l'ancienne écurie est disponible pour de divers évènements.

Este encantador cortijo andaluz de 4 estrellas quedó perfectamente acondicionado como hotel en 1991 y dispone de excelentes habitaciones y suites junior. Cada habitación se distingue por su decoración y nombre propios; dispone de mobiliario pintado a mano y de suntuosos tapices que adornan sus paredes. Sus platos caseros se elaboran a partir de productos frescos locales y cultivados en la propia granja del hotel. El nuevo comedor, provisto de paneles de cristal desmontables, proporciona vistas a sus relajantes jardines y a otros paisajes más lejanos. Una amplia sala insonorizada, que antaño fueron los establos, puede dar acogida a variados eventos.

Our inspector loved: *The lights of Sevilla in the distance after dark.*

  13    300    

Directions: Please contact the hotel for detailed directions.

Web: www.johansens.com/cortijoaguilareal
E-mail: hotel@aguilareal.com
Tel: +34 955 78 50 06
Fax: +34 955 78 43 30

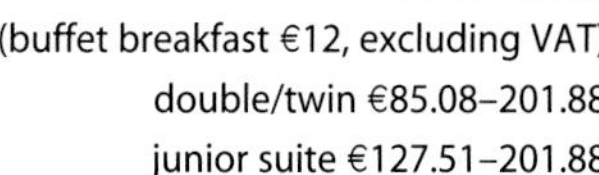

Price Guide:
(buffet breakfast €12, excluding VAT)
double/twin €85.08–201.88
junior suite €127.51–201.88

Cortijo Soto Real

CTRA. LAS CABEZAS VILLAMARTIN KM 13, 41730 - LAS CABEZAS (SEVILLA), SPAIN

Perfectly located amongst hills and valleys, this 5-star country house is an oasis of peace set within 5,000 acres of natural countryside. Soothing pastel colours and charming interior design create a welcoming atmosphere that is enhanced by large windows and stunning views of the rural Andalucían landscapes. Guests will enjoy swimming, horse and horse-carriage rides, quad and mountain bike excursions, small game shooting and many other outdoor activities as well as the indoor wellness centre and gym facilities.

Idéalement situé parmi des collines et des vallées, ce manoir 5 étoiles est un havre de paix au cœur de 2,500 ha de campagne. Des couleurs pastels et une décoration intérieure de charme créent une atmosphère accueillante qui est renforcée par de larges fenêtres offrant de superbes vues sur les paysages andalous ruraux. Les hôtes apprécieront la natation, les promenades à cheval et en voiture à cheval, les excursions en V.T.T, les sessions de tir et beaucoup d'autres activités extérieures ainsi que le centre de santé intérieure et les installations du gym.

Perfectamente ubicado entre colinas y valles, este antiguo cortijo de 5 estrellas es un oasis de paz entre 2,500 ha de paisaje natural. Sus serenos colores pastel y su encantador y armonioso diseño interior crean un espacio equilibrado que se realza con sus grandes ventanales y las sorprendentes vistas del paisaje rural andaluz. Sus huéspedes podrán disfrutar de la natación, paseos a caballo y en enganche, excursiones de bicicletas de montaña, sessiones de tiro y muchas otras actividades al aire libre así como el centro de la salud interior y las instalaciones del gym.

***Our inspector loved:** The sheer breadth of the estate which offers tranquillity as well as a wealth of activities.*

Directions: From Sevilla > A4 towards Cádiz > exit at Las Cabezas de San Juan > follow the road to Villamartin > hotel is on the right at km 13.

Web: www.johansens.com/sotoreal
E-mail: reservas@hotelcortijosotoreal.com
Tel: +34 955 869 200
Fax: +34 955 869 202

Price Guide: (room only, excluding VAT)
single €232-290
double €290-350
suite €390-680

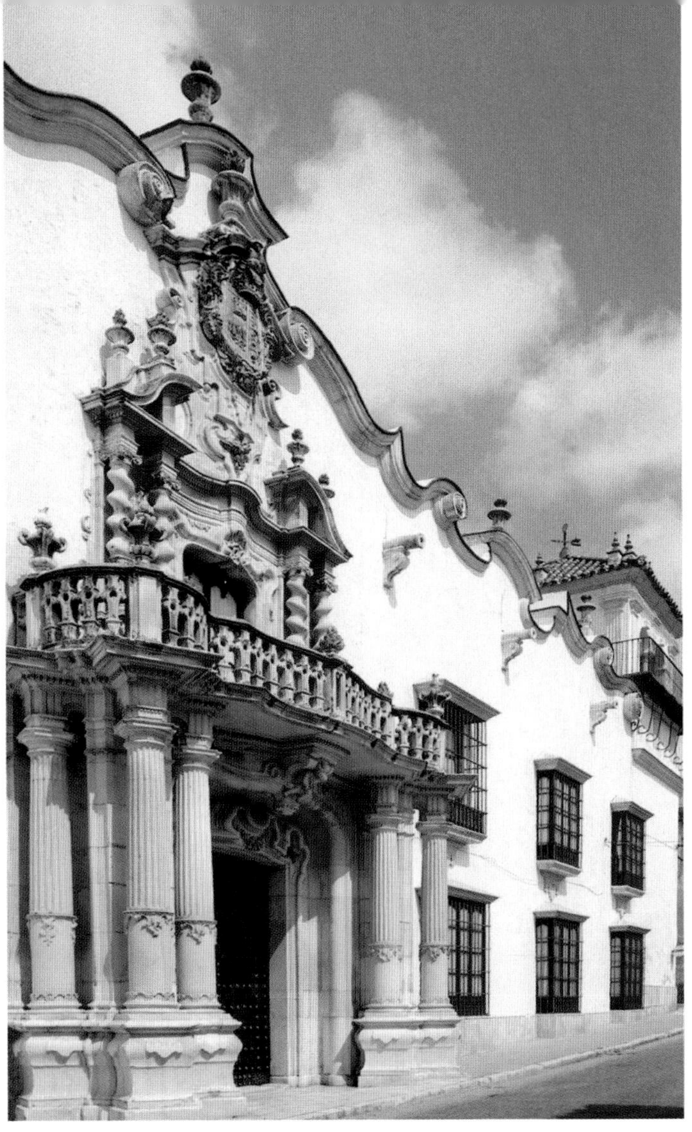

Palacio Marqués de la Gomera

C/ San Pedro 20, 41640 Osuna, Sevilla, Spain

Set in a street full of wonderful old aristocratic houses, the façade of the Palace is one of the best examples of 18th-century Baroque architecture. Walking into its typical Andalucían central courtyard is like stepping back in time. Behind graceful colonnade arches lie public rooms filled with antiques and paintings and bedrooms all with their own special atmosphere and features, from wooden beams to stone walls, French windows and the classic Suite 7 as used in Zeffirelli's film "Callas Forever".

Situé dans une rue pleine de vieilles maisons aristocratiques, la façade du Palace est l'un des meilleurs exemples du Baroque XVIIIe siècle et entrer dans sa cour intérieure typiquement andalouse est un saut dans le passé. Derrière de belles arches à colonnades, se tiennent des pièces communes emplies d'antiquités et de particularités, des poutres en bois aux murs de pierre, portes-fenêtres et au Suite 7 classique comme celui du film de Zeffirelli "Callas Forever".

Ubicado en una calle llena de antiguas mansiones aristocráticas, la fachada de este palacio constituye una de las mejores muestras de la arquitectura barroca del siglo XVIII. Entrar a su patio central típico andaluz es como retroceder en el tiempo. Los elegantes arcos sobre columnas dan paso a los salones repletas de antigüedades y lienzos así como a las habitaciones, cada una de ellas con un ambiente y rasgos propios: las hay con vigas de madera; otras con muros de piedra; otras con ventanas francesas o está la clásica Suite 7 tal y como aparece en la película "Callas Forever" de Zeffirelli.

Our inspector loved: *The unique charm of each bedroom that makes one feel like staying in a different one each night.*

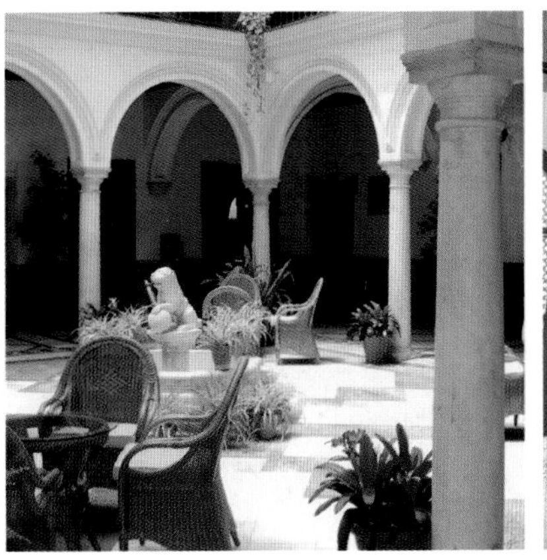

Directions: From Sevilla > A92 to Osuna. From Málaga > Granada > Antequera > A92 to Osuna.

Web: www.johansens.com/palaciomarquesdelagomera
E-mail: info@hotelpalaciodelmarques.com
Tel: +34 95 4 81 22 23
Fax: +34 95 4 81 02 00

Price Guide: (room only, excluding VAT)
double (single occupancy) €68-95
standard double €88-125
upper-class double €108-150
suite €156-210

HACIENDA BENAZUZA EL BULLI HOTEL

C/VIRGIN DE LAS NIEVES S/N, 41800 SANLÚCAR LA MAYOR, SEVILLE, SPAIN

Directions: Seville Airport > Huelva > exit no 16 / Sanlucar La Mayor > hotel.

Web: www.johansens.com/haciendabenazuza
E-mail: hbenazuza@elbullihotel.com
Tel: +34 955 70 33 44
Fax: +34 955 70 34 10

Price Guide:
(closed 3rd January - 28th February)
double/twin €310-410
suite €415-1,130

Dating back, in part, to the 10th century, this is one of Sevilla's most spectacular hotels that regularly plays host to a number of high-profile guests. There are delightful courtyards and gardens and a stunning swimming pool, which is arranged as a series of "water terraces" creating an instant sense of tranquillity and relaxation. The gourmet restaurant is the only establishment in Andalucía to currently hold 2 Michelin stars, and the staff take great pleasure to ensure exceptional levels of service.

Datant en partie du Xe siècle, c'est l'un des hôtels les plus spectaculaires de Séville qui accueille régulièrement des hôtes de prestige. Des cours et jardins charmants ainsi qu'une superbe piscine, arrangée comme une suite de "pièces d'eau" crées immédiatement un sentiment de tranquillité et de relaxation. Le restaurant gastronomique est le seul établissement d'Andalousie à détenir 2 étoiles au Michelin, et le personnel prend grand soin d'assurer un service exceptionnel.

He aquí uno de los hoteles más espectaculares de Sevilla, parte del cual se remonta al siglo X, que aloja a un gran número de visitantes de alto nivel. Dispone de encantadores patios y jardines, así como de una espléndida piscina dividida en "terrazas de agua" que proporcionan una inmediata sensación de tranquilidad y relax. Su restaurante gastronómico es hoy el único establecimiento de Andalucía galardonado con 2 estrellas Michelín. Para el personal del hotel supone un verdadero placer garantizar un nivel de servicio realmente excepcional.

Our inspector loved: *Taking a siesta in the gardens amongst silk cushions with gauze curtains swaying in the breeze.*

Casa No 7

CALLE VIRGENES NO 7, 41004 SEVILLA, SPAIN

Winner of Tatler's Travel Award 2001 for the Best Small Hotel of the World, this is a charming, quiet and comfortable property situated in one of Seville's narrow, winding streets close to the quaint old Jewish quarter and just a short stroll from the cathedral. The 6 well-appointed bedrooms and public rooms are on the upper 2 floors surrounding a lovely inner courtyard. All are tastefully decorated, delightfully furnished with antiques and little extras that help guests feel they are staying at a friend's house rather than a hotel.

Cet hôtel a reçu le prix du Meilleur Petit Hôtel du monde remis en 2001 par la revue Tatler. Ce charmant bâtiment, calme et confortable est situé dans l'une des rues étroites et tortueuses de Séville, proche du vieux et pittoresque quartier juif et à quelques pas de la cathédrale. Les 6 chambres et salles communes bien équipées se trouvent sur les 2 étages supérieurs qui entourent une adorable cour intérieure. Toutes joliment décorées avec des vieux meubles et des petits extras qui laissent penser aux hôtes qu'ils sont chez des amis plutôt qu'à l'hôtel.

Ganador en 2001 del premio al Mejor Hotel Pequeño del mundo de la revista Tatler, este es un hotel, tranquilo, atractivo y cómodo, Casa No 7 está situada en una de las sinuosas y angostas calles de Sevilla, muy cerca del pintoresco y antiguo barrio judío y a sólo unos minutos andando de la Catedral. Sus 6 habitaciones así como sus salas comunes tienen un buen terminado y se encuentran en las dos plantas superiores, las cuales rodean un precioso patio interior. Todas ellas están elegantemente decoradas y amuebladas con piezas de anticuario y pequeños detalles que hacen al cliente sentirse como en casa de un amigo más que en un hotel.

Our inspector loved: *The warm ambience and the lovely décor - a perfect blend of elegance and comfort.*

Directions: Seville > Sevilla city and Barrio de Santa Cruz.

Web: www.johansens.com/casanumero7
E-mail: info@casanumero7.com
Tel: +34 954 221 581
Fax: +34 954 214 527

Price Guide: (excluding VAT)
double €177

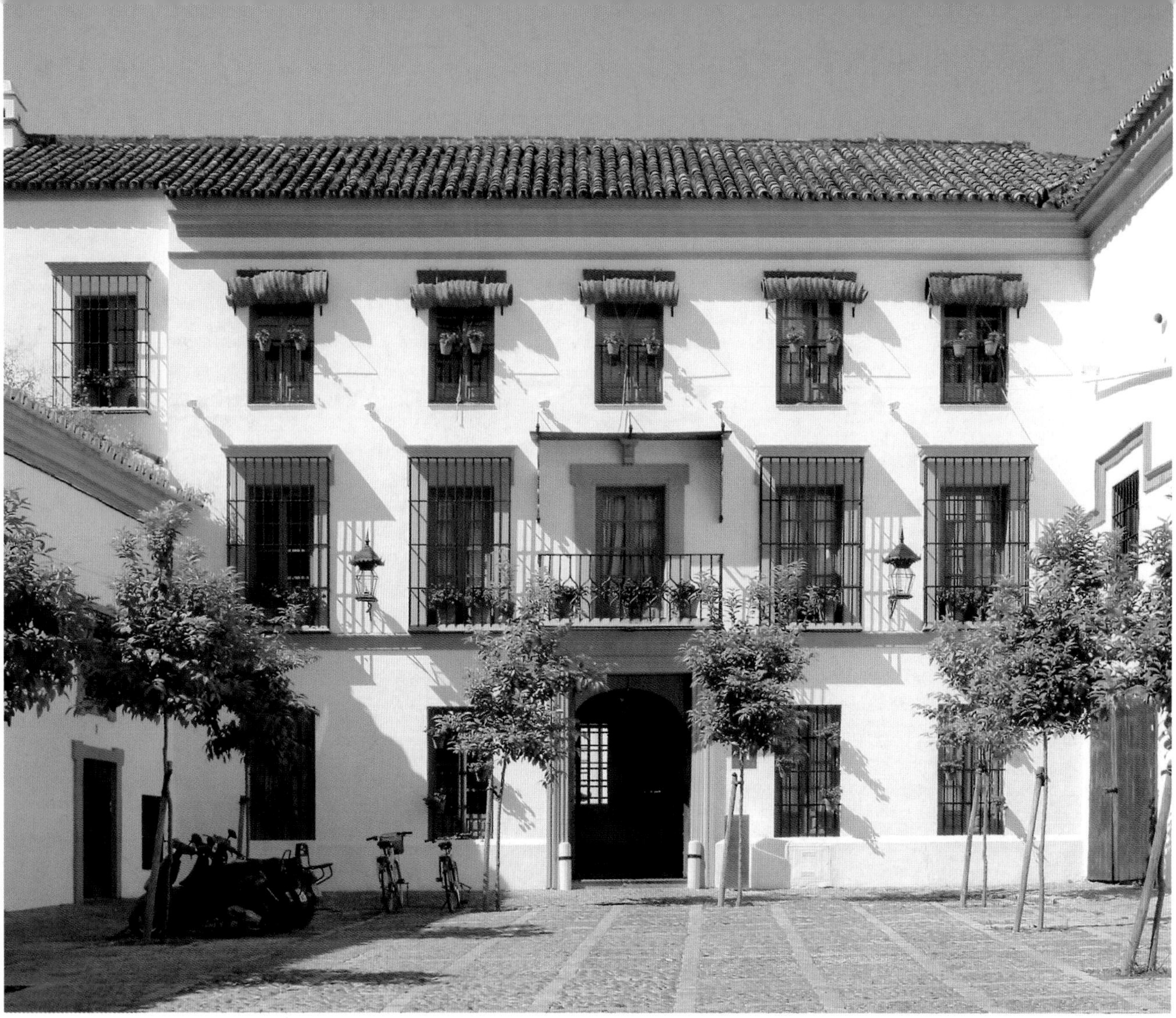

SPAIN / ANDALUCÍA (SEVILLA)

Hospes Las Casas del Rey de Baeza

C/SANTIAGO, PLAZA JESÚS DE LA REDENCIÓN 2, 41003 SEVILLA, SPAIN

Surrounded by churches, palaces and monuments in the old quarter of Seville stands this charming hotel, minutes from the business centre. Walk through one of the cobbled courtyards, with its blue wooden pillars and cascading flowers, into the relaxing public rooms, which are filled with light. Natural fabrics, iron and dark woods furnish the softly lit bedrooms in a minimalist style. Senzone restaurant offers local cuisine prepared from fresh produce. Relax on the patio or in a deckchair on the roof terrace with swimming pool where views of Seville's rooftops are enchanting.

Entouré d'églises, de palais et de monuments dans le vieux quartier de Séville, ce charmant hôtel n'est qu'à quelques minutes du centre d'affaires. L'accès aux agréables pièces communes envahies de lumière se fait en traversant l'une des cours pavées aux piliers en bois bleu et cascades de fleurs. Tissus naturels, fer et bois foncés meublent les chambres au style minimaliste et à l'éclairage doux. Le restaurant Senzone propose une cuisine locale préparée à partir de produits locaux. Les clients peuvent se relaxer dans le patio ou sur une chaise longue sur le toit avec piscine, d'où les vues sur Séville sont magiques.

Rodeado de iglesias, palacios y monumentos, en el casco antiguo de Sevilla, este encantador hotel esta a pocos minutos del centro comercial. El acceso a los confortables salones llenos de luz se hace a través de uno de los patios con adoquines, columnas de madera pintadas de azul y cascadas de flores. De estilo minimalista y luz tenue, las habitaciones estan amuebladas con telas naturales, hierro forjado y maderas oscuras. El restaurante Senzone ofrece productos frescos y ligeros. Para el descanso: uno de los patios o la piscina-solarium del ultimo piso con sus encantadoras vistas sobre Sevilla.

Our inspector loved: *The small, carefully chosen details.*

Directions: Seville Airport > city centre > hotel is signposted.

Web: www.johansens.com/casasdelrey
E-mail: reydebaeza@hospes.es
Tel: +34 954 561 496
Fax: +34 954 561 441

Price Guide: (room only, excluding VAT)
single €140-275
double €160-320
suite €300-500

Hotel Almenara

A-7 (NATIONAL ROAD), 11310 SOTOGRANDE, SPAIN

Located in the centre of the superb 27-hole Almenara golf course, each of the 148 spacious rooms, including 12 suites, has been decorated in an exquisite, modern design and maintains a warm and local ambience and look out over the green, the gardens or the Mediterranean Sea. There are 2 restaurants, a piano bar, the award-winning Spa Elysium with Sotogrande Health Experience, outdoor and indoor swimming pools, beach club, Sotogrande Golf Academy, equestrian centre, tennis and paddle courts and water sports at La Marina.

Situé au cœur du superbe golf 27 trous d'Almenara, chacune des 148 chambres spacieuses, y compris les 12 suites, a été décorée dans un design moderne et superbe duquel dégage une atmosphère locale chaleureuse, et a vue sur le green, les jardins ou la Méditerranée. L'hôtel dispose de 2 restaurants, un piano bar, du Spa Elysium qui a été primé avec son Sotogrande Health Experience, piscine intérieure et extérieure, club de plage, de l'Académie de Golf Sotogrande, d'un centre équestre, de cours de tennis et de paddle ainsi que de ports nautiques à la Marina.

Este hotel, situado en el centro del magnífico campo de golf de 27 hoyos de Almenara, cuenta con 148 amplias habitaciones, incluidas 12 suites. Todas ellas han sido decoradas con elegante y moderno diseño, conservan el cálido ambiente lugareño y tienen vistas al campo de golf, a los jardines o al mar Mediterráneo. Dispone de 2 restaurantes, un piano bar, el galardonado Spa Elysium con Sotogrande Health Experience, piscina interior y exterior, club de playa, Academia de Golf de Sotogrande, un centro de equitación, pistas de tenis y pádel al tiempo que ofrece la posibilidad de disfrutar de diversos deportes acuáticos en La Marina.

Our inspector loved: *The outdoor aspect in this lovely natural setting.*

Directions: Málaga to Cádiz coast road A7/AP7 > exit 130 > signposted.

Web: www.johansens.com/almenara
E-mail: info@sotogrande.com
Tel: +34 956 58 20 00 or +34 902 18 18 36
Fax: +34 956 58 20 01

Barcelona
Madrid
Málaga

Price Guide: (excluding VAT, enquire for special offers)
single €150–215
double €165–230
junior suite €263–368

Palacio de la Rambla

PLAZA DEL MARQUÉS 1, 23400 ÚBEDA~JAÉN, SPAIN

Directions: Málaga - Granada > motorway to Jaén > A316 toward Úbeda.

Web: www.johansens.com/rambla
E-mail: hotel@palaciodelarambla.com
Tel: +34 953 75 01 96
Fax: +34 953 75 02 67

Price Guide: (excluding VAT, closed 16th July - 10th August)
single €90
double €115
suite €125

In the heart of the peaceful city of Úbeda stands this exclusive 16th-century palace, within walking distance of many local monuments and sights. Built in 1575, many original features remain and the air of relaxation is ensured by the friendly and attentive staff. Beyond the courtyard, with its archways and ivy-clad walls, special touches such as displays of fresh flowers pervade the palace, making this a unique place to stay. With only 8 bedrooms, a quiet, tranquil experience is guaranteed.

Au cœur de la paisible ville d'Úbeda, à quelques pas des nombreux sites et monuments locaux se dresse cet unique palace du XVIe siècle. Construit en 1575, de nombreuses caractéristiques subsistent et l'atmosphère reposante est renforcée par le personnel amical et attentif. Au delà de la cour, avec ses voûtes et ses murs couverts de lierre, des attentions particulières telles que la présence de fleurs fraîches se répandent dans le palace, en faisant ainsi un lieu de séjour unique. Avec seulement 8 chambres, calme et tranquillité sont garantis.

Ubicado en el centro de la tranquila ciudad de Úbeda data este selecto palacio del siglo XVI, desde el que se pueden visitar a pie muchos monumentos y curiosidades locales. Construido en 1575 muchos de sus rasgos originales se han mantenido y su ambiente relajado está asegurado por el personal atento y acogedor. Más allá del patio con sus arcadas y paredes cubiertas de hiedra, toques especiales como arreglos florales frescos impregnan el palacio, lo que lo convierten en un lugar único. Con solamente 8 habitaciones el silencio y la tranquilidad están garantizados.

Our inspector loved: *This Renaissance palace, that exudes period charm with antique furnishings and a four-poster bed.*

Hotel el Privilegio de Tena

PLAZA MAYOR, 22663 TRAMACASTILLA DE TENA, ARAGÓN, SPAIN

Built using 15th-century stone from an ancient abbey, this elegant modern hotel stands in a beautiful setting. With a no-smoking bar and restaurant and newly created spa with double massage facilities and a hydrotherapy bath in one of the recently created suites, there is an emphasis on health and wellness. The vast Red Suite comprises 100m² and has its own private serving hatch, and a beautiful attic meeting room can accommodate up to 12. Music enthusiasts will love the soprano and pianist that sometimes perform in the restaurant.

Construit avec les pierres d'une ancienne abbaye du XVe siècle, cet élégant et moderne hôtel se situe dans un cadre magnifique. Avec son bar, son restaurant non-fumeurs et son nouveau spa avec équipements pour massage double et bain d'hydrothérapie dans l'une des suites récemment crées, l'accent est définitivement mis sur la santé et le bien-être. La spacieuse Suite Rouge a une surface de 100m² et possède son propre accès. Une superbe salle de réunion sous les toits peut contenir jusqu'à 12 personnes. Les mélomanes adoreront le soprano et le pianiste qui offrent parfois des représentations dans le restaurant.

Construido con piedra del siglo XV procedente de una antigua abadía, este elegante y moderno hotel se erige en un bello entorno. Dispone de un bar para no fumadores y de un spa de nueva creación con dobles instalaciones para servicio de masajes así como de un baño de hidroterapia en una de sus más recientes suites con el fin de dar la importancia que merece a la salud y el bienestar. La amplia Suite Roja abarca 100 m², dispone de su propia puerta de servicio y de un bello salón de reuniones en su ático con una capacidad de hasta 12 personas. Los amantes de la música disfrutarán del soprano y pianista que en ocasiones actúan en el restaurante.

Our inspector loved: *The compact wellness centre.*

Directions: Airport > Zaragoza/Pau or Torbes, France. The hotel is on the A136 road, close to the French border.

Web: www.johansens.com/elprivilegiodetena
E-mail: info@elprivilegio.com
Tel: +34 974 487 206
Fax: +34 974 487 270

Price Guide:
double €114-146
suite €166-600

La Torre del Visco

44587 FUENTESPALDA, TERUEL, SPAIN

This beautiful 15th-century estate house in the undiscovered "Spanish Provence" is surrounded by lovely gardens and patios with fountains, at the end of 5km of forest track in a remote river valley. The Mediterranean cuisine, for which it is renowned, uses herbs and vegetables, olive oil and truffles from the 220-acre farm, and is complemented by wines from the well-stocked wine cellar. Cooking courses are available. British owners and Spanish staff create a friendly and peaceful atmosphere enjoyed all year round.

Ce beau domaine romantique qui date du XVe siècle est entouré de beaux jardins et terrasses avec fontaines et est situé au bout de 5 km d'un chemin forestier dans une vallée écartée la "Provence la espagne" non découverte. La cuisine méditerranéenne renommée emploie des herbes et légumes, huile d'olives et truffes de la ferme de 90 ha et elle est arrosée de vins de la cave bien fournie. Des cours de cuisine sont disponibles. Les propriétaires britanniques et le personnel espagnol offrent une ambiance accueillante et tranquille tout au long de l'année.

Esta preciosa mansión del siglo XV se encuentra en la "Provenza española" aún sin descubrir, rodeada de encantadores jardines y patios al final de un camino forestal de 5 km en un remoto valle fluvial. En su cocina mediterránea, por la que es famosa, se usan hierbas, verduras, aceite de oliva y trufas procedentes de la finca de 90 ha, y se complementa con vinos de su bien surtida bodega. Tienen a disposición cursos de cocina. Los dueños británicos y el personal español crean un ambiente amistoso y pacífico del que se puede disfrutar todo el año.

Our inspector loved: *Being surrounded by nature.*

Directions: The nearest airports are Zaragoza, Reus, Valencia and Barcelona. A7 > N420 - Calaceite > Valderrobres > the hotel is signposted on the road to Fuentespalda.

Web: www.johansens.com/torredelvisco
E-mail: torredelvisco@torredelvisco.com
Tel: +34 978 76 90 15
Fax: +34 978 76 90 16

Price Guide: (including dinner for 2, excluding VAT)
double €245-295
suite €330-370

Hotel La Cepada

AVENIDA CONTRANQUIL S/N, 33550 CANGAS DE ONÍS, SPAIN

Located on the edge of a charming village and boasting spectacular mountain views, Hotel La Cepada invites guests into a professional, friendly environment. The spacious, individual bedrooms are bathed in light, which also filters through an impressive window-wall. The elegant restaurant, which has a designated no-smoking area, serves traditional Asturian cuisine with a contemporary twist. Meals may be taken on the outside decking which enables diners to delight in the breathtaking views. Nearby Picos de Europa offers salmon fishing and canoeing.

Situé sur les bords d'un charmant village et offrant de superbes vues sur les montagnes, Hôtel La Cepada reçoit ses hôtes dans un environnement amical et professionnel. Les chambres spacieuses ont toutes leur propre style et baignent dans la lumière par le biais d'impressionnants murs-fenêtres. L'élégant restaurant, avec sa salle non-fumeur, sert une cuisine traditionnelle des Asturies préparée avec une touche contemporaine. Les repas peuvent être pris sur le terrasse afin que les clients puissent admirer les somptueuses vues. Picos de Europa, à proximité, propose pêche au saumon et canoë.

En las afueras de un encantador pueblo, ostentando espectaculares vistas montañosas, el Hotel La Cepada le invita a disfrutar de un ambiente cordial y profesional. Las espaciosas habitaciones llenas de luz, poseen un estilo propio, y gran luminosidad procede también de la impresionante pared-ventana. En el elegante restaurante, donde no se puede fumar, sirven cocina tradicional asturiana con un toque contemporáneo, y si prefiere comer en la terraza de madera al aire libre, disfrutará al máximo de las espectaculares vistas. Los cercanos Picos de Europa ofrecen la posibilidad de pescar salmón y de practicar piragüismo.

Our inspector loved: *The frescoes on the restaurant walls.*

Directions: The nearest airports are Asturias or Santander. A8 > junction with N634 > N625 to Cangas de Onís.

Oviedo
Barcelona
Madrid
Málaga

Web: www.johansens.com/cepada
E-mail: info@hotellacepada.com
Tel: +34 985 84 94 45
Fax: +34 985 84 95 66

Price Guide: (excluding VAT)
single €65-126
double €82-158

Palacio de Cutre

LA GOLETA S/N, VILLAMAYOR, 33583 INFIESTO, ASTURIAS, SPAIN

Directions: The nearest airports are Asturia and Santander. A8 > N634 > at Villamayor exit Borines > signposted.

Web: www.johansens.com/palaciodecutre
E-mail: hotel@palaciodecutre.com
Tel: +34 985 70 80 72
Fax: +34 985 70 80 19

Price Guide: (excluding VAT)
single €78-85.60
double €108.07-145.52
suite €177.62-204.37

Built on a hill with incredible views of the surrounding mountains and farmland, this 16th-century farmhouse, with its own chapel, has been recently renovated and has a peaceful and friendly atmosphere. Great attention to detail, antique doll collections and small artefacts make every corner interesting. There is a delicious menu offering the region's seasonal specialities. Outdoor activities include canoeing, rafting, horse riding and hiking.

Construite sur une colline avec une vue imprenable sur les montagnes environnantes et les terres agricoles, cette ferme du XVIe siècle avec sa propre chapelle, a récemment été rénovée et bénéficie d'une atmosphère paisible et amicale. Une attention particulière au détail, des poupées antiques et de petits artefacts en rendent chaque recoin particulièrement intéressant. Un délicieux menu sert des spécialités régionales de saison. Pour activités de plein air, canoë, raft, randonne équestre et marche sont à disposition.

Construido sobre una colina ofrece increíbles vistas de las montañas y de la finca que lo circunda, ésta casa-palacio del siglo XVI con su propia capilla, ha sido recientemente renovada, creando un ambiente tranquilo y acogedor. Una atención cuidadosa y detallista, una importante colección de muñecas antiguas, y pequeños objetos convierten cada rincón en un auténtico museo. Además, cuenta con un delicioso menú que ofrece especialidades regionales de temporada. En las actividades al aire libre se incluye canoa, rafting, equitación y senderismo.

Our inspector loved: *The peaceful, country views.*

SPAIN / BALEARIC ISLANDS (IBIZA)

Atzaró Agroturismo

CTRA. SAN JUAN, KM 15, 07840 SANTA EULALIA, IBIZA, BALEARIC ISLANDS

This century-old converted finca stands within exotic, tranquil gardens and a fragrant orange grove, surrounded by magnificent statues and fountains. The modern interior features exciting splashes of red, and each bedroom has a private terrace and bathroom decorated in colourful marble. The private spacious villa, located 100m from the finca comprises 6 superior and de luxe suites. International-Mediterranean cuisine is served in the intimate restaurant, and weddings/events can be accommodated in the Pavilion. The Oriental spa, in the gardens, offers treatments, massages, hammam, sauna and a gym.

Cette finca restaurée du siècle dernier, entourée de superbes statues et fontaines, se dresse au cœur de jardins exotiques et tranquilles et d'une orangeraie parfumée. L'intérieur moderne est composé de touches de rouge et chaque chambre possède sa propre terrasse et une salle de bains en marbre de couleur. A 100m de la finca, la spacieuse villa privée comprend 6 suites de catégorie supérieure et de luxe. Une cuisine d'inspiration internationale et méditerranéenne est servie dans le restaurant intime et raffiné, et des noces/événements peuvent être arrangés au pavillon. Le spa oriental situé dans le jardin propose soins, massages, hammam, sauna et gym.

Esta finca centenaria se encuentra en unos jardines exóticos y tranquilos junto a un naranjal, rodeada de magníficas estatuas y fuentes. El interior es de estilo moderno con pinceladas en rojo, y cada una de las habitaciones esta dotada de terraza privada y baño con mármol de color. La espaciosa villa privada, a 100m de la finca, se compone de 6 suites superiors y de lujo. Cocina internacional-mediterránea se sirve en el restaurante refinado e íntimo y las bodas y eventos se pueden celebrar en el Pabellón. En los jardines, encontrara el Spa Oriental, donde puede disfrutar de tratamientos, masajes, hammam, sauna y gimnasio.

Our inspector loved: *The spa, housed in hand-carved wooden pavilions.*

Directions: Ibiza - San Joan de Labritja > hotel is signposted.

Web: www.johansens.com/atzaroagroturismo
E-mail: agroturismo@atzaro.com
Tel: +34 971 33 88 38
Fax: +34 971 33 16 50

Price Guide: (excluding VAT)
double €260-340
suite €300-520

Can Lluc

CRTA. SANTA INÉS, KM 2, 07816 SAN RAFAEL, IBIZA, BALEARIC ISLANDS

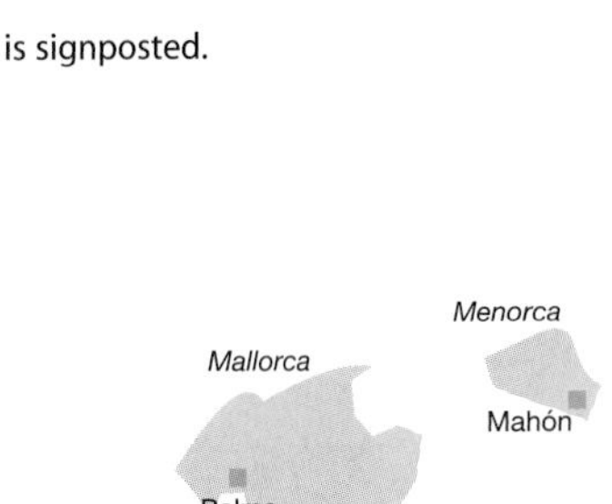

Located in San Rafael, a valley in the heart of the island, Can Lluc perfectly captures the tranquillity and magic of rural Ibiza. The main old farm building has retained sturdy stone walls and wooden beams, whilst skylights let in plenty of natural sunlight. Many bedrooms are housed in out-buildings, such as small houses with little terraces, and some feature fireplaces and hydromassage baths or showers. There is a restaurant service in summer. Guests can enjoy water sports, rambling and cycling, and the new outdoor Jacuzzi.

Situé à San Rafael, une vallée au cœur de l'île, Can Lluc représente parfaitement la tranquillité et la magie du véritable Ibiza. Ses anciens bâtiments fermiers ont gardé leurs robustes murs de pierre et poutres en bois tandis que les lucarnes au plafond laissent entrer un flot de lumière naturelle. La plupart des chambres sont situées dans des bâtiments extérieurs, sortes de petites maisons avec terrasses dont certaines offrent cheminées, bains ou douches à jets massant. L'été un service de restauration est disponible. Les clients peuvent pratiquer des sports nautiques, du vélo, des randonnées ou profiter du nouveau jacuzzi extérieur.

Situada en el valle de San Rafael en el centro de la isla, Can Lluc refleja la tranquilidad y la magia de la Ibiza rural. El edificio principal que fue una antigua casa de campo, mantiene los fuertes muros de piedra y las vigas de madera mientras que la luz natural penetra por las claraboyas. Muchas de las habitaciones están emplazadas en edificios adyacentes, como casitas con pequeñas terrazas, algunas poseen chimeneas y baños o duchas hidromasajes. Existe servicio de restaurante solamente en verano. Se pueden practicar deportes acuáticos, senderismo, ciclismo y disfrutar del nuevo Jacuzzi exterior.

Our inspector loved: *Listening to the birdsong in the gardens.*

Directions: Road to Santa Agnés > hotel is signposted.

Web: www.johansens.com/canlluc
E-mail: info@canlluc.com
Tel: +34 971 198 673
Fax: +34 971 198 547

Price Guide: (excluding VAT)
double €225-500

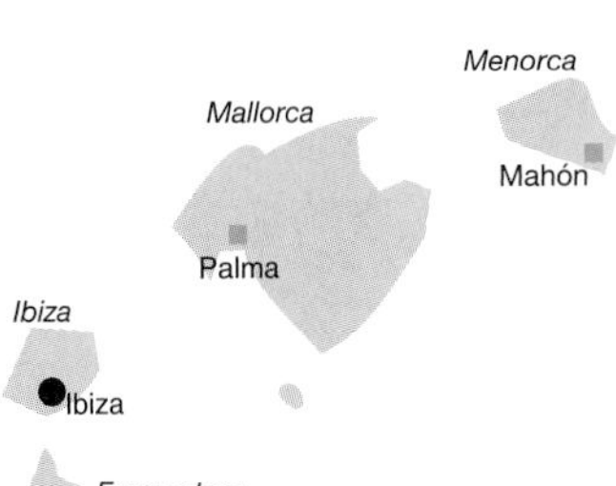

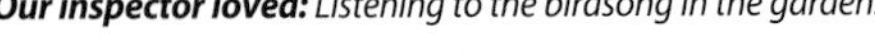

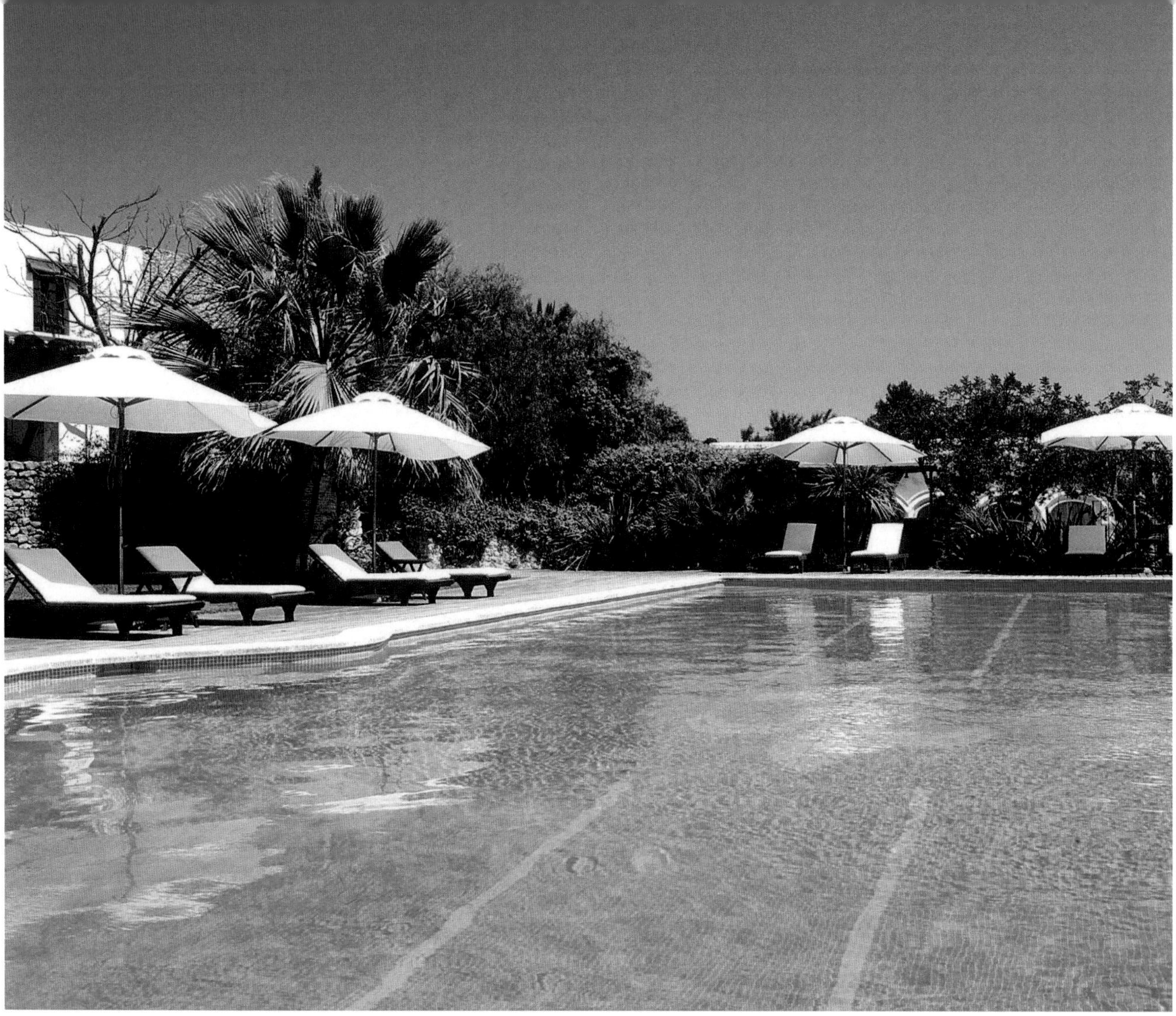

Cas Gasi

CAMINO VIEJO DE SANT MATEU S/N, PO BOX 117, 07814 SANTA GERTRUDIS, IBIZA, BALEARIC ISLANDS

Set amidst pretty gardens, almond trees, orchards and olive groves, this former farmhouse has been completely renovated to offer guests an exclusive stay in tranquil surroundings. The beautifully decorated bedrooms provide every modern comfort and are adorned with hand-painted tiles. In the summer guests will enjoy the nightlife and beaches, and exploring the countryside on foot or by bicycle during the winter. The wellness area features a Jacuzzi, sauna and fitness centre. A private yacht is available for excursions.

Au sein de charmants jardins, d'amandiers, de vergers et d'oliveraies, cet ancien corps de ferme a été complètement rénové pour offrir à ses hôtes un séjour exclusif dans un environnement tranquille. Les chambres joliment décorées offrent tout le confort et sont ornées avec des carrelages peints à la main. En été, les hôtes peuvent profiter des plages et de la vie nocturne, alors qu'en hiver ils peuvent explorer la campagne à pied ou bicyclette. Le centre de bien-être offre un jacuzzi, un sauna et un centre de remise en forme. Un bateau à moteur privé est disponible pour des promenades.

Ubicada entre preciosos jardines, almendros, huertas y olivares, esta antigua granja ha sido totalmente renovada con el propósito de ofrecer a los clientes una estancia exclusiva en un entorno tranquilo. Las habitaciones, de magnífica decoración, proporcionan todo el confort moderno y están adornadas de azulejos pintados a mano. En el verano los huéspedes podrán disfrutar de la vida nocturna y de las playas, así como explorar el campo a pie o en bicicleta durante el invierno. La zona de wellness dispone de jacuzzi, sauna y centro de fitness. Hay un yacht privado para excursiones a disposición de los clientes.

Our inspector loved: *The scent of the roses in the rooms and gardens.*

Directions: Ibiza Airport > Ibiza > Santa Eulalia > Santa Gertrudis > Sant Mateu > hotel is signposted.

Web: www.johansens.com/casgasi
E-mail: info@casgasi.com
Tel: +34 971 197 700
Fax: +34 971 197 899

Price Guide: (excluding VAT)
double €254-333
suite €450-620

  10  40       

Blau Porto Petro Beach Resort & Spa

AVENIDA DES FAR 12, 07691 PORTO PETRO (SANTANYI), MALLORCA, BALEARIC ISLANDS

This new 5-star resort is located next to picturesque Porto Petro and the Mondrago Nature Reserve. Each of the modern-style guest rooms, suites and villas has a sun terrace and magnificent sea views. Villas have a pool or outdoor Jacuzzi. Excellent gourmet, Japanese, Spanish or buffet dining are available. Leisure facilities include 2 semi-private beaches, 3 pools, a wide range of sports including sailing and diving, spa treatments and a beauty centre. Children are warmly welcome and there is even a special area for them.

Ce nouveau complexe hôtelier 5-étoiles est situé à côté du pittoresque Porto Petro et de la réserve naturelle de Mondràgo. Toutes les chambres, suites et villas sont décorées dans un style moderne et ont des terrasses qui offrent de splendides vues sur la mer. Les villas sont équipées de piscine ou de Jacuzzi exterieur. Sont proposées au choix, une cuisine gastronomique, Japonaise et Espagnole ainsi qu'un buffet. Les équipements de loisir comprennent 2 plages semi-privées, 3 piscines; un éventail d'activités sportives incluant la voile et la plongée; des traitements thermaux et un centre de soins de beauté. Une zone est réservée aux enfants qui sont chaleureusement acceuillis.

Este nuevo hotel complejo hotelero de 5-estrellas está espléndidamente situado junto al pintoresco Port Petro y la reserva natural Mondragó. Cada una de sus habitaciones, suites y villas de estilo contemporáneo tiene una terraza y vistas magníficas del mar. Las villas cuentan con piscina o jacuzzi descubierta. Se dispone asimismo de excelente servicio de cena gourmet, japonesa, española o buffet. Sus magnificas instalaciones incluyen 2 playas semi-privadas, 3 piscinas, una amplia gama de deportes, incluyendo escuela de vela y de submarinismo, circuito de hidroterapia y centro de salud y belleza. Los niños son muy bienvenidos, con un área especial reservada para ellos.

Our inspector loved: *The wonderful location with 2 semi-private beaches.*

Directions: Palma Airport > motorway to Santanyi > Porto Petro > turn right at the entrance to the village > the hotel is signposted.

Web: www.johansens.com/blaupivilege
E-mail: venportopetro@blau-hotels.com
Tel: +34 971 648 282
Fax: +34 971 648 283

Price Guide: (closed November - January)
single from €200
double from €250
suite from €390

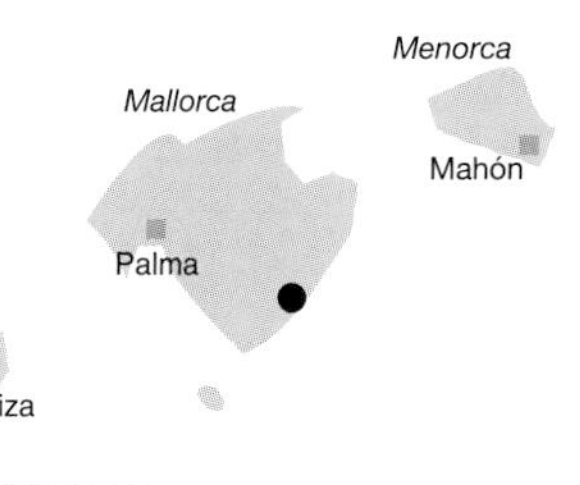

319

550

Ca's Xorc

CARRETERA DE DEIÀ, KM 56.1, 07100 SÓLLER, MALLORCA, BALEARIC ISLANDS

Majorcan tradition and contemporary style have been combined throughout this captivating hotel, surrounded by landscaped gardens. Stunning vistas of the Tramuntana mountains and the Mediterranean are enjoyed from the terrace, where guests can sample a weekly changing menu. Inside, the rooms with stone floors, exposed beams and white fabrics create a romantic ambience. The hotel's enviable seclusion ensures a peaceful yet invigorating stay. A Moroccan pavilion accommodates private functions and gatherings such as meetings (max 40) and wedding receptions (max 100).

Tradition majorquine et style contemporain se complètent à merveille dans cet hotel d'exception, qui est entouré de jardins dessinés. De la terrasse, les visiteurs profitent d'une vue spectaculaire sur la Sierra de Tramuntana et la Méditerranée tout en dégustant des mets délicats chaque semaine différents. Les sols dallés, les poutres apparentes et les tissus blancs créent une ambiance romantique. Grâce à son endroit retiré, l'hôtel offre des séjours paisibles et vivifiants. Un pavillon marocain est disponible aux conférences (40 places) et aux mariages (100 places).

Este delicioso hotel rodeado de jardines paisajistas ha sabido combinar en su totalidad la tradición mallorquina con un estilo contemporáneo. Espléndidas vistas de las montañas Tramuntana y del Mediterráneo se pueden disfrutar desde la terraza donde los clientes pueden degustar un menú que cambia cada semana. En su interior destacan suelos de piedra, vigas vistas y telas blancas que le otorgan un ambiente romántico. El retiro envidiable asegura una estancia sosegada a la vez que vigorizante. Un pabellón marroquí aloja funciones como conferencias (capacidad para 40) y bodas (para 100).

Our inspector loved: *Taking dinner on the terrace overlooking the coast.*

Directions: Palma Airport > Sóller > Deià > the hotel is on the left-hand side.

Web: www.johansens.com/casxorc
E-mail: stay@casxorc.com
Tel: +34 971 63 82 80
Fax: +34 971 63 29 49

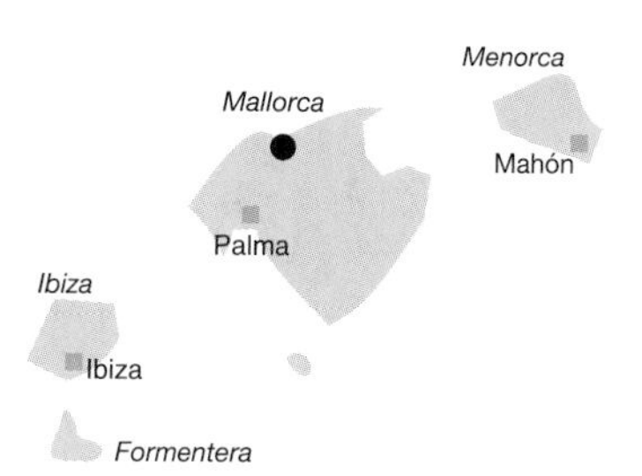

Price Guide: (excluding VAT, closed November - February)
interior room €180
vista room €195
superior room €225
de luxe room (with terrace) €290

Can Simoneta

CTRA. DE ARTÁ A CANYAMEL KM 8, FINCA TORRE DE CANYAMEL, 07580 CAPDEPERA, MALLORCA, BALEARIC ISLANDS

Directions: Palma Airport > Manacor > Canyamel > the hotel entrance is marked.

Web: www.johansens.com/simoneta
E-mail: info@cansimoneta.com
Tel: +34 971 816 110
Fax: +34 971 816 111

Price Guide: (closed during November)
double €225-300
suite €350-410

Perched on the edge of a cliff with stunning sea views, this is a charming, lovingly restored and modernised country hotel. Subtle colour co-ordination creates a relaxing interior where guests enjoy lying back and allowing the warm sea breezes to pass by. Spiral stairs cut into the cliff to reach a beautiful secluded sea-bathing cove. The restaurant hosts weekly barbecues and gala dinners, and private meals can be taken on the terrace or in the gardens. Activities include cycling and diving.

Perché sur le bord d'une falaise avec de magnifiques vues sur la mer, Can Simoneta est un ravissant et charmant hôtel de campagne restauré et modernisé. Une coordination de couleurs douces créée une atmosphère relaxante ou les hôtes aiment à se reposer et à sentir l'air de la mer. Un escalier en spirale taillé dans la falaise permet d'accéder à une magnifique crique isolée. Le restaurant propose chaque semaine des barbecues et des dîners de gala tandis que les repas privés sont servis sur la terrasse ou dans les jardins. Les activités comprennent le cyclisme et la plongée.

Situado al borde de un acantilado con impresionantes vistas al mar, este es un encantador hotel rural que ha sido restaurado y modernizado con mucho cariño. Los colores tenues del interior crean una atmósfera tranquila donde los huéspedes pueden relajarse, descansar y disfrutar de la cálida brisa. Una escalera excavada en el acantilado da acceso a una bella y apartada cala donde se puede tomar un baño en el mar. Cada semana se ofrecen barbacoas y cenas de gala en el restaurante, pudiéndose cenar privadamente en la terraza o en el jardín. Entre otras actividades se puede hacer buceo y ciclismo.

Our inspector loved: *The unspoilt location.*

Hospes Maricel

CARRETERA D'ANDRATX 11, 07181 CAS CATALÀ, (CALVIÀ) MALLORCA, BALEARIC ISLANDS

This stunning hotel is an eclectic fusion of old and new with captivating views over the Mediterranean Sea. The high ceiling and glass windows of the lobby enhance the magnificent scenery and the contemporary bedrooms have bathrooms with traditional bathtubs. Dine al fresco or in the Senzone Restaurant where gourmet breakfasts are also served. Enjoy jazz nights at the bar, mid-week live music on the pool terrace, yacht charters, and the new Bodyna Spa & Sensations, which offers an extensive menu of treatments.

Ce superbe hôtel est un mélange éclectique de l'ancien et du moderne avec de captivantes vues sur la mer Méditerranée. Les hauts plafonds et grandes fenêtres de l'impressionnant lobby mettent en valeur le magnifique décor. Les chambres sont contemporaines et les salles de bain ont des baignoires traditionnelles. Les hôtes dînent au fresco ou dedans le Senzone restaurant où peuvent déguster le délicieux petit-déjeuner. Les hôtes peuvent profiter des soirées jazz au bar, des concerts en semaine sur la terrasse de la piscine, du yacht et du nouveau Bodyna Spa & Sensations qui offre un grand nombre de soins.

Este deslumbrante hotel, que combina de forma ecléctica lo nuevo con lo antiguo, goza de cautivadoras vistas al Mediterráneo. Su impactante vestíbulo, tiene altos techos y ventanas de cristal que proporcionan una impresión de grandeza. Las habitaciones, contemporáneas, tienen cuartos de baño con bañeras al estilo tradicional. Los clientes pueden cenar dentro o al aire libre en el Senzone restaurant y gozar de sus desayunos gastronómicos. Disfrute de las noches de jazz en el bar, música en vivo entre semana en la terraza de la piscina, servicio de alquiler de yates, y el nuevo Bodyna Spa & Sensations con su extenso menú de tratamientos.

Our inspector loved: *The massage area overlooking the sea.*

Directions: Palma Airport > motorway to Palma > exit Andratx > exit Bendinat > turn left to Palma > hotel is on the right.

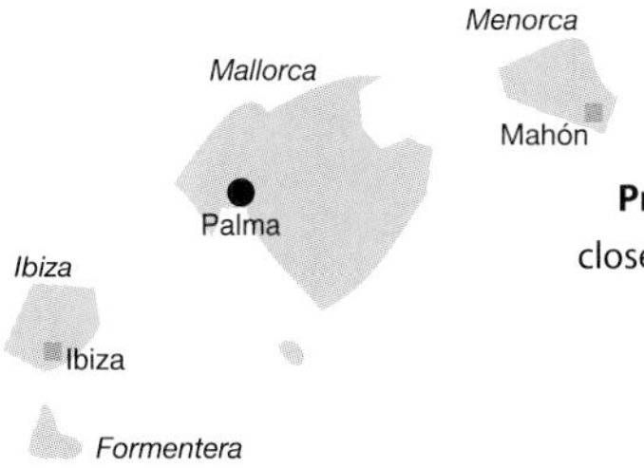

Web: www.johansens.com/maricel
E-mail: maricel@hospes.es
Tel: +34 971 707 744
Fax: +34 971 707 745

Price Guide: (room only, excluding VAT, closed end of December - end of February)
single €250-370
double €250-560
suite €425-800

Hotel Aimia

SANTA MARIA DEL CAMÍ, 1 07108 PORT DE SÓLLER, MALLORCA, SPAIN

Directions: Palma Airport > Andratx. Turn off for Sóller > Port de Sóller. The hotel is behind the promenade.

Web: www.johansens.com/aimia
E-mail: info@aimiahotel.com
Tel: +34 971 631 200
Fax: +34 971 638 040

Price Guide:
single €67-83
double €125-165

This charming hotel is delightfully situated in a small port and beach resort in northern Mallorca. Totally renovated in 2005, it is stunningly attractive with an ultra modern interior that offers total relaxation for the discerning visitor. Décor is contemporary with dark wood floors complementing the beige, lilac and yellow pastel surrounds. Each of the 43 air-conditioned bedrooms offers every comfort and facility. Excellent cuisine is served in an elegant restaurant and guests can enjoy relaxing treatments in the fully-equipped spa.

Cet hôtel de charme est idéalement situé dans un petit port et station balnéaire au nord de Majorque. Complètement rénové en 2005, l'hôtel est absolument magnifique avec un intérieur moderne qui offre une relaxation totale aux visiteurs. La décoration est contemporaine avec des parquets foncés qui mettent en valeur les couleurs beiges, lilas et jaunes environnantes. Les 43 chambres climatisées offrent tout le confort ainsi qu'un équipement moderne. Une délicieuse cuisine est servie dans l'élégant restaurant et les hôtes peuvent profiter des soins relaxants dans le spa.

Este encantador hotel goza de un espléndido emplazamiento en un pueblo del norte de Mallorca que dispone de un pequeño puerto y playa. Totalmente renovado en 2005, resulta excepcionalmente atractivo por sus interiores ultramodernos destinados a proporcionar al cliente más exigente un relax absoluto. Su decoración es contemporánea, con suelos de madera oscura que se complementan con el beige, lila y amarillo pastel del entorno. Cada una de sus 43 habitaciones, provistas de aire acondicionado, proporcionan todo tipo de comodidades y confort. Su excelente carta se sirve en un elegante restaurante. Los clientes pueden disfrutar de relajantes tratamientos en su spa.

Our inspector loved: *The sheltered pool area.*

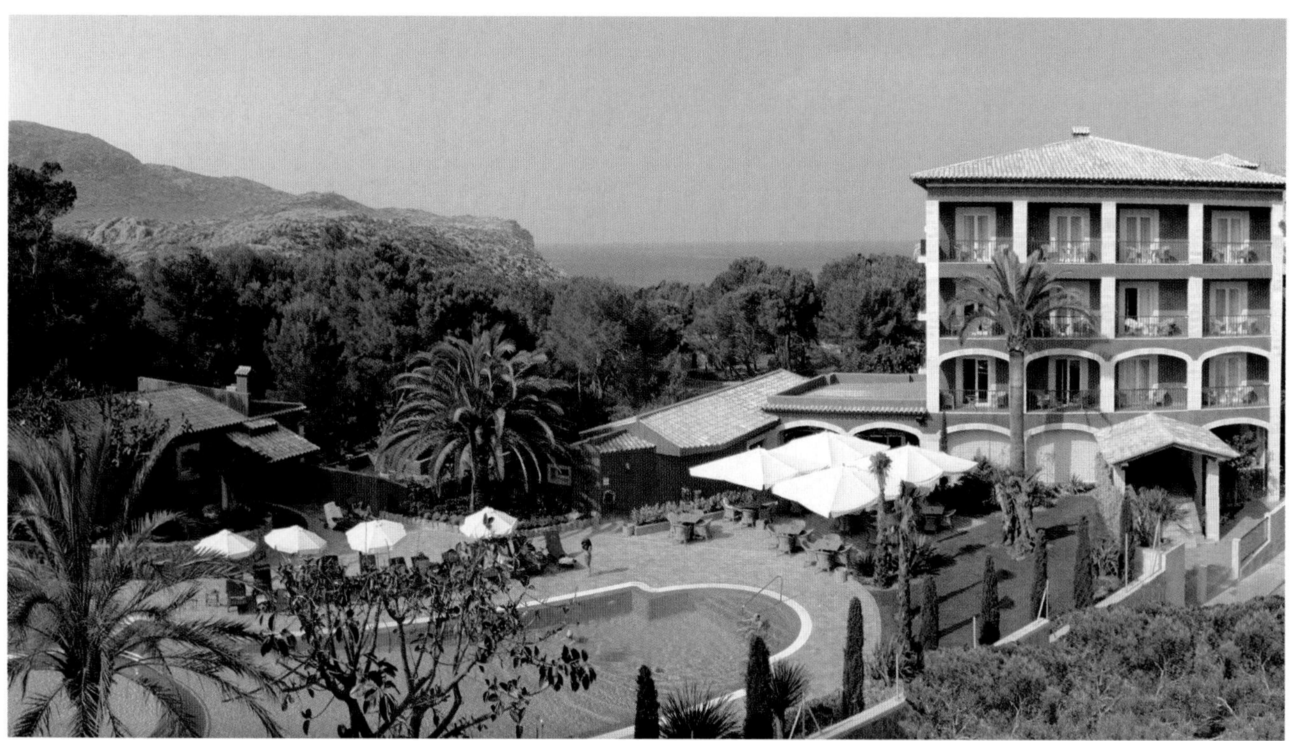

Hotel Cala Sant Vicenç

C/MARESSERS 2, CALA SANT VICENÇ, 07469 POLLENÇA, MALLORCA, SPAIN

Situated in a small, peaceful village, surrounded by superb gardens with a scenic backdrop of mountains sloping down to the calm, blues waters of the Mediterranean, this charming terracotta hotel with stone-coloured arches is an idyllic, restful retreat, just a 200-metre walk to the soft sands of a tiny, picturesque cove. The delightfully decorated bedrooms, many with balconies, provide every modern comfort and delicious cuisine is offered at the elegant gastronomic restaurant or the Italian Trattoria.

Situé dans un petit village tranquille, entouré de superbes jardins avec en arrière-plan des montagnes plongeant dans les eaux bleu calmes de la Méditerranée, ce charmant hôtel terracotta avec des arches couleur de pierre est un lieu idyllique et reposant à 200 mètres des sables blancs d'une crique pittoresque. Les chambres délicieusement décorées, dont beaucoup avec balcons, offrent tout le confort moderne. Une cuisine délicieuse est servie à l'élégant restaurant gastronomique ou la Trattoria italien.

Situado en una pequeña y tranquila aldea, rodeado de sorprendentes jardines con un espectacular fondo de montañas que se deslizan suavemente hacia las pacíficas y azules aguas del Mediterráneo, este encantador hotel de color rojizo con arcos de mares constituye un idílico refugio para el descanso, a sólo 200 metros a pie de las suaves arenas de una pequeña y pintoresca cala. Sus habitaciones de primorosa decoración, muchas de ellas provistas de balcones, proporcionan todas las modernas comodidades. Su deliciosa cocina puede degustarse en su elegante restaurante gastronómico o la Trattoria italia.

Our inspector loved: *The helpful staff.*

Directions: Palma Airport > motorway > Inca > Pollença > Puerto de Pollença > Hotel Cala Sant Vicenç hotel is signposted.

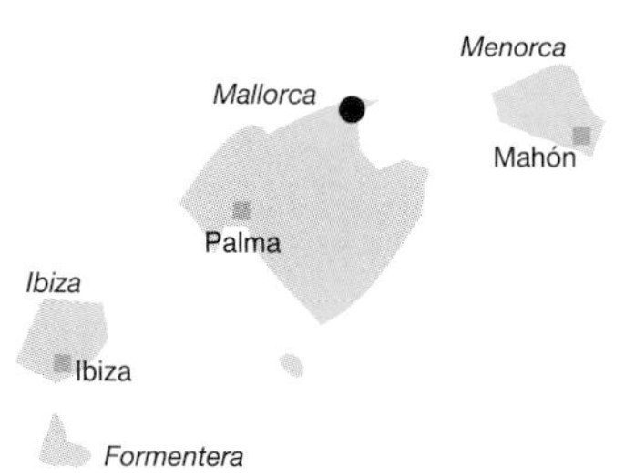

Web: www.johansens.com/hotelcala
E-mail: info@hotelcala.com
Tel: +34 971 53 02 50
Fax: +34 971 53 20 84

Price Guide: (excluding VAT, closed December - 21st March)
single €69-155
double €135-310

HOTEL DALT MURADA

C/ ALMUDAINA 6-A, 07001 PALMA DE MALLORCA, MALLORCA, BALEARIC ISLANDS

Situated in the gothic quarter of Palma and just a few metres away from the cathedral, this delightfully restored house dates back to the 16th century. A warm and friendly welcome awaits guests at this family-run hotel, which offers a simple Mediterranean chic combined with modern day luxuries. The rooms are carefully furnished with oil paintings, rugs, tapestries, traditional Majorcan glass lamps and antiques, and most incorporate giant Jacuzzi baths in the bathrooms.

Située dans le quartier gothique de Palma, à quelques mètres de la cathédrale, cette charmante maison restaurée du XVIe siècle offre à ses hôtes un accueil amical et chaleureux. Cet hôtel familial offre une élégance méditerranéenne sans prétentions à laquelle se mélange le confort moderne. Les chambre sont meublées avec soin: peintures à l'huile, plaids, tapisseries, lampes traditionnelles majorquines, antiquités, et la plupart des salles de bains possèdent une grande baignoire jacuzzi.

Situado en el barrio gótico de Palma y a pocos metros de la catedral, esta casa señorial data del siglo XVI. Administrado por una familia que le da una bienvenida cálida y amistosa, este hotel se caracteriza por un estilo mediterráneo combinado con todos los lujos modernos. Las habitaciones están amuebladas con todo esmero y con muebles de época: óleos, alfombras, tapices y lámparas del tradicional vidrio mallorquín. La mayoría de ellas tienen en los cuartos de baño enormes bañeras jacuzzi.

Our inspector loved: *The private house charm.*

Directions: Palma Airport > centre of the old town.

Web: www.johansens.com/daltmurada
E-mail: info@daltmurada.com
Tel: +34 971 425 300
Fax: +34 971 719 708

Price Guide:
double from €140
suite €236
penthouse €332

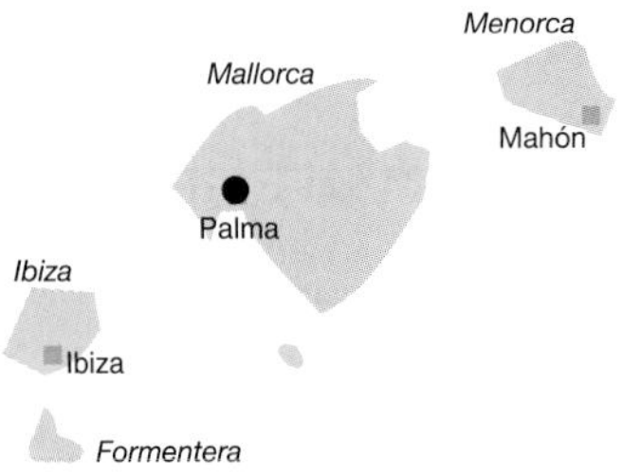

Menorca
Mallorca
Mahón
Palma
Ibiza
Ibiza
Formentera

Hotel Migjorn

POLIGONO 18, PARCELA 477, CAMPOS, MALLORCA, SPAIN

Set amidst 35 acres of beautiful countryside, this former farmhouse has been superbly converted into a luxurious, rural 4-star hotel with a warm family atmosphere. All of the 10 suites are decorated in a rustic, minimalist style and have kitchens as well as private terraces overlooking the gardens or swimming pool. A wide range of massages and facial treatments is available. Numerous secluded coves and white beaches are within easy reach, and guests may hire bicycles, practice water sports or play golf at a nearby golf course.

Situé au coeur d'une magnifique campagne de 14 ha, cette ancienne ferme a été transformée en un luxueux hôtel rural 4 étoiles à l'ambiance familiale chaleureuse. Chacune des 10 suites est décorée dans un style rustique minimaliste et possède cuisine et terrasse privée surplombant les jardins et la piscine. Un choix complet de soins du visage et de massages est disponible. De nombreuses criques sauvages et plages de sable blanc sont à proximité et les hôtes peuvent louer des vélos, pratiquer des sports nautiques ou jouer au golf sur le parcours voisin.

Emplazado en medio de 14 ha de bello paisaje rural, esta antigua granja ha sido magistralmente reconvertida en un lujoso hotel rural de 4 estrellas con un cálido ambiente familiar. Sus 10 suites están decoradas con estilo rústico minimalista y dispone tanto de cocinas como de terrazas privadas con vistas a jardines o a la piscina. El cliente tiene a su disposición una amplia variedad de masajes y tratamientos faciales. Existen también numerosas y recónditas bahías y blancas playas de fácil acceso. Los clientes pueden alquilar bicicletas, practicar deportes acuáticos o jugar al golf en un campo de golf cercano.

***Our inspector loved:** The enthusiasm of the owners to please their guests.*

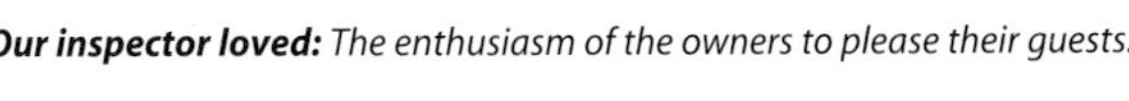

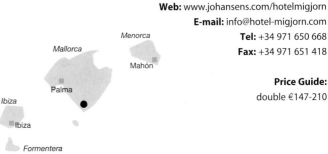

Directions: Palma Airport > motorway > Santanyi. Exit Campos > Calonia de Sant Jordi. Hotel is signposted on this road.

Web: www.johansens.com/hotelmigjorn
E-mail: info@hotel-migjorn.com
Tel: +34 971 650 668
Fax: +34 971 651 418

Price Guide:
double €147-210

SPAIN / BALEARIC ISLANDS (MALLORCA)

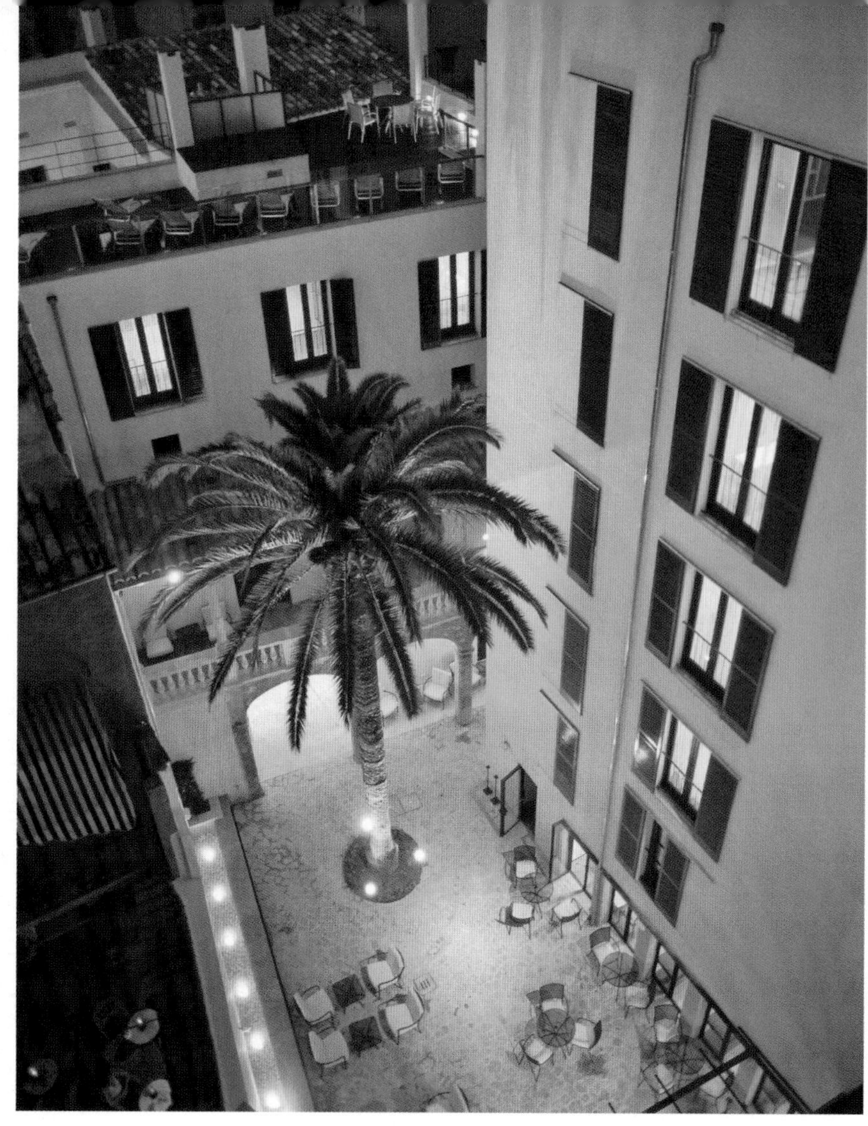

Hotel Tres

C/ APUNTADORES 3, 07012 PALMA DE MALLORCA, BALEARIC ISLANDS, SPAIN

450m from Palma's beautiful cathedral, this former 16th-century palace is a 4-star hotel that cleverly combines contemporary design with centuries-old remains. Original beams feature alongside marble flooring and modern white lines in the bedrooms. The honeymoon suite boasts a private roof terrace and Jacuzzi. Light meals and drinks are served in Hotel Tres Lounge Bar and a buffet breakfast is prepared each morning. Sun lovers will enjoy the roof terrace. A meeting room, filled with natural light and ergonomic chairs, accommodates 20.

A 450 m de la superbe cathédrale de Palma, cet ancien palais du XVIe siècle est un hôtel 4 étoiles qui combine astucieusement un design contemporain aux structures centenaires. Les poutres d'origine se mélangent aux sols en marbre et aux lignes modernes blanches de la chambre. La suite lune de miel possède une terrasse sur le toit et un jacuzzi. Des repas légers et des boissons sont servis au Lounge Bar de l'hôtel et un petit-déjeuner buffet est préparé tous les matins. Les amoureux du soleil profiteront de la terrasse. La salle de réunion avec lumière naturelle et sièges ergonomiques peut accueillir 20 personnes.

A 450 m de la bella catedral de Palma, este antiguo palacio del siglo XVI es hoy un hotel de 4 estrellas que combina con inteligencia el diseño contemporáneo con restos de varios siglos de antigüedad. Las vigas originales se juntan con suelos de mármol y modernas líneas blancas en las habitaciones. La suite de luna de miel dispone de azotea privada y jacuzzi. En el Hotel Tres Lounge Bar se sirven bebidas y comidas ligeras y todas las mañanas se prepara un desayuno buffet. Los amantes del sol disfrutarán de la azotea. La sala para reuniones, con luz natural y sillas ergonómicas, tiene capacidad para 20 personas.

***Our inspector loved:** Relaxing in the courtyard.*

Directions: Palma Airport > Palma > city centre.

Web: www.johansens.com/hoteltres
E-mail: reservation@hoteltres.com
Tel: +34 971 717 333
Fax: +34 971 717 372

Price Guide: (excluding VAT)
single from €140
double from €195
suite from €450

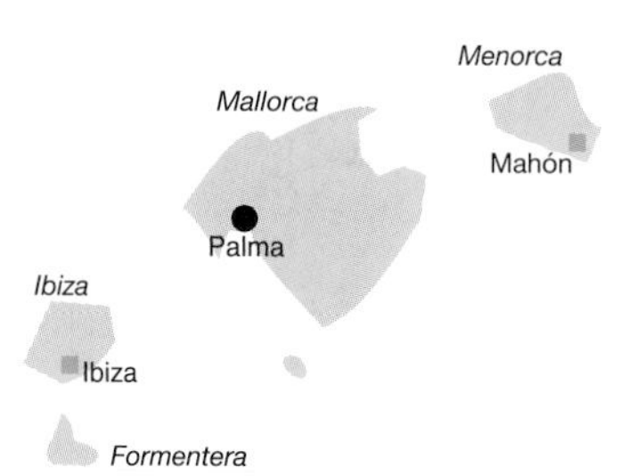

La Reserva Rotana

CAMI DE SA VALL, KM 3, APART. CORREOS 69, 07500 MANACOR, MALLORCA, SPAIN

Authentic Majorcan style, décor and furnishings combined with modern comforts and facilities have transformed this 17th-century mansion into a hotel of charm and elegance. Situated on a hill in the heart of a 300-acre finca, and surrounded by its own vineyard, olive groves and private 9-hole golf course, La Reserva Rotana offers the utmost in hospitality, service and relaxation. The interior is stunning, guest rooms are a delight and the international cuisine is of the highest quality served in the cool restaurant.

Un style, un décor et un mobilier majorquins authentiques combiné au confort et équipements moderne ont transformé cette demeure du XVIIe siècle en un hôtel de charme et d'élégance. Situé sur une colline au cœur d'une finca de près de 120 ha, entourée de son vignoble, oliveraie et d'un golf 9 trous. La Reserva Rotana offre le plus haut degré d'hospitalité, un excellent service et la meilleure détente possible. L'intérieur est superbe, les chambres sont un plaisir et la cuisine internationale, servie dans un restaurant délicieusement frais, est de la meilleure qualité.

El genuino estilo, decoración y mobiliario mallorquín combinado con la modernidad de sus instalaciones y comodidades han convertido esta mansión del siglo XVII en un encantador y elegante hotel. Situada sobre una colina en el corazón de una finca de 120 ha y rodeada de su propio viñedo, olivares y privado campo de golf de 9 hoyos, La Reserva Rotana ofrece lo mejor en hospitalidad, servicio y relax. Su interior es sorprendente, sus habitaciones son una maravilla y la cocina internacional, servida en su refrescante restaurante, es de una calidad suprema.

Our inspector loved: *The relaxed atmosphere.*

Directions: Palma Airport > Manacor > take the lateral lanes through the town > road to hotel is signposted.

Web: www.johansens.com/reservarotana
E-mail: info@reservarotana.com
Tel: +34 971 84 56 85
Fax: +34 971 55 52 58

Price Guide: (closed during January)
single €189-230
double €270-440
suite €418-475

           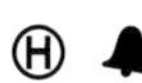

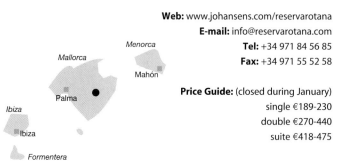

Palacio Ca Sa Galesa

CARRER DE MIRAMAR 8, 07001 PALMA DE MALLORCA, BALEARIC ISLANDS

This 16th-century palacio is located in the heart of the Gothic quarter in the centre of Palma and is only a 2-minute walk from the cathedral. Original stained glass, floor tiles, chandeliers and tapestries adorn the beautiful public rooms, whilst the comfortable bedrooms are classically decorated, some with a very cosy feel. Bathrooms offer a "bath menu" which features a choice of salts, oils, candles and music whilst the "massage menu" includes yoga and Tai Chi classes. The hotel boasts a small spa area complete with sauna and gymnasium; mountain bikes are available for excursions.

Ce palais du XVIe siècle est situé au cœur du quartier gothique de Palma et à deux pas de la cathédrale. Les vitraux originaux, des carreaux, des lustres et des tapisseries ornent les belles salles publiques, alors que les chambres sont décorées de façon classique, quelques-unes avec une ambiance très intime. Des hôtes ont le choix entre le "menu de bain" avec une sélection de sels, huiles, bougies et musique, et le "menu massage" qui incluit yoga et Tai Chi. L'hôtel s'enorgueillit d'un petit spa comprenant un sauna et une salle de remise en forme; des VTT sont disponibles pour des excursions.

Este palacio del siglo XVI se encuentra en el corazón del barrio gótico en pleno centro de Palma y a sólo 2 minutos de la catedral. Originales vidrieras de colores, un suelo embaldosado, lámparas de araña y tapices adornan sus salones comunes. Las cómodas habitaciones están decoradas al estilo clásico, algunas con un toque muy acogedor. Sus cuartos de baños ofrecen un "menú de baño" de sales de baño, aceites, velas y música así como un "menú de masajes" que incluye clases de yoga y Tai Chi. El hotel cuenta con una pequeña zona de spa completo con sauna y gimnasio, y bicicletas de montaña están disponibles para las excursiones.

***Our inspector loved:** Enjoying tea and cake at 4pm in the Monet kitchen.*

Directions: The nearest airport is Palma. Take the motorway to Palma Port and enter the old town behind the cathedral. At Plaça Santa Eulália press the button at the police bollard to gain entry to the street. Valet parking available.

Web: www.johansens.com/casagalesa
E-mail: reservas@palaciocasagalesa.com
Tel: +34 971 715 400
Fax: +34 971 721 579

Price Guide: (breakfast €21, excluding 7% VAT)
single €237
double €301-359
suite €403-435

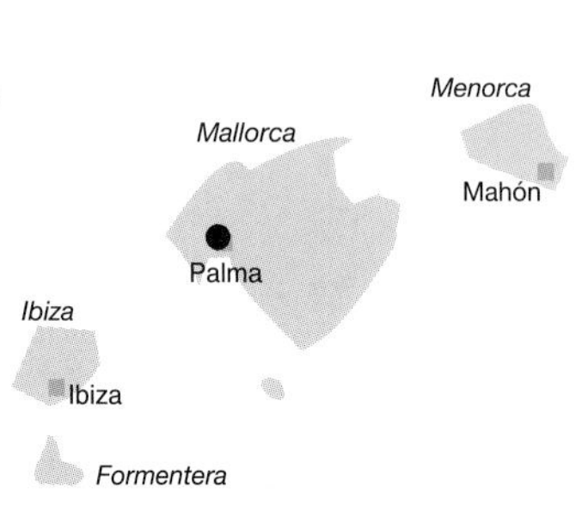

Read's Hotel & Vespasian Spa

CARRETERA VIEJO DE ALARO S/N, SANTA MARÍA 07320, MALLORCA, BALEARIC ISLANDS

Only 15 mins from Palma at the foot of the Tramuntana Mountains, surrounded by 20,000m² of wonderful landscaped gardens, its own vineyard and total tranquillity, this 500-year-old manor house, with stunning interior and beautiful frescoed walls, is a totally unique hotel. The perfect combination of beauty and ultimate luxury. Relax in the 600m² Vespasian Spa and restore mind and body to its natural harmony. Whether dining in the Michelin-starred restaurant or Bistro33, with summer terrace, the cuisine alone will persuade guests to return.

A seulement 15mn de Palma, au pied du massif montagneux de Tramuntana, au coeur de 20000m² de merveilleux jardins aménagés, de son vignoble et d'une tranquillité totale, cette demeure vieille de 500 ans au décor intérieur superbe et aux fresques murales remarquables, est un hôtel extraordinaire qui combine parfaitement beauté et luxe. Le Spa Vespasian avec ses 600m², invite à la relaxation, restaurant ainsi l'harmonie naturelle entre le corps et l'esprit. Sa cuisine seule, que ce soit au restaurant recommandé par Michelin ou au Bistro33 à la terrasse estivale, persuadera ses hôtes à revenir.

Esta casa señorial de 500 años de antigüedad, con su sorprendente decoración interior y los bellos frescos de las paredes, a sólo 15 minutos de Palma, al pie de las Montañas de Tramontana, rodeada de 20.000 m² de maravillosos jardines panorámicos, con su propio viñedo y con un ambiente de la más absoluta tranquilidad, constituye un singular y excepcional hotel. Es la perfecta combinación de belleza y lo último en lujo. El cliente podrá relajarse en su Vespasian Spa de 600 m² y descansar el cuerpo y el espíritu hasta lograr su perfecta armonía. Tanto si decide cenar en su restaurante galardonado con una estrella por Michelín, como si lo hace en su Bistro33, provisto de terraza de verano, será su carta por sí sola la que conseguirá convencerle para que regrese.

Our inspector loved: *The expanse of the green lawns.*

Directions: Palma Airport > motorway to Palma > motorway exit to Inca to Santa María.

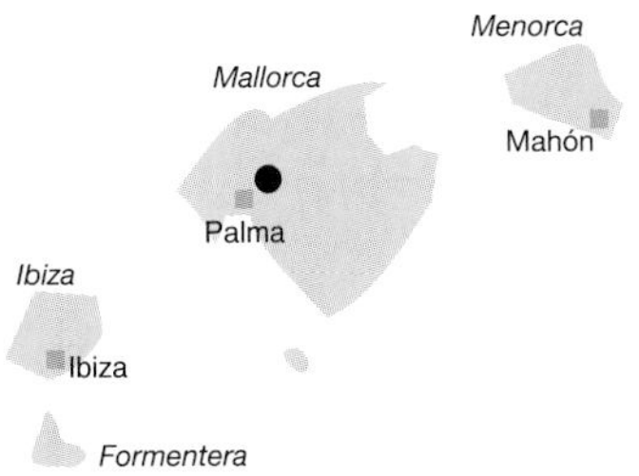

Menorca
Mallorca
Mahón
Palma
Ibiza
Ibiza
Formentera

Web: www.johansens.com/reads
E-mail: readshotel@readshotel.com
Tel: +34 971 14 02 61
Fax: +34 971 14 07 62

Price Guide: (excluding VAT)
double €250–460
suite €330–910

  23      35   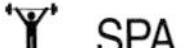  SPA 

Son Brull Hotel & Spa

CTRA. PALMA - POLLENÇA, MA 2200 - KM 49.8, 07460 POLLENÇA, MALLORCA, SPAIN

Directions: The nearest airport is Palma. Motorway > Inca > Pollença > hotel is signposted.

Web: www.johansens.com/sonbrull
E-mail: info@sonbrull.com
Tel: +34 971 53 53 53
Fax: +34 971 53 10 68

Price Guide: (excluding VAT, closed December - January)
single €210-293
double €247-345
suite €399-510

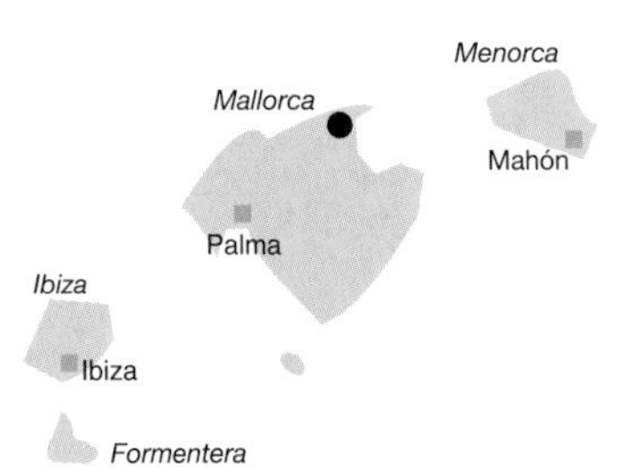

Originally a monastery dating back to the 18th century, this beautiful building has been painstakingly restored resulting in a stunning combination of contemporary design lovingly incorporated into this graceful building. A small meeting room can host receptions for up to 20 people, and the beautiful spa has both indoor and outdoor pools as well as 2 treatment rooms and sauna. There are many local markets to explore as well as the fascinating monastery at Lluc. A member of Relais & Châteaux since 2005.

A l'origine un monastère du XVIIIe siècle, ce magnifique bâtiment a été restauré avec une extrême précision créant un sublime mélange de design contemporain parfaitement intégré à cet élégant édifice. Une petite salle de réunion peut accueillir jusqu'à 20 personnes et le superbe spa possède piscines intérieure et extérieure ainsi que 2 salles de traitements et un sauna. Il y a de nombreux marchés locaux à explorer et le fascinant monastère de Lluc. Membre de Relais & Châteaux depuis 2005.

Este impresionante edificio, originalmente un monasterio del siglo XVIII se transformo tras un minucioso proceso de restauración en una perfecta combinación de diseño contemporáneo y elegancia. Dispone de un pequeño salón de reuniones con capacidad hasta 20 personas y un precioso spa que cuenta con piscina cubierta y exterior así como 2 salas de tratamientos y sauna. En los alrededores se pueden explorar los numerosos mercados locales así como el fascinante monasterio de Lluc. Miembro de la prestigiosa cadena Relais & Châteaux desde 2005.

Our inspector loved: *The contrast of ancient exteriors with minimalist interiors.*

Valldemossa Hotel & Restaurant

CTRA. VIEJA DE VALLDEMOSSA S/N, 07170 VALLDEMOSSA, MALLORCA, BALEARIC ISLANDS

This romantic stone-built Majorcan house offers spectacular views over the village, the Bay of Palma and the Tramuntana mountain range. Built over 100 years ago, it has been converted into a luxurious hotel with superb facilities. No expense has been spared in the bedrooms, which vary in size and décor and display wonderful touches such as specially made hand-painted lamps. Superb cuisine is served in the Valldemossa restaurant, and there is a large outdoor pool, a spa pool, sauna and various treatments for men and women available.

Cette maison majorquine romantique construite en pierre offre des vues spectaculaires sur le village, la baie de Palma et les montagnes de Tramuntana. Construite il y a plus de 100 ans, la maison a été convertie en hôtel luxueux avec des facilités superbes. Les chambres opulentes, qui ne manque aucun détail, varient en taille et décor et ont des agréments comme des lampes peintes à la main. Une cuisine superbe est servie dans le restaurant Valldemossa. L'hôtel dispose d'une grande piscine extérieure, d'une petite piscine de spa, d'un sauna ainsi que de nombreux soins pour hommes et femmes.

Esta romántica casa mallorquina de piedra proporciona espectaculares vistas al pueblo, a la Bahía de Palma y a la cordillera Tramuntana. Construida hace más de 100 años, ha sido convertida en un lujoso hotel de excelentes instalaciones. No se ha reparado en gastos en las habitaciones, que varían de tamaño y decoración y que despliegan detalles tales como las exclusivas lámparas pintadas a mano. El restaurante Valldemossa sirve excelentes platos culinarios, y el hotel también cuenta con una gran piscina exterior, una piscina cubierta en el spa, sauna y varios tratamientos disponibles para hombres y mujeres.

Our inspector loved: *The pretty gardens with ancient olive trees.*

Directions: Palma Airport > motorway to Palma > exit Valldemossa > hotel is signposted upon entry to the village.

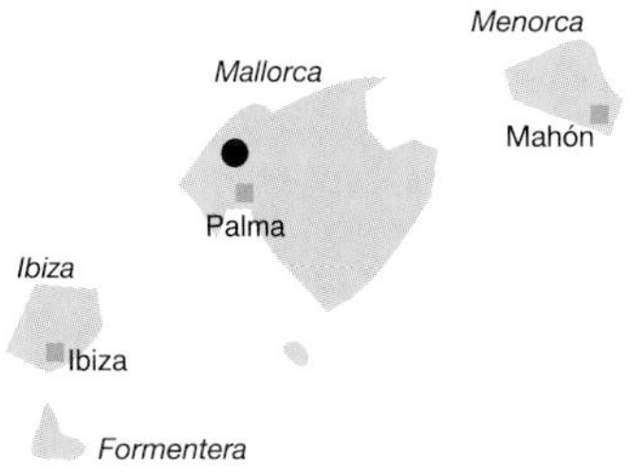

Web: www.johansens.com/valldemossa
E-mail: info@valldemossahotel.com
Tel: +34 971 61 26 26
Fax: +34 971 61 26 25

Menorca
Mallorca
Mahón
Palma
Ibiza
Ibiza
Formentera

Price Guide: (excluding VAT)
single €170-210
double €265-410
suite €313.79-390

Hotel Elba Palace Golf

URB. FUERTEVENTURA GOLF CLUB, CTRA. DE JANDIA, KM11, 35610 ANTIGUA, FUERTEVENTURA, CANARY ISLANDS

Directions: 8km from Fuerteventura Airport > Caleta de Fuste > golf course and hotel are signposted on the right.

Web: www.johansens.com/elbapalacegolfhotel
E-mail: epg@hoteleselba.com
Tel: +34 928 16 39 22
Fax: +34 928 16 39 23

Price Guide:
single €280-440
double €280–440
suite €380–540

Lanzarote
Arrecife
Tenerife
Santa Cruz
Las Palmas
Puerto del Rosario
Fuerteventura
Gran Canaria

This elegant hotel is surrounded by a garden and has its own swimming pool and an on-site 18-hole golf course. The warm and welcoming décor reflects traditional Canarian style, with wooden furniture and floors alongside hand-crafted ceilings and doors; a wonderful 4m spider lamp welcomes guests into the hall. The cellar, library and cards room are the perfet venues for meetings. The hotel also offers various beauty treatments, a fitness centre, sauna and Jacuzzi. Additional activities include windsurfing, diving, sea fishing and sailing.

Cet hôtel élégant est entouré d'un jardin et a son propre piscine et un terrain de golf de 18 trous sur site. Le décor est sobre et élégant grâce à une combinaison entre autres de parquets, de meubles, portes et plafonds en bois travaillés à la main. Dans l'entrée se tient un chandelier incroyable de près de 4 mètres. Le cellier à vin souterrain, la bibliothèque et la salle de jeu, sont les rendez-vous parfaits pour des réunions. L'hotel offre des traitements de beauté, un gymnase, le sauna et jacuzzi. La planche à voile, le plongée, le pêche en mer et voile sont disponibles aussi.

Este elegante hotel esta rodeado por una zona ajardinada y tiene su propia piscina y un campo de golf de 18 hoyos in situ. La decoración cálida y acogedora, está marcada por el tradicional estilo canario. Los suelos y muebles de madera noble, los techos y puertas artesanales se mezcian con una maravillosa araña de 4 metros que da la bienvenida al Hall. La bodega, la biblioteca y el salón para jugar a las cartas son los lugares ideales para las reuniones. Cuenta además con distintos tratamientos de belleza y con gimnasio, sauna y un jacuzzi. Actividades adicionales incluyen windsurf, submarinismo, pesca submarina o navegación.

Our inspector loved: *The classic English style of the bedrooms.*

Kempinski Atlantis Bahía Real

AVENIDA GRANDES PLAYAS S/N, 35660 CORRALEJO, FUERTEVENTURA, CANARY ISLANDS

Owned by the reputable Atlantis Hotels and Resorts Group in co-partnership with Kempinski Hotels & Resorts, Kempinski Hotel Atlantis Bahía Real opened on 1st November 2003. Adjacent to the sea and Las Dunas National Park, this Canarian hotel boasts magnificent views across Lobos Island and Lanzarote. All 242 bedrooms have terraces or balconies, and 5 restaurants serve national, gourmet, Italian and Japanese cuisine. The Spa Bahia Vital offers a wide range of health and beauty treatments (clients must be 16 years old and over) specialising in hydrotherapy.

Kempinski Hotel Atlantis Bahía Real, qui appartient au groupe bien connu Atlantis Hotels and Resorts, en co-gestion avec Kempinski Hotels & Resorts, a ouvert le 1er novembre 2003. Juste à coté de la mer et du Parc National de Las Dunas, cet hôtel canarien offre des vues imprenables sur l'île de Lobos et Lanzarote. Les 242 chambres sont dotées de terrasses ou balcons et 5 restaurants servent une cuisine nationale, gourmet, italienne et japonaise. Le Spa Bahia Vital offre toute une gamme de traitements de beauté et de santé, spécialisés en hydrothérapie (l'âge minimum est de 16 ans).

Perteneciente al afamado grupo Atlantis Hotels y Resorts y co-gestionado con Kempinski Hotels & Resorts, el Kempinski Hotel Atlantis Bahía Real se inauguró el 1 de noviembre del 2003. Contiguo al mar y al Parque Nacional Las Dunas, este hotel canario exhibe magníficas vistas de la isla Lobos y Lanzarote. Sus 242 habitaciones tienen terrazas o balcones, 5 restaurantes donde se sirven comida nacional, gourmet, italiana y japonesa. El Spa Bahía Vital ofrece una amplia variedad de tratamientos de salud y belleza (entrada a mayores de 16 años) con especialidad en hidroterapia.

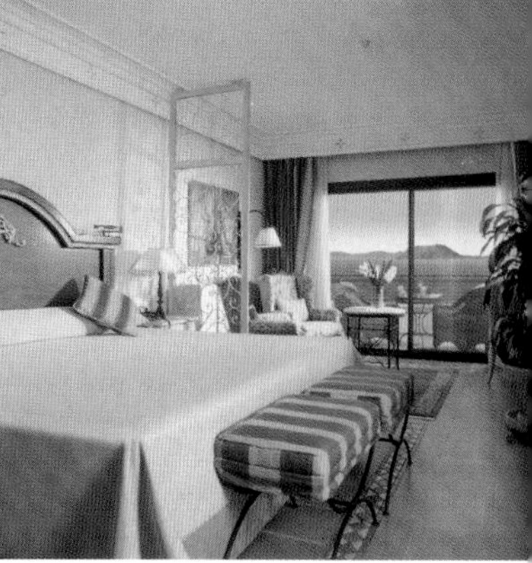

Directions: Fuerteventura Airport Puerto del Rosario > Corralejo > hotel.

Web: www.johansens.com/atlantisbahiareal
E-mail: info.bahiareal@kempinski.com
Tel: +34 928 53 64 44
Fax: +34 928 53 75 75

Lanzarote
Arrecife
Tenerife
Santa Cruz
Las Palmas
Puerto del Rosario
Fuerteventura
Gran Canaria

Price Guide:
upon request

Our inspector loved: *Relaxing in the spa.*

 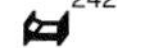 242     350       SPA 

Gran Hotel Lopesan Costa Meloneras

C/MAR MEDITERRÁNEO 1, 35100 MASPALOMAS, GRAN CANARIA, CANARY ISLANDS

This hotel retains a sense of individuality and reflects the Colonial and Canarian architecture of the island. Spacious public areas with exotic furniture and painted tile floors lead to beautifully landscaped gardens covering 76,000m², numerous swimming pools and the beach. Activities such as golf and water sports are nearby and the spa offers a superb variety of water, massage and innovative treatments. A wide selection of restaurants and bars all offer their own distinctive ambience.

Cet hôtel retient un sens d'individualité et ses décors reflètent l'architecture coloniale et canarienne de l'île. Les espaces publiques spacieux emplis de meubles exotiques et aux carrelages peints conduisent à de beaux jardins aménagés de 76 000 m² à de nombreuses piscines et à la plage. Des activités telles que golf et sports nautiques sont à potée, ainsi qu'un spa offrant une variété superbe comprenant des traitements innovatifs, d'eau et de massage. Il existe également une vaste sélection de restaurants et de bars qui offrent tous leur propre ambience.

Este hotel mantiene una cierta singularidad y refleja la arquitectura colonial y canaria de la isla. Las espaciosas zonas comunes con su exótico mobiliario y los suelos de baldosas pintadas nos llevan a bonitos jardines paisajistas de 76.000 m², a numerosas piscinas y a la playa. La práctica del golf y de los deportes acuáticos están muy próximos al hotel, tambien hay un spa que ofrece una gran variedad de masajes, agua y tratamientos innovadores. Existen además una selección de restaurantes y bares con una gran oferta de selecto ambiente.

Our inspector loved: *The extensive gardens.*

Directions: From Gran Canaria Airport > motorway GCI to Pasito Blanca > follow signs to Meloneras.

Web: www.johansens.com/costameloneras
E-mail: info.ghcm@lopesanhr.com
Tel: +34 928 12 81 00
Fax: +34 928 12 81 22

Price Guide: (half board, per person)
single from €126
double from €73
junior suite from €101

Lanzarote
Arrecife
Tenerife
Santa Cruz
Las Palmas
Puerto del Rosario
Fuerteventura
Gran Canaria

Gran Hotel Lopesan Villa del Conde

C/Mar Mediterráneo 7, Urbanización Costa Meloneras, 35100 Maspalomas, Gran Canaria, Canary Islands

This 5-star complex stands within a beautiful tropical garden at the southernmost tip of the island. Designed as a replica Canarian village, the brightly coloured houses comprise spacious, elegantly furnished rooms and suites, all with a dressing room and balcony. 4 restaurants and 5 bars provide a variety of cuisine including an Italian à la carte menu and freshly prepared grilled food. Savour spectacular views of the coast whilst playing on the new 18 hole par 71 golf course, and enjoy the golf school, club house, golf shop, putting green and driving range.

Ce complexe 5 étoiles se dresse au milieu de magnifiques jardins tropicaux à l'extrémité sud de l'île. Conçu comme un village des Canaries, les maisons aux couleurs vives sont spacieuses et élégamment meublées et chaque chambre et suite possèdent un dressing et balcon. 4 restaurants et 5 bars proposent un vaste choix de cuisines comprenant des mets Italiens et des produits fraîchement grillés. Les hôtes peuvent admirer les vues spcectaculaires de la côte tout en jouant sur le nouveau parcours de golf par 71 ou profiter de l'école de golf, le club house, le pro shop, le putting green et le practice.

Este complejo de 5 estrellas se ubica en un majestuoso jardín tropical en el punto más sureño de la isla. Diseñado como una réplica de un pueblo canario con casas de vivos colores que albergan habitaciones y suites espaciosas, elegantemente amuebladas y incluyen vestidor y balcón. 4 restaurantes y 5 bares ofrecen gran variedad culinaria, incluyendo un menú italiano y alimentos frescos a la plancha. Deléitese con vistas espectaculares mientras juega en el nuevo campo de golf de 18 hoyos par 71 y aprovéchese de la escuela de golf, del club y tienda de golf, del putting green y del campo de practicas.

Our inspector loved: *The elegant new Thalasso.*

Directions: Gran Canaria Airport > GCI motorway to Pasito Blanco > follow signs to Meloneras.

Web: www.johansens.com/lopesanconde
E-mail: info.ghvc@lopesanhr.com
Tel: +34 928 563 200
Fax: +34 928 563 222

Lanzarote
Arrecife
Tenerife
Santa Cruz
Las Palmas
Puerto del Rosario
Fuerteventura
Gran Canaria

Price Guide: (half board, per person)
single from €141
double from €83
junior suite from €123

  561   120       SPA

Caserío de Mozaga

MOZAGA 8, 35562 SAN BARTOLOMÉ, LANZAROTE, CANARY ISLANDS

Directions: Lanzarote Airport > Arecife > follow signs to San Bartolomé > Mozaga > hotel is signposted upon entering the village.

Web: www.johansens.com/caseriodemozaga
E-mail: reservas@caseriodemozaga.com
Tel: +34 928 520 060
Fax: +34 928 522 029

Price Guide: (room only, excluding VAT) prices on request.

In the heart of the agricultural centre of Lanzarote, this former farmhouse, constructed at the end of the 18th century, is now a home from home for travellers searching for peaceful, rustic accommodation providing every modern convenience. Each double room and the single are filled with antique furnishings and feature exposed beams. The restaurant, which is popular with locals, provides an excellent contemporary, Mediterranean seasonal menu that is both traditional and healthy. Local fishing, riding and cycling excursions can be arranged.

Au cœur du centre agricole de Lanzarote, cette ancienne ferme, construite à la fin du XVIIIe siècle abrite maintenant un second chez-soi aux voyageurs à la recherche d'un logement paisible, rustique et équipé de tout le confort moderne. Toutes les chambres, doubles et simples, ont un mobilier ancien et des poutres apparentes. Le restaurant, populaire auprès des habitants de la région, sert une excellente et saine cuisine méditerranéenne, mélange de contemporain et traditionnel. Pêche locale, randonnées cyclistes et équestres peuvent être organisées.

Sito en el corazón agrícola de Lanzarote, fue una casa de campo construida a finales del siglo XVIII que ahora ofrece un ambiente hogareño a los viajeros que buscan alojamiento tranquilo y rústico con todo el confort moderno. Cada habitación doble y sencilla está decorada con mobiliario antiguo y vigas vistas. El restaurante popular con la gente local ofrece un excelente menú mediterráneo que es a la vez tradicional y sano. Excursiones para pescar, montar a caballo y hacer ciclismo se pueden organizar.

***Our inspector loved:** Taking lunch in the elegant restaurant overlooking Lanzarote's wild countryside.*

Princesa Yaiza Suite Hotel Resort

Avenida Papagayo S/N, 35570 Playa Blanca, Yaiza, Lanzarote, Canary Islands

This modern resort with towers, domes, and spacious balconies overlooks Playa Blanca beach. With restful gardens and a stylish interior, Princesa Yaiza provides everything for the discerning guest. All suites and superior double rooms have tasteful décor, luxury bathrooms and extensive facilities; many enjoy sea views. The variety of restaurants offers everything from Oriental to Mediterranean cuisine; Isla de Lobos has an à la carte menu. The spa offers Thalasso therapy, a variety of massages, chocolate wraps and numerous treatments.

Ce complexe moderne avec ses tours, ses dômes et ses larges balcons surplombe la plage de Playa Blanca. Avec ses jardins reposants et une décoration de goût, le Princesa Yaiza offre tout ce que désire un client avisé. Les suites et chambres doubles de catégorie supérieure ont de somptueuses salles de bains et de nombreux équipements; beaucoup offrent la vue sur la mer. La grande variété de cuisines proposée, d'orientale à méditerrannéenne, satisfait tout les goûts. Le restaurant Isla de Lobos propose un menu à la carte. Le centre thermal offre thalassothérapie, cacaothérapie, divers massages et de nombreux autres traitements.

En este moderno resort destacan torres, cúpulas y balcones que dan a Playa Blanca. Con sus tranquilos jardines y un estilo interior, Princesa Yaiza ofrece a su entendido huésped todo lo que pudiera desear. Todas las suites y las habitaciones dobles superiores están amuebladas y decoradas con un exquisito gusto además de poseer baños lujosos y un sinfín de instalaciones, muchas tienen vistas al mar. Hay una gran variedad de restaurantes, que ofrecen desde la cocina oriental hasta la mediterránea; Isla de Lobos tiene un menu a la carta. En el spa, puede disfrutar de talasoterapia, una variedad de masajes, coberturas de chocolate y numerosos tratamientos.

Our inspector loved: *The warm welcome.*

Directions: Lanzarote Airport > Yaiza > Playa Blanca.

Web: www.johansens.com/yaiza
E-mail: info@princesayaiza.com
Tel: +34 928 519 222
Fax: +34 928 519 179

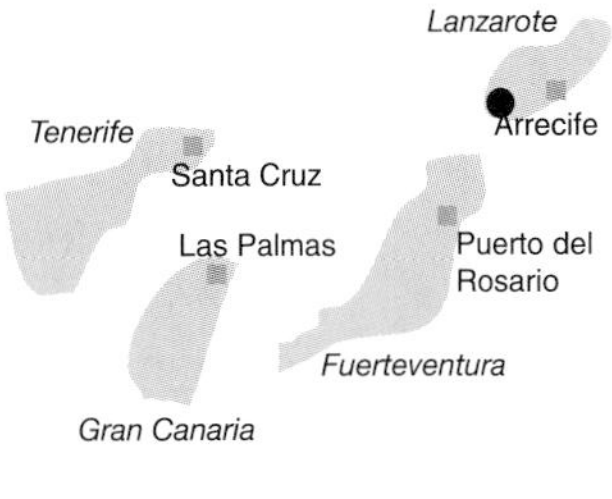

Lanzarote
Arrecife
Tenerife
Santa Cruz
Las Palmas
Puerto del Rosario
Fuerteventura
Gran Canaria

Price Guide: (room only, excluding VAT)
single €167-247
double €227-323
suite €317-1,502

ABAMA

CARRETERA GENERAL TF-47, KM 9, 38687 GUÍA DE ISORA, TENERIFE, CANARY ISLANDS

Directions: In Guía de Isora, on the West Coast of Tenerife. Take the motorway to Adeje > Playa de San Juan. Transfers from the airport can be arranged.

Web: www.johansens.com/abama
E-mail: info@abamahotelresort.com
Tel: +34 922 126 000
Fax: +34 922 126 100

Price Guide: (room only, excluding VAT)
citadele: double from €308
suite from €600
villa: double from €526
suite from €750

Located on the ocean front, on the west coast of Tenerife, Abama stands in a charming, green setting surrounded by banana plantations. Built into hills that lead down to a semi-private beach, which is only accessed via the hotel's private road, the beautifully appointed rooms are decorated in beige, dark brown and rust colours inspired by African design. Attentive, personal service and great attention to detail are guaranteed. Abama includes a golf course, Wellness & Spa Centre and fine gastronomy supervised by 3-Star Michelin Chef Martín Berasategui.

Situé en bord de mer, Abama se dresse dans un environnement rural entouré de plantations de bananiers. Construites sur des collines qui mènent à une plage semi-privée seulement accessible par la route de l'hôtel, les superbes chambres sont décorées dans des tons de beige, de marrons foncés et de couleurs rouille d'inspiration Africaine. Un service personnel, attentif et un grand souci du détail sont garantis. Abama dispose, entre autre, d´un terrain de golf, d´un Wellness & Spa Centre et gastronomique dirigé par le grand chef 3 étoiles Michelin Martín Berasategui.

Frente al océano, en la costa oeste de Tenerife, Abama se encuentra en un encantador entorno natural rodeado de plantaciones plataneras. Las habitaciones, de bello acabado, construidas sobre unas colinas que descienden hasta una playa semi-privada a la que sólo se tiene acceso por el camino privado del hotel, están decoradas en colores beige, marrón oscuro y teja de inspiración africana. Abama garantiza un servicio atento y personalizado así como una escrupulosa atención a los pequeños detalles. Abama cuenta con un campo de golf, un Centro Wellness y Spa y alta cocina supervisada por el chef 3 estrellas Michelín, Martín Berasategui.

Our inspector loved: *The hand-laid mosaic floors on the terraces.*

420    400    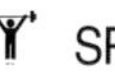  SPA   

Hotel Jardín Tropical

Calle Gran Bretaña, 38670 Costa Adeje, Tenerife, Canary Islands

Built just 15 years ago, and recently completely renovated, this magnificent Moorish palace with its brilliant white walls is enveloped by the exotic green foliage of its subtropical garden interspersed with blue pools and colourful flowers. All the rooms have been glamorously redecorated, displaying cool luxury, and the exclusive Las Adelfas Suites are phenomenal. Guests are spoilt for choice with the cuisine and may enjoy everything from poolside snacks to a gourmet feast. Beauty treatments are available in Tropical Wellness.

Construit il y a tout juste 15 ans et récemment renové en totalité magnifique palais mauresque avec ses murs blancs se dresse au milieu d'un jardin exotique parsemé de bassins azurs et de fleurs colorées. Toutes les chambres ont été redécorées d'un style splendide et affichent un luxe sobre, et les prestigieuses suites Las Adelfas sont remarquables. Les hôtes sont gâtés au niveau culinaire et pourront se régaler du simple snack au bord de la piscine jusqu'au festin gastronomique. Le centre Tropical Wellness offre des soins de beauté.

Este magnífico palacio árabe con sus impresionantes paredes blancas envueltas por el exótico follaje verde de su jardín tropical entremezclado con el azul de las piscinas y las flores multicolores, fue construido hace sólo 15 años y acaba de ser completamente renovado. Todas las habitaciones han sido lujosamente redecoradas y las exclusivas suites Las Adelfas son impresionantes. Los huéspedes gozan de tal variedad culinaria que pueden degustar desde unas tapas junto a la piscina hasta un festín gourmet. Tratamientos de belleza están disponibles en el centro Tropical Wellness.

Our inspector loved: *Enjoying a massage whilst basking in the sun.*

Directions: Airport > Tenerife South > motorway - Playa Americas > exit 29, San Eugenio.

Lanzarote
Tenerife
Arrecife
Santa Cruz
Las Palmas
Puerto del Rosario
Fuerteventura
Gran Canaria

Web: www.johansens.com/jardintropical
E-mail: reservas@jardin-tropical.com
Tel: +34 922 74 60 00
Fax: +34 922 74 60 60

Price Guide: (excluding VAT)
single €72-196
double/twin €102-340
junior suite €202-482
suite €238-566

403 400

SPAIN / CANARY ISLANDS (TENERIFE)

Gran Hotel Bahía del Duque Resort ★★★★★ G.Lujo

C/ALCALDE WALTER PAETZMANN, S/N, 38660 COSTA ADEJE, TENERIFE, CANARY ISLANDS

Directions: The nearest airport is Tenerife South. Motorway to Playa de las Américas > San Eugenio exit.

Web: www.johansens.com/granhotelbahiadelduque
E-mail: reservations@bahia-duque.com
Tel: +34 922 74 69 00
Fax: +34 922 74 69 16

Price Guide: (room only, excluding VAT)
single €229–415
double/twin €248–444
suite €452–2,103

This hotel is a private romantic village created on a gentle hill sloping down to the sea. 20 houses in turn-of-the-century Canarian architecture form this prestigious complex in a large estate with sculptured terraces and pools. The furniture has been specially designed, the floors are cool Spanish tiles and the bathrooms are luxurious. Descending towards the coast, guests will find a patio surrounded by 10 restaurants. The newly opened "El Mirador" section, decorated in soft, understated colours, offers its own restaurants and 8 swimming pools.

Cet hôtel est un village romantique privé créé sur une pente douce descendant sur la mer. 20 maisons qui reflètent l'architecture canarienne du début du siècle forment un complexe prestigieux au milieu d'une grande propriété agrémentée de terrasses ornées et de piscines. Les meubles ont été spécialement conçus, les sols sont de céramiques espagnoles et les salles de bain sont luxueuses. En descendant vers la côte, les visiteurs trouveront un patio et 10 restaurants. La nouvelle section "El Mirador" est décorée en couleurs douces et dispose de ses propres restaurants et 8 piscines.

Este hotel es en realidad una aldea romántica creada sobre una suave colina que desciende hacia el mar. 20 casas construidas al estilo Canario de fin de siglo forman este prestigioso complejo hotelero en una grande finca repleta de esculturales terrazas y piscinas. Los muebles han sido diseñados expresamente para el hotel, los suelos son de frescos azulejos y los baños son lujosos. Bajando hacia la costa se encuentra un patio rodeado de 10 restaurantes. Una zona nueva, El Mirador, decorada con colores tenues, dispone de sus propios restaurantes y 8 piscinas.

Our inspector loved: *Taking an evening stroll around the illuminated gardens.*

Hotel Las Madrigueras

GOLF LAS AMÉRICAS, 38660 PLAYA DE LAS AMÉRICAS, TENERIFE, CANARY ISLANDS

Surrounded by the 222-acre Las Américas golf course, this 5-star hotel is 10 minutes from Playa de Las Américas. Furnished with wooden flooring and marble against soothing colour schemes, the bedrooms and luxury suites are spacious and enjoy magnificent views. Light lunch may be taken in Belle Vue terrace restaurant whilst Bogey restaurant serves an à la carte menu in the evening. Enjoy the free spa facilities and fitness centre or simply stroll down to the beach. Guests are entitled to discounts on green fees and complimentary use of a golf buggy.

Entouré par les 90 ha du parcours de golf Las Americas, cet hôtel 5* est à 10 minutes de la Playa de las Américas. Equipées de parquets et de marbre et décorées dans des tons apaisants, les chambres et suites sont spacieuses et offrent de superbes vues. La terrasse du restaurant Belle Vue est idéale pour un déjeuner léger tandis que le restaurant Bogey propose un service à la carte le soir. Les clients peuvent profiter du spa gratuit et du centre de remise en forme ou se balader jusqu'à la plage. Ils peuvent également bénéficier de remise sur les green fees et d'un buggy de golf gratuit.

Rodeado por el campo de golf Las Américas, de 90 ha, este hotel de 5 estrellas está a 10 minutos de la Playa de las Américas. Con suelos de madera y mármol que contrastan con una gama de colores suaves, las habitaciones y suites de lujo son espaciosas y disfrutan de magníficas vistas. Se pueden degustar comidas ligeras a mediodía en el restaurante-terraza Belle Vue mientras que por la noche se sirve menú a la carta en el restaurante Bogey. Disfrute de las prestaciones del spa gratuitas y del centro fitness o simplemente baje a dar un paseo a la playa. Los huéspedes tienen derecho a descuentos especiales en los green fees y uso gratuito de una calesa de golf.

Our inspector loved: *The quiet and exclusive atmosphere.*

Directions: Tenerife South Airport > TF1 motorway > exit 29 > hotel is situated on the golf course, Las Américas.

Web: www.johansens.com/madrigueras
E-mail: reservas@hotel-lasmadrigueras.com
Tel: +34 922 77 78 18
Fax: +34 922 77 78 19

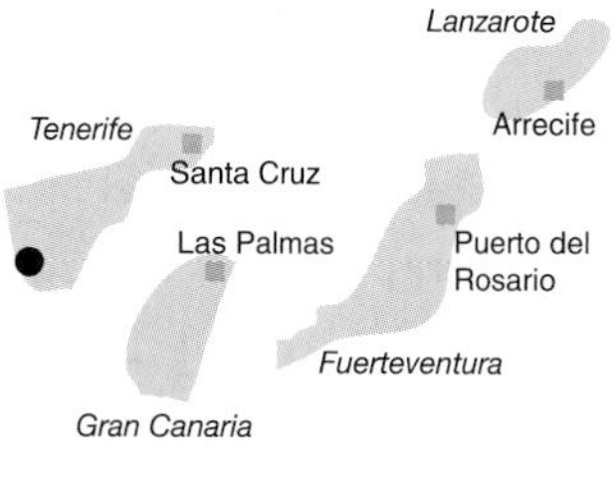

Lanzarote
Arrecife
Tenerife
Santa Cruz
Las Palmas
Puerto del Rosario
Fuerteventura
Gran Canaria

Price Guide:
(closed during August, excluding VAT)
double (single occupancy) €175
double €225
suite €475-700

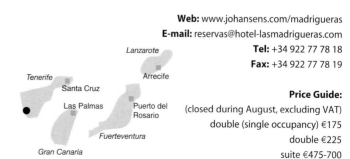

  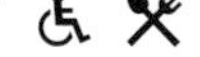        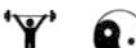   

JARDÍN DE LA PAZ

CALLE DE ACENTEJO 48-52, 38370 LA MATANZA, TENERIFE, CANARY ISLANDS

Directions: Airport >Tenerife north > motorway - Puerto de la Cruz > at La Matanza take road parallel to the sea > the hotel is signposted.

Web: www.johansens.com/jardindelapaz
E-mail: info@jardin-de-la-paz.com
Tel: +34 922 578 818
Fax: +34 922 578 436

Price Guide: (room only)
studio €170
apartment (1 bedroom) €180-190
apartment (2 bedrooms) €200
half villa (2 bedrooms) €240
villa (2 bedrooms) €390

Lanzarote
Arrecife
Tenerife
Santa Cruz
Las Palmas
Puerto del Rosario
Fuerteventura
Gran Canaria

Located within quiet terraced gardens overlooking the ocean, Jardín de la Paz features gorgeous 1 and 2-bedroom apartments and villas that are spacious and filled with light. Each has a balcony or garden with awe-inspiring views, fully-equipped modern kitchens and is complemented by warm pastel hues. For complete relaxation, there is a beauty room where guests can enjoy a massage or manicure. 2 crystal clear pools are ideal for cooling off on a warm day.

Situé sur de calmes jardins en terrasses surplombant l'océan, Jardín de la Paz offre de sublimes appartements et villas 1 ou 2 chambres, spacieux et remplis de lumière. Chacun possède balcon ou jardin avec des vues impressionnantes, des cuisines équipées modernes et sont décorés de chaleureuses nuances de pastels. Pour une relaxation totale, il y a un salon de beauté où les hôtes peuvent s'offrir un massage ou une manucure. Les 2 piscines cristallines sont l'endroit idéal pour se rafraîchir après une chaude journée.

Inmerso en una zona tranquila de jardines en terraza y con vistas al océano, Jardín de la Paz pone a disposición de sus clientes excelentes apartamentos y villas de 1 y 2 habitaciones, todos ellos espaciosos y luminosos. Todos los apartamentos, acabados en cálidos tonos pastel, tienen un balcón o jardín con sobrecogedoras vistas y cocina moderna totalmente equipada. Para conseguir una total relajación, Jardín de la Paz dispone también de un salón de belleza donde los clientes pueden disfrutar de un masaje o hacerse la manicura. Sus 2 piscinas de agua cristalina son ideales para refrescarse en los días de calor.

Our inspector loved: *The tropical gardens overlooking the ocean.*

Finca Canturias

CTRA. ALCAUDETE - CALERA, KM 12, 45660 BELVÍS DE LA JARA, TOLEDO, SPAIN

Overlooking the River Tajo and magnificent rolling countryside and distant mountains, Finca Canturias is a spectacular rural retreat. Set within a country estate in the province of Toledo, the 12 guest rooms provide extremely comfortable accommodation decorated in a rustic style featuring wooden timber beams and ceramic tiles. The restaurant serves imaginative regional cuisine and a varied wine list, whilst the café/bar provides lighter meals. An extensive range of outdoor activities can be arranged, such as rambling and 4x4 excursions. There is also an equestrian centre.

Surplombant la rivière Tajo et le superbe paysage vallonné, Finca Canturias est un magnifique refuge de campagne. Situé dans la province de Toledo, dans un domaine, les 12 chambres offrent un hébergement très confortable et sont décorées dans un style rustique composé de poutres en bois et de carrelage. Une cuisine régionale imaginative et une liste de vins variés sont proposés au restaurant et des plats plus légers sont offerts au café/bar. De nombreuses activités extérieures peuvent être organisées telles que des randonnées à pied ou en 4x4. Il y a aussi un centre équestre.

Finca Canturias es un espectacular refugio rural en una finca rústica de la provincia de Toledo, con vistas al río Tajo, al magnífico paisaje ondulado y a las montañas más lejanas. Sus 12 habitaciones decoradas en un estilo rústico con vigas de madera y baldosas de cerámica proporcionan un confort extremado. El restaurante sirve cocina regional imaginativa y una variada lista de vinos, mientras que el café bar ofrece comidas ligeras. Todo esto se complementa con una extensa variedad de actividades al aire libre que se pueden organizar, tales como senderismo y excursiones 4 X 4. También existe un centro ecuestre.

Directions: From Madrid > N-V motorway heading west > pass Talavera de la Reina > Calera y Chozas > follow Alcaudete de la Jara > the hotel is on a country estate at Km 12.

Web: www.johansens.com/canturias
E-mail: reservas@canturias.com
Tel: +34 925 59 41 08
Fax: +34 925 59 4107

Price Guide:
double €100
suite €150-200

Our inspector loved: *The unique hand-crafted chestnut wood bed heads.*

Hotel Rector

C/RECTOR ESPERABÉ 10–APARTADO 399, 37008 SALAMANCA, SPAIN

Directions: The nearest airports are Madrid and Valladolid. The hotel is within walking distance of the city centre.

Web: www.johansens.com/rector
E-mail: hotelrector@telefonica.net
Tel: +34 923 21 84 82
Fax: +34 923 21 40 08

Price Guide: (breakfast €11, excluding VAT, parking €12 per day)
double/twin €116-145
double/twin de luxe €140-175
suite €152-190

This exclusive hotel stands by the walls of the citadel looking up to the cathedral, a magnificent golden vision at night when floodlit. The interior looks cool and elegant with archways between the spacious reception hall and the welcoming bar. Unique features in the main salon are 2 exquisite modern stained glass windows. There are 13 bedrooms, delightfully furnished with marble bathrooms. Breakfast is served in the hotel, and for dinner, there are numerous restaurants in the vicinity. Salamanca has been named City of Culture.

Cet hôtel exclusif se dresse à côté des remparts de la citadelle; elle même dominée par la cathédrale, qui devient une vision magique lorsqu'illuminée la nuit. L'intérieur est frais et élégant, avec de belles voûtes qui séparent le spacieux hall de réception et le bar accueillant. Le salon principal est orné de 2 ravissants vitraux modernes. L'hôtel compte 13 chambres, délicieusement meublées avec salles de bain en marbre. Le petit déjeuner est servi à l'hôtel et de nombreux restaurants sont situés à proximité. Salamanca a été appellé Ville Culturelle.

Este exclusivo hotel junto a las murallas del alcázar con vistas a la catedral, ofrece una magnifica panorámica nocturna cuando ésta encendida. El interior tiene un aspecto elegante y tranquilo con arcos entre la espaciosa zona de recepción y el acogedor bar. En el salón principal tiene como característica única 2 exquisitas vidrieras de colores, modernas. Consta de 13 habitaciones amuebladas esmeradamente con cuartos de baño en mármol. El desayuno se sirve en el hotel y para cenar existen numerosos restaurantes próximos. Salamanca ha sido nombrada Ciudad de la Cultura.

Our inspector loved: *The impeccable neatness of this hotel.*

Castillo de Buen Amor

CARRETERA NATIONAL 630 KM 317.6, 37799 TOPAS, SALAMANCA, SPAIN

This is a 15th-century castle with enough elegance, charm and atmosphere to satisfy the most discerning visitor. Majestic stone walls are topped with imposing battlements, a moat with swimming pool. The cool interior has all the attributes of a tranquil past era combined with the luxurious comforts of the 21st century. Public rooms are tall and spacious, their natural walls decorated with fine paintings and ancient artwork. Furnishings are in-keeping with the castle's age but the superb en-suite bedrooms are more contemporary.

Ce château du XVe siècle démontre de suffisamment d'élégance, de charme et d'atmosphère pour satisfaire les visiteurs les plus exigeants avec ses murs de pierre imposants surplombés de créneaux, ses douvres offrant une piscine. L'intérieur frais combine les attributs d'une époque passée au confort luxueux du XXIe siècle. Les salles communes sont hautes et spacieuses, leurs murs naturels décorés avec des tableaux de goût et d'anciennes œuvres d'art. Les tentures sont en accord avec l'âge du château mais les chambres superbes sont plus contemporaines.

Este es un castillo del siglo XV con suficiente elegancia, encanto y ambiente para satisfacer al visitante más exigente. Majestuosos muros de piedra coronados con impresionantes almenas y un foso con piscina. La frescura interior tiene todos los atributos de un pasado tranquilo combinado con las comodidades lujosas del siglo XXI. Los salones son espaciosos y de altura con paredes naturales decoradas con estupendas pinturas y arte antiguo. El mobiliario ha sido elegido acorde con la época del castillo, pero sus excelentes habitaciones en-suite son más contemporáneas.

Our inspector loved: *The castle's authenticity, and amazing food.*

Directions: Madrid or Valladolid Airport > N630 - Salamanca - Zamora Road.

Web: www.johansens.com/buenamor
E-mail: castillo@buenamor.net
Tel: +34 923 355 002
Fax: +34 923 355 112

Price Guide: (excluding VAT)
double €182-245
suite €245-285

Hacienda Zorita

CARRETERA SALAMANCA-LEDESMA, KM 8.7, 37115 VALDERÓN, SALAMANCA, SPAIN

Towering redwood sequoias surrounded by vineyards are some of the striking gems that this landscape has to offer. Inside the impressive stone building, the 29 bedrooms are simple yet stylish whilst the hacienda's chapel is the ideal spot for historians. Here, 16th-18th century artworks are complemented by 176 barrels of mature wines. Gastronomic treats are served alongside wines of the Duero in the Refectory and al fresco in the Pergola Patio for those wanting to savour the spectacular views.

Des séquoias géants entourés de vignes sont des exemples frappants de ce que ce paysage peut offrir. A l'intérieur de cet impressionnant bâtiment en pierre, les 29 chambres sont simple mais élégantes et la chapelle de l'hacienda est l'endroit idéal pour les historiens. Ici les illustrations du XVIe au XVIIIe siècle côtoient les 176 tonneaux de vins arrivés à maturation. Des délices gastronomiques accompagnés de vins du Duero sont servis au réfectoire ou à l'extérieur sur le Pergola Patio d'où l'on peut admirer de magnifiques vues.

Unas gigantescas secuoyas rojas rodeadas de viñedos son algunas de las sorprendentes joyas que ofrece el paisaje. En el interior de este impresionante edificio de piedra, sus 29 habitaciones son simples pero elegantes, siendo la capilla de la hacienda el lugar ideal para el historiador. Aquí las obras de arte de los siglos XVI-XVIII se complementan con 176 barricas de vino añejo. Las delicias gastronómicas se sirven acompañadas de vinos del Duero en el Refectorio y al aire libre en el Pérgola Patio para los que quieran saborear los espectaculares paisajes.

***Our inspector loved:** The "Tormes" River running under the hotel, the spectacular views, and very good rooms. This is a special place.*

Directions: Madrid or Valladolid airport - A62 - Salamanca - SA300 (Ledesma road).

Web: www.johansens.com/haciendazorita
E-mail: zorita@haciendas-espana.com
Tel: +34 923 129 400
Fax: +34 923 129 401

Price Guide: (excluding VAT)
double €132
junior suite €193

Tancat de Codorniu

CTRA. N340, KM 1059, 43530 ALCANAR, SPAIN

This 19th-century country house is set amongst orange groves and is a short walk from stunning beaches. The simple interiors are filled with colourful modern artworks and relaxing armchairs. The cool bedrooms are peaceful and 3 new suites, with sun terraces, are now available; one has a sauna. The restaurant serves freshly caught fish and lobster. Facilities include 2 pools, one for children, small shady pavilions, mini golf and a pool bar. The meeting room has a walled garden and the Pavillion is ideal for weddings or special events.

Cette maison de campagne du XIXe siècle entourée d'orangeraies n'est qu'à quelques minutes de belles plages. Les intérieurs superbes, sont remplis d'illustrations modernes et colorées ainsi que de fauteuils confortables. Les chambres sont tranquilles et les 3 nouvelles suites avec leur propre solarium sont dorénavant disponibles; l'une d'elle a un sauna. Le restaurant sert des poissons et des homards fraîchement pêchés. L'hôtel propose 2 piscines dont une pour enfant, des petits pavillons ombragés, un mini golf et un bar de piscine. La salle de réunion a un jardin clos et le Pavillon est idéal pour les mariages et les occasions spéciales.

Esta masía del siglo XIX está enclavada entre campos de naranjos y a sólo un paso de unas playas virginales. Sus interiores bellos están decorados con modernas obras de arte llenas de colorido y con relajantes sillones a la vez que sus habitaciones fomentan la meditación, y 3 suites de reciente construcción tienen terrazas para tomar el sol, una con su propia sauna. El hotel tiene 2 piscinas, una para niños, y pequeños pabellones que proporcionan sombra. El restaurante ofrece pescado y langostas frescas. Podrá disfrutar del mini-golf y de la nueva piscina-bar. La sala de reuniones cuenta ahora con un jardín amurallado y el Pabellón es el lugar ideal para celebras bodas y otros eventos.

Our inspector loved: *The bedroom lighting: soft, atmospheric and adjustable.*

Directions: The nearest airports are Barcelona, Valencia and Reus. A7 > exit 41 > N340 > Les Cases d'Alcanar > the hotel is signposted.

Web: www.johansens.com/tancat
E-mail: info@tancatdecodorniu.com
Tel: +34 977 737 194
Fax: +34 977 737 231

Price Guide: (room only, excluding VAT)
double €120-170
suite €140-220
special double €200-300

Barcelona

Hotel location shown in red (hotel) or purple (spa hotel) with page number

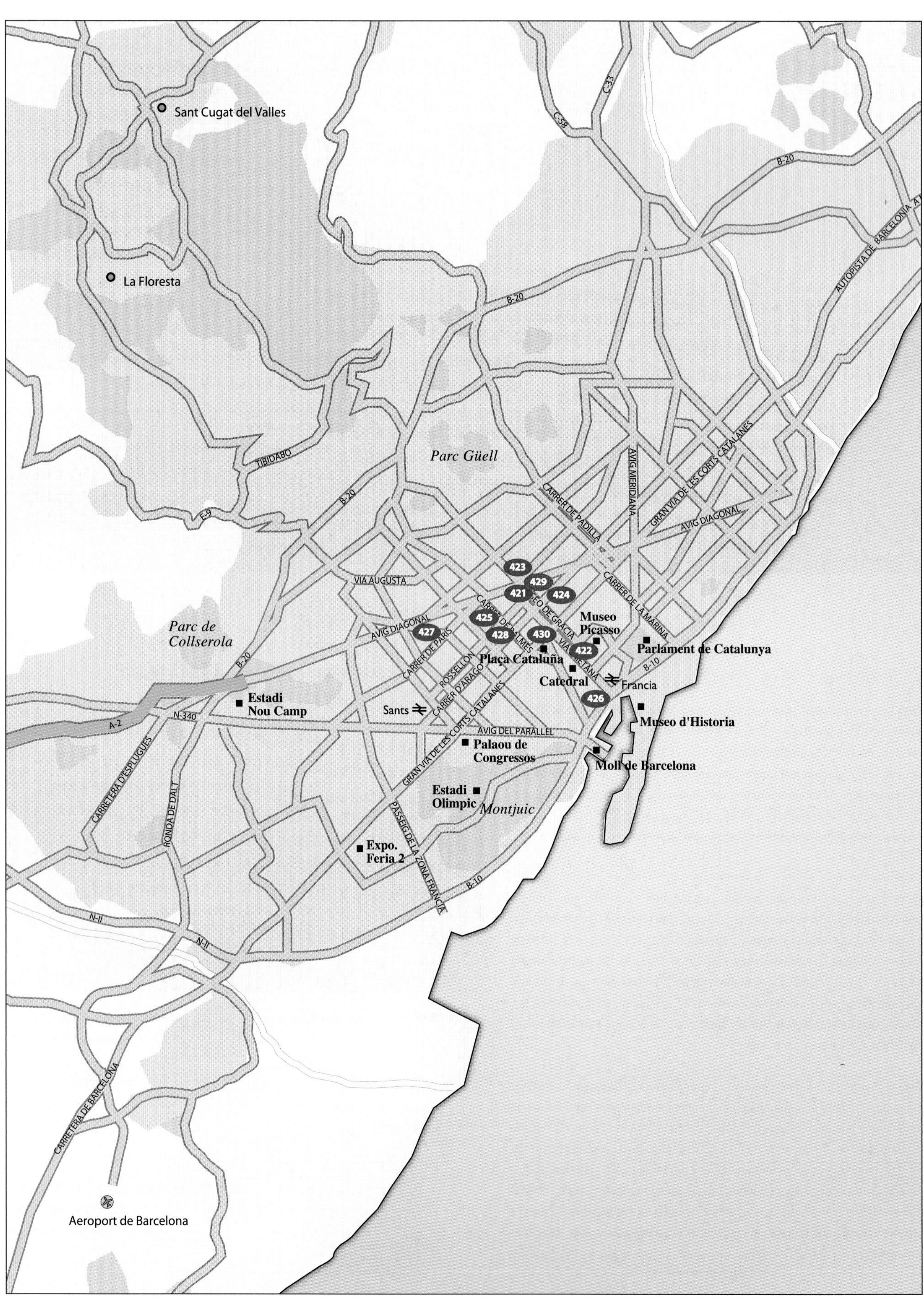

GALLERY HOTEL

C/ ROSSELLÓ 249, 08008 BARCELONA, SPAIN

Visitors to the Gallery Hotel are enveloped by a warm ambience and are treated to a personal service whilst enjoying the fine standards of accommodation. Featuring a stylish blend of modern and classic décor, the bedrooms offer every amenity including fax. The Bar is ideal for a preprandial drink after which fine cuisine may be enjoyed in the atmospheric Café Del Gallery. A garden terrace, fitness centre and separate saunas offer revitalisation to visitors returning from a day exploring vibrant Barcelona. A business centre is available.

Les visiteurs du Gallery découvrent une atmosphère chaleureuse et un service personalisé, tout en profitant de cet établissement de grand standing. Les chambres, savant mélange d'éléments modernes et classiques, offrent tout le confort possible (incluant fax). Le Bar est idéal pour prendre l'apéritif à la suite de quoi une excellente cuisine vous est proposée au Café Del Gallery. Une terrasse au jardin, des saunas et un club de remise en forme attendent les visiteurs en quête de revitalisation après une journée de visite de Barcelone. Un centre d'affaires est disponible.

Los visitantes en el Gallery Hotel se sentirán arropados por un cálido ambiente y un trato personalizado a la vez que disfrutarán del alojamiento al más alto nivel. Con una elegante mezcla de decoración moderna y clásica, las habitaciones proporcionan todo tipo de confort, incluido fax. El Bar es ideal para tomar un aperitivo previo a la excelente comida que puede degustarse en el Café Del Gallery o en la terraza jardín. Un gimnasio, un solarium y sus saunas independientes les permitirán relajarse después de haber pasado el día explorando la emocionante ciudad de Barcelona. Dispone de business centre.

Our inspector loved: *Looking out to the interior terrace with a morning coffee.*

Directions: Between Rambla de Cataluña and Paseo de Gracia in the centre of the shopping district. Transfers are available from the airport to the hotel.

Web: www.johansens.com/gallery
E-mail: galleryhotel@galleryhoteles.com
Tel: +34 934 15 99 11
Fax: +34 934 15 91 84

Barcelona
Madrid
Málaga

Price Guide: (room only, excluding VAT)
single €200-255
double €290
suite €375

  115     200     

Grand Hotel Central

VIA LAIETANA 30, 08003 BARCELONA, SPAIN

This impressive, beautifully renovated 1920s hotel is set in the heart of Barcelona with views over the cathedral and the cultural Gothic quarter. Close by is bustling, commercial Las Ramblas and the narrow streets and lively squares of trendy Barrio del Born with its shops, restaurants, cafés and exciting nightlife. There are 147 superbly decorated and furnished bedrooms, comfortably relaxing lounge areas, a fitness and leisure centre with large swimming pool and an elegant restaurant.

Cet impressionnant hôtel des années 20, situé au cœur de Barcelone, a été magnifiquement restauré et offre des vues sur la cathédrale et sur le quartier gothique. A quelques pas se trouve le quartier commercial de Las Ramblas ainsi que le nouveau quartier à la mode Barrio del Born avec ses magasins, cafés et restaurants disséminés dans des ruelles étroites et places animées. L'hôtel propose 147 chambres superbement meublées et décorées, des salons confortables et accueillants, un centre de loisirs et de remise en forme doté d'une grande piscine et un élégant restaurant.

Este imponente hotel de la década de los 20 de exquisita renovación está situado en pleno corazón de Barcelona con vistas a la catedral y a su cultural Barrio Gótico. En las inmediaciones se encuentran la bulliciosa y comercial avenida de Las Ramblas y las estrechas calles y animadas plazas del típico Barrio del Born, repleto de tiendas, restaurantes, cafeterías y una excitante vida nocturna. Dispone de 147 habitaciones admirablemente decoradas y amuebladas, cómodas salas de estar para el relax, un centro de fitness y ocio provisto de una amplia piscina, y un elegante restaurante.

Directions: Located in the city centre. Chauffeur driven transportation to and from Barcelona Airport can be arranged.

Web: www.johansens.com/grandhotelcentral
E-mail: info@grandhotelcentral.com
Tel: +34 93 295 79 00
Fax: +34 93 268 12 15

Price Guide: (room only, excluding VAT)
single €245
double €272
executive €265
suite €340-700

Our inspector loved: *The views across the old town from the rooftop pool.*

HOTEL CASA FUSTER

PASSEIG DE GRÀCIA 132, 08008 BARCELONA, SPAIN

Enjoying a central location, this impressive early 20th-century property affords stunning views over the city. The bedrooms and suites are decorated in a 1930s theme, painted in sumptuous shades of chocolate brown and blue tones and embellished with potted plants and art déco furniture. The restaurant serves contemporary Mediterranean cuisine and boasts similar modernist décor. After dining guests may relax in the bar, on the rooftop pool area, sink into huge, red sofas adorned with plush velvet cushions.

Bénéficiant d'un emplacement central, cet impressionnant bâtiment du XXe siècle offre de superbes vues sur la ville. Les chambres et suites sont décorées dans un style 1930, peintes dans de somptueux tons de bleu et marron chocolat et embellies par des plantes et des meubles art déco. Le restaurant sert une cuisine méditerranéenne contemporaine dans un décor moderniste similaire. Après dîner, les clients peuvent se relaxer sur la terrasse sur le toit avec piscine, ou se détendre dans le bar qui a des enormes canapés rouge couverts de coussins en velour violets.

Ubicado en el centro de la ciudad, este edificio del siglo XX, ofrece unas vistas impresionantes de la ciudad. Las habitaciones y suites, decoradas al estilo de los años 30 en suntuosos colores marrón chocolate y tonos de azul, estan adornadas con plantas y muebles tipo art déco. El restaurante sirve cocina Mediterránea contemporanea y está decorado del mismo estilo modernista. Después de la cena, puede relajarse en el bar de la azotea donde se encuentra la piscina y descansar en enormes sofás rojos adornados con cojines de terciopelo.

Our inspector loved: *The magnificent, pillared bar.*

Directions: The hotel is in the city centre. The nearest airport is Barcelona.

Web: www.johansens.com/fuster
E-mail: casafuster@hotelescenter.es
Tel: +34 93 255 30 00
Fax: +34 93 255 30 02

Barcelona
Madrid
Málaga

Price Guide: (room only, excluding VAT)
single €400
double €400-525
suite €650-2,800

96

200

HOTEL CLARIS

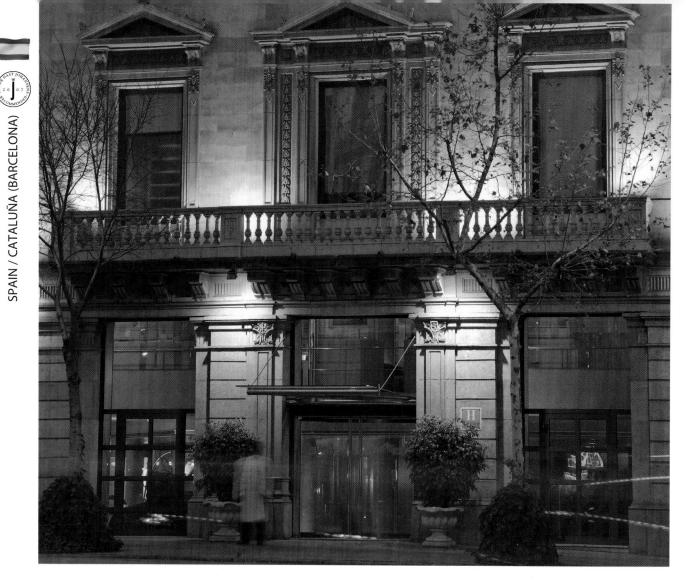

PAU CLARIS 150, 08009 BARCELONA, SPAIN

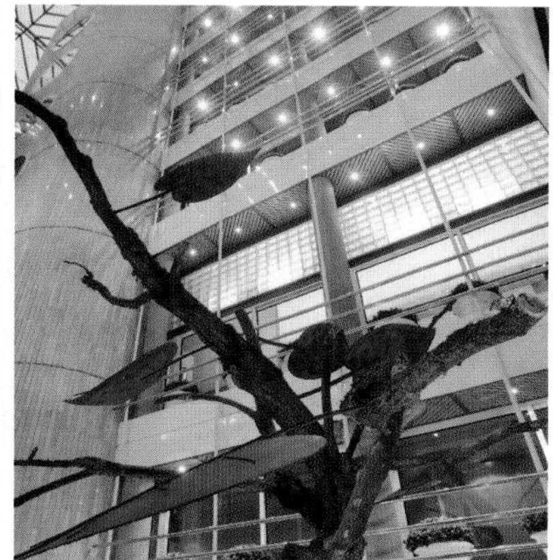

This former palace, close to Paseo de Gracia, still retains its graceful neo-classical façade whilst the interior is avant-garde with marble, glass and rare timbers. Art pieces and 5th-century Roman mosaics abound, and there is a collection of Egyptian art. The bedrooms are modern with antique objets d'art. Creative Mediterranean cuisine and Spanish and French wines can be sampled in the gourmet restaurant and cocktail bar, East 47. There are also 2 other restaurants, La Terraza del Claris and the Claris. A pool, solarium and sauna are available.

Cet ancien palais, près du Paseo de Gracia, conserve toujours sa gracieuse façade néo-classique alors que l'intérieur est un exemple d'avant-garde avec du marbre, du verre et des bois rares. Des œuvres d'art et des mosaïques romaines du Ve siècle abondent, et il y a une collection d'art égyptien. Les chambres ont un décor contemporain avec des objets d'art antiques. Une cuisine méditerranéenne créative peut être dégustée au restaurant gourmet et bar-cocktail East 47, accompagnée des vins espagnols et français. Il existe également 2 autres restaurants, La Terraza del Claris et le Claris. Une piscine, un solarium et un sauna sont disponibles.

Este antiguo palacio cercano al Paseo de Gracia mantiene aún su elegante fachada neo-clásica mientras su interior representa un vanguardista diseño con mármol, vidrio y vigas poco comunes. Abundan los objetos de arte y los mosaicos romanos del siglo V. Posee asimismo una colección de arte egipcio. Las habitaciones combinan el diseño contemporáneo con antigüedades artísticas. Puede degustarse la cocina mediterránea creativa así como los vinos españoles y franceses en el restaurante gourmet y en el cóctel-bar, East 47. Hay otros 2 restaurantes, La Terraza del Claris y el Claris. El hotel también tiene piscina, solarium y sauna.

***Our inspector loved:** The efficient reception staff.*

Directions: From Barcelona Airport take a taxi, train or bus to the city centre.

Web: www.johansens.com/claris
E-mail: claris@derbyhotels.com
Tel: +34 93 487 62 62
Fax: +34 93 215 79 70

Price Guide: (breakfast €14-20, excluding VAT)
single €387
double €430
suite €508-1,096

Hotel Cram

C/ ARIBAU 54, 8011 BARCELONA, SPAIN

Beyond the restored 19th-century façade lies innovative and exciting design. Interiors with black ceilings and bright colours, circular walls and inspiration taken from the Tibetan monks combine to provide a bold statement whilst maintaining extreme comfort. Interactive TVs with over 80 films, video games, Internet access and personal adjustment controls for sound and light feature in the guest rooms. The Michelin-starred GAIG offers Spanish dishes, there is a roof terrace and pool area with solarium and state-of-the-art meeting rooms.

Sous une façade du XIXe siècle restaurée, on découvre un design innovateur et sensationnel. Plafonds noirs et couleurs vives, pièces circulaires et influence des moines Tibétains la décoration intérieure est audacieuse mais aussi êxtremement confortable. Les chambres disposent de TV interactives avec plus de 80 films, jeux vidéo, et accès à l'internet ainsi que des touches de contrôle pour l'ajustement personnel du son et de la lumière. Le GAIG primé au Michelin sert des plats espagnols ; également dans l'hôtel une terrasse sur le toit, une piscine avec solarium et des salles de réunions ultra moderne.

Detrás de la afinadamente restaurada fachada del siglo XIX se encuentra un impresionante diseño innovador. En el interior, techos negros y colores vivos, paredes circulares e inspiración de los monjes tibetanos se combinan para resultar en un ambiente atrevido pero al mismo tiempo de extremo confort. Las habitaciones tienen televisores interactivos, con mas de 80 películas, juegos, y acceso a Internet, así como ajustes personales para controlar el sonido y la luz. En el conocido restaurante GAIG, galardonado por la guía Michelin, se sirven platos de cocina española. El hotel también cuenta con una terraza solarium, y salas para reuniones equipadas con todo lo último

Our inspector loved: *The trendy design with guests' comfort in mind.*

Directions: The nearest airport is Barcelona. The hotel is in the city centre.

Web: www.johansens.com/hotelcram
E-mail: info@hotelcram.com
Tel: +34 93 216 77 00
Fax: +34 93 216 77 07

Price Guide: (excluding VAT)
single €148-280
double €168-300
superior €184-350
junior suite €260-580

  67     100      

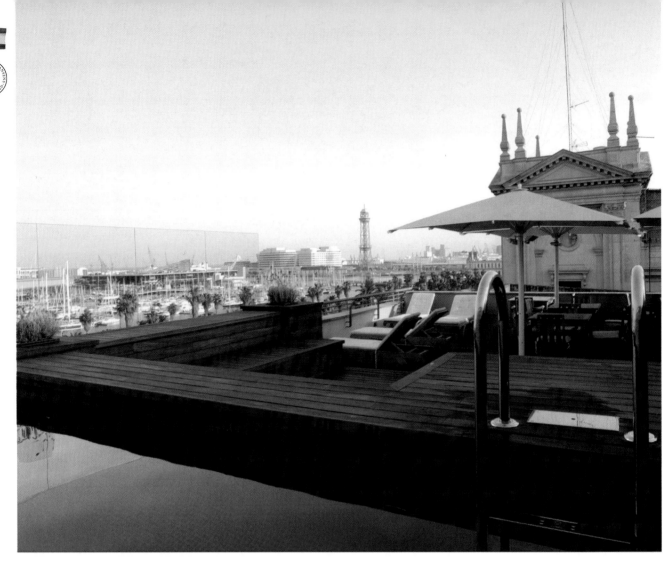

Hotel Duquesa de Cardona

PASEO COLON 12, 08002 BARCELONA, SPAIN

Directions: The nearest airport is Barcelona. The hotel is opposite the marina.

Web: www.johansens.com/duquesadecardona
E-mail: info@hduquesadecardona.com
Tel: +34 93 268 90 90
Fax: +34 93 268 29 31

Price Guide: (room only, excluding VAT)
single €215
double €250
junior suite €345

This stylish hotel is a restored 19th-century palace, once the home of nobility and refuge of royalty. Ideally situated opposite the marina in the heart of Barcelona's cultural Gothic quarter, the hotel is discreetly furnished and delightfully decorated with original features combined with 21st-century comforts. New services include an "Ask Me" information desk in the lobby and interactive TVs. The restaurant is charming and offers delicious Mediterranean cuisine. The rooftop pool enjoys a spectacular view of Barcelona harbour.

Cet hôtel élégant est un ancien palais du XIXe siècle entièrement restauré et qui fut la résidence de nobles et de familles royales. Situé en face du port, au cœur du quartier culturel Gothique de Barcelone, l'hôtel est discrètement meublé et délicieusement décoré, mélangeant ses caractéristiques d'origine avec le confort du XXIe siècle. Les nouveaux services comprennent un bureau d'information "Ask Me" et des téléviseurs interactifs. Le restaurant charmant sert une délicieuse cuisine méditerranéenne. De la piscine, qui est situé sur le toit de l'hôtel les clients peuvent apprécier une vue spectaculaire du port de Barcelone.

Este elegante hotel ha sido, restaurado a partir de un palacio del siglo XIX, morada en el pasado de la nobleza y refugio de la realeza. El hotel, situado en frente al puerto deportivo en pleno corazón del barrio cultural gótico, está discretamente amueblado a la vez que decorado con sumo encanto a base de elementos originales que se combinan con las comodidades propias del siglo XXI. Novedades del hotel son el mostrador de información "Ask Me" y las pantallas de televisión interactivas. El restaurante, con una deliciosa cocina mediterránea, ofrece un ambiente encantador. La piscina que se encuentra en el ático tiene una vista espectacular del puerto de Barcelona.

Our inspector loved: *The harbour views from the roof terrace.*

Hotel Gran Derby

CALLE LORETO 28, 08029 BARCELONA, SPAIN

This stunning hotel has been beautifully designed to create a contemporary and sophisticated style, whilst ensuring all modern comforts are available. Designed for the 21st-century guest there is a distinct fusion of business and leisure, with all rooms able to accommodate small meetings as well as luxurious accommodation. The surrounding pool area is a popular spot for coffee breaks and guests may also use the bar and restaurant facilities at the sister Hotel Derby Barcelona with complimentary hire of a Smart car.

Cet hôtel incroyable a été superbement décoré afin de créer un style contemporain et sophistiqué, avec tout le confort. Créé pour les hôtes du XXIe siècle, la fusion entre affaires et loisirs est évidente toutes les chambres peuvent accommoder des petites réunions tout en étant des logements luxueux. L'endroit populaire pour prendre un café est autour de la piscine et les hôtes peuvent aussi utiliser le bar et le restaurant de l'hôtel partenaire Derby Barcelona en profitant du prêt d'une voiture Smart.

Este excelente hotel ha sido magníficamente diseñado al estilo contemporáneo y sofisticado sin descuidar todas las modernas comodidades de la actualidad. Diseñado con el cliente del siglo XXI en mente, presenta una singular combinación de profesionalidad y ocio en todas sus habitaciones, las cuales están preparadas tanto para dar cabida a pequeñas reuniones como para proporcionar lujoso alojamiento. La zona que rodea a la piscina es muy frecuentada para tomar café durante los descansos. Los clientes pueden asimismo hacer uso de las instalaciones del bar y del restaurante del idéntico Hotel Derby Barcelona con préstamo gratuito de un automóvil Smart.

Our inspector loved: *The Head Receptionist's comment, "The most important thing for us is to remain in the hearts of our guests."*

Directions: The nearest airport is Barcelona. The hotel is located in a residential district near Place de Francesco Macia.

Barcelona
Madrid
Málaga

Web: www.johansens.com/granderby
E-mail: granderby@derbyhotels.com
Tel: +34 93 445 2544
Fax: +34 93 419 6820

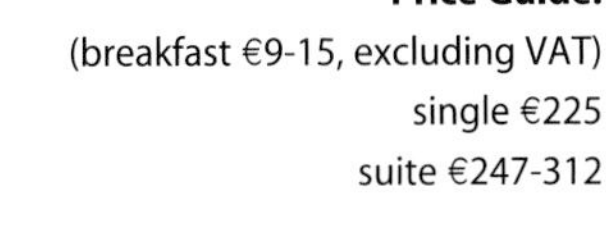

Price Guide:
(breakfast €9-15, excluding VAT)
single €225
suite €247-312

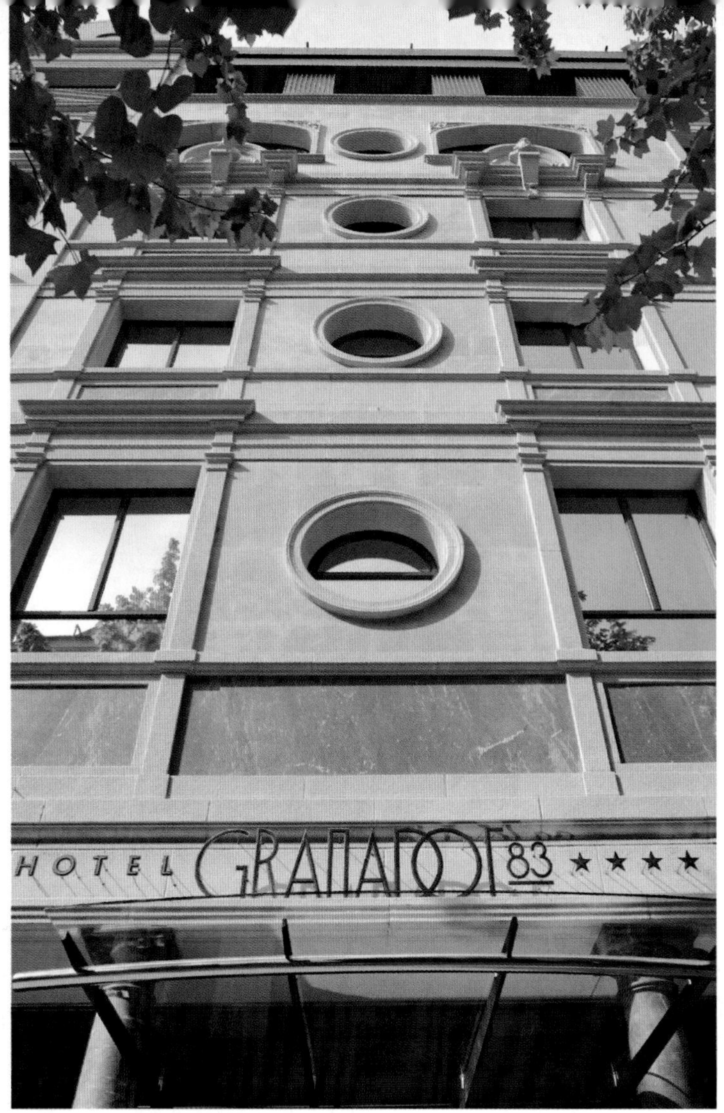

Hotel Granados 83

C/ Enric Granados 83, 08008 Barcelona, Spain

This is a unique 4-star superior hotel full of surprises situated on a quiet street in the city centre. The classic façade hides a contemporary, avant-garde interior of minimalist elegance, eye-catching décor and Zen design. At its heart is a central courtyard with spectacular glass roof. Some of the superbly furnished and decorated guest accommodation of New York-style lofts, suites, split-level and 3-level rooms have private pools and terraces. The restaurant, "3", serves creative Mediterranean cuisine and the 2 bars, the rooftop "8" and minimalist "GBar" serve cocktails.

Cet unique hôtel 4 étoiles, situé dans une rue calme du centre ville, est plein de surprises. La façade classique cache un intérieur contemporain et avant-gardiste, à l'élégance minimaliste, au décor attirant et au design Zen. Au cœur de l'hôtel, on trouve une cour au toit en verre spectaculaire. Des terrasses et des piscines privées équipent certaines des chambres organisés sur 2 ou 3 étages ainsi que des suites et des lofts de style New-Yorkais. On retrouve partout un intérieur magnifiquement meublé et décoré. Le restaurant "3" sert une cuisine Méditerranéenne créative et les 2 bars, le "8" sur le toit et le "GBar" servent des cocktails.

He aquí un singular hotel de 4 estrellas superior lleno de sorpresas y situado en una tranquila calle del centro de la ciudad. Su clásica fachada esconde unos interiores contemporáneos y vanguardistas de elegancia minimalista, impactante decoración y diseño Zen. El corazón del hotel es un patio central con espectacular techo de cristal. Algunas de las magníficamente amuebladas y decoradas habitaciones, tipo duplex y de 3 pisos, áticos al estilo de Nueva York y suites, disponen de piscinas y terrazas privadas. En el restaurante "3" se sirve cocina creativa mediterránea, y existen 2 bares para degustar cócteles: el "8" en lo alto del edificio y el minimalista "GBar".

Our inspector loved: *The pool terraces.*

Directions: The nearest airport is Barcelona. The hotel is in the city centre.

Web: www.johansens.com/granados83
E-mail: granados83@derbyhotels.com
Tel: +34 93 492 96 70
Fax: +34 93 492 96 90

Price Guide: (breakfast €10-16, excluding VAT)
single €231-389
double €389
suite €508

HOTEL OMM

ROSSELLÓ 265, 08008 BARCELONA, SPAIN

This stylishly modern hotel lies discreetly hidden among the many main streets of cosmopolitan Barcelona. The vast bedrooms are elegantly decorated with a minimal theme, and each has CD player and Internet access, with great emphasis being placed on soft, mood lighting. The restaurant Moo is run by the Roca brothers of Celler de Can Roca in Girona and each course comes with a recommended wine by the glass. The new spa comprises a plunge pool, Jacuzzi, treatment rooms offering European and Oriental massages and relaxing areas.

Cet hôtel moderne de style est discrètement caché parmi les rues principales de la cosmopolite Barcelone. Les vastes chambres sont élégamment décorées sur un thème minimaliste et ont toutes lecteur CD et accès Internet. L'accent est mis sur une ambiance et un éclairage doux. Le restaurant Moo est géré par les frères Roca du Celler de Can Roca à Girona et chaque plat est accompagné d'un vin recommandé, servi au verre. Le nouveau spa est équipé d'une piscine profonde, d'un jacuzzi, de salles de repos et de salles de soins offrant des massages Européens et Orientaux.

Este moderno y elegante hotel se esconde discretamente entre las numerosas calles principales de las cosmopolita ciudad de Barcelona. Sus enormes habitaciones están decoradas con estilo y con motivos temáticos minimalistas, disponiendo cada una de ellas de equipo de CD y acceso a Internet. Se ha puesto especial interés en su suave iluminación ambiental. El restaurante Moo está regentado por los hermanos Roca de Celler de Can Roca (Girona) y cada plato viene acompañado de una copa de vino recomendado. Un Jacuzzi, piscina de inmersión, salas para tratamientos que incluyen masajes europeos y orientales así como zonas de relajación, forman parte del nuevo spa.

Our inspector loved: *The stylish and elegant new city spa.*

Directions: Barcelona Airport > centre of the city.

Web: www.johansens.com/hotelomm
E-mail: reservas@hotelomm.es
Tel: +34 93 445 40 00
Fax: +34 93 445 40 04

Price Guide: (room only, excluding VAT)
single €295-375
double €295-375
superior €350-420
junior suite €450-550
suite €600-800

Hotel Pulitzer

C/BERGARA 8, 08002 BARCELONA, SPAIN

Directions: Situated in the city centre, off the Plaça Cataluña.

Web: www.johansens.com/pulitzer
E-mail: info@hotelpulitzer.es
Tel: +34 93 481 67 67
Fax: +34 93 481 64 64

Price Guide: (room only, excluding VAT)
single €255
double €270

Ideally located in the centre of Barcelona, Hotel Pulitzer is elegant and modern with carefully designed, stylish décor and a welcoming atmosphere. Cosy white sofas complement the spectacular black and red lacquer Chinese cabinets and the display of large prints on the walls of the public area. Creative Mediterranean dishes are freshly prepared each day and sushi is served in the bar on Wednesdays. A charming roof terrace has tables and chairs and is overflowing with beautiful plants, perfect to enjoy the city's panorama.

Idéalement situé au centre de Barcelone, l'hôtel Pulitzer est élégant et moderne avec un décor stylé et une atmosphère accueillante. Les canapés blancs confortables mettent en valeur les meubles chinois laqués rouge et noir ainsi que l'exposition de tableaux sur les murs des parties communes. Une cuisine méditerranéenne créative est fraîchement préparée chaque jour et des sushis sont servis au bar le mercredi. La charmante terrasse sur le toit, équipée de tables et de chaises et ornées de superbes plantes est idéale pour apprécier les panoramas de la ville.

Estratégicamente situado en el centro de Barcelona, el hotel Pulitzer es elegante y moderno con un décor diseñado cuidadosamente para recibir con calidez. Unos cómodos sofás blancos complementan las espectaculares vitrinas chinas, lacadas en rojo y negro y la exhibición de grandes grabados en las paredes de las zonas comunes. Platos de cocina creativa mediterránea se preparan con productos frescos cada día y los miércoles se sirve sushi en el bar. En el aspecto culinario ofrece deliciosos platos creativos mediterráneos preparados diariamente. La encantadora terraza sobre el tejado dispone de sillas y mesas, que rebosante de hermosas plantas es el lugar perfecto para disfrutar del panorama ciudadano.

Our inspector loved: *The lobby bar: stylish and comfortable.*

El Convent Begur

C/DEL RACÓ 2, SA RIERA, 17255 BEGUR, SPAIN

This former 18th-century convent has been renovated to offer 25 individual bedrooms with en-suite facilities. Vestiges of the past include original arched ceilings and an impressive ancient stone staircase. Stroll through the surrounding pine woods, walk down to the nearby cove or simply laze around the pool and outside bar. The dining experience is enhanced by the well-stocked cellar and enthusiastic in-house wine expert. Functions can be arranged in the chapel, which can also be used as a meeting room.

Cet ancien couvent du XVIIIe siècle a été rénové pour accueillir 25 chambres individuelles avec en suite. Comme vestiges du passé, on trouve d'originaux plafonds voûtés et un vieil escalier de pierre impressionnant. Il est possible de se promener dans les pinèdes et de descendre vers la crique de sable toute proche, ou bien de lézarder au bord de la piscine et au bar extérieur. Le dîner est mis en valeur par l'excellente cave et l'expert en vins de la maison. Des cérémonies peuvent être organisées dans la chapelle qui est également utilisée comme salle de réunion.

Este antiguo convento del siglo XVIII ha sido totalmente renovado para conseguir 25 bonitas habitaciones con cuartos de baño. Como vestigios del pasado se conservan los techos abovedados originales y una impresionante escalera de piedra. Pasee por el bosque de pinos que rodean el hotel, baje hasta la cercana cala arenosa, o descanse simplemente al lado de la piscina y del bar exterior. La experiencia de la cena se realza gracias a la presencia de un entusiasta experto en vinos y una extensa bodega. Se organizan eventos en la capilla, que también se puede utilizar como sala de reuniones.

Our inspector loved: *The ancient stone staircase, lined with candles.*

Directions: Barcleona or Gerona Airport > A7 > exit La Bisbal > Begur > Sa Riera > hotel is signposted at Begur village.

Web: www.johansens.com/conventbegur
E-mail: info@conventbegur.com
Tel: +34 972 62 30 91
Fax: +34 972 62 31 04

Barcelona
Madrid
Málaga

Price Guide:
(closed January and February)
single €85-140
double €115-210
suite €195-290

Torre del Remei

CAMÍ REIAL S/N, 17539 BOLVIR DE CERDANYA, GERONA, SPAIN

Torre del Remei lies within easy reach of the French Pyrenees and is a haven for walking enthusiasts. Rooms combine a perfect fusion of style and comfort, with the overall décor paying homage to the building's art deco heritage. The restaurant has won many accolades; the cuisine is supported by impeccable yet discreet service, which is evident throughout the hotel. 2 new treatment rooms are located in the tower, golf is a 15-minute walk away and walking packages with a guide can be arranged.

Torre del Remei est proche des Pyrénées françaises, c'est un paradis pour les amateurs de randonnées. Les chambres conjuguent parfaitement style et confort en respectant l'harmonie du patrimoine art déco du bâtiment. La renommé du restaurant grandit rapidement et a été acclamé à plusieurs reprises par les critiques. Les ingrédients du jardin sont utilisés dans la cuisine. Le service est impeccable et discret. 2 nouvelles salles de traitement sont situées dans la tour, un golf est situé à 15 minutes à pied et des randonnées pédestres guidées peuvent être organisées.

Torre del Remei se encuentra muy cerca de los Pirineos franceses, siendo todo un remanso para quienes gustan de pasear. Sus habitaciones combinan plenamente estilo y confort y toda la decoración en su conjunto rinde homenaje a la tradición Art Deco del edificio. El restaurante, de rápida y creciente fama, ha recibido numerosos elogios. La cocina, que hace uso de los ingredientes que produce su propio huerto, cuenta con un servicio impecable y discreto que se hace evidente en todo el hotel. En la torre se encuentran 2 nuevas salas para tratamientos de salud y belleza, a 15 minutos a pie hay un campo de golf, y se pueden organizar paseos con guia.

Our inspector loved: *The polite and friendly welcome upon entering the hotel.*

Directions: The nearest airports are Barcelona, Gerona and Perpignan. Travel to Puigcerdà > N260 to Bolvir de Cerdanya.

Web: www.johansens.com/torredelremei
E-mail: torreremei@relaischateaux.com
Tel: +34 972 140 182
Fax: +34 972 140 449

Price Guide: (room only, excluding VAT)
double €220-270
suite €340-620

Hotel Rigat

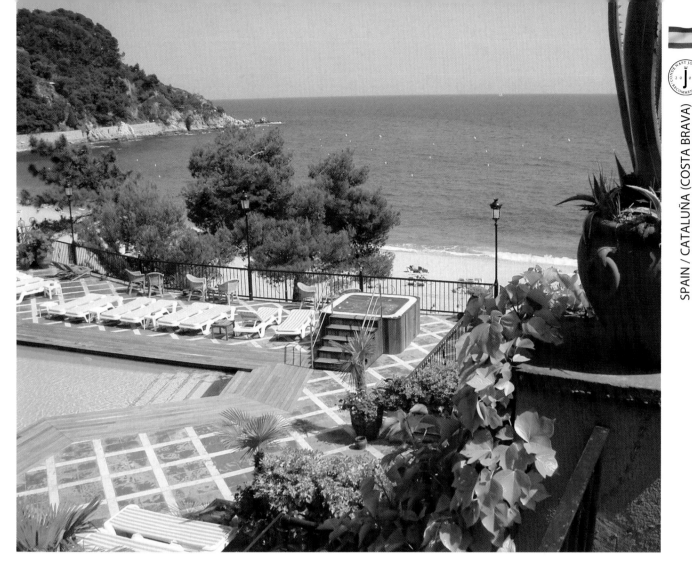

AV. AMERICA 1, PLAYA DE FENALS, 17310 LLORET DE MAR, COSTA BRAVA, GERONA, SPAIN

Surrounded by lush gardens and pine trees exuding their distinctive aroma, the Rigat Park is an ideal base for exploring the beaches of Costa Brava and the nearby Catalan towns. The 21 beautiful Mediterranean-style suites have tiled floors and marble bathrooms and 3 have motorised posturing beds. Guests may play billiards, swim in the pool or take advantage of the spa that offers sauna, Jacuzzi, mineralised water and indoor heated pool.

Entouré de jardins luxuriants et de pins exsudant leur senteur particulière, le Rigat Park Hôtel est une base idéale pour explorer les plages de la Costa Brava et les viles catalanes proches. Les 21 belles suites méditerranéennes ont un sol carrelés et des salles de bain en marbre et 3 ont des lits à position réglable motorisés. Les hôtes peuvent jouer au billard, profiter de la piscine ou des Bains avec sauna, jacuzzi, eau minérale et piscine intérieure chauffée.

Rodeado de exuberantes jardines y pinares que exhalan su característico aroma, el Rigat Park es el punto de partida ideal para explorar las playas de la Costa Brava y las localidades catalanas de los alrededores. Sus 21 bellas suites de estilo mediterráneo disponen de suelos embaldosados y cuartos de baño de mármol y 3 de ellas tienen camas con regulador que permite distintas posiciones. Los clientes pueden jugar al billar, nadar en la piscina o hacer uso de su spa que pone a su disposición sauna, jacuzzi, agua mineralizada y piscina climatizada cubierta.

Our inspector loved: *The secluded atmosphere yet close to all amenities.*

Directions: A7 > exit 9 > Lloret de Mar > Fenals Beach. Barcelona and Gerona Airports are nearby.

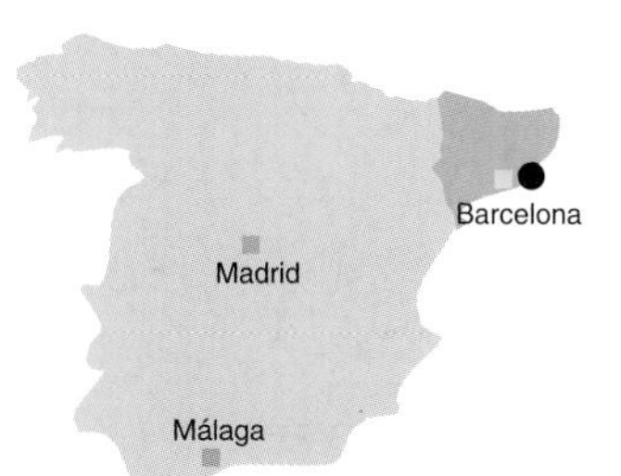

Web: www.johansens.com/rigatpark
E-mail: info@rigat.com
Tel: +34 972 36 52 00
Fax: +34 972 37 04 11

Price Guide: (excluding VAT, closed during November)
single €187-242
double €209-330
suite €330-1,430

99 210 SPA

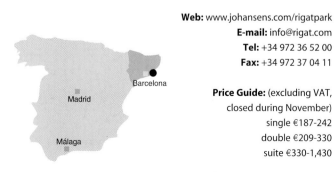

HOTEL SANTA MARTA

PLAYA DE SANTA CRISTINA, 17310 LLORET DE MAR, SPAIN

Surrounded by pine-covered hills and with extensive gardens sloping down to a spectacular sandy beach and the Mediterranean's warm, translucent waters, this attractive hotel offers tranquillity and comfort together with an extensive range of sport and leisure facilities. Furnishings and décor are classic, public rooms spacious, en-suite guest rooms light and with shaded balconies from which to enjoy sea, garden or hillside views. First-class cuisine is served in a traditional-style restaurant with charming features such as wall displays of copper pans.

Entouré de collines de pins et avec de vastes jardins descendants directement sur une superbe plage de sable blanc et sur les eaux tièdes et transparentes de la Méditerranée, ce bel hôtel offre tranquillité et confort mais également un large choix d'activités de sports et de loisirs. Ameublements et décoration sont de style classique, les salons sont spacieux et les chambres offrent un balcon ombragé d'où l'on peut admirer la mer, le jardin ou les collines. Une cuisine de premier ordre est servie dans un cadre traditionnel avec de charmants détails tels qu'un mur de casseroles en cuivre.

Rodeado de colinas de pinares y de extensos jardines que acaban deslizándose hacia una playa de arena y hacia las cálidas y cristalinas aguas del Mediterráneo, este atractivo hotel proporciona tranquilidad y confort junto a una gran variedad de instalaciones deportivas y de ocio. Sus muebles y decoración son clásicos, sus salones comunes amplios, las habitaciones repletas de luz y con balcones en sombra desde los que se puede disfrutar de vistas al mar, al jardín o a las colinas. Su excelente cocina se sirve en un restaurante tradicional con encantadores detalles tales como una exhibición de recipientes de cocina de cobre sobre sus paredes.

Our inspector loved: *The fragrance of the pine trees that surround the hotel.*

Directions: The nearest airports are Gerona and Barcelona. A7 > exit 9 > hotel is signposted before entering Lloret de Mar.

Web: www.johansens.com/santamarta
E-mail: info@hotelsantamarta.net
Tel: +34 972 364 904
Fax: +34 972 369 280

Price Guide: (breakfast €14, excluding VAT, closed December and January)
single €104-170
double €114-280
suite €190-390

Gran Hotel Balneario Blancafort

MINA 7, 08530 LA GARRIGA (BARCELONA), SPAIN

Located in a privileged, modernist area that boasts fascinating links to the arts and literature that have existed since the 19th century, this luxury spa hotel offers the ultimate in amenities and excellent customer service. Exquisite décor is complemented by striking original artworks that are displayed throughout the resort. The exclusive spa is one of a kind and is the ideal place to unwind from the pressures of everyday life.

Situé dans lieu moderniste et privilégié qui peut-être fier de ses liens fascinants avec l'art et la littérature qui existent depuis le XIXe siècle, cet hôtel spa de luxe offre le summum en équipements ainsi qu'un excellent service client. La superbe décoration est sublimée par les impressionnantes œuvres d'arts originales exposées à travers tout le resort. Le spa exclusif est unique et est l'endroit idéal pour échapper aux pressions de la vie de tous les jours.

Situado en una privilegiada zona modernista vinculada de manera fascinante al arte y la literatura del siglo XIX, este hotel–spa de lujo ofrece lo último en servicios así como una excelente atención al cliente. La refinada decoración incluye sorprendentes obras de arte originales expuestas por todo el recinto. Su exclusivo e inigualable spa es el lugar ideal para descansar y olvidarse de las tensiones de la vida cotidiana.

Our inspector loved: *The romantic Rincón de Lola restaurant set in the beautiful resort gardens.*

Directions: The nearest airports are Barcelona and Gerona. A7 > exit Granollers/Parets del Vallés.

Web: www.johansens.com/blancafort
E-mail: info@balnearioblancafort.com
Tel: +34 93 860 56 00
Fax: +34 93 861 23 90

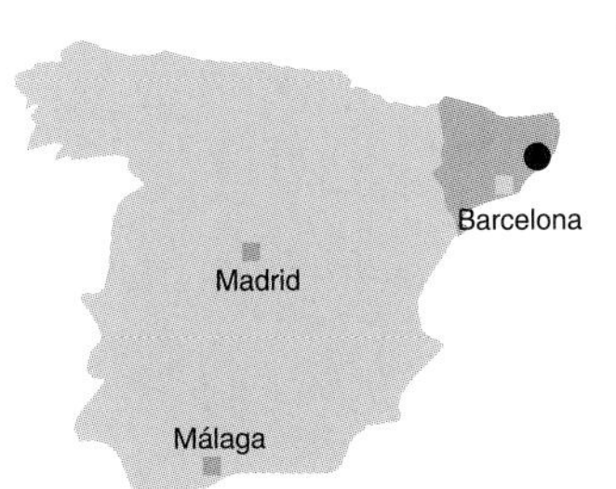

Price Guide: (room only)
single €185-250
double €220-395
suite €430-1,300

Mas Passamaner

CAMÍ DE LA SERRA 52, 43470 LA SELVA DEL CAMP (TARRAGONA), SPAIN

Close to the Costa Daurada beaches, the ruins of Tarragona and near to a Roman amphi-theatre, vineyards and Port Aventura theme park, this contemporary 5-star hotel is in a prime location for enjoying an array of activities and attractions. Constructed in 1922, the hotel recently underwent a refurbishment based on Modernism. Each bedroom is named after a Catalonian modernist architect and displays a brief biography representing their work. The highly acclaimed chef serves a "vintage" menu in La Gigantea, and the spa offers hydrotherapy and numerous treatments.

Prés des plages de la Costa Daurada, des ruines de Tarragona et proche d'un amphithéâtre Romain, de vignobles et du parc d'aventures "Port Aventura," cet hôtel contemporain 5 étoiles est idéalement situé pour profiter d'un large choix d'attractions et d'activités. Construit en 1922, l'hôtel a récemment subi une rénovation basée sur le Modernisme. Chaque chambre porte le nom d'un architecte moderniste Catalan et affiche une rapide biographie de leur travail. Le chef, très renommé, sert un menu 'Vintage' au restaurant La Gigantea. De nombreux traitements et de l'hydrothérapie sont proposés au spa.

Cerca de las playas de Costa Daurada, de las ruinas de Tarragona y próximo a un anfiteatro romano, zonas de viñedos y al parque temático de Port Aventura, este moderno hotel de 5 estrellas se encuentra en un lugar ideal para disfrutar de una gama variada de actividades y atracciones. Construido en 1922, el hotel ha sido recientemente objeto de una renovación de carácter modernista. Cada una de las habitaciones lleva el nombre de un arquitecto modernista catalán y exhibe una breve biografía de su obra artística. Su aclamado chef sirve un excelente menú "tradicional" en la Gigantea y su spa ofrece hidroterapia además de numerosos tratamientos.

***Our inspector loved:** Being surrounded by almond orchards.*

Directions: The nearest airports are Barcelona and Reus. From A7 > exit 34 towards Reus Airport > C14 towards Montblanc > exit at La Selva del Camp/Constantí > head towards Constantí > after 2.5km turn right.

Web: www.johansens.com/passamaner
E-mail: hotel@maspassamaner.com
Tel: +34 977 766 333
Fax: +34 977 766 336

Price Guide: (breakfast €15, excluding 7% VAT)
single €145-188
double €215-270
junior suite €260-320
suite €423-540

SPAIN / CATALUÑA (ROSES)

ROMANTIC VILLA - HOTEL VISTABELLA

CALA CANYELLES PETITES, PO BOX 3, 17480 ROSES (GERONA), SPAIN

Overlooking a spectacular sandy beach, this tranquil hotel offers 29 bedrooms, including 8 suites. The Royal Suite has 2 bedrooms. All rooms are individually decorated; most with sea view and the restaurant serves a variety of delicious and imaginative dishes. Vistabella is near the Dalí museum, the home of the painter Cadaqués and between the natural parks of Aiguamolls of l'Empordà and the CAP of Creus. The region is ideal for enjoying many leisure activities such as golf, walking, horseriding and a variety of water sports.

Avec ses vues magnifiques de la plage, cet hôtel tranquille propose 29 chambres dont 8 sont des suites. La Suite Royale dispose de 2 chambres. Toutes les chambres sont individuellement décorées; la plupart ont une vue sur la mer et le restaurant sert une variété de plats délicieux et imaginatifs. Vistabella se situe près du musée de Dalí, la maison du peintre à Cadaqués et entre les parcs de l'Aiguamolls de l'Empordà et du Cap de Creus. La région est idéale pour apprécier beaucoup d'activités de loisirs telles que le golf, marches dans la campagne, l'équitation et une variété de sports nautique.

Este tranquilo hotel con vistas a una espectacular playa de arena pone a su disposición 29 habitaciones, incluidas 8 suites. La Royal Suite consta de 2 habitaciones. Todas están decoradas individualmente; la mayoría tienen vistas al mar. El restaurante sirve una variedad de platos deliciosos e imaginativos. El hotel se encuentra cerca del museo Dalí y de la casa del pintor en Cadaqués, así como entre los parques naturales de los Aiguamolls de l'Empordà y del Cap de Creus. La región es ideal para gozar de muchas actividades del oció tales como el golf, senderismo, montar a caballo y una variedad de deportes de náutico.

Our inspector loved: *The uninterrupted sea views.*

Directions: The nearest airport is Gerona or Perpignan. Alternatively Barcelona Airport is still nearby. A7 > exit 4 > Roses > travel 2km through village > hotel is signposted.

Barcelona
Madrid
Málaga

Web: www.johansens.com/vistabella
E-mail: info@vistabellahotel.com
Tel: +34 972 25 62 00
Fax: +34 972 25 32 13

Price Guide: (excluding VAT)
double €110–270
suite €270–890

Dolce Sitges Hotel

AV. CAMI DE MIRALPEIX 12, SITGES 08870, SPAIN

The Dolce Sitges Hotel offers modern design, fine dining and extensive spa facilities. Standing on a hilltop overlooking the Mediterranean Sea and the city of Sitges, Barcelona is only 30 minutes away. Elegant guest rooms have terraces with sea or pool views, and Mediterranean cuisine is provided in the intimate Esmarris Restaurant whilst private dining is hosted in Racó de la Calma. The spa comprises 8 treatment rooms; there is over 2,175m² of meeting space, and various excursions discovering the local area can be organised.

L'Hôtel Dolce Sitges offre un design moderne, une cuisine fine et des équipements de loisirs. Situé sur une colline avec vue sur la Méditerranée et la ville de Sitges, il n'est qu'à 30 mn de Barcelone. Les chambres élégantes disposent de terrasses avec vue sur la mer ou la piscine, et l'intime restaurant Esmarris propose une cuisine méditerranéenne et des dîners privés dans la salle Racó de la Calma. Le spa comprend 8 salles de soins; l'hôtel dispose de 2,175m² de salles de réunions et peut organiser toute sorte d'excursions pour découvrir la région.

El Hotel Dolce Sitges, de moderno y actual diseño, ofrece a sus clientes la posibilidad de disfrutar de excelentes cenas así como de las amplias instalaciones de su spa. Situado en la cima de una colina con vistas al mar Mediterráneo y a la ciudad de Sitges, se encuentra a tan sólo 30 minutos de Barcelona. Las terrazas de las elegantes habitaciones dan al mar o a la piscina. Los clientes podrán disfrutar de una innovadora cocina mediterránea en el ambiente íntimo del Restaurante Esmarris o de cenas privadas en Racó de la Calma. Su spa tiene 8 salas de tratamientos. El hotel dispone de 2175 m² de salones de reunión y pueden organizarse diferentes rutas vinícolas y excursiones o actividades en los alrededores.

***Our inspector loved:** The bright, attractive business centre.*

Directions: Barcelona, International Airport Barcelona - El Prat, Sitges.

Web: www.johansens.com/doclesitges
E-mail: info_sitges@dolce.com
Tel: +34 938 109 000
Fax: +34 938 109 001

Price Guide: (excluding VAT)
single €230-425
double €230-425
suite €800

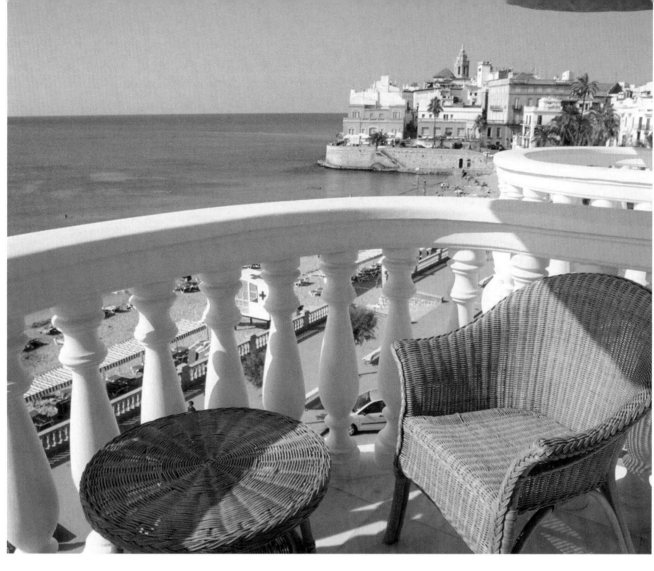

San Sebastian Playa Hotel

CALLE PORT ALEGRE 53, 08870 SITGES (BARCELONA), SPAIN

Located in the cosmopolitan town of Sitges, this hotel offers a sense of peace and tranquillity and extremely friendly Spanish hospitality. The spacious bedrooms have balconies, whilst the bathrooms boast thermostatic showers. El Posit, set directly on the sea, specialises in seafood dishes and uses the finest of local produce. With no less than 17 beaches and an abundance of restaurants and museums, activities for all tastes are catered for. Extensive, state-of-the-art audio-visual equipment is available with a professional conference team on hand to help organise a variety of events.

Situé dans la ville cosmopolite de Sitges, cet hôtel offre un sentiment de paix et de tranquillité et l'extrêmement amicale hospitalité espagnole. Chaque chambre est spacieuse et a un balcon, et les salles de bain bénéficient de douches thermostatiques. El Posit, qui donne directement sur la mer, sert poissons et fruits de mer et utilise les meilleurs produits locaux. Avec 17 plages et un grand nombre de restaurants et musées, il y a des activités pour tous les goûts. Des équipements audio-visuels ultramodernes et un personnel professionnel aident à l'organisation de divers évènements.

Situado en la ciudad cosmopolita de Sitges, en este hotel reina un ambiente de paz y tranquilidad al mismo tiempo que una hospitalidad española extremadamente acogedora. Las espaciosas habitaciones tienen balcones y los cuartos de baño duchas termostáticas El Posit, ubicado en la misma playa se especializa en pescados y mariscos, usando productos locales de gran calidad. En la ciudad hay más de 17 playas, gran cantidad de restaurantes y museos, actividades muy diversas para todos los gustos. El hotel posee también un extenso equipo audiovisual de última generación y personal profesional a disposición para organizar congresos y todo tipo de eventos.

Our inspector loved: *The newly decorated bedrooms.*

Directions: Barcelona or Reus Airports > motorway to Sitges > hotel is located on the seafront in the centre of Sitges.

Web: www.johansens.com/sebastian
E-mail: hotelsansebastian@hotelsansebastian.com
Tel: +34 93 894 86 76
Fax: +34 93 894 04 30

Barcelona
Madrid
Málaga

Price Guide: (room only, excluding VAT)
single €118-214
double €129-305
suite €205-350

SPAIN / EXTREMADURA (BADAJOZ - ZAFRA)

Casa Palacio Conde de la Corte

PLAZA PILAR REDONDO 2, 06300 ZAFRA (BADAJOZ), SPAIN

Directions: From Seville take the N-630 to Merida (Zafra is 130km). From Madrid take N-V to Badajoz and in Merida turn to N-630 to Sevilla.

Web: www.johansens.com/condedelacorte
E-mail: reservas@condedelacorte.com
Tel: +34 924 563 311
Fax: +34 924 563 072

Price Guide:
single €85
double €105-130
suite €160

Step inside this small palace on the picturesque town square in Zafra and admire the local architecture and inviting private mansion ambience. The opulent carpets, paintings and décor lend an aristocratic feel to the property and the bedrooms are bedecked with period furnishings, wall friezes and hand-painted trinkets. The comfortable living room with armchairs and fireplace is a perfect spot to relax whilst outside there is the terraced garden with pool and tiled fountain. The formal dining room is dominated by a large mahogany table and high-backed chairs.

Pénétrez dans ce petit palais dans la ville pittoresque de Zafra et admirez l'architecture Andalouse ainsi que l'ambiance d'une demeure privée. Les superbes tapis, tableaux et décors donnent une touche aristocratique à la maison et les chambres sont remplies de meubles d'époque, de frises murales et babioles artisanales. Le salon confortable avec ses fauteuils et cheminée est l'endroit idéal pour se relaxer, tandis qu'à l'extérieur se trouvent la terrasse avec la piscine et la fontaine carrelée. La salle à manger est dominée par une grande table en acajou et des chaises à hauts dossiers.

Entre por la puerta de este pequeño palacio ubicado en una pintoresca plazuela de la ciudad de Zafra y admire la arquitectura típica de la zona y el atractivo ambiente de una mansión privada. Las suntuosas alfombras, cuadros, y decoración dan un aire aristocrático a la casa y las habitaciones están adornadas con muebles de época, paredes con decorados pintados a mano y otras piezas de artesanía. El cómodo salón con sofás y chimenea es un lugar ideal para descansar, mientras que si se prefiere el exterior, tiene el jardín con terrazas, piscina y fuente de azulejos. El comedor tradicional tiene una mesa central de caoba con sillas de respaldo alto.

***Our inspector loved:** The comfort and service, and family home ambience.*

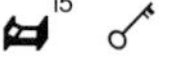

TUNEL DEL HADA HOTEL & SPA

TRAVESÍA DE LA FUENTE NUEVA 2, 10612 JERTE (CÁCERES), SPAIN

A nature lover's paradise, Tunel del Hada Hotel & Spa is situated in the heart of the Nature Reserve of Garganta de los Infiernos, with flora and wildlife, natural swimming pools and hillsides full of cherry and chestnut trees. Soak up the views from the comfortably modern rooms where antique furniture mixes with contemporary and the latest technology. In the Spa, a great variety of massages, beauty treatments, and personalized circuits ensure relaxation. Breakfast is served in the attractive conservatory, which opens out to the valley.

C'est l'endroit rêvé pour les amoureux de la nature. L'Hôtel et Spa Tunel Del Hada se trouve au cœur de la Réserve Naturelle de Garganta de los Infiernos, et de son abondante flore et vie sauvage, ses piscines naturelles et ses coteaux couverts de cerisiers et de châtaigniers. Il faut s'imprégner de la vue tout en profitant du confort moderne et du décor interieur des chambres qui allie meubles anciens et modernes avec les dernières technologies. Le Spa offre une grande variété de massages, de soins de beauté et des circuits personnalisés vous débarrasserons de tout stress. Le petit-déjeuner se prend dans la véranda qui s'ouvre sur la vallée.

Un paraíso para los amantes de la naturaleza, el Hotel-Spa Tunel del Hada está situado en pleno corazón de la Reserva Natural de la Garganta de los Infiernos, rodeado de flora y fauna, piscinas naturales y con laderas repletas de cerezos y castaños. Déjese seducir por las vistas desde sus modernas y cómodas habitaciones donde muebles de anticuario se mezclan con los de vanguardia y con la ultima tecnología. En el Spa, una gran variedad de masajes y tratamientos de belleza, así como baños y circuitos personalizados, le liberaran del estrés. El desayuno se sirve en una atractiva terraza acristalada abierta al valle.

Our inspector loved: *The suite above the spa.*

Directions: Madrid > motorway to Avila > exit N-110 towards Plasencia > at Jerte the hotel is signposted.

Web: www.johansens.com/tuneldelhada
E-mail: info@tuneldelhada.com
Tel: +34 927 470 000
Fax: +34 927 470 021

Barcelona
Madrid
Badajoz
Málaga

Price Guide: (room only, excluding VAT)
double (single use) €56-70
double €80-125
suite €124-185

 17
 30

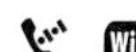

Madrid

Hotel location shown in red (hotel) or purple (spa hotel) with page number

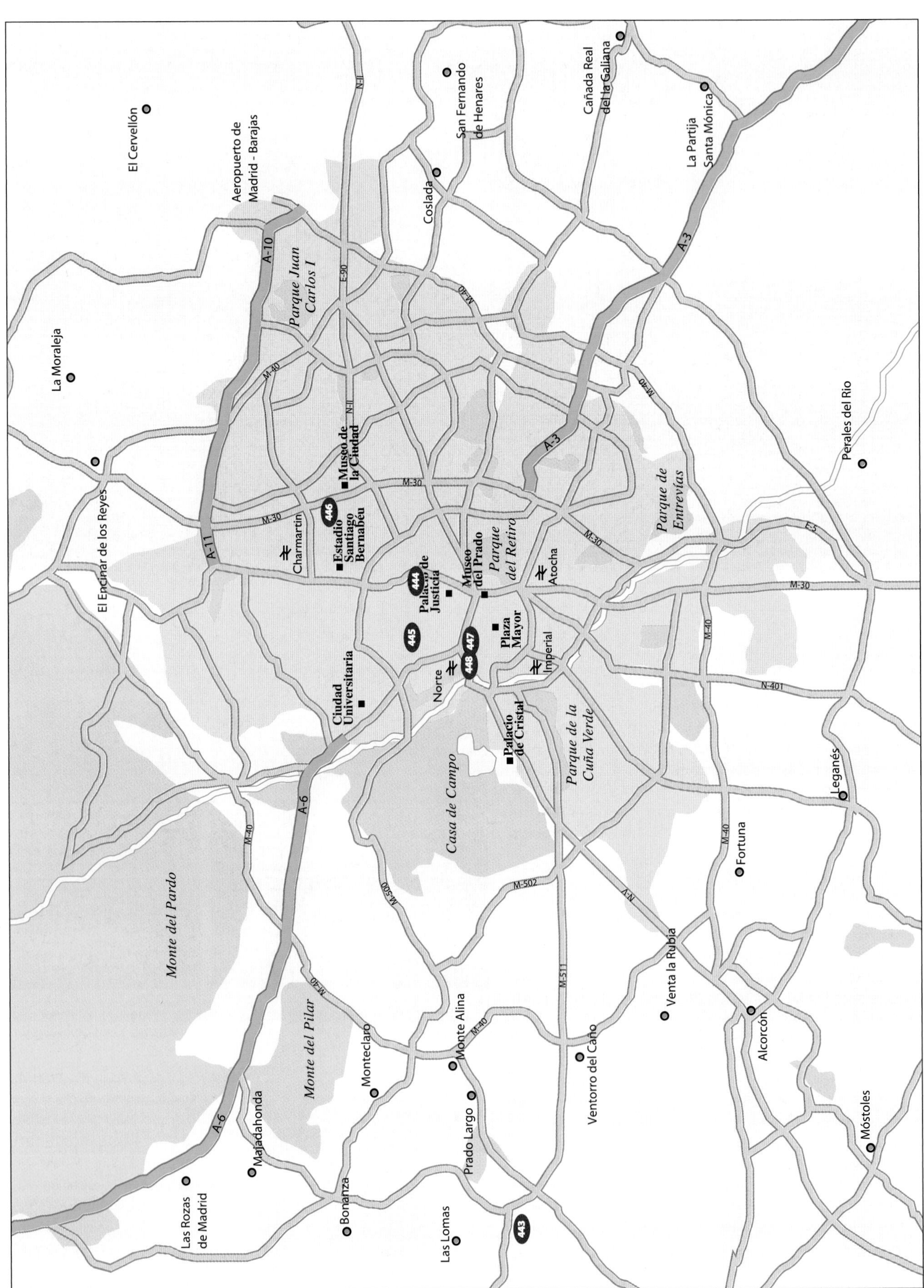

Antiguo Convento

C/ DE LAS MONJAS, S/N BOADILLA DEL MONTE, 28660 MADRID, SPAIN

Dating from the 17th century, this old convent has been beautifully refurbished with modern fittings, antiques and harmonious period details. The former nun cells have been imaginatively decorated as bedrooms and guests can enjoy a stroll through the exquisite ornamental gardens. Impressive skylights and a large covered patio create light and space. The new restaurant offers superb cuisine and extensive business facilities are provided. Madrid is nearby with excellent shopping and tourist attractions.

Ce vieux couvent du XVIIe siècle a été admirablement rénové avec des installations modernes, antiquités et d'harmonieux détails d'époque. La décoration des anciennes cellules des nonnes en chambres est originale et les hôtes peuvent se promener dans les charmants jardins ornementaux. Des lucarnes impressionnantes associées à un grand patio couvert créent lumière et espace. Une cuisine superbe est servie dans le nouveau restaurant, et l'hôtel dispose d'un centre d'affaires. Madrid est proche pour du shopping de qualité et des visites touristiques.

En un edificio del siglo XVII este antiguo convento ha sido maravillosamente restaurado con accesorios modernos, antigüedades y detalles de la época. Las antiguas celdas conventuales han sido decoradas imaginativamente como habitaciones y sus magníficos jardines ornamentales invitan a pasear por ellos. La luz y el espacio están generados por impresionantes claraboyas y un gran patio cubierto. El nuevo restaurante ofrece una esmerada cocina y también unas excelentes facilidades para los negocios. Madrid está muy próximo con sus magníficas zonas comerciales y atracciones turísticas.

Our inspector loved: *The exceptional fine dining and service in the Hosteria del Convento restaurant.*

Directions: M40 out of Madrid towards A Coruña > M511 to Boadilla del Monte.

Web: www.johansens.com/elconvento
E-mail: informacion@elconvento.net
Tel: +34 91 632 22 20
Fax: +34 91 633 15 12

Price Guide: (excluding VAT)
single €138.23
double €156.26
suite €300.50

Gran Meliá Fénix

HERMOSILLA 2, 28001 MADRID, SPAIN

Directions: Located on the Castellana, central Madrid.

Web: www.johansens.com/granmeliafenix
E-mail: gran.melia.fenix@solmelia.com
Tel: +34 91 431 67 00
Fax: +34 91 576 06 61

Price Guide: (per person, breakfast €25, excluding VAT)
de luxe €180-350
premium €195-365
suite €475-3,000

This superb hotel is the epitome of elegance and luxury with standards of comfort and service that exceed its 5-star rating. Behind a grand exterior are opulently decorated public and guest rooms. Each en-suite bedroom and suite has every modern facility, and the Presidential Suite is exceptionally luxurious. Veritas serves Mediterranean/Mallorcan gastronomic cuisine. The new wellness centre comprises a gym, lounge, a hairdressers and 2 treatment rooms.

Cet hôtel superbe est l'exemple même de l'élégance et du luxe avec des standards de confort et de service excédant son classement 5 *. L'extérieur magnifique cache des salles et des chambres somptueusement décorées, chacune a sa salle de bain et bénéficie, comme les suites, de tout le confort moderne. La Suite Présidentielle est probablement la plus luxueuse de la ville. Le restaurant Veritas sert une cuisine gastronomique d'inspiration méditerranéenne/majorquine. Le nouveau centre de remise en forme comprend une salle de gym, un salon, un coiffeur et 2 salles de soins.

Este grandioso hotel, compendio de elegancia y lujo con unos estándares de confort y servicio muy por encima de sus 5 estrellas. Detrás de un gran exterior encontramos las zonas comunes y las habitaciones suntuosamente decoradas. Cada habitación y suite poseen todo tipo de instalaciones modernas y la suite Presidencial probablemente la más lujosa de la ciudad. En el restaurante Veritas, se puede degustar cocina gastronómica mediterránea-mallorquina. El recientemente inaugurado centro Wellness se compone de un gimnasio, salón, peluquería y 2 salas para tratamientos.

Our inspector loved: *The "Royal Service" exclusive to suites and the VIP floor.*

214 120

Hotel Orfila

C/ORFILA, NO 6, 28010 MADRID, SPAIN

Located in a quiet residential area and surrounded by stately residences within minutes of the city centre, this 19th-century palace has been converted into a hotel and refurbished to a high standard. Each bedroom is individually decorated with antique pieces and equipped with hydro-massage baths. Guests can savour haute cuisine in the small restaurant, which opens onto a terrace and pretty garden, whilst the cocktails served in the intimate bar are reputed to be amongst the best in Madrid. Guests can enjoy the facilities of a nearby fitness centre with indoor pool.

Situé dans un quartier résidentiel calme et entouré par des résidences majestueuses à quelques minutes du centre ville, ce palais datant du XIXe siècle a été converti en hôtel et remis à neuf. Chaque chambre est ornée de façon individuelle avec des antiquités et équipée avec bain hydro-massage. Les hôtes peuvent savourer la haute cuisine dans le petit restaurant qui donne sur une terrasse et joli jardin, alors que les cocktails servis dans le bar intime sont réputés être parmi les meilleurs à Madrid. Les hôtes peuvent profiter d'un centre de remise en forme avec piscine couverte tout près.

Ubicado en una tranquila zona residencial y rodeado de residencias majestuosas a unos minutos del centro, este palacio del siglo XIX ha sido convertido en un hotel y restaurado a un alto estándar. Cada habitación está decorada individualmente con antigüedades y equipada con baños hidromasaje. Su alta cocina se puede saborear en el pequeño restaurante que da a una terraza y a un bonito jardín, al mismo tiempo que los cócteles que se sirven en el bar íntimo son conocidos como los mejores de Madrid. Existe un gimnasio y una piscina en las inmediaciones del hotel.

Our inspector loved: *The landscaped terrace garden with central wall-mounted fountain; charming for candle-lit al fresco dining.*

  32     120   

Directions: The hotel is located within minutes of the city centre.

Web: www.johansens.com/orfila
E-mail: inforeservas@hotelorfila.com
Tel: +34 91 702 77 70
Fax: +34 91 702 77 72

Barcelona
Madrid
Málaga

Price Guide: (breakfast €25, excluding VAT)
double €310-380
suite €420-1,250

HOTEL QUINTA DE LOS CEDROS

C/ALLENDESALAZAR 4, 28043 MADRID, SPAIN

Directions: The hotel is north of Madrid's centre, adjacent to C/Arturo Soria. Close to Chamartin train station and 10km from Madrid Airport.

Web: www.johansens.com/loscedros
E-mail: reservas@quintadeloscedros.com
Tel: +34 91 515 2200
Fax: +34 91 415 2050

Price Guide: (breakfast from €10.50, excluding 7% VAT)
single €100-144.40
double €100-181.45
superior double €177.60-210.90
suite €226.40-268.85

Surrounded by cedar trees and affording fine views across the city, this charming hotel was built in the elegant style of a Tuscan villa and provides an impeccably high standard of service and the utmost in comfort. Each of its 22 bedrooms and 10 terraced bungalows, which have direct access to the gardens, is themed differently and features all modern amenities. The intimate and romantic Los Cedros restaurant serves traditional and modern cuisine with Mediterranean flavours under the direction of prestigious Spanish Chef Pedro Larumbe. Guests may enjoy meals on the terrace overlooking the gardens.

Entouré de cèdres et offrant des vues spectaculaires sur la ville, cet hôtel de charme fut construit dans le style élégant d'une villa toscane et offre un excellent niveau de service et de confort. Chacune des 22 chambres et des 10 pavillons en terrasses, qui ont un accès direct aux jardins, sont décorés sur des thèmes différents et équipés de tout le confort moderne. "Los Cedros", restaurant intime et romantique dirigé par le célèbre chef espagnol Pedro Larumbe, sert des plats traditionnels et modernes aux saveurs Méditerranéennes. Les hôtes peuvent dîner sur la terrasse dominant les jardins.

Rodeado de cedros y con estupendas vistas a la ciudad, este encantador hotel, construido con el elegante estilo de una villa toscana, ofrece a sus clientes un servicio impecable así como un confort supremo. Cada una de sus 22 habitaciones, así como sus 10 bungalows adosados con acceso directo al jardín, están decoradas con motivos temáticos diferentes y dotadas de toda clase de modernas comodidades. Su íntimo y romántico restaurante, Los Cedros, sirve platos tradicionales y modernos con sabor mediterráneo. Las comidas se pueden disfrutar en la terraza con vistas a los jardines.

Our inspector loved: *The bungalow suites in the immaculate gardens.*

Hotel Urban

CARRERA DE SAN JERÓNIMO 34, 28014 MADRID, SPAIN

Hotel Urban is ideally located to explore the sights and cultural exhibitions of Madrid. Stunning eclectic design combines chrome, iron, glass, light and wood to create a warm, contemporary ambience. There are superior rooms available including junior suites and duplex accommodations with 2 split-levels. Light snacks and delicious Japanese apéritifs can be enjoyed in the most fashionable oyster bar in Madrid, and Europa Decó restaurant serves fantastic Mediterranean cuisine; reservations are necessary. La Terraza del Urban offers stunning city views.

Hotel Urban est idéalement situé pour explorer les monuments et expositions culturelles de Madrid. Un design éclectique qui mélange chrome, fer, verre, lumière et bois, crée une atmosphère chaleureuse et contemporaine. Les chambres supérieures incluent des junior suites et des duplex avec 2 étages. Une cuisine légère et de délicieux apéritifs japonais peuvent être dégustés dans le plus à la mode des bar à huitres de Madrid et le restaurant Europa Decó sert une succulente cuisine méditerranéenne, sur réservation uniquement. La Terraza del Urban offre de superbes vues sur la ville.

El Hotel Urban posee la ubicación ideal para explorar las geniales vistas y exposiciones culturales de Madrid. Su maravilloso diseño ecléctico combina cromo, con hierro, vidrio, luz y madera para crear un ambiente acogedor y contemporáneo. Las habitaciones superiores incluyen unas junior suites y unas duplex de 2 niveles. En el bar de ostras, el bar mas de moda de Madrid, se pueden probar comidas ligeras y deliciosos aperitivos japoneses, y en el restaurante Europa Deco: fantástica cocina mediterránea. Es necesario reservar con anterioridad. La Terraza del Urban ofrece unas impresionantes vistas de la ciudad.

Our inspector loved: *Enjoying cocktails and apéritifs in the "hip" Glass Bar.*

Directions: The hotel is situated in the city centre.

Web: www.johansens.com/urban
E-mail: urban@derbyhotels.com
Tel: +34 91 787 77 70
Fax: +34 91 787 77 99

Price Guide: (breakfast €14-20, excluding VAT)
single €387
double €430
suite €586-1,096

 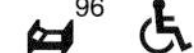       

Hotel Villa Real

PLAZA DE LAS CORTES 10, 28014 MADRID, SPAIN

Surrounded by cultural attractions, this prestigious hotel offers impeccable service and a palatial interior, filled with wonderful antiques and mirrors, handsome rugs on marble floors, Roman mosaics and Greek ceramics. The newly refurbished Royal and Imperial Suites offer hydro-massage baths; one of the suites has a small sauna. Guests can sample exquisite dishes in the gourmet restaurant Europa or enjoy creative cuisine in the East 47. Wireless Internet connection available.

Entouré des attractions culturelles, ce prestigieux hôtel bénéficie d'un service impeccable et d'un intérieur grandiose, orné des antiquités et des miroirs, de beaux tapis sur des sols de marbre, des mosaïques romaines et céramiques grecques. Les suites Royale et Impériale disposent d'un bain hydro-massage; une a un sauna. Il y a 2 restaurants: le restaurant gastronomique Europa et l'East 47, où une cuisine créative est servie. Service internet sans fil disponible.

Rodeado de atracciones culturales, este prestigioso hotel ofrece un servicio impecable y un interior palaciego lleno de maravillosas antigüedades y espejos, hermosas alfombras sobre suelos de mármol, mosaicos romanos y cerámicas griegas. Las recién renovadas suites Real e Imperial ofrecen baños-hidromasajes, una de ellas incluso tiene una pequeña sauna. Los huéspedes pueden degustar platos exquisitos en el restaurante gourmet Europa o degustar la cocina creativa en el East 47. También está disponible la conexión a internet inalámbrica.

Our inspector loved: *The original Marilyn prints by Andy Warhol in the fashionable, atmospheric East 47 where drinks and snacks are served.*

Directions: Located in the centre of the city.

Web: www.johansens.com/villareal
E-mail: villareal@derbyhotels.com
Tel: +34 914 20 37 67
Fax: +34 914 20 25 47

Price Guide: (breakfast €14-20, excluding VAT)
single €349
double €389
suite €586-1,096

115 200

Hotel Arresi

PORTUGANE 7, 48620 ARMINTZA, SPAIN

This captivating house retains all the charm and privacy one would expect from a family-owned hotel. The magnificent flower-filled gardens and terraces are the ideal place to relax during the day, and there are many beautiful walks and hikes to enjoy. All of the bedrooms are light and airy, and the food and wine is exceptional. Guests have use of the outdoor pool, tennis courts, children's play area and golf 12km away. Alternatively, the Rioja Vineyards and Bilbao's cultural sites such as the Guggenheim are nearby.

Cette étonnante maison a gardé tout le charme et l'intimité d'un hôtel géré en famille. Les superbes terrasses et jardins remplis de fleurs sont l'endroit idéal pour se reposer pendant la journée et il y a de nombreuses promenades et randonnées à faire. Toutes les chambres sont claires et spacieuses et la cuisine et les vins sont exceptionnels. Les clients peuvent profiter de la piscine extérieure, des courts de tennis, de l'aire de jeux pour enfants et d'un parcours de golf à 12 kms. Il y a également les vignobles du Rioja et les sites culturels de Bilbao tels que le Guggenheim à proximité.

Esta deliciosa casa mantiene todo el encanto y la intimidad que se espera de un hotel regido por la propia familia. Los magníficos jardines y terrazas rebosantes de flores son lugares ideales para relajarse durante el día, y se pueden dar agradables paseos y caminatas por los bellos alrededores. Todas las habitaciones son luminosas y espaciosas. La comida y el vino son excepcionales. El hotel tiene piscina, cancha de tenis, parque para niños y hay un campo de golf a 12 Km. También puede visitar los viñedos de Rioja y el museo Guggenheim y otros lugares culturales de Bilbao.

Our inspector loved: *The views over the tiny port.*

Directions: Located 15 minutes from Bilbao Airport. Bilbao Airport > N631 > Mungia > Plentzia. Follow signs to Armintza > hotel is signposted.

Bilbao
Barcelona
Madrid
Málaga

Web: www.johansens.com/arresi
E-mail: hotelarresi@hotelarresi.com
Tel: +34 94 68 79 208
Fax: +34 94 68 79 310

Price Guide: (special weekend breaks available during low season)
single €80-97
double €100-122
suite €156

Hospes Amérigo

C/ Rafael Altamira 7, 03002 Alicante, Spain

The interior of this restored 16th-century convent features marble, stone, leather and chrome to create a luxurious yet functional 21st-century ambience. Spacious bedrooms and bathrooms boast contemporary décor and possess all modern amenities. Enjoy the roof terrace with Bodyna Spa, which offers a variety of beauty and therapeutic massage treatments, an indoor pool with retractable roof, fitness centre and sauna. There are 2 dining options: Senzone Restaurant and Senzone Tapas Bar.

L'intérieur de ce convent restauré du XVIe siècle est composé de marbre, de pierres, de bois, de cuir, de verre et de chrome habilement mélangés pour créer une atmosphère luxueuse et fonctionnelle du XXIe siècle. Les chambres et salles de bain spacieuses s'enorgueillissent d'un décor contemporain avec toute la technologie moderne. Profitez de la terrasse sur le toit où se trouvent un centre de remise en forme, sauna, le Bodyna Spa qui offre une variété de massages thérapeutiques et de soins de beauté, ainsi qu'une piscine intérieure à toit rétractable. Pour le dîner, 2 options : le restaurant Senzone et le Bar à Tapas Senzone.

En el interior de este convento del siglo XVI restaurado, mármol, piedra, madera, cuero, vidrio y cromo se mezclan para crear un ambiente lujoso y al mismo tiempo funcional. Sus espaciosas habitaciones y cuartos de baño de decoración contemporánea poseen todas la amenidades modernas. Disfruten del Bodyna Spa en la terraza del último piso, con su piscina interior de techo retractable, sauna, gimnasio y donde se ofrece una gran variedad de masajes de belleza y terapéuticos. Para cenar, 2 opciones: el restaurante Senzone y el bar de tapas Senzone.

Our inspector loved: *The innovation and design.*

Directions: Alicante Airport > city centre > city council/hall street.

Web: www.johansens.com/amerigo
E-mail: amerigo@hospes.es
Tel: +34 965 14 65 70
Fax: +34 965 14 65 71

Price Guide: (room only, excluding VAT, parking is available at the hotel)
single €185-255
double €185-255
suite €360-720

Hotel Sidi San Juan & Spa

PLAYA DE SAN JUAN, 03540 ALICANTE, SPAIN

This excellent hotel is situated on a long, sandy beach near Cabo de Las Huertas, 10 minutes from Alicante, renowned for its cultural activities and sights. With beautiful gardens filled with over 250 palm trees, this is just the place for a relaxing stroll. All rooms and suites have magnificent sea views. Grill Sant Joan offers international specialities and exquisite wines. The hotel has a new gym, 5 tennis, 2 paddle courts, indoor and outdoor pools and a spa with 3 new health and beauty treatment rooms. Free shuttle bus service to the centre of Alicante.

Cet excellent hôtel est situé sur une longue plage de sable près de Cabo de Las Huertas, à 10 minutes d'Alicante, célèbre pour ses attractions culturelles. Avec ses jardins merveilleux remplis de plus de 250 palmiers, c'est un endroit parfait pour des longues promenades relaxantes. Toutes les chambres et suites ont des vues sur la mer. Le Grill Sant Joan offre des spécialités internationales et des vins exquis. L'hôtel dispose d'une nouvelle salle de gym, de 5 courts de tennis, de 2 de paddle, piscines intérieure et extérieure, ainsi que d'un spa avec 3 nouvelles salles de traitements pour les soins de beauté et du corps. Service de navette gratuit au centre d'Alicante.

Este excelente hôtel situado en una arenosa y larga playa próxima al Cabo de las Huertas está sólo a 10 minutos de Alicante, famoso por sus actividades culturales y sus vistas. Cuenta con preciosos jardines llenos de palmeras,más de 250 ejemplares, es el lugar ideal para disfrutar de un largo y relajante paseo. Todas las habitaciones y suites ofrecen magníficas vistas al mar. En el Grill Sant Joan se pueden saborear una extensa gama de especialidades internacionales y excelentes vinos. El hotel tiene un nuevo gimnasio, 5 canchas de tenis, 2 de paddle, piscina exterior e interior y un spa con 3 nuevas salas de tratamientos saluz y belleza. Servicio de minibús gratuito al centro de Alicante.

Our inspector loved: *The family activities: sun, sea, spa, sports and relaxation.*

Directions: From Alicante follow the signs to Playa San Juan. 12km from the city centre, the hotel is on the beachfront.

Web: www.johansens.com/sanjuan
E-mail: reservas@sidisanjuan.com
Tel: +34 96 516 13 00
Fax: +34 96 516 33 46

Price Guide: (room only, excluding VAT)
single €160-186
double €199-232
suite €697-795

SPAIN / VALENCIA (ALQUERIAS - CASTELLÓN)

TORRE LA MINA

C/ LA REGENTA 1, 12539 ALQUERIAS-CASTELLÓN, SPAIN

This 19th-century mansion, set amidst extensive landscaped grounds featuring sculptures created by the acclaimed local artist Juan Ripolles, has the sophisticated ambience of a private stately home. Stone, marble, ceramic tiles and exposed beams create a sleek décor and the 8 individually styled bedrooms provide hydromassage. Regional and Mediterranean cuisine is served in the restaurant, where candle-lit banquets with live jazz in the gardens takes place every Friday evening during summer. A large conference building is available. Special offers available.

De cette demeure du XIXe siècle, au cœur d'un grand parc où se dressent des sculptures créées par l'artiste local Juan Ripolles, émane l'atmosphère sophistiquée d'une propriété aristocratique. Pierres, marbre, carrelages et poutres apparentes créent un décor soigné et les 8 chambres aménagées individuellement disposent d'hydromassage. Une cuisine régionale et méditerranéenne est servie au restaurant, où des banquets aux chandelles avec du jazz dans les jardins se tiennent les vendredis soirs en été. Un bâtiment pour les conférences ainsi que des offres spéciales sont disponibles.

Esta mansión del siglo XIX, situada en medio de una vasta zona verde y con esculturas del aclamado artista local Juan Ripolles, ofrece el ambiente sofisticado de una casa aristocrática. La piedra, el mármol, los azulejos de cerámicos y las vigas al descubierto creen una décoración elegante y las 8 habitaciones individualmente diseñados ofrecen hidromassage. El restaurante sirve platos regionales y mediterráneos, en cuyos jardines todos los noches de viernes durante el verano se celebran banquetes a la luz de las velas amenizados con jazz vivo. Un edificio para los congresos y ofertas especiales están disponibles.

Our inspector loved: *The fine gourmet dining and excellent service.*

Directions: From Valencia > A7 north > exit Burriana/Villa Real > follow signs to Alquerias.

Web: www.johansens.com/torrelamina
E-mail: info@torrelamina.com
Tel: +34 964 57 1746/0180
Fax: +34 964 57 0199

Price Guide: (excluding 7% VAT)
single €150
double €150
suite €210

Hotel Termas Marinas el Palasiet

PARTIDA CANTALLOPS S/N, 12560 BENICÀSSIM, CASTELLÓN, COSTA DEL AZAHAR, SPAIN

Dating back to the 1800s, this hotel houses the first thalasso therapeutic spa of its kind to be opened in Spain, and offers a wide range of health and beauty treatments. Set in spacious grounds and landscaped gardens it is an oasis of tranquillity, and the décor is elegant with a touch of Old World charm. All bedrooms have balconies overlooking the bay, and furnishings include Spanish tiles, wooden floors, antiques and wall frescoes. The restaurant serves Mediterranean cuisine with a focus on healthy eating.

Datant du XIXe siècle, cet hôtel de charme héberge le premier centre de thalassothérapie de son genre en Espagne, et propose une grande variété de traitements de soins de beauté. Au sein d'un grand parc et de jardins aménagés, c'est un havre de paix dont le décor élégant s'allie au charme d'autrefois. Toutes les chambres ont des balcons surplombant la baie. La décoration intérieure est composée de carrelage espagnol, de parquets, d'antiquités et de fresques murales. Le restaurant met l'accent sur une nourriture saine et sert une cuisine méditerranéenne.

El hotel, que data del siglo XIX, dispone del primer spa de talasoterapia de su clase que se abrió en España y ofrece una amplia gama de tratamientos de salud y belleza. Su situación en una amplia zona verde ajardinada lo convierte en un oasis de paz y tranquilidad. Su elegante decoración conserva cierto toque que recuerda los encantos del Viejo Mundo. Todas las habitaciones tienen balcones con vistas a la bahía y entre los elementos que las decoran están la teja española, los suelos de madera, las piezas de anticuario y los frescos en las paredes. El restaurante sirve cocina mediterránea con especial interés en proporcionar una dieta saludable.

Our inspector loved: *The philosophy behind this family-run thalasso spa/hotel: health, wellbeing, relaxation and tranquillity in a perfect climate.*

Directions: From Valencia > coastal motorway north towards Barcelona > exit Castellón north > follow signs to Benicàssim.

Web: www.johansens.com/termasmarinas
E-mail: reservas@termasmarinas.com
Tel: +34 964 300 250
Fax: +34 964 302 236

Price Guide:
single €125-151
double €162-187
suite €163-209

La Posada del Mar

PLAÇA DE LES DRASSANES, 1-2 03700 DÉNIA, SPAIN

Situated opposite the marina in the midst of the cosmopolitan town of Dénia with the magnificent fortified hill of the town to its rear, this charming building dates back over 800 years and perfectly combines period features with luxurious contemporary comfort. Beautiful bedrooms enjoy marvellous views and are decorated with terracotta, wood and marble for a cool and comfortable feel. Guests will enjoy the hotel's excellent seafood cuisine in the new Sal de Mar restaurant, the abundance of shops in the vicinity, the gym and sauna.

La Posada del Mar est située en face de la marina au cœur de la ville cosmopolite de Dénia. Avec une magnifique colline fortifiée à son arrière, ce batiment charmant date de plus de 800 ans et combine parfaitement des décors d'époque avec un confort luxueux contemporain. De belles chambres offrent des vues magnifiques et sont ornées en terracotta, en bois et en marbre pour créer une ambiance fraîche et confortable. Les hôtes pourront profiter de la délicieuse cuisine de poissons et de fruits de mer d'inspiration dans le nouveau restaurant Sal de Mar, de la salle de gym, du sauna et de l'abondance de boutiques à proximité.

La Posada del Mar está situada frente a la marina en medio del pueblo cosmopolita que es Dénia. Con el magnífico monte fortificado a sus espaldas, este edificio de más de 800 años es hoy un encantador hotel que combina perfectamente detalles de época con un lujoso confort contemporáneo. Las bonitas habitaciones ofrecen maravillosas vistas y están decoradas con terracota, madera y mármol, proporcionando un ambiente fresco y cómodo. Los clientes apreciarán la excelente cocina basada en mariscos que se sirve en el nuevo restaurante Sal de Mar, la cantidad de tiendas muy próximos, el gimnasio y la sauna.

__Our inspector loved:__ The location for exploring the town centre and marina.

Directions: The hotel is situated in Dénia midway between Alicante and Valencia. Take the A7 and turn off at the Dénia exit.

Web: www.johansens.com/posadadelmar
E-mail: info@laposadadelmar.com
Tel: +34 96 643 29 66
Fax: +34 96 642 01 55

Price Guide:
(room only, excluding VAT)
single €100
double €110-160
junior suite €130
suite €210-260

Hotel Mont Sant

SUBIDA AL CASTILLO, S/N JÁTIVA - XÀTIVA, 46800 VALENCIA, SPAIN

Originally a Moorish palace on whose foundations a monastery was built, this hotel has stunning views of the "mini Alhambra" hilltop fortification which was the residence of the Borgia family and birthplace of 2 Spanish popes. Extensive gardens overlook the valley and are surrounded by ancient city walls. Careful attention to detail and rustic décor have created a cosy ambience whilst superb international and Mediterranean cuisine is served in the hotel's attractive restaurant. There is an abundance of walking and sightseeing in the area.

A l'origine un palais Mauresque sur les fondations duquel un monastère fût construit, cet hôtel a une vue superbe sur le "mini Alhambra", fortification sur un sommet, qui fut la résidence de la famille Borgia et le lieu de naissance de 2 papes espagnol. De grands jardins surplombent la vallée et sont entourés par les anciens murs de la ville. Une attention particulière au détail et un décor rustique ont créé une ambiance chaleureuse alors qu'une délicieuse cuisine internationale et méditerranéenne est servie dans l'élégant restaurant. Les possibilités de randonnées et visites sont nombreuses dans la région.

Este hotel, originariamente un palacio árabe en cuyos cimientos se levantó un monasterio, tiene impresionantes vistas de una mini-Alhambra. Esta fortificación, en la cima de un monte, fue la residencia de la familia Borgia y el lugar donde nacieron 2 Papas españoles. Sus grandes jardines, rodeados por la antigua muralla de la ciudad, miran al valle. El esmero por el detalle y su estilo rústico proporcionan un ambiente acogedor. A la vez puede disfrutarse de su excelente cocina internacional y mediterránea en el bello restaurante del hotel. El lugar cuenta con numerosas zonas de paseo y de interés paisajístico.

Our inspector loved: *The great views of Xàtiva's mini-Alhambra fortification.*

Directions: Valencia > A7 to Albacete > turn off for Xàtiva.

Web: www.johansens.com/montsant
E-mail: mont-sant@mont-sant.com
Tel: +34 962 27 50 81
Fax: +34 962 28 19 05

Barcelona
Valencia
Madrid
Málaga

Price Guide: (room only, excluding VAT, closed 7th - 20th January)
single €80-140
double €110-160
suite €320

Casa Lehmi

EL BUSCARRÓ 1-3, E-03518 TÁRBENA, ALICANTE, SPAIN

This beautifully restored hacienda nestles in a fertile valley high in the unspoiled mountains of inland Alicante, 30km from the busy Costa Blanca beaches. A relaxing, peaceful environment within a 16-acre estate of landscaped gardens, pine woods and fruit groves, guests can enjoy lazing in the sun or engaging in a range of sports. Bedrooms are luxurious, and guests dine together at one long table or under the garden pergola.

Cette hacienda superbement restaurée est nichée dans une vallée fertile, haut dans les montagnes restées naturelles de l'arrière pays d'Alicante, à 30km des plages touristique de la Costa Blanca. Dans un havre de paix de 6.5 ha de jardins aménagés, de pinède et de vergers, les hôtes peuvent lézarder au soleil ou se lancer dans diverses activités sportives. Les chambres sont luxueuses et les hôtes peuvent dîner ensemble autour d'une grande table ou sous la pergola.

Esta hacienda magníficamente restaurada se encuentra en medio de un fértil valle entre las altas y virginales montañas del interior de la provincia de Alicante, a sólo 30 kms de las bulliciosas playas de la Costa Blanca. En este tranquilo y sosegado lugar, ubicado en una propiedad 6'5 ha con zonas ajardinadas, pinares y huertas frutales, los clientes podrán disfrutar tomando el sol o practicando distintos deportes. Las habitaciones son lujosas, y los clientes cenan todos juntos en una larga mesa o bajo la pérgola del jardín.

Our inspector loved: *The inspired restoration of this country house, and its privileged location.*

Directions: From A7 Alicante-Valencia > exit Callosa d en Sarria > in Callosa d en Sarria head towards Tarbena > follow the signs.

Web: www.johansens.com/casalehmi
E-mail: hotel@casalehmi.com
Tel: +34 96 588 4018
Fax: +34 96 588 4106

Price Guide:
double €170-270

Hospes Palau de la Mar

NAVARRO REVERTER 14, 46004 VALENCIA, SPAIN

In the heart of Valencia, this renovated aristocratic property creatively blends luxury and style. Comprising 2 buildings, only visible from the exterior due to the different façades, inside the ambience is homogenous. Each floor is individually designed; some of the rooms are situated around an open landscaped patio. The exceptional staircase has a magnificent stained-glass skylight depicting the waves of the sea. Bodyna Oriental massage and therapies can be enjoyed in the specially created new cabins.

Situé au cœur de la ville de Valencia, cette noble demeure rénovée est un créatif mélange de luxe et de style. L'hôtel est composé de 2 bâtiments attenants, aux façades différentes mais dont l'ambiance intérieure est homogène. Chaque étage a son propre design et certaines chambres se trouvent autour d'une cour intérieure paysagée. L'escalier est un élément exceptionnel avec un magnifique vitrail au plafond représentant les vagues de la mer. Les hôtes peuvent profiter de massages orientaux Bodyna et autres thérapies dans nouvelles cabines spécialement conçues.

Este renovado aristocrático hotel que se encuentra en el corazón de Valencia es una combinación creativa de lujo y estilo. Consta de 2 edificios contiguos visibles solamente desde el exterior por sus distintas fachadas, su ambiente interior es totalmente homogéneo. Cada planta posee un diseño individual y algunas de sus estancias se encuentran alrededor de un patio abierto y paisajista. La escalera es un rasgo excepcional con su magnífica claraboya de vidriera representando las olas del mar. Un nuevo Bodyna Spa ha sido creado para ofrecer masajes y múltiples terapias.

Our inspector loved: *The exceptional guest amenities, and attention to detail in the bedrooms.*

Directions: Valencia Airport > city centre > Plaza Porta de la Mar.

Web: www.johansens.com/palaudelamar
E-mail: palaudelamar@hospes.es
Tel: +34 96 316 2884
Fax: +34 96 316 2885

Price Guide: (room only, excluding VAT, private hotel parking available)
single €200-300
double €200-350
suite €600-650

        SPA

Hotel Sidi Saler & Spa

PLAYA EL SALER, 46012 VALENCIA, SPAIN

This 5-star hotel is situated on the long sandy beach of El Saler, within the Albufera Nature Park, which features a lake and habitat for all kinds of birds. All rooms and suites enjoy magnificent views of the Mediterranean. The Les Dunes à la carte restaurant offers a wide range of regional and international dishes accompanied by live music. Enjoy a ride on a mountain bike, a swim in the outdoor or indoor swimming pool, a game of tennis, golf on El Saler golf course or a session in the completely renovated beauty salon with new facilities and treatments. Free shuttle bus service to the centre of Valencia.

Cet hôtel 5 étoiles est situé sur la longue plage de sable de El Saler, au parc naturel d'Albufera avec son lac et sa grande variété d'oiseaux. Toutes les chambres et suites ont des vues merveilleuses de la Méditerranée. Le restaurant Les Dunes offre un menu à la carte de plats régionaux et internationaux accompagnés de musique sur scène. Les hôtes peuvent faire du VTT, nager dans la piscine couverte ou en plein air, jouer au tennis et au golf au parcours El Saler ou jouir des facilités et traitements nouveaux au salon de beauté complètement renové. Service de navette au centre de Valencia.

En la extensa y arenosa playa de El Saler, dentro del Parque Natural Albufera, con un lago y hábitat para toda clase de aves, se ubica este hôtel de 5 estrellas. Todas las habitaciones y suites disfrutan de magníficas vistas al Mediterráneo. El restaurante à la carte Les Dunes ofrece una amplia variedad de platos regionales e internacionales acompañados de música en vivo. Los huéspedes pueden acceder a montar en mountain bike, nadar en piscina interior o exterior, jugar al tenis o al golf en el campo El Saler Golf así como también a una sesión en el renovado salón de belleza con nuevas instalaciones y tratamientos. Servicio de minibús gratuito al centro de Valencia.

Directions: From Valencia take the coastal road and follow signs to El Saler. The hotel is 15km further on.

Web: www.johansens.com/saler
E-mail: reservas@sidisaler.com
Tel: +34 961 61 04 11
Fax: +34 961 61 08 38

Price Guide: (room only, excluding VAT)
single €134-245
double €172-290
suite €735-902

Our inspector loved: *The new luxury spa with very friendly and attentive staff.*

SPA

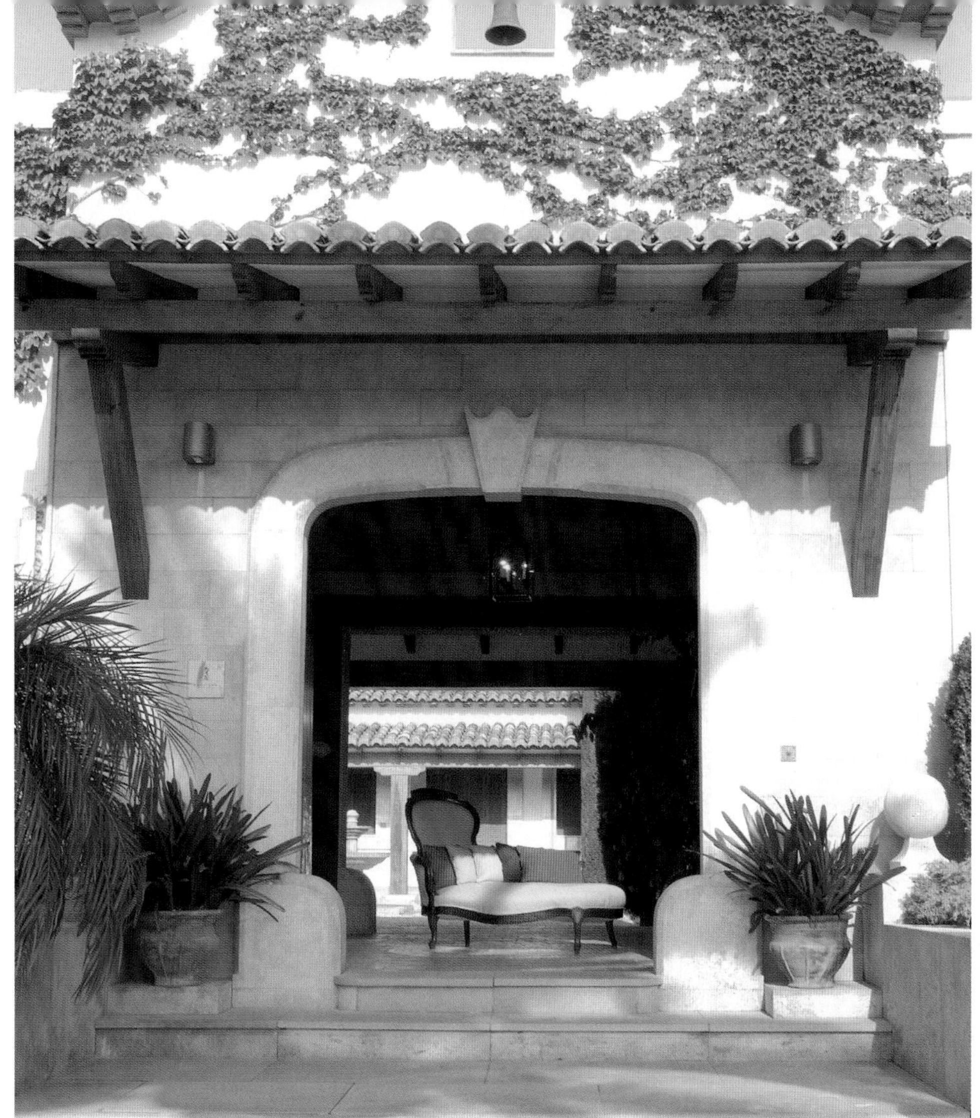

Mas de Canicattí

CTRA. DE PEDRALBA, KM 2.9, 46191 VILAMARXANT, VALENCIA, SPAIN

Idyllically situated amongst 128 acres of citrus trees and landscaped gardens, this delightful hotel offers guests a unique and luxurious experience. This beautifully restored property combines the period features of a traditional country house with the latest designs to create a light, spacious and elegant retreat. The outdoor pool lies within beautiful terraced gardens opening onto orange groves with far-reaching views towards the distant town of Vilamarxant, and the exciting gastronomic creations emerging from the El Càdec restaurant will delight even the most discerning palete.

Idéallement situé au sein de 52 ha de cultures d'agrumes et de jardins aménagés, ce charmant hôtel offre à ses hôtes une expérience unique et luxueuse. Cette propriété superbement restaurée combine les caractéristiques d'époque d'une maison de campagne traditionnelle aux derniers designs afin de créer une retraite lumineuse, spacieuse et élégante. La piscine extérieure se tient au milieu des beaux jardins en terrasse qui donnent sur les orangeraies avec vue sur le lointain en direction de la ville de Vilamarxant. Les créations gastronomiques du restaurant El Càdec enchanteront les palais les plus délicats.

Situado idílicamente entre 52 ha de cítricos y jardines paisajistas, este encantador hotel ofrece a los huéspedes una experiencia lujosa y única. Magníficamente restaurado combina rasgos de época de una casa de campo tradicional con los últimos diseños para crear luz, espacio y elegancia. La piscina exterior entre bonitos jardines colgantes lleva a los naranjales con vistas lejanas al pueblo de Vilamarxant. Sus excelentes creaciones gastronómicas procedentes del restaurante El Càdec deleitarán al más exigente paladar.

Our inspector loved: *The 101 hidden charms, that make this an exceptional hotel.*

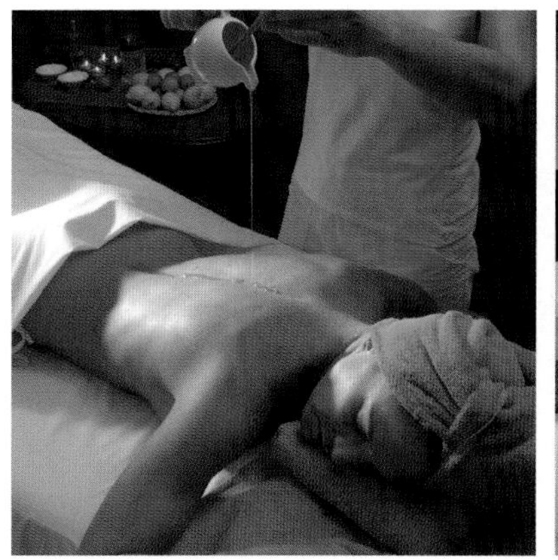

Directions: Valencia Airport is 20km away. A3 towards Madrid > turn off for Ribaroja (331) > follow signs to Vilamarxant > follow signs to Pedralba.

Web: www.johansens.com/canicatti
E-mail: hotel@masdecanicatti.com
Tel: +34 96 165 05 34
Fax: +34 96 165 05 35

Price Guide:
single €196
double €234
suite €318-446

SWITZERLAND

Hotel location shown in red (hotel) or purple (spa hotel) with page number

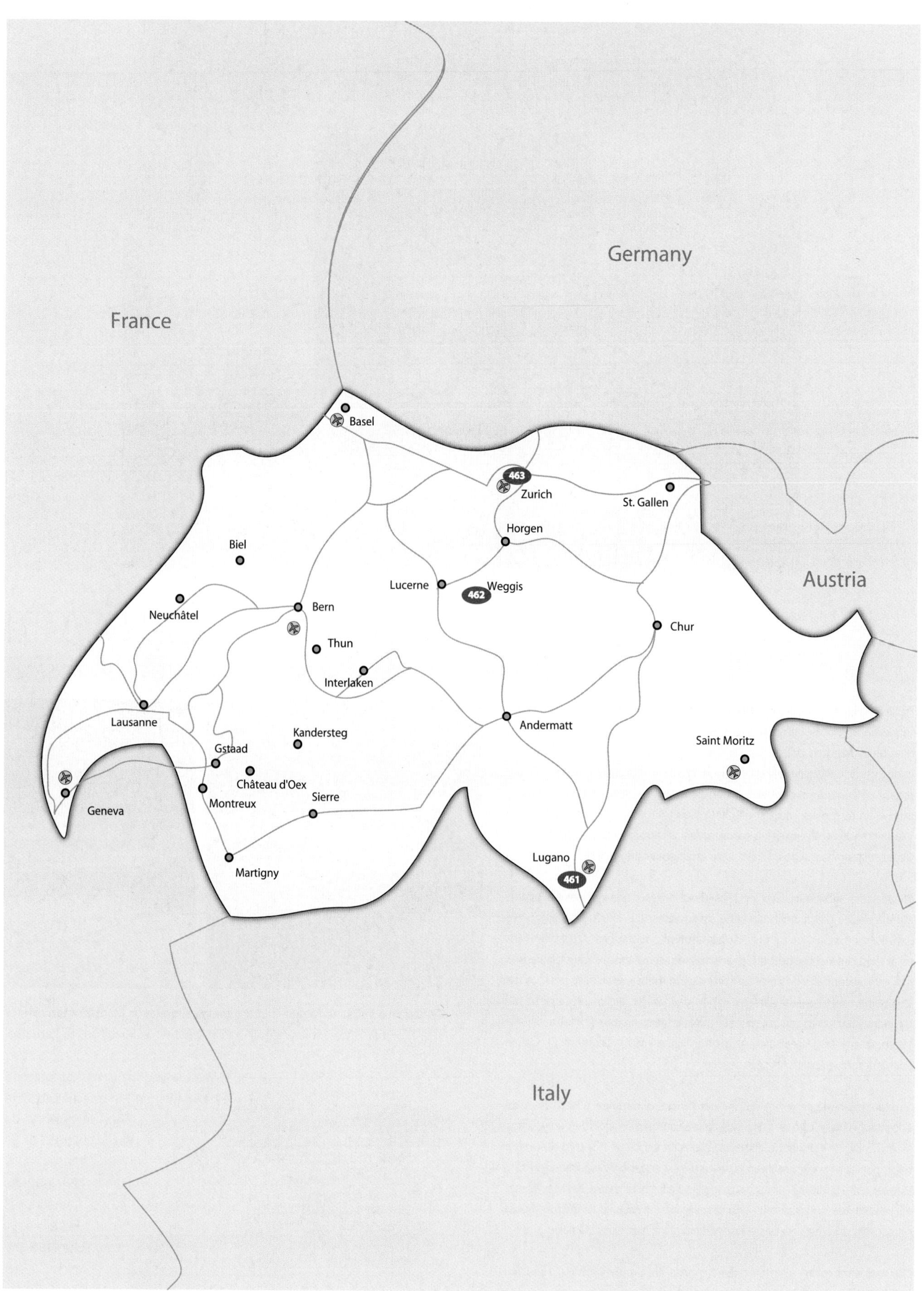

Villa Sassa - Hotel & Spa

VIA TESSERETE 10, 6900 LUGANO, SWITZERLAND

The 4-star Villa Sassa enjoys a prime position on the hills of Lugano with breathtaking views of the Lake, city and mountains. Bright open areas and modern, home-from-home furnishings create a wonderful ambience of tranquillity and spaciousness. The extended and comfortable bedrooms benefit from large terraces, and the 3,000m² of fitness, health and Spa Club offers a vast array of beauty treatments and massages. Delicious Mediterranean cuisine is served in the gourmet restaurant with its spectacular outlook. There is also a Bar Lounge and discotheque.

Cet hôtel 4 étoiles bénéficie d'un emplacement idéal sur les collines de Lugano et offre des vues à couper le souffle sur le lac, la ville et les montagnes. De grands espaces clairs et un mobilier moderne créent une superbe atmosphère de tranquillité. Les chambres spacieuses et confortables jouissent d'une grande terrasse. 3000m² d'espace fitness, santé et thermes offrent une grande variété de soins de beauté et de massages. Une succulente cuisine méditerranéenne est servie dans le restaurant gastronomique d'où la vue est spectaculaire. Sur place on trouve également un salon bar et une boîte de nuit.

Villa Sassa, de 4 estrellas, disfruta de una posición privilegiada en las colinas de Lugano con fabulosas vistas del lago, la ciudad y las montañas. Sus zonas luminosas y modernas, amuebladas para que se sienta como en casa, crean un maravilloso ambiente de tranquilidad y amplitud. Las confortables habitaciones has sido ampliadas y gozan de grandes terrazas, y el Spa Club, con sus 3.000 m², ofrece una grande variedad de tratamientos de belleza y de masajes para el bienestar y la salud. En el idílico restaurante del hotel con sus espectaculares vistas, se sirve una deliciosa cocina mediterránea. El hotel también tiene Bar Lounge y discoteca.

Our inspector loved: *The bright and spacious ambience.*

Directions: Less than 1hr from Milan-Malpensa Italian Intl Airport. Close to Milan's exhibition and trade-show area. Italian border (Como-Chiasso) > Lugano Nord > signs to hospital/railway station. Free pick-up from Lugano-Agno Airport available.

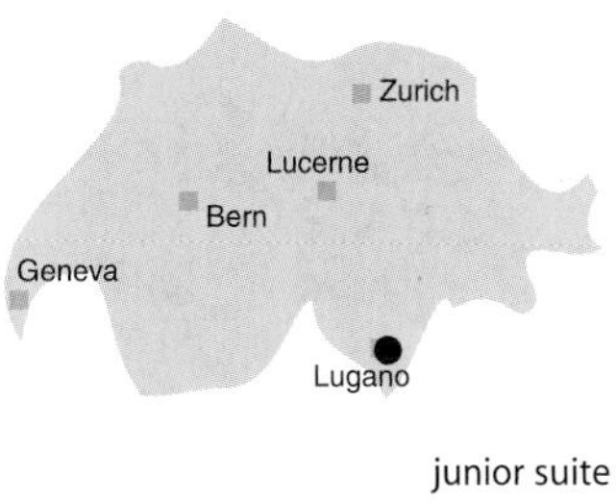

Zurich
Lucerne
Bern
Geneva
Lugano

Web: www.johansens.com/villasassa
E-mail: info@villasassa.ch
Tel: +41 91 911 41 11
Fax: +41 91 922 05 45

Price Guide: (including access to the Health and Spa Club)
standard/superior €190-290
studio/executive suite €260-360
junior suite €330-430 royal/diplomat suite €400-500

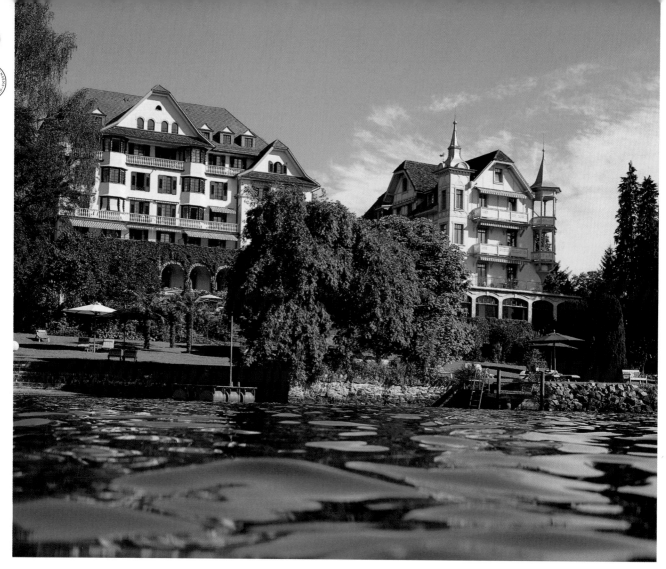

Park Hotel Weggis

HERTENSTEINSTRASSE 34, 6353 WEGGIS, SWITZERLAND

Directions: 60 minutes by car from Zurich Airport. The hotel is in the resort town of Weggis, on the shores of Lake Lucerne.

Web: www.johansens.com/weggis
E-mail: info@phw.ch
Tel: +41 41 392 05 05
Fax: +41 41 392 05 28

Price Guide: (per person)
single €180-225
double €128-205
suite €228-392

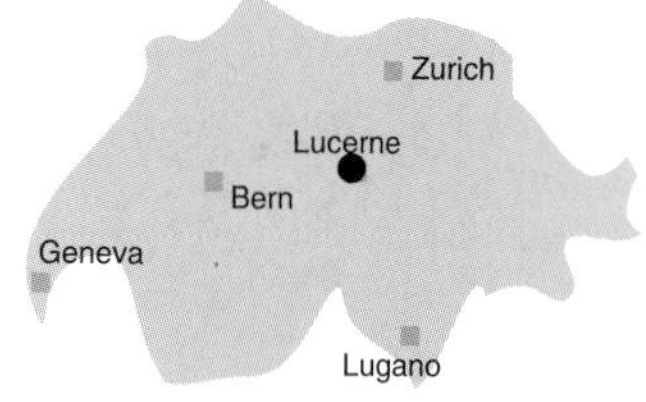

Set in magnificent parkland with a private beach and breathtaking views over Lake Lucerne and the Alps, this unique hotel blends traditional charm and elegance with modern flair. Emphasis is on relaxation, and the 6 private SPA-Cottages offer a full range of beauty and massage treatments. The award-winning Annex restaurant serves French cuisine, whilst the bedrooms and suites are stylishly decorated with Designers Guild fabrics, Philippe Starck lighting and Molteni furniture.

Situé dans un magnifique parc avec une plage privée et des vues imprenables sur le lac Lucerne et les Alpes, cet hôtel unique marie à merveille le charme et l'élégance traditionnels avec un style moderne. L'accent est sur la détente, et les 6 villas-SPA offrent un choix complet de soins et traitements de beauté et massage. Une Cuisine française est servie au restaurant primé Annex. Les chambres et suites élégantes sont ornées avec goût avec des tissus de Designers Guild, lampes de Philippe Starck et meubles de Molteni.

Situado en una magnífica zona verde con playas privadas y espectaculares vistas al Lago Lucerna y a los Alpes, este hotel único combina el encanto y la elegancia tradicional con la tendencia moderna. Sus 6 casitas rurales-Spa, privadas, ofrecen una completa gama de tratamientos de belleza y masaje, enfatizando la relajación. El restaurante galardonado Annex sirve cocina francesa, mientras que las habitaciones y suites ofrecen un gran estilo, decoradas con telas del Designers Guild, alumbrado de Philippe Starck y mobiliario de Molteni.

Our inspector loved: *The Bonsai trees in the Japanese meditation garden and the Rachmaninoff Suite.*

ALDEN HOTEL SPLÜGENSCHLOSS

SPLÜGENSTRASSE 2, GENFERSTRASSE, 8002 ZÜRICH, SWITZERLAND

This charming, family-run 5-star hotel is effortlessly well organised and extremely welcoming. The stunning authentic façade is a unique reflection of the thoughtfully refurbished interior, which is stylishly contemporary whilst maintaining many original period features: ornate stucco decorations and impressive painted ceilings. Natural colour schemes create an ambience that is wonderfully restful and cosy. The latest high-tech equipment can be found in the spacious suites, most of which have balconies or terraces.

Ce charmant hôtel familial 5 étoiles est naturellement organisée et très accueillant. La superbe façade authentique est simplement le reflet de son intérieur soigneusement re-décoré, dans un style contemporain chic tout en ayant conservé de nombreux éléments d'époque : stuc orné et impressionants plafonds peints. Des tons naturels créent une ambiance merveilleusement reposante et douillette. Chaque suite est spacieuse, la plupart avec balcon ou terrasse, et dispose d'un équipement haute-technologie des plus modernes.

Este encantador hotel de 5 estrellas de regencia familiar es enormemente acogedora y organizada sin aparente esfuerzo. La impresionante fachada original constituye una singular muestra de un interior renovado con esmero, elegantemente moderno a la vez que conserva numerosos elementos originales de época, tales como las vistosas decoraciones en estuco o sus impresionantes techos pintados. Las naturales combinaciones de color crean un ambiente increíblemente tranquilo y acogedor. Las espaciosas suites, la mayoría con balcones o terrazas, disponen de lo último en equipos de alta tecnología.

Directions: Zürich > city centre > cross the river towards the main train station > remain parallel to the river > financial district.

Web: www.johansens.com/aldenhotel
E-mail: welcome@alden.ch
Tel: +41 44 289 99 99
Fax: +41 44 289 99 98

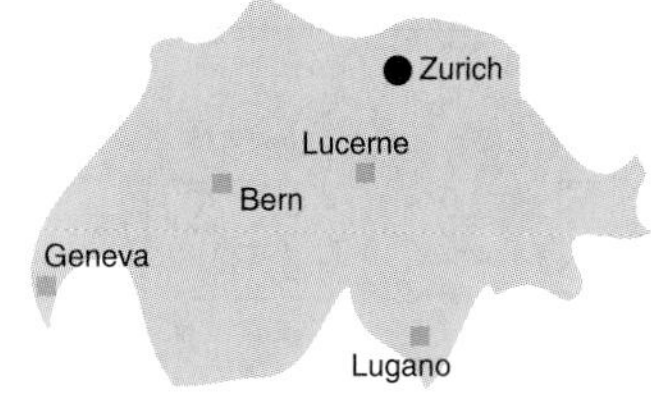

Price Guide:
suite CHF700-1,500

Our inspector loved: *The superb atmosphere, comfort, and service.*

  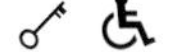       

TURKEY

Hotel location shown in red (hotel) or purple (spa hotel) with page number

THE MARMARA ANTALYA

ESKI LARA YOLU NO 136, SIRINYALI, ANTALYA, TURKEY

Boasting one of the largest conference centres in the region, not to mention a private beach with a plethora of waterside activities, this new hotel is ideal for both business and leisure travellers alike. Decorated in a contemporary style, there are 208 rooms in the main complex and 24 lofts in the rotating annex, which smoothly revolves to offer magnificent views of the Mediterranean. Dining options are plentiful and at Tuti Restaurant, one of the youngest and highly acclaimed chefs in the country displays his culinary talents.

Possédant l'un des plus grand centre de conférences de la région, sans parler de sa plage privée avec une abondance d'activités nautiques, ce nouvel hôtel est idéal aussi bien pour les affaires que pour les loisirs. Décoré dans un style contemporain, l'hôtel comporte 208 chambres dans le complexe principal et 24 lofts dans l'annexe rotative, qui tourne doucement offrant ainsi de magnifiques vues sur la Méditerranée. Les options dînatoires sont nombreuses et au restaurant Tuti. Le chef le plus jeune et le plus reconnu du pays expose ses talents culinaires.

Este nuevo hotel, provisto de uno de los mayores centros de congresos de la región así como de una playa privada con un gran despliegue de actividades acuáticas, resulta ideal tanto para los viajeros de negocios como para los turistas. Decorado en estilo contemporáneo, cuenta con 208 habitaciones en el complejo principal y 24 áticos en el anexo rotativo, que gira lenta y suavemente para ofrecer magníficas vistas al Mediterráneo. Las alternativas para cenar son abundantes, y en el Tuti Restaurant uno de los chefs mas jóvenes y cotizados del país demuestra su talento gastronómico.

Directions: Antalya Airport > Lara > city centre.

Web: www.johansens.com/marmaraantalya
E-mail: info@themarmarahotels.com
Tel: +90 242 249 36 00
Fax: +90 242 316 81 04

Price Guide:
single €170-260
double €190-370

Istanbul
Ankara
Antalya

Our inspector loved: *The revolving loft bedroom; one of a kind!*

  232    1000       

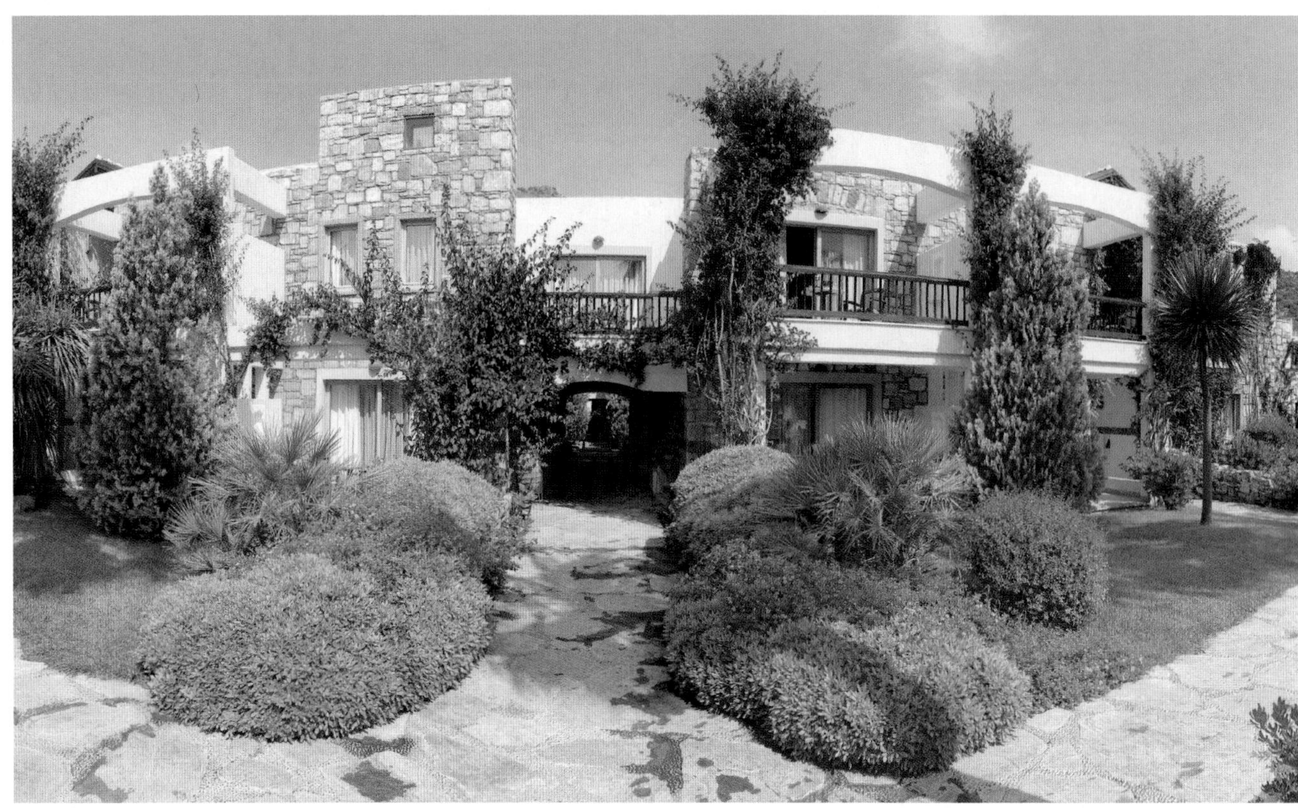

Divan Bodrum Palmira

KELESHARIM CADDESI 6, GÖLTÜRKBÜKÜ, MUGLA, 48483 BODRUM, TURKEY

Directions: Bodrum-Milas Airport > follow signs for Türkbükü > follow signs for Divan Palmira towards beach.

Web: www.johansens.com/divanpalmira
E-mail: divan@divanpalmira.com.tr
Tel: +90 252 377 5601
Fax: +90 252 377 5952

Price Guide:
rooms €235-525

Stone walls and wooden balconies give real charm to this wonderful beachfront hotel, which has a lovely colourful garden and a bright lobby with eye-catching paintings. The comfortable rooms are spacious and beautifully decorated; some have sea views. Tasty Mediterranean cuisine is served either al fresco by the swimming pool or in the cosy restaurant. Guests can take advantage of the excellent fitness facilities, water sports, tennis, snooker and basketball or explore the many historical sights nearby.

Des murs de pierre et balcons en bois ajoutent au charme de ce merveilleux hôtel de bord de plage, qui a un ravissant jardin coloré et un hall clair avec des tableaux accrocheurs. Les chambres douillettes sont spacieuses et joliement décorées; certaines ont vue sur la mer. Une cuisine méditerranéenne délicieuse est servie au frais au bord de la piscine ou dans le confortable restaurant. Les hôtes peuvent profiter des excellents équipements de remise en forme, des sports nautiques, tennis, billard et basket ou explorer les sites historiques proches.

Muros de piedra y balcones de madera confieren un verdadero encanto a este maravilloso hotel situado en primera línea de playa. El hotel cuenta con un bello y vistoso jardín así como de un luminoso vestíbulo con llamativos lienzos. Las cómodas habitaciones, algunas con vistas al mar, son espaciosas y están magníficamente decoradas. Los clientes podrán saborear la sabrosa cocina mediterránea bien al aire libre a la vera de la piscina o en el acogedor restaurante. Asimismo, podrán hacer uso de las excelentes instalaciones de fitness deportes acuáticos, tenis, snooker y baloncesto o explorar los numerosos lugares de interés histórico que ofrecen los alrededores.

***Our inspector loved:** The energetic and friendly management.*

The Marmara Bodrum

SULUHASAN CADDESI, YOKUSBASI, MAHALLESI NO 18, PO BOX 199, 48400 BODRUM, TURKEY

Overlooking Bodrum, with medieval castle and harbour, this is the ideal base from which to enjoy the area's non-stop nightlife, shopping and museums. Surrounded by gardens, this hilltop hotel features Japanese-influenced bedrooms; all have balconies. Enjoy Mediterranean and Turkish cuisine and cocktails in the 2 bars. The spa offers an array of massages and treatments, includes a floating tank, Turkish bath and sauna. This is the only SLH member in Turkey and the only hotel in the south awarded a Star Diamond Award.

Surplombant Bodrum, avec son port et son château médiéval, cet hôtel est idéal pour profiter des boutiques, des musées et de la vie nocturne de la région. Entouré de jardins, cet hôtel au sommet d'une colline a été décoré avec d'intéressants objets artisanaux et des peintures. Les chambres aux influences japonaises sont faites avec du bois clair, des sols en pierre et possèdent des balcons. Les clients peuvent apprécier une cuisine méditerranéenne et Turque et siroter des cocktails dans les 2 bars. Le spa offre un large choix de soins dont la caisse à eau, le bain turque et le sauna. L'hôtel est le seul membre de SLH en Turquie et le seul hôtel dans le sud qui s'est vu attribuer un Star Diamond Award.

Con vistas a la localidad de Bodrum, con su castillo medieval y puerto, esta es una base ideal para disfrutar de las tiendas, los museos y la interminable vida nocturna de la zona. Rodeado de jardines, este hotel sitado en la cima de una colina, tiene habitaciones de inspiracion japonesa, todas con balcones. Podrá disfrutar de cocina mediterránea y turca y tomarse un cóctel en uno de sus 2 bares. El spa proporciona una variedad de masajes y tratamientos, e incluye un tanque de flotación, baño turco y sauna. Este es el único hotel de SLH en Turquía y el único hotel del sur que ha ganado un Star Diamond Award.

Our inspector loved: *The spacious, well designed bedrooms.*

Directions: Bodrum Airport is 30km away. From the airport head towards Bodrum and turn right just before travelling downhill to Bodrum then turn right before the Nissan showroom.

Web: www.johansens.com/marmarabodrum
E-mail: bodrum-sales@themarmarahotels.com
Tel: +90 252 313 8130
Fax: +90 252 313 8131

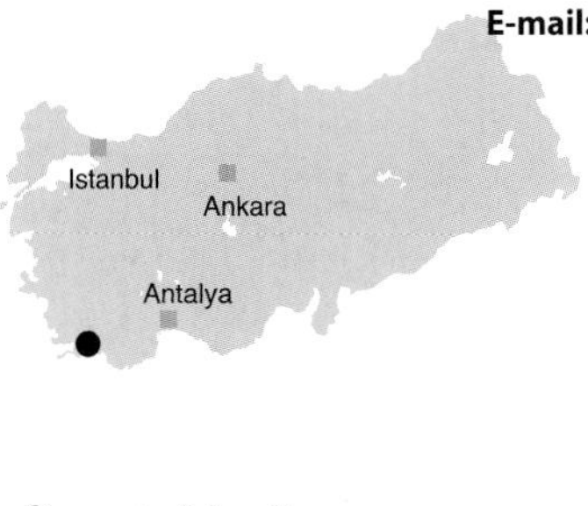

Istanbul
Ankara
Antalya

Price Guide:
single €250
double €300
party animal €920

 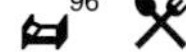 96   150      

Degirmen Otel

DEGIRMEN SOK 3, ALAÇATI, ÇESME, IZMIR, TURKEY

Directions: Izmir to Çesme > turn right to Alaçati > 90km.

Web: www.johansens.com/degirmen
E-mail: info@alacatidegirmen.com
Tel: +90 232 716 6714
Fax: +90 232 716 8936

Price Guide:
double €110-160

Re-built in the old Aegean style using local stone and reclaimed wood, this hotel comprises 4 windmills containing 2 rooms each. All have open fireplaces, regional handicrafts and artefacts and some feature waterbeds. Only breakfast is served at the hotel, but the small town of Alaçati is just a short walk away and offers many nice restaurants, shops and cafés, as well as excellent beaches. Horse riding and water sports are available nearby.

Reconstruit dans le vieux style égéen utilisant la pierre locale et du bois ancien, cet hôtel comprend 4 moulins avec seulement 2 chambres chacun. Toutes les chambres ont une cheminée et sont décorées d'objets d'artisanat local. Certains lits sont équipés de matelas à eau. Seuls les petits-déjeuners sont servis à l'hôtel, mais la petite ville d'Alaçati n'est qu'à quelques minutes à pied et offre une grande sélection de bons restaurants, magasins et cafés, ainsi que de très belles plages. Equitation et sports nautiques sont disponibles à proximité.

Reconstruido al estilo antiguo del Egeo utilizando la piedra local y madera antigua recuperada, este hotel se compone de 4 molinos de viento con 2 habitaciones en cada uno. Cada habitación goza de chimenea, artesanía regional y alguna tiene cama de agua. Solo el desayuno se sirve en el hotel, pero a corta distancia se halla la pequeña aldea de Alaçati, donde encontrara buenos restaurantes, tiendas y cafeterías así como unas playas excelentes. Se pueden practicar deportes acuáticos y también montar a caballo.

Our inspector loved: *The bedrooms in the windmills.*

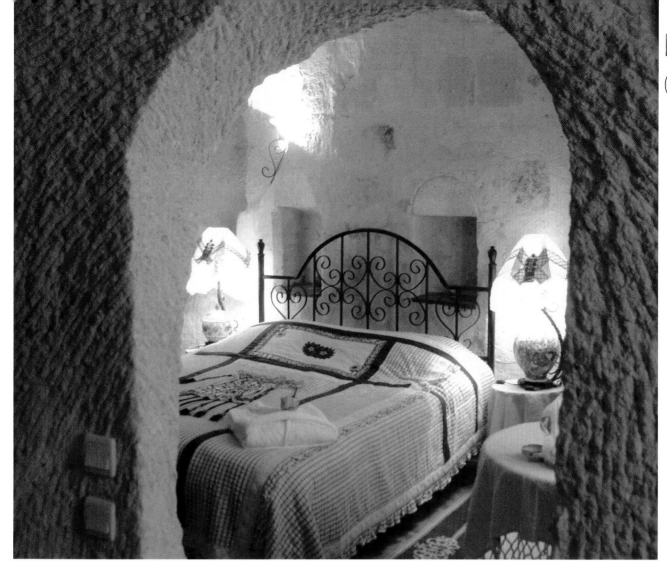

Cappadocia Cave Suites

GAFFERLI MAHALLESI, UNLÜ SOKAK, 50180 GÖREME - NEVSEHIR, TURKEY

This truly unique hotel is like something from a mythological era. Situated in an incredible landscape rich in history and mystery, this intriguing retreat has been transformed from a series of centuries-old caves and architectural formations into award-winning luxury accommodation offering everything to everyone. Local handicrafts, antiques and expertly selected furniture combine with modern amenities to make the cool caves stylish and comfortable, and excellent local delicacies can be enjoyed in the cosy restaurant.

Cet hôtel absolument unique semble venir tout droit de la mythologie. Situé dans un paysage incroyable riche en histoire et en mystère, ce refuge intrigant a été transformé à partir d'une série de caves centenaires et des formations architecturales en un hébergement luxueux primé offrant tout ce que les clients désirent. Des produits artisanaux, des antiquités et des meubles choisis avec soins se mélangent aux équipements modernes donnant à ces caves fraîches confort et élégances. De délicieux mets locaux peuvent être dégustés au restaurant.

Este hotel verdaderamente singular parece procedente de la época mitológica. Situado en medio de un increíble paisaje plagado de historia y misterio, este impresionante remanso de paz, originalmente un conjunto de cuevas y estructuras arquitectónicas de varios siglos de antigüedad, ha sido transformado en un galardonado hotel de lujo para todo tipo de clientes y grado de exigencia. La artesanía local, las antigüedades y el mobiliario seleccionado por expertos se combinan con sus modernas instalaciones para convertir las refrescantes cuevas en lugares de suma comodidad y elegancia. En su acogedor restaurante se pueden degustar las excelentes especialidades del lugar.

Directions: Kayseri Airport > Ürgüp > Nevsehir. 10km before Nevsehir, enter Göreme centre > follow hotel signs.

Web: www.johansens.com/cappadociacaves
E-mail: info@cappadociacavesuites.com
Tel: +90 384 271 2800
Fax: +90 384 271 27 99

Price Guide:
single US$120-150
double US$150-180
suite US$200-300

Our inspector loved: *This wonderful setting in the midst of history.*

TURKEY (ISTANBUL)

AJIA HOTEL

AHMET RASIM PASA YALISI, ÇUBUKLU CADDESI, NO 27, KANLICA, ISTANBUL, TURKEY

The sparkling white façade of this superbly restored Ottoman period mansion, standing on the shores of the Bosporus Sea, contrasts beautifully with the deep blue waters over which it regally rises. This is a hotel that comfortably blends the old with the new. While its exterior and surrounds are elegantly traditional the interior is tastefully modern, reflecting an almost minimalist style. Guest rooms have every facility, and indoor and outdoor dining is an experience to savour.

La façade blanche immaculée de cette demeure d'époque ottomane superbement restaurée qui se tient sur les bords du Bosphore, contraste superbement avec les eaux bleues profondes au dessus desquelles elle s'élève majestueusement. C'est un hôtel qui marie confortablement l'ancien et le neuf. Alors que son extérieur et ses environs sont traditionnellement élégants, l'intérieur a été décoré avec goût dans un style moderne presque minimaliste. Les chambres sont toutes confortables, et dîner que ce soit à l'intérieur ou à l'extérieur est une expérience à apprécier plainement.

La fachada de blanco inmaculado de esta mansión del periodo otomano, magníficamente restaurada y situada a orillas del mar del Bósforo, proporciona un bello contraste con las profundas y azules aguas sobre las que majestuosamente se erige. Es un hotel que conjuga de forma natural lo nuevo con lo antiguo. Mientras su exterior y aledaños emanan un sabor de elegante tradición, su interior se expresa con un fino toque moderno, reflejo de un estilo casi minimalista. Las habitaciones disponen de todas las comodidades. Las cenas tanto en el interior como en el exterior son todo una experiencia que hay que saborear.

Directions: Ataturk Airport to Ajia via Fatih Sultan > Mehmet Bridge > turn right for A Hisari > Kanlica.

Web: www.johansens.com/aijahotel
E-mail: info@ajiahotel.com
Tel: +90 216 413 9300
Fax: +90 216 413 9355

Price Guide:
single/double €250-850
suite €450-650

Our inspector loved: *The view of the Bosphorus from the bath.*

The Marmara Istanbul

TAKSIM MEYDANI, TAKSIM, 34437 ISTANBUL, TURKEY

This prestigious city hotel offers comfort and luxury. Stunning views of the Bosporus and Istanbul can be experienced from the Panorama Restaurant and the rooftop swimming pool. All rooms and suites are fully equipped with modern facilities; there is a fitness centre, and numerous bars and places to eat nearby. Located within the heart of the city, the hotel provides the perfect base for leisure or business travellers alike.

Cet hôtel prestigieux offre confort et luxe. De magnifiques vues du Bosphore et d'Istanbul peuvent être admirées depuis le restaurant Panorama et la piscine sur le toit. Toutes les chambres et suites sont parfaitement équipées de tout le confort moderne ; il y a un centre de remise en forme ainsi que de nombreux bars et restaurants aux alentours. Situé au cœur de la ville, l'hôtel est une base idéale pour les clients en vacances ou ceux qui sont en voyages d'affaires.

Este prestigioso hotel ofrece confort y lujo. Vistas impresionantes del Bósforo y de Estambul se pueden apreciar desde el restaurante Panorama y la zona de la piscina que se sitúan en la azotea. Las habitaciones y suites están equipadas con todas las comodidades modernas. El hotel dispone de gimnasio, y una gran variedad de bares y restaurantes se encuentran en la vecindad. Situado en el centro de la ciudad, el hotel es una base perfecta para viajes de placer o de negocios.

Our inspector loved: *The great panoramic view from the restaurant.*

Directions: 24km from Ataturk Airport. The hotel is in the centre of the city, to the right of Taksim Square.

Web: www.johansens.com/maramaraistanbul
E-mail: istanbul-info@themarmarahotels.com
Tel: +90 212 251 4696
Fax: +90 212 244 0509

Istanbul
Ankara
Antalya

Price Guide: (room only, excluding VAT)
single €240
double €275
suite €395-1,050

The Marmara Pera

MESRUTIYET CADDESI, TEPEBASI, 34430 ISTANBUL, TURKEY

The Marmara Pera's tall façade prominently stands out in the former social quarter of Istanbul: the Beyoglu district, now the city's most fashionable area. Bedrooms are comfortable with modern décor and offer diverse views of the city. The hotel's stylish interior includes Turkish antiques, and an art gallery on the second floor displays fascinating exhibitions. Café Marmara, on the ground floor, is the ideal place to unwind after experiencing Istanbul's endless cultural sites and social life.

La grande façade du Marmara Pera se détache dans la partie historique d'Istanbul : le Beyoglu, devenu aujourd'hui le quartier le plus en vue de la ville. Les chambres à la décoration moderne sont confortables et offrent d'intéressantes vues sur la ville. L'intérieur élégant de l'hôtel met en avant des antiquités Turques et une galerie d'art au deuxième étage propose des expositions passionnantes. Le Café Marmara est l'endroit idéal pour se relaxer après avoir expérimenté la vie sociale et les innombrables sites d'Istanbul.

La alta fachada del Marmara Pera destaca en esta antigua zona social de Estambul, el distrito Beyoglu, hoy día el mas de moda de la ciudad. Las habitaciones son cómodas con decoración moderna y ofrecen variadas vistas de la ciudad. El elegante interior incluye antigüedades turcas, y una galería de arte ubicada en el segundo piso expone colecciones fascinantes. El Café Marmara, al pie calle, es un lugar ideal para relajarse después de un día disfrutando de la vida social de Estambul y los muchos monumentos que hay que ver.

Our inspector loved: *The relaxed atmosphere of the Café Marmara.*

Directions: 25km from Ataturk Airport.

Web: www.johansens.com/marmarapera
E-mail: pera-info@themarmarahotels.com
Tel: +90 212 251 4646
Fax: +90 212 249 8033

Price Guide: (room only, excluding VAT)
single €190
double €210
suite €315

Sumahan On The Water

KULELÍ CADDESI NO 51, ÇENGELKÖY, 34684 ISTANBUL, TURKEY

Originally a 19th-century factory, Sumahan On The Water is a very modern, small hotel in an historic setting. All bedrooms have marble bathrooms, views directly onto the Bosphorus, and most have fireplaces. The atmosphere is relaxed, and the facilities include a health club, Turkish bath and award-winning seafood restaurant. A 10-minute boat ride from major transport hubs and a 5-minute walk to Çengelköy, a traditional neighbourhood of wooden houses, shops and restaurants.

A l'origine une usine du XIXe siècle, Sumahan On The Water est un petit hôtel très moderne dans un cadre historique. Toutes les chambres ont des salles de bains en marbre, des vues directes sur le Bosphore et la plupart ont des cheminées. L'atmosphère est décontractée et les équipements comprennent un centre de remise en forme, un bain turc et un restaurant de poissons primé. L'hôtel est à 10 minutes en bateau des principaux centres de transports et à 5 minutes à pied de Çengelköy, un quartier traditionnel avec maisons en bois, magasins et restaurants.

Originariamente una fábrica del siglo XIX, Sumahan On The Water es hoy un pequeño hotel muy moderno situado en un enclave histórico. Todas las habitaciones cuentan con baños de mármol, vistas al Bósforo y la mayoría disponen además de chimenea. El ambiente es relajado y entre sus instalaciones hay un club de salud, baño turco y un galardonado restaurante especializado en mariscos. A 10 minutos en barco de los principales centros de transporte y a sólo 5 minutos a pie de Çengelköy, podrá encontrar un barrio tradicional de casas de madera, tiendas y restaurantes.

Our inspector loved: *The dramatic views of the Bosphorus from the bedrooms.*

Directions: 35km from Istanbul Ataturk Airport. From the airport travel to the Asian Side then follow signs to the Kuleli District.

Web: www.johansens.com/sumahan
E-mail: info@sumahan.com
Tel: +90 216 422 8000
Fax: +90 216 422 8008

Price Guide:
double US$220-280
suite US$265-490

Tuvana Residence

TUZCULAR MAHALLESI, KARANLIK SOKAK 7, 07100 KALEIÇI - ANTALYA, TURKEY

Set in Kaleiçi, Antalya's old quarter, this is the newest of the 3 distinct Tuvana hotels. All rooms are beautifully decorated and offer all modern amenities, and wooden floors and ceilings create a warm and cosy atmosphere. Delightful Turkish cuisine can be sampled in one of the 3 restaurants, and guests have full use of the swimming pool and gardens of the Tuvana Hotel across the road. The historic parts of Antalya such as the old harbour as well as numerous shops, restaurants and beaches are within easy reach.

Situé à Kaleiçi, le vieux quartier d'Antalya, celui-ci est le plus récent des 3 différents hôtels Tuvana. Toutes les chambres sont superbement décorées et offrent toutes les facilités modernes. Planchers et plafonds en bois créent une atmosphère chaleureuse et douillette. Une délicieuse cuisine turque peut être dégustée dans l'un des 3 restaurants et les hôtes peuvent utiliser la piscine et les jardins de l'hôtel Tuvana de l'autre côte de la route. Les quartiers historiques d'Antalya tel que le vieux port, ainsi que de nombreux magasins, restaurants et plages sont d'accès facile.

Situado en Kaleiçi, la parte antigua de Antalya, este es el más nuevo de los 3 hoteles Tuvana. Todas las habitaciones, bellamente decoradas ofrecen las últimas comodidades, y los suelos y techos de madera, crean un ambiente cálido y acogedor. Hay 3 restaurantes que ofrecen estupenda cocina turca, y los clientes pueden disfrutar de la piscina y de los jardines del Hotel Tuvana situado enfrente. La zona histórica de Antalya, el puerto antiguo, y numerosas tiendas, restaurantes y playas se encuentran a pocos pasos del hotel.

Our inspector loved: *The calming atmosphere.*

Directions: The nearest airport is Antalya. From the clock tower turn left > left again after 200 metres.

Web: www.johansens.com/tuvanaresidence
E-mail: tuvanaotel@superonline.com
Tel: +90 242 247 60 15
Fax: +90 242 241 19 81

Price Guide:
single US$110–135
double US$140–250

Villa Mahal

PO BOX 4 KALKAN, 07960 ANTALYA, TURKEY

This intimate, hillside hotel overlooks the bay of Kalkan, surrounded by olive trees. Stone steps plunge to the villa's own beach platforms, and the pool suite has a private pool and terrace. The bright, airy bedrooms, all with seaview, cater up to 26 guests. The ambience is more like a private house than a hotel. Breakfast is a delicious buffet taken on the rooftop terrace, and the Beach Restaurant serves succulent Turkish specialities for lunch and dinner. Enjoy the new infinity pool, with integrated Jacuzzi, and relax with a massage by the sea.

Cet hôtel intime, entouré d'oliviers et perché sur une colline, surplombe la baie de Kalkan. Un escalier en pierre donne accès au ponton privé, et la suite piscine possède une terrasse et une piscine privées. Les chambres spacieuses et lumineuses, pouvant accueillir jusqu'à 26 hôtes, ont toutes vue sur la mer et l'ambiance ressemble plus à celle d'une maison particulière qu'à celle d'un hôtel. Le petit-déjeuner est un superbe buffet servi sur la terrasse sur le toit et le restaurant de la plage propose de délicieuses spécialités turques pour le déjeuner et le dîner. Les hôtes peuvent profiter de la nouvelle piscine à débordement avec jacuzzi intégré et d'un massage de relaxation en bord de mer.

Este hotel íntimo, rodeado de olivos, está situado en la ladera de una colina con vistas a la espectacular bahía de kalkan. Escalones de piedra dan acceso a la playa privada en forma de plataformas y la piscina-suite posee terraza privada con piscina. Las habitaciones amplias y luminosas, todas con vistas al mar, pueden alojar a un máximo de 26 personas y el ambiente es más propio de una casa particular que de un hotel. El desayuno, un delicioso buffet, se degusta en la terraza de la azotea y el beach restaurant sirve suculentas especialidades turcas para el el almuerzo y la cena. Disfrute en la nueva piscina con jacuzzi y relajese con un masaje al lado del mar.

Our inspector loved: *Watching the fantastic sunset from the terrace.*

Directions: Dalaman Airport > Kas > Kalkan sign > left > beach.

Web: www.johansens.com/villamahal
E-mail: info@villamahal.com
Tel: +90 242 844 32 68
Fax: +90 242 844 21 22

Price Guide:
(closed 3rd November - 1st March)
single €135
double/twin €150–250
suite €270–300

  13      

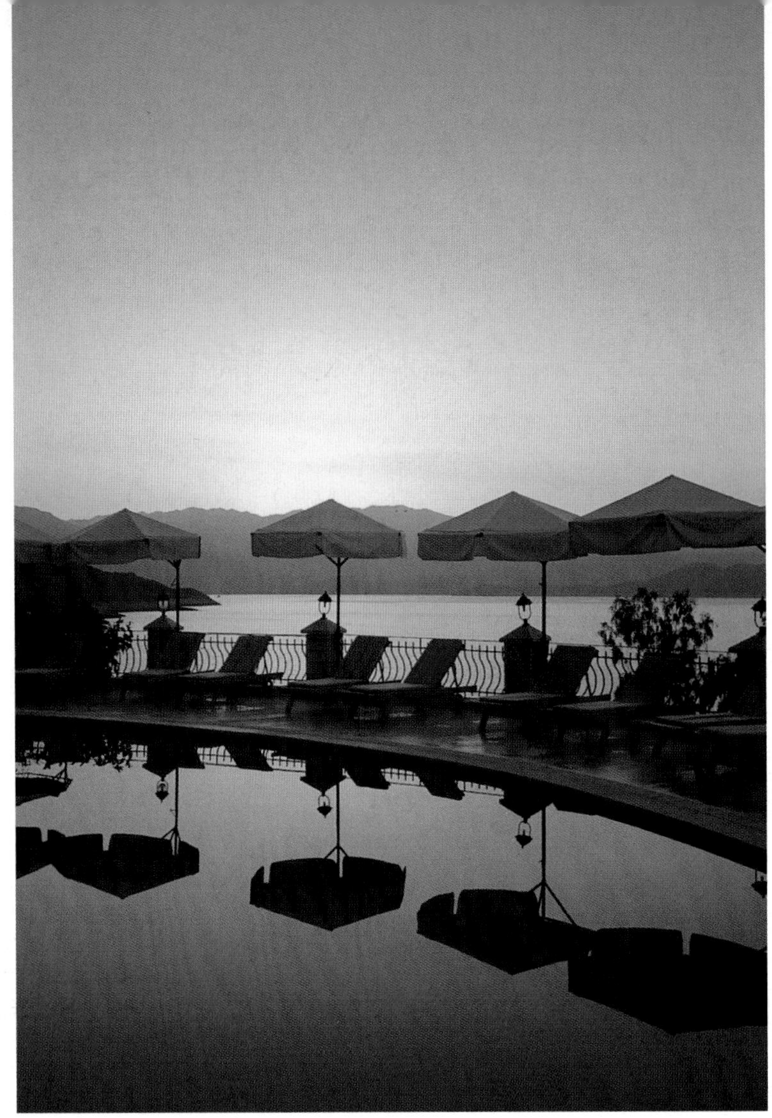

VILLA HOTEL TAMARA

ÇURURBAG YARIMADASI, KAS, ANTALYA, TURKEY

Overlooking the Kas peninsula, this elegant, peaceful hotel has 30 luxury suites, all decorated in a different style to reflect local sites of ancient historic interest. They also have large private balconies with sea views and are fitted with air conditioning and a mini bar. A bar and outdoor restaurant serve drinks and meals on the terrace, whilst 2 swimming pools and walkways below allow guests to take full advantage of the stunning coastline.

Donnant sur la Péninsule de Kas, cet hôtel élégant et paisible a 30 suites luxueuses, toutes décorées dans un style différent pour refléter les sites locaux d'intérêt historiques anciens. Elles ont également de grands balcons privés, l'air conditionné et un mini bar. Un bar et un restaurant extérieur servent des boissons et repas sur la terrasse, alors que 2 piscines et des terrasses donnant sur la mer permettent aux hôtes de profiter pleinement de la superbe côte.

Mirando a la península de Kas, este pacifico y elegante hotel se compone de 30 suites de lujo decoradas con estilos diferentes para reflejar lugares locales de interés histórico antiguo. Gozan de grandes balcones privados con vistas al mar y están equipados con aire acondicionado y mini bar. Existe un restaurante y bar al aire libre donde se sirven comidas y bebidas en la terraza y que, junto con las 2 piscinas y las plataformas sobre el mar, permite beneficiarse al máximo de este impresionante litoral.

Our inspector loved: *The view of the great blue Mediterranean.*

Directions: Balaman Airpot > Kas > turn right before Marina on Peninsula.

Web: www.johansens.com/villahoteltamara
E-mail: info@hoteltamara.com.tr or tamara1@superonline.com
Tel: +90 242 836 3273
Fax: +90 242 836 2112

Price Guide:
double €60
suite €100

30

Richmond Nua Wellness - Spa

SAHILYOLU, 54600 SAPANCA, ADAPAZARI, TURKEY

This modern building sits serenely by the Sapanca Lake, and features a sleek, minimal interior design as well as a brand new state-of-the-art spa complex. Most bedrooms have lake views, and the atrium-style lobby has walkways over water leading to spacious restaurants, relaxed reading rooms or a bar with live piano music during the winter season. Treatments and facilities at the spa include hot stone and Ayurvedic massage, natural baths, Aqua Cave with rain and thunder and a vitamin bar.

Ce bâtiment moderne qui se tient sereinement sur les bords du lac de Sapanca offre un design intérieur minimaliste et chic ainsi qu'un tout nouveau complexe de spa d'un style artistic des plus modernes. La plupart des chambres ont vue sur le lac, et la réception dans le style d'un atrium a des passerelles au-dessus de l'eau qui mènent aux restaurants spacieux, salles de lecture relaxantes et au bar avec pianiste durant l'hiver. Les traitements et équipements du spa incluent pierres chaudes et massages ayurvédiques, bains naturels, L'Aqua Cave avec pluie, tonnerre et un bar à vitamines.

Este moderno edificio se encuentra junto al apacible lago Sapanca y destaca por su elegante estilo interio rminimalista así como por un complejo spa totalmente nuevo y vanguardista. La mayoría de las habitaciones tienen vistas al lago y a un vestíbulo similar a un atrio que cuenta con pasarelas sobre el agua conducentes a espaciosos restaurantes, tranquilas y silenciosas salas de lectura o un bar con música de piano en directo durante el invierno. Entre las instalaciones y tratamientos que ofrece el spa se encuentran los masajes ayurvedas y masajes de piedras calientes, baños naturales, L'Aqua Cave con lluvia y niebla y trueno y bar vitaminas.

Our inspector loved: *The rainforest shower in the spa.*

Directions: Ataturk Airport > exit Ankara Highway > turn left at Sapanca > hotel signs. Alternatively fly into Sabiha Gokcen Airport.

Web: www.johansens.com/richmondnua
E-mail: info@richmondnua.com
Tel: +90 264 582 2100
Fax: +90 264 582 2101

Price Guide:
single €215-275
double €255-315
suite €455-515

    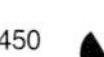     

Sacred House

KARAHANDERE MAHALLESI, BARBAROS HAYRETTIN SOKAK, NO 25, 50400 ÜRGÜP, TURKEY

Directions: Kayseri Airport > Nevsehir > turn left for Ürgüp > take the road opposite historical Hamam.

Web: www.johansens.com/sacredhouse
E-mail: info@sacred-house.com
Tel: +90 384 341 7102
Fax: +90 384 341 6986

Price Guide:
double US$130-200

Stylish, elegant and private, Sacred House, a former medieval mansion, is a boutique hotel that has lost none of its historic charm. History, art and modern comforts combine with attentive service to provide guests with a relaxing and luxurious visit in a refined setting with beautiful décor and antique furnishings throughout. 4 of the bedrooms open onto a vine-hung courtyard, 5 have fireplaces and all are furnished to a high standard. Excellent meals created from ancient recipes are served in the unique, cave-style restaurant.

Chic, élégant et prive, Sacred House, ancienne demeure médiévale, est un hôtel boutique qui n'a perdu aucun de son charme historique. Histoire, art et confort moderne sont associés à un service attentif, procurant aux hôtes une visite luxueuse et de détente dans une location raffinée aux superbes décors et un mobilier ancien. 4 des chambres donnent sur une cour où pend la vigne vierge, 5 ont des cheminées et toutes sont meublées dans les meilleurs goûts. D'excellents repas basés sur des recettes anciennes sont servis dans l'exceptionnel restaurant cave.

Refinada, elegante e íntima, Sacred House, una antigua mansión medieval, es un hotel boutique que aún conserva todo su encanto histórico. La historia, el arte y sus modernas comodidades se combinan con un servicio atento con el objetivo de poder obsequiar a los clientes una relajada estancia de lujo en un entorno refinado, magníficamente decorado y amueblado con antigüedades por doquier. 4 de sus habitaciones dan a un patio del que pende una parra, 5 disponen de chimenea y todas están amuebladas al más alto nivel. El restaurante, un lugar único al estilo de una cueva, sirve excelentes platos inspirados en antiguas recetas.

Our inspector loved: *The charming setting of the hotel.*

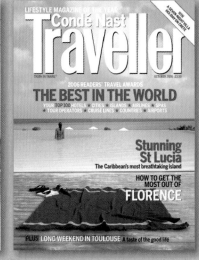

Mini Listings Great Britain & Ireland

Condé Nast Johansens are delighted to recommend over 500 properties across Great Britain and Ireland. These properties can be found in *Recommended Hotels & Spas - GB & I 2007* and *Recommended Country Houses, Small Hotels, Inns & Restaurants - GB & I 2007.* Call +44 1323 649350 or see the Order Form on page 523 to order Guides.

Recommended Hotels & Spas Great Britain & Ireland 2007

England

The Bath Priory Hotel and Restaurant	B&NE Somerset	+44 (0)1225 331922
The Bath Spa Hotel	B&NE Somerset	+44 (0)1225 444424
Dukes Hotel	B&NE Somerset	+44 (0)1225 787960
Homewood Park	B&NE Somerset	+44 (0)1225 723731
Hunstrete House	B&NE Somerset	+44 (0)1761 490490
The Park	B&NE Somerset	+44 (0)117 937 2251
The Royal Crescent & Bath House Spa	B&NE Somerset	+44 (0)1225 823333
Moore Place Hotel	Bedfordshire	+44 (0)1908 282000
The Bear Hotel	Berkshire	+44 (0)1488 682512
Cliveden	Berkshire	+44 (0)1628 668561
The Crab at Chieveley	Berkshire	+44 (0)1635 247550
Donnington Valley Hotel & Golf Club	Berkshire	+44 (0)1635 551199
Fredrick's - Hotel Restaurant Spa	Berkshire	+44 (0)1628 581000
The French Horn	Berkshire	+44 (0)1189 692204
The Great House	Berkshire	+44 (0)118 9692277
Oakley Court Hotel	Berkshire	+44 (0)1753 609988
The Regency Park Hotel	Berkshire	+44 (0)1635 871555
The Vineyard At Stockcross	Berkshire	+44 (0)1635 528770
New Hall	Birmingham	+44 (0)121 378 2442

▼

Danesfield House Hotel and Spa	**Buckinghamshire**	**+44 (0)1628 891010**
Hartwell House Hotel, Restaurant & Spa	Buckinghamshire	+44 (0)1296 747444
Stoke Park Club	Buckinghamshire	+44 (0)1753 717171
Hotel Felix	Cambridgeshire	+44 (0)1223 277977
The Alderley Edge Hotel	Cheshire	+44 (0)1625 583033
The Chester Grosvenor and Spa	Cheshire	+44 (0)1244 324024
Green Bough Hotel	Cheshire	+44 (0)1244 326241
Hillbark Hotel	Cheshire	+44 (0)151 625 2400
Mere Court Hotel	Cheshire	+44 (0)1565 831000
Nunsmere Hall	Cheshire	+44 (0)1606 889100
Rowton Hall Hotel, Health Club & Spa	Cheshire	+44 (0)1244 335262
Alverton Manor	Cornwall	+44 (0)1872 276633
Budock Vean - The Hotel on the River	Cornwall	+44 (0)1326 252100
Fowey Hall Hotel & Restaurant	Cornwall	+44 (0)1726 833866
The Garrack Hotel & Restaurant	Cornwall	+44 (0)1736 796199
Hell Bay	Cornwall	+44 (0)1720 422947
The Idle Rocks Hotel	Cornwall	+44 (0)1326 270771
The Lugger Hotel	Cornwall	+44 (0)1872 501322
Meudon Hotel	Cornwall	+44 (0)1326 250541
The Nare Hotel	Cornwall	+44 (0)1872 501111
The Rosevine Hotel	Cornwall	+44 (0)1872 580206
St Michael's Hotel & Spa	Cornwall	+44 (0)1326 312707
Talland Bay Hotel	Cornwall	+44 (0)1503 272667
Treglos Hotel	Cornwall	+44 (0)1841 520727
The Well House	Cornwall	+44 (0)1579 342001
Armathwaite Hall Hotel	Cumbria	+44 (0)17687 76551
Farlam Hall Hotel	Cumbria	+44 (0)16977 46234
Gilpin Lodge	Cumbria	+44 (0)15394 88818
Holbeck Ghyll Country House Hotel	Cumbria	+44 (0)15394 32375
The Inn on the Lake	Cumbria	+44 (0)17684 82444
Lakeside Hotel on Lake Windermere	Cumbria	+44 (0)15395 30001
Linthwaite House Hotel	Cumbria	+44 (0)15394 88600
The Lodore Falls Hotel	Cumbria	+44 (0)17687 77285
Lovelady Shield Country House Hotel	Cumbria	+44 (0)1434 381203
Netherwood Hotel	Cumbria	+44 (0)15395 32552
Rampsbeck Country House Hotel	Cumbria	+44 (0)17684 86442
Rothay Manor	Cumbria	+44 (0)15394 33605
Sharrow Bay Country House Hotel	Cumbria	+44 (0)17684 86301
Tufton Arms Hotel	Cumbria	+44 (0)17683 51593
Callow Hall	Derbyshire	+44 (0)1335 300900
East Lodge Country House Hotel	Derbyshire	+44 (0)1629 734474
Hassop Hall	Derbyshire	+44 (0)1629 640488
The Izaak Walton Hotel	Derbyshire	+44 (0)1335 350555
The Peacock at Rowsley	Derbyshire	+44 (0)1629 733518
Riber Hall	Derbyshire	+44 (0)1629 582795
The Arundell Arms	Devon	+44 (0)1566 784666
Bovey Castle	Devon	+44 (0)1647 445000
Buckland-Tout-Saints	Devon	+44 (0)1548 853055
Burgh Island	Devon	+44 (0)1548 810 514
Combe House Hotel & Restaurant	Devon	+44 (0)1404 540400
Gidleigh Park	Devon	+44 (0)1647 432367
The Horn of Plenty Country House Hotel & Restaurant	Devon	+44 (0)1822 832528
Hotel Riviera	Devon	+44 (0)1395 515201
Ilsington Country House Hotel	Devon	+44 (0)1364 661452
Langdon Court Hotel & Restaurant	Devon	+44 (0)1752 862358
Lewtrenchard Manor	Devon	+44 (0)1566 783222
Northcote Manor Country House Hotel	Devon	+44 (0)1769 560501
Orestone Manor & The Restaurant at Orestone Manor	Devon	+44 (0)1803 328098
The Palace Hotel	Devon	+44 (0)1803 200200
Soar Mill Cove Hotel	Devon	+44 (0)1548 561566
The Tides Reach Hotel	Devon	+44 (0)1548 843466
Watersmeet Hotel	Devon	+44 (0)1271 870333
Woolacombe Bay Hotel	Devon	+44 (0)1271 870388
Avonmouth Hotel and Restaurant	Dorset	+44 (0)1202 483434
Moonfleet Manor	Dorset	+44 (0)1305 786948
Norfolk Royale Hotel	Dorset	+44 (0)1202 551521
Plumber Manor	Dorset	+44 (0)1258 472507
The Priory Hotel	Dorset	+44 (0)1929 551666

MINI LISTINGS GREAT BRITAIN & IRELAND

Condé Nast Johansens are delighted to recommend over 500 properties across Great Britain and Ireland.

These properties can be found in *Recommended Hotels & Spas - GB & I 2007* and *Recommended Country Houses, Small Hotels, Inns & Restaurants - GB & I 2007.*

Call +44 1323 649350 or see the Order Form on page 523 to order Guides.

Stock Hill Country House	Dorset	+44 (0)1747 823626
Summer Lodge Country House Hotel, Restaurant & Spa	Dorset	+44 (0)20 7589 2412
Headlam Hall	Durham	+44 (0)1325 730238
Five Lakes Hotel, Golf, Country Club & Spa	Essex	+44 (0)1621 868888
Burleigh Court	Gloucestershire	+44 (0)1453 883804
Calcot Manor Hotel & Spa	Gloucestershire	+44 (0)1666 890391
Corse Lawn House Hotel	Gloucestershire	+44 (0)1452 780479
Cotswold House Hotel	Gloucestershire	+44 (0)1386 840330
The Dial House	Gloucestershire	+44 (0)1451 822244
The Grapevine Hotel	Gloucestershire	+44 (0)1451 830344
The Greenway	Gloucestershire	+44 (0)1242 862352
The Hare and Hounds Hotel	Gloucestershire	+44 (0)1666 880233
Hotel On The Park	Gloucestershire	+44 (0)1242 518898
Lords of the Manor Hotel	Gloucestershire	+44 (0)1451 820243
Lower Slaughter Manor	Gloucestershire	+44 (0)1451 820456
The Noel Arms Hotel	Gloucestershire	+44 (0)1386 840317
The Painswick Hotel & Old Rectory Restaurant	Gloucestershire	+44 (0)1452 812160
Stonehouse Court Hotel	Gloucestershire	+44 (0)1453 794950
The Swan Hotel At Bibury	Gloucestershire	+44 (0)1285 740695
Washbourne Court Hotel	Gloucestershire	+44 (0)1451 822143
Thornbury Castle	South Gloucestershire	+44 (0)1454 281182
Audleys Wood	Hampshire	+44 (0)1256 817555
Careys Manor Hotel & Senspa	Hampshire	+44 (0)8707 512305
Chewton Glen	Hampshire	+44 (0)1425 275341
Chilworth Manor	Hampshire	+44 (0)23 8076 7333
Esseborne Manor	Hampshire	+44 (0)1264 736444
Lainston House Hotel	Hampshire	+44 (0)1962 863588
Le Poussin at Whitley Ridge	Hampshire	+44 (0)1590 622354
The Montagu Arms Hotel	Hampshire	+44 (0)1590 612324
New Park Manor & Bath House Spa	Hampshire	+44 (0)1590 623467
Passford House Hotel	Hampshire	+44 (0)1590 682398
Tylney Hall	Hampshire	+44 (0)1256 764881
Castle House	Herefordshire	+44 (0)1432 356321
Down Hall Country House Hotel	Hertfordshire	+44 (0)1279 731441
The Grove Hotel	Hertfordshire	+44 (0)1923 807807
St Michael's Manor	Hertfordshire	+44 (0)1727 864444
Sopwell House	Hertfordshire	+44 (0)1727 864477
West Lodge Park Country House Hotel	Hertfordshire	+44 (0)20 8216 3900
The Priory Bay Hotel	Isle of Wight	+44 (0)1983 613146
Eastwell Manor	Kent	+44 (0)1233 213000
The Spa	Kent	+44 (0)1892 520331
Eaves Hall	Lancashire	+44 (0)1200 425 271
The Gibbon Bridge Hotel	Lancashire	+44 (0)1995 61456
Stapleford Park Country House Hotel & Sporting Estate	Leicestershire	+44 (0)1572 787 000
41	London	+44 (0)20 7300 0041
51 Buckingham Gate	London	+44 (0)20 7769 7766
Beaufort House	London	+44 (0)20 7584 2600
Cannizaro House	London	+44 (0)208 879 1464
The Capital Hotel & Restaurant	London	+44 (0)20 7589 5171
The Cranley	London	+44 (0)20 7373 0123
Dorset Square Hotel	London	+44 (0)20 7723 7874
The Egerton House Hotel	London	+44 (0)20 7589 2412
Grim's Dyke Hotel	London	+44 (0)20 8385 3100
Hendon Hall Hotel	London	+44 (0)20 8203 3341
Jumeirah Carlton Tower	London	+44 (0)20 7235 1234
Jumeirah Lowndes Hotel	London	+44 (0)20 7823 1234
Kensington House Hotel	London	+44 (0)20 7937 2345
The Mandeville Hotel	London	+44 (0)20 7935 5599
The Mayflower Hotel	London	+44 (0)20 7370 0991
The Milestone Hotel & Apartments	London	+44 (0)20 7917 1000
The Richmond Gate Hotel and Restaurant	London	+44 (0)20 8940 0061
The Royal Park	London	+44 (0)20 7479 6600
Sofitel St James	London	+44 (0)20 7747 2200
The Sumner	London	+44 (0)20 7723 2244
Twenty Nevern Square	London	+44 (0)20 7565 9555
Etrop Grange	Greater Manchester	+44 (0)161 499 0500
Congham Hall	Norfolk	+44 (0)1485 600250
The Hoste Arms	Norfolk	+44 (0)1328 738777

▼

Fawsley Hall	**Northamptonshire**	**+44 (0)1327 892000**
Rushton Hall	Northamptonshire	+44 (0)1536 713001
Whittlebury Hall	Northamptonshire	+44 (0)1327 857857
Marshall Meadows Country House Hotel	Northumberland	+44 (0)1289 331133
Matfen Hall	Northumberland	+44 (0)1661 886500
Tillmouth Park	Northumberland	+44 (0)1890 882255
Colwick Hall Hotel	Nottinghamshire	+44 (0)115 950 0566
Lace Market Hotel	Nottinghamshire	+44 (0)115 852 3232
Le Manoir Aux Quat' Saisons	Oxfordshire	+44 (0)1844 278881
Phyllis Court Club	Oxfordshire	+44 (0)1491 570500
The Springs Hotel & Golf Club	Oxfordshire	+44 (0)1491 836687
Weston Manor	Oxfordshire	+44 (0)1869 350621
Hambleton Hall	Rutland	+44 (0)1572 756991
Dinham Hall	Shropshire	+44 (0)1584 876464
Bindon Country House Hotel	Somerset	+44 (0)1823 400070
The Castle at Taunton	Somerset	+44 (0)1823 272671
Combe House Hotel	Somerset	+44 (0)1278 741382
Mount Somerset Country House Hotel	Somerset	+44 (0)1823 442500
Ston Easton Park	Somerset	+44 (0)1761 241631
Hoar Cross Hall Spa Resort	Staffordshire	+44 (0)1283 575671
Brudenell Hotel	Suffolk	+44 (0)1728 452071
Hintlesham Hall	Suffolk	+44 (0)1473 652334
Ravenwood Hall Country Hotel & Restaurant	Suffolk	+44 (0)1359 270345
Seckford Hall	Suffolk	+44 (0)1394 385678

Mini Listings Great Britain & Ireland

Condé Nast Johansens are delighted to recommend over 500 properties across Great Britain and Ireland.
These properties can be found in *Recommended Hotels & Spas - GB & I 2007* and *Recommended Country Houses, Small Hotels, Inns & Restaurants - GB & I 2007.*
Call +44 1323 649350 or see the Order Form on page 523 to order Guides.

The Swan Hotel	Suffolk	+44 (0)1502 722186
The Swan Hotel	Suffolk	+44 (0)1787 247477
The Westleton Crown	Suffolk	+44 (0)1728 648777
Foxhills	Surrey	+44 (0)1932 872050
Grayshott Spa	Surrey	+44 (0)1428 602020
Great Fosters	Surrey	+44 (0)1784 433822
Lythe Hill Hotel & Spa	Surrey	+44 (0)1428 651251
Pennyhill Park Hotel & The Spa	Surrey	+44 (0)1276 471774
Ashdown Park Hotel and Country Club	East Sussex	+44 (0)1342 824988
Dale Hill	East Sussex	+44 (0)1580 200112
Deans Place Hotel	East Sussex	+44 (0)1323 870248
The Grand Hotel	East Sussex	+44 (0)1323 412345
Horsted Place Country House Hotel	East Sussex	+44 (0)1825 750581
Lansdowne Place, Boutique Hotel & Spa	East Sussex	+44 (0)1273 736266
Newick Park	East Sussex	+44 (0)1825 723633
The PowderMills	East Sussex	+44 (0)1424 775511
Rye Lodge	East Sussex	+44 (0)1797 223838
Amberley Castle	West Sussex	+44 (0)1798 831992
Bailiffscourt Hotel & Health Spa	West Sussex	+44 (0)1903 723511
Millstream Hotel	West Sussex	+44 (0)1243 573234
Ockenden Manor	West Sussex	+44 (0)1444 416111
The Spread Eagle Hotel & Health Spa	West Sussex	+44 (0)1730 816911
The Vermont Hotel	Tyne & Wear	+44 (0)191 233 1010
Ardencote Manor Hotel, Country Club & Spa	Warwickshire	+44 (0)1926 843111

▼

Billesley Manor	**Warwickshire**	**+44 (0)1789 279955**
Ettington Park	Warwickshire	+44 (0)1789 450123
The Glebe at Barford	Warwickshire	+44 (0)1926 624218
Mallory Court	Warwickshire	+44 (0)1926 330214
Nailcote Hall	Warwickshire	+44 (0)2476 466174
The Shakespeare Hotel	Warwickshire	+44 (0)1789 293636
Wroxall Abbey Estate	Warwickshire	+44 (0)1926 484470
Bishopstrow House & Spa	Wiltshire	+44 (0)1985 212312
Howard's House	Wiltshire	+44 (0)1722 716392
Lucknam Park, Bath	Wiltshire	+44 (0)1225 742777
The Pear Tree At Purton	Wiltshire	+44 (0)1793 772100
Whatley Manor	Wiltshire	+44 (0)1666 822888
Woolley Grange	Wiltshire	+44 (0)1225 864705
Brockencote Hall	Worcestershire	+44 (0)1562 777876
Buckland Manor	Worcestershire	+44 (0)1386 852626
The Cottage in the Wood	Worcestershire	+44 (0)1684 575859
Dormy House	Worcestershire	+44 (0)1386 852711
The Elms	Worcestershire	+44 (0)1299 896666
The Evesham Hotel	Worcestershire	+44 (0)1386 765566
Willerby Manor Hotel	East Riding of Yorkshire	+44 (0)1482 652616
The Boar's Head Hotel	North Yorkshire	+44 (0)1423 771888
The Crown Spa Hotel	North Yorkshire	+44 (0)1723 357400
The Devonshire Arms Country House Hotel & Spa	North Yorkshire	+44 (0)1756 718111
The Feversham Arms Hotel	North Yorkshire	+44 (0)1439 770766
The Grange Hotel	North Yorkshire	+44 (0)1904 644744
Grants Hotel	North Yorkshire	+44 (0)1423 560666
Hackness Grange	North Yorkshire	+44 (0)1723 882345
Hob Green Hotel, Restaurant & Gardens	North Yorkshire	+44 (0)1423 770031
Judges Country House Hotel	North Yorkshire	+44 (0)1642 789000
Middlethorpe Hall Hotel, Restaurant & Spa	North Yorkshire	+44 (0)1904 641241
Monk Fryston Hall Hotel	North Yorkshire	+44 (0)1977 682369
The Pheasant	North Yorkshire	+44 (0)1439 771241
The Royal Hotel	North Yorkshire	+44 (0)1723 364333
Rudding Park	North Yorkshire	+44 (0)1423 871350
Simonstone Hall	North Yorkshire	+44 (0)1969 667255
The Worsley Arms Hotel	North Yorkshire	+44 (0)1653 628234
Wrea Head Country Hotel	North Yorkshire	+44 (0)1723 378211
Whitley Hall Hotel	South Yorkshire	+44 (0)114 245 4444
42 The Calls	West Yorkshire	+44 (0)113 244 0099
Holdsworth House Hotel & Restaurant	West Yorkshire	+44 (0)1422 240024

Channel Islands

The Atlantic Hotel and Ocean Restaurant	Jersey	+44 (0)1534 744101
The Club Hotel and Spa	Jersey	+44 (0)1534 876500
Longueville Manor	Jersey	+44 (0)1534 725501

Northern Ireland

Bushmills Inn Hotel	Antrim	+44 (0)28 2073 3000

Ireland

Gregans Castle	Clare	+353 65 7077005
Longueville House & Presidents' Restaurant	Cork	+353 22 47156
Harvey's Point	Donegal	+353 74 972 2208
Rathmullan House	Donegal	+353 74 915 8188
Merrion Hall Hotel	Dublin	+353 1 668 1426
The Schoolhouse Hotel	Dublin	+353 1 667 5014
Cashel House	Galway	+353 95 31001
Renvyle House Hotel	Galway	+353 95 43511
Ballygarry House	Kerry	+353 66 7123322
Cahernane House Hotel	Kerry	+353 64 31895
Park Hotel Kenmare & Sámas	Kerry	+353 64 41200

Mini Listings Great Britain & Ireland

Condé Nast Johansens are delighted to recommend over 500 properties across Great Britain and Ireland.
These properties can be found in *Recommended Hotels & Spas - GB & I 2007* and *Recommended Country Houses, Small Hotels, Inns & Restaurants - GB & I 2007.*
Call +44 1323 649350 or see the Order Form on page 523 to order Guides.

Parknasilla Hotel	Kerry	+353 1 2144800
Sheen Falls Lodge	Kerry	+353 64 41600
Killashee House Hotel & Villa Spa	Kildare	+353 45 879277
Mount Juliet Conrad	Kilkenny	+353 56 777 3000
Ashford Castle	Mayo	+353 94 95 46003
Knockranny House Hotel & Spa	Mayo	+353 98 28600
Nuremore Hotel and Country Club	Monaghan	+353 42 9661438
Marlfield House	Wexford	+353 53 94 21124

Scotland

Darroch Learg	Aberdeenshire	+44 (0)13397 55443
Ardanaiseig	Argyll & Bute	+44 (0)1866 833333
Loch Melfort Hotel & Restaurant	Argyll & Bute	+44 (0)1852 200233
Kirroughtree House	Dumfries & Galloway	+44 (0)1671 402141
Channings	Edinburgh	+44 (0)131 274 7401
Le Monde Hotel	Edinburgh	+44 (0)131 270 3900
Mar Hall Hotel & Spa	Glasgow	+44 (0)141 812 9999
One Devonshire Gardens	Glasgow	+44 (0)141 3392001
Bunchrew House Hotel	Highland	+44 (0)1463 234917
Cuillin Hills Hotel	Highland	+44 (0)1478 612003
Culloden House	Highland	+44 (0)1463 790461
Drumossie Hotel	Highland	+44 (0)1463 236451
Inverlochy Castle	Highland	+44 (0)1397 702177
Loch Torridon Country House Hotel	Highland	+44 (0)1445 791242
Rocpool Reserve	Highland	+44 (0)1463 240089
Royal Marine Hotel	Highland	+44 (0)1408 621252
Dalhousie Castle and Spa	Midlothian	+44 (0)1875 820153
Ballathie House Hotel	Perth & Kinross	+44 (0)1250 883268
Cromlix House	Perth & Kinross	+44 (0)1786 822125
Kinnaird	Perth & Kinross	+44 (0)1796 482440
The Royal Hotel	Perth & Kinross	+44 (0)1764 679200
Cringletie House	Scottish Borders	+44 (0)1721 725750
Glenapp Castle	South Ayrshire	+44 (0)1465 831212

Wales

Miskin Manor Country House Hotel	Cardiff	+44 (0)1443 224204
Falcondale Mansion Hotel	Ceredigion	+44 (0)1570 422910
Bodysgallen Hall & Spa	Conwy	+44 (0)1492 584466
St Tudno Hotel & Restaurant	Conwy	+44 (0)1492 874411
Wild Pheasant Hotel	Denbighshire	+44 (0)1978 860629
Palé Hall	Gwynedd	+44 (0)1678 530285
Penmaenuchaf Hall	Gwynedd	+44 (0)1341 422129
Allt-Yr-Ynys Hotel	Monmouthshire	+44 (0)1873 890307
Llansantffraed Court Hotel	Monmouthshire	+44 (0)1873 840678
Lamphey Court Hotel	Pembrokeshire	+44 (0)1646 672273
Penally Abbey	Pembrokeshire	+44 (0)1834 843033
Warpool Court Hotel	Pembrokeshire	+44 (0)1437 720300
The Lake Country House and Spa	Powys	+44 (0)1591 620202
Lake Vyrnwy Hotel	Powys	+44 (0)1691 870 692
Llangoed Hall	Powys	+44 (0)1874 754525

Recommended Country Houses, Small Hotels, Inns & Restaurants Great Britain & Ireland 2007

England

The County Hotel	B&NE Somerset	+44 (0)1225 425003

▼

The Ring O' Roses	**B&NE Somerset**	**+44 (0)1761 232478**
Cornfields Restaurant & Hotel	Bedfordshire	+44 (0)1234 378990
Mill House Hotel with Riverside Restaurant	Bedfordshire	+44 (0)1234 781678
Cantley House	Berkshire	+44 (0)118 978 9912
The Christopher Hotel	Berkshire	+44 (0)1753 852359
The Cottage Inn	Berkshire	+44 (0)1344 882242
The Inn on the Green, Restaurant with Rooms	Berkshire	+44 (0)1628 482638
L'ortolan Restaurant	Berkshire	+44 (0)1189 888 500
The Leatherne Bottel Riverside Restaurant	Berkshire	+44 (0)1491 872667
The Royal Oak Restaurant	Berkshire	+44 (0)1628 620541
Stirrups Country House Hotel	Berkshire	+44 (0)1344 882284
Bull & Butcher	Buckinghamshire	+44 (0)1491 638283
The Dinton Hermit	Buckinghamshire	+44 (0)1296 747473
The Ivy House	Buckinghamshire	+44 (0)1494 872184
The Tickell Arms	Cambridgeshire	+44 (0)1223 833128
Broxton Hall	Cheshire	+44 (0)1829 782321
Chandlers Waterside Apartment	Cornwall	+44 (0)1726 810800
Highland Court Lodge	Cornwall	+44 (0)1726 813320
The Hundred House Hotel & Fish in the Fountain Restaurant	Cornwall	+44 (0)1872 501336
Lower Barn	Cornwall	+44 (0)1726 844881
The Old Coastguard Hotel	Cornwall	+44 (0)1736 731222
Primrose Valley Hotel	Cornwall	+44 (0)1736 794939
Rose-In-Vale Country House Hotel	Cornwall	+44 (0)1872 552202
Tredethy House	Cornwall	+44 (0)1208 841262
Trehellas House Hotel & Restaurant	Cornwall	+44 (0)1208 72700
Trelawne Hotel - The Hutches Restaurant	Cornwall	+44 (0)1326 250226
Trevalsa Court Country House Hotel & Restaurant	Cornwall	+44 (0)1726 842468
Wisteria Lodge & Apartments	Cornwall	+44 (0)1726 810800

Mini Listings Great Britain & Ireland

Condé Nast Johansens are delighted to recommend over 500 properties across Great Britain and Ireland.
These properties can be found in *Recommended Hotels & Spas - GB & I 2007* and *Recommended Country Houses, Small Hotels, Inns & Restaurants - GB & I 2007.*
Call +44 1323 649350 or see the Order Form on page 523 to order Guides.

Broadoaks Country House	Cumbria	+44 (0)1539 445566
Crosby Lodge Country House Hotel	Cumbria	+44 (0)1228 573618

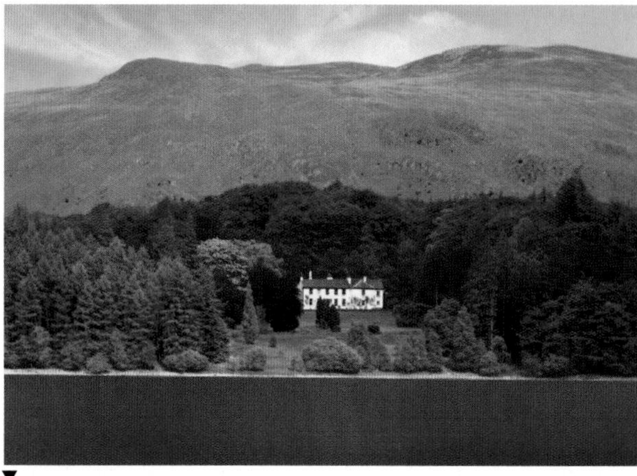

▼

Dale Head Hall Lakeside Hotel	**Cumbria**	**+44 (0)17687 72478**
Fayrer Garden House Hotel	Cumbria	+44 (0)15394 88195
Hipping Hall	Cumbria	+44 (0)15242 71187
Lake House Hotel	Cumbria	+44 (0)15394 32360
The Leathes Head	Cumbria	+44 (0)17687 77247
Linthwaite House Hotel	Cumbria	+44 (0)15394 88600
Nent Hall Country House Hotel	Cumbria	+44 (0)1434 381584
The Pheasant	Cumbria	+44 (0)17687 76234
The Queen's Head Hotel	Cumbria	+44 (0)15394 36271
Temple Sowerby House Hotel and Restaurant	Cumbria	+44 (0)17683 61578
Underwood	Cumbria	+44 (0)1229 771116
West Vale Country House & Restaurant	Cumbria	+44 (0)1539 442 817
The Wheatsheaf @ Brigsteer	Cumbria	+44 (0)15395 68254
The Chequers Inn	Derbyshire	+44 (0)1433 630231
Dannah Farm Country House	Derbyshire	+44 (0)1773 550273
The Plough Inn	Derbyshire	+44 (0)1433 650319
The Wind in the Willows	Derbyshire	+44 (0)1457 868001
Combe House Hotel & Restaurant	Devon	+44 (0)1404 540400
Heddon's Gate Hotel	Devon	+44 (0)1598 763481
Hewitt's - Villa Spaldi	Devon	+44 (0)1598 752293
Home Farm Hotel	Devon	+44 (0)1404 831278
Ilsington Country House Hotel	Devon	+44 (0)1364 661452
Kingston House	Devon	+44 (0)1803 762 235
Lydford House	Devon	+44 (0)1822 820347
Mill End	Devon	+44 (0)1647 432282
The New Inn	Devon	+44 (0)1363 84242
Yeoldon House Hotel	Devon	+44 (0)1237 474400
The Bridge House Hotel	Dorset	+44 (0)1308 862200
The Grange at Oborne	Dorset	+44 (0)1935 813463
La Fleur de Lys	Dorset	+44 (0)1747 853717
Yalbury Cottage	Dorset	+44 (0)1305 262382
The Crown House	Essex	+44 (0)1799 530515
The Pump House Apartment	Essex	+44 (0)1277 656579
Bibury Court	Gloucestershire	+44 (0)1285 740337
Charlton Kings Hotel	Gloucestershire	+44 (0)1242 231061
Lower Brook House	Gloucestershire	+44 (0)1386 700286
Lypiatt House	Gloucestershire	+44 (0)1242 224994
The Malt House	Gloucestershire	+44 (0)1386 840295
Three Choirs Vineyards Estate	Gloucestershire	+44 (0)1531 890223
The Wild Duck Inn	Gloucestershire	+44 (0)1285 770310
Langrish House	Hampshire	+44 (0)1730 266941
The Mill At Gordleton	Hampshire	+44 (0)1590 682219
The Nurse's Cottage	Hampshire	+44 (0)1590 683402
Aylestone Court	Herefordshire	+44 (0)1432 341891
Ford Abbey	Herefordshire	+44 (0)1568 760700
Glewstone Court	Herefordshire	+44 (0)1989 770367
Moccas Court	Herefordshire	+44 (0)1981 500 019
Seven Ledbury	Herefordshire	+44 (0)1531 631317
The Swan at Hay	Herefordshire	+44 (0)1497 821188
The Verzon	Herefordshire	+44 (0)1531 670381
Wilton Court Hotel	Herefordshire	+44 (0)1989 562569
Redcoats Farmhouse Hotel and Restaurant	Hertfordshire	+44 (0)1438 729500
The White House and Lion & Lamb Bar & Restaurant	Hertfordshire	+44 (0)1279 870257
The Hambrough	Isle of Wight	+44 (0)1983 856333
Koala Cottage	Isle of Wight	+44 (0)1983 842031
Rylstone Manor	Isle of Wight	+44 (0)1983 862806
Winterbourne Country House	Isle of Wight	+44 (0)1983 852535
Little Silver Country Hotel	Kent	+44 (0)1233 850321
Romney Bay House Hotel	Kent	+44 (0)1797 364747
Wallett's Court Hotel & Spa	Kent	+44 (0)1304 852424
Ferrari's Restaurant & Hotel	Lancashire	+44 (0)1772 783148
The Inn at Whitewell	Lancashire	+44 (0)1200 448222
Springfield House Hotel	Lancashire	+44 (0)1253 790301
Tree Tops Country House Restaurant & Hotel	Lancashire	+44 (0)1704 572430
Horse & Trumpet	Leicestershire	+44 (0)1858 565000
Sysonby Knoll Hotel	Leicestershire	+44 (0)1664 563563
Bailhouse Hotel	Lincolnshire	+44 (0)1522 520883
The Crown Hotel	Lincolnshire	+44 (0)1780 763136
The Dower House Hotel	Lincolnshire	+44 (0)1526 352588
Washingborough Hall	Lincolnshire	+44 (0)1522 790340
Beechwood Hotel	Norfolk	+44 (0)1692 403231
Broom Hall Country Hotel	Norfolk	+44 (0)1953 882125
Brovey Lair	Norfolk	+44 (0)1953 882706
Elderton Lodge Hotel & Langtry Restaurant	Norfolk	+44 (0)1263 833547
The Gin Trap Inn	Norfolk	+44 (0)1485 525264
The Great Escape Holiday Company	Norfolk	+44 (0)1485 518717
Idyllic Cottages At Vere Lodge	Norfolk	+44 (0)1328 838261
The Kings Head Hotel	Norfolk	+44 (0)1485 578 265
The Neptune Inn & Restaurant	Norfolk	+44 (0)1485 532122
The Old Rectory	Norfolk	+44 (0)1603 700772
The Stower Grange	Norfolk	+44 (0)1603 860210
The Falcon Hotel	Northamptonshire	+44 (0)1604 696200
The New French Partridge	Northamptonshire	+44 (0)1604 870033
The Windmill at Badby	Northamptonshire	+44 (0)1327 702363
Waren House Hotel	Northumberland	+44 (0)1668 214581
Cockliffe Country House Hotel	Nottinghamshire	+44 (0)1159 680179
Langar Hall	Nottinghamshire	+44 (0)1949 860559
Restaurant Sat Bains with Rooms	Nottinghamshire	+44 (0)115 986 6566
Burford Lodge Hotel & Restaurant	Oxfordshire	+44 (0)1993 823354
The Dashwood Hotel & Restaurant	Oxfordshire	+44 (0)1869 352707
Duke Of Marlborough Country Inn	Oxfordshire	+44 (0)1993 811460
Fallowfields	Oxfordshire	+44 (0)1865 820416
The Feathers	Oxfordshire	+44 (0)1993 812291
The Jersey Arms	Oxfordshire	+44 (0)1869 343234

MINI LISTINGS GREAT BRITAIN & IRELAND

Condé Nast Johansens are delighted to recommend over 500 properties across Great Britain and Ireland.
These properties can be found in *Recommended Hotels & Spas - GB & I 2007* and *Recommended Country Houses, Small Hotels, Inns & Restaurants - GB & I 2007.*
Call +44 1323 649350 or see the Order Form on page 523 to order Guides.

The Kings Head Inn & Restaurant	Oxfordshire	+44 (0)1608 658365
The Lamb Inn	Oxfordshire	+44 (0)1993 823155
The Plough Hotel, Game & Seafood Restaurant	Oxfordshire	+44 (0)1367 810222
The Spread Eagle Hotel	Oxfordshire	+44 (0)1844 213661
Barnsdale Lodge	Rutland	+44 (0)1572 724678
The Lake Isle Restaurant & Townhouse Hotel	Rutland	+44 (0)1572 822951
Pen-Y-Dyffryn Country Hotel	Shropshire	+44 (0)1691 653700
Soulton Hall	Shropshire	+44 (0)1939 232786
Ashwick Country House Hotel	Somerset	+44 (0)1398 323868
Bellplot House Hotel & Thomas's Restaurant	Somerset	+44 (0)1460 62600
Beryl	Somerset	+44 (0)1749 678738
Compton House	Somerset	+44 (0)1934 733944
Farthings Country House Hotel & Restaurant	Somerset	+44 (0)1823 480664
Glencot House	Somerset	+44 (0)1749 677160
Karslake Country House & Restaurant	Somerset	+44 (0)1643 851242
Three Acres Country House	Somerset	+44 (0)1398 323730
Clarice House	Suffolk	+44 (0)1284 705550
The Ickworth Hotel and Apartments	Suffolk	+44 (0)1284 735350
Chase Lodge	Surrey	+44 (0)20 8943 1862
Great Tangley Manor	Surrey	+44 (0)20 7526 4852
The Hope Anchor Hotel	East Sussex	+44 (0)1797 222216
Crouchers Country Hotel & Restaurant	West Sussex	+44 (0)1243 784995
The Mill House Hotel	West Sussex	+44 (0)1903 892426
Nuthurst Grange	Warwickshire	+44 (0)1564 783972
Beechfield House	Wiltshire	+44 (0)1225 703700
The George Inn	Wiltshire	+44 (0)1985 840396
The Lamb at Hindon	Wiltshire	+44 (0)1747 820 573
The Old Manor Hotel	Wiltshire	+44 (0)1225 777393
Stanton Manor Hotel & Gallery Restaurant	Wiltshire	+44 (0)1666 837552
Widbrook Grange	Wiltshire	+44 (0)1225 864750
The Broadway Hotel	Worcestershire	+44 (0)1386 852401
Colwall Park	Worcestershire	+44 (0)1684 540000
The Old Rectory	Worcestershire	+44 (0)1527 523000
The Peacock Inn	Worcestershire	+44 (0)1584 810506
The White Lion Hotel	Worcestershire	+44 (0)1684 592551
The Austwick Traddock	North Yorkshire	+44 (0)15242 51224
The Devonshire Fell	North Yorkshire	+44 (0)1756 729111
Dunsley Hall	North Yorkshire	+44 (0)1947 893437
Hob Green Hotel, Restaurant & Gardens	North Yorkshire	+44 (0)1423 770031
The Red Lion	North Yorkshire	+44 (0)1756 720204
Stow House Hotel	North Yorkshire	+44 (0)1969 663635
The Wensleydale Heifer	North Yorkshire	+44 (0)1969 622322
Hey Green Country House Hotel	West Yorkshire	+44 (0)1484 844235

Channel Islands

La Sablonnerie	Guernsey	+44 (0)1481 832061
The White House	Guernsey	+44 (0)1481 722159

Ireland

St Clerans Manor House	Galway	+353 91 846 555
Brook Lane Hotel	Kerry	+353 64 42077
Coopershill House	Sligo	+353 71 9165108

Scotland

Castleton House Hotel	Angus	+44 (0)1307 840340
Highland Cottage	Argyll & bute	+44 (0)1688 302030
Balcary Bay Hotel	Dumfries & Galloway	+44 (0)1556 640217
The Peat Inn	Fife	+44 (0)1334 840206
The Bridge Hotel	Highland	+44 (0)1431 821100
Corriegour Lodge Hotel	Highland	+44 (0)1397 712685

Dunain Park Hotel	**Highland**	**+44 (0)1463 230512**
Forss House Hotel	Highland	+44 (0)1847 861201
Greshornish House Hotel	Highland	+44 (0)1470 582266
Hotel Eilean Iarmain	Highland	+44 (0)1471 833332
Ruddyglow Park	Highland	+44 (0)1571 822216
The Steadings at The Grouse & Trout	Highland	+44 (0)1808 521314
Toravaig House	Highland	+44 (0)1471 833231
Knockomie Hotel	Moray	+44 (0)1309 673146
Cairn Lodge Hotel	Perth & Kinross	+44 (0)1764 662634
The Four Seasons Hotel	Perth & Kinross	+44 (0)1764 685 333
Castle Venlaw	Scottish Borders	+44 (0)1721 720384
Culzean Castle - The Eisenhower Apartment	South Ayrshire	+44 (0)1655 884455
Amhuinnsuidhe Castle	Western Isles	+44 (0)1859 560200

Wales

The Inn at the Elm Tree	Cardiff	+44 (0)1633 680225
Ty Mawr Country Hotel	Carmarthenshire	+44 (0)1267 202332
Conrah Country House Hotel	Ceredigion	+44 (0)1970 617941
Sychnant Pass House	Conwy	+44 (0)1492 596868
Tan-Y-Foel Country House	Conwy	+44 (0)1690 710507
Egerton Grey	Glamorgan	+44 (0)1446 711666
Bae Abermaw	Gwynedd	+44 (0)1341 280550
Hotel Maes-Y-Neuadd	Gwynedd	+44 (0)1766 780200
Plas Dolmelynllyn	Gwynedd	+44 (0)1341 440273
Porth Tocyn Country House Hotel	Gwynedd	+44 (0)1758 713303
The Bell At Skenfrith	Monmouthshire	+44 (0)1600 750235
The Crown At Whitebrook	Monmouthshire	+44 (0)1600 860254
Wolfscastle Country Hotel & Restaurant	Pembrokeshire	+44 (0)1437 741225
Glangrwyney Court	Powys	+44 (0)1873 811288

Historic Houses, Castles & Gardens

Incorporating Museums & Galleries

We are pleased to feature over 140 places to visit during your stay at a Condé Nast Johansens recommended hotel.

England

Bedfordshire

▼

Woburn Abbey - Woburn, Bedfordshire MK17 9WA. Tel: 01525 290333

Berkshire

Mapledurham House - The Estate Office, Mapledurham, Reading, Berkshire RG4 7TR. Tel: 01189 723350

Buckinghamshire

Doddershall Park - Quainton, Aylesbury, Buckinghamshire HP22 4DF. Tel: 01296 655238

Nether Winchendon Mill - Nr Aylesbury, Buckinghamshire HP18 0DY. Tel: 01844 290199

Stowe Landscape Gardens - Stowe, Buckingham, Buckinghamshire MK18 5EH. Tel: 01280 822850

Waddesdon Manor - Waddesdon, Nr Aylesbury, Buckinghamshire HP18 0JH. Tel: 01296 653226

Cambridgeshire

The Manor - Hemingford Grey, Huntingdon, Cambridgeshire PE28 9BN. Tel: 01480 463134

Oliver Cromwell's House - 29 St Mary's Street, Ely, Cambridgeshire CB7 4HF. Tel: 01353 662062

Cheshire

Arley Hall & Gardens - Arley, Northwich, Cheshire CW9 6NA. Tel: 01565 777353

Dorfold Hall - Nantwich, Cheshire CW5 8LD. Tel: 01270 625245

Rode Hall and Gardens - Rode Hall, Scholar Green, Cheshire ST7 3QP. Tel: 01270 873237

Co Durham

The Bowes Museum - Barnard Castle, Co Durham DL12 8NP. Tel: 01833 690606

Raby Castle - Staindrop, Darlington, Co Durham DL2 3AH. Tel: 01833 660202

Cumbria

Isel Hall - Cockermouth, Cumbria CA13 0QG.

Muncaster Castle , Gardens & Owl Centre- Ravenglass, Cumbria CA18 1RQ. Tel: 01229 717614

Derbyshire

Haddon Hall - Bakewell, Derbyshire DE45 1LA. Tel: 01629 812855

Melbourne Hall & Gardens - Melbourne, Derbyshire DE73 8EN. Tel: 01332 862502

Renishaw Hall Gardens - Renishaw, Nr Sheffield, Derbyshire S21 3WB. Tel: 01246 432310

Devon

Bowringsleigh - Kingbridge, Devon TQ7 3LL. Tel: 01548 852014

Downes Estate at Crediton - Devon EX17 3PL. Tel: 01392 439046

Dorset

Moignes Court - Moreton Road, Owermoigne, Dorchester, Dorset DT2 8HY. Tel: 01305 853 300

Essex

The Gardens of Easton Lodge - Warwick House, Easton Lodge, Gt Dumnow, Essex CM6 2BB. Tel: 01371 876979

Ingatestone Hall - Hall Lane, Ingatestone, Essex CM4 9NR. Tel: 01277 353010

Gloucestershire

Cheltenham Art Gallery & Museum - Clarence Street, Cheltenham, Gloucestershire GL50 3JT. Tel: 01242 237431

Hardwicke Court - Nr Gloucester, Gloucestershire GL2 4RS. Tel: 01452 720212

Mill Dene Garden - Blockley, Moreton-in-Marsh, Gloucestershire GL56 9HU. Tel: 01386 700 457

Sezincote - Nr Moreton-in-Marsh, Gloucestershire GL56 9AW. Tel: 01386 700444

Hampshire

Beaulieu - John Montagu Building, Beaulieu, Hampshire SO42 7ZN. Tel: 01590 612345

Beaulieu Vineyard and Estate - Beaulieu Estate, John Montagu Building, Beaulieu, Hampshire SO42 7ZN. Tel: 01590 612345

Gilbert White's House and The Oates Museum - Selborne, Nr Alton, Hampshire GU34 3JH. Tel: 01420 511275

Greywell Hill House - Greywell, Hook, Hampshire RG29 1DG. Tel: 01256 703565

Pylewell House - South Baddesley, Lymington, Hampshire SO41 5SJ. Tel: 01725 513004

Herefordshire

Kentchurch Court - Kentchurch, Nr Pontrilas, Hereford, Herefordshire HR2 0DB. Tel: 01981 240228

Hertfordshire

Ashridge - Ringshall, Berkhamsted, Hertfordshire HP4 1NS. Tel: 01442 841027

Hatfield House, Park & Gardens - Hatfield, Hertfordshire AL9 5NQ. Tel: 01707 287010

Isle of Wight

Deacons Nursery - Moor View, Godshill, Isle of Wight PO38 3HW. Tel: 01983 840750

Kent

Belmont House and Gardens - Belmont Park, Throwley, Nr Faversham, Kent ME13 0HH. Tel: 01795 890202

Cobham Hall - Cobham, Kent DA12 3BL. Tel: 01474 823371

Groombridge Place Gardens - Groombridge, Tunbridge Wells, Kent TN3 9QG. Tel: 01892 861444

Hever Castle & Gardens - Hever, Nr Edenbridge, Kent TN8 7NG. Tel: 01732 865224

Knole - Sevenoaks, Kent TN15 0RP. Tel: 01732 462100

Marle Place Gardens and Gallery - Marle Place Road, Brenchley, Nr Tonbridge, Kent TN12 7HS. Tel: 01892 722304

Mount Ephraim Gardens - Hernhill, Nr Faversham, Kent ME13 9TX. Tel: 01227 751496

The New College of Cobham - Cobhambury Road, Cobham, Nr Gravesend, Kent DA12 3BG. Tel: 01474 814280

Penshurst Place & Gardens - Penshurst, Nr Tonbridge, Kent TN11 8DG. Tel: 01892 870307

Lancashire

Stonyhurst College - Stonyhurst, Clitheroe, Lancashire BB7 9PZ. Tel: 01254 827084/826345

Townhead House - Slaidburn, Via CLitheroe, Lancashire BBY 3AG. Tel: 01772 421566

London

Dulwich Picture Gallery - Gallery Road, London SE21 7AD. Tel: 020 8299 8711

Handel House Museum - 25 Brook Street, London W1K 4HB. Tel: 020 7495 1685

Pitzhanger Manor House and Gallery - Walpole Park, Mattock Lane, Ealing, London W5 5EQ. Tel: 020 8567 1227

Sir John Soane's Museum - 13 Lincoln's Inn Fields, London WC2A 3BP. Tel: 020 7405 2107

Merseyside

Knowsley Hall - Knowsley Park, Prescot, Merseyside L32 4AG. Tel: 0151 489 4827

Middlesex

Syon House - Syon Park, London Road, Brentford, Middlesex TW8 8JF. Tel: 020 8560 0882

Norfolk

Fairhaven Woodland and Water Garden - School Road, South Walsham, Norwich, Norfolk NR13 6EA. Tel: 01603 270449

Walsingham Abbey Grounds - , Walsingham, Norfolk NR22 6BP. Tel: 01328 820259

Northamptonshire

Cottesbrooke Hall and Gardens - Cottesbrooke, Northampton, Northamptonshire NN6 8PF. Tel: 01604 505808

Haddonstone Show Garden - The Forge House, Church Lane, East Haddon, Northamptonshire NN6 8DB. Tel: 01604 770711

Northumberland

Chillingham Castle - Nr Wooler, Northumberland NE66 5NJ. Tel: 01668 215359

Chipchase Castle - Chipchase, Wark on Tyne, Hexham, Northumberland NE48 3NT. Tel: 01434 230203

Seaton Delaval Hall - Seaton Sluice, Whitley Bay, Northumberland NE26 4QR. Tel: 0191 237 1493 / 0786

Nottinghamshire

Newstead Abbey - Ravenshead, Nottinghamshire NG15 8NA. Tel: 01623 455 900

Oxfordshire

Blenheim Palace - Woodstock, Oxfordshire OX20 1PX. Tel: 08700 602080

Kingston Bagpuize House - Kingston Bagpuize, Abingdon, Oxfordshire OX13 5AX. Tel: 01865 820259

Sulgrave Manor - Manor Road, Sulgrave, Banbury, Oxfordshire OX17 2SD. Tel: 01295 760205

Wallingford Castle Gardens - Castle Street, Wallingford, Oxfordshire OX10 0AL. Tel: 01491 835373

Shropshire

Shipton Hall - Shipton, Much Wenlock, Shropshire TF13 6JZ. Tel: 01746 785225

Weston Park - Weston-under-Lizard, Nr Shifnal, Shropshire TF11 8LE. Tel: 01952 852100

Somerset

The American Museum in Britain - Claverton Manor, Bath, Somerset BA2 7BD. Tel: 01225 460503

Cothay Manor & Gardens - Greenham, Wellington, Somerset TA21 0JR. Tel: 01823 672283

Great House Farm - Wells Road, Theale, Wedmore, Somerset BS28 4SJ. Tel: 01934 713133

Number 1 Royal Crescent - 1 Royal Crescent, Bath, Somerset BA1 2LR. Tel: 01225 428126

Staffordshire

The Ancient High House - Greengate Street, Stafford, Staffordshire ST16 2JA. Tel: 01785 619131

Izaak Walton's Cottage - Shallowford, nr. Stafford, Staffordshire ST15 0PA. Tel: 01785 760 278

Stafford Castle - Newport Road, Stafford, Staffordshire ST16 1DJ. Tel: 01785 257 698

Whitmore Hall - Whitmore, Newcastle-under-Lyme, Staffordshire ST5 5HW. Tel: 01782 680478

Suffolk

Kentwell Hall - Long Melford, Sudbury, Suffolk CO10 9BA. Tel: 01787 310207

Newbourne Hall - Newbourne, Nr. Woodbridge, Suffolk IP12 4NP. Tel: 01473 736277

Otley Hall - Hall Lane, Otley, Suffolk IP6 9PA. Tel: 01473 890264

Surrey

Claremont House - Claremont Drive, Esher, Surrey KT10 9LY. Tel: 01372 473623

Guildford House Gallery - 155, High Street, Guildford, Surrey GU1 3AJ. Tel: 01483 444740

Loseley Park - Guildford, Surrey GU3 1HS. Tel: 01483 304440

Painshill Park - Portsmouth Road, Cobham, Surrey KT11 1JE. Tel: 01932 868113

East Sussex

Bentley Wildfowl & Motor Museum - Halland, Nr Lewes, Sussex BN8 5AF. Tel: 01825 840573

Charleston - Firle, Lewes, East Sussex BN8 6LL. Tel: 01323 811626

Firle Place - Firle, Nr Lewes, East Sussex BN8 6LP. Tel: 01273 858307

Garden and Grounds of Herstmonceux Castle - Herstmonceux Castle, Hailsham, East Sussex BN27 1RN. Tel: 01323 833816

Merriments Gardens - Hurst Green, East Sussex TN19 7RA. Tel: 01580 860666

Preston Manor - Preston Drove, Brighton, East Sussex BN1 6SD. Tel: 01273 292770

Royal Pavilion - Brighton, East Sussex BN1 1EE. Tel: 01273 290900

West Sussex

Denmans Garden - Clock House, Denmans Lane, Fontwell, West Sussex BN18 0SU. Tel: 01243 542808

Goodwood House - Goodwood, Chichester, West Sussex PO18 0PX. Tel: 01243 755000

High Beeches Gardens - High Beeches, Handcross, West Sussex RH17 6HQ. Tel: 01444 400589

Leonardslee - Lakes & Gardens - Lower Beeding, Horsham, West Sussex RH13 6PP. Tel: 01403 891212

Uppark - South Harting, Petersfield, West Sussex GU31 5QR. Tel: 01730 825415

West Dean Gardens - West Dean , Chichester, West Sussex PO18 0QZ. Tel: 01243 818210

Worthing Museum & Art Gallery - Chapel Road, Worthing, West Sussex BN11 1HP. Tel: 01903 239999

Warwickshire

Arbury Hall - Nuneaton, Warwickshire CV10 7PT. Tel: 024 7638 2804

The Shakespeare Houses - The Shakespeare Birthplace Trust, The Shakespeare Centre, Henley Street, Stratford-upon-Avon, Warwickshire CV37 6QW. Tel: 01789 201845

West Midlands

Barber Institute of Fine Arts - The University of Birmingham, Edgbaston, Birmingham, West Midlands B15 2TS. Tel: 0121 414 7333

The Birmingham Botanical Gardens and Glasshouses - Westbourne Road, Edgbaston, Birmingham, West Midlands B15 3TR. Tel: 0121 454 1860

Wiltshire

▼

Salisbury Cathedral - Visitor Services, 33 The Close, Salisbury, Wiltshire SP1 2EJ. Tel: 01722 555120

Worcestershire

Harvington Hall - Harvington, Kidderminister, Worcestershire DY10 4LR. Tel: 01562 777846

Little Malvern Court - Nr Malvern, Worcestershire WR14 4JN. Tel: 01684 892988

Spetchley Park Gardens - Spetchley, Worcester, Worcestershire WR5 1RS. Tel: 01453 810303

East Riding of Yorkshire

Burton Agnes Hall & Gardens - Burton Agnes, Driffield, East Yorkshire YO25 4NB. Tel: 01262 490324

Historic Houses, Castles & Gardens

Incorporating Museums & Galleries

www.historichouses.co.uk

North Yorkshire

Duncombe Park - Helmsley, York, North Yorkshire YO62 5EB. Tel: 01439 770213

The Forbidden Corner - Tupgill Park Estate, Coverham, Nr Middleham, North Yorkshire DL8 4TJ. Tel: 01969 640638

Fountains Abbey & Studley Royal - Ripon, North Yorkshire HG4 3DY. Tel: 01765 608888

Norton Conyers - Wath, Nr Ripon, North Yorkshire HG4 5EQ. Tel: 01765 640333

Ripley Castle - Ripley Castle Estate, Harrogate, North Yorkshire HG3 3AY. Tel: 01423 770152

Skipton Castle - Skipton, North Yorkshire BD23 1AW. Tel: 01756 792442

West Yorkshire

Bramham Park - Bramham, Wetherby, West Yorkshire LS23 6ND. Tel: 01937 846000

Harewood House - Harewood, Leeds, West Yorkshire LS17 9LG. Tel: 0113 218 1010

Ledston Hall - Hall Lane, Ledstone, Castleford, West Yorkshire WF10 2BB. Tel: 01423 523 423

Northern Ireland

Co Down

Seaforde Gardens - Seaforde, Downpatrick, Co Down BT30 8PG. Tel: 028 4481 1225

Ireland

Co Cork

Bantry House & Gardens - Bantry, Co Cork. Tel: 00 353 2 750 047

Co Dublin

Ardgillan Castle - Balbriggan, Co Dublin. Tel: 00 353 1 849 2212

Co Kildare

The Irish National Stud, Garden & House Museum - Tully, Kildare Town, Co Kildare. Tel: 00 353 45 521617

Co Offaly

Birr Castle Demesne & Ireland's Historic Science Centre - Birr, Co Offaly. Tel: 00 353 57 91 20336

Co Waterford

Lismore Castle Gardens - Lismore, Co Waterford. Tel: 00 353 58 54424

Co Wexford

Kilmokea Country Manor & Gardens - Great Island, Campile, Co Wexford. Tel: 00 353 51 388109

Co Wicklow

Mount Usher Gardens - Ashford, Co Wicklow. Tel: +353 404 40205

Scotland

Argyll

Inveraray Castle - Inveraray, Argyll PA32 8XE. Tel: 01499 302203

Ayrshire

Kelburn Castle and Country Centre - South Offices, Kelburn, Fairlie, Ayrshire KA29 0BE. Tel: 01475 568685

Dumfries

Drumlanrig Castle, Gardens and Country Park - Thornhill, Dumfries DG3 4AQ. Tel: 01848 330248

Orkney Islands

Balfour Castle - Shapinsay, Orkney Islands KW17 2DY. Tel: 01856 711282

Peebles

Traquair House - Innerleithen, Peebles EH44 6PW. Tel: 01896 830323

Perthshire

Scone Palace - Perth, Perthshire PH2 6BD. Tel: 01738 552300

Scottish Borders

Bowhill House & Country Park - Bowhill, Selkirk, Scottish Borders TD7 5ET. Tel: 01750 22204

Manderston - Duns, Berwickshire, Scottish Borders TD11 3PP. Tel: 01361 882636

Strathclyde

Mount Stuart - Isle of Bute, Strathclyde PA20 9LR. Tel: 01700 503877

West Lothian

Hopetoun House - South Queensferry, Nr Edinburgh West Lothian EH30 9SL. Tel: 0131 331 2451

Newliston - Kirkliston, West Lothian EH29 9EB. Tel: 0131 333 3231

Wigtownshire

Ardwell Estate Gardens - Ardwell House, Stranraer DG9 9LY. Tel: 01776 860227

Wales

Conway

Bodnant Garden - Tal-y-Cafn, Nr Colwyn Bay, Conway LL28 5RE. Tel: 01492 650460

Dyfed

Pembroke Castle - Pembroke, Dyfed SA71 4LA. Tel: 01646 681510

Flintshire

Golden Grove - Llanasa, Nr. Holywell, Flintshire CH8 9NA. Tel: 01745 854452

Gwynedd

Plas Brondanw Gardens - Menna Angharad, Plas Brondanw, Llanfrothen, Gwynedd LL48 6SW. Tel: 01766 770484

Monmouthshire

Usk Castle - Castle House, Monmouth Road, Usk, Monmouthshire NP15 1SD. Tel: 01291 672563

Pembrokeshire

St Davids Cathedral - The Close, St. David's, Pembrokeshire SA62 6RH. Tel: 01437 720199

France

Château de Chenonceau - Chenonceaux, 37150. Tel: 00 33 2 47 23 90 07

Château de Thoiry - Thoiry, Yvelines 78770 . Tel: 00 33 1 34 87 53 65

Mini Listings The Americas

Condé Nast Johansens are delighted to recommend 310 properties across The Americas, Atlantic, Caribbean and Pacific.

Call +44 1323 649 349 or see the order forms on pages 523-527 to order guides.

Recommendations in Canada

CANADA - BRITISH COLUMBIA (SALT SPRING ISLAND)

Hastings House Country Estate
160 Upper Ganges Road, Salt Spring Island,
British Columbia V8K 2S2
Tel: +1 250 537 2362
Fax: +1 250 537 5333
Web: www.johansens.com/hastingshouse

CANADA - BRITISH COLUMBIA (TOFINO)

The Wickaninnish Inn
Box 250, Tofino, British Columbia V0R 2Z0
Tel: +1 250 725 3100
Fax: +1 250 725 3110
Web: www.johansens.com/wickaninnish

CANADA - BRITISH COLUMBIA (VANCOUVER)

The Sutton Place Hotel Vancouver
845 Burrard Street, Vancouver, British Columbia V6Z 2K6
Tel: +1 604 682 5511
Fax: +1 604 682 5513
Web: www.johansens.com/suttonplacebc

CANADA - BRITISH COLUMBIA (VANCOUVER)

Wedgewood Hotel & Spa
845 Hornby Street, Vancouver, British Columbia V6Z 1V1
Tel: +1 604 689 7777
Fax: +1 604 608 5348
Web: www.johansens.com/wedgewoodbc

CANADA - BRITISH COLUMBIA (VICTORIA)

Villa Marco Polo Inn
1524 Shasta Place, Victoria, British Columbia V8S 1X9
Tel: +1 250 370 1524
Fax: +1 250 370 1624
Web: www.johansens.com/villamarcopolo

CANADA - NEW BRUNSWICK (ST ANDREWS BY-THE-SEA)

Kingsbrae Arms
219 King Street, St. Andrews By-The-Sea,
New Brunswick E5B 1Y1
Tel: +1 506 529 1897
Fax: +1 506 529 1197
Web: www.johansens.com/kingsbraearms

CANADA - ONTARIO (CAMBRIDGE)

Langdon Hall Country House Hotel & Spa
1 Langdon Drive, Cambridge, Ontario N3H 4R8
Tel: +1 519 740 2100
Fax: +1 519 740 8161
Web: www.johansens.com/langdonhall

CANADA - ONTARIO (NIAGARA-ON-THE-LAKE)

Riverbend Inn & Vineyard
16104 Niagara River Parkway, Niagara-on-the-Lake,
Ontario L0S 1J0
Tel: +1 905 468 8866
Fax: +1 905 468 8829
Web: www.johansens.com/riverbend

CANADA - ONTARIO (TORONTO)

Windsor Arms
18 St. Thomas Street, Toronto, Ontario M5S 3E7
Tel: +1 416 971 9666
Fax: +1 416 921 9121
Web: www.johansens.com/windsorarms

CANADA - QUÉBEC (QUÉBEC CITY)

Auberge Saint-Antoine
8, Rue Saint-Antoine, Québec City, Québec G1K 4C9
Tel: +1 418 692 2211
Fax: +1 418 692 1177
Web: www.johansens.com/saintantoine

CANADA - QUÉBEC (MONT-TREMBLANT)

Hôtel Quintessence
3004 chemin de la chapelle, Mont-Tremblant,
Québec J8E 1E1
Tel: +1 819 425 3400
Fax: +1 819 425 3480
Web: www.johansens.com/quintessence

CANADA - QUÉBEC (LA MALBAIE)

La Pinsonnière
124 Saint-Raphaël, La Malbaie, Québec G5A 1X9
Tel: +1 418 665 4431
Fax: +1 418 665 7156
Web: www.johansens.com/lapinsonniere

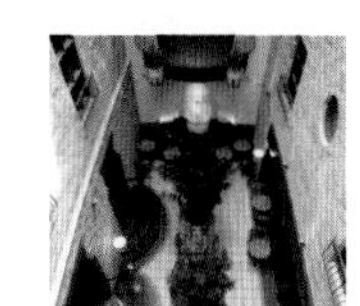

CANADA - QUÉBEC (MONTRÉAL)

Hôtel Nelligan
106 rue Saint-Paul Ouest, Montréal, Québec H2Y 1Z3
Tel: +1 514 788 2040
Fax: +1 514 788 2041
Web: www.johansens.com/nelligan

CANADA - QUÉBEC (MONTRÉAL)

Le Place d'Armes Hôtel & Suites
55 rue Saint-Jacques Ouest, Montréal, Québec H2Y 3X2
Tel: +1 514 842 1887
Fax: +1 514 842 6469
Web: www.johansens.com/hotelplacedarmes

Recommendations in Mexico

MEXICO - BAJA CALIFORNIA NORTE (TECATE)

Rancho La Puerta
Tecate, Baja California Norte
Tel: +52 665 654 9155
Fax: +52 665 654 1108
Web: www.johansens.com/rancholapuerta

MEXICO - BAJA CALIFORNIA SUR (CABO SAN LUCAS)

Esperanza
Km. 7 Carretera Transpeninsular, Punta Ballena,
Cabo San Lucas, Baja California Sur 23410
Tel: +52 624 145 6400
Fax: +52 624 145 6499
Web: www.johansens.com/esperanza

MEXICO - BAJA CALIFORNIA SUR (LOS CABOS)

Marquis Los Cabos
Lote 74, Km. 21.5 Carretera Transpeninsular, Fraccionamiento
Cabo Real, Los Cabos, Baja California Sur 23400
Tel: +52 624 144 2000
Fax: +52 624 144 2001
Web: www.johansens.com/marquisloscabos

MEXICO - BAJA CALIFORNIA SUR (SAN JOSE DEL CABO)

Casa Natalia
Blvd. Mijares 4, San Jose Del Cabo, Baja California Sur 23400
Tel: +52 624 14671 00
Fax: +52 624 14251 10
Web: www.johansens.com/casanatalia

Mini Listings The Americas

Condé Nast Johansens are delighted to recommend 310 properties across The Americas, Atlantic, Caribbean and Pacific.

Call +44 1323 649 349 or see the order forms on pages 523-527 to order guides.

MEXICO - BAJA CALIFORNIA SUR (SAN JOSE DEL CABO)

One & Only Palmilla

Km 7.5 Carretera Transpeninsular, San Jose Del Cabo, Baja California Sur 23400
Tel: +52 624 146 7000
Fax: +52 624 146 7001
Web: www.johansens.com/oneandonlypalmilla

MEXICO - COLIMA (COLIMA)

Hacienda de San Antonio

Municipio de Comala, Colima, Colima 28450
Tel: +52 312 314 9554
Fax: +52 312 313 4254
Web: www.johansens.com/sanantonio

MEXICO - DISTRITO FEDERAL (MEXICO CITY)

Casa Vieja

Eugenio Sue 45 (Colonia Polanco), Mexico Distrito Federal 11560
Tel: +52 55 52 82 0067
Fax: +52 55 52 81 3780
Web: www.johansens.com/casavieja

MEXICO - ESTADO DE MEXICO (MALINALCO)

Casa Limon

Rio Lerma 103, Barrio de Santa María, Malinalco, Estado de Mexico 524040
Tel: +52 714 147 0256
Fax: +52 714 147 0619
Web: www.johansens.com/casalimon

MEXICO - GUANAJUATO (GUANAJUATO)

Quinta Las Acacias

Paseo de la Presa 168, Guanajuato, Guanajuato 36000
Tel: +52 473 731 1517
Fax: +52 473 731 1862
Web: www.johansens.com/acacias

MEXICO - GUANAJUATO (SAN MIGUEL DE ALLENDE)

Dos Casas

Calle Quebrada 101, San Miguel de Allende, Guanajuato 37700
Tel: +52 415 154 4073
Fax: +52 415 154 4958
Web: www.johansens.com/doscasas

MEXICO - GUANAJUATO (SAN MIGUEL DE ALLENDE)

La Puertecita Boutique Hotel

Santo Domingo 75 Col. Los Arcos, San Miguel de Allende, Guanajuato 37740
Tel: +52 415 152 5011
Fax: +52 415 152 5505
Web: www.johansens.com/lapuertecita

MEXICO - GUERRERO (ZIHUATANEJO)

Villa del Sol

Playa La Ropa, P.O. Box 84, Zihuatanejo, Guerrero 40880
Tel: +52 755 555 5500
Fax: +52 755 554 2758
Web: www.johansens.com/villadelsol

MEXICO - JALISCO (PUERTA VALLARTA / COSTA ALEGRE)

Las Alamandas Resort

Carretera Barra de Navidad - Puerto Vallarta km 83.5, Col. Quemaro, Jalisco 48850
Tel: +52 322 285 5500
Fax: +52 322 285 5027
Web: www.johansens.com/lasalamandas

MEXICO - JALISCO (PUERTO VALLARTA)

Casa Velas

Pelicanos 311, Fracc. Marina Vallarta, Puerto Vallarta, Jalisco 48354
Tel: +52 322 226 9585
Fax: +52 322 226 6690
Web: www.johansens.com/casavelas

MEXICO - JALISCO (PUERTO VALLARTA)

Hacienda San Angel

Miramar 336, Col. Centro Puerto Vallarta, Jalisco 48300
Tel: +52 322 222 2692
Fax: +52 322 223 1941
Web: www.johansens.com/sanangel

MEXICO - MICHOACÁN (MORELIA)

Hotel Los Juaninos

Morelos Sur 39, Centro, Morelia, Michoacán 58000
Tel: +52 443 312 00 36
Fax: +52 443 312 00 36
Web: www.johansens.com/juaninos

MEXICO - MICHOACÁN (MORELIA)

Hotel Virrey de Mendoza

Av. Madero Pte. 310, Centro Histórico, Morelia, Michoacán 58000
Tel: +52 44 33 12 06 33
Fax: +52 44 33 12 67 19
Web: www.johansens.com/hotelvirrey

MEXICO - MICHOACÁN (MORELIA)

Villa Montaña Hotel & Spa

Patzimba 201, Vista Bella, Morelia, Michoacán 58090
Tel: +52 443 314 02 31
Fax: +52 443 315 14 23
Web: www.johansens.com/montana

MEXICO - NAYARIT (NUEVO VALLARTA)

Grand Velas All Suites & Spa Resort

Av. Cocoteros 98 Sur, Nuevo Vallarta, Nayarit 63735
Tel: +52 322 226 8000
Fax: +52 322 297 2005
Web: www.johansens.com/grandvelas

MEXICO - OAXACA (OAXACA)

Casa Oaxaca

Calle García Vigil 407, Centro, Oaxaca, Oaxaca 68000
Tel: +52 951 514 4173
Fax: +52 951516 4412
Web: www.johansens.com/oaxaca

MEXICO - OAXACA (OAXACA)

Hacienda Los Laureles - Spa

Hidalgo 21, San Felipe del Agua, Oaxaca, Oaxaca 68020
Tel: +52 951 501 5300
Fax: +52 951 501 5301 or +52 951 520 0890
Web: www.johansens.com/laureles

MEXICO - PUEBLA (CHOLULA)

La Quinta Luna

3 sur 702, San Pedro Cholula, Puebla 72760
Tel: +52 222 247 8915
Fax: +52 222 247 8916
Web: www.johansens.com/quintaluna

MEXICO - QUERÉTARO (QUERÉTARO)

La Casa de la Marquesa

Madero 41, Querétaro, Centro Histórico 7600
Tel: +52 442 212 0092
Fax: +52 442 212 0098
Web: www.johansens.com/marquesa

MEXICO - QUINTANA ROO (PLAYA DEL CARMEN)

Royal Hideaway Playacar

Lote Hotelero No. 6, Mza 6 Fracc., Playacar, Playa del Carmen, Quintana Roo 77710
Tel: +52 984 873 4500
Fax: +52 984 873 4507
Web: www.johansens.com/royalhidewaway

MINI LISTINGS THE AMERICAS

Condé Nast Johansens are delighted to recommend 310 properties across The Americas, Atlantic, Caribbean and Pacific.
Call +44 1323 649 349 or see the order forms on pages 523-527 to order guides.

MEXICO - QUINTANA ROO (PUERTO MORELOS)

Ceiba del Mar Spa Resort
Costera Norte Lte. 1, S.M. 10, MZ. 26, Puerto Morelos, Quintana Roo 77580
Tel: +52 998 872 8060
Fax: +52 998 872 8061
Web: www.johansens.com/ceibademar

MEXICO - QUINTANA ROO (TULUM)

Casa Nalum
Sian Ka'an Biosphere Reserve, Quintana Roo
Tel: +52 984 806 4905
Web: www.johansens.com/casanalum

MEXICO - YUCATÁN (MÉRIDA)

Hacienda Xcanatun - Casa de Piedra
Carretera Mérida-Progreso, Km 12, Mérida, Yucatán 97302
Tel: +52 999 941 0273
Fax: +52 999 941 0319
Web: www.johansens.com/xcanatun

Recommendations in U.S.A

U.S.A. - ARIZONA (GREER)

Hidden Meadow Ranch
620 Country Road 1325, Greer, Arizona 85927
Tel: +1 928 333 1000
Fax: +1 928 333 1010
Web: www.johansens.com/hiddenmeadow

U.S.A. - ARIZONA (PARADISE VALLEY / SCOTTSDALE)

The Hermosa Inn
5532 North Palo Cristi Road, Paradise Valley, Arizona 85253
Tel: +1 602 955 8614
Fax: +1 602 955 8299
Web: www.johansens.com/hermosa

U.S.A. - ARIZONA (PARADISE VALLEY / SCOTTSDALE)

Sanctuary on Camelback Mountain
5700 East McDonald Drive, Scottsdale, Arizona 85253
Tel: +1 480 948 2100
Fax: +1 480 483 7314
Web: www.johansens.com/sanctuarycamelback

U.S.A. - ARIZONA (SEDONA)

Amara Creekside Resort
310 North Highway 89A, Sedona, Arizona 86336
Tel: +1 928 282 4828
Fax: +1 928 282 4825
Web: www.johansens.com/amaracreekside

U.S.A. - ARIZONA (SEDONA)

L'Auberge de Sedona
301 L'Auberge Lane, Sedona, Arizona 86336
Tel: +1 928 282 1661
Fax: +1 928 282 2885
Web: www.johansens.com/laubergedesedona

U.S.A. - ARIZONA (SEDONA)

Sedona Rouge Hotel & Spa
2250 West Highway 89A, Sedona, Arizona 86336
Tel: +1 928 203 4111
Fax: +1 928 203 9094
Web: www.johansens.com/sedonarouge

U.S.A. - ARIZONA (TUCSON)

Arizona Inn
2200 East Elm Street, Tucson, Arizona 85719
Tel: +1 520 325 1541
Fax: +1 520 881 5830
Web: www.johansens.com/arizonainn

U.S.A. - ARIZONA (TUCSON)

Tanque Verde Ranch
14301 East Speedway Boulevard, Tucson, Arizona 85748
Tel: +1 520 296 6275
Fax: +1 520 721 9427
Web: www.johansens.com/tanqueverde

U.S.A. - ARIZONA (WICKENBURG)

Rancho de los Caballeros
1551 South Vulture Mine Road, Wickenburg, Arizona 85390
Tel: +1 928 684 5484
Fax: +1 928 684 9565
Web: www.johansens.com/caballeros

U.S.A. - CALIFORNIA (ATASCADERO)

The Carlton Hotel
6005 El Camino Real, Atascadero, California 93422
Tel: +1 805 461 5100
Fax: +1 805 461 5116
Web: www.johansens.com/carltoncalifornia

U.S.A. - CALIFORNIA (BIG SUR)

Post Ranch Inn
Highway 1, P.O. Box 219, Big Sur, California 93920
Tel: +1 831 667 2200
Fax: +1 831 667 2512
Web: www.johansens.com/postranchinn

U.S.A. - CALIFORNIA (BIG SUR)

Ventana Inn and Spa
Highway 1, Big Sur, California 93920
Tel: +1 831 667 2331
Fax: +1 831 667 2419
Web: www.johansens.com/ventana

U.S.A. - CALIFORNIA (CARMEL-BY-THE-SEA)

L'Auberge Carmel
Monte Verde at Seventh, Carmel-by-the-Sea, California 93921
Tel: +1 831 624 8578
Fax: +1 831 626 1018
Web: www.johansens.com/laubergecarmel

U.S.A. - CALIFORNIA (CARMEL-BY-THE-SEA)

Tradewinds Carmel
Mission Street at Third Avenue, Carmel-by-the-Sea, California 93921
Tel: +1 831 624 2776
Fax: +1 831 624 0634
Web: www.johansens.com/tradewinds

U.S.A. - CALIFORNIA (EUREKA)

The Carter House Inns
301 L Street, Eureka, California 95501
Tel: +1 707 444 8062
Fax: +1 707 444 8067
Web: www.johansens.com/carterhouse

U.S.A. - CALIFORNIA (GLEN ELLEN)

The Gaige House
13540 Arnold Drive, Glen Ellen, California 95442
Tel: +1 707 935 0237
Fax: +1 707 935 6411
Web: www.johansens.com/gaige

Mini Listings The Americas

Condé Nast Johansens are delighted to recommend 310 properties across The Americas, Atlantic, Caribbean and Pacific.
Call +44 1323 649 349 or see the order forms on pages 523-527 to order guides.

U.S.A. - CALIFORNIA (HEALDSBURG)

The Grape Leaf Inn

539 Johnson Street, Healdsburg, California 95448
Tel: +1 707 433 8140
Fax: +1 707 433 3140
Web: www.johansens.com/grapeleaf

U.S.A. - CALIFORNIA (KENWOOD)

The Kenwood Inn and Spa

10400 Sonoma Highway, Kenwood, California 95452
Tel: +1 707 833 1293
Fax: +1 707 833 1247
Web: www.johansens.com/kenwoodinn

U.S.A. - CALIFORNIA (LA JOLLA)

Estancia La Jolla Hotel & Spa

9700 North Torrey Pines Road, La Jolla, California 92037
Tel: +1 858 202 3389
Fax: +1 858 202 3399
Web: www.johansens.com/estancialajolla

U.S.A. - CALIFORNIA (LOS ANGELES)

Hotel Bel-Air

701 Stone Canyon Road, Los Angeles, California 90077
Tel: +1 310 472 1211
Fax: +1 310 909 1611
Web: www.johansens.com/belair

U.S.A. - CALIFORNIA (LOS OLIVOS)

The Fess Parker Wine Country Inn

2860 Grand Avenue, Los Olivos, California 93441
Tel: +1 805 688 7788
Fax: +1 805 688 1942
Web: www.johansens.com/fessparker

U.S.A. - CALIFORNIA (MENDOCINO)

The Stanford Inn By The Sea

Coast Highway One & Comptche-Ukiah Road, Mendocino, California 95460
Tel: +1 707 937 5615
Fax: +1 707 937 0305
Web: www.johansens.com/stanford

U.S.A. - CALIFORNIA (MILL VALLEY)

Mill Valley Inn

165 Throckmorton Avenue, Mill Valley, California 94941
Tel: +1 415 389 6608
Fax: +1 415 389 5051
Web: www.johansens.com/millvalleyinn

U.S.A. - CALIFORNIA (MONTEREY)

Old Monterey Inn

500 Martin Street, Monterey, California 93940
Tel: +1 831 375 8284
Fax: +1 831 375 6730
Web: www.johansens.com/oldmontereyinn

U.S.A. - CALIFORNIA (NAPA VALLEY)

1801 First Inn

1801 First Street, Napa, California 94559
Tel: +1 707 224 3739
Fax: +1 707 224 3932
Web: www.johansens.com/1801inn

U.S.A. - CALIFORNIA (NAPA)

Milliken Creek Inn & Spa

1815 Silverado Trail, Napa, California 94558
Tel: +1 707 255 1197
Fax: +1 707 255 3112
Web: www.johansens.com/milliken

U.S.A. - CALIFORNIA (OAKHURST)

Château du Sureau & Spa

48688 Victoria Lane, Oakhurst, California 93644
Tel: +1 559 683 6860
Fax: +1 559 683 0800
Web: www.johansens.com/chateausureau

U.S.A. - CALIFORNIA (PASO ROBLES)

The Villa Toscana

4230 Buena Vista, Paso Robles, California 93446
Tel: +1 805 238 5600
Fax: +1 805 238 5605
Web: www.johansens.com/villatoscana

U.S.A. - CALIFORNIA (RANCHO SANTA FE)

The Inn at Rancho Santa Fe

5951 Linea del Cielo, Rancho Santa Fe, California 92067
Tel: +1 858 756 1131
Fax: +1 858 759 1604
Web: www.johansens.com/ranchosantafe

U.S.A. - CALIFORNIA (SAN DIEGO)

Tower23 Hotel

723 Felspar, San Diego, California 92109
Tel: +1 858 270 2323
Fax: +1 858 274 2333
Web: www.johansens.com/tower23

U.S.A. - CALIFORNIA (SAN FRANCISCO BAY AREA)

Inn Above Tide

30 El Portal, Sausalito, California 94965
Tel: +1 415 332 9535
Fax: +1 415 332 9535
Web: www.johansens.com/innabovetide

U.S.A. - CALIFORNIA (SAN FRANCISCO)

The Union Street Inn

2229 Union Street, San Francisco, California 94123
Tel: +1 415 346 0424
Fax: +1 415 922 8046
Web: www.johansens.com/unionstreetsf

U.S.A. - CALIFORNIA (SANTA BARBARA)

Harbor View Inn

28 West Cabrillo Boulevard, Santa Barbara, California 93101
Tel: +1 805 963 0780
Fax: +1 805 963 7967
Web: www.johansens.com/harborview

U.S.A. - CALIFORNIA (SANTA YNEZ)

The Santa Ynez Inn

3627 Sagunto Street, Santa Ynez, California 93460-0628
Tel: +1 805 688 5588
Fax: +1 805 686 4294
Web: www.johansens.com/santaynez

U.S.A. - CALIFORNIA (SONOMA)

Ledson Hotel & Harmony Restaurant

480 First Street East, Sonoma, California 95476
Tel: +1 707 996 9779
Fax: +1 707 996 9776
Web: www.johansens.com/ledsonhotel

U.S.A. - CALIFORNIA (ST. HELENA)

Meadowood

900 Meadowood Lane, St. Helena, California 94574
Tel: +1 707 963 3646
Fax: +1 707 963 3532
Web: www.johansens.com/meadowood

MINI LISTINGS THE AMERICAS

Condé Nast Johansens are delighted to recommend 310 properties across The Americas, Atlantic, Caribbean and Pacific.
Call +44 1323 649 349 or see the order forms on pages 523-527 to order guides.

U.S.A. - COLORADO (BOULDER)

The Bradley Boulder Inn
2040 16th Street, Boulder, Colorado 80302
Tel: +1 303 545 5200
Fax: +1 303 440 6740
Web: www.johansens.com/bradleyboulderinn

U.S.A. - COLORADO (DENVER)

Castle Marne Bed & Breakfast Inn
1572 Race Street, Denver, Colorado 80206
Tel: +1 303 331 0621
Fax: +1 303 331 0623
Web: www.johansens.com/castlemarne

U.S.A. - COLORADO (ESTES PARK)

Taharaa Mountain Lodge
P.O. Box 2586, Estes Park, Colorado 80517
Tel: +1 970 577 0098
Fax: +1 970 577 0819
Web: www.johansens.com/taharaa

U.S.A. - COLORADO (MANITOU SPRINGS)

The Cliff House at Pikes Peak
306 Cañon Avenue, Manitou Springs, Colorado 80829
Tel: +1 719 685 3000
Fax: +1 719 685 3913
Web: www.johansens.com/thecliffhouse

U.S.A. - COLORADO (MONTROSE)

Elk Mountain Resort
97 Elk Walk, Montrose, Colorado 81401
Tel: +1 970 252 4900
Fax: +1 970 252 4913
Web: www.johansens.com/elkmountain

U.S.A. - COLORADO (STEAMBOAT SPRINGS)

Vista Verde Guest Ranch
P.O. Box 770465, Steamboat Springs, Colorado 80477
Tel: +1 970 879 3858
Fax: +1 970 879 6814
Web: www.johansens.com/vistaverderanch

U.S.A. - COLORADO (VAIL)

The Tivoli Lodge at Vail
386 Hanson Ranch Road, Vail, Colorado 81657
Tel: +1 970 476 5615
Fax: +1 970 476 6601
Web: www.johansens.com/tivoli

U.S.A. - COLORADO (VAIL)

Vail Mountain Lodge & Spa
352 East Meadow Drive, Vail, Colorado 81657
Tel: +1 970 476 0700
Fax: +1 970 476 6451
Web: www.johansens.com/vailmountain

U.S.A. - CONNECTICUT (GREENWICH)

Delamar Greenwich Harbor
500 Steamboat Road, Greenwich, Connecticut 06830
Tel: +1 203 661 9800
Fax: +1 203 661 2513
Web: www.johansens.com/delamar

U.S.A. - CONNECTICUT (STONINGTON)

The Inn at Stonington
60 Water Street, Stonington, Connecticut 06378
Tel: +1 860 535 2000
Fax: +1 860 535 8193
Web: www.johansens.com/stonington

U.S.A. - DELAWARE (REHOBOTH BEACH)

The Bellmoor
Six Christian Street, Rehoboth Beach, Delaware 19971
Tel: +1 302 227 5800
Fax: +1 302 227 0323
Web: www.johansens.com/thebellmoor

U.S.A. - DELAWARE (REHOBOTH BEACH)

Boardwalk Plaza Hotel
Olive Avenue & The Boardwalk, Rehoboth Beach, Delaware 19971
Tel: +1 302 227 7169
Fax: +1 302 227 0561
Web: www.johansens.com/boardwalkplaza

U.S.A. - DELAWARE (WILMINGTON)

Inn at Montchanin Village
Route 100 & Kirk Road, Montchanin, Delaware 19710
Tel: +1 302 888 2133
Fax: +1 302 888 0389
Web: www.johansens.com/montchanin

U.S.A. - DISTRICT OF COLUMBIA (WASHINGTON)

The Hay Adams
Sixteenth & H. Streets N.W., Washington D.C. 20006
Tel: +1 202 638 6600
Fax: +1 202 638 2716
Web: www.johansens.com/hayadams

U.S.A. - FLORIDA (COCONUT GROVE)

Grove Isle Hotel & Spa
Four Grove Isle Drive, Coconut Grove, Florida 33133
Tel: +1 305 858 8300
Fax: +1 305 858 5908
Web: www.johansens.com/groveisle

U.S.A. - FLORIDA (DAYTONA BEACH SHORES)

The Shores Resort & Spa
2637 South Atlantic Avenue, Daytona Beach Shores, Florida 32118
Tel: +1 386 767 7350
Fax: +1 386 760 3651
Web: www.johansens.com/shoresresort

U.S.A. - FLORIDA (FISHER ISLAND)

Fisher Island Hotel & Resort
One Fisher Island Drive, Fisher Island, Florida 33109
Tel: +1 305 535 6000
Fax: +1 305 535 6003
Web: www.johansens.com/fisherisland

U.S.A. - FLORIDA (JUPITER)

Jupiter Beach Resort & Spa
5 North A1A, Jupiter, Florida 33477-5190
Tel: +1 561 746 2511
Fax: +1 561 744 1741
Web: www.johansens.com/jupiterbeachresort

U.S.A. - FLORIDA (KEY WEST)

Ocean Key Resort
Zero Duval Street, Key West, Florida 33040
Tel: +1 305 296 7701
Fax: +1 305 292 7685
Web: www.johansens.com/oceankey

U.S.A. - FLORIDA (KEY WEST)

Simonton Court Historic Inn & Cottages
320 Simonton Street, Key West, Florida 33040
Tel: +1 305 294 6386
Fax: +1 305 293 8446
Web: www.johansens.com/simontoncourt

Mini Listings The Americas

Condé Nast Johansens are delighted to recommend 310 properties across The Americas, Atlantic, Caribbean and Pacific.
Call +44 1323 649 349 or see the order forms on pages 523-527 to order guides.

U.S.A. - FLORIDA (KEY WEST)

Sunset Key Guest Cottages
245 Front Street, Key West, Florida 33040
Tel: +1 305 292 5300
Fax: +1 305 292 5395
Web: www.johansens.com/sunsetkey

U.S.A. - FLORIDA (MARCO ISLAND/NAPLES)

Marco Beach Ocean Resort
480 South Collier Boulevard, Marco Island, Florida 34145
Tel: +1 239 393 1400
Fax: +1 239 393 1401
Web: www.johansens.com/marcobeach

U.S.A. - FLORIDA (MIAMI BEACH)

Hotel Victor
1144 Ocean Drive, Miami Beach, Florida 33139
Tel: +1 305 428 1234
Fax: +1 305 421 6281
Web: www.johansens.com/hotelvictor

U.S.A. - FLORIDA (NAPLES)

LaPlaya Beach & Golf Resort
9891 Gulf Shore Drive, Naples, Florida 34108
Tel: +1 239 597 3123
Fax: +1 239 597 8283
Web: www.johansens.com/laplaya

U.S.A. - FLORIDA (ORLANDO)

Portofino Bay Hotel
5601 Universal Boulevard, Orlando, Florida 32819
Tel: +1 407 503 1000
Fax: +1 407 503 1010
Web: www.johansens.com/portofinobay

U.S.A. - FLORIDA (PONTE VEDRA BEACH)

The Lodge & Club at Ponte Vedra Beach
607 Ponte Vedra Boulevard, Ponte Vedra Beach,Florida 32082
Tel: +1 904 273 9500
Fax: +1 904 273 0210
Web: www.johansens.com/ponteverdrabeach

U.S.A. - FLORIDA (SANTA ROSA BEACH)

WaterColor Inn and Resort
34 Goldenrod Circle, Santa rosa Beach, Florida 32459
Tel: +1 850 534 5000
Fax: +1 850 534 5001
Web: www.johansens.com/watercolor

U.S.A. - FLORIDA (ST. PETE BEACH)

Don CeSar Beach Resort
3400 Gulf Boulevard, St. Pete Beach, Florida 33706
Tel: +1 727 360 1881
Fax: +1 727 367 3609
Web: www.johansens.com/doncesar

U.S.A. - GEORGIA (ADAIRSVILLE)

Barnsley Gardens Resort
597 Barnsley Gardens Road, Adairsville, Georgia 30103
Tel: +1 770 773 7480
Fax: +1 770 877 9155
Web: www.johansens.com/barnsleygardens

U.S.A. - GEORGIA (CUMBERLAND ISLAND)

Greyfield Inn
Cumberland Island, Georgia
Tel: +1 904 261 6408
Fax: +1 904 321 0666
Web: www.johansens.com/greyfieldinn

U.S.A. - GEORGIA (SAVANNAH)

The Ballastone
14 East Oglethorpe Avenue, Savannah, Georgia 31401-3707
Tel: +1 912 236 1484
Fax: +1 912 236 4626
Web: www.johansens.com/ballastone

U.S.A. - GEORGIA (SAVANNAH)

Eliza Thompson House
5 West Jones Street, Savannah, Georgia 31401
Tel: +1 912 236 3620
Fax: +1 912 238 1920
Web: www.johansens.com/elizathompsonhouse

U.S.A. - GEORGIA (SAVANNAH)

The Gastonian
220 East Gaston Street, Savannah, Georgia 31401
Tel: +1 912 232 2869
Fax: +1 912 232 0710
Web: www.johansens.com/gastonian

U.S.A. - HAWAII (BIG ISLAND)

The Palms Cliff House
28-3514 Mamalahoa Highway 19, P.O. Box 189, Honomu, Hawaii 96728-0189
Tel: +1 808 963 6076
Fax: +1 808 963 6316
Web: www.johansens.com/palmscliff

U.S.A. - HAWAII (BIG ISLAND)

Shipman House
131 Ka'iulani Street, Hilo, Hawaii 96720
Tel: +1 808 934 8002
Fax: +1 808 934 8002
Web: www.johansens.com/shipman

U.S.A. - HAWAII (MAUI)

Hotel Hana-Maui and Honua Spa
5031 Hana Highway, Hana, Maui, Hawaii 96713
Tel: +1 808 248 8211
Fax: +1 808 248 7202
Web: www.johansens.com/hanamaui

U.S.A. - IDAHO (KETCHUM)

Knob Hill Inn
960 North Main Street, P.O. Box 800, Ketchum, Idaho 83340
Tel: +1 208 726 8010
Fax: +1 208 726 2712
Web: www.johansens.com/knobhillinn

U.S.A. - KANSAS (LAWRENCE)

The Eldridge Hotel
701 Massachusetts, Lawrence, Kansas 66044
Tel: +1 785 749 5011
Fax: +1 785 749 4512
Web: www.johansens.com/eldridge

U.S.A. - LOUISIANA (NEW ORLEANS)

Hotel Maison de Ville
727 Rue Toulouse, New Orleans, Louisiana 70130
Tel: +1 504 561 5858
Fax: +1 504 528 9939
Web: www.johansens.com/maisondeville

U.S.A. - LOUISIANA (NEW ORLEANS)

The Lafayette Hotel
600 St. Charles Avenue, New Orleans, Louisiana 70130
Tel: +1 504 524 4441
Fax: +1 504 962 5537
Web: www.johansens.com/lafayette

Mini Listings The Americas

Condé Nast Johansens are delighted to recommend 310 properties across The Americas, Atlantic, Caribbean and Pacific.
Call +44 1323 649 349 or see the order forms on pages 523-527 to order guides.

U.S.A. - LOUISIANA (NEW ORLEANS)

The St. James Hotel

330 Magazine Street, New Orleans, Louisiana 70130
Tel: +1 504 304 4000
Fax: +1 504 304 4444
Web: www.johansens.com/stjamesno

U.S.A. - MAINE (GREENVILLE)

The Lodge At Moosehead Lake

Lily Bay Road, P.O. Box 1167, Greenville, Maine 04441
Tel: +1 207 695 4400
Fax: +1 207 695 2281
Web: www.johansens.com/lodgeatmooseheadlake

U.S.A. - MAINE (KENNEBUNKPORT)

The White Barn Inn

37 Beach Avenue, Kennebunkport, Maine 04043
Tel: +1 207 967 2321
Fax: +1 207 967 1100
Web: www.johansens.com/whitebarninn

U.S.A. - MAINE (PORTLAND)

Portland Harbor Hotel

468 Fore Street, Portland, Maine 04101
Tel: +1 207 775 9090
Fax: +1 207 775 9990
Web: www.johansens.com/portlandharbor

U.S.A. - MARYLAND (EASTON)

Inn at 202 Dover

202 E. Dover Street, Easton, Maryland 21601
Tel: +1 410 819 8007
Fax: +1 410 819 3368
Web: www.johansens.com/innat202dover

U.S.A. - MARYLAND (FROSTBURG)

Savage River Lodge

1600 Mt. Aetna Road, Frostburg, Maryland 21532
Tel: +1 301 689 3200
Fax: +1 301 689 2746
Web: www.johansens.com/savageriver

U.S.A. - MARYLAND (ST. MICHAELS)

Five Gables Inn & Spa

209 North Talbot Street, St. Michaels, Maryland 21663
Tel: +1 410 745 0100
Fax: +1 410 745 2903
Web: www.johansens.com/fivegables

U.S.A. - MASSACHUSETTS (BOSTON)

The Charles Street Inn

94 Charles Street, Boston, Massachusetts 02114
Tel: +1 617 314 8900
Fax: +1 617 371 0009
Web: www.johansens.com/charlesstreetinn

U.S.A. - MASSACHUSETTS (BOSTON)

Clarendon Square Inn

198 West Brookline Street, Boston, Massachusetts 02118
Tel: +1 617 536 2229
Fax: +1 617 536 2993
Web: www.johansens.com/clarendonsquare

U.S.A. - MASSACHUSETTS (BOSTON)

Hotel Commonwealth

500 Commonwealth Avenue, Boston, Massachusetts 02215
Tel: +1 617 933 5000
Fax: +1 617 266 6888
Web: www.johansens.com/commonwealth

U.S.A. - MASSACHUSETTS (BOSTON)

The Lenox

61 Exeter Street at Boylston, Boston, Massachusetts 02116
Tel: +1 617 536 5300
Fax: +1 617 267 1237
Web: www.johansens.com/lenox

U.S.A. - MASSACHUSETTS (BOSTON)

Nine Zero Hotel

90 Tremont Street, Boston, Massachusetts 02108
Tel: +1 617 772 5800
Fax: +1 617 772 5810
Web: www.johansens.com/ninezero

U.S.A. - MASSACHUSETTS (CAMBRIDGE)

Hotel Marlowe

25 Edwin H. Land Boulevard, Cambridge,
Massachusetts 02141
Tel: +1 617 868 8000
Fax: +1 617 868 8001
Web: www.johansens.com/marlowe

U.S.A. - MASSACHUSETTS (CAPE COD)

The Crowne Pointe Historic Inn & Spa

82 Bradford Street, Provincetown, Cape Cod,
Massachusetts 02657
Tel: +1 508 487 6767
Fax: +1 508 487 5554
Web: www.johansens.com/crownepointe

U.S.A. - MASSACHUSETTS (CAPE COD)

Wequassett Inn Resort and Golf Club

On Pleasant Bay, Chatham, Cape Cod, Massachusetts 02633
Tel: +1 508 432 5400
Fax: +1 508 430 3131
Web: www.johansens.com/wequassett

U.S.A. - MASSACHUSETTS (EDGARTOWN)

The Charlotte Inn

27 South Summer Street, Edgartown, Massachusetts 02539
Tel: +1 508 627 4151
Fax: +1 508 627 4652
Web: www.johansens.com/charlotte

U.S.A. - MASSACHUSETTS (IPSWICH)

The Inn at Castle Hill

280 Argilla Road, Ipswich, Massachusetts 01938
Tel: +1 978 412 2555
Fax: +1 978 412 2556
Web: www.johansens.com/castlehill

U.S.A. - MASSACHUSETTS (LENOX)

Blantyre

16 Blantyre Road, P.O. Box 995, Lenox,
Massachusetts 01240
Tel: +1 413 637 3556
Fax: +1 413 637 4282
Web: www.johansens.com/blantyre

U.S.A. - MASSACHUSETTS (LENOX)

Cranwell Resort, Spa & Golf Club

55 Lee Road, Route 20, Lenox, Massachusetts 01240
Tel: +1 413 637 1364
Fax: +1 413 637 4364
Web: www.johansens.com/cranwell

U.S.A. - MASSACHUSETTS (MARTHA'S VINEYARD)

Winnetu Oceanside Resort

31 Dunes Road, Edgartown, Massachusetts 02539
Tel: +1 978 443 1733
Fax: +1 978 443 0479
Web: www.johansens.com/winnetu

Mini Listings The Americas

Condé Nast Johansens are delighted to recommend 310 properties across The Americas, Atlantic, Caribbean and Pacific.
Call +44 1323 649 349 or see the order forms on pages 523-527 to order guides.

U.S.A. - MISSISSIPPI (JACKSON)

Fairview Inn & Restaurant

734 Fairview Street, Jackson, Mississippi 39202
Tel: +1 601 948 3429
Fax: +1 601 948 1203
Web: www.johansens.com/fairviewinn

U.S.A. - MISSISSIPPI (NATCHEZ)

Monmouth Plantation

36 Melrose Avenue, Natchez, Mississippi 39120
Tel: +1 601 442 5852
Fax: +1 601 446 7762
Web: www.johansens.com/monmouthplantation

U.S.A. - MISSISSIPPI (NESBIT)

Bonne Terre Country Inn

4715 Church Road West, Nesbit, Mississippi 38651
Tel: +1 662 781 5100
Fax: +1 662 781 5466
Web: www.johansens.com/bonneterre

U.S.A. - MISSISSIPPI (VICKSBURG)

Anchuca Historic Mansion & Inn

1010 First East Street, Vicksburg, Mississippi 39183
Tel: +1 601 661 0111
Fax: +1 601 631 0501
Web: www.johansens.com/anchuca

U.S.A. - MISSOURI (BRANSON)

Chateau on the Lake

415 North State Highway 265, Branson, Missouri 65616
Tel: +1 417 334 1161
Fax: +1 417 339 5566
Web: www.johansens.com/chateaulake

U.S.A. - MISSOURI (KANSAS CITY)

The Raphael Hotel

325 Ward Parkway, Kansas City, Missouri 64112
Tel: +1 816 756 3800
Fax: +1 816 802 2131
Web: www.johansens.com/raphael

U.S.A. - MISSOURI (RIDGEDALE)

Big Cedar Lodge

612 Devil's Pool Road, Ridgedale, Missouri 65739
Tel: +1 417 335 2777
Fax: +1 417 335 2340
Web: www.johansens.com/bigcedar

U.S.A. - MONTANA (BIG SKY)

The Big EZ Lodge

7000 Beaver Creek Road, Big Sky, Montana 59716
Tel: +1 406 995 7000
Fax: +1 406 995 7007
Web: www.johansens.com/bigez

U.S.A. - MONTANA (DARBY)

Triple Creek Ranch

5551 West Fork Road, Darby, Montana 59829
Tel: +1 406 821 4600
Fax: +1 406 821 4666
Web: www.johansens.com/triplecreek

U.S.A. - NEW HAMPSHIRE (JACKSON VILLAGE)

The Wentworth

Jackson Village, New Hampshire 03846
Tel: +1 603 383 9700
Fax: +1 603 383 4265
Web: www.johansens.com/wentworth

U.S.A. - NEW HAMPSHIRE (PLAINFIELD)

Home Hill

703 River Road, Plainfield, New Hampshire 03781
Tel: +1 603 675 6165
Fax: +1 603 675 5220
Web: www.johansens.com/homehill

U.S.A. - NEW HAMPSHIRE (WHITEFIELD / WHITE MOUNTAINS)

Mountain View, The Grand Resort & Spa

Mountain View Road, Whitefield, New Hampshire 03598
Tel: +1 603 837 2100
Fax: +1 603 837 8884
Web: www.johansens.com/mountainview

U.S.A. - NEW MEXICO (ESPAÑOLA)

Rancho de San Juan

P.O. Box 4140, Highway 285, Española, New Mexico 87533
Tel: +1 505 753 6818
Fax: +1 505 753 6818
Web: www.johansens.com/ranchosanjuan

U.S.A. - NEW MEXICO (SANTA FE)

Inn and Spa at Loretto

211 Old Santa Fe Trail, Santa Fe, New Mexico 87501
Tel: +1 505 988 5531
Fax: +1 505 984 7968
Web: www.johansens.com/innatloretto

U.S.A. - NEW MEXICO (TAOS)

El Monte Sagrado Living Resort & Spa

317 Kit Carson Road, Taos, New Mexico 87571
Tel: +1 505 758 3502
Fax: +1 505 737 2985
Web: www.johansens.com/elmontesagrado

U.S.A. - NEW YORK (BANGALL)

The Inn at Bullis Hall

P.O. Box 630, Bangall (Stanfordville), New York 12506
Tel: +1 845 868 1665
Fax: +1 845 868 1441
Web: www.johansens.com/bullishall

U.S.A. - NEW YORK (BOLTON LANDING)

The Sagamore

110 Sagamore Road, Bolton Landing, New York 12814
Tel: +1 518 644 9400
Fax: +1 518 644 2851
Web: www.johansens.com/sagamore

U.S.A. - NEW YORK (BUFFALO)

Mansion on Delaware

414 Delaware Avenue, Buffalo, New York 14202
Tel: +1 716 886 3300
Fax: +1 716 883 3923
Web: www.johansens.com/mansionondelaware

U.S.A. - NEW YORK (EAST AURORA)

The Roycroft Inn

40 South Grove Street, East Aurora, New York 14052
Tel: +1 716 652 5552
Fax: +1 716 655 5345
Web: www.johansens.com/roycroftinn

U.S.A. - NEW YORK (LAKE PLACID)

Whiteface Lodge

7 Whiteface Inn Lane, Lake Placid, New York 12946
Tel: +1 518 523 0500
Fax: +1 518 523 0559
Web: www.johansens.com/whiteface

Mini Listings The Americas

Condé Nast Johansens are delighted to recommend 310 properties across The Americas, Atlantic, Caribbean and Pacific.
Call +44 1323 649 349 or see the order forms on pages 523-527 to order guides.

U.S.A. - NEW YORK (NEW YORK CITY)

Hotel Plaza Athénée

37 East 64th Street, New York, New York 10021
Tel: +1 212 734 9100
Fax: +1 212 772 0958
Web: www.johansens.com/athenee

U.S.A. - NEW YORK (NEW YORK CITY)

The Inn at Irving Place

56 Irving Place, New York, New York 10003
Tel: +1 212 533 4600
Fax: +1 212 533 4611
Web: www.johansens.com/irvingplace

U.S.A. - NEW YORK (TARRYTOWN)

Castle On The Hudson

400 Benedict Avenue, Tarrytown, New York 10591
Tel: +1 914 631 1980
Fax: +1 914 631 4612
Web: www.johansens.com/hudson

U.S.A. - NEW YORK (VERONA)

The Lodge at Turning Stone

5218 Patrick Road, Verona, New York 13478
Tel: +1 315 361 8525
Fax: +1 315 361 8686
Web: www.johansens.com/turningstone

U.S.A. - NEW YORK/LONG ISLAND (EAST HAMPTON)

The Baker House 1650

181 Main Street, East Hampton, New York 11937
Tel: +1 631 324 4081
Fax: +1 631 329 5931
Web: www.johansens.com/bakerhouse

U.S.A. - NEW YORK/LONG ISLAND (EAST HAMPTON)

The Mill House Inn

31 North Main Street, East Hampton, New York 11937
Tel: +1 631 324 9766
Fax: +1 631 324 9793
Web: www.johansens.com/millhouse

U.S.A. - NEW YORK/LONG ISLAND (SOUTHAMPTON)

1708 House

126 Main Street, Southampton, New York 11968
Tel: +1 631 287 1708
Fax: +1 631 287 3593
Web: www.johansens.com/1708house

U.S.A. - NORTH CAROLINA (ASHEVILLE)

Inn on Biltmore Estate

One Antler Hill Road, Asheville, North Carolina 28803
Tel: +1 828 225 1600
Fax: +1 828 225 1629
Web: www.johansens.com/biltmore

U.S.A. - NORTH CAROLINA (BLOWING ROCK)

Gideon Ridge Inn

202 Gideon Ridge Road, Blowing Rock,
North Carolina 28605
Tel: +1 828 295 3644
Fax: +1 828 295 4586
Web: www.johansens.com/gideonridge

U.S.A. - NORTH CAROLINA (CHARLOTTE)

Ballantyne Resort

10000 Ballantyne Commons Parkway, Charlotte,
North Carolina 28277
Tel: +1 704 248 4000
Fax: +1 704 248 4005
Web: www.johansens.com/ballantyneresort

U.S.A. - NORTH CAROLINA (DUCK)

The Sanderling Resort & Spa

1461 Duck Road, Duck, North Carolina 27949
Tel: +1 252 261 4111
Fax: +1 252 261 1638
Web: www.johansens.com/sanderling

U.S.A. - NORTH CAROLINA (HIGHLANDS)

Inn at Half Mile Farm

P.O. Box 2769, 214 Half Mile Drive, Highlands,
North Carolina 28741
Tel: +1 828 526 8170
Fax: +1 828 526 2625
Web: www.johansens.com/halfmilefarm

U.S.A. - NORTH CAROLINA (HIGHLANDS)

Old Edwards Inn and Spa

445 Main Street, Highlands, North Carolina 28741
Tel: +1 828 526 8008
Fax: +1 828 526 8301
Web: www.johansens.com/oldedwards

U.S.A. - NORTH CAROLINA (NEW BERN)

The Aerie Inn

509 Pollock Street, New Bern, North Carolina 28562
Tel: +1 252 636 5553
Fax: +1 252 514 2157
Web: www.johansens.com/aerieinn

U.S.A. - NORTH CAROLINA (PITTSBORO)

The Fearrington House

2000 Fearrington Village Center, Pittsboro,
North Carolina 27312
Tel: +1 919 542 2121
Fax: +1 919 542 4202
Web: www.johansens.com/fearrington

U.S.A. - NORTH CAROLINA (RALEIGH - DURHAM)

The Siena Hotel

1505 E. Franklin Street, Chapel Hill, North Carolina 27514
Tel: +1 919 929 4000
Fax: +1 919 968 8527
Web: www.johansens.com/siena

U.S.A. - NORTH CAROLINA (TRYON)

Pine Crest Inn and Restaurant

85 Pine Crest Lane, Tryon, North Carolina 28782
Tel: +1 828 859 9135
Fax: +1 828 859 9136
Web: www.johansens.com/pinecrestinn

U.S.A. - OHIO (CINCINNATI)

The Cincinnatian Hotel

601 Vine Street, Cincinnati, Ohio 45202-2433
Tel: +1 513 381 3000
Fax: +1 513 651 0256
Web: www.johansens.com/cincinnatian

U.S.A. - OKLAHOMA (OKLAHOMA CITY)

Colcord Hotel

15 North Robinson, Oklahoma City, Oklahoma 73102
Tel: +1 405 601 4300
Fax: +1 405 208 4399
Web: www.johansens.com/colcord

U.S.A. - OKLAHOMA (TULSA)

Hotel Ambassador

1345 South Main Street, Tulsa, Oklahoma 74119
Tel: +1 918 587 8200
Fax: +1 918 587 8208
Web: www.johansens.com/ambassador

Mini Listings The Americas

Condé Nast Johansens are delighted to recommend 310 properties across The Americas, Atlantic, Caribbean and Pacific.
Call +44 1323 649 349 or see the order forms on pages 523-527 to order guides.

U.S.A. - OREGON (ASHLAND)

The Winchester Inn & Restaurant

35 South Second Street, Ashland, Oregon 97520
Tel: +1 541 488 1113
Fax: +1 541 488 4604
Web: www.johansens.com/winchester

U.S.A. - OREGON (PORTLAND)

The Benson Hotel

309 Southwest Broadway, Portland, Oregon 97205
Tel: +1 503 228 2000
Fax: +1 503 471 3920
Web: www.johansens.com/benson

U.S.A. - OREGON (PORTLAND)

The Heathman Hotel

1001 S.W. Broadway, Portland, Oregon 97205
Tel: +1 503 241 4100
Fax: +1 503 790 7110
Web: www.johansens.com/heathman

U.S.A. - PENNSYLVANIA (BRADFORD)

Glendorn

1000 Glendorn Drive, Bradford, Pennsylvania 16701
Tel: +1 814 362 6511
Fax: +1 814 368 9923
Web: www.johansens.com/glendorn

U.S.A. - PENNSYLVANIA (FARMINGTON)

Nemacolin Woodlands

1001 LaFayette Drive, Farmington, Pennsylvania 15437
Tel: +1 724 329 8555
Fax: +1 724 329 6947
Web: www.johansens.com/nemacolin

U.S.A. - PENNSYLVANIA (HERSHEY)

The Hotel Hershey & Spa

100 Hotel Road, Hershey, Pennsylvania 17033
Tel: +1 717 533 2171
Fax: +1 717 534 3165
Web: www.johansens.com/hershey

U.S.A. - PENNSYLVANIA (LEOLA)

Leola Village Inn & Suites

38 Deborah Drive, Route 23, Leola, Pennsylvania 17540
Tel: +1 717 656 7002
Fax: +1 717 656 7648
Web: www.johansens.com/leolavillage

U.S.A. - PENNSYLVANIA (PHILADELPHIA)

Rittenhouse 1715, A Boutique Hotel

1715 Rittenhouse Square, Philadelphia, Pennsylvania 19103
Tel: +1 215 546 6500
Fax: +1 215 546 8787
Web: www.johansens.com/rittenhouse

U.S.A. - PENNSYLVANIA (POCONOS)

Skytop Lodge

One Skytop, Skytop, Pennsylvania 18357
Tel: +1 570 595 8905
Fax: +1 570 595 7285
Web: www.johansens.com/skytop

U.S.A. - RHODE ISLAND (NEWPORT)

The Chanler at Cliff Walk

117 Memorial Boulevard, Newport, Rhode Island 02840
Tel: +1 401 847 1300
Fax: +1 401 847 3620
Web: www.johansens.com/chanler

U.S.A. - RHODE ISLAND (PROVIDENCE)

Hotel Providence

311 Westminster Street, Providence, Rhode Island 02903
Tel: +1 401 861 8000
Fax: +1 401 861 8002
Web: www.johansens.com/providence

U.S.A. - SOUTH CAROLINA (BLUFFTON)

The Inn at Palmetto Bluff

476 Mount Pelia Road, Bluffton, South Carolina 29910
Tel: +1 843 706 6500
Fax: +1 843 706 6550
Web: www.johansens.com/palmettobluff

U.S.A. - SOUTH CAROLINA (CHARLESTON)

The Boardwalk Inn at Wild Dunes Resort

5757 Palm Boulevard, Isle of Palms, South Carolina 29451
Tel: +1 843 886 6000
Fax: +1 843 886 2916
Web: www.johansens.com/boardwalk

U.S.A. - SOUTH CAROLINA (CHARLESTON)

Charleston Harbor Resort & Marina

20 Patriots Point Road, Charleston, South Carolina 29464
Tel: +1 843 856 0028
Fax: +1 843 856 8333
Web: www.johansens.com/charlestonharbor

U.S.A. - SOUTH CAROLINA (CHARLESTON)

Woodlands Resort & Inn

125 Parsons Road, Summerville, South Carolina 29483
Tel: +1 843 875 2600
Fax: +1 843 875 2603
Web: www.johansens.com/woodlandssc

U.S.A. - SOUTH CAROLINA (KIAWAH ISLAND)

The Sanctuary at Kiawah Island Golf Resort

One Sanctuary Beach Drive, Kiawah Island,
South Carolina 29455
Tel: +1 843 768 6000
Fax: +1 843 768 5150
Web: www.johansens.com/sanctuary

U.S.A. - SOUTH CAROLINA (PAWLEYS ISLAND)

Litchfield Plantation

Kings River Road, Box 290, Pawleys Island,
South Carolina 29585
Tel: +1 843 237 9121
Fax: +1 843 237 1688
Web: www.johansens.com/litchfieldplantation

U.S.A. - SOUTH CAROLINA (TRAVELERS REST)

La Bastide

10 Road Of Vines, Travelers Rest, South Carolina 29210
Tel: +1 864 836 8463
Fax: +1 864 836 4820
Web: www.johansens.com/labastide

U.S.A. - TENNESSEE (WALLAND)

Blackberry Farm

1471 West Millers Cove Road, Walland,
Great Smoky Mountains, Tennessee 37886
Tel: +1 865 380 2260
Fax: +1 865 681 7753
Web: www.johansens.com/blackberryfarm

U.S.A. - TEXAS (AUSTIN)

The Mansion at Judges' Hill

1900 Rio Grande, Austin, Texas 78705
Tel: +1 512 495 1800
Fax: +1 512 691 4461
Web: www.johansens.com/judgeshill

Mini Listings The Americas

Condé Nast Johansens are delighted to recommend 310 properties across The Americas, Atlantic, Caribbean and Pacific.
Call +44 1323 649 349 or see the order forms on pages 523-527 to order guides.

U.S.A. - TEXAS (GRANBURY)

The Inn on Lake Granbury

205 West Doyle Street, Granbury, Texas 76048
Tel: +1 817 573 0046
Fax: +1 817 573 0047
Web: www.johansens.com/lakegranbury

U.S.A. - TEXAS (SAN ANTONIO)

The Havana Riverwalk Inn

1015 Navarro, San Antonio, Texas 78205
Tel: +1 210 222 2008
Fax: +1 210 222 2717
Web: www.johansens.com/havanariverwalkinn

U.S.A. - TEXAS (WAXAHACHIE)

The Chaska House

716 West Main Street, Waxahachie, Texas 75165
Tel: +1 972 937 3390
Fax: +1 972 937 1780
Web: www.johansens.com/chaskahouse

U.S.A. - UTAH (MOAB)

Sorrel River Ranch Resort & Spa

Highway 128 Mile 17, H.C. 64 BOX 4000, Moab, Utah 84532
Tel: +1 435 259 4642
Fax: +1 435 259 3016
Web: www.johansens.com/sorrelriver

U.S.A. - VERMONT (BARNARD)

Twin Farms

P.O. Box 115, Barnard, Vermont 05031
Tel: +1 802 234 9999
Fax: +1 802 234 9990
Web: www.johansens.com/twinfarms

U.S.A. - VERMONT (KILLINGTON)

Mountain Top Inn & Resort

195 Mountain Top Road, Chittenden, Vermont 05737
Tel: +1 802 483 2311
Fax: +1 802 483 6373
Web: www.johansens.com/mountaintopinn

U.S.A. - VERMONT (WARREN)

The Pitcher Inn

275 Main Street, P.O. Box 347, Warren, Vermont 05674
Tel: +1 802 496 6350
Fax: +1 802 496 6354
Web: www.johansens.com/pitcherinn

U.S.A. - VIRGINIA (ABINGDON)

The Martha Washington Inn

150 West Main Street, Abingdon, Virginia 24210
Tel: +1 276 628 3161
Fax: +1 276 628 8885
Web: www.johansens.com/themartha

U.S.A. - VIRGINIA (CHARLOTTESVILLE)

200 South Street Inn

200 South Street, Charlottesville, Virginia 22901
Tel: +1 434 979 0200
Fax: +1 434 979 4403
Web: www.johansens.com/200southstreetinn

U.S.A. - VIRGINIA (GLOUCESTER)

The Inn at Warner Hall

4750 Warner Hall Road, Gloucester, Virginia 23061
Tel: +1 804 695 9565
Fax: +1 804 695 9566
Web: www.johansens.com/warnerhall

U.S.A. - VIRGINIA (IRVINGTON)

Hope and Glory Inn

65 Tavern Road, Irvington, Virginia 22480
Tel: +1 804 438 6053
Fax: +1 804 438 5362
Web: www.johansens.com/hopeandglory

U.S.A. - VIRGINIA (MIDDLEBURG)

The Goodstone Inn & Estate

36205 Snake Hill Road, Middleburg, Virginia 20117
Tel: +1 540 687 4645
Fax: +1 540 687 6115
Web: www.johansens.com/goodstoneinn

U.S.A. - VIRGINIA (STAUNTON)

Frederick House

28 North New Street, Staunton, Virginia 24401
Tel: + 1 540 885 4220
Fax: +1 540 885 5180
Web: www.johansens.com/frederickhouse

U.S.A. - VIRGINIA (WASHINGTON METROPOLITAN AREA)

Morrison House

116 South Alfred Street, Alexandria, Virginia 22314
Tel: +1 703 838 8000
Fax: +1 703 684 6283
Web: www.johansens.com/morrisonhouse

U.S.A. - WASHINGTON (BELLINGHAM)

The Chrysalis Inn and Spa

804 10th Street, Bellingham, Washington 98225
Tel: +1 360 756 1005
Fax: +1 360 647 0342
Web: www.johansens.com/chrysalis

U.S.A. - WASHINGTON (FRIDAY HARBOR)

Friday Harbor House

130 West Street, Friday Harbor, Washington 98250
Tel: +1 360 378 8455
Fax: +1 360 378 8453
Web: www.johansens.com/fridayharbor

U.S.A. - WASHINGTON (LEAVENWORTH)

Run of the River Inn and Refuge

9308 E. Leavenworth Road, Leavenworth, Washington 98826
Tel: +1 509 548 7171
Fax: 1 509 548 7547
Web: www.johansens.com/runoftheriver

U.S.A. - WASHINGTON (SPOKANE)

The Davenport Hotel and Tower

10 South Post Street, Spokane, Washington 99201
Tel: +1 509 455 8888
Fax: +1 509 624 4455
Web: www.johansens.com/davenport

U.S.A. - WASHINGTON (UNION)

Alderbrook Resort & Spa

10 East Alderbrook Drive, Union, Washington 98592
Tel: +1 360 898 2200
Fax: +1 360 898 4610
Web: www.johansens.com/alderbrook

U.S.A. - WASHINGTON (WOODINVILLE)

The Herbfarm

14590 North East 145th Street, Woodinville, Washington 98072
Tel: +1 425 485 5300
Fax: +1 425 424 2925
Web: www.johansens.com/herbfarm

Mini Listings The Americas

Condé Nast Johansens are delighted to recommend 310 properties across The Americas, Atlantic, Caribbean and Pacific.
Call +44 1323 649 349 or see the order forms on pages 523-527 to order guides.

U.S.A. - WEST VIRGINIA (WHITE SULPHUR SPRINGS)

The Greenbrier

300 West Main Street, White Sulphur Springs, West Virginia 24986
Tel: +1 304 536 1110
Fax: +1 304 536 7818
Web: www.johansens.com/greenbrier

U.S.A. - WISCONSIN (CHETEK)

Canoe Bay

P.O. Box 28, Chetek, Wisconsin 54728
Tel: +1 715 924 4594
Fax: +1 715 924 2078
Web: www.johansens.com/canoebay

U.S.A. - WISCONSIN (DELAFIELD)

The Delafield Hotel

415 Genesee Street, Delafield, Wisconsin 53018
Tel: +1 262 646 1600
Fax: +1 262 646 1613
Web: www.johansens.com/delafield

U.S.A. - WYOMING (CHEYENNE)

Nagle Warren Mansion

222 East 17Th Street, Cheyenne, Wyoming 82001
Tel: +1 307 637 3333
Fax: +1 307 638 6879
Web: www.johansens.com/naglewarrenmansion

U.S.A. - WYOMING (DUBOIS)

Brooks Lake Lodge

458 Brooks Lake Road, Dubois, Wyoming 82513
Tel: +1 307 455 2121
Fax: +1 307 455 2221
Web: www.johansens.com/brookslake

U.S.A. - WYOMING (GRAND TETON NATIONAL PARK)

Jenny Lake Lodge

Inner Park Loop Road, Grand Teton National Park, Wyoming 83013
Tel: +1 307 543 3300
Fax: +1 307 543 3358
Web: www.johansens.com/jennylake

U.S.A. - WYOMING (TETON VILLAGE)

Teton Mountain Lodge

3385 W. Village Drive, Teton Village, Wyoming 83025
Tel: +1 307 734 7111
Fax: +1 307 734 7999
Web: www.johansens.com/teton

Recommendations in Central America

COSTA RICA - GUANACASTE (ISLITA)

Hotel Punta Islita

Guanacaste
Tel: +506 231 6122
Fax: +506 231 0715
Web: www.johansens.com/hotelpuntaislita

COSTA RICA - GUANACASTE (PLAYA CONCHAL)

Paradisus Playa Conchal

Bahía Brasilito, Playa Conchal, Santa Cruz, Guanacaste
Tel: +506 654 4123
Fax: +506 654 4181
Web: www.johansens.com/paradisusplayaconchal

COSTA RICA - PUNTARENAS (MANUEL ANTONIO)

Gaia Hotel & Reserve

Km 2.7 Carretera Quepos, Manuel Antonio
Tel: +506 777 9797
Fax: +506 777 9126
Web: www.johansens.com/gaiahr

HONDURAS - ATLÁNTIDA (LA CEIBA)

The Lodge at Pico Bonito

A. P. 710, La Ceiba, Atlántida, C. P. 31101
Tel: +504 440 0388
Fax: +504 440 0468
Web: www.johansens.com/picobonito

Recommendations in South America

ARGENTINA - BUENOS AIRES (CIUDAD DE BUENOS AIRES)

1555 Malabia House

Malabia 1555, C1414DME Buenos Aires
Tel: +54 11 4832 3345
Fax: +54 11 4832 3345
Web: www.johansens.com/malabiahouse

ARGENTINA - BUENOS AIRES (CIUDAD DE BUENOS AIRES)

LoiSuites Recoleta Hotel

Vicente López 1955 – C1128ACC, Ciudad de Buenos Aires
Tel: +54 11 5777 8950
Fax: +54 11 5777 8999
Web: www.johansens.com/loisuites

ARGENTINA - PATAGONIA (ISLA VICTORIA)

Hosteria Isla Victoria

Isla Victoria, Parque Nacional Nahuel Huapi, C.C. 26 (R8401AKU)
Tel: +54 43 94 96 05
Fax: +54 11 43 94 95 99
Web: www.johansens.com/islavictoria

ARGENTINA - PATAGONIA (VILLA LA ANGOSTURA)

Correntoso Lake & River Hotel

Av. Siète Lagos 4505, Villa La Angostura, Neuquén
Tel: +54 2944 15 619728
Web: www.johansens.com/correntoso

BRAZIL - ALAGOAS (SÃO MIGUEL DOS MILAGRES)

Pousada do Toque

Rua Felisberto de Ataide, Povoado do Toque, São Miguel dos Milagres, Alagoas
Tel: +55 82 3295 1127
Fax: +55 82 3295 1127
Web: www.johansens.com/pousadadotoque

BRAZIL - BAHIA (ITACARÉ)

Txai Resort

Rod. Ilhéus-Itacaré km 48, Itacaré, Bahia 45530-000
Tel: +55 73 2101 5000
Fax: +55 73 2101 5251
Web: www.johansens.com/txairesort

BRAZIL - BAHIA (PORTO SEGURO FRANCOSO)

Estrela d'Agua

Estrada Arraial d'Ajuda - Trancoso S/No, Trancoso Porto Seguro, Bahia 45818-000
Tel: +55 73 3668 1030
Fax: +55 73 3668 1030
Web: www.johansens.com/estreladagua

Mini Listings South America

Condé Nast Johansens are delighted to recommend 310 properties across The Americas, Atlantic, Caribbean and Pacific.
Call +44 1323 649 349 or see the order forms on pages 523-527 to order guides.

BRAZIL - BAHIA (PRAIA DO FORTE)

Praia do Forte Eco Resort & Thalasso Spa

Avenida do Farol, Praia do Forte - Mata de São João, Bahia
Tel: +55 71 36 76 40 00
Fax: +55 71 36 76 11 12
Web: www.johansens.com/praiadoforte

BRAZIL - MINAS GERAIS (TIRADENTES)

Pousada dos Inconfidentes

Rua João Rodrigues Sobrinho 91, 36325-000, Tiradentes, Minas Gerais
Tel: +55 32 3355 2135
Fax: +55 32 3355 2135
Web: www.johansens.com/inconfidentes

BRAZIL - MINAS GERAIS (TIRADENTES)

Solar da Ponte

Praça das Mercês S/N, Tiradentes, Minas Gerais 36325-000
Tel: +55 32 33 55 12 55
Fax: +55 32 33 55 12 01
Web: www.johansens.com/solardaponte

BRAZIL - PERNAMBUCO (PORTO DE GALINHAS)

Nannai Beach Resort

Rodovia PE-09, acesso à Muro Alto, Km 3, Ipojuca, Pernambuco 55590-000
Tel: +55 81 3552 0100
Fax: +55 81 3552 1474
Web: www.johansens.com/nannaibeach

BRAZIL - RIO DE JANEIRO (ANGRA DOS REIS)

Sítio do Lobo

Ponta do Lobo, Ilha Grande, Angra dos Reis, Rio de Janeiro
Tel: +55 21 2227 4138
Fax: +55 21 2267 7841
Web: www.johansens.com/sitiodolobo

BRAZIL - RIO DE JANEIRO (ARMAÇÃO DOS BÚZIOS)

Pérola Búzios

Av. José Bento Ribeiro Dantas, 222, Armação dos Búzios, Rio de Janeiro 28950-000
Tel: +55 22 2620 8507
Fax: +55 22 2623 9015
Web: www.johansens.com/perolabuzios

BRAZIL - RIO DE JANEIRO (BÚZIOS)

Casas Brancas Boutique-Hotel & Spa

Alto do Humaitá 10, Armação dos Búzios, Rio de Janeiro 28950-000
Tel: +55 22 2623 1458
Fax: +55 22 2623 2147
Web: www.johansens.com/casasbrancas

BRAZIL - RIO DE JANEIRO (BÚZIOS)

Glenzhaus Lodge

Rua 1 - Quadra F - Lote 27/28, Armação dos Búzios, Rio de Janeiro 28950-000
Tel: +55 22 2623 2823
Fax: +55 22 2623 5293
Web: www.johansens.com/glenzhaus

BRAZIL - RIO DE JANEIRO (ENGENEIRO PAULO DE FRONTIN)

Vivenda Les 4 Saisons

Rua João Cordeiro da Costa E silva, 5, Caixa Postal 127, Engenheiro Paulo de Frontin, Rio de Janeiro 26650-000
Tel: +55 24 2463 2892
Fax: +55 24 2463 1395
Web: www.johansens.com/4saisons

BRAZIL - RIO DE JANEIRO (PETRÓPOLIS)

Parador Santarém Marina

Estrada Correia da Veiga, 96, Petrópolis, Rio de Janeiro 25745-260
Tel: +55 24 2222 9933
Fax: +55 24 2222 9933
Web: www.johansens.com/paradorsantarem

BRAZIL - RIO DE JANEIRO (PETRÓPOLIS)

Solar do Império

Koeler Avenue, 376- Centro, Petrópolis, Rio de Janeiro
Tel: +55 24 2103 3000
Fax: +55 24 2242 0034
Web: www.johansens.com/solardoimperio

BRAZIL - RIO DE JANEIRO (PETRÓPOLIS)

Tankamana EcoResort

Estrada Júlio Cápua, S/N Vale Do Cuiabá, Itaipava - Petrópolis, Rio De Janeiro 25745-050
Tel: +55 24 2222 9181
Fax: +55 24 2222 9181
Web: www.johansens.com/tankamana

BRAZIL - RIO DE JANEIRO (RIO DE JANEIRO)

Hotel Marina All Suites

Av. Delfim Moreira, 696, Praia do Leblon, Rio de Janeiro 22441-000
Tel: +55 21 2172 1001
Fax: +55 21 2172 1110
Web: www.johansens.com/marinaallsuites

BRAZIL - RIO GRANDE DO SUL (SAO FRANCISCO DE PAULA)

Pousada Do Engenho

Rua Odon Cavalcante, 330, São Francisco de Paula 95400-000, Rio Grande do Sul
Tel: +55 54 3244 1270
Fax: +55 54 3244 1270
Web: www.johansens.com/pousadadoengenho

BRAZIL - RIO GRANDE DO SUL (GRAMADO)

Kurotel

Rua Nacões Unidas 533, P.O. Box 65, Gramado, Rio Grande do Sul 95670-000
Tel: +55 54 3295 9393
Fax: +55 54 3286 1203
Web: www.johansens.com/kurotel

BRAZIL - SANTA CATARINA (GOVERNADOR CELSO RAMOS)

Ponta dos Ganchos

Rua Eupídio Alves do Nascimento, 104, Governador Celso Ramos, Santa Catarina 88190-000
Tel: +55 48 3262 5000
Fax: +55 48 3262 5046
Web: www.johansens.com/pontadosganchos

BRAZIL - SÃO PAULO (CAMPOS DO JORDÃO)

Hotel Frontenac

Av. Dr. Paulo Ribas, 295 Capivari, Campos do Jordão 12460-000
Tel: +55 12 3669 1000
Fax: +55 12 3669 1009
Web: www.johansens.com/frontenac

CHILE - ARAUCANIA (PUCON)

Hotel Antumalal

Carretera Pucon-Villarka Highway at Km 2 from Pucon
Tel: +5645 441 011
Fax: +5645 441 013
Web: www.johansens.com/antumalal

CHILE - COLCHAGUA (SAN FERNANDO)

Hacienda Los Lingues

Km 124.5, Ruta 5 Sur + 5km Al Oriente, 6a Region, Colchagua
Tel: +562 431 0510
Fax: +562 431 0501
Web: www.johansens.com/loslingues

CHILE - PATAGONIA (PUERTO GUADAL)

Hacienda Tres Lagos

Carretera Austral Sur Km 274, Localidad Lago Negro, Puerto Guadal
Tel: + 56 2 333 41 22 and + 56 67 411 323
Fax: + 56 2 334 52 94 and + 56 67 411 323
Web: www.johansens.com/treslagos

Mini Listings Atlantic / Caribbean

Condé Nast Johansens are delighted to recommend 310 properties across The Americas, Atlantic, Caribbean and Pacific.
Call +44 1323 649 349 or see the order forms on pages 523-527 to order guides.

PERU - LIMA PROVINCIAS (YAUYOS)
Refugios Del Peru - Viñak Reichraming
Santiago de Viñak, Yauyos, Lima
Tel: +51 1 421 6952
Fax: +51 1 421 8476
Web: www.johansens.com/refugiosdelperu

Recommendations in the Atlantic

ATLANTIC - BAHAMAS (GRAND BAHAMA ISLAND)
Old Bahama Bay Resort & Yacht Harbour
West End, Grand Bahama Island, Bahamas
Tel: +1 242 350 6500
Fax: +1 242 346 6546
Web: www.johansens.com/oldbahamabay

ATLANTIC - BAHAMAS (HARBOUR ISLAND)
Rock House
Bay & Hill Street, Harbour Island, Bahamas
Tel: +1 242 333 2053
Fax: +1 242 333 3173
Web: www.johansens.com/rockhouse

ATLANTIC - BERMUDA (HAMILTON)
Rosedon Hotel
P.O. Box Hm 290, Hamilton Hmax, Bermuda
Tel: +1 441 295 1640
Fax: +1 441 295 5904
Web: www.johansens.com/rosedonhotel

ATLANTIC - BERMUDA (HAMILTON)
Waterloo House
P.O. Box H.M. 333, Hamilton H.M. B.X., Bermuda
Tel: +1 441 295 4480
Fax: +1 441 295 2585
Web: www.johansens.com/waterloohouse

ATLANTIC - BERMUDA (PAGET)
Horizons and Cottages
33 South Shore Road, Paget, P.G.04, Bermuda
Tel: +1 441 236 0048
Fax: +1 441 236 1981
Web: www.johansens.com/horizonscottages

ATLANTIC - BERMUDA (SOMERSET)
Cambridge Beaches
Kings Point, Somerset, Bermuda
Tel: +1 441 234 0331
Fax: +1 441 234 3352
Web: www.johansens.com/cambridgebeaches

ATLANTIC - BERMUDA (SOUTHAMPTON)
The Reefs
56 South Shore Road, Southampton, Bermuda
Tel: +1 441 238 0222
Fax: +1 441 238 8372
Web: www.johansens.com/thereefs

ATLANTIC - BERMUDA (WARWICK)
Surf Side Beach Club
90 South Shore Road, Warwick, Bermuda
Tel: +1 441 236 7100
Fax: +1 441 236 9765
Web: www.johansens.com/surfside

Recommendations in the Caribbean

CARIBBEAN - ANGUILLA (RENDEZVOUS BAY)
CuisinArt Resort & Spa
P.O. Box 2000, Rendezvous Bay, Anguilla
Tel: +1 264 498 2000
Fax: +1 264 498 2010
Web: www.johansens.com/cuisinartresort

CARIBBEAN - ANTIGUA (ST. JOHN'S)
Blue Waters
P.O. Box 257, St. John's Antigua
Tel: +44 870 360 1245
Fax: +44 870 360 1246
Web: www.johansens.com/bluewaters

CARIBBEAN - ANTIGUA (ST. JOHN'S)
The Inn at English Harbour
English Harbour, Antigua
Tel: +1 268 460 1014
Fax: +1 268 460 1603
Web: www.johansens.com/innatenglishharbour

CARIBBEAN - ANTIGUA (ST. JOHN'S)
Curtain Bluff
P.O. Box 288, St. John's, Antigua
Tel: +1 268 462 8400
Fax: +1 268 462 8409
Web: www.johansens.com/curtainbluff

CARIBBEAN - ANTIGUA (ST. JOHN'S)
Galley Bay
Five Islands, St. John's, Antigua
Tel: +1 954 481 8787
Fax: +1 954 481 1661
Web: www.johansens.com/galleybay

CARIBBEAN - BARBADOS (CHRIST CHURCH)
Little Arches
Enterprise Beach Road, Christ Church, Barbados
Tel: +1 246 420 4689
Fax: +1 246 418 0207
Web: www.johansens.com/littlearches

CARIBBEAN - BARBADOS (ST. JAMES)
Coral Reef Club
St. James, Barbados
Tel: +1 246 422 2372
Fax: +1 246 422 1776
Web: www.johansens.com/coralreefclub

CARIBBEAN - BARBADOS (ST. JAMES)
Lone Star
Mount Standfast, St. James, Barbados
Tel: +1 246 419 0599
Fax: +1 246 419 0597
Web: www.johansens.com/lonestar

CARIBBEAN - BARBADOS (ST. JAMES)
The Sandpiper
Holetown, St. James, Barbados
Tel: +1 246 422 2251
Fax: +1 246 422 0900
Web: www.johansens.com/sandpiper

Mini Listings Caribbean / Pacific

Condé Nast Johansens are delighted to recommend 310 properties across The Americas, Atlantic, Caribbean and Pacific.

Call +44 1323 649 349 or see the order forms on pages 523-527 to order guides.

CARIBBEAN - BARBADOS (ST. PETER)

Cobblers Cove

Speightstown, St. Peter, Barbados
Tel: +1 246 422 2291
Fax: +1 246 422 1460
Web: www.johansens.com/cobblerscove

CARIBBEAN - BARBADOS (ST. PETER)

Little Good Harbour

Shermans, St. Peter, Barbados
Tel: +1 246 439 3000
Fax: +1 246 439 2020
Web: www.johansens.com/goodharbour

CARIBBEAN - BONAIRE

Harbour Village Beach Club

Kaya Gobernador N. Debrot No. 71, Bonaire, Netherlands Antilles
Tel: +1 305 567 9509
Fax: +1 305 648 0699
Web: www.johansens.com/harbourvillage

CARIBBEAN - BRITISH VIRGIN ISLANDS (VIRGIN GORDA)

Biras Creek Resort

North Sound, Virgin Gorda, British Virgin Islands
Tel: +1 310 440 4225
Fax: +1 310 440 4220
Web: www.johansens.com/birascreek

CARIBBEAN - CURAÇAO (WILLEMSTAD)

Avila Hotel on the beach

Penstraat 130, Willemstad, Curaçao, Netherlands Antilles
Tel: +599 9 461 4377
Fax: +599 9 461 1493
Web: www.johansens.com/avilabeach

CARIBBEAN - DOMINICAN REPUBLIC (PUERTO PLATA)

Casa Colonial Beach & Spa

P.O. Box 22, Puerto Plata, Dominican Republic
Tel: +1 809 320 3232
Fax: +1 809 320 3131
Web: www.johansens.com/casacolonial

CARIBBEAN - GRENADA (ST. GEORGE'S)

Spice Island Beach Resort

Grand Anse Beach, St. George's, Grenada
Tel: +1 473 444 4423/4258
Fax: +1 473 444 4807
Web: www.johansens.com/spiceisland

CARIBBEAN - JAMAICA (MONTEGO BAY)

Half Moon

Montego Bay, Jamaica
Tel: +1 876 953 2211
Fax: +1 876 953 2731
Web: www.johansens.com/halfmoongolf

CARIBBEAN - JAMAICA (MONTEGO BAY)

Round Hill Hotel and Villas

P.O. Box 64, Montego Bay, Jamaica
Tel: +1 876 956 7050
Fax: +1 876 956 7505
Web: www.johansens.com/roundhill

CARIBBEAN - JAMAICA (MONTEGO BAY)

Tryall Club

P.O. Box 1206, Montego Bay, Jamaica
Tel: +1 800 238 5290
Fax: +1 876 956 5673
Web: www.johansens.com/tryallclub

CARIBBEAN - JAMAICA (ORACABESSA)

Goldeneye

Oracabessa, St. Mary, Jamaica
Tel: +1 876 975 3354
Fax: +1 876 975 3620
Web: www.johansens.com/goldeneye

CARIBBEAN - MARTINIQUE (LE FRANÇOIS)

Cap Est Lagoon Resort & Spa

97240 Le François, Martinique
Tel: +596 596 54 80 80
Fax: +596 596 54 96 00
Web: www.johansens.com/capest

CARIBBEAN - NEVIS (CHARLESTOWN)

Montpelier Plantation Inn

Montpelier Estate, Charlestown, Nevis
Tel: +1 869 469 3462
Fax: +1 869 469 2932
Web: www.johansens.com/montpelierplantation

CARIBBEAN - PUERTO RICO (RINCÓN)

Horned Dorset Primavera

Apartado 1132, Rincón, Puerto Rico 00677
Tel: +1 787 823 4030
Fax: +1 787 823 5580
Web: www.johansens.com/horneddorset

CARIBBEAN - SAINT-BARTHÉLEMY (GRAND CUL DE SAC)

Hotel Guanahani & Spa

Grand Cul de Sac, 97133 Saint-Barthélemy
Tel: +590 590 27 66 60
Fax: +590 590 27 70 70
Web: www.johansens.com/guanahani

CARIBBEAN - SAINT-BARTHÉLEMY (GRAND CUL DE SAC)

Le Toiny

Anse de Toiny 97133, Saint-Barthélemy
Tel: +590 590 27 88 88
Fax: +590 590 27 89 30
Web: www.johansens.com/letoiny

CARIBBEAN - SAINT-BARTHÉLEMY (GUSTAVIA)

Carl Gustaf Hotel

Rue des Normands, Gustavia, 97099 Saint-Barthélemy
Tel: +590 590 29 79 00
Fax: +590 590 27 82 37
Web: www.johansens.com/carlgustaf

CARIBBEAN - ST. LUCIA (SOUFRIÈRE)

Ladera

Soufrière, St. Lucia
Tel: +1 758 459 7323
Fax: +1 758 459 5156
Web: www.johansens.com/ladera

CARIBBEAN - ST. LUCIA (SOUFRIÈRE)

Anse Chastanet

Soufrière, St. Lucia
Tel: +1 758 459 7000
Fax: +1 758 459 7700
Web: www.johansens.com/ansechastanet

CARIBBEAN - ST. LUCIA (SOUFRIÈRE)

Jade Mountain at Anse Chastanet

Soufrière, St. Lucia
Tel: +1 758 459 4000
Fax: +1 758 459 4002
Web: www.johansens.com/jademountain

MINI LISTINGS CARIBBEAN / PACIFIC

Condé Nast Johansens are delighted to recommend 310 properties across The Americas, Atlantic, Caribbean and Pacific.
Call +44 1323 649 349 or see the order forms on pages 523-527 to order guides.

CARIBBEAN - ST. MARTIN (BAIE LONGUE)

La Samanna

P.O. Box 4077, 97064 St. Martin - CEDEX
Tel: +590 590 87 64 00
Fax: +590 590 87 87 86
Web: www.johansens.com/lasamanna

CARIBBEAN - THE GRENADINES (MUSTIQUE)

Firefly

Mustique Island, St. Vincent & The Grenadines
Tel: +1 784 488 8414
Fax: +1 784 488 8514
Web: www.johansens.com/firefly

CARIBBEAN - THE GRENADINES (PALM ISLAND)

Palm Island

St. Vincent & The Grenadines
Tel: +1 954 481 8787
Fax: +1 954 481 1661
Web: www.johansens.com/palmisland

CARIBBEAN - TURKS & CAICOS (PROVIDENCIALES)

Grace Bay Club

P.O. Box 128, Providenciales, Turks & Caicos Islands
Tel: +1 649 946 5050
Fax: +1 649 946 5758
Web: www.johansens.com/gracebayclub

CARIBBEAN - TURKS & CAICOS (PROVIDENCIALES)

Parrot Cay

P.O. Box 164, Providenciales, Turks & Caicos Islands
Tel: +1 649 946 7788
Fax: +1 649 946 7789
Web: www.johansens.com/parrotcay

CARIBBEAN - TURKS & CAICOS (PROVIDENCIALES)

Point Grace

P.O. Box 700, Providenciales, Turks & Caicos Islands
Tel: +1 649 946 5096
Fax: +1 649 946 5097
Web: www.johansens.com/pointgrace

CARIBBEAN - TURKS & CAICOS (PROVIDENCIALES)

Turks & Caicos Club

P.O. Box 687, West Grace Bay Beach, Providenciales, Turks & Caicos Islands
Tel: +1 649 946 5800
Fax: +1 649 946 5858
Web: www.johansens.com/turksandcaicos

CARIBBEAN - TURKS & CAICOS (PROVIDENCIALES)

The Somerset

Princess Drive, Providenciales, Turks & Caicos Islands
Tel: +1 649 946 5900
Fax: +1 649 946 5944
Web: www.johansens.com/somersetgracebay

Recommendations in the Pacific

PACIFIC - FIJI ISLANDS (LABASA)

Nukubati Island

P.O. Box 1928, Labasa, Fiji Islands
Tel: +61 2 93888 196
Fax: +61 2 93888 204
Web: www.johansens.com/nukubati

PACIFIC - FIJI ISLANDS (LAUTOKA)

Blue Lagoon Cruises

183 Vitogo Parade, Lautoka, Fiji Islands
Tel: +679 6661 622
Fax: +679 6664 098
Web: www.johansens.com/bluelagooncruises

PACIFIC - FIJI ISLANDS (QAMEA ISLAND)

Qamea Resort & Spa

P.A. Matei, Tavenui, Fiji Islands
Tel: +679 888 0220
Fax: +679 888 0092
Web: www.johansens.com/qamea

PACIFIC - FIJI ISLANDS (SAVUSAVU)

Jean-Michel Cousteau Fiji Islands Resort

Lesiaceva Point, SavuSavu, Fiji Islands
Tel: +415 788 5794
Web: www.johansens.com/jean-michelcousteau

PACIFIC - FIJI ISLANDS (SIGATOKA)

Myola Plantation

P.O. Box 638, Sigatoka, Fiji Islands
Tel: +679 652 1084
Fax: +679 652 0899
Web: www.johansens.com/myola

PACIFIC - FIJI ISLANDS (TOBERUA ISLAND)

Toberua Island Resort

P.O. Box 3332, Nausori, Fiji Islands
Tel: +679 347 2777
Fax: +679 347 2888
Web: www.johansens.com/toberuaisland

PACIFIC - FIJI ISLANDS (UGAGA ISLAND)

Royal Davui

P.O. Box 3171, Lami, Fiji Islands
Tel: +679 336 1624
Fax: +679 336 1253
Web: www.johansens.com/royaldavui

PACIFIC - FIJI ISLANDS (YAQETA ISLAND)

Navutu Stars Resort

P.O. Box 1838, Lautoka, Fiji Islands
Tel: +679 664 0553 and +679 664 0554
Fax: +679 666 0807
Web: www.johansens.com/navutustars

PACIFIC - FIJI ISLANDS (YASAWA ISLAND)

Yasawa Island Resort

P.O. Box 10128, Nadi Airport, Nadi, Fiji Islands
Tel: +679 672 2266
Fax: +679 672 4456
Web: www.johansens.com/yasawaisland

avon data systems
hospitality solutions

Index by Property

Austria

Belgium

Croatia

Czech Republic

Estonia

France

▼

Index by Property

Great Britain

Greece

▼

Ireland

Italy

Index by Property

▼

Index by Property

Index by Property

▼

Switzerland

Turkey

Index by Activity

Golf course on-site

▼

Property has indoor swimming pool

▼

Skiing on-site

▼

Skiing nearby (within 50kms)

▼

Tennis court at property

▼

▼

Fishing on-site

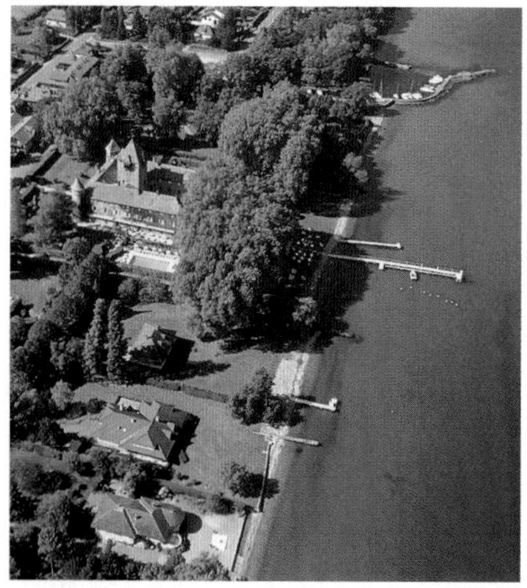

▼

Shooting on-site

SPA Dedicated Spa

▼

Wellness area

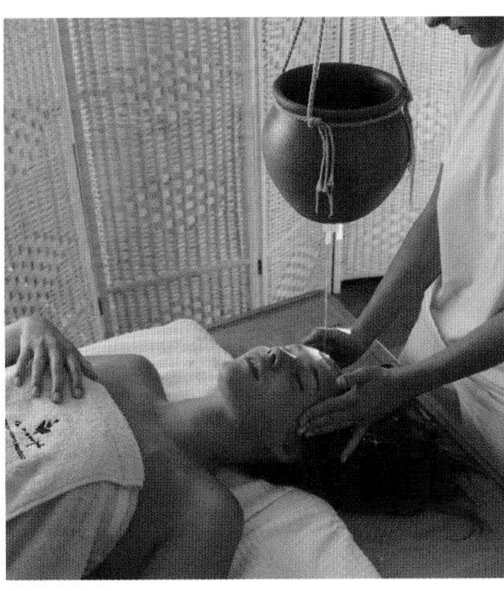

Gym facilities on-site

Index by Activity

▼

Licensed for wedding ceremonies

▼

Index by Activity

▼

▼

Index by Activity

Gastronomic restaurant

▼

Conference facilities for 100 delegates or more

▼

Index by Activity / Hotel Organisation

Hotel Organisations

Abitare la Storia

Authentic Hotels

Charme & Relax

Chateaux & Hotels de France

Index by Hotel Organisation

Design Hotels

Hospes Maricel .... Spain 393

Great Hotels of the World

Luxury Lifestyle Hotels & Resorts

Relais & Châteaux

Park Hotel Weggis .... Switzerland 462

Romantik Hotels

Rusticae

Index by Hotel Organisation / Group

Small Luxury Hotels of the World

▼

Symboles de France

Yades

Hotel Groups

Derby Hotels

Grandes Etapes Françaises

▼

HOSPES

Hospes Hotels & Moments

Un Cadeau Idéal...

Les Chèques-Cadeaux de Condé Nast Johansens

Les chèques-cadeaux "Gift Vouchers" de Condé Nast Johansens sont une idée originale et unique pour célébrer les anniversaires, les mariages, les occasions spéciales ou comme prime d'encouragement.

Les chèques-cadeaux "Gift Vouchers" sont disponibles en coupure de £100, £50, 140€, 70€, $150, $75 et peuvent être utilisé comme payement partiel ou complet de votre séjour ou d'un repas à tout les hôtels recommandés par Condé Nast Johansens en 2007.

Pour passer votre commande, appellez le +44 (0) 207 152 3558

Ou commandez en ligne sur www.johansens.com

BON DE COMMANDE

30€ de remise si vous commandez au moins 2 Guides

Commandez 4 Guides et recevez une remise de 30€,
3 Guides et une remise de 15€, 2 Guides et une remise de 8€

Hotels & Spas
Great Britain & Ireland
29€

QUANTITY	€

Country Houses, Small Hotels
Inns & Restaurants, Great
Britain & Ireland - 25€

QUANTITY	€

Hotels & Spas
Europe & Mediterranean
29€

QUANTITY	€

Hotels, Inns, Resorts & Spas
The Americas, Atlantic,
Caribbean, Pacific - 26€

QUANTITY	£

Business Venues
(édité en Février 2007)
38€

QUANTITY	€

Economisez 78€ en commandant la **Collection Internationale**

La Collection Internationale
€100.00

QUANTITÉ	€

une présentation en coffret des 4 Guides de loisirs,

PLUS le guide des lieux de conférence,

PLUS notre exclusif marque bagage en argent.

Une superbe offre pour seulement 100€

(178€ prix public conseillé)

(Prix public conseillé du marque bagage 23€, de la boîte 8€)

REMISE - 2 Guides = 8€ de remise ☐ 3 Guides = 15€ de remise ☐ 4 Guides = 30€ de remise ☐

FRAIS D'ENVOI - Merci d'ajouter 9€ par guide pour toute commande en dehors du Royaume-Uni et 38€ pour la Collection Internationale. €

GRAND TOTAL - N'oubliez pas de déduire vos remises €

☐ Je joint un chèque à l'ordre de Condé Nast Johansens

☐ Merci de débiter ma carte Visa/Mastercard/Amex. CB No.:______________________________

Le Cryptogramme Visuel : Expire le:

Le Cryptogramme Visuel est composé des 3 derniers chiffres du numéro inscrit à l'arrière de la carte de crédit.
Pour American Express le code à 4 chiffres est inscrit juste au-dessus du numéro de la carte, à gauche.

Titulaire: Signature:

Adresse:

Code postal/ville: Tel: E-mail:

Merci de cocher si vous souhaitez recevoir des informations de The Condé Nast Publications Ltd par téléphone ☐ ou SMS ☐ ou E-mail ☐
Merci de cocher si vous souhaitez recevoir des informations ou des offres de sociétés sélectionnées par téléphone ☐ ou SMS ☐ ou E-mail ☐
Merci de cocher si vous ne souhaitez pas recevoir des informations ou des offres de The Condé Nast Publications Ltd ☐ ou d'autres sociétés sélectionnées ☐

Envoyez à Condé Nast Johansens Condé Nast Johansens, Unit 1, 16 Maple Road, Eastbourne, BN23 6NY, Great Britain
ou faxez votre bon de commande au +44 1323 649 350

Appelez notre Numéro 24h/24 au +44 1323 649 349
OU VISITEZ NOTRE SITE WEB – www.cnjguides.co.uk – Réf: K008

ENQUÊTE DE SATISFACTION

Evaluez votre séjour dans un hotel recommendé par Condé Nast Johansens

Nous espérons que vous avez apprécié votre séjour dans cet établissement recommandé par Johansens. Merci de nous accorder un peu de votre temps pour compléter le questionnaire d'évaluation ci-joint. Ce document est essentiel pour Condé Nast Johansens, non seulement pour maintenir les standards de qualité de nos Recommandations, mais également afin d'aider le travail de nos inspecteurs. C'est aussi la meilleure source pour les nominations aux Prix d'Excellence que remet chaque année Condé Nast Johansens aux établissements qui représentent les meilleurs standards et valeurs de l'hébergement indépendant de luxe à travers le monde.

Vos détails

Votre nom: ________________

Votre adresse: ________________

Code Postal: ________ Ville: ________

Téléphone: ________________

E-mail: ________________

Votre évaluation de l'hotel

	Excellent	Bon	Décevant	Inférieure
Chambres	❍	❍	❍	❍
Lieux publiques	❍	❍	❍	❍
Cuisine/Restaurant	❍	❍	❍	❍
Service	❍	❍	❍	❍
Accueil	❍	❍	❍	❍
Rapport qualité prix	❍	❍	❍	❍

Détails de l'hôtel

Nom de l'hôtel: ________________

Ville/Lieu: ________________

Date de séjour: ________________

Commentaires

Pour de plus amples commentaires, merci de nous écrire séparément à Condé Nast Johansens Ltd, 6-8 Old Bond Street, London W1S 4PH, Grande-Bretagne

Merci de cocher si vous souhaitez recevoir des informations de The Condé Nast Publications Ltd par téléphone téléphone☐ ou SMS☐ ou E-mail☐
Merci de cocher si vous souhaitez recevoir des informations ou des offres de sociétés selectionnées par téléphone☐ ou SMS☐ ou E-mail☐

Merci de faxer ce questionnaire au +44 (0) 207 152 3566
ou connectez-vous sur www.johansens.com (E-Club login) et vous pourrez compléter ce questionnaire en ligne

ENQUÊTE DE SATISFACTION

Evaluez votre séjour dans un hotel recommendé par Condé Nast Johansens

Nous espérons que vous avez apprécié votre séjour dans cet établissement recommandé par Johansens. Merci de nous accorder un peu de votre temps pour compléter le questionnaire d'évaluation ci-joint. Ce document est essentiel pour Condé Nast Johansens, non seulement pour maintenir les standards de qualité de nos Recommandations, mais également afin d'aider le travail de nos inspecteurs. C'est aussi la meilleure source pour les nominations aux Prix d'Excellence que remet chaque année Condé Nast Johansens aux établissements qui représentent les meilleurs standards et valeurs de l'hébergement indépendant de luxe à travers le monde.

Vos détails

Votre nom: ________________

Votre adresse: ________________

Code Postal: ________ Ville: ________

Téléphone: ________________

E-mail: ________________

Votre évaluation de l'hotel

	Excellent	Bon	Décevant	Inférieure
Chambres	❍	❍	❍	❍
Lieux publiques	❍	❍	❍	❍
Cuisine/Restaurant	❍	❍	❍	❍
Service	❍	❍	❍	❍
Accueil	❍	❍	❍	❍
Rapport qualité prix	❍	❍	❍	❍

Détails de l'hôtel

Nom de l'hôtel: ________________

Ville/Lieu: ________________

Date de séjour: ________________

Commentaires

Pour de plus amples commentaires, merci de nous écrire séparément à Condé Nast Johansens Ltd, 6-8 Old Bond Street, London W1S 4PH, Grande-Bretagne

Merci de cocher si vous souhaitez recevoir des informations de The Condé Nast Publications Ltd par téléphone téléphone☐ ou SMS☐ ou E-mail☐
Merci de cocher si vous souhaitez recevoir des informations ou des offres de sociétés selectionnées par téléphone☐ ou SMS☐ ou E-mail☐

Merci de faxer ce questionnaire au +44 (0) 207 152 3566
ou connectez-vous sur www.johansens.com (E-Club login) et vous pourrez compléter ce questionnaire en ligne

FORMULARIO DE PEDIDA

Descuento de hasta €30 si compra más de una Guía

Compre 4 Guías - €30 de descuento, 3 Guías - €15 de descuento, 2 Guías - €8 de descuento

Hotels & Spas
Great Britain & Ireland
€29.00

Quantity	€

Country Houses, Small Hotels
Inns & Restaurants, Great
Britain & Ireland - €25.00

Quantity	€

Hotels & Spas
Europe & Mediterranean
€29.00

Quantity	€

Hotels, Inns, Resorts & Spas
The Americas, Atlantic,
Caribbean, Pacific - €26.00

Quantity	£

Business Venues
(publicado Febrero de 2007)
€38.00

Quantity	€

Ahorre €78 comprando **The International Collection...**

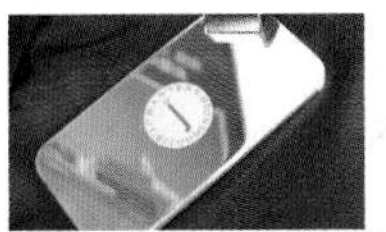

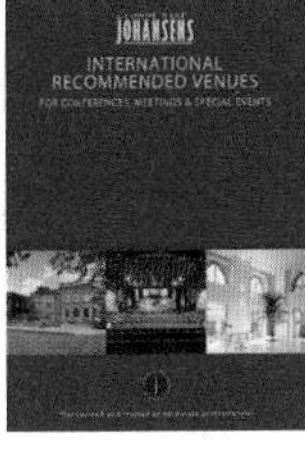

The International Collection
€100.00

Cantidad	€

Las 4 Guías de ocio presentadas con estuche

MÁS La Guía de Business

MÁS nuestra etiqueta de maletas chapada en plata

Una magnífica oferta – solo €100

(precio normal: €178.00)

(etiqueta de maletas chapada en plata, precio normal: €23, estuche €8)

DESCUENTOS - no incluye The International Collection 2 Guías = €8 de descuento ☐ 3 Guías = €15 de descuento ☐ 4 Guías = €30 de descuento ☐

EMBALAJE Y PORTE - para pedidos fuera del Reino Unido añader €9 por guía y €38 por The International Collection €

GRAN TOTAL - no olviden deducir el descuento €

☐ Adjunto un cheque pagable a Condé Nast Johansens

☐ Adeuden mi tarjeta Visa/Mastercard/Amex

Numero de tarjeta: Fecha de caducidad: Número de seguridad:

El numero de seguridad se compone de los 3 últimos dígitos del numero que aparece sobre la firma al dorso de la tarjeta de credito.
En Amex, el código de 4 dígitos aparece en la parte frontal, a la derecha y encima del numero de la tarjeta.

Nombre: Firma:

Dirección: Código postal:

Ciudad: Tel: E-mail:

Por favor, indique si desea recibir información u ofertas de Condé Nast Publications Ltd por teléfono ☐ o SMS ☐ o E-mail ☐
Por favor, indique si desea recibir información u ofertas de otras compañías selectas por teléfono ☐ o SMS ☐ o E-mail ☐
Por favor, indique si no quiere recibir información de Condé Nast Publications Ltd ☐ o de otras compañías selectas ☐

Envie por correo a Condé Nast Johansens, Unit 1, 16 Maple Road, Eastbourne, Great Britain, BN23 6ZW
o envie este formulario por fax a +44 1323 649 350

LLAME A NUESTRO TELÉFONO 24 HORAS +44 1323 649 349
O VAYA A NUESTRO SITIO WEB www.cnjguides.co.uk - ref: K008

CUESTIONARIO DE CALIDAD

Evaluación de su estancia en un hotel recomendado por Condé Nast Johansens.

Esperamos que su estancia en este hotel haya sido agradable. Le agradeceríamos nos dedicara algunos minutos para contestar a las siguientes preguntas con el fin no solo de mantener los altos niveles de los hoteles que recomendamos pero también para apoyar el trabajo de nuestro equipo de inspectores. Sus comentarios seran utilizados asimismo para decidir cuales serán los hoteles nominados a nuestros premios anuales de excelencia. Estos premios son concedidos a los establecimientos que ofrecen excelencia y buena relación calidad-precio.

Sus señas

Nombre: ________

Dirección: ________

Código postal: ____ Ciudad: ____ País: ____

Teléfono: ________

E-mail: ________

El Hotel

Nombre del hotel: ________

Ciudad y País: ________

Fecha de su visita: ________

Su evalaución

	Excelente	Buena	Decepcionante	Mala
Habitaciones	❍	❍	❍	❍
Salones	❍	❍	❍	❍
Comida/Restaurante	❍	❍	❍	❍
Servicio del hotel	❍	❍	❍	❍
Acogida/Amabilidad	❍	❍	❍	❍
Relación calidad-precio	❍	❍	❍	❍

Comentarios

Si necesita más espacio para sus comentarios, por favor dirijarse a:
Condé Nast Johansens Ltd, 6-8 Old Bond Street, London W1S 4PH, Great Britain

____

____

Por favor, indique si desea recibir información u ofertas de Condé Nast Publications Ltd por teléfono ☐ o SMS ☐ o E-mail ☐
Por favor, indique si desea recibir información u ofertas de otras compañías selectas por teléfono ☐ o SMS ☐ o E-mail ☐

Por favor, envie por fax a +44 (0) 207 152 3566
o vaya a nuestro sitio web www.johansens.com (E-Club login) donde se puede también comletar el cuestionario

CUESTIONARIO DE CALIDAD

Evaluación de su estancia en un hotel recomendado por Condé Nast Johansens.

Esperamos que su estancia en este hotel haya sido agradable. Le agradeceríamos nos dedicara algunos minutos para contestar a las siguientes preguntas con el fin no solo de mantener los altos niveles de los hoteles que recomendamos pero también para apoyar el trabajo de nuestro equipo de inspectores. Sus comentarios seran utilizados asimismo para decidir cuales serán los hoteles nominados a nuestros premios anuales de excelencia. Estos premios son concedidos a los establecimientos que ofrecen excelencia y buena relación calidad-precio.

Sus señas

Nombre: ________

Dirección: ________

Código postal: ____ Ciudad: ____ País: ____

Teléfono: ________

E-mail: ________

El Hotel

Nombre del hotel: ________

Ciudad y País: ________

Fecha de su visita: ________

Su evalaución

	Excelente	Buena	Decepcionante	Mala
Habitaciones	❍	❍	❍	❍
Salones	❍	❍	❍	❍
Comida/Restaurante	❍	❍	❍	❍
Servicio del hotel	❍	❍	❍	❍
Acogida/Amabilidad	❍	❍	❍	❍
Relación calidad-precio	❍	❍	❍	❍

Comentarios

Si necesita más espacio para sus comentarios, por favor dirijarse a:
Condé Nast Johansens Ltd, 6-8 Old Bond Street, London W1S 4PH, Great Britain

____

____

Por favor, indique si desea recibir información u ofertas de Condé Nast Publications Ltd por teléfono ☐ o SMS ☐ o E-mail ☐
Por favor, indique si desea recibir información u ofertas de otras compañías selectas por teléfono ☐ o SMS ☐ o E-mail ☐

Por favor, envie por fax a +44 (0) 207 152 3566
o vaya a nuestro sitio web www.johansens.com (E-Club login) donde se puede también comletar el cuestionario